Joan Holub
Illustrator
Page 188

Joe Kelly
Editor
Page 268

Chris Crutcher
Novelist
Page 84

Sharon Draper
Author
Page 104

1996 Children's Writer's & Illustrator's Market

Distributed in Canada by McGraw-Hill Ryerson, 300 Water St., Whitby, Ontario L1N 9B6. Also distributed in Australia by Kirby Books, Private Bag No. 19, P.O. Alexandria NSW 2015.

Managing Editor, Market Books Department: Constance J. Achabal;
Supervising Editor: Michael Willins;
Production Editor: Anne Bowling.

Children's Writer's & Illustrator's Market.

Published by F&W Publications,
1507 Dana Ave., Cincinnati, Ohio 45207.
Printed and bound in the United States of America.

International Standard Serial Number
0897-9790
International Standard Book Number
0-89879-714-4

Cover design: Lamson Design
Cover illustration: Chris O'Leary
Portraits: Ann Barrow

Attention Booksellers: This is an annual directory of F&W Publications. Return deadline for this edition is April 30, 1997.

1996 Children's Writer's & Illustrator's Market

Edited by
Alice P. Buening

WRITER'S DIGEST BOOKS
Cincinnati, Ohio

Contents

Page 36

The Markets

Page 127

Resources

© The Standard Publishing Company

Page 200

From the Editor

Some weeks ago, I received a wonderful postcard which I immediately hung in my office. The card features a photo of Dr. Seuss, Judy Blume and Maurice Sendak taken in 1978. At that time I was well past *Fox in Socks* and *In The Night Kitchen* and reading *Are You There, God? It's Me, Margaret*, and every other Blume title I could get my young hands on. As a kid these authors inspired me to read and imagine.

Today, when I glance at their faces above my desk, they inspire me to work—to put together the best book I can—because one of you reading this may be the next Seuss, Blume or Sendak, and I want to be your inspirator. To do this, I've put together the 1996 *Children's Writer's & Illustrator's Market*, a book of up-to-date listings (including more than 175 new ones), instructive articles, useful indexes, and other valuable tools to guide you in finding publishers for your writing, artwork and photos.

To start with, instead of the long business article we've had in the past editions, you'll find four separate articles dealing with the essential elements of getting published, such as Guide to Submitting Your Work (page 13), and Tips on Contracts and Negotiations (page 17). We'll also help you answer the "agent question" (Do you need one to get published?) with opinions from both sides. You'll find An Agent's View: Representation Is Important, on page 7; and A Writer's View: Be Your Own Agent, on page 10. (Look for the phrase "only interested in agented material" in bold within some listings in Book Publishers and Magazines.)

A great deal of advice and insights into the children's publishing world can be gained from reading Telling Tales From Around the World: an Interview with **Eric Kimmel** (page 25). Kimmel talks about the struggles of breaking in, the magazine market, the challenges of writing picture books, and more. (He was also inspired by Dr. Seuss.)

Once again, we bring you First Books (page 33) for inspiration from those just starting out. We talked to two authors (including Newbery Honor Medal winner **Karen Cushman**), an illustrator, and a photographer. Hear about the different courses they took to get their first children's books published.

In this year's Insider Reports, there's a little something for everyone. We talked to a poet, **J. Patrick Lewis** (page 48); an award-winning young adult novelist, **Chris Crutcher** (page 84); a Caldecott Honor-medalist author/illustrator, **Denise Fleming** (page 88); and a renowned photographer, **William Wegman** (page 96), among others.

We've again included artwork with each Insider Report interview (as well as within the listings). Note the wonderful portraits of the subjects by artist **Ann Barrow**, of South Dartmouth, Massachusetts. Barrow, who also illustrates children's books and greeting cards, sent us samples of her work, and we fell in love with her soft, realistic style. Flip open the front or back cover of the book for a look at all of her portraits. So you can quickly locate the Insider Reports, page numbers and descriptions are also included (thanks to our first-ever hard cover!).

Especially for illustrators, we've put all illustration information under a single subheading within the listings in Book Publishers and Magazines, with clear contact information for sending only illustration samples as well as manuscript/illustration packages. For photographers, we've added a Photography Index, so you can easily find which book and magazine publishers and special markets (like greeting card and puzzle producers) buy freelance photos.

We've also continued to add editorial comments within the listings to give you more information about certain publishers, such as policy changes or awards they've won.

So dive right in. But before you turn to the listings, turn the page and read How to Use This Book. When you've read the articles, used the indexes, and submitted to the listings, let me know how it's going (write a letter, call, e-mail to wdigest@aol.com—or you could even send a postcard). Tell me what else you'd like to see in the book, what issues you'd like us to cover, who you'd like us to interview. Most of all, tell me when you get your first book published, your first illustration assignment, or your first magazine article in print. For me, hearing your success stories is the greatest source of inspiration.

How to Use This Book

As a writer, illustrator or photographer first picking up *Children's Writer's & Illustrator's Market*, you may not know quite how to start using the book. Your impulse may be to flip through the book and quickly make a mailing list, then submit to everyone in hopes someone will take interest in your work. Well, there's more to it. Finding the right market takes some time and research. The more you know about a company that interests you, the better chance you have of getting work accepted. We've made your job easier by putting a wealth of information at your fingertips. Besides providing listings, this directory includes tools to help you determine which markets are the best ones for your work.

Using the indexes

This book has more than 675 buyers of freelance material. To learn which companies want the type of material you're interested in submitting, start with the indexes.

The Age-Level Index

Age-groups are broken down into these categories in the Age-Level Index:

- **Picture books** or **picture-oriented material** are for preschoolers to 8-year-olds.
- **Young readers** are written and illustrated for 5- to 8-year-olds.
- **Middle readers** are for 9- to 11-year-olds.
- **Young adults** are for ages 12 and up.

These age breakdowns may vary slightly from publisher to publisher, but using them as guidelines will help you target appropriate markets. For example, if you've written an article about the latest teen fashions, check the Magazines Age-Level Index under the Young Adult subheading. Using this list, you'll quickly find the listings for young adult magazines.

The Subject Index

But let's narrow the search further. Take your list of young adult magazines, turn to the Subject Index, and find the Fashion subheading. Then highlight the names that appear on both lists (Young Adult and Fashion). Now you have a smaller list of all the magazines that would be interested in your teen fashion article. Read through those listings and decide which ones sound best for your work.

Illustrators and photographers can use the Subject Index as well. If you specialize in painting animals, for instance, consider sending samples to book and magazine publishers listed under Animals and, perhaps, Nature/Environment. Illustrators, however, can simply send general examples of their style (in the form of tearsheets or postcards) to art directors to keep on file. The indexes may be more helpful to artists sending manuscript/illustration packages. Always read the listings for the potential markets to see the type of work art directors prefer and what type of samples they'll keep on file.

The Photography Index

New this year is an index especially for photographers. The Photography Index lists book and magazine publishers, as well as special markets (such as greeting card and puzzle manufacturers) that buy photos from freelancers. Copy the lists and read the listings for specific needs.

Using the listings

Many listings begin with one or more symbols. Here's what each stands for:

(*) symbol indicates a listing is new in this edition.

(■) symbol indicates a listing subsidy or co-op publishes.

(🍁) symbol indicates a listing is Canadian.

(‡) symbol indicates a contest or organization is open to students.

(●) symbol introduces special comments by the editor of this book.

The subheadings under each listing contain valuable information about such things as age-levels, subjects needed, how to submit your work, payments and response time. The Tips section contains special advice straight from an editor or art director about what their company wants or doesn't want, or other helpful advice.

Publishers also state the average word lengths for the fiction and nonfiction material they need. Many listings indicate whether submission guidelines are available. If a publisher you're interested in offers them, send for them and read them. The same is true with catalogs. Sending for catalogs and seeing and reading about the books a publisher produces give you a better idea of how your work would fit in. (You may even want to look at a few of the books in the catalog at a library or bookstore.)

In researching listings you'll also find payment information. Some markets pay on acceptance, others on publication. Some pay a flat rate for manuscripts and artwork, others pay advances and royalties.

Especially for artists and photographers

Along with information for writers, listings provide information for photographers and illustrators. Illustrators will find numerous markets that maintain files of samples for possible future assignments. If you're both a writer and illustrator, look for markets that accept manuscript/illustration packages. If you're a photographer, after consulting the Photography Index, read the information under the Photography subhead within listings to see what format a buyer prefers. Note the type of photos a buyer wants to purchase and the procedures for submitting. It's not uncommon for a market to want a résumé and promotional literature, as well as tearsheets from previous work. Listings also note whether model releases and/or captions are required.

Especially for young writers

If you're a parent, teacher or student, you may be interested in Young Writer's & Illustrator's Markets. The markets in this section encourage submissions from young writers and artists. Young people should also check Contests & Awards for contests that accept work by young people. These are marked with a double dagger (‡). Some listings in Clubs & Organizations, also marked with a double dagger (‡), accept or are especially for students.

Common abbreviations

Throughout the listings, the following abbreviations are used:

- **ms** or **mss** stands for manuscript or manuscripts.
- **SASE** refers to a self-addressed, stamped envelope.
- **SAE** refers to a self-addressed envelope.
- **IRC** stands for International Reply Coupon. These are required with SAEs sent to markets in countries other that your own.

For information on submission procedures and formats, turn to Guide to Submitting Your Work on page 13.

The Facts About Agents & Reps

Many children's writers, illustrators and photographers, especially those just beginning, are confused about whether to enlist the services of an agent or representative. The decision is strictly one that each writer, illustrator or photographer must make for herself. Some are confident with their own negotiation skills and believe acquiring an agent or rep is not in their best interest. Others feel uncomfortable in the business arena or are not willing to sacrifice valuable creative time for marketing.

It's estimated that about half of children's publishers accept unagented work, so it is possible to break into children's publishing without an agent. Some agents avoid working with children's books because traditionally low advances and trickling royalty payments over long periods of time make children's books less lucrative. Writers targeting magazine markets do not need the services of an agent. In fact, it's practically impossible to find an agent interested in marketing articles and short stories—there simply isn't enough financial incentive.

One benefit of having an agent, though, is it may speed up the process of getting your work reviewed, especially by publishers who don't accept unagented submissions (a policy becoming more and more common in children's publishing). If an agent has a good reputation and submits your manuscript to an editor, that manuscript may actually bypass the first-read stage (which is done by editorial assistants and junior editors) and end up on the editor's desk sooner.

When agreeing to have a reputable agent represent you, remember that she should be familiar with the needs of the current market and evaluate your manuscript/artwork/photos accordingly. She should also determine the quality of your piece and whether it is saleable. When your manuscript sells, your agent should negotiate a favorable contract and clear up any questions you have about monetary payments.

Keep in mind that however reputable the agent or rep is, she has limitations. Representation does not guarantee sale of your work. It just means an agent or rep sees potential in your writing, art or photos. Though an agent or rep may offer criticism or advice on how to improve your work, she can't make you a better writer, artist or photographer or give you fame.

What they charge

Literary agents typically charge a 15 percent commission from the sale of writing; art and photo representatives usually charge a 25 to 30 percent commission. Such fees are taken from advances and royalty earnings. If your agent sells foreign rights to your work, she will deduct a higher percentage because she will most likely be dealing with an overseas agent with whom she must split the fee.

Be advised that not every agent is open to representing a writer, artist or photographer who lacks an established track record. Just as when approaching a publisher, the manuscript, artwork or photos, and query or cover letter you submit to a potential agent must be attractive and professional looking. Your first impression must be that of an organized, articulate person.

The two articles that follow offer opinions from both sides of the "do-you-need-an-agent?" fence. First, hear from literary agent Ethan Ellenberg as he gives the lowdown on what an agent does and why you may need one. Next is an article by writer Ruth Turk who does her own marketing and successfully published ten books without the aid of an agent. She shares her marketing strategies, and tells you how to be your own agent.

For a detailed directory of literary agents, refer to *Guide to Literary Agents*; for listings of art reps, consult *Artist's & Graphic Designer's Market*; and for photo reps, see *Photographer's Market* (all Writer's Digest Books).

An Agent's View: Representation Is Important

by Ethan Ellenberg

Finding and working with an agent is an important part of many published authors' and illustrators' careers. At best, an agent is a business partner and a colleague. A good agent will immeasurably increase both your earnings and your enjoyment of your career, as he handles all the business of being an author or illustrator.

An agent's role can be broken down into three main areas: editorial, marketing and expertise/management. Editorial work includes reading, evaluating and working with a writer to make sure his work is ready to market. Although some books reach me ready to sell and some of my working writers are so consistent that I don't have to check their work, most of what I sell I read and evaluate first. Since I take on only new clients I believe in, reading and evaluating work is part of the entire process of choosing the right clients to represent and building my agency.

Selling a manuscript is seldom easy, especially for new writers. Editors are less and less available to do editorial work, so a flawed manuscript, even from a very talented writer, could well be rejected. Because I am continually involved in selling books and talking to editors, I have a firm grip on both the market and what inherently makes a good book good.

Before I try to sell a book I must make sure it's ready to be bought. Some agents do little or no editorial work. They feel they're only "salesmen." They may take only writers with established careers who don't need editorial work. If you feel you need only a "salesperson," such an agent may suit your needs.

It's important that an agent knows an author's work to represent him well, so I put special emphasis on the editorial work—even when it's minimal. Editorial work I do includes such things as choosing the best manuscript of three or four for submission; or critiquing a novel to eliminate weak areas in the plot or adjust characters that need to be more sympathetic. If you don't have a professional reading and evaluating your work before it's offered for sale, your odds of success drastically decrease.

Marketing and management

The second important area is marketing. This is absolutely fundamental in an agent's role. Although children's publishing is still relatively open to unsolicited manuscripts, this is changing quickly. Unsolicited manuscripts simply don't get the attention that agented manuscripts do. Because agents know editors, have track records, and have ongoing business with a house, they can demand and receive more attention, more quickly.

Ethan Ellenberg *founded and has run The Ethan Ellenberg Literary Agency in New York City for almost a dozen years. He's formerly held positions with both Bantam and Berkley/Jove publishers and has written articles for* Guide to Literary Agents, Romance Writers of America Report, Gothic Journal *and* The Literary Times. *Children's publishing is a major focus of his agency, which represents about 70 writers and illustrators.*

However, marketing goes far beyond the clout of ongoing business and personal relationships with editors. Agents keep up with who is buying what, who is hungry for new talent and who is full. Agents know all the publishing houses and have a talent for selling. If you are a bit shy or self-conscious about your work, your agent certainly won't be. And when a publisher is interested in your work, an agent knows how to close the deal and what kind of advance and royalty you should receive.

The final part of an agent's role is expertise/career management. The truth is, publishing is a difficult, complex and dynamic business. Most authors, even authors with long track records, are not experts in publishing contracts, subsidiary rights sales, marketing plans, etc. Agents are involved in all these activities on a regular basis. They negotiate publishing agreements, sell rights such as translation rights in foreign countries and movie rights in Hollywood. They know the significance of your book's first printing. They can advise you on how to market yourself. They have a depth of knowledge and experience that covers every aspect of an author's working life. When you hire an agent, you get the benefit of all that experience.

Different 'authors,' different needs

Something unique to children's publishing is that there are really three kinds of children's "authors"—the writer, the writer/illustrator and the illustrator.

If you write children's books (but do not illustrate), you can consider using the services of a literary agent. Literary agents routinely sell the manuscripts of children's books. If you write and illustrate, a literary agent could handle all your manuscripts for children's books, while your illustration could be handled by an illustration agent or a commercial art agent. If you are solely an illustrator, you may want to have a literary agent involved in your children's book illustration work and an illustration agent or commercial art agent handling other illustration work. Each of these working "authors" has different needs and you must be clear about what your needs are when shopping for an agent.

Writers' and illustrators' reasons for using the services of an agent vary. Some feel it's tough earning a living as a writer or illustrator, and it's great to have a successful professional who believes in their work on their side. Some writers and illustrators need a partner in business to complement their skills—they need agents who possess the business skills they don't. Some simply like to have someone to talk to about how their career is going and what's going to happen next—as they say, two heads are better than one and a good agent is that invaluable "second head." Some writers and illustrators simply find that although they may not *need* an agent's expertise, there's a lot of career business that must be taken care of and they'd prefer someone else do it.

If you're a working writer and can relate to some of the above reasons, an agent might be just what your career needs. If you're unpublished and feel strongly that you have a manuscript ready to sell or that your illustrations are ready to appear in the books of top children's publishers, you may also want to find an agent.

Choosing an agent

Finding an agent, especially a good one, may be difficult. Good agents have good businesses—they're busy with established clients and represent first-rate talent. They get referrals and established writers come to them, so it's harder for them to take newcomers (it's often hardest to sell that first book) or writers whose track records are spotty.

Nevertheless, you can find a good agent. All agents want talented writers with big futures, and when they find someone new who they're excited about, it makes their day. A few years ago I found a new writer/illustrator named Eric Rohmann in my unsolicited pile. In 1995, I attended a dinner in Chicago where he was honored—he won the Caldecott Silver Medal for his first book *Time Flies* (Crown). After that experience, I'm paying very close attention to the unsolicited work that arrives in my office.

Be aware that you may run across "bad agents"—people who take advantage of writers and illustrators. If your prospective agent is charging tens or hundreds of dollars in fees (often called reading fees, marketing fees, housekeeping fees) just to read your manuscript and market it, beware. This person may not be a "real" literary agent, but someone who makes his living charging fees. In my opinion, "real agents" make their livings solely on commissions generated by sales. You must decide if it's worth several hundred dollars to simply have someone read and critique your book. Your money may be better spent at a writing workshop, college writing course or writers' conference.

Fees aside, you need to ask a prospective agent the same types of questions you'd ask a doctor or a lawyer you were considering hiring: How long have you been in business? What's your background? How many books did you sell this year? To whom? How many clients do you have? Can I speak to a few of them? (Note: the Association of Authors' Representatives offers "Suggested Agent Checklist for Authors," the organization's list of questions for potential agents. Send a SASE to: AAR, 10 Astor Place, 3rd Floor, New York NY 10003.) If your prospective agent has never sold a book, never worked in professional publishing, doesn't know any editors, etc., keep looking. Also, if you have an agent who isn't performing properly, change agents until you find someone who's a good match for you and who has all the skills you need—that way you'll be sure to get the most out of the author/agent relationship.

A Writer's View: Be Your Own Agent

by Ruth Turk

I had a literary agent who worked from a large agency representing more than 200 authors. My agent's time was divided between me and her share of the clients. But I wanted an agent who would devote 100 percent of her time to marketing my work—so I became my own agent.

Since then, I've sold ten books (among them picture books, fiction and nonfiction titles), as well as short stories, poetry and magazine articles, proving that writers can achieve modest publishing goals without agents if they are willing to give the time, initiative and energy required. Will it take some time away from your writing? Of course. But the more active marketing you do, the greater results you will ultimately achieve.

Using marketing tools

A writer without an agent needs to research appropriate markets with perseverance and dedication. Stay abreast of the market by consulting invaluable sources such as *Writer's Market*, *Literary Market Place* (*LMP*), *Children's Writer's & Illustrator's Market*, *Writer's Digest*, *The Writer*, *Publishers Weekly* and *The Horn Book*, among others. Though all of these references are available for use in public libraries, if you plan to be your own agent, you may want to consider subscribing or purchasing current editions of some of these resources. These publications will keep you up-to-date on publishing needs and give you useful tips, leads and changes in the industry.

Because today's markets are constantly changing and reorganizing, it's important to find just the right home for your particular manuscript. One way to ensure you're targeting appropriate markets is to send for free catalogs and writer's guidelines offered by many houses. (Include a SASE when requested.) Postage and stationery are not inexpensive, but they are part of the investment you must make to further your publishing goals. When you receive a catalog, study it carefully to see if your work fits in with the kind of books described. Follow up by looking at examples of a few of these books in your public library or local bookstores.

Libraries and bookstores are also good places to learn about the children's market. Browse the shelves in the children's reading room; talk to librarians and booksellers in the children's department. These are the people who know what's being read by what age-groups. The children's reference librarian can tell you which books are most requested or needed, and which subjects in fiction and nonfiction have been overdone. In my years of self-marketing, some of my best sources have been cooperative librarians.

Ruth Turk, *a former English teacher and guidance counselor, has had ten books published for both children and adult readers. Among her work is* Lillian Hellman: Rebel Playwright *(Lerner, 1995). She's currently working on a biography of Ray Charles for Lerner, a biography of Rosalynn Carter for Franklin Watts, and several picture books. When she's not writing books, magazine articles and poetry, she frequently lectures to new writers. Turk lives in Lake Worth, Florida.*

Books in Print can also be a valuable tool. You can check this annual directory to find whether books similar to yours have been published, and the dates of publication. Of course, a few books on the same topic don't necessarily preclude one more, providing the approach and format are different, and a publisher is interested.

Making a good impression

Once you become familiar with appropriate markets, the job of being your own agent becomes highly specialized. The strongest impression you make on an editor is your first written communication—your query letter or cover letter. For help with writing good queries, refer to *How to Write Irresistible Query Letters*, by Lisa Collier Cool (Writer's Digest Books).

Address your letter to a specific editor, otherwise it may get lost beneath the slush pile. Names can be found in this book, or the latest *Writer's Market. LMP* usually lists the names of publishing house staff members, as well as their titles. It's always a good idea to call the publisher's office to make sure the information you have is current, as editors change quickly in this business. You can save some money by finding out if the publishers you're calling have 800 numbers. (This information often appears in *LMP*.)

Don't forget to limit your first letter to a single typed page, and write in your best style, because to an editor, your letter will be an indication of your overall writing ability. Open your letter with a statement that "hooks" the editor. For example, when your proposed book has an intriguing title it helps attract attention, or at least, curiosity. The publisher who accepted *Fifteen Is the Pits* (New Win Publishing, 1993), my young adult novel, told me the title made him interested in learning more about that particular stage of adolescence.

For nonfiction, a well-written proposal can frequently sell a book. Though your research may not be complete, present information that will convince the editor your material has potential. When an editor requests an outline and sample chapter, be prepared to submit your finest work along with an enthusiastic response. While an editorial invitation doesn't necessarily mean acceptance at this point, it's important to let the editor know you're excited about your writing. Editors enjoy working with authors who are enthusiastic as well as dedicated and flexible. Once a manuscript is accepted, pay attention to constructive suggestions for revision with a spirit of cooperation. After all, an editor's job is to help a writer's work be as good as possible. A cordial author/editor relationship ensures a smoothly finished product, a published book of which you both can be proud.

Simultaneous submissions

Since some editors may take 10-12 weeks to respond to a manuscript, it doesn't make sense for a writer to make exclusive submissions. Although some editors don't like simultaneous submissions, it's in the best interest of a writer who is her own agent to circulate her work among a number of publishers. It's important, however, to inform each publisher that you've sent the same manuscript elsewhere.

Will there be rejections? You can count on it. It's all part of the process. Every now and then you may receive a little note (sometimes handwritten) that invites future submission, even though the rejected manuscript was not appropriate at the time. Don't be shy! Recognize this bit of encouragement for what it is and act upon it. Go back to the publisher's catalog, study it again, write something new, then polish it with your hard work and enthusiasm until it shines. Send the story back to the encouraging editor with a "thank you" that is not long and effusive, but brief and sincere. Editors need writers as much as writers need editors. The name of the game is working together.

When the moment arrives that genuine publishing contracts come in such numbers that no time remains for writing, it's a good idea to look for an agent. Until that time, providing you are willing and able to do lots of homework, you may discover the rewards of being your own agent.

Guide to Submitting Your Work

Editors and art directors hate to receive inappropriate submissions—handling them wastes their time, not to mention your time and money. By sending out material without knowing a market's needs, you're sure to meet with rejection.

If you're interested in submitting to a particular magazine, write to request a sample copy. For a book publisher, obtain a book catalog and check a library or bookstore for titles produced by that publisher. Studying such materials carefully, you better acquaint yourself with that market's writing and illustration styles and formats.

Most of the book publishers and magazines listed in this book (as well as many special markets such as greeting card and paper product companies) offer some sort of writer's, artist's or photographer's guidelines for a SASE. It's important to send for guidelines and study them before submitting work. You'll get a better understanding of what a particular publisher wants. You may even decide, after reading the submission guidelines, that your work isn't right for a company you considered.

Important submission elements

Throughout the listings you'll read requests for particular elements to include when contacting markets. Here are explanations of some of these submission components.

- **Query letters for nonfiction.** A query letter is a no-more-than-one-page, well-written piece to arouse an editor's or art director's interest in your work. Queries are usually required when submitting nonfiction material to a publisher, in which case, your goal is to convince the editor your idea is perfect for her readership and that you're the writer qualified to do the job. Note any previous writing experience and include published samples to prove your credentials, especially samples related to the subject matter you're querying about.

Many query letters start with leads similar to those of actual manuscripts. In the rest of the letter, briefly outline the work you're proposing and include facts, anecdotes, interviews or other pertinent information that give the editor a feel for the manuscript's premise—entice her to want to know more. End your letter with a straightforward request to write (or submit) the work, and include information on its approximate length, date it could be completed, and whether accompanying photos or artwork is available. *Always enclose a SASE.*

- **Query letters for fiction.** More and more, queries are being requested for fiction manuscripts. For a fiction query, explain the story's plot, main characters, conflict and resolution, and make the editor eager to see more. For more information on writing good queries, consult *How to Write Irresistible Query Letters*, by Lisa Collier Cool (Writer's Digest Books).
- **Cover letters for writers.** Some editors prefer complete manuscripts, especially for fiction. In such cases, the cover letter (no longer than one page) serves as an introduction, establishes your credentials as a writer, and gives an overview of the manuscript.

If an editor asked for a manuscript because of a query, note this in your cover letter. Also, if an earlier rejection letter included an invitation to submit other work, mention that as well. Editors should know the work was solicited.

- **Cover letters for illustrators and photographers.** For an illustrator or photographer, the cover letter serves as an introduction to the art director and establishes credentials. Explain what services you can provide and the type of follow-up contact you plan to make, if any. When sending samples of your work, indicate whether they should be returned or filed. *Never* send original work. If you wish to have the samples returned, include a SASE.

- **Résumés.** Often writers, illustrators and photographers are asked to submit résumés with their cover letters and samples. They can be created in a variety of formats, from a single page listing information, to color brochures featuring your work. Keep your résumé brief, and focus on your achievements, including your clients and the work you've done for them, as well as your educational background and any awards you've received.
- **Book proposals.** Throughout the listings in the Book Publishers section, publishers refer to submitting a synopsis, outline and sample chapters. Depending on an editor's preference, some or all of these components, along with a cover letter, make up a book proposal.

Advice from editorial

In addition to helping sort through the 350 or so manuscripts received each week by Peachtree Publishers, Ltd., in Atlanta, Helen L. Harriss, of Peachtree's editorial department, takes calls from authors one afternoon each week. The following list includes some important suggestions she shares with callers. Her advice comes from four years of looking over "a stack of manuscripts that never diminishes."

1. *Know your audience—write from knowledge about, understanding of, and appreciation for them.*
2. *Understand that children are savvy people; do not talk down to them.*
3. *Test-read your work to children. Ask for honest answers. If possible read it to children in schools or in libraries; you'll know quickly if they like your story.*
4. *Get into writers' groups—read your work aloud, listen to critical comments from other writers.*
5. *Do your homework. Read books such as* Children's Writer's & Illustrator's Market *and others as though they were texts for your most important final.*
6. *Learn how to write a good query letter. Give a succinct account of the story, and your target age-group. Give a brief account of your experience and background, and your published works, if any. Spell and punctuate well. Remember, this is your introduction to someone in a publishing house.*
7. Always *send a self-addressed, stamped envelope.*
8. *Send manuscripts in sturdy envelopes that fit the material.*

A *synopsis* summarizes the book, covering the basic plot (including the ending). It should be easy to read and flow well.

An *outline* covers your book chapter by chapter and provides highlights of each. If you're developing an outline for fiction include major characters, plots and subplots, and length of the book.

Sample chapters give a more comprehensive idea of your writing skill. Some editors may request the first two or three chapters to see how your material is set up. Find out what the editor wants before writing or revising sample chapters.

Formats for manuscripts

When submitting a complete manuscript, follow some basic guidelines. In the upper-left corner of your title page, type your legal name (not pseudonym), address, phone number and Social Security number (publishers need this to file payment records with the government). In the upper-right corner, type the approximate word length. All material in the upper corners should be typed single-spaced. Then type the title (centered) almost halfway down the page with the word "by" two spaces under that and your name or pseudonym two spaces under "by."

The first page should also include the title (centered) one-third of the way down. Two spaces under that type "by" and your name or pseudonym. To begin the body of your manuscript, drop down two double spaces and indent five spaces for each new paragraph. There should be 1-inch margins around all sides of a full typewritten page.

Set your computer or typewriter on double-space for the manuscript body. From page two to the end of your manuscript include your last name followed by a comma and the title (or key words of the title) in the upper-left corner. The page number should go in the top right corner. Drop down two double spaces to begin the body of each page. If you're submitting a novel, type each chapter title one-third of the way down the page. For more information on manuscript formats read *Writer's Digest Guide to Manuscript Formats*, by Dian Dinein Buchman and Seli Groves, or *Manuscript Submission*, by Scott Edelstein (both Writer's Digest Books). The Society of Children's Book Writers and Illustrators offers submission guidelines to members for a SASE. Request "From Typewriter to Printed Page . . . Facts You Need to Know."

Picture books formats

The majority of editors prefer to see complete manuscripts for picture books. When typing the text of a picture book, *do not* include page breaks or supply art. Editors will find their own illustrators for picture books. Most of the time, a writer and an illustrator who work on the same book never meet. The editor acts as their go-between. *How to Write and Sell Children's Picture Books*, by Jean E. Karl (Writer's Digest Books), offers advice on preparing text and marketing your work.

If you're an illustrator who has written your own book, create a dummy or storyboard containing both art and text. Then submit it along with your complete manuscript and sample pieces of final art (color photocopies or slides—never originals). Publishers interested in picture books specify in their listings what should be submitted. For a step-by-step guide on creating a good dummy, refer to *How to Write and Illustrate Children's Books and Get Them Published*, edited by Treld Pelkey Bicknell and Felicity Trotman (North Light Books), or Frieda Gates's book, *How to Write, Illustrate, and Design Children's Books* (Lloyd-Simone Publishing Company).

Mailing submissions

Your main concern when packaging material is to be sure it arrives undamaged. If your manuscript is less than six pages, simply fold it in thirds and send it in a #10 (business-size) envelope. For a SASE, either fold another #10 envelope in thirds or insert a #9 (reply) envelope which fits in a #10 neatly without any folding.

Another option is folding your manuscript in half in a 6×9 envelope, with a #9 or #10 SASE enclosed. For larger manuscripts use a 9×12 envelope both for mailing the submission and as a SASE (which can be folded in half). Book manuscripts require a sturdy box for mailing. Include a self-addressed mailing label and return postage.

Artwork or photographs require a bit more care in packaging to guarantee they arrive in good condition. Sandwich illustrations and photos between heavy cardboard slightly larger than the work, and tape the cardboard together. Write your name and address on the back of each piece of art or each photo in case the inside material becomes separated. For the packaging use either a manila envelope, foam-padded envelope, brown paper or a mailer lined with plastic air bubbles. Bind non-joined edges with reinforced mailing tape and affix a typed mailing label or clearly write your address.

Mailing material first class ensures quick delivery. Also, first-class mail is forwarded for one year if the addressee has moved, and can be returned if undeliverable. If you're concerned about your original material safely reaching its destination, consider other mailing options, such as UPS or certified mail. If material needs to reach your editor or art director quickly, you can elect to use overnight delivery services.

Remember, markets outside your own country can't use your country's postage when returning a manuscript to you. When mailing a submission to another country, include a self-addressed envelope and International Reply Coupons or IRCs. (You'll see this term in many Canadian listings.) Your post office can help you determine, based on a package's weight, the correct number of IRCs to include to ensure its return.

If it's not necessary for an editor to return your work, don't include return postage. You can track the status of your submission by enclosing a postage-paid reply postcard with options for the editor to check, such as "Yes, I'm interested," "I'll keep the material on file," or "No, the material isn't appropriate for current needs."

Some writers, illustrators and photographers simply include a deadline date. If you don't hear from the editor or art director by the specified date, your work is automatically withdrawn from consideration. Because many publishing houses and companies are overstocked with material, a minimum deadline should be at least three months.

It's never a good idea to use a company's fax number or e-mail address to send lengthy manuscript submissions. This can disrupt a company's internal business.

Keeping submission records

It's important to keep track of the material you submit. When recording each submission, include the date it was sent, the business and contact name, and any enclosures (such as samples of writing, artwork or photography). Keep copies of the article or manuscript you send together with related correspondence to make follow-up easier. When you sell rights to a manuscript, artwork or photos you can "close" your file on a particular submission by noting the date the material was accepted, what rights were purchased, the publication date and payment.

If you don't hear from a market within its stated response time, wait another month and follow up with a note inquiring about the status of your submission. Include the title or description, date sent, and a SASE for response. Ask the contact person when she anticipates making a decision. At the very least you'll receive a definite "no," and free yourself to send the material to another market.

Simultaneous submissions

If you opt for simultaneous (also called "multiple") submissions—sending the same material to several editors at the same time—be sure to inform each editor your work is being considered elsewhere. Many editors are reluctant to receive simultaneous submissions but understand that for hopeful freelancers, waiting several months for a response can be frustrating. In some cases, an editor may actually be more inclined to read your manuscript sooner if she knows it's being considered by another publisher.

SCBWI cautions writers against simultaneous submissions. They recommend submitting to one publisher at a time, but waiting only three months (state you'll do so in your cover letter). If no response is received, send a note withdrawing your manuscript from consideration. SCBWI considers simultaneous submissions acceptable only if you have a manuscript dealing with a timely issue.

It is especially important to keep track of submissions when you are submitting simultaneously. This way if you get an offer on that manuscript, you can instruct the other publishers to withdraw your work from consideration.

Tips on Contracts & Negotiation

Before you see your work in print, before you even begin working with an editor or art director on a project, there is negotiation. And whether negotiating a book contract, a magazine article assignment, or an illustration or photo assignment, remember these tips: First, if you find any clauses vague or confusing in a contract, get legal advice. The time and money invested in counseling up front could protect you from problems later. If you have an agent or rep, she will review any contract.

A contract is an agreement between two or more parties that specifies the fees to be paid, services rendered, deadlines, rights purchased and, for artists and photographers, whether original work is returned. Most companies have standard contracts for writers, illustrators and photographers. The specifics (such as royalty rates, advances, delivery dates, etc.) are typed in after negotiations.

Though it's okay to conduct negotiations over the phone, get a written contract once both parties have agreed on terms. Never depend on oral stipulations; written contracts protect both parties from misunderstandings. Watch for clauses that may not be in your best interest, such as "work-for-hire." When you do work for hire, you give up all rights to your creations.

Some reputable children's magazines, such as *Highlights for Children*, buy all rights, and many writers and illustrators believe it's worth the concession in order to break into the field. However, once you've entered the field, it's in your best interest to keep rights to your work.

When negotiating a book deal, find out whether your contract contains an option clause. This clause requires the author to give the publisher a first look at her next work before offering it to other publishers. Though it's editorial etiquette to give the publisher the first chance at publishing your next work, be wary of statements in the contract which could trap you. Don't allow the publisher to consider the next project for more than 30 days and be specific about what type of work should actually be considered "next work." (For example, if the book under contract is a young adult novel, specify that the publisher will receive an exclusive look at only your next young adult novel.)

Book publishers' payment methods

Book publishers pay authors and artists in royalties, a percentage of either the wholesale or retail price of each book sold. From large publishing houses, the author usually receives an advance issued against future royalties before the book is published. Half of the advance amount is issued upon signing the book contract; the other half is issued when the book is finished. For illustrations, one-third of the advance should be collected upon signing the contract; one-third upon delivery of sketches; and one-third upon delivery of finished art.

After your book has sold enough copies to earn back your advance, you'll start to get royalty checks. Some publishers hold a reserve against returns, which means a percentage of royalties is held back in case books are returned from bookstores. If you have a reserve clause in your contract, find out the exact percentage of total sales that will be withheld and the time period the publisher will hold this money. You should be reimbursed this amount after a reasonable time period, such as a year. Royalty percentages vary with each publisher, but there are standard ranges.

Book publishers' rates

According to the latest figures from the Society of Children's Book Writers and Illustrators (SCBWI), picture book writers can expect advances of $3,500-5,000; picture book illustrators' advances range from $7,000-10,000; text and illustration packages can score $8,000-10,000. Royalties for picture books are generally about 5 percent (split between the author and illustrator), but can go as high as 10 percent. Those who both write and illustrate a book, of course, receive the full royalty.

Advances for chapter books and middle-grade novels vary slightly from picture books. Hardcover titles can fetch authors advances of $4,000-6,000 and 10 percent royalties; paperbacks bring in slightly lower advances of $3,000-5,000 and royalties of 6-8 percent. Fees for young adult novels are generally the same, but additional length may increase fees and royalties.

As you might expect, advance and royalty figures vary from house to house and are affected by the time of year, the state of the economy, and other factors. Some smaller houses may not even pay royalties, just flat fees. First-time writers and illustrators generally start on the low end of the scale, while established and high-profile writers are paid more.

Remaindering

When a book goes out of print, a publisher will sell any existing copies to a wholesaler who, in turn, sells the copies to stores at a discount. When the books are "remaindered" to a wholesaler, they are usually sold at a price just above the cost of printing. When negotiating a contract with a publisher you may want to discuss the possibility of purchasing the remaindered copies before they are sold to a wholesaler. Then you can market the copies you purchased and still make a profit.

Pay rates for magazines

For writers, price structures for magazines are based on a per-word rate or range for a specific article length. Artists and photographers have a few more variables to contend with before contracting their services.

Payment for illustrations and photos can be set by such factors as whether the piece(s) will be black and white or four-color, how many are to be purchased, where the work appears (cover or inside), circulation, and the artist's or photographer's prior experience.

You can determine an hourly rate by using the annual salary of a staff artist or photographer doing similar work in an economically similar geographic area (try to find an artist or photographer willing to share this information), then dividing that salary by 52 (the number of weeks in a year) and again by 40 (the number of hours in a work week). To figure in overhead expenses such as rent, utilities, supplies, etc., multiply the hourly rate you came up with by 2.5. Research again to be sure your rate is competitive. Members of SCBWI can get additional information on contracts—send a SASE to SCBWI, 22736 Vanowen St., Suite 106, West Hills CA 91307 and request "Answers to Some Questions About Contracts."

Know Your Rights

A copyright is protection provided to creators of original works, published or unpublished. In general, copyright protection gives a writer, illustrator or photographer the exclusive right to decide how her work is used and allows her to receive payment for each use.

Essentially, copyright also encourages the creation of new works by guaranteeing the creator power to sell rights to the work in the marketplace. The copyright holder can print, reprint or copy her work; sell or distribute copies of her work; or prepare derivative works such as plays, collages or recordings. The Copyright Law is designed to protect a writer's, illustrator's or photographer's work (created on or after January 1, 1978) for her lifetime plus 50 years. (Note: Canadians can consult *Canadian Copyright Law*, by Lesley Ellen Harris [McGraw-Hill Ryerson] for information specific to their country's laws.)

If you collaborate with someone else on a written or artistic project, the copyright will last for the lifetime of the last survivor plus 50 years. The creators' heirs may hold a copyright for an additional 50 years. After that, the work becomes public domain. Works created anonymously or under a pseudonym are protected for 100 years, or 75 years after publication. Under work-for-hire agreements, you relinquish your copyright to your "employer."

The copyright notice

Some feel a copyright notice should be included on all work, registered or not. Others feel it's not necessary and a copyright notice will only confuse publishers about whether the material is registered (acquiring rights to previously registered material is a more complicated process).

Although it's not necessary to include a copyright notice on unregistered work, if you don't feel your work is safe without the notice, it's your right to include one. Including a copyright notice—© (year of work, your name)—should help safeguard against plagiarism.

Lawsuits and registration

Registration is a legal formality intended to make copyright public record. Registration can help you win in a court case. By registering work within three months of publication or before an infringement occurs, you are eligible to collect statutory damages and attorney's fees. If you register later than three months after publication, you will qualify only for actual damages and profits.

Ideas and concepts are not copyrightable, only expressions of those ideas and concepts. A character type or basic plot outline, for example, is not subject to a copyright infringement lawsuit. Also, titles, names, short phrases or slogans, and lists of contents are not subject to copyright protection, though titles and names may be protected through the Trademark Office.

You can register a group of articles, illustrations or photos if it meets these criteria:

- the group is assembled in order, such as in a notebook;
- the works bear a single title, such as "Works by (your name)";
- it's the work of one writer, artist or photographer;
- the material is the subject of a single claim to copyright.

It's a publisher's responsibility to register your book for copyright. If you have previously registered the same material, you must inform your editor and supply the previous copyright information, otherwise, the publisher can't register the book in its published form.

Getting the facts and forms

For more information about the proper procedure to register works, contact the Copyright Office, Library of Congress, Washington DC 20359. The forms available are TX for writing (books, articles, etc.); VA for pictures (photographs, illustrations); and PA for plays and music. (To order copyright forms by phone, call (202)707-9100.) For information about how to use the copyright forms, request a copy of Circular I on Copyright Basics. All of the forms and circulars are free. Send the completed registration form along with the stated fee and a copy of the work to the Copyright Office.

For specific answers to questions about copyright (but not legal advice), call the Copyright Public Information Office at (202)707-3000 weekdays between 8:30 a.m. and 5 p.m. EST. Copyright information is also available over the internet. Call the Information Services Referral Desk at (800)444-4354 for a list of providers.

For members of the Society of Children's Book Writers and Illustrators, information about copyrights and the law is available. Send a SASE to SCBWI, 22736 Vanowen St., Suite 106, West Hills CA 91307. Request "Copyright Facts for Writers."

The rights you sell

The copyright law specifies that a writer, illustrator or photographer generally sells one-time rights to her work unless she and the buyer agree otherwise in writing. Many publications will want more exclusive rights to your work than just one-time usage; some will even require you to sell all rights. Be sure you are monetarily compensated for the additional rights you relinquish. If you must give up all rights to a work, carefully consider the price you're being offered to determine whether you'll be compensated for the loss of other potential sales.

Writers who only give up limited rights to their work can then sell reprint rights to other publications, foreign rights to international publications, or even movie rights, should the opportunity arise. Artists and photographers can sell their work to other markets such as paper product companies who may use an image on a calendar, greeting card or mug. Illustrators and photographers may even sell original work after it has been published. And there are now galleries throughout the U.S. that display the work of children's illustrators.

Rights acquired through the sale of a book manuscript are explained in each publisher's contract. Take time to read relevant clauses to be sure you understand what rights each contract is specifying before signing. Be sure your contract contains a clause allowing all rights to revert back to you in the event the publisher goes out of business.

The following are the rights you'll most often be selling to publishers, periodicals and producers in the marketplace:

- **One-time rights.** The buyer has no guarantee that she is the first to use a piece. One-time permission to run written work, illustrations or photos is acquired, then the rights revert back to the creator.
- **First rights.** The creator sells the rights to use the work for the first time in any medium. All other rights remain with the creator. When material is excerpted from a soon-to-be-published book for use in a newspaper or periodical, first serial rights are also purchased.
- **First North American serial rights.** This is similar to first rights, except that companies who distribute both in the U.S. and Canada will stipulate these rights to ensure that a company in the other country won't come out with simultaneous usage of the same work.

- **Second serial (reprint) rights.** In this case newspapers and magazines are granted the right to reproduce a work that has already appeared in another publication. These rights are also purchased by a newspaper or magazine editor who wants to publish part of a book after the book has been published. The proceeds from reprint rights for a book are often split 50/50 between the author and his publishing company.
- **Simultaneous rights.** More than one publication buys one-time rights to the same work at the same time. Use of such rights occurs among magazines with circulations that don't overlap, such as many religious publications.
- **All rights.** Just as it sounds, the writer, illustrator or photographer relinquishes all rights to a piece—she no longer has any say in who acquires rights to use it. All rights are purchased by publishers who pay premium usage fees, have an exclusive format, or have other book or magazine interests from which the purchased work can generate more mileage. If a market insists on acquiring all rights to your work, see if you can negotiate for the rights to revert back to you after a reasonable period of time. If they agree to such a proposal, get it in writing.
- **Foreign serial rights.** Be sure before you market to foreign publications that you have sold only North American—not worldwide—serial rights to previous markets. If so, you are free to market to publications that may be interested in material that's appeared in a North American-based periodical.
- **Syndication rights.** This is a division of serial rights. For example, if a syndicate prints portions of a book in installments in its newspapers, it would be syndicating second serial rights. The syndicate would receive a commission and leave the remainder to be split between the author and publisher.
- **Subsidiary rights.** These include serial rights, dramatic rights, book club rights or translation rights. The contract should specify what percentage of profits from sales of these rights go to the author and publisher.
- **Dramatic, television and motion picture rights.** During a specified time the interested party tries to sell a story to a producer or director. Many times options are renewed because the selling process can be lengthy.
- **Display rights.** They're also known as "Electronic Publishing Rights" or "Data, Storage and Retrieval." Usually listed under subsidiary rights, they're not clearly spelled out and may refer to means of publication not yet fully developed. If a display rights clause is listed in your contract, it's a good idea to try to negotiate its elimination. Otherwise, demand the clause be restricted to things designed to be read only. By doing this, you maintain your rights to use your work for things such as games and interactive software.

A final note: Writers, illustrators and photographers should be wary of "work-for-hire" arrangements. If you sign an agreement stipulating that your work will be done as work for hire, you will not control the copyright of the completed work—the company that hired you will be the copyright owner.

Business Basics

An important part of being a freelance writer, illustrator or photographer is running your freelance business. It's imperative you maintain accurate business records to determine if you're making a profit as a freelancer. Keeping correct, organized records will also make your life easier as you approach tax time.

When setting up your system, begin by keeping a bank account and ledger for your business finances apart from your personal finances. Also, if writing, illustrating or photography is secondary to another freelance career, keep separate business records for each.

You will likely accumulate some business expenses before showing any profit when you start out as a freelancer. To substantiate your income and expenses to the IRS, keep all invoices, cash receipts, sales slips, bank statements, canceled checks and receipts related to travel expenses and entertaining clients. For entertainment expenditures, record the date, place and purpose of the business meeting as well as gas mileage. Keep records for all purchases, big and small—don't take the small purchases for granted; they can add up to a substantial amount.

File all receipts in chronological order. Maintaining a separate file for each month simplifies retrieving records at the end of the year.

Keeping the books

When setting up a single-entry bookkeeping system, record income and expenses separately. Use some of the subheads that appear on Schedule C (the form used for recording income from a business) of the 1040 tax form so you can easily transfer information onto the tax form when filing your return. In your ledger include a description of each transaction—the date, source of income (or debts from business purchases), description of what was purchased or sold, the amount of the transaction, and whether payment was by cash, check or credit card.

Don't wait until January 1 to start keeping records. The moment you first make a business-related purchase or sell an article, book manuscript, illustration or photo, begin tracking your profits and losses. If you keep records from January 1 to December 31, you're using a calendar-year accounting period. Any other accounting period is called a fiscal year.

There are two types of accounting methods you can choose from—the cash method and the accrual method. The cash method is used more often: You record income when it is received and expenses when they're disbursed.

Using the accrual method, you report income at the time you earn it rather than when it's actually received. Similarly, expenses are recorded at the time they're incurred rather than when you actually pay them. If you choose this method, keep separate records for "accounts receivable" and "accounts payable."

Those inevitable taxes

To successfully—and legally—work as a freelancer, you must know what income you should report and what deductions you can claim. But before you can do that, you must prove to the IRS you're in business to make a profit, that your writing, illustrating or photography is not merely a hobby.

The Tax Reform Act of 1986 says you should show a profit for three years out of a five-year period to attain professional status. The IRS considers these factors as proof of your professionalism:

- accurate financial records;
- a business bank account separate from your personal account;
- proven time devoted to your profession;
- whether it's your main or secondary source of income;
- your history of profits and losses;
- the amount of training you have invested in your field;
- your expertise.

If your business is unincorporated, you'll fill out tax information on Schedule C of Form 1040. If you're unsure of what deductions you can take, request the IRS publication containing this information. Under the Tax Reform Act, only 30 percent of business meals, entertainment and related tips, and parking charges are deductible. Other deductible expenses allowed on Schedule C include: car expenses for business-related trips; professional courses and seminars; depreciation of office equipment, such as a computer; dues and publications; and miscellaneous expenses, such as postage used for business needs.

If you're working out of a home office, a portion of your mortgage interest (or rent), related utilities, property taxes, repair costs and depreciation may be deducted as business expenses—under special circumstances. To learn more about the possibility of home office deductions, consult IRS Publication 387, Business Use of Your Home.

The method of paying taxes on income not subject to withholding is called "estimated tax" for individuals. If you expect to owe more than $500 at year's end and if the total amount of income tax that will be withheld during the year will be less than 90% of the tax shown on the current year's return, you'll generally make estimated tax payments. Estimated tax payments are made in four equal installments due on April 15, June 15, September 15 and January 15 (assuming you're a calendar-year taxpayer). For more information, request Publication 505, Self-Employment Tax.

Social Security tax

Depending on your net income as a freelancer, you may be liable for a Social Security tax. This is a tax designed for those who don't have Social Security withheld from their paychecks. You're liable if your net income is $400 or more per year. Net income is the difference between your income and allowable business deductions. Request Schedule SE, Computation of Social Security Self-Employment Tax, if you qualify.

If completing your income tax return proves to be too complex, consider hiring an accountant (the fee is a deductible business expense) or contact the IRS for assistance (look in the White Pages under U.S. Government—Internal Revenue Service). In addition to numerous publications to instruct you in various facets of preparing a tax return, the IRS also has walk-in centers in some cities.

Getting insurance

As a self-employed professional be aware of what health and business insurance coverage is available to you. Unless you're a Canadian who is covered by national health insurance or a fulltime freelancer covered by your spouse's policy, health insurance will no doubt be one of your biggest expenses. Under the terms of a 1985 government act (COBRA), if you leave a job with health benefits, you're entitled to continue that coverage for up to 18 months—you pay 100 percent of the premium and sometimes a small administration fee.

Eventually, you must search for your own health plan. You may also need disability and life insurance. Disability insurance is offered through many private insurance companies and state governments. This insurance pays a monthly fee that covers living and business expenses during periods of long-term recuperation from a health problem. The amount of money paid is based on the recipient's annual earnings.

Before contacting any insurance representative, talk to other writers, illustrators or photographers to find which insurance companies they recommend. If you belong to a writers' or artists' organization, ask the organization if it offers insurance coverage for professionals. (SCBWI has a plan available. Look through the Clubs & Organizations section for other groups that may offer coverage.) Group coverage may prove less expensive and provide more comprehensive coverage than an individual policy.

Telling Tales From Around the World: An Interview with Eric Kimmel

by Alice P. Buening

In his line of work, Eric Kimmel often employs props. He'll tote a tambourine, miniature tools, his banjo—whatever it takes to keep an audience's attention. He wants them to listen to the story he's telling.

His calling as a storyteller has led him to travel throughout the United States. He's even taken to having a few of his tales published (more than 30 at last count). Among his books are fairytales and folktales gathered from all over the world. His first picture book for Holiday House was an African tale, *Anansi and the Moss-Covered Rock*, illustrated by Janet Stevens (1988). He's adapted tales from the Brothers Grimm such as *The Four Gallant Sisters*, illustrated by Tatyana Yuditskaya (Henry Holt, 1992). He's written several Hanukkah tales including Caldecott Honor Book *Hershel and the Hanukkah Goblins*, illustrated by Trina Schart Hyman (Holiday House, 1989). He's found Mexican, Japanese, Middle Eastern, Hungarian and Norwegian stories, among others, to adapt and retell in picture books. He's written chapter books including *I-know-not-what, I-know-not-where: a Russian Tale*, illustrated by Robert Sauber (Holiday House, 1990). He's even written a novel, *One Good Tern Deserves Another* (Holiday House, 1994).

But Kimmel isn't a "multicultural" author—he's simply a storyteller. The versions he writes are his own unique takes on traditional tales, most of which have been around for centuries, changing as they are told from generation to generation, culture to culture. For instance, he'll rewrite Grimm verse, which can be "horribly clunky" in translation from the original German, to more pleasing, rhythmic English. That's what Kimmel finds so exciting about telling stories. "It allows me to add something of myself to each story, just as each story adds something of itself to me."

Most recently, Kimmel has retold *The Adventures of Hershel of Ostropol*, a follow-up to his first Hershel book, as well as *The Goose Girl*, one of the author's favorite childhood stories from the Brothers Grimm (both Holiday House, 1995, illustrated by Hyman and Sauber respectively). And there are others on the horizon.

In what follows, the author/storyteller shares the story of how he broke into publishing. He talks about finding stories, starting in the magazine market, and writing picture books, and gives advice to children's writers who want to get published.

How did you develop your love of stories? What led you to tell and write them?

It goes back to when I was very young, even before school. My grandma lived with us and I spent a lot of time with her. She was from Eastern Europe and she loved to tell stories about all kinds of things. Some were Bible stories, some were folktales, some were stories about herself. I have lots of memories of just lying on the floor or sitting in the garden pulling weeds listening to her. Years later, I discovered that this was something they call storytelling—they actually teach courses in it.

One of my favorite books was *Grimm's Fairy Tales*. In fact, a friend of our family picked up three astonishingly wonderful books for me at an American Legion yard sale for almost nothing. One was the Grosset Junior Illustrated Library edition of *Grimm's Fairy Tales* with Fritz Kredel illustrations, another was the Grosset *Hans Christian Andersen's Fairy Tales* with Arthur Szyk illustrations, and this incredible two-volume version of the King James Bible with Jacques Tissot paintings. It was like opening up a whole world. I was about seven or eight at the time so I was old enough to read. I would go through the Tissot Bible or the story collections and I'd see these strange and wonderful pictures. I wanted to know what the story was. I think that started a lifelong love of stories. I read that *Grimm* until it fell apart.

When I was a graduate student at the University of Illinois, there was a class in storytelling. And I thought, why not take it? It was a wonderful class with a wonderful instructor, and she took us all over the place [to tell stories]. Really, that's all there is to storytelling—you find a group and you tell them some stories. If they sit still through the whole thing you did pretty well.

As for writing stories, I always wanted to be an author. Again that goes back very, very early. My inspiration was Dr. Seuss. I didn't care about Mickey Mouse—give me Seuss! And this was classic Seuss—not *The Cat in the Hat*, but *Horton Hatches the Egg*, a wonderful book! I wanted to hear it again and again and again. A teacher pointed out that there really is a man named Dr. Seuss who writes books. People who do that are authors—they get their names on the front of books. And I thought, "Oh that's wonderful! I want that." And that's really all I ever wanted to be. But I never knew that I wanted to write for kids.

Then how did you come to be a children's author?

It's funny. Every writer and artist I know tells the same story—they just kind of blunder into it. And so did I. I started to write after college. I didn't know any more about writing than I read in *Writer's Market* or *Writer's Digest*. That's where everybody begins. You go to the library: "Got anything about writing?" and they give you that book and those journals. You read the chapters and say "Oh, I can do that." But you have no idea how difficult it is. Writers are kind of like sailors in the time of Columbus—we set sail, but we don't know where we're going or what we're doing—and we just land somewhere.

When I started I wrote everything. I started writing for magazines, and wrote mysteries, cowboy stories, science fiction, sex stories for men's magazines, even true romance stories. I was actually getting pretty good at those—the editors were starting to write back and give me critiques. I tell kids, maybe if I kept it up, I could've been the queen of Harlequin Romance.

But one day my mother sent me an ad—Harper & Row was looking for people to write children's books. I was teaching and working in the children's room of the public library, so I thought why not try it? They didn't accept what I had ultimately sent them, but they were encouraging so I kept doing it. And I found I liked it. It's like you find a glove that fits your hand, and this was it. Since then I've never wanted to do anything other than children's books, and I really never have.

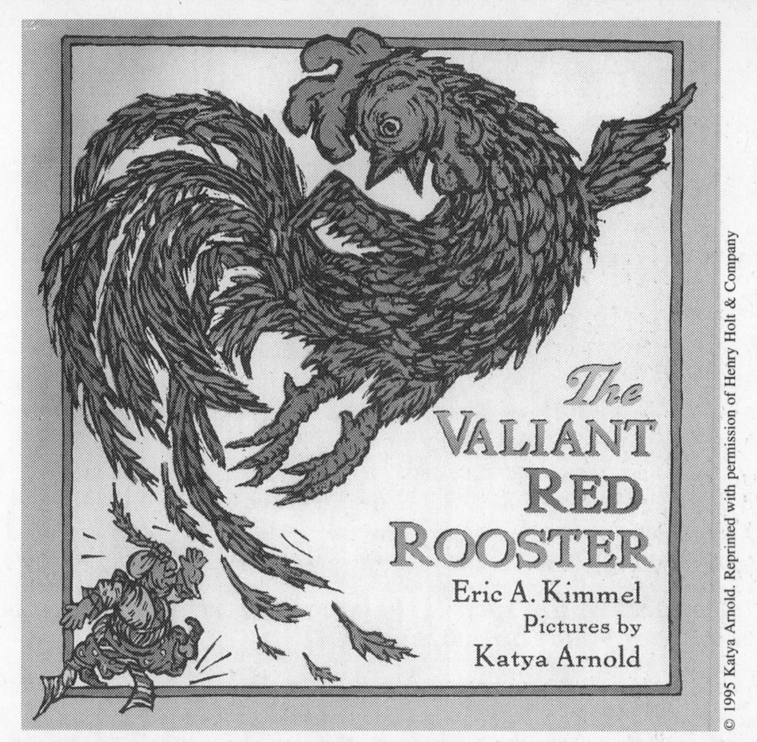

Kimmel retells a Hungarian tale of a hungry rooster, a greedy sultan, and a diamond button in* The Valiant Red Rooster *(Henry Holt & Co., 1995), boldly illustrated by Russian artist Katya Arnold. His retelling is full of fun phrases (great for reading aloud) like Red Rooster's screech "ku-keri-keri" and the oft repeated rhythmic names of the sultan's court, "the bondarjis, the sipahis, and the bashi-bazouks." Other versions of this story can be found throughout Europe, such as the Spanish tale "Medio Pollito" ("Half Chicken").

You had a few books published in the early '70s, then about 30 or so starting in the late '80s. Why the big gap?

The big gap wasn't because of me. I didn't stop writing, I just stopped publishing. I was limping along in those early years. I might get one book in print then a year or two would go by and somebody would buy another one. None of them did very well, the reviews were mediocre, and the books sank like rocks.

Finally by 1985, the only person that was keeping me going was Marianne Carus at *Cricket Magazine*. She was always encouraging and would always buy a story or an article and ask for more. I really wouldn't have a career in children's publishing today if it wasn't for *Cricket*.

So you think the magazine market is a good place to start?

Magazines are a great market. The competition is less ferocious because you're not competing with the established people. Most magazines don't pay enough for a writer like myself to want to write for them with the exception of *Cricket*, *Highlights* and a couple of others. It's a wide open field for people who are beginning.

Also, writing for magazines is great practice in learning how to work with an editor, how to revise a manuscript, how to get it in shape for publication. When editors say the story has to be 1,800 words, they mean 1,800—not 1,801. That takes practice, too. So when you submit a book manuscript, you can say "I have published stories in

Cricket, *Highlights* and *Jack and Jill*," and that means a lot to editors because they know they're not dealing with a rank amateur. That's a plus.

How then did you finally start to have books published again?

I was at the point where I was so sick of rejections and discouraged, I thought I was going nowhere. I put 15 years in—how much longer was I going to do this? Ah, maybe I'll just hang it up, find something else to do with my time. This lasted for about three months, then my fingers started to itch; I started to think about things I'd like to do. This was one of those moments of revelation, and really writing is essentially a process of self-discovery. I thought to myself, "You were meant to be a writer. You were put on this earth to write stories. Maybe you weren't meant to be a successful one, but you were meant to write them." So I decided to just keep writing them and sending them out, and if they came back, so what?

That was the moment I got a letter from Holiday House accepting *Hershel and the Hanukkah Goblins*, which had previously appeared in *Cricket*. It's been since I hooked up with Holiday House that I've had a career [in children's book publishing]. *Hershel* was a Caldecott honor book and then Anansi the spider came along—and I had a career. I was at the point of giving up and suddenly everything fell into place.

What are some of the special challenges in writing picture books, which most of your books have been?

Most people, when they decide they want to be a children's writer, start with picture books. That's like saying "I want to be a poet, so I'll start writing sonnets because they are short." Picture books are short, but they're also very compact. And you have to write a story around illustrations that aren't even there yet. You have to assume that a lot of what's important in telling the story is going to be portrayed by the pictures. The text for a good picture book is almost like a Chinese painting. The empty space—what you don't write—is just as important as what you do.

When I write, usually the longest draft is the first. Then it's a process of cutting it down, cutting it down, cutting it down and throwing away, until I'm down to the core of a story, and everything that's there is essential. You're laying the foundation for the rest of the building. An author doesn't see the illustrations until the book is finished. Often artists come up with things I would never have thought of.

The editor is very important to the process [of writing a picture book]. You can work on a manuscript and refine it up to a certain point, then you really need somebody who stands outside to give you a critique. I think that's one of the things that goes into making you a better writer, as you get that sense of what makes a manuscript very strong.

How do you decide, from all of the stories you've heard and read, which would make good books?

A story has to grab me. Sometimes in criticism I've been introduced as Eric Kimmel, a multicultural author, and I'm really not. Because when you're in the multicultural bag, it's that Andy Warhol world where every culture gets 15 minutes. "I did a Serbian story, now I have to do a Croatian story. I did one for the Romanians; I have to do one for the Ukranians," and so on. You end up with a grab bag of stories—good, bad and indifferent. I don't go by that. I like good stories from all over the world and I don't care where they come from, because stories are international.

If a story is good, then it speaks to me. I may understand the story differently than somebody in the culture, but I definitely understand it in a unique way. The story clicks with me, it makes me laugh, or it has an image that I really like. But what it comes

What do you get when you add a touch of Halloween—in the form of a bunch of ugly, mean-spirited goblins—to a Hanukkah story? Kimmel came up with **Hershel and the Hanukkah Goblins** ***(Holiday House, 1985), the tale of a sad town that can't celebrate Hanukkah because of the nasties haunting its synagogue. Hershel, the hero, outsmarts the fang-laden, sharp-clawed, anti-holiday fellows, brought to life by both Kimmel's text and the Caldecott-Honor-winning illustrations of Trina Schart Hyman.*** **Hershel,** ***Kimmel's first book for Holiday House, first appeared in*** **Cricket Magazine. The Adventures of Hershel of Ostropol,** ***another adventure featuring the popular character (also illustrated by Hyman) was released by Holiday House in September 1995.***

down to is this is a story that I would have liked to have read to me when I was a kid. I think in a lot of ways I and many of the other children's authors and illustrators I know are still big kids—we never grow up. Who wants to be a grown-up? Grown-ups are so dull and solemn. I haven't read anything in 30 years that didn't have pictures.

Where do all the stories come from?

I collect volumes of folktales from around the world. I may find I like the beginning of one, but the end of another, so I put them together. I do a lot of mixing and matching. Sometimes I don't even remember where they come from. To phrase it in terms of playing the banjo, you have a tune with a little gap that you'd like to fill, so you throw in a lick from something else and it works. As long as it's in the proper measure, you can get away with it. That's what I do with a fairytale. I have a hole in the story and I fill it.

What do you say to critics who dislike your changing traditional stories?

I don't think the story is static—it's fluid. You can tell the same story 50 times and it will be different every time. Storytellers, before things were written down, would wander from village to village and they did whatever they had to to hold their audience. If I want to change a story, then I do it. That may not be kosher from a folklore point of view, but then, I'm not a folklorist. I'm just a storyteller. The only thing that counts is the story. And since the story is being told to kids, they're the important audience.

If someone gets upset, then I know that person is not a storyteller. Yes, you should be true to a story if you retell it—but you should be true to the spirit of the story rather than the details. A story is changed forever as it's passed from one culture to another, that's why you have the same stories all over the world. What's the original *Cinderella*? You can't find it. If you open up *Grimm's Fairy Tales* and point to the story there, I say "No. That's the version the Grimm Brothers wrote down." Had they gone down the road and talked to another person, or had they lived 100 years earlier, they might have written another version. The original version is lost. It probably goes back to those cave paintings they found in France.

It's like this whole tapestry to which generations and generations of people have added a stitch, and I'm the latest in the chain. Thousands of people have told this story before me, now I'm telling it. This is the Eric Kimmel version. If you like it, take it. If you don't like it, change it. I'm not writing for academics or folklorists or professors, I'm writing for kids and my job is to tell a story that kids will listen to.

In the beginning of **Boots and His Brothers** *(Holiday House, 1992) you included a note explaining that the ax and spade in the story are tiny because you found tiny tools in a store that you used when telling the story. Does the way you verbally tell a story often have an effect on what you end up writing?*

More and more lately I've been coming to think that stories have less to do with literature and more to do with music. It's not like really singing the performance, but the story has definite rhythms. When you tell a story you're conscious of those rhythms; you see it in your audience. You build them up to a peak and then you bring them down with the ending.

Iron John, a story Kimmel first read as an eight-year-old, was adapted from the Brothers Grimm, a major source of inspiration for the author. In his adaptation, Kimmel changed the story considerably from Grimm's version, including cutting the lengthy tale to suit a picture book, and naming Grimm's characters. He even revamped the ending. In Kimmel's version, Walter the prince marries Elsa the garden girl instead of the princess. "I always resented the idea that a princess who despised the hero when he was poor would love him when he became rich," Kimmel explains. "Fie on princesses. Elsa loves Walter truly so she will have him." Trina Schart Hyman illustrated the tale, her first foray using oil paint for a picture book.

When I tell *Anansi and the Moss-Covered Rock*, I use a tambourine and that's the "KPOM!" in the story. "KPOM! Everything went black. Down fell Anasi, senseless." When you're reading a story, you don't have a tambourine, so the writer has to convey that experience through the written word. In one sense, the artist fleshes out the tale with pictures, and when I'm telling it, I flesh it out with words. When I tell my stories, I don't show pictures. I just say to the kids, "You can see it in your own mind."

A lot of artists draw [at appearances]. That's something kids love. But I can't draw. I can't sing. I tell stories, or I play my banjo a little bit. You do whatever you can to keep them interested.

So you're a traveling, banjo-playing storyteller?

I'm just a minstrel show! I have the banjo; I have a tambourine. I bring my laptop; we write a little bit. I do all kinds of stuff, and I have a great time with it.

How important is it that kids hear stories?

Oh, I think it's enormously important because they don't do enough of it. I was formerly a professor of education at Portland State, so I'm very interested in educational issues. Schools are 19th century places in the 20th century. What's most important in the world of kids and teenagers? Video, film and music. Yet studying music, studying the arts, is regarded as frills. Kids spend much more of their time visually and orally than they do literarily.

If a book wins a Caldecott or a Newbery they say that it's guaranteed to sell something like 100,000 copies. In the video, Nintendo and CD business, 100,000 is a flop. Children's books is a funny area. Everything relating to children and teenagers generates millions of dollars in profits, except for books. I think we're coming to a generation that, for one reason or another, does not read anymore.

The world is changing. It's going back to what it used to be. People learned by seeing and hearing and expressed themselves in these ways rather than in the printed word. Remember, the printed word was a revolution when it came along. First the printing press then universal literacy. Now everybody's got a computer and video camera. I don't necessarily think the future includes the book as we know it, which would be a great tragedy.

We are on the cusp of some very profound changes—I think everybody in publishing realizes this. When you negotiate a contract, holding onto electronic rights is a very important issue. It doesn't necessarily include CDs, video tape and computer applications, but technology that hasn't even been invented yet. These are interesting times, for better or worse.

In these interesting times, what would you say to someone who wants to be a children's book author?

First of all, you have to understand that this is a ferociously competitive business. A lot of people start writing children's books because they think it's easy. They don't think they have the talent or perseverance to write an adult novel, but anybody can knock out a children's book. Well, not anybody can. If you want to do them, you have to understand that you're in competition not just with everybody else who's trying to get a book published, but with all the established people, too. If a publisher publishes 20 or 30 books a year, two or three of those slots might be open to a newcomer. And a publisher will receive 6,000 to 7,000 unsolicited manuscripts a year, so figure what your chances are.

There's a great saying that I've always remembered: "It's not good enough to be as good as somebody else. You've got to be better." You've got to be the author that only you can be. And that means giving 110 percent of your effort for years. It was 15 years before I got anywhere and I almost gave up.

Actually, I think it's easier to spend years paying your dues than to have instant success. With an instant success, you hear "Oh, well now come up with another one." But you don't even know how you did the first one. When the door finally opened for me, I had lots of stuff written. The editor wanted to see more—boy, I had files of it.

Also, I'd known the business, been involved in it for years. So when the door opened, I could walk through. Just like in the music business, they say a lot of people can have one hit, but the real trick is having two or three. So for a beginning writer, it's very difficult. You've got to give it everything you've got and be prepared to write for the long run.

A mistake many beginning writers make is they write one story then they wait for it to get into print. Well, if you do get into print, it might not be your first manuscript, it might be your tenth. This is a business where success comes through persistence and volume. The more things you have out there, the more possibilities are open.

Anansi and the Talking Melon ***is Kimmel's third book telling the adventures of trickster Anansi the spider, a character from African folklore. In this book readers find him toying with a gullible elephant, hippo and warthog, among other jungle dwellers, delightfully illustrated by Janet Stevens. The spider crawls through a hole in a melon, eats more than his fill, and gets stuck, then passes the time fooling the animals into thinking they found a talking melon, which they set out to present to the king.*** **Anansi and the Talking Melon** ***first appeared in*** **Spider.**

The question I would ask of someone who wants to write children's books is "Why?" If the answer is "Well, I hear it's easier to get into print," or "I hear you can make a lot of money," these are wrong answers. Would you still do it if I could tell you you're not going to get into print ever? Would you still do it if you're not going to make a dime at it? A committed writer will say "Yes, because I've got these stories that I have to write. I need to write them." The others will try for a while and then they'll go away.

First Books

by Christine Martin

Thousands of people dream of writing or illustrating children's books. But many refrain from pursuing those dreams because they're afraid they will never get their work published. Here are four individuals who not only always wanted to create children's books, but whose dedicated pursuit of their dreams has led them to see their books on store shelves. They say that, with a little hard work, dreams do come true.

Shelley Moore Thomas

Putting the World to Sleep (Houghton Mifflin Co.)

Shelley Moore Thomas, an elementary school teacher in Albuquerque, New Mexico, wanted to write for children most of her life. In fact, it was in fourth grade that she began writing a book. But it wasn't until the summer of 1987, when she attended a branch of the National Writing Project, that she began to write on a fairly regular basis.

© James Daniels

The National Writing Project, a program in which teachers can learn to improve their students' writing by improving their own, proved to be just what Thomas needed. She not only realized how much she loved writing but she discovered her own voice—and a strong desire to submit her work for publication. Then she had two children of her own and says, "what I gained in experience I lost in time."

Yet Thomas remained committed. By carrying her writing book everywhere, she kept "stealing" moments in which to write. Then, in the summer of 1993, the purchase of a computer made thoughts of submitting her work resurface. "I decided I should just send off the stuff I liked—maybe someone else would like it too," she says. "And if nobody liked it, well, at least I had fun writing it!"

Though Thomas had five manuscripts by that time, she says she was "completely clueless" about how to submit them for publication. So she purchased *Children's Writer's & Illustrator's Market*. "I read it cover to cover, highlighted publishers who I thought might like my writing, and bought a big box of envelopes and lots of stamps." Then she started submitting—learning about the different publishers as she sent different pieces to different places.

While shuffling her work from one publisher to the next, Thomas got the idea for her sixth manuscript. It came as she was putting her older daughter, Noel, to bed one night. "We had listened to some tape about bears going to bed for about the zillionth time and were making up our own little songs. We sang about 'putting Noel to sleep'

Christine Martin *is editor of* Poet's Market, *and former editor of* Children's Writer's & Illustrator's Market. *She also wrote the interview of children's poet J. Patrick Lewis on page 48 of this edition.*

and 'putting Mommy to sleep' and, finally, 'putting the whole world to sleep.' I liked the idea of 'putting the world to sleep' so I wrote it in my writing book."

She played with that phrase for about two weeks and then wrote a very gentle, *House that Jack Built* type story, one in which old phrases are repeated as new details are added. It begins: "The moon climbs over the mountain each night, putting the world to sleep. The crickets start singing farewell to the day, as the moon climbs over the mountain each night, putting the world to sleep." The bedtime story continues as the stars shine, darkness falls, the fireplace glows, a big dog lounges, a mommy hums a lullaby, and a baby yawns.

Once the manuscript was finished, Thomas thumbed through *Children's Writer's & Illustrator's Market* looking for a publisher. When her eyes stopped at Houghton Mifflin, she read the editor's name, liked it, and sent the editor, Matilda Welter, her manuscript. Though Thomas admits that her method was less than scientific, she says, "I figured it would take a while to be published, if it ever did happen. So, I thought I would probably end up sending something to every publisher eventually."

As it turned out, Thomas was pleasantly surprised. In December of 1993, she received a letter from Houghton Mifflin asking if they could hold the manuscript for a while. In February of 1994, she got another letter saying they would like to publish the book but needed to find an artist. The next month Vermont-based illustrator Bonnie Christensen was contacted and by spring the contract was signed. A year later Thomas got her first look at the full-color illustrations, and *Putting the World to Sleep* was finally published in the fall of 1995.

Shelley Moore Thomas got inspiration for her first book as she put her daughter to bed one evening—they were tired of the same old bedtime stories and began to make up their own. Their efforts evolved into the picture book* Putting the World to Sleep, *illustrated by Bonnie Christensen. Thomas's text begins with one sentence which is added to and added to as the story progresses, creating soothing repetition for drowsy young readers.

Looking back, Thomas remembers her husband predicting that, because of its simplicity, *Putting the World to Sleep* would be the first manuscript to sell. And while he was right, and she is delighted to have one of her manuscripts published, she has not given up on the others. In fact, they are still being considered by publishers. But whatever happens, Thomas knows there's little chance she'll stop writing.

"I write; that's what I do. The best advice I would give would be to write because you like to write, *not* because you want to be 'published.' If you love *writing*, you will never quit. If you only dream of getting published, you will get discouraged and possibly quit. And as golf instructor Harvey Penick once wrote, you have to give luck a chance to work for you. You have to try—and you have to keep trying."

Shelley Jackson
Great-Aunt Martha (Dutton Children's Books)

© Caroline Janiak

"There was never a time when I didn't make pictures," says Shelley Jackson. "As little kids my sister and I would spread out paper on the dining room table and tell each other stories while we drew pictures of what we were talking about—pirate girls steering ships, knight girls laying siege to castles. My parents kept me in pencils, crayons and paints. As a child it was one way of playing."

As Jackson grew older, she continued to enjoy drawing and began to train her eyes and hands. By the time she went off to Stanford University to major in studio art, she had already spent hours "doing drawing after drawing from life, most of them of sleeping dogs and my sisterreading—the only subjects I could get to hold still for me!"

While she was making charcoal drawings of semi-abstracted human figures in her classes at Stanford, she also started writing and began to experience what she calls "the first yanks of the tug-of-war between pictures and words." A few years later her determination to persist in a fine art career was foundering, partly because she was more and more serious about writing—and she wanted to do both.

Then Jackson realized there *were* people who made a living pursuing both writing and art: children's book authors who drew their own illustrations. The answer, then, was to enter that field. To prepare herself, she took a children's book illustration class with Daniel San Souci and began to put together a portfolio while working at a used bookstore. As luck would have it, she also managed to obtain an agent.

"Meeting Kendra Marcus was a combination of chance and a moment of daring on my part," Jackson says. "I had brought one of my drawings to the bookstore with me to show my friend and co-worker. I stopped to ring up a sale and recognized the customer's name from his check. It was Robert D. San Souci, the brother of my teacher and a children's book writer himself. I introduced myself and asked somewhat brazenly if he wanted to see one of my drawings. He kindly said yes and gave me some encouragement, and with it Kendra's name and address."

After reviewing some of her work, Marcus agreed to represent Jackson and requested a few more drawings to take around to publishers. Shortly thereafter, Jackson received her first illustration project, a chapter book about a little girl in Zimbabwe, entitled *Do You Know Me*, written by Nancy Farmer (Orchard Books, 1993). Jackson created the color cover and a pencil illustration for each chapter. At the same time she started studying creative writing in graduate school at Brown University.

Then while still in school, Jackson was contacted by Dutton regarding *Great-Aunt Martha*, a story written by Rebecca C. Jones about a young girl whose life becomes restricted—no television or playing with the dog, for instance—because her great-aunt is visiting and "needed her rest." As it turns out, much to the delight of the young girl, Great-Aunt Martha doesn't want to rest.

Since Jackson viewed her own grandmothers as "energetic, sometimes uproarious people with many interests," she found the story particularly appealing but wondered whether she was the right illustrator for the project. "I saw myself illustrating moodier or more fantastical stories. What they saw in my work was its playfulness and the expressive looks and gestures of my characters."

Of course, Jackson accepted the offer, and because *Great-Aunt Martha* was her first picture book, she worked very closely with the art director. First she created a rather finished dummy in black and white. Then, after making revisions, she created color illustrations, one after another, in Caran D'ache crayons, which are soft enough to blend, but hard enough to make a clean line.

"*Great-Aunt Martha* called up a fairly realistic style. Even in my most realistic drawings, though, I want to surprise the eye with lively compositions or unexpected angles," Jackson says. "I can't speak for children in general, but I know that as a child I spent a lot of time both on top of very high things and way down under low things, checking out how the world looked from there. I thought grown-ups were missing a lot by staying planted on solid ground."

In Great-Aunt Martha, *Shelley Jackson's first foray into picture book illustration, the artist employs lively compositions, unusual angles and expressive faces to give life to young girl and her family as they are visited by her great-aunt. Rebecca C. Jones's story ends as the girl realizes that Aunt Martha is fun and lively (not the drag she expected her to be) as Jackson depicts the whole crew kicking up their heels with their energetic elder.*

Though the project took about two years—"in which spurts of intense hard work alternated with periods of waiting for feedback"—when *Great-Aunt Martha* was published in the fall of 1995, *The Horn Book Magazine* noted the "strong, stylized illustrations that successfully play with perspective." And *Publishers Weekly* said "her characters' expressive faces convincingly move from frustration to jubilation."

In many respects Jackson, who now resides in San Francisco, California, and works in another used bookstore, is well on her way to fulfilling her dream. She is currently finishing the illustrations for her second picture book, *Willie's Silly Grandma* by Cynthia DeFelice, to be published by Orchard Books in 1996. Next, she will create the illustrations for the first picture book she has written herself, tentatively titled *The Old Woman and the Wave* and also scheduled to be published by Orchard.

Throughout, Jackson says she found *Writing With Pictures*, by Uri Shulevitz, to be a very useful general guide but recommends reading picture books. "Read them like a child before anything else, with your heart and your imagination, as if you were watching something not made by craft but born and running wild. Then read them again like a writer, like an illustrator, slantwise, with an eye to how and why they were made. Then, draw like crazy," she says. "The absolute best advice I've ever been given: Be willing to throw away anything. The permission to blithely make horrible mistakes is the one best guarantee that you won't stifle your own imagination out of fear that it will embarrass you. Few people fail by risking too much."

Karen Cushman
Catherine, Called Birdy (Clarion Books)

© Herrington-Olson Photography

Though Karen Cushman began writing at a very young age, it took her more than 50 years to become a writer, and while her path to publication seems easy, it's only because she did a lot of work beforehand. "As long as I can remember I was writing things," Cushman says. "I didn't exactly know what a writer did, or what a writer was, but I was writing. I have some fragments of poems and plays and things that I wrote when I was six, seven, eight. I was born in a working-class family, and writing wasn't really something to aspire to as a profession. It was always something I did kind of separately."

In fact, when Cushman won a scholarship to college, she didn't think of majoring in creative writing. She graduated with a combined degree in Greek and English. Later she received a Master's in Human Behavior and, after that, one in Museum Studies. Except for some writing and editing of the museum studies journal, writing fell by the wayside as Cushman became a teacher in the Museum Studies Department at John F. Kennedy University in the San Francisco Bay Area.

Eventually thoughts of writing resurged and Cushman, who lives in Oakland, California, began occasionally attending meetings of children's book writers. "I didn't do much writing at all, but I always had these great ideas and I'd say to my husband, 'Oh, listen, I have a great idea for a children's book.' For some reason, I was always interested in children's books and sometimes the ideas were picture book ideas, sometimes they were nonfiction ideas. But I would tell him and we'd talk about what a great idea it was, and it was like the pressure was off. Once I verbalized it, I didn't have to write it."

That was until a few years ago. Cushman had another idea for a book and asked her husband to listen to it. He refused, saying that when he listened, she didn't write. So he handed her a paper and pencil and told her to write the idea down. When Cushman was done, she had the outline for her first book, *Catherine, Called Birdy*, a work of historical fiction about a teenage girl in medieval England—the daughter of a country knight—who tries to resist being sold as a bride to the highest bidder.

One thing that makes the story interesting is Cushman's use of a diary format, which she got from reading the Adrian Mole books by British writer Sue Townsend. The books are diaries of a contemporary, British teenage boy, and the humor in them is in the difference between how he sees himself and how the books' readers see him, Cushman says. "And I thought that would be very interesting with a historical character."

So, for about three and a half years, Cushman wrote Catherine's story—researching as she went along. "Coming from museum studies, what I really knew was how to look for information and how to use objects, how to find things out about a time [period] from objects, and how to extrapolate from details and specifics. But I had to find out about the Middle Ages." To do so, she did a lot of reading—starting with general history books about the period and using the bibliographies from those to discover books that discussed more of a domestic history.

Once the manuscript was on its way, she called Sandy Boucher, a local writer who runs writing groups, and requested to see her individually. Then after meeting with

***Newbery-Honor-winner* Catherine, Called Birdy, *Karen Cushman's first book, is a witty, delightful story told in charming and honest detail through a 13-year-old girl's fictional diary entries. Catherine, the daughter of a 13th-century country knight, is trying her best to escape an arranged marriage which her father insists upon, as she copes with day-to-day life. Cushman studied medieval English history, especially what ordinary life was like for young people of the time, in preparation for writing* Catherine.**

Cushman's novel* The Midwife's Apprentice, *her follow-up to* Catherine, Called Birdy, *tells the story of a poor, nameless orphan girl in early 14th-century England who's taken in by a sharp-tongued midwife in need of a helper. Through the course of the story, the young waif chooses a name for herself (Alyce) and learns lessons in compassion, as she becomes a midwife in her own right and makes a place for herself in the world. Cushman's third book,* The Ballad of Lucy Whipple, *will be published in 1996.

Boucher a few times, Cushman located a woman through the Society of Children's Book Writers and Illustrators who did manuscript consultation. She sent the woman her manuscript and met with her as well. "But almost more than their help, I really needed some kind of outside reinforcement," she says. The need for professional feedback was just one of a series of tiny steps on the path to publication.

Cushman also heard from people who said she'd never see her manuscript published because historical fiction didn't sell or nobody was interested in the Middle Ages. But Cushman continued to work on her story. "I was writing it whether it got published or not," she says. "I didn't know what would happen, but I thought it was a great idea."

What *did* happen was that, almost by chance, Cushman got an agent. With her husband's help, she found an agent who offered to look at her manuscripts. The agent decided to represent her and gave the text to Dorothy Briley, the editor-in-chief at Clarion, an imprint of Houghton Mifflin. Cushman soon received a publishing contract for her first book.

After some revision, *Catherine, Called Birdy* was published in the spring of 1994 and was named a Newbery Honor book the following year. Cushman's first book was so well received that she has already published a second, and her third is due out this year. *The Midwife's Apprentice*, her follow-up to *Catherine*, the story of a homeless girl who's taken in by a midwife, is also set in medieval England, and was published by Clarion in 1995. *The Ballad of Lucy Whipple*, set in the California gold rush, will by published by Clarion in 1996.

In many ways, Cushman's whole publishing experience has been overwhelming. "It was like I spent the first 50 years of my life getting all this input, and when I felt like I had enough, then I could give it out," she says. "It's not too late [to write]. It's not like us have to go out there and do something that we're physically incapable of doing at 53 or 54. Maybe we're better prepared. I'm beginning to think I couldn't have done it before, and now I can."

Though she still works part-time in the Museum Studies Department, Cushman is committed to writing, however long it takes. "It's not enough in this world to have an idea, even a good idea, about anything. We have to make a commitment, take a stand, write it down. And I think that's true both literally and figuratively about writing—that we make a commitment," she says. "I'm a writer."

Doug Wechsler
Bizarre Bugs (Cobblehill Books)

By the time Doug Wechsler finished the manuscript for his first children's book, he had a publisher quite interested in the project. But the contract fell through. At first it was a disappointment, Wechsler says, but then it became an opportunity to find a publisher who produced better books and offered more favorable terms.

From the start, it was a long journey. Wechsler graduated from Ohio's Oberlin College with a biology degree and went straight to work in the Amazon rain forest, assisting with a study of birds that follow army ants. Afterward, he moved to Seattle, Washington, and began working as a naturalist and, later, a wildlife biologist.

At the same time, Wechsler started writing articles forthe Seattle Audubon Society newsletter. "I proved to myself what my college composition professor probably never would have guessed," he says. "I can be a good writer if motivated by an interesting subject." He was also taking numerous photographs, intending to use them to illustrate nature courses for adults.

Eventually, Wechsler began selling his photographs, beginning with a regional nature magazine. Then he met wildlife photographer Michael Fogden while doing research in Costa Rica and decided to make freelance nature photography a career. After three years, and some nice publication credits, including an article and accompanying photographs in *International Wildlife*, Wechsler opted for a position which allows him to combine both biology and photography.

In 1987, he became Director of Visual Resources for Ornithology (VIREO), the world's largest collection of bird photographs, at The Academy of Natural Sciences of Philadelphia, Pennsylvania. As director, Wechsler oversees the staff, sells photo rights to publishers "for just about any use imaginable," and photographs birds once or twice a year on expeditions to tropical forests.

In his spare time on those expeditions, and during vacations, he photographs other wildlife and continues to sell his photographs, sometimes through stock agencies, sometimes directly to publishers with articles he has written. His work has appeared in hundreds of publications, including children's magazines such as *Chickadee*, *Owl* and, most often, *Ranger Rick*.

Particularly interested in teaching children about nature, Wechsler had long thought about writing and photographing a children's book. In fact, his first thought was to do a book on rain forests—before the subject was so popular. "But by the time I was ready to write, 10 or 20 others were on the market," he says. So Wechsler chose insects, not only because they were one of his own interests (note the praying mantis on his chin) but also because he already had a large collection of insect photos and "it seemed like a logical place to start."

It took Wechsler two months to write the first two chapters, which he submitted with 20 sample photographs (actually duplicate slides) as a proposal to a publisher to whom he had provided photographs from VIREO. Three and a half months later the publisher responded, saying the material looked promising but she needed to see the entire manuscript. Wechsler took a few months to finish the manuscript and the publisher took a few more months to respond—this time requesting revisions.

The publisher wanted more details, more facts, and more explanations, Wechsler says. So he added information and, a few weeks later, was told she wanted to go to contract. "We briefly discussed their proposed advance and royalties, both of which seemed inadequate. This gave me a great deal of concern," he says. "I wrote a two-page letter asking all kinds of questions about where and how the book would be sold, what kind of subsidiary rights they were requesting, how many copies I would get. . . . I soon received word that their research showed it wasn't the time to do a book on this subject."

Not to be discouraged, Wechsler did his own research—to find another publisher. He went to the local nature center and studied the photo-illustrated books in search of a company "who did a nice job of reproducing and laying out photographs in books with informative texts." The publisher Cobblehill fit the bill and, fortunately for Wechsler, he had recently sent photos from VIREO to Rosanne Lauer, an editor there.

In Bizarre Bugs, his first book for kids, photographer/writer Doug Wechsler introduces young readers to the world of some common—and some very unusual—insects. Wechsler's fun, full-color photos are accompanied by facts about the life cycles, feeding habits, and survival techniques of a number of truly odd-looking bugs. He also explains the flashy colors and weird shapes of some of his subjects.

"Having had some contact, I felt comfortable calling to inquire whether she would care to review the text and a selection of the photographs," he says. Lauer did. And, after a few months, Wechsler received a note asking whether he would be willing to make some changes in the manuscript. When he agreed, he then was asked what kind of advance he would like and "suddenly I was glad to have been rejected the first time around."

Ironically, the changes Lauer requested meant deleting much of the detailed information Wechsler had added at the request of the previous publisher. The goal was to simplify the text for a younger age-group. After a year of revisions—and after having the manuscript reviewed by a couple of entomologists—the text was complete and *Bizarre Bugs* was published by Cobblehill in the spring of 1995.

The book takes the idea of the bizarre and uses it to illustrate common themes that are important in biology and that ultimately will be important in conservation, Wechsler says. "Insects are a much maligned group. By presenting some of the most interesting forms from both our backyard and exotic locales I hope to build an appreciation for them and ultimately a better attitude about how we relate to them."

To keep kids interested in the subject, Wechsler not only illustrated the text with numerous, full-color, close-up photographs, but he also incorporated extraordinary facts and a number of visual (and often humorous) references, such as comparing a swarm of army ants to a professional football game. Reading *Ranger Rick*, he says, proved most instructional in terms of how to write nonfiction for kids.

"The real inspiration has been being able to live in the jungle for years and having a lot of access to the natural world," he says. "I think soon after I began writing, I thought seriously about writing a book. I just didn't actually act on it until about ten years later."

Now, Wechsler is at work on a children's book about birds (which will use pictures from VIREO as well as his own photographs) and is collaborating on a children's wetlands book. His advice to other writers is simple: "Don't wait ten years. Start writing now. Start with a subject that means something to you and that you are well-versed in. Produce something you are proud of. Then market it with confidence."

Key to Symbols & Abbreviations

** Symbol indicating a listing is new in this edition*
🍁 *Symbol indicating a listing is Canadian*
■ *Symbol indicating a market subsidy or co-op publishes manuscripts*
‡ *Symbol indicating a contest or organization is open to students*
● *Symbol indicating a comment from the editor of* Children's Writer's & Illustrator's Market
ms *or* **mss** *stands for manuscript or manuscripts.*
SASE *refers to a self-addressed stamped envelope.*
SAE *refers to a self-addressed envelope.*
IRC *stands for International Reply Coupon. These are required with SAEs sent to markets in countries other than your own.*

Important Market Listing Information

● *Listings are based on questionnaires, phone calls and updated copy. They are not advertisements nor are markets reported here necessarily endorsed by the editor of this book.*
● *Information in the listings comes directly from the companies and is as accurate as possible, but situations may change and needs may fluctuate between the publication of this directory and the time you use it.*
● Children's Writer's & Illustrator's Market *reserves the right to exclude any listing that does not meet its requirements.*

The Markets

Book Publishers

Things are looking up for children's booksellers. Sales have been promising in the past year and the prognosis for the next few years is good. The Book Industry Study Group's *Trends 95* report shows a small increase in hardcover sales and predicts sales will rise to a total increase of 14% (over 1994 sales) by 1999. Paperback sales, too, are on the rise—BISG forecasts a 46% increase in the next four years.

How these numbers will affect publishers' buying habits is hard to say. The fact remains that publishers want titles that will attract both bookstore owners and prospective book buyers, so houses deluged with thousands of submissions are still selective in determining which manuscripts to buy. Children's writers and illustrators must study the market carefully, submit highly polished work and be tenacious.

Ever-changing policies

Although a number of larger houses still abide by "does not accept unsolicited manuscripts" policies, some, including Simon & Schuster, have gone back to accepting unsolicited work and continue to publish from their slush piles.

So the question remains: Do *you* need an agent? For opinions from both sides of the issue, see An Agent's View: Representation Is Important on page 7 and A Writer's View: Be Your Own Agent on page 10. And note that this year, the phrase "Accepts only agented material" appears in bold within listings.

Make the most of indexes

As always, the key to marketing children's writing, illustration and photography is to match your interests with those of the publisher. To help you locate publishers seeking your type of work, we've included several indexes at the back of this book.

The Subject Index lists book and magazine publishers according to their fiction and nonfiction needs or interests. The Age-Level Index indicates which age-groups publishers cater to. And, for the first time we've compiled a Photography Index, indicating which markets buy photography for children's publications.

Use the indexes to hone your list of markets. For instance, if you write contemporary fiction for young adults and you're trying to place a book manuscript, go first to the Subject Index. Locate the fiction categories under Book Publishers, find Contemporary, and copy the list. Now go to the Age-Level Index and find all the publishers on the Contemporary list that are included under the Young Adults heading and highlight them. Read the listings for the highlighted publishers and see if your work matches their needs.

Photographers can also use the indexes to narrow their list of possible publishers. If you are interested in selling nature photos to book publishers for example, first copy the Book Publishers list in the Photography Index. Next check the Subject Index under the Nature/Environment (you could check fiction, nonfiction or both). Highlight those markets on both the Book Publishers list and the Nature/Environment list. Again, read the highlighted listings to determine which publishers are most appropriate for your work.

Be aware of what's popular

It's important writers and illustrators pay attention to trends in the marketplace—what's selling, what's not, which publishers are doing what. However, keep in mind that what you're seeing in the bookstores may be a year or two behind what publishers are working on right now. While a house's offerings may not change drastically, don't base your writing decisions solely on the trend of the day.

That said, some types of children's books are more popular than others. Traditional picture book sales are experiencing sluggish growth so houses that focus on them aren't doing as well as those offering a broader fare.

Licensed products from mass-market publishers (Lion King-, Barney-, and Power Rangers-based books, for example) still enjoy the most sales overall. And with an emphasis on merchandise and "book plus" packages (books that include extras such as toys, stuffed animals or audiotapes), and products being offered in outlets such as superstores, media stores, warehouses and gift stores, strong sales will no doubt continue.

The awareness of the need for multicultural offerings is still alive in the children's book market. Native American folktales and myths are still popular, and can be found in fiction for all age-groups. Books dealing with the African-American, Hispanic, and Asian-American experiences are also being published in increasing numbers. "Editors are looking for more multicultural picture book stories and novels with broad appeal," says *Children's Book Insider.*

Series still selling

Middle reader chapter books—in the form of paperback series—are still enjoying a boom. Horror series like genre leader R.L. Stine's Goosebumps, whose sales have reached the 90 million mark, and Christopher Pike's books, which have also sold well into the millions, still dominate the bestseller lists.

Sales are still healthy for other series too, such as the Babysitter's Club (which was even made into a movie), Sweet Valley University and American Girls. One reason these series, as well as the horror books, do so well is that consumers know exactly what they're going to get. Kids know they'll like the next book in a familiar series, and so do parents and grandparents who buy books for kids.

Resurgence of romance

Romance for preteens and teens seems to be making a comeback after dwindling since a boom in the '80s. According to Gwen Montgomery, editorial director for Avon Books for Young Readers, "The market for so long has been heavily teen horror and suspense, I think at the expense of everything else. Not every girl wants to read slasher books. Publishers are looking into other untapped areas."

As publishers return to updated versions of classic romances, they are coming up with different slants. Look for historical romance, as well as romance/horror combinations, and fantasies woven around love stories, says *Children's Writer.*

Nonfiction markets

Nonfiction picture books are expanding their audience and their slice of the educational market as the interest in homeschooling and supplementing traditional education continues to blossom. No longer are picture books with nonfiction subjects just for preschoolers and elementary school children. Artwork and photographs are being integrated into nonfiction books aimed at even older readers.

And taking a cue from mass-market "book plus" packages, publishers such as Planet Dexter are finding ways to make learning more fun by including "extras" with nonfiction titles—for example, a book about math that includes a calculator. (See the Insider Report with Planet Dexter Editor Liz Doyle in page 134 for more on the nonfiction market.)

Subsidy publishing

Some writers who are really determined to get their work into print, but who receive rejections from royalty publishers, may look to subsidy and co-op publishers as an option. These publishers ask writers to pay all or part of the costs of producing a book. Some of the listings in this section give percentages of subsidy- or co-op-published material and are marked with a solid block (■).

If you consider working with a subsidy publisher, in addition to book production service, here's what to expect: the publisher will edit your work for grammatical and spelling errors only, not content; they'll hire an illustrator, and design and print the book; for the most part, authors are responsible for the entire production costs (which are set so that the publisher makes a profit), as well as all marketing and distribution.

Aspiring writers should strongly consider working solely with publishers who pay. Such publishers will be active in marketing work because they profit only through these efforts. Having a subsidy publisher's name on your book may stigmatize it with reviewers, making your promotional efforts more difficult. Before entering into any contract with a subsidy publisher, have it checked out by a lawyer or someone qualified to scrutinize such documents.

Co-op and self-publishing

Co-op publishers operate a little differently than subsidy publishers. When working with a co-op publisher, authors pay anywhere from 25-100% of production costs, but co-op publishers handle all the marketing and distribution. Authors then receive up to 40% royalty until their initial investment is recovered, then 10-15% royalty. Co-op publishers work editorially more like traditional publishers.

If you're interested in publishing your book just to share it with friends and relatives, self-publishing is a viable option. In the long run it's often cheaper to self-publish than to work with a subsidy publisher. But self-publishing involves a lot more time and energy—you oversee all of the book production details. A local printer may be able to help you, or you may want to arrange some type of desktop computer publishing.

Whatever path you choose to take, remember that the road to publication is not easy. The business is competitive, and everyone gets his or her share of rejections. It took Eric Kimmel, now author of more than 30 children's books, 15 years before he got a break. Kimmel always keeps in mind a favorite saying: "It's not good enough to be as good as somebody else—you've got to be better." As he says, "You've got to be the author that only you can be. And that means giving 110 percent of your effort for years." (For more from Kimmel, see the Telling Tales From Around the World: An Interview with Eric Kimmel on page 25.)

ADVOCACY PRESS, P.O. Box 236, Santa Barbara CA 93102. (805)962-2728. Fax: (805)963-3580. Division of The Girls Incorporated of Greater Santa Barbara. Book publisher. Editorial Contact: Bill Sheehan. Publishes 2-4 children's books/year.

Fiction: Picture books, young readers, middle readers: adventure, animal, concepts in self-esteem, contemporary, fantasy, folktales, gender equity, multicultural, nature/environment, poetry. "Illustrated children's stories incorporate self-esteem, gender equity, self-awareness concepts."

Published *Nature's Wonderful World in Rhyme* (birth-age 12, collection of poems); *Shadow and the Ready Time* (32-page picture book). "Most publications are 32-48 page picture stories for readers 4-11 years. Most feature adventures of animals in interesting/educational locales."
Nonfiction: Middle readers, young adults: careers, multicultural, self-help, social issues, textbooks.
How to Contact/Writers: "Because of the required focus of our publications, most have been written inhouse." Reports on queries/mss in 1-2 months. Include SASE.
Illustration: "Require intimate integration of art with story. Therefore, almost always use local illustrators." Average about 30 illustrations per story. Reviews ms/illustration packages from artists. Submit ms with dummy. Contact: William Sheehan. Reports in 1-2 months. Samples returned with SASE.
Terms: Authors paid by royalty or outright purchase. Pays illustrators by project or royalty. Book catalog and ms guidelines for SASE.
Tips: "We are not presently looking for new titles."

AFRICA WORLD PRESS, P.O. Box 1892, Trenton NJ 08607. (609)844-9583. Fax: (609)844-0198. Book publisher. Editor: Kassahun Checole. Publishes 5 picture books/year; 15 young reader and young adult titles/year; 8 middle readers/year. Books concentrate on African-American life.
Fiction: Picture books, young readers: adventure, concept, contemporary, folktales, history, multicultural. Middle readers, young adults: adventure, contemporary, folktales, history, multicultural.
Nonfiction: Picture books, young readers, middle readers, young adults: concept, history, multicultural. Does not want to see self-help, gender or health books.
How to Contact/Writers: Query; submit outline/synopsis and 2 sample chapters. Reports on queries in 30-45 days; mss in 3 months. Will consider previously published work.
Illustration: Works with 10-20 illustrators/year. Reviews ms/illustration packages from artists. Query. Contact: Kassahun Checole, editor. Illustrations only: Query with samples. Reports in 3 months.
Terms: Pays authors royalty based on retail price. Pays illustrators by the project or royalty based on retail price. Book catalog available for SAE; ms and art guidelines available for SASE.

AFRICAN AMERICAN IMAGES, 1909 W. 95th St., Chicago IL 60643. (312)445-0322. Fax: (312)445-9844. Book publisher. Editor: Jawanza Kunjufu. Publishes 2 picture books/year; 1 young reader title/year; 1 middle reader title/year. 90% of books by first-time authors.
Fiction: Picture books, young readers, middle readers: history, multicultural. "We publish books from an Africentric frame of reference that promote self-esteem, collective values, liberation and skill development." Does not want to see poetry, essays, novels, autobiographies, biographies, religious materials or mss exclusively addressing the continent of Africa.
Nonfiction: Picture books, young readers, middle readers: multicultural, social issues.
How to Contact/Writers: Fiction/Nonfiction: Query or submit complete ms. Reports on queries in 1 week; mss in 2 months. Publishes a book 9 months after acceptance. Will consider simultaneous submissions. Include SASE for return of ms.
Illustration: Works with 4 children's illustrators/year. Illustrations only: Submit tearsheets. Reports on art samples in 2 weeks. Samples returned with SASE. Original artwork returned at job's completion.
Terms: Pays 10% royalty based on wholesale price or buys ms outright. Illustrators paid by the project ($100-$1,000 range). Book catalog, ms/artist's guidelines free on request.

ALADDIN PAPERBACKS, 1230 Avenue of the Americas, 4th Floor, 866 Third Avenue, New York NY 10020. (212)698-2711. Paperback imprint of Simon & Schuster Children's Publishing Division.

- Aladdin publishes primarily reprints of successful hardcovers from other Simon & Schuster imprints. They publish very little original material. Send SASE for writer's and artist's guidelines.

ALYSON PUBLICATIONS, INC., P.O. 4371, Los Angeles CA 90078. (213)871-1788. Book publisher. Editorial Contact: Helen Eisenbach. Publishes 4 (projected) picture books/year; 3 (projected) young adult titles/year. "Alyson Wonderland is the line of children's books. We are looking for diverse depictions of family life for children of gay and lesbian parents."

• Alyson has recently been purchased and moved from Boston to L.A. There may be more changes in store. To learn more about Alyson, see Insider Report with Sasha Allyson in the 1995 edition of *Children's Writer's & Illustrator's Market*.

Fiction: All levels: adventure, anthology, contemporary and multicultural. "We like books that incorporate all racial, religious and body types, as well as dealing with children with gay and lesbian parents—which all our books must deal with. Our YA books should deal with issues faced by kids growing up gay or lesbian." Published *Anna Day and the O-Ring*, by Elaine Wickens; and *One Dad, Two Dads, Brown Dad, Blue Dads*, by Johnny Valentine.

How to Contact/Writers: Submit outline/synopsis and sample chapters (young adults); submit complete manuscript (picture books/young readers). Reports on queries in 1 month; on mss in 6 weeks. Include SASE.

Illustration: Works with 4 illustrators/year. Reviews mss/illustration packages from artists. Illustrations only: Submit "representative art that can be *kept on file*. Good quality photocopies are OK."

Terms: Pays authors and illustrators royalties. Prefers to discuss terms with the authors and artists. "We *do* offer advances." Book catalog and/or ms guidelines free on request.

Tips: "We only publish kids' books aimed at the children of gay or lesbian parents."

AMERICAN BIBLE SOCIETY, 1865 Broadway, New York NY 10023. (212)408-1235. Fax: (212)408-1435. Book publisher. Estab. 1816. Product Development Coordinator: Christina Murphy. Publishes 2 picture books/year; 4 young readers/year; 4 young adults/year. Publishes books with spiritual/religious themes based on the Bible.

Nonfiction: All levels: activity books, multicultural, religion, self-help, nature/environment, reference, social issues and special needs. Multicultural needs include intercity lifestyle; African-American, Hispanic/Latino, Native American, Asian; mixed groups (such as choirs, classrooms, church events). "Unsolicited manuscripts will be returned unread! We prefer published writing samples with résumés so that we can contact copywriters when an appropriate project comes up." Published *God Loves You: Proverbs from the Bible* (ages 4-6, full color cover and 42 full color interior illustrations).

How to Contact/Writers: All mss developed inhouse. Query with résumé and writing samples. Contact: Barbara Bernstengel. Unsolicited mss rejected. No credit lines given.

Illustration: Works with 2-5 illustrators/year. "Would be more interested in artwork for children and teens which is influenced by the visual 'vocabulary' of videos." Reviews ms/illustration packages from artists. Contact: Christina Murphy. Illustrations only: Query with samples; arrange a personal interview to show portfolio; send "résumés, tearsheets and promotional literature to keep; slides will be returned promptly." Reports on queries in 2 months. Original artwork returned at job's completion. Book catalog free on request.

Photography: Contact: Christina Murphy. Buys stock and assigns work. Looking for "nature, scenic, multicultural, intergenerational people shots." Model/property releases required. Uses any size b&w prints; 35mm, 2¼×2¼ and 4×5 transparencies. Photographers should query with samples; arrange a personal interview to show portfolio; provide résumé, promotional literature or tearsheets.

Terms: Photographers paid by the project (range: $800-5,000); per photo (range $150-1,500). Credit line given on most projects. Most photos purchased on one-time use basis. Factors used to determine payment for ms/illustration package include "nature and scope of project; complexity of illustration and continuity of work; number of illustrations." Pays illustrators $200-30,000; based on fair market value. Sends 2 complimentary copies of published work to illustrators. ABS owns all publication rights to illustrations and mss.

AMERICAN EDUCATION PUBLISHING, 150 E. Wilson Bridge Rd., Suite 145, Columbus OH 43085-2328. (614)848-8866. Book publisher. Publishes 6-8 picture books/year. 20% of books by first-time authors; 80% of books developed inhouse.

***A bullet within a listing introduces special comments by the editor of* Children's Writer's & Illustrator's Market.**

INSIDER REPORT

Poetry Publication Demands Dedication

It might seem strange to ask an economics professor how to publish a children's book. But not if the professor is J. Patrick Lewis, an instructor at Otterbein College in Westerville, Ohio, who is also the author of a dozen published children's books and has another dozen books in various stages of production at a number of publishing companies. In fact, the question isn't as surprising as Lewis's answer.

J. Patrick Lewis

"Expect to run the gauntlet of rejection," he says. "If that's too painful, time-consuming or inconvenient, then get out of the game early. But if you believe in what you've done, send out the manuscript, even if the cows *don't* come home very soon."

Though his publishing record may indicate otherwise, Lewis knows of what he speaks. His first published book, *The Tsar and the Amazing Cow*, an original folktale set in Russia, was rejected 13 times before it was accepted by Dial and published in 1988. His second book, *A Hippopotamusn't*, his first collection of animal poems, was rejected 20 times before Dial published the picture book in 1990. And even today, he says, one of his manuscripts can be rejected three or four times before it's finally accepted by a publisher.

Indeed, for Lewis, and most children's writers, perseverance paves the path to publication—particularly when the manuscript being submitted is poetry, as is much of Lewis's work. In fact, when Lewis began sending out his poetry manuscripts, he was told that a half dozen children's poets—Dr. Seuss and Shel Silverstein among them—had the market pretty much to themselves. "But I persevered," says the then-unknown children's poet.

Before he ever submitted his work, however, Lewis also learned the importance of craft. "I first began writing poetry around 1980—terrible stuff—treacly, didactic, forced rhyme doggerel. Of course, I thought it was pretty good . . . until I came to my senses. Enthusiasm is a necessary but not a sufficient condition for writing poetry," he says. "There must be first and always a sense of craft."

After sharing his early poetry with his three children, who were his first critics, Lewis stopped writing for three years and immersed himself in metrics and the masters—both adult's and children's poets. "Only when I felt solidly grounded there did I presume to try again. Most of my poems for children follow strict metrics, but that matters little. Quality ought to be the sole criterion, which means that poems should be wonderfully eccentric and unexpected."

Having taken to heart what author Samuel Johnson once said, "Never trust anyone who writes more than he reads," Lewis encourages beginning children's poets to read every children's poet they can get their hands on—to find their own voices. Yet Lewis refrains from developing a distinctive voice. "I don't want people to be able to say 'That's a Pat Lewis poem,' the way you can tell a Dr. Seuss poem. I want to write as wildly and widely as possible, in as many different verse forms and genres as I can."

To understand how Lewis stretches himself, review a list of his recently published and forthcoming titles: *Ridicholas Nicholas*, his fourth collection of animal poems, was published in the fall of 1995 by Dial. At the same time, *Black Swan/White Crow*, a collection of haiku for children, was published by Atheneum. In the spring of 1996 *Riddle-icious*, a collection of riddle poems, will be published by Knopf. And in fall 1996 *The Boat of Many Rooms*, the story of Noah's Ark in narrative verse, will be published by Atheneum, and Creative Editions will publish *Boshblobberbosh: A Runcible Life of Edward Lear*, verse about incidents from the life of the Victorian nonsense writer and children's poet (who has been Lewis's inspiration).

In many ways, Lewis has proven there is not just a market for children's poetry, but a market for all types of children's poetry. Today, the most difficult task for aspiring children's writers and poets is overcoming the desire for instant gratification, he says. "If a half dozen rejections are enough to make you want to bury your head in the sand, then perhaps there are other, less stressful pursuits that would interest you. If, on the other hand, you are in for the long haul, it's just possible that patience and hard work will find their rewards."

—Christine Martin

J. Patrick Lewis expounds in verse on the changing seasons and the wonders of nature in his month-by-month poetry collection* July is a Mad Mosquito. *The book wraps up with a longer, lyrical poem bringing all the months of the year together—from "January's polar bear" to "June's a thousand bees" to "the deer that is December."

Fiction: Picture books: adventure, animal, concept, contemporary. Young readers: adventure, animal, concept, contemporary, fantasy, folktales, humor. Does not want to see dinosaurs, talking animals and environment. Published *The Wind*, *The Alphabet* and *The Colors*, all by Monique Felix (8×8 softcover for toddlers).
Nonfiction: Picture books: activity books, animal, concept and science. Young readers: activity books, animal, concept, hobbies and science. Does not want to see dinosaurs, environment. Published *Gnat* and *Fire* both by Kitty Benedict (8×8 softcover for beginners).
How to Contact/Writers: Fiction/Nonfiction: Submit outline/synopsis and 3 sample chapters. Reports on queries in 2 months; mss in 3-4 months. Publishes a book 6-8 months after acceptance. Will consider simultaneous submissions and previously published work.
Illustration: Works with 5 illustrators/year. Reviews ms/illustration packages from artists. Submit ms with 2 pieces of final art. Illustrations only: Query with samples, résumé, tearsheets. Reports in 2 months. Samples returned with SASE; samples kept on file. Original artwork returned at job's completion.
Terms: Pays authors royalty of 5-10% based on wholesale price or work purchased outright. Pays illustrators by the project or royalty of 5-10% based on wholesale price. Sends galleys to authors.

ARCHWAY/MINSTREL BOOKS, 1230 Avenue of the Americas, New York NY 10020. (212)698-7000. Fax: (212)698-7337. Imprint of Pocket Books. Book publisher—Minstrel Books (ages 7-11) and Archway Paperbacks (ages 12-16). Editorial Director: Patricia MacDonald. Publishes originals and reprints.
Fiction: Middle readers: animal stories, adventures, fantasy, funny school stories, thrillers. Young adults: adventure, romance, romantic suspense, contemporary stories, horror, suspense. Recently published (Archway) *The Midnight Club*, by Christopher Pike and *Fear Street* cheerleaders trilogy, by R.L. Stine; *Someone at the Door*, by Richie Tankersley Cusick. Published (Minstrel) *Aliens Are My Homework*, by Bruce Coville; *French Fries Up My Nose*, by M.M. Rogz; and *My Crazy Cousin Courtney*, by Judi Miller.
Nonfiction: Middle readers: environment, sports. Young adults: sports, popular media figures.
How to Contact/Writers: Fiction/Nonfiction: Query; submit outline/synopsis and sample chapters. SASE mandatory.
Terms: Pays authors in royalties.

ATHENEUM BOOKS FOR YOUNG READERS, 866 Third Ave., New York NY 10022. (212)702-2000. Simon & Schuster Children's Publishing Division. Book publisher. Vice President/Associate Publisher and Editorial Director: Jonathan Lanman. Editorial Contacts: Anne Schwartz, editorial director of Anne Schwartz books; Marcia Marshall, senior editor; Sarah Caquiat, editor; Ana Cerro, associate editor. Publishes 15-20 picture books/year; 4-5 young readers/year; 20-25 middle readers/year; 10-15 young adults/year. 10% of books by first-time authors; 50% of books from agented writers.

- Atheneum won a Boston Globe-Horn Book Award for nonfiction for *Abigail Adams: Witness to a Revolution*, by Natalie S. Bober.

Fiction: Picture books and middle readers: animal, contemporary, fantasy. Young readers and young adults: contemporary, fantasy.
Nonfiction: All levels: animal, biography, education, history.
How to Contact/Writers: Fiction/Nonfiction: Query; will consider complete picture book ms. Reports on queries in 6-8 weeks; mss in 3 months. Publishes a book 18-24 months after acceptance. Will consider simultaneous submissions from previously unpublished authors; "we request that the author let us know it is a simultaneous submission."
Illustration: Editorial reviews ms/illustration packages from artists. Query first. Illustrations only: Submit résumé, tearsheets. Reports on art samples only if interested. Original artwork returned at job's completion.
Terms: Pays authors in royalties of 8-10% based on retail price. Illustrators paid royalty or flat fee depending on the project. Sends galleys to authors; proofs to illustrators. Book catalog available for 9×12 SAE and 5 first-class stamps; ms guidelines for #10 SAE and 1 first-class stamp.

AUGSBURG FORTRESS, PUBLISHERS, 426 S. Fifth St., Box 1209, Minneapolis MN 55440. (612)330-3300. Fax: (612)330-3455. Acquisition Editor: Alice Peppler. Managing Editor: Pam

McClanahan. Publishes 3-4 Christian picture books/year; 2 Bible information books/year; 3-4 devotionals/year. 5% of books by first-time authors.
Fiction: Looking for picture books of Christian children from American multicultural homes and single parent homes. Also interested in Christmas and Easter picture books.
Nonfiction: Looking for Christian devotions for children; Christian information books on the Bible, people in the Bible, etc.
How to Contact/Writers: Query. Reports in 3 weeks. Publishes a book 1½ years after acceptance. Will consider simultaneous and previously published submissions.
Illustration: Works with 6 illustrators/year. Reviews ms/illustration packages from artists. Contact: Pam McClanahan. Illustrations only: Query with samples, résumé, promo sheet and client list. Reports back in 3 months only if interested. Samples are not returned; samples filed. Originals not returned.
Terms: Pays authors royalty. Pays illustrators by the project (range: varies). Book catalog, ms and artist's guidelines available for SASE.
Tips: "Devotion authors must be familiar with Lutheran and other mainline church denominations. Bible information book authors must have educational or comparable criteria for writing this genre. Picture books must be unique and have a message within the plot. Prefer no animal picture book stories. Be sure to get our ms guidelines before mailing a proposal."

***A/V CONCEPTS CORP.**, 30 Montauk Blvd., Oakdale NY 11769. (516)567-7227. Fax: (516)567-8745. Educational book publisher. Editor: Laura Solimene. President: Phil Solimene. Publishes 6 young readers/year; 6 middle readers/year; 6 young adult titles/year. 20% of books by first-time authors. Primary theme of books and multimedia is classic literature, math, science, language arts, self esteem.
Fiction: Picture books, young readers, middle readers and young adults: hi-lo. "We hire writers to adapt classic literature."
Nonfiction: Average word length: middle readers—300-400; young adults—500-950.
How to Contact/Writers: Fiction: Submit outline/synopsis and 1 sample chapter. Reports on queries in 2-4 weeks.
Illustration: Works with 4-6 illustrators/year. Reviews ms/illustration packages from artists. Submit ms with 3-4 pieces of final art. Contact: Phil Solimene, president. Illustrations only: Query with samples. Contact: Phil Solimene, president. Reports in 2-4 weeks. Samples returned with SASE; samples filed.
Terms: Work purchased outright from authors (range $700-1,000). Pays illustrators by the project (range: $35-1,000). Ms and art guidelines available for SASE.

AVON BOOKS/BOOKS FOR YOUNG READERS (Avon Flare, Avon Camelot and Young Camelot), 1350 Avenue of the Americas, New York NY 10019. (212)261-6817. Division of The Hearst Corporation. Book publisher. Editorial Director: Gwen Montgomery. Senior Editor: Anne E. Dunn. Assistant Editor: Stephanie Siegel. Publishes 25-30 middle readers/year; 20-25 young adults/year. 10% of books by first-time authors; 20% of books from agented writers.
Fiction: Middle readers: comedy, contemporary, problem novels, sports, spy/mystery/adventure. Young adults: contemporary, problem novels, romance. Average length: middle readers—100-150 pages; young adults—150-250 pages. Avon does not publish preschool picture books.
Nonfiction: Middle readers: hobbies, music/dance, sports. Young adults: music/dance, "growing up." Average length: middle readers—100-150 pages; young adults—150-250 pages.
How to Contact/Writers: Fiction: Submit complete ms. Nonfiction: Submit outline/synopsis and sample chapters. Reports on queries in 1 month; mss in 3-4 months. Publishes a book 18-24 months after acceptance. Will consider simultaneous submissions.
Illustration: Very rarely will review ms/illustration packages. Illustrations only: "Send samples we can keep. Need line art and cover art."
Terms: Pays authors in royalties of 6% based on retail price. Average advance payment is "very open." Sends galleys to authors; sometimes sends dummies to illustrators. Book catalog available

The asterisk before a listing indicates the listing is new in this edition.

for 9×12 SAE and 4 first-class stamps; ms guidelines for #10 SASE.
Tips: "We have three young readers imprints: Young Camelot, books for beginner readers; Avon Camelot, books for the middle grades; and Avon Flare, young adults. Our list includes both individual titles and series, with the emphasis in our paperback originals on high quality recreational reading—a fresh and original writing style; identifiable, three-dimensional characters; a strong, well-paced story that pulls readers in and keeps them interested." Writers: "Make sure that you really know what a company's list looks like before you submit work. Is your work in line with what they usually do? Is your work appropriate for the age group that this company publishes for? Keep aware of what's in your bookstore (but not what's in there for too long!)" Illustrators: "Submit work to art directors and people who are in charge of illustration at publishers. This is usually not handled entirely by the editorial department."

BANDANNA BOOKS, 319-B Anacapa St., Santa Barbara CA 93101. (805)962-9915. Fax: (805)564-3278. E-mail: bbooks@eworld.com. Book Publisher. Editor: Sasha Newborn. Fiction Editor: Joan Blake. Publishes 1 young adult title/year. "Most books have been translations in the humanist tradition. Looking for themes of intellectual awakening."
Fiction: Young adults (16 and older): history and autobiographical. No religious, fantasy. Average word length: 60,000. Published *Benigna Machiavelli*, by Charlotte Perkins Gilman.
Nonfiction: Young adult: social issues, history, biography, textbooks.
How to Contact/Writers: Fiction: Submit outline/synopsis and 1 sample chapter. Reports on queries/mss in 2 months. Publishes a book up to a year after acceptance. Will consider simultaneous submissions.
Illustration: Works with 1 illustrator/year. Uses b&w artwork only. Prefers woodblock, scratchboard artwork. Reviews ms/illustration packages from artists. Submit ms with dummy. Contact: Sasha Newborn, publisher. Illustrations only: Query with samples, portfolio and tearsheets. Reports back in 2 months only if interested. Samples not returned; samples filed. Originals are not returned.
Terms: Pays authors royalty of 5-10% based on retail price; also advances (average amount: $200). Pays illustrators by the project (range: $25-200). Sends galleys to authors. Book catalog available for SASE. Ms and art guidelines not available.
Tips: "Our market is 16 and older (high school) and college. No kid stuff. Our list is primarily classics."

B&B PUBLISHING, INC., Interactive Education Technologies, 820 Wisconsin St., P.O. Box 96, Wallworth WI 53184. (414)275-9474. Fax: (414)275-9530. Book publisher, independent book producer/packager. Managing Director: Katy O'Shea. Publishes 8 young adult titles/year. All titles are nonfiction, educational, usually curriculum related. "We do not do fiction unless it is based on fact (i.e., historical), has an educational theme, and could fit a curriculum area."
Nonfiction: Middle readers, young adults: biography, careers, concept, geography, history, multicultural, nature/environment, reference, science, social issues. Multicultural needs include smaller ethnic groups, sociological perspective, true stories; no folktales. "Please no personal war experiences, most such material is unsuitable for younger readers." Average word length: middle readers—15,000; young adults—20,000. Recently published *Awesome Almanac*™ *Ohio*, by Margie Benson and *Awesome Almanac Texas*™, by Suzanne Martin.
How to Contact/Writers: Fiction/Nonfiction: Query. Submit outline/synopsis and 1 sample chapter. Reports in 3 months. Usually publishes a book 1 year after acceptance. Will consider simultaneous and previously published submissions. "Send SASE or submission will not be acknowledged."
Illustration: Works with 3-4 illustrators/year. Reviews ms/illustration packages from artists. Query. Submit sample chapter with illustration. Contact: Katy O'Shea, managing director. Reports back in 3 months. Illustrations only: Query with samples, resume, promo sheet and tearsheets. Reports only if interested on non-manuscript sample submissions. Samples returned with SASE; samples filed. Original artwork returned at job's completion.
Photography: Buys photos from freelancers. Contact: Margie Benson, photo editor. Buys stock and assigns work. Photos used vary by project—wonders of the world, nature/environment, etc. Uses color or b&w prints and 35mm, 2¼×2¼, 4×4 or 8×10 transparencies. Submit cover letter, resume, published samples, stock photo list and promo piece.
Terms: Pays authors royalty of 1-10% on net receipts. Work purchased outright from authors ($500-4,000). Offers advances (up to $2,000). Pays illustrators by the project. Pays photographers

by the project or per photo. Sends galleys to authors; dummies to illustrators. Ms guidelines available for SASE.

BANTAM DOUBLEDAY DELL, 1540 Broadway, New York NY 10036. (212)354-6500. Book publisher Vice President/Publisher: Craig Virden. Deputy Publisher/Editor-in-Chief: Beverly Horowitz. Publishes 12 picture books/year; 12 young reader titles/year; 60 middle reader books/year; 60 young adult titles/year. 10% of books by first-time authors; 70% of books from agented writers.

- Bantam won a Coretta Scott King Honor Award in 1995 for *I Hadn't Meant to Tell You This*, by Jacqueline Woodson. They rank the 8th based on net sales, of the top 15 children's publishers.

Fiction: Picture books: adventure, animal, contemporary, easy-to-read, fantasy, humor. Young readers: animal, contemporary, humor, easy-to-read, fantasy, sports, suspense/mystery. Middle readers: adventure, animal, contemporary, humor, easy-to-read, fantasy, sports, suspense/mystery. Young adults: adventure, contemporary issues, humor, coming-of-age, suspense/mystery. Published *Spite Fences*, by Trudy Krisher; *Driver's Ed*, by Caroline Cooney; *Bill*, by Chap Reaver.
Nonfiction: "Bantam Doubleday Dell Books for Young Readers publishes a very limited number of nonfiction titles."
How to Contact/Writers: Submit through the agent only. "All unsolicited manuscripts returned unopened with the following exceptions: Unsolicited manuscripts are accepted for the Delacorte Press Prize for a First Young Adult Novel contest (see Contests and Awards section) and the Marguerite de Angeli Prize for a First Middle Grade Novel contest (see Contests and Awards section)." Reports on queries in 6-8 weeks; mss in 3 months.
Illustration: Number of illustrations used per fiction title varies considerably. Reviews ms/illustration packages from artists. Query first. Do not send originals. "If you submit a dummy, please submit the text separately." Reports on ms/art samples only if interested. Cannot return samples; samples filed. Illustrations only: Submit tearsheets, rèsumè, samples that do not need to be returned. Original artwork returned at job's completion.
Terms: Pays authors advance and royalty. Pays illustrators advance and royalty or flat fee.

***■BARBOUR & CO., INC.**, 1810 Barbour Dr., Uhrichsville OH 44683. (614)922-6045. Fax: (614)922-5948. Book publisher. Vice President: Stephen Reginald. Publishes 2 picture books/year; 6 middle readers/year. 10% of books by first-time authors; .5% subsidy published.
Fiction: Picture books: humor, religion. Middle readers: history, religion. Average word length: middle readers—16,000. Recently published *Pete, Feet, and Fish to Eat*, written and illustrated by Phil A. Smouse; and *KJV Bible for Toddlers*, written by Randy Kryszewski, illustrated by Caren Jurina.
Nonfiction: Picture books: religion. Middle readers: biography, history, religion.
How to Contact/Writers: Fiction/Nonfiction: Query. Reports on queries in 1 month; mss in 2 months. Publishes a book 1 year after acceptance. Will consider simultaneous submissions and previously published work.
Illustration: Works with 5 illustrators/year. Reviews ms/illustration packages from artists. Query. Contact: Stephen Reginald, vice president editorial. Illustrations only: Query with samples. Contact: Stephen Reginald, vice president editorial. Reports only if interested. Samples returned with SASE; samples filed. Originals not returned.
Photography: Buys photos from freelancers. Contact: Stephen Reginald, vice president editorial. Buys stock images. Model/property release required. Uses $2\frac{1}{4} \times 2\frac{1}{4}$ transparencies. Submit cover letter.
Terms: Work purchased outright from authors (range: $500-2,500). Pays illustrators by the project (range: $250-800). Pays photographers by the project. Book catalog available for $2. Ms guidelines available for SASE.

The solid block before a listing indicates the market subsidy or co-op publishes manuscripts.

BARRON'S EDUCATIONAL SERIES, 250 Wireless Blvd., Hauppauge NY 11788. (516)434-3311. Fax: (516)434-3723. Book publisher. Estab. 1945. Managing/Acquisitions Editor: Grace Freedson. Publishes 20 picture books/year; 20 young readers/year; 20 middle reader titles/year; 10 young adult titles/year. 25% of books by first-time authors; 25% of books from agented writers.

Fiction: Picture books: animal, concept, multicultural, nature/environment. Young readers: Adventure, multicultural, nature/environment, suspense/mystery. Middle readers: adventure, horror, multicultural, nature/environment, problem novels, suspense/mystery. Young adults: horror, problem novels. Recently published *The Truth About Sharks*, by Carol Amaro, illustrated by David Wenzel (Young Reader's series); *Gardening Wizardry For Kids*, by Patricia Kite, illustrated by Yvette Santiago Banek; and *Computer Dictionary For Kids*, by Jani Lynne Borman.

Nonfiction: Picture books: concept, reference. Young readers: how-to, reference, self help, social issues. Middle readers: hi-lo, how-to, reference, self help, social issues. Young adults: how-to, self help, social issues.

How to Contact/Writers: Fiction: Query. Nonfiction: Submit outline/synopsis and sample chapters. "Submissions must be accompanied by SASE for response." Reports on queries in 1 month; mss in 6-8 months. Publishes a book 1 year after acceptance. Will consider simultaneous submissions.

Illustration: Works with 10 illustrators/year. Reviews ms/illustration packages from artists. Query first; 3 chapters of ms with 1 piece of final art, remainder roughs. Contact: Grace Freedson. Illustrations only: Submit tearsheets or slides plus résumé. Reports in 3-8 weeks.

Terms: Pays authors in royalties of 10-16% based on wholesale price or buys ms outright for $2,000 minimum. Pays illustrators by the project based on retail price. Sends galleys to authors; dummies to illustrators. Book catalog, ms/artist's guidelines for 9×12 SAE.

Tips: Writers: "We are predominately on the lookout for preschool storybooks and concept books. No YA fiction/romance or novels." Illustrators: "We are happy to receive a sample illustration to keep on file for future consideration. Periodic notes reminding us of your work are acceptable." Children's book themes "are becoming much more contemporary and relevant to a child's day-to-day activities."

■**BEAUTIFUL AMERICA PUBLISHING COMPANY**, 9725 S.W. Commerce Circle, Wilsonville OR 97070. (503)682-0173. Fax: (503)682-0175. Imprint of Little America (children's). Book publisher. Editor: Jaime Thoreson. Art Director: Heather Kier. Publishes 2 middle readers titles/year. 50% of books by first-time authors; 50% subsidy published.

Fiction: Middle readers: animal, environmentally and/or morally conscious. Average length: middle readers—60-90 pages. Published *The Christmas Collie*.

Nonfiction: Middle readers: animal, environmentally and/or morally conscious. Average length: 60-90 pages. Published *Melody's Mystery*.

How to Contact/Writers: Fiction/Nonfiction: Query. Submit outline/synopsis. Reports on mss in 6 months. Publishes a book 1-2 years after acceptance.

Illustration: Works with 3 illustrators/year. Reviews ms/illustration packages from artists. Submit ms with dummy. Illustrations only: Query with samples. Contact: Heather Kier, art director. Reports only if interested. Samples returned with SASE; samples filed if artist doesn't want samples back. Original artwork returned at job's completion.

Photography: Buys photos from freelancers. Contact: Jaime Thoreson, photo-librarian. Buys stock and assigns work. Model/property releases required; captions required. "Absolutely no prints accepted." Uses 35mm, 2¼×2¼, 4×5 or 8×10 transparencies. Submit résumé, published samples and promo piece.

Terms: Pays authors royalty on retail price. Offers advances. Pays illustrators by the project. Pays photographers by the project, per photo, royalty. Book catalog available for 9×12 SAE and 2 first-class stamps.

BEHRMAN HOUSE INC., 235 Watchung Ave., West Orange NJ 07052. (201)669-0447. Fax: (201)669-9769. Book publisher. Project Editor: Adam Siegel. Publishes 3 young reader titles/year; 3 middle reader titles/year; 3 young adult titles/year. 12% of books by first-time authors; 2% of books from agented writers. Publishes books on all aspects of Judaism: history, cultural, textbooks, holidays.

Nonfiction: All levels: Judaism, Jewish educational textbooks. Average word length: young reader—1,200; middle reader—2,000; young adult—4,000. Published *My Jewish Year*, by Adam Fisher (ages 8-9); and *It's a Mitzvah!*, by Bradley Arlson (adult).
How to Contact/Writers: Fiction/Nonfiction: Submit outline/synopsis and sample chapters. Reports on queries in 1 month; mss in 2 months. Publishes a book 2½ years after acceptance. Will consider simultaneous submissions.
Illustration: Works with 6 children's illustrators/year. Reviews ms/illustration packages from artists. "Query first." Illustrations only: Query with samples; send unsolicited art samples by mail. Reports on queries in 1 month; mss in 2 months.
Photography: Purchases photos from freelancers. Contact: Adam Siegel. Buys stock and assigns work. Uses photos of families involved in Jewish activities. Uses color and b&w prints. Photographers should query with samples. Send unsolicited photos by mail. Submit portfolio for review.
Terms: Pays authors in royalties of 3-8% based on retail price or buys ms outright for $1,000-5,000. Offers advance. Pays illustrators by the project (range: $500-5,000). Sends galleys to authors; dummies to illustrators. Book catalog free on request.
Tips: Looking for "religious school texts" with Judaic themes.

BERKLEY PUBLISHING GROUP, 200 Madison Ave., New York NY 10016. Imprints: Berkley, Jove, Diamond, Ace. Book publisher. Senior Editor: Gary Goldstein. "We are mainly publishing young adult horror, thrillers and romance."
Fiction: Young adults: problem novels, romance, suspense/horror. Average word length: young adults—55,000.
How to Contact/Writers: Fiction: Submit outline/synopsis and 3 sample chapters. Reports on queries in 2 weeks; mss in 2-3 months. Publishes a book in 12-18 months after acceptance.
Terms: Pays authors royalty based on retail price. Offers advance. Sends galleys to authors.

BESS PRESS, P.O. Box 22388, Honolulu HI 96823. (808)734-7159. Editor: Revé Shapard. Publishes 1-2 picture books/year; 1-2 young readers/year; 0-1 middle readers/year. 60% of books by first-time authors. "Books must be about Hawaii, Asia or the Pacific."
Fiction: Picture books, young readers: adventure, animal, anthology, concept, contemporary, folktales, hi-lo, history, humor, multicultural, nature/environment, sports, suspense/mystery. Middle readers: adventure, animal, anthology, contemporary, folktales, hi-lo, history, humor, multicultural, nature/environment, problem novels, sports, suspense/mystery. Young adults: adventure, anthology, contemporary, hi-lo, history, humor, multicultural, problem novels, sports, suspense/mystery. Published *The Little Makana*, by Helen M. Dano, illustrated by Wren (ages 3-8); *Too Many Curls*, by Marilyn Kahalewai (ages 3-8, picture book); *Let's Call Him Lau-wili-wili-humu-humu-nukunuku-nukunuku-apuaa-oioi*, by Tim Myers, illustrated by Daryl Arakaki (ages 3-8, picture book).
Nonfiction: Picture books: activity books, biography, concept, geography, hi-lo, history, multicultural, reference, sports, textbooks. Young readers: activity books, biography, geography, hi-lo, history, multicultural, reference, sports, textbooks. Middle readers, young adults: biography, geography, hi-lo, history, multicultural, reference, sports, textbooks. Published *Filipino Word Book*, by Teresita V. Ramos and Josie Clausen, illustrated by Jerri Asuncion and Boboy Betco (ages 5-11, introductory language book); *Flowers of Hawaii Coloring Book*, by Wren (ages 3-8, coloring book); Keiki's First Books, by Maile and Wren (toddlers, concept books).
How to Contact/Writers: Fiction/Nonfiction: Submit complete ms. Reports on queries in 2 weeks; on mss in 3-4 weeks. Publishes a book 6-12 months after acceptance. Will consider simultaneous submissions and previously published work.
Illustration: Works with 3 illustrators/year. Reviews ms/illustration packages from artists. Submit ms with dummy. Contact: Revé Shapard, editor. Illustrations only: Query with samples. Reports in 3 weeks. Samples returned with SASE; samples filed. Original artwork returned at job's completion.
Terms: Pays authors royalty of 2½-10% based on wholesale price or work purchased outright. Pays illustrators by the project, royalty of 2½-5% based on wholesale price. Sends galleys to authors; dummies to illustrators. Book catalog available for SASE; ms and art guidelines available for SASE.
Tips: Looks for "books with commercial or educational appeal in our primary markets—Hawaii, Asia, the Western United States and libraries."

BETHANY HOUSE PUBLISHERS, 11300 Hampshire Ave. S., Minneapolis MN 55438. (612)829-2500. Book publisher. Children's Book Editor: Barbara Lilland. Managing Editor: Lance Wubbels. Publishes 16 young readers/year; 16 young adults/year. Publishes books with spiritual and religious themes.

Fiction: Middle readers, young adults: adventure, contemporary, problem novels, romance, suspense/mystery. Does not want to see poetry or science fiction. Average word length: young readers—20,000; young adults—35,000. Published *Too Many Secrets*, by Patricia H. Rushford (young adult/teens, mystery-adventure series); *Becky's Brainstorm*, by Elaine L. Schulte (young readers, adventure series with strong Christian values theme); *Mandie and the Fiery Rescue*, by Lois Leppard (young readers, adventure series).

Nonfiction: Middle readers, young adults: religion, self-help, social issues. Published *Can I Be a Christian Without Being Weird?*, by Kevin Johnson (early teens, devotional book); *Dear Judy, Did You Ever Like a Boy (who didn't like you?)*, by Judy Baer (young adult/teen, advice book on social issues).

How to Contact/Writers: Fiction/Nonfiction: Query. Reports on queries in 1 month; mss in 2 months. Publishes a book 9-12 months after acceptance. Will consider simultaneous submissions and previously published work.

Illustration: Works with 4 illustrators/year. Reviews ms/illustration packages from artists. Query. Illustrations only: Query with samples. Reports in 6 weeks. Samples returned with SASE.

Terms: Pays authors royalty based on retail price. Pays illustrators by the project. Sends galleys to authors. Book catalog available for 11×14 SAE and 5 first-class stamps.

Tips: "Research the market, know what is already out there. Study our catalog before submitting material. We look for an evangelical message woven delicately into a strong plot and topics that seek to broaden the reader's experience and perspective."

BETHEL PUBLISHING, 1819 S. Main, Elkhart IN 46516. (219)293-8585. Book publisher. Contact: Senior Editor. Publishes 1-2 young readers/year; 1-2 middle readers/year.

Fiction: Young readers: animal, religion. Middle readers and young adults: adventure, religion. Does not want to see "New-Age—Dungeon & Dragons type." Published *The Great Forest*, by Jean Springer (ages 9-14, religion); *Pordy's Prickly Problem*, by Janette Oke (ages 7-12, religion); *Peace Porridge*, by Marjie Douglas (ages 8-13, religion). Does not want to see workbooks, cookbooks, coloring books, books on theological studies, poetry or preschool/elementary age stories. Average word length: 30,000-50,000.

Nonfiction: Young readers, middle readers and young adults: religion.

How to Contact/Writers: Fiction/Nonfiction: Query. Submit complete ms. Reports on queries in 3 weeks; mss in 3 months. Publishes a book 1 year after acceptance. Will consider simultaneous submissions and previously published work.

Illustration: Works with 2 illustrators/year. Reviews ms/illustration packages from artists. Ms/illustration packages and illustrations only: Query. Reports in 1 month. Samples returned with SASE. Originals not returned.

Photography: Purchases photos from freelancers. Contact: Senior Editor. Buys stock. Model/property releases required. Uses color and b&w glossy prints; 35mm and 2¼×2¼ transparencies. Photographers should send cover letter.

Terms: Pays authors royalty of 5-10% on wholesale price. Pays illustrators by the project. Photographers paid by the project. Sends galleys to authors. Book catalog available for 9×12 SAE and 3 first-class stamps. Ms guidelines available for SASE. Artist's guidelines not available.

***BLACKBIRCH PRESS, INC./BLACKBIRCH GRAPHICS, INC.**, 260 Amity Rd., Woodbridge CT 06525. Fax: (203)389-1596. Book publisher, independent book producer/packager. Senior Editor: Nicole Bowen. Art Director: Sonja Kalter. Publishes 20 middle readers; 70 young adult titles. 15% of books by first-time authors.

Nonfiction: Picture books: animal, concept, geography, history, nature/environment, science. Young readers: animal, biography, geography, multicultural, nature/environment, special needs. Middle readers and young adults: geography, nature/environment, reference, special needs. Does not want to see dogs, spiritual, medical themes. Average word length: young adult readers—8,000-10,000; middle readers—5,000-7,000. Recently published *Mount Rushmore*, *Marine Biologist* (ages 8-10); and *Lennon & McCartney* (ages 11-15).

How to Contact/Writers: Nonfiction: Query. SASE "if material needs to be returned." Reports on queries in 2 months. Publishes a book 1 year after acceptance. Will consider simultaneous submissions.
Illustration: Works with 10 illustrators/year. Uses color artwork only. Reviews ms/illustration packages from artists. Submit query. Contact: Nicole Bowen, senior editor. Illustrations only: Query with samples; send résumé, promo sheet. Reports in 1 month. Samples not returned; samples filed. Original artwork returned at job's completion.
Photography: Buys photos from freelancers. Contact: Sonja Kalter, art director. Buys stock and assigns work. Uses animal, human culture, geography. Captions required. Uses 35mm, 2¼×2¼, 4×5 transparencies. Submit cover letter, published samples and promo piece.
Terms: Pays authors royalty or work purchased outright from author. Offers advances. Pays illustrators by the project or royalty. Pays photographers by the project, per photo or royalty. Book catalog available for 8×10 SAE and 2 first-class stamps. Ms guidelines available for SASE.
Tips: "Submit *only* nonfiction in age-appropriate subjects."

*🍁**BLIZZARD PUBLISHING**, 73 Furby St., Winnipeg, Manitoba R3L 2A2 Canada. (204)775-2923. Fax: (204)775-2947. Book publisher. Acquisitions Assistant: Todd Scarth. Publishes 2-3 picture books/year; 1-2 young readers/year; 1-2 middle readers/year; 1-2 young adult titles/year. 20% of books by first-time authors.
Fiction: Picture books: contemporary, humor, multicultural, nature/environment, special needs. Young readers, middle readers, young adult/teens: contemporary, folktales, humor, multicultural, nature/environment, special needs.
How to Contact/Writers: Query; submit outline/synopsis. Reports on queries in 1 month; mss in 2-3 months. Publishes a book 1 year after acceptance. Will consider electronic submissions via disk or modem.
Illustration: Works with 2-3 illustrators/year. Reviews ms/illustration packages from artists. Send ms with dummy. Contact: Todd Scarth, acquisitions editor. Illustrations only: Query with samples. Reports in 2-3 months. Samples returned with SASE; samples filed. Original artwork returned at job's completion.
Terms: Pays authors royalty based on retail price. Offers advances. Pays illustrators royalty. Sends galleys to authors. Book catalog free for legal-size SAE and 2 Canadian stamps (or IRC); ms guidelines available for SASE.
Tips: "Secondary materials (reviews, etc.) are important to us."

***BLUE SKY PRESS**, 555 Broadway, New York NY 10012. (212)343-6100. Book publisher. Imprint of Scholastic Inc. Contact: Editorial Submissions. Publishes 8 picture books/year; 2 young adult titles/year. 1% of books by first-time authors. Publishes various categories.
Fiction: Picture books: adventure, animal, concept, contemporary, fantasy, folktales, history, humor, multicultural, nature/environment, poetry. Young readers: adventure, anthology, contemporary, fantasy, folktales, history, humor, multicultural, nature/environment, poetry. Young adults: adventure, anthology, contemporary, fantasy, history, humor, multicultural, poetry. Multicultural needs include "strong fictional or nonfictional themes featuring non-white characters and cultures." Does not want to see mainstream religious, bibliotherapeutic, adult. Average length: picture books—varies; young adults—150 pages. Recently published *The Sorcerer's Apprentice*, by Nancy Willard, illustrated by Leo and Diane Dillon (ages 7 and up, picture book); *Freak the Mighty*, by Rodman Philbrick (ages 8 and up, young adult, middle readers); and *How Georgie Radbourn Saved Baseball*, by David Shannon (ages 5 and up, picture book).
Nonfiction: Picture books: animal, biography, concept, history, multicultural, nature/environment. Young readers: biography, history, multicultural, nature/environment. Young adults: biography, history, multicultural. Nonfiction multicultural themes "usually best handled in biography format." Average length: picture books—varies; young adults 150 pages. "Often there is a nonfiction element to Blue Sky Press fiction picture books; otherwise we have not yet published nonfiction."
How to Contact/Writers: "Due to large numbers of submissions, we are discouraging unsolicited submissions—send query (don't call!) only if you feel certain we publish the type of book you have written." Fiction: Query (novels), submit complete ms (picture books). Reports on queries/mss in 6 months. Publishes a book 1-3 years after acceptance; depending on chosen illustrator's schedule. Will not consider simultantous submissions.

Illustration: Works with 10 illustrators/year. Uses both b&w and color artwork. Reviews ms/illustration packages "only if illustrator is the author." Submit ms with dummy. Contact: Editorial Submissions. Illustrations only: Query with samples, tearsheets. Reports only if interested. Samples returned with SASE. Original artwork returned at job's completion.
Photography: Buys photos from freelancers. Contact: Photo Research Department. Buys stock and assigns work. Uses photos to accompany nonfiction. Model/property releases required. Captions required. Submit cover letter, résumé, client list, stock photo list.
Terms: Author's royalty varies by project—usually standard trade rates. Offers variable advance. Pays illustrators by the project or standard royalty based on retail price. Pays photographers by the project or royalty.
Tips: "Read currently published children's books. Revise—never send a first draft. Find your own voice, style, and subject. With material from new people we look for a theme or style strong enough to overcome the fact that the author/illustrator is unknown in the market. Children's book publishers are becoming more selective, looking for irresistible talent and fairly broad appeal; yet most are still willing to take risks, just to keep the game interesting."

***BOINGO BOOKS, INC.**, 3857 Coral Tree Circle, Suite 208, Coconut Creek FL 33073. (305)979-1085. Fax: (305)979-1354. Book producer. Creative Director: Lisa McCourt. Produces juvenile titles and series for major children's book publishers, focusing on novelty formats and original book-plus-product packages for pre-school through middle-grade. Averages 30 titles/year. 50% by first-time authors.
Fiction: Juvenile. "Subjects include any topic of interest to children age 3-12 handled in a new and innovative manner, or submitted with an original idea for book manufacturing or packaging with an inexpensive product."
Nonfiction: Juvenile. "Subjects include any topic of interest to children 3-12 handled in a new and innovative manner, or submitted with an original idea for book manufacturing or packaging with an inexpensive product."
How to Contact/Writers: Fiction/Nonfiction: Send queries, series proposals, or entire mss to Aimee Foster, Submissions Editor, 339 Park Ave., Park Ridge NJ 07656. Reports within 3 months. All submissions must include SASE. Guidelines available for #10 SASE.
Illustration: Works with 15-20 illustrators/year. Uses color artwork only. "We use a wide variety of styles." Reviews mss/illustration packages from artists. Query, submit with dummy or submit ms with some final art. Illustrations only: Send samples, résumé, promo sheet, client list. Samples are filed unless illustrator has included a SASE and "requested the return of the materials." Contact: Lisa McCourt.
Photography: Buys photos from freelancers. Contact: Lisa McCourt. Works on assignment only. Submit résumé, client list, samples or promo pieces.
Terms: All contracts negotiated separately; offers variable advance.
Tips: "Please send only submissions that are very different from the things you already see on the market. We specialize in innovative formats and unique book-plus-product packages."

***DON BOSCO MULTIMEDIA**, 130 Main St., New Rochelle NY 10801. (914)576-0122. Fax: (914)654-0443. Book publisher. Editorial Director: Dr. James T. Morgan. Production Manager: Michelle Whiton.
Nonfiction: Needs include "how various cultural groups influence the growth of the church communities; how young people shape the church of the future." Does not want to see stories about heavenly apparitions, pious poetry; doomsday chronicles. Recently published *Spirituality of Relationships*, by Don Kimball (young adult/adult).
How to Contact/Writers: Nonfiction: Submit outline/synopsis. Reports on mss in 3 weeks. Publishes a book 9-12 months after acceptance. Will consider electronic submissions via disk or modem.
Terms: Pays authors royalty of 5-10% based on retail price. Sends galleys to authors. Book catalog available for SAE; ms and art guidelines available for SASE.

BOYDS MILLS PRESS, 815 Church St., Honesdale PA 18431. (800)949-7777. Fax: (717)253-0179. Imprint: Wordsong (poetry). Book publisher. Manuscript Coordinator: Beth Troop. Art Director: Tim Gillner. 5% of books from agented writers.

- Boyds Mills appeared on a 1995 Hot List® compiled by *Children's Book Insider*. This

Combining the techniques of sponging, collage and acrylic painting, artist Cheryl Nathan created a charming array of critters for* Holiday Bugs and Birthday Beasties*. Published by Boingo Books, Inc. of Coconut Creek, Florida, the book is a collection of all-occasion greeting cards that can be removed, folded, and sealed with accompanying stickers. Creative Director Lisa McCourt says Nathan's illustrations "respect children. Too-cute artwork can be as patronizing as didactic text, so I look for art that will intrigue and captivate young readers." McCourt spotted Nathan's work at a local art show, and has since worked with her on several book projects.

list of "10 Book and Magazine Publishers Most Receptive to New Writers" is updated every few months, and available to new and renewing subscribers.

Fiction: All levels: adventure, animal, contemporary, folktales, history, humor, multicultural, poetry, problem novels, special needs, sports. Middle readers, young adults: problem novels. Multicultural themes vary. "Please query us on the appropriateness of suggested topics for middle grade and young adult. For all other submissions send entire manuscript." Does not want to see talking animals, coming-of-age novels, romance and fantasy/science fiction. Recently published *I Don't Want To Got To Camp*, by Eve Bunting (ages 4-6, contemporary picture book); *The Fall of the Red Star*, by Helen M. Szablya and Peggy King Anderson (ages 12 and up, multicultural novel); and *A Thousand Cousins*, by David L. Harrison (ages 6-10, poetry).

Nonfiction: All levels: animal, history, multicultural, nature/environment. Young readers, middle readers, young adult: geography, health, science. Does not want to see reference/curricular text. Recently published *Taking Care of the Earth*, by Laurence Pringle (ages 7-10, middle readers, nature/environment); and *Faces Only a Mother Could Love* by Jennifer Owings Dewey (ages 6-9, young readers, animals).

How to Contact/Writers: Fiction/Nonfiction: Submit complete manuscript or submit through agent. Query on middle reader, young adult and nonfiction. Reports on queries/mss in 1 month.

Illustration: Works with 50 illustrators/year. Reviews ms/illustration packages from artists. Submit complete ms with 1 or 2 pieces of art. Illustrations only: Query with samples; send résumé and slides.

Photography: Buys photos from freelancers. Contact: Tim Gillner, art director. Assigns work.

Terms: Authors paid royalty or work purchased outright. Offers advances. Illustrators paid by the project; varies. Photographers paid by the project; varies. Catalog available for 9×12 SASE. Manuscript and art guidelines available for free.

Tips: "Picture books—with fresh approaches, not work themes—are our strongest need at this time. Check to see what's already on the market before submitting your story. An increasing number of publishers seem to be closing their doors to unsolicited submissions, but at the same time, many new publishing houses are starting. Sometimes a new author can get a foot in the door with a new or small house, then develop credentials for approaching bigger houses. Authors should keep this in mind when looking for a publisher."

BRIGHT RING PUBLISHING, 1900 N. Shore Dr., Box 31338, Bellingham WA 98228-3338. (360)734-1601 or (800)480-4278. Fax: (360)676-1271. Estab. 1985. Editor: MaryAnn Kohl. Publishes 1 young reader title/year. 50% of books by first-time authors. Uses only recipe format—"but no cookbooks unless woven into another subject like art, music, science."

- Bright Rings accepts no picture books, no poetry, no stories of any kind and no crafts—strictly nonfiction.

Nonfiction: Young readers and middle readers: activity books involving art ideas, hobbies, cooking, how-to, multicultural, music/dance, nature/environment, science. Average length: "about 125 ideas/book." Multicultural needs include: arts of world cultures or relate to kids' literature. "We are moving into only recipe-style resource books in any variety of subject areas—useful with children 2-12. 'Whole language' is the buzz word in early education—so books to meet the new demands of that subject will be needed." Published: SCRIBBLE ART: *Independent Creative Art Experiences for Children*; MUDWORKS: *Creative Clay, Dough, and Modeling Experiences*; and SCIENCE ARTS: *Discovering Science Through Art Experiences*.

How to Contact/Writers: Nonfiction: submit complete ms. Reports on queries in 2 weeks; mss in 6 weeks. Publishes a book 1 year after acceptance. Will consider simultaneous submissions.

Illustration: Works with 2 illustrators/year. Prefers to review "black line (drawings) for text." Reviews ms/illustration packages from artists. "Query first." Illustrations only: Query with samples; send tearsheets and "sample of ideas I request after query." Reports in 6-8 weeks.

Terms: Pays authors in royalties of 3-10% based on net sales. Work purchased outright (range: $500-2,000). Pays illustrators $500-2,000. Also offers "free books and discounts for future books." Book catalog, ms/artist's guidelines for business-size SAE and 32¢ postage.

Tips: "Bright Ring Publishing is not looking for picture books, juvenile fiction, or poetry at this time. We are, however, highly interested in creative activity and resource books for children to use independently or for teachers and parents to use with children. Must work for pre-school through age 12." We cannot accept book ideas which require unusual packaging such as attached toys or unique binding or paper."

***BROADMAN & HOLMAN PUBLISHERS**, Baptist Sunday School Board, 127 Ninth Ave. N., Nashville TN 37234. Book publisher. Acquisitions & Development Editor: Janis M. Whipple. Publishes 4 middle readers/year; 4 young adult titles/year. 25% of books by first-time authors. "All books have Christian values/themes."

Nonfiction: Middle readers: biography, religion, self help, social issues, special needs, devotional. Young adults: biography, careers, religion, self help, social issues special needs, devotional. Special needs include books on parenting or friendship with special-needs children. Average word length: middle readers—30,000; young adults—45,000-60,000. Recently published *258 Great Dates While You Wait*, by Susie Shellenberger and Greg Johnson (dating book for teens); *First Days in High School* and *First Days of College*, both by Mary Sayler (devotional books for young adult/teens); *Real Kids, Real Adventures*, by Deborah Morris (real life adventure stories about kids for middle readers).

How to Contact/Writers: Nonfiction: Query, submit outline/synopsis and 2 sample chapters. Reports on queries in 4-6 weeks; mss in 2 months. Publishes a book 1 year after acceptance. Will consider simultaneous submissions.

Terms: Pays authors royalty 12-20% based on wholesale price. Offers variable advance. Sends galleys to authors. Book catalog available for 9×12 SAE and 2 first-class stamps. Ms guidelines available for SASE.

Tips: "We're looking specifically for nonfiction Christian issues/devotions for middle readers and teens."

CAMBRIDGE EDUCATIONAL, P.O. Box 2153, Charleston WV 25328-2153. (800)468-4227. Fax: (800)FAX-ONUS (329-6687). Contact: Editor. Publishes 10-20 middle readers/year; 20-40 young adult titles/year. 15-20% of books by first-time authors.

Nonfiction: Middle readers and young adults: activity books, arts/crafts, careers, concept, geography, history, how-to, nature/environment, science, self-help, social issues, sports. Published *Underdeveloped and Overexposed: Putting Your Self-Esteem in Focus*, by K. Lordan (ages 9-adult, self-help); and *Basic Office Skills*, by DeFaila (ages 9-adult, self-help).

How to Contact/Writers: Submit outline/synopsis. Reports on queries in 1-2 weeks; mss in 1-2 months. Publishes a book 6 months after acceptance. Will consider simultaneous submissions, electronic submissions via disk or modem, and previously published work.

Illustration: Uses b&w and color artwork. Reviews ms/illustration packages from artists. Query. Illustrations only: Query with samples and tearsheets. Samples returned with SASE; samples not filed. Originals not returned.

Photography: Buys photos from freelancers. Contact: Charlotte Angel, production director. Buys stock and assigns work. Model/property releases required. Uses 5×7 glossy b&w prints, 35mm, 2¼×2¼, or 4×5 transparencies. Submit letter.

Terms: Pays authors royalty of 15-20% based on retail price. Work purchased outright from authors (range: $1,500-5,000). Offers advances (average amount: $1,000). Pays illustrators by the project (range: $250-1,000). Pays photographers by the project (range: $250-1,000); per photo (range: $50-500). Book catalog available for 9×12 SAE and 7 first-class stamps; ms and art guidelines available for SASE.

Tips: Looking for "more titles to break down cultural diversity barriers; self-help or career oriented titles; more titles dealing with controversial issues facing children."

CANDLEWICK PRESS, 2067 Massachusetts Ave., Cambridge MA 02140. (617)661-3330. Fax: (617)661-0565. Book publisher. Editorial Assistant: Bruce Frost. Design Coordinator: Aimee Smith. Publishes 120 picture books/year; 6 young readers/year; 10 middle readers/year; and 6 young adult titles/year. 5% of books by first-time authors.

• Candlewick won a Boston Globe-Horn Book Honor Award for nonfiction for *It's Perfectly Normal: Changing Bodies, Growing Up, Sex, and Sexual Health*, by Robie H. Harris, illustrated by Michael Emberley. They cannot accept unsolicited manuscripts.

Fiction: Picture books, young readers: animal, contemporary, fantasy, folktales, history. Middle readers, young adults: adventure, animal, anthology, contemporary, fantasy, folktales, history, poetry.

Nonfiction: Picture book, young readers, middle readers: animal, biography, history, music/dance, nature/environment. Young adults: animal, biography, history, music/dance.

How to Contact/Writers: Only interested in agented material. Reports on queries in 3 weeks; mss in 3 months. Publishes a book 12-18 months after acceptance. Will consider simultaneous submissions.

Illustration: Works with 50 illustrators/year. "We prefer to see a variety of the artist's style." Reviews ms/illustration packages from artists. "General samples only please." Illustrations only: Submit résumé and portfolio. Samples returned with SASE; samples filed. Original artwork returned at job's completion.

Terms: Pays authors royalty of 5-10% based on retail price. Offers advances. Pays illustrators 5-10% royalty based on retail price. Sends galleys to authors; dummies to illustrators. Book catalog available for 9×12 SAE and $1.67 postage.

CAROLINA WREN PRESS/LOLLIPOP POWER BOOKS, 120 Morris St., Durham NC 27701. (919)560-2738. Book publisher. Carolina Wren, Estab. 1976; Lollipop Power, Estab. 1971. Both are nonprofit, small presses. Children's Editor: Ruth A. Smullin. Designer: Martha Scotford. Publishes an average of 1 picture book/year.

• Carolina Wren will not be reviewing manuscripts until 1997. Contact them at that time for current status.

Fiction: Picture books: bilingual (English/Spanish), multicultural, multiracial, nonsexist. Average length: 30 pages.

How to Contact/Writers: "Query and request guidelines; enclose SASE with request. All manuscripts must be typed, double-spaced and accompanied by SASE of appropriate size with sufficient postage. If you do not wish your manuscript returned, you may simply enclose SASE for our response. Do not send illustrations." Reports on queries/ms in 3 months. Publishes a book 2-3 years after acceptance.

Illustration: Reviews ms/illustration packages from artists. Contact: Martha Scotford, designer. Illustration only: Query with tearsheets. Reports on art samples only if SASE enclosed. Original artwork returned at job's completion.

Terms: Pays authors in royalties of 5% of print-run based on retail price, or cash, if available. Pays illustrators in royalties of 5% of print-run based on retail price, or cash, if available.

Tips: "Lollipop Power Books offer alternative points of view to prevailing stereotypes. Our books show children: girls and women who are self-sufficient, with responsibilities beyond those of home and family; boys and men who are emotional and nurturing and involved in domestic responsibilities; families that use day care or alternative child care; families that consist of one parent only, working parents, or extended families; realistic portrayals of children of all races and ethnic groups, who have in common certain universal feelings and experiences. We believe that children must be taken seriously. Our books present their problems honestly and without condescension. Lollipop Power Books must be well-written stories that will appeal to children. We are not interested in preachy tales where message overpowers plot and character. We are looking for good stories told from a child's point of view. Our current publishing priorities are: a) African-American, Hispanic or Native American characters; b) bilingual books (English/Spanish); c) books that show gay men or lesbian women as ordinary people who can raise children. To request a catalog, send a 9×12 envelope with postage sufficient for 2 ounces."

CAROLRHODA BOOKS, INC., 241 First Ave. N., Minneapolis MN 55401. (612)332-3344. Book publisher. Estab. 1969. Submissions Editor: Rebecca Poole. Publishes 5 picture books/year; 25 young reader titles/year; 30 middle reader titles/year. 20% of books by first-time authors; 10% of books from agented writers.

Fiction: Picture books: folktales, multicultural, nature/environment. Young readers, middle readers: historical, special needs. Average word length: picture books—1,000-1,500; young readers—2,000. Published *Pug, Slug, and Doug the Thug*, by Carol Saller; and *A Place to Belong*, by Emily Crofford.

Nonfiction: Young readers, middle readers: animal, biography, history, hobbies, multicultural, nature/environment, science, social issues, special needs. Multicultural needs include biographies. Average word length: young readers— 2,000; middle readers—6,000. Published *What I Had Was Singing: The Story of Marian Anderson*, by Jeri Ferris; and *Grand Canyon*, by Patrick Cone.
How to Contact/Writers: Fiction/Nonfiction: Submit complete ms. Reports on queries in 3-4 weeks; mss in 3 months. Publishes a book 18 months after acceptance. Will consider simultaneous submissions. Must enclose SASE.
Illustration: "Do not send originals. We like illustrators to send samples we can keep on file." Reviews ms/illustration packages from artists. Submit at least 1 sample illustration (in form of photocopy, slide, duplicate photo) with full ms. Contact: Rebecca Poole, submissions editor. Illustrations only: Query with samples; send résumé/slides. Reports on art samples only if interested. Samples kept on file.
Photography: Purchases photos from freelancers. Buys stock and assigns work.
Terms: Buys ms outright for variable amount. Factors used to determine final payment for illustrations: color vs. b&w, number of illustrations, quality of work. Sends galleys to authors; dummies to illustrators. Book catalog available for 9×12 SAE and 3 first-class stamps; ms guidelines for #10 SAE and 1 first-class stamp.
Tips: Writers: "Research the publishing company to be sure it is in the market for the type of book you're interested in writing. Familiarize yourself with the company's list. We specialize in beginning readers, photo essays and books published in series. We do very few single-title picture books and no novels. For more detailed information about our publishing program, consult our catalog. We do not publish any of the following: textbooks, workbooks, songbooks, puzzles, plays and religious material. In general, we suggest that you steer clear of alphabet books; preachy stories with a moral to convey; stories featuring anthropomorphic protagonists ('Amanda the Amoeba,' 'Frankie the Fire Engine,' 'Tonie the Tornado'); and stories that revolve around trite, unoriginal plots. Be sure to avoid racial and sexual stereotypes in your writing, as well as sexist language." (See also Lerner Publications.)

CHARIOT BOOKS, 4050 Lee Vance View, Colorado Springs CO 80918. (719)536-3280. An imprint of Chariot Family Products and a division of David C. Cook Publishing Co. Book publisher. Managing Editor: Julie Smith. Publishes 20-30 picture books/year; 6-8 young readers/year; 10-15 middle readers/year; 4-6 young adult titles/year. Less than 5% of books by first-time authors; 15% of books from agented authors. "All books have overt Christian values, but there is no primary theme."

- Chariot does not read unsolicited manuscripts.

Illustration: Works with 20 illustrators/year. "Send color material I can keep." Query with samples; send résumé, promo sheet, portfolio, tearsheets. Reports only if interested. Samples returned with SASE; samples filed. Original artwork returned at job's completion.
Terms: Pays illustrators by the project, royalty or work purchased outright. Sends dummies to illustrators. Ms guidelines available for SASE.

CHARLESBRIDGE, 85 Main St., Watertown MA 02172. (617)926-0329. Fax: (617)926-5720. Subsidiary of Mastery Education. Book publisher. Publishes 14 picture books/year. Managing Editor: Elena Dworkin Wright. Publishes nature or science picture books.

- Charlesbridge appeared on a 1995 Hot List® compiled by *Children's Book Insider*. This list of "10 Book and Magazine Publishers Most Receptive to New Writers" is updated every few months, and available to new and renewing subscribers.

Fiction: Picture books: nature/environment, animal, humor, multicultural. Multicultural needs include Hispanic, Latino.
Nonfiction: Picture books: animal, concept, geography, math/counting, multicultural, nature/environment, science, textbooks. "We look for accurate biological and behavioral information about animals in their appropriate environment." Average word length: picture books—1,500. Recently published: *The M&M Counting Book*, by Barbara McGrath (picture book); *Can We Be Friends? Partners in Nature*, by Alexandra Wright (picture book); and *Families of the Deep Blue Sea*, by Kenneth Mallory.
How to Contact/Writers: Nonfiction: Submit complete ms. Reports on queries/mss in 1 month. Publishes a book 1-2 years after acceptance.

Illustration: Works with 10 illustrators/year. Uses color artwork only. Reviews ms/illustration packages from artists. Illustrations only: Query with samples; provide résumé, tearsheets to be kept on file. Reports back only if interested.
Terms: Pays authors in royalties or work purchased outright. Pays illustrators by the project. Book catalog, ms/art guidelines available for SASE.
Tips: Wants "picture books that have humor and are factually correct."

CHELSEA HOUSE PUBLISHERS, 300 Park Ave. S., New York NY 10010. (212)677-4010. Fax: (212)677-9414. Creative Director: Bob Mitchell. Art Director: Joan Ferrigno. Publishes 40 middle readers/year; 80 young adult titles/year. 50% of books by first-time authors.
Nonfiction: Middle readers, young adults: biography, history, multicultural, science, sports. Average word length: middle readers—10,000; young adults—20,000.
How to Contact/Writers: Nonfiction: Submit outline/synopsis and 1 sample chapter. Reports on queries/mss in 1 month. Publishes a book 9 months after acceptance. Will consider electronic submissions via disk or modem.
Illustration: Works with 40 illustrators/year. Uses color artwork only. Illustrations only: Arrange personal portfolio review. Reports in 1 month. Samples returned with SASE; samples filed. Original artwork returned at job's completion.
Terms: Work purchased outright from authors. Pays illustrators by the project. Sends galleys to authors. Book catalog and ms guidelines available for SAE.

***■CHERUBIC PRESS**, P.O. Box 5036, Johnstown PA 15904-5036. Phone/fax: (814)535-4300. Acquisitions Editor: Juliette Gray. Director: Anna Dorin. Publishes 2-3 picture books/year; 2-3 middle readers/year. 50% of books by first-time authors; 10% subsidy published. "All books must teach children something—answer children's questions, address their fears."
Fiction: Picture books and young readers: adventure, animal, concept, contemporary, folktales, health, history, humor, nature/environment, special needs, sports, suspense/mystery. Middle readers: adventure, animal, contemporary, folktales, health, history, humor, nature/environment, problem novels, romance, special needs, sports, suspense/mystery. Does not want to see fantasy or science fiction, but New Age spirituality is a possibility. Average word length: picture books—100-400; young readers—100-400; middle readers—100-800. Recently published *Grandpa's Berries—A Story to Help Children Understand Grief and Loss*, by Julie G. Dickerson, illustrated by Patricia Brant (ages 6-12, picture book).
How to Contact/Writers: Fiction: Submit complete ms. Reports on queries/mss in 1-2 months. Publishes a book 1 year after acceptance. Will consider simultaneous submissions "when noted as such."
Illustration: Works with 2-3 illustrators/year. Uses primarily b&w artwork; color for covers. Prefers pencil, charcoal or pen & ink for interior art. Reviews ms/illustration packages from authors. Submit ms with dummy. Contact: Anna Dorin, director. Illustration only: Query with samples (copies—no originals) or samples of portrait art (copies only) with model releases. Uses primarily b&w artwork. Reports in 2 months. Samples returned with SASE; samples filed.
Terms: Pays authors minimum royalty of 10% based on wholesale price. Pays illustrators minimum royalty of 10% based on wholesale price. Sends galleys to authors; dummies to illustrators. Book catalog for legal size SAE.
Tips: "Read books on how to write and sell children's books to get a background on how books are chosen, how manuscripts are submitted, the purpose of a dummy, etc."

CHICAGO REVIEW PRESS, 814 N. Franklin St., Chicago IL 60610. (312)337-0747. Book publisher. Editorial Director: Amy Teschner. Art Director: Joan Sommers. Publishes 1 middle reader/year; "about 4" young adult titles/year. 50% of books by first-time authors; 30% of books from agented authors. "We publish art activity books for young children and project books in the arts and sciences for ages 10 and up (our Ziggurat Series). We do not publish fiction."
Nonfiction: Young readers, middle readers and young adults: activity books, arts/crafts. "We're interested in hands-on, educational books; anything else probably will be rejected." Average length: young readers and young adults—175 pages. Recently published *Kids Camp/Activities for the Backyard or Wilderness*, by Laurie Carlson (ages 4-12); *Why Design? Activities & Projects From The National Building Museum*, by Anna Slafer and Kevin Cahill (ages 12 and up) and *Video Cinema: Techniques and Projects for Beginning Filmmakers*, by John Parris Frantz (ages

11 and up). Reports on queries/mss in 2 months. Publishes a book 1-2 years after acceptance. Will consider simultaneous submissions and previously published work.
How to Contact/Writers: Reports on queries/mss in 2 months.
Illustration: Works with 4 illustrators/year. Uses primarily b&w artwork. Reviews ms/illustration packages from artists. Submit 1-2 chapters of ms with corresponding pieces of final art. Illustrations only: Query with samples, résumé. Contact: Joan Sommers, art director. Reports back only if interested. Samples not returned; samples filed. Original artwork "usually" returned at job's completion.
Photography: Buys photos from freelancers ("but not often"). Contact: Joan Summers, art director. Buys stock and assigns work. Wants "instructive photos. We consult our files when we know what we're looking for on a book-by-book basis." Uses b&w prints.
Terms: Pays authors royalty of 7½-12½% based on retail price. Offers advances ("but not always") of $500-1,500. Pays illustrators by the project (range varies considerably). Pays photographers by the project (range varies considerably). Sends galleys to authors. Book catalog/ms guidelines available for $3.
Tips: "We're looking for original activity books for small children and the adults caring for them—new themes and enticing projects to occupy kids' imaginations and promote their sense of personal creativity. We like activity books that are as much fun as they are constructive. For older kids, age 10 and up, we publish Ziggurat Books—activity books geared to teach a discipline in the arts or sciences. Our Ziggurat books are intended to encourage children to pursue interests and talents inspired but not thoroughly covered by their schoolwork or other influences. When a kid becomes curious about say, videography or graphic design, we want to provide the challenging hands-on book that will cultivate enthusiasm while teaching him or her all about that intriguing subject. We are also providing teachers with a myriad of projects for various subjects taught in the classroom. Please write for guidelines so you'll know what we're looking for."

CHILDREN'S BOOK PRESS, 6400 Hollis St., Suite 4, Emeryville CA 94608. (510)655-3395. Contact: Submissions Editor. Publishes 3 picture books/year. 50% of books by first-time authors. "Children's Book Press is a nonprofit publisher of bilingual and multicultural children's literature. We publish folktales and contemporary stories reflecting the traditions and culture of the emerging majority in the United States and from countries around the world. Our goal is to help broaden the base of children's literature in this country to include more stories from the African-American, Asian-American, Hispanic and Native American communities as well as the diverse Spanish-speaking communities throughout the Americas."
Fiction: Picture books, middle readers, young adults: contemporary, multicultural. Average word length: picture books—800-1,600.
How to Contact/Writers: Fiction: Submit complete ms to Submissions Editor. Reports on queries in 2-4 months, mss in 1-4 months. Publishes a book 1 year after acceptance. Will consider simultaneous submissions.
Illustration: Works with 4 illustrators/year. Uses color artwork only. Reviews ms/illustration packages from artists. Send ms with 3 or 4 color photocopies. Illustrations only: Send slides. Reports in 1-12 months. Samples returned with SASE. Original artwork returned at job's completion.
Terms: Pays authors royalty. Pays illustrators by the project. Book catalog available for SAE; ms guidelines available for SASE.
Tips: "Vocabulary level should be approximately third grade (eight years-old) or below. Keep in mind, however, that many of the young people who read our books may be nine, ten, or eleven years old or older. Their life experiences are often more advanced than their reading level, so try to write a story that will appeal to a fairly wide age range. We are especially interested in humorous stories and original stories about contemporary life from the multicultural communities mentioned above by writers *from* those communities."

"Picture books" are for preschoolers to 8-year-olds; "Young readers" are for 5- to 8-year-olds; "Middle readers" are for 9- to 11-year-olds; and "Young adults" are for those ages 12 and up.

CHILDRENS PRESS, Sherman Turnpike, Danbury CT 06816. (203)797-3500. Book publisher. Vice President/Publisher: John Selfridge. Publishes more than 100 titles/year. 5% of books by first-time authors. Publishes informational (nonfiction) for K-6; picture books for young readers K-3.

Fiction: Picture books, young readers: adventure, animal, concept, contemporary, folktales, multicultural. Middle readers: contemporary, hi-lo, humor, multicultural. Young adults: hi-lo. Does not want to see young adult fiction, romance or science fiction. Average word length: picture book—300; middle readers—4,000.

Nonfiction: Picture books: arts/crafts, biography, concept, geography, hi-lo, history, hobbies, how-to, multicultural, nature/environment, science, special needs. Young readers: animal, arts/crafts, biography, careers, concept, geography, health, hi-lo, history, hobbies, multicultural, nature/environment, science, social issues, sports. Middle readers: hi-lo, history, multicultural, reference, science. Average word length: picture books—400; young readers—2,000; middle readers—8,000; young adult—12,000.

How to Contact/Writers: Fiction: Query; submit outline/synopsis or submit outline/synopsis and 1 sample chapter. Nonfiction: Query; submit outline/synopsis. SASE required for response. Reports in 2-3 months. Publishes book 18 months after acceptance. Will consider simultaneous submissions.

Illustration: Works with 14 illustrators/year. Uses color artwork only. Reviews ms/illustration packages from artists. Illustrations only: Query with samples or arrange personal portfolio review. Contact: V. Fischman, art director. Reports back only if interested. Samples returned with SASE. Samples filed. Originals not returned.

Photography: Purchases photos from freelancers. Contact: Photo Editor. Buys stock and assigns work. Model/property releases and captions required. Uses color and b&w prints; $2\frac{1}{4} \times 2\frac{1}{4}$, 35mm transparencies. Photographers should send cover letter and stock photo list.

Terms: Pays authors royalty of 5% based on net or work purchased outright (range: $500-1,000). Offers average advances of $1,000. Pays illustrators by the project (range: $1,800-3,500). Photographers paid per photo (range: $50-100). Sends galleys to authors; dummies to illustrators. Book catalog available for SAE; ms guidelines for SASE.

Tips: "Never write down to reader; keep language lively."

CHILDREN'S WRITER'S & ILLUSTRATOR'S MARKET, 1507 Dana Ave., Cincinnati OH 45207. (513)531-2690, ext. 546. E-mail: wdigest@aol.com. Publication of Writer's Digest Books. Editor: Alice P. Buening. Annual directory of freelance markets for children's writers, illustrators and photographers.

Illustration: Send samples—photographs, tearsheets or good quality photocopies of artwork. Continuous tone b&w artwork reproduces best. Since *Children's Writer's & Illustrator's Market* is published only once a year, submissions are kept on file for the upcoming edition until selections are made. Material is then returned by SASE.

Terms: Buys one-time rights to 8-12 illustrations/year. Pays $50 to holder of reproduction rights and free copy of *CWIM* when published.

Tips: "I need examples of art that have been sold to one of the listings in *CWIM*. Thumb through the book for examples. The art must have been freelanced; it cannot have been done as staff work. Include the name of the listing that purchased the work, what the art was used for and the payment you received."

***CHRISTIAN ED. PUBLISHERS**, P.O. Box 26639, San Diego CA 92196. (619)578-4700. Book publisher. Managing Editor: Carol Rogers. Publishes 64 curriculum titles/year.

Fiction: Picture books and young readers: contemporary. Middle readers: adventure, contemporary, suspense/mystery. "We also publish fiction for Bible club take-home papers."

Nonfiction: Publishes Bible curriculum and take-home papers for all ages.

How to Contact/Writers: Fiction/Nonfiction: Query. Reports on queries in 3-4 weeks. Publishes a book 1 year after acceptance.

Illustration: Works with 4-5 illustrators/year. Uses primarily b&w artwork. Query; include a SASE; we'll send an application form. Contact: Carol Rogers, managing editor. Reports in 3-4 weeks. Samples returned with SASE.

Terms: Work purchased outright from authors for 3¢/word. Pays illustrators by the project (range: $200-300/book). Book catalog available for 9×12 SAE and 5 first-class stamps; ms and art guidelines available for SASE.

Tips: "Read our guidelines carefully before sending us a manuscript or illustrations. All writing and illustrating is done on assignment only, and must be age-appropriate (preschool through sixth grade)."

CHRONICLE BOOKS, 275 Fifth St., San Francisco CA 94103. (415)777-7240. Fax: (415)495-2478. Book publisher. Director of Children's Books: Victoria Rock. Editorial Assistant: Erica Jacobs. Publishes 25-40 (both fiction and nonfiction) picture books/year; 2-4 middle readers nonfiction titles/year; 2-4 beginning readers or middle readers fiction/year. 10-50% of books by first-time authors; 10-50% of books from agented writers.

Fiction: Picture books: animal, folktales, history, multicultural, nature/environment. Young readers: animal, folktales, history, multicultural, nature/environment, poetry. Middle readers: animal, history, multicultural, nature/environment, poetry, problem novels. Young adults: multicultural needs include "projects that feature diverse children in everyday situations." Recently published *Little Vampire's Diary*, by Sonia Holleyman; and *The Trouble with Mister*, by Debbie Keller and Shannon McNeil.

Nonfiction: Picture books: animal, history, multicultural, nature/environment, science. Young readers: animal, arts/crafts, cooking, geography, history, multicultural and science. Middle readers: animal, arts/crafts, biography, cooking, geography, history, multicultural and nature/environment. Young adults: biography and multicultural. Recently published *Any Bear Can Wear Glasses*, by Sylvia Thomas and Matthew Long; and *Waiting for Filippo*, by Michael Bender.

How to Contact/Writers: Fiction/Nonfiction: Submit complete ms (picture books); submit outline/synopsis and 3 sample chapters (for older readers). Reports on queries/mss in 2-18 weeks. Publishes a book 1-3 years after acceptance. Will consider simultaneous submissions, as long as they are marked "multiple submission." Will not consider submissions by fax.

Illustration: Works with 15-20 illustrators/year. Wants "unusual art, something that will stand out on the shelves. Either bright and modern or very traditional. Fine art, not mass market." Reviews ms/illustration packages from artists. "Indicate if project *must* be considered jointly, or if editor may consider text and art separately." Illustrations only: Submit samples of artist's work (not necessarily from book, but in the envisioned style). Slides, tearsheets and color photocopies OK. (No original art.) Dummies helpful. Résumé helpful. "If samples sent for files, generally no response—unless samples are not suited to list, in which case samples are returned. Queries and project proposals responded to in same time frame as author query/proposals."

Photography: Purchases photos from freelancers. Works on assignment only. Wants nature/natural history photos.

Terms: Generally pays authors in royalties based on retail price "though we do occasionally work on a flat fee basis." Advance varies. Illustrators paid royalty based on retail price or flat fee. Sends proofs to authors and illustrators. Book catalog for 9×12 SAE and 8 first-class stamps; manuscript guidelines for #10 SASE.

Tips: "Chronicle Books publishes an eclectic mixture of traditional and innovative children's books. We are interested in taking on projects that have a unique bent to them—be it in subject matter, writing style, or illustrative technique. As a small list, we are looking for books that will lend our list a distinctive flavor. Primarily we are interested in fiction and nonfiction picture books for children ages infant-8 years, and nonfiction books for children ages 8-12 years. We are also interested in developing a middle grade/YA fiction program, and are looking for literary fiction that deals with relevant issues. Our sales reps are witnessing a resistance to alphabet books. And the market has become increasingly competitive. The '80s boom in children's publishing has passed, and the market is demanding high-quality books that work on many different levels."

CLARION BOOKS, 215 Park Ave. S., New York NY 10003. (212)420-5889. Houghton Mifflin Co. Book publisher. Editor and Publisher: Dorothy Briley. Art Director: Anne Diebel. Publishes 20 picture books/year; 7 young reader titles/year; 14 middle reader titles/year; 4 young adult titles/year. 10% of books by first-time authors; 15% of books from agented writers.

- Clarion won a Newbery Honor Medal in 1995 for *Catherine, Called Birdy*, by Karen Cushman. See First Books for an interview with the author.

Fiction: All levels: adventure, contemporary, folktales, history, humor, multicultural, poetry, science fiction. Average word length: picture books—50-1,000; young readers—1,000-2,500; middle readers—10,000-30,000; young adults—20,000-30,000. Recently published *The Midwife's Apprentice*, by Karen Cushman, (young adult fiction); and *Piggie Pie*, by Margie Palatini and Howard Fine (ages 5-8, picture book).

Nonfiction: All levels: animal, biography, concept, history, multicultural, nature/environment, science, social issues. Average word length: picture books—750-1,000; young readers—1,000-2,500; middle readers—10,000-30,000. Recently published *Across America on an Emigrant Train*, by Jim Murphy (nonfiction).
How to Contact/Writers: Fiction: Send complete ms. Nonfiction: Query. Reports on queries in 1 month; mss in 2-3 months. Publishes a book 18-24 months after acceptance. Will consider simultaneous submissions. "Address all submissions to Dorothy Briley."
Illustration: Works with 30 illustrators/year. Uses primarily color artwork. Reviews ms/illustration packages from artists. Send ms with dummy. "No original art." Illustrations only: Query with samples. Samples returned with SASE; samples filed "if interested." Reports on art samples only if interested. Original artwork returned at job's completion.
Terms: Pays in royalties of 10% based on retail price, shared 50/50 by author and illustrator. Offers advance (average amount: $2,500-5,000). Sends galleys to authors; dummies to illustrators. Ms/artist's guidelines free on request with #10 SASE; book catalog and guidelines free on request with 9×12 SASE ($1.24 postage).

COBBLEHILL BOOKS, 375 Hudson St., New York NY 10014. (212)366-2628. Affiliate of Dutton Children's Books, a division of Penguin Books USA Inc. Book publisher. Editorial Director: Joe Ann Daly. Executive Editor: Rosanne Lauer.

- See First Books for an interview with Cobblehill photographer/author Doug Wechsler on his book *Bizarre Bugs*.

Fiction: Picture books, young readers: adventure, animal, contemporary, easy-to-read, sports, suspense/mystery. Middle readers: adventure, contemporary, problem novels, sports, suspense/mystery. Young adults: adventure, suspense/mystery.
Nonfiction: Picture books, young readers: animal, nature/environment, sports. Middle readers: nature/environment.
How to Contact/Writers: Fiction/Nonfiction: Query. Will consider simultaneous submissions "if we are informed about them."
Illustration: Illustrations only: Submit samples to keep on file, no original artwork. Original artwork returned at job's completion.
Terms: Pays authors in royalties. Pays illustrators royalties or a flat fee. Book catalog available for 8½×11 SAE and 2 first-class stamps; ms guidelines available for #10 SASE.

CONCORDIA PUBLISHING HOUSE, 3558 S. Jefferson Ave., St. Louis MO 63118. (314)268-1000. Book publisher. Family and Children's Resources Editor: Ruth Geisler. Art Director: Ed Luhmann. "Concordia Publishing House publishes a number of quality children's books each year. Most are fiction, with some nonfiction, based on a religious subject."
Fiction/Nonfiction: "Reader interest ranges from picture books to young adults. All books must contain explicit Christian content." Published *Little Visits on the Go*, by Mary Manz Simon (family devotional book and audio tape); *The Biggest Bully in Brookdale*, by Carol Gormon (The Tree House Kids series, grades 2-3, first chapter books); *God Loves Me—So What*, by Guy Doud (preteen and teen, Christian living).
How to Contact/Writers: Fiction: Query. Submit complete ms (picture books); submit outline/synopsis and sample chapters (novel-length). Reports on queries in 1 month; mss in 2 months. Publishes a book 1 year after acceptance. Will consider simultaneous submissions.
Illustration: Illustrations only: Query with samples. Contact: Ed Luhmann, art director.
Terms: Pays authors in royalties based on retail price or outright purchase (minimum $500). Sends galleys to author. Ms guidelines for 1 first-class stamp and a #10 envelope.
Tips: "Do not send finished artwork with the manuscript. If sketches will help in the presentation of the manuscript, they may be sent. If stories are taken from the Bible, they should follow the Biblical account closely. Liberties should not be taken in fantasizing Biblical stories."

✤COTEAU BOOKS LTD., 401-2206 Dewdney Ave., Regina, Saskatchewan S4R 1H3 Canada. (306)777-0170. Thunder Creek Publishing Co-op Ltd. Book publisher. Managing Editor: Shelley Sopher. Publishes 1-2 juvenile and/or young adult books/year, 9-12 books/year. 10% of books by first-time authors.
Fiction: Middle readers, young adults: adventure, contemporary, fantasy, history, humor, multicultural, nature/environment, suspense/mystery. "No didactic, message pieces, nothing religious."

How to Contact/Writers: Fiction: Submit complete ms. Reports on queries in 3 months; mss in 5 months. Publishes a book 1-2 years after acceptance. Coteau Books publishes Canadian writers only; mss from the US are returned unopened.
Illustration: Only Canadian illustrators are used. Illustrations only: Submit nonreturnable samples. Contact: Ruth Linka, production coordinator. Reports only if interested. Original artwork returned at job's completion.
Photography: "Very occasionally buys photos from freelancers." Buys stock and assigns work.
Terms: Pays authors in royalties of 5-12½% based on retail price. Other method of payment: "signing bonus." Pays illustrators by the project (range: $500-2,000) or royalty of 5% maximum based on retail price. Sends galleys to authors; dummies to illustrators. Book catalog free on request with 9×12 SASE.

CRESTWOOD HOUSE, 250 James St., Morristown NJ 07960. Imprint of Silver Burdett Press, Simon & Schuster Education Group. Book publisher. Editor: Debby Biber. See Silver Burdett Press listing.

CROCODILE BOOKS, USA, 46 Crosby St., Northhampton MA 01060. (413)582-7054. Imprint of Interlink Publishing Group, Inc. Book publisher. Vice President: Ruth Moushabeck. Publishes 16 picture books/year. 25% of books by first-time authors.

- Crocodile does not accept unsolicited manuscripts.

Fiction: Picture books: animal, contemporary, history, spy/mystery/adventure.
Nonfiction: Picture book: history, nature/environment.
Terms: Pays authors in royalties. Sends galleys to author; dummies to illustrator.

CROSSWAY BOOKS, Good News Publishers, 1300 Crescent, Wheaton IL 60187. (708)682-4300. Fax: (708)682-4785. Book Publisher. Editorial Director: Leonard Goss. Publishes 1-2 picture books/year; 2-4 middle readers/year; 2-4 young adult titles/year. "Crossway Books is committed to publishing books that bring Biblical reality to readers and that examine crucial issues through a Christian world view."
Fiction: Picture books: religion. Middle readers: adventure, contemporary, fantasy, history, humor, religion, suspense/mystery, supernatural, Christian realism. Young adults: contemporary, fantasy, history, humor, religion, suspense/mystery, supernatural, Christian realism. Does not want to see horror novels, romance or prophecy novels. Published *Tell Me the Secrets*, by Max Lucado, illustrated by Ron DiCianni.
How to Contact/Writers: Fiction: Submit outline/synopsis. Reports on queries/mss in 4-6 weeks. Publishes a book 12-18 months after acceptance. Will consider simultaneous submissions.
Illustration: Works with 5 illustrators/year. Reviews ms/illustration packages from artists. Query. Illustrations only: Query with samples; provide resume, promo sheet and client list.
Terms: Pays authors royalty based on net sales. Pays illustrators by the project. Sends galleys to authors; dummies to illustrators. Book catalog available; ms guidelines available for SASE.

CROWN PUBLISHERS (CROWN BOOKS FOR CHILDREN), 201 E. 50th St., New York NY 10022. (212)940-7742. Imprint of Random House, Inc. See Random House listing.

- Crown won a Caldecott Honor Medal in 1995 for *Time Flies*, illustrated and written by Eric Rohmann.

***CRUMB ELBOW PUBLISHING**, P.O. Box 294, Rhododendron OR 97049. Book publisher. Publisher: Michael P. Jones. Publishes 5 picture books/year; 5 young readers/year; 5 middle readers/year; 5 young adult titles/year. 40% of books by first-time authors. Primary subjects include history, nature, environment and criminal justice.
Fiction: Picture books, young readers, middle readers and young adults: adventure, animal, anthology, contemporary, fantasy, folktales, health, hi-lo, history, humor, multicultural, nature/

The maple leaf before a listing indicates that the market is Canadian.

environment, poetry, problem novels, religion, romance, science fiction, special needs, sports, suspense/mystery. Also picture books and young readers: concept.

Nonfiction: Picture books, young readers, middle readers and young adults: activity books, animal, arts/crafts, biography, careers, concept, cooking, geography, health, hi-lo, history, hobbies, how-to, multicultural, music/dance, nature/environment, reference, religion, science, self help, social issues, special needs, sports, textbooks.

How to Contact/Writers: Fiction/Nonfiction: Submit complete ms. Reports on queries in 2 weeks; mss in 1 month. Considers simultaneous submissions and previously published work.

Illustration: Works with 10 illustrators/year. Uses primarily b&w artwork. Prefers 5×7 or 8×10 vertical. Reviews ms/illustration packages from authors. Submit ms with 5 or more pieces of final art. Contact: Michael P. Jones, publisher. Illustration only: Query with samples, résumé, promo sheet, portfolio, slides, client list, tearsheets. Reports in 3 weeks. Samples returned with SASE; samples filed. Original artwork returned at job's completion.

Photography: Buys photos from freelancers. Contact: Michael P. Jones, publisher. Buys stock and assigns work Uses history, nature, environment photos. Model/property releases required. Uses 5×7 and 8×10 b&w prints; 35mm transparencies. Submit cover letter, résumé, published samples, slides, client list, stock photo list, portfolio.

Terms: Authors, illustrators and photographers paid copies of published work. Book catalog available for $2; ms and art guidelines available for SASE.

Tips: "Be flexible! Don't be afraid to try something different. In all correspondence, include SASE. We're looking mostly for nature, environmental and historical themes."

CSS PUBLISHING, 517 S. Main St., P.O. Box 4503, Lima OH 45802-4503. (419)227-1818. Book publisher. Editor: Terry Rhoads. Publishes books with religious themes.

Fiction: Picture books, young readers, middle readers, young adults: religion. Needs children's sermons (object lesson) for Sunday morning worship services; dramas for Advent, Christmas or Epiphany involving children for church services; activity and craft ideas for Sunday school or mid-week services for children (particularly pre-school and first and second grade). Does not want to see secular picture books. Published *That Seeing, They May Believe*, by Kenneth Mortonson (lessons for adults to present during worship services to pre-schoolers-third graders); *What Shall We Do With This Baby?*, by Jan Spence (Christmas Eve worship service involving youngsters from newborn babies-high school youth); *Miracle in the Bethlehem Inn*, by Mary Lou Warstler (Advent or Christmas drama involving pre-schoolers-high school youth and adult).

Nonfiction: Picture books, young readers, middle readers, young adults: religion. Needs children's sermons (object lesson) for Sunday morning workship services; dramas for Advent, Christmas or Epiphany involving children for church services; activity and craft ideas for Sunday school or mid-week services for children (particularly pre-school and first and second grade). Does not want to see secular picture books. Published *Mustard Seeds*, by Ellen Humbert (activity/bulletins for pre-schoolers-first graders to use during church); *This Is The King*, by Cynthia Cowen.

Terms: Work purchased outright from authors. Ms guidelines available for SASE.

How to Contact/Writers: Reports on queries in 1 month; mss in 4-6 months. Publishes a book 9 months after acceptance. Will consider simultaneous submissions.

Tips: "We are seeking material for use by clergy, Christian education directors and Sunday school teachers for mainline Protestant churches. Our market is mainline Protestant clergy."

MAY DAVENPORT, PUBLISHERS, 26313 Purissima Rd., Los Altos Hills CA 94022. (415)948-6499. Independent book producer/packager. Estab. 1976. Editor: May Davenport. Publishes 1-2 picture books/year; 2-3 young adult titles/year. 99% of books by first-time authors. Seeks books with literary merit. "We are overstocked with picture book/elementary reading material."

Fiction: Young adults: contemporary. Average word length: 40,000-60,000. Recently published *Something in the Air*, by Anne Derson (A Migg McClue Mystery, grades 4-5, paper); *Mickey Steals the Show*, by Diane Harris-Filderman; illustrations Miriam Sagasti (grades 2-4, hardback); *Eyes in the Attic*, by Nadine McKinney, illustrations by Renee Deprey (grades 4-5, paper); and *Tug of War*, by Barbara A. Scott (grades 8-12, paper).

Nonfiction: Young readers: special needs activity books to read alone or aloud, or to color. Special needs include dislexia, tricks to develop for reading skills. Published *History of Papa Frog*, by William F. Meisburger (Spanish/English, grades 1-2, paper); *Sumo, The Wrestling Elephant*, by Esther Lee (Spanish/English, grades 1-2, paper).

How to Contact/Writers: Fiction: Query. Reports on queries/mss in 2-3 weeks. "We do not answer queries or manuscripts which do not have SASE attached." Publishes a book 6-12 months after acceptance.
Illustration: Works with 1-2 illustrators/year. Reviews ms/illustration packages from artists. Submit ms with 2-3 pieces of final art. Reports in 2 weeks. Samples returned with SASE. Illustrations only: "We have enough samples for our files for future reference."
Terms: Pays authors in royalties of 15% based on retail price. Pays "by mutual agreement, no advances." Pays illustrators by the project (range: $75-300). Book listing, ms guidelines free on request with SASE.
Tips: "Avoid TV's true to life stories with music and special effects. Just entertain youthful readers with your own literary pizzazz."

DAVIS PUBLICATIONS, INC., 50 Portland St., Worcester MA 01608. (508)754-7201. Fax: (508)753-3834. E-mail: davispub@aol.com. Book publisher. Acquisitions Editors: Claire M. Golding (grades K-8) and Helen Ronan (grades 9-12). Publishes 10 titles total/year. 30% of books by first-time authors. "We publish books for the art education market (elementary through high school), both technique-oriented and art appreciation resource books and textbooks."
Nonfiction: Middle readers, young adults: activity books about art and art-related textbooks; multicultural books detailing the arts of other cultures (Hispanic, Native American, African-American, Asian); textbooks. Recently published *Puppets and Masks: Stagecraft & Storytelling*, by Nan Rump; *African Arts and Cultures*, by Jacqueline Chanda; *Helen Cordova and the Storytellers of Cochiti Pueblo*, by Nancy Howard; *3-D Wizardry: Design in Papier-Mâché, Plaster and Form*, by George Wolfe.
How to Contact/Writers: Submit outline/synopsis and 1 sample chapter. Reports on queries in 3 months; mss in 6 months. Publishes a book 1 year after acceptance. Will consider simultaneous submissions and electronic submissions via disk.
Illustration: Works with 2 illustrators/year. We use a combination of photos and line drawings (200-300/nonfiction title). "We are not major purchasers of illustrations; we generally need clear, informative line art that can be used to explain, demonstrate and elucidate art procedures and materials." Reviews ms/illustration packages from artists. Ms/illustration packages and illustration only: Query with samples. Reports only if interested. Samples returned with SASE or kept on file. Originals returned at job's completion.
Photography: "Rarely" purchases photos from freelancers. Contact: Holly Hanson. "Usually need photos of particular artists, artworks or art forms." Model/property releases required; captions required. Publishes photo concept books. Uses 5×7 and 8×10 glossy, b&w prints and 4×5 and 8×10 transparencies.
Terms: Pays authors royalties of ½-12½% based on retail price or by outright purchase ($1,000-2,000). Pays illustrators by the project (range $50-300). Sends galleys to authors. Book catalog available for 8½×11 SASE; ms guidelines available for 6×9 SASE.
Tips: "Look at our catalog and get a feel for the kind of books we publish. The majority of our books are for *teachers* of children, but are used as resources that children may peruse in the classroom. We do occasional resource books that are written *for* children (A Closer Look Series, *Pictures & Poetry*) plus textbooks that children use. Most of our textbooks are written by art teachers/professors, not freelance writers."

DAWN PUBLICATIONS, 14618 Tyler Foote, Nevada City CA 95959. (916)292-3482. Fax: (916)292-4258. Book publisher. Publisher: Bob Rinzler. Publishes works with holistic themes dealing with nature..
Fiction: Picture books: animal, nature/environment.
Nonfiction: Picture books: animal, nature/environment. Recently published *A Tree in the Ancient Forest*, by Carol Reed-Jones, illustrated by Christopher Canyon; and *Little Brother Moose*, by James Kasperson, illustrated by Karlyn Holman.
How to Contact/Writers: Fiction/Nonfiction: Query; submit complete ms; submit outline/synopsis and sample chapters. Reports on queries/mss in 2 month maximum. Publishes a book 1 year after acceptance. Will consider simultaneous submissions and previously published work.
Illustration: Works with 4 illustrators/year. Will review ms/illustration packages from artists. Query; send ms with dummy. Contact: Glenn Hovemann, editor. Illustrations only: Query with samples, résumé.

Terms: Pays authors royalty based on wholesale price. Offers advance. Pays illustrators by the project or royalties based on wholesale price. Sends galleys to authors; dummies to illustrators. Book catalog available for 6×9 SASE; ms guidelines available for SASE.
Tips: Looking for "picture books expressing nature awareness with inspirational quality leading to enhanced self-awareness. Usually no animal dialogue."

T.S. DENISON CO. INC., 9601 Newton Ave. S., Minneapolis MN 55431. Fax: (612)888-6318. Editor: Danielle Gregory. 25% of books by first-time authors. "We publish only teacher resource/activity books."
Nonfiction: Young readers, middle readers: activity books, animal, geography, health, history, multicultural, nature/environment, reference, social issues, textbooks, teacher resource. Average length: middle readers—150 pages. Published *Let's Meet Famous Composers*, by Harriet Kinghorn, illustrated by Margo De Paulis (grades 3-6, teacher resource); *Toddler Calendar*, by Elaine Commins, illustrated by Anita Nelson (Pre-K, teacher resource); *FairyTale Mask*, by Gwen Rives Jones, illustrated by Darcy Myers (grades 1-3, teacher resource).
How to Contact/Writers: Query; submit complete ms; submit outline/synopsis and 2 sample chapters. Reports on queries/mss in 3 months. Publishes a book 12-18 months after acceptance. Will consider simultaneous submissions and electronic submissions via disk.
Illustration: Works with 15 illustrators/year. Illustrations only: Query with samples; arrange a personal interview to show portfolio. Reports back only if interested. Samples returned with SASE or kept on file. Original artwork not returned at job's completion.
Terms: Work purchased outright from authors. Pays illustrators by the project (range: $300-400 for covers; $20-25 for b&w interior). Book catalog available for 9×12 SAE and 3 first-class stamps; ms guidelines available for SASE.

DIAL BOOKS FOR YOUNG READERS, 375 Hudson St., New York NY 10014. (212)366-2800. Imprint of Penguin Books USA Inc. Editor-in-Chief: Phyllis J. Fogelman. Publishes 70 picture books/year; 10 young reader titles/year; 5 middle reader titles/year; 10 young adult titles/year.

- Dial won both a Caldecott Honor Medal and a Boston Globe-Horn Book Award in 1995 for *John Henry*, illustrated by Jerry Pinkney, retold by Julius Lester. They no longer accept unsolicited manuscripts; only agented material will be read.

Fiction: Picture books: adventure, animal, contemporary, fantasy, folktales, history, nature/environment, poetry, religion, science fiction, sports, suspense/mystery. Young readers: animal, contemporary, easy-to-read, fantasy, folktales, history, nature/environment, poetry, science fiction, sports, mystery/adventure. Middle readers, young adults: animal, contemporary, fantasy, folktales, history, health-related, nature/environment, poetry, problem novels, religion, science fiction, sports, spy/mystery/adventure. Published *Brother Eagle, Sister Sky*, illustrated by Susan Jeffers (all ages, picture book); *Amazing Grace*, by Mary Hoffman (ages 4-8, picture book); and *Soul Looks Back in Wonder*, by Tom Feelings, Maya Angelou, et al (ages 7 and up, poetry picture book.)
Nonfiction: Uses very little nonfiction but will consider submissions of outstanding artistic and literary merit. Picture books: animal, biography, history, nature/environment, sports. Young readers: activity books, animal, biography, history, nature/environment, religion, sports. Middle readers: animal, biography, careers, health, history, nature/environment, religion, sports. Young adults: animal, biography, careers, health, history, hobbies, music/dance, nature/environment, religion, sports. Recently published *Big-Top Circus*, by Neal Porter (ages 4-8, picture book); *Hand, Heart, and Mind*, by Lou Ann Walker (middle readers).
How to Contact/Writers: Only interested in agented material.
Illustration: To arrange a personal interview to show portfolio, send samples and a letter requesting an interview.
Photography: Only interested in agented material.
Terms: Pays authors and illustrators in royalties based on retail price. Average advance payment "varies." Ms guidelines for SASE.

DILLON PRESS, INC., 250 James St., Morristown NJ 07960. Imprint of Silver Burdett Press, Simon & Schuster Education Group. Book Publisher. Editor: Debbie Biber. See Silver Burdett listing.

■**DISCOVERY ENTERPRISES, LTD.**, 31 Laurelwood Dr., Carlisle MA 01741-1205. (508)287-5401. Fax: (508)287-5402. E-mail: delljbw@aol.com. Book publisher and independent book producer/packager. Executive Director: JoAnne Weisman. Publishes 10 middle readers books/year. 40% of books by first-time authors; subsidy publishes 10%. Publishes all nonfiction—serious histories and biographies, 15,000-20,000 words for ages 12-adult. Needs pen & ink drawings for history series.

Nonfiction: Young adults: biography, history, plays, science. "No sports figures, religious leaders, pop stars or current entertainers for biographies." Average word length: middle readers 15,000-20,000; young adults 15,000-20,000. Published *Marjory Stoneman Douglas: Guardian of the Everglades*, by Kem Knapp Sawyer, illustrated by Leslie Carow (ages 10-adult, biography); *Pride and Promise: The Harlem Renaissance*, by Kathryn Cryan-Hicks (ages 12-adult, historical); *Humor in the Classroom: A New Approach to Critical Thinking*, by Prof. Fred Stopsky (guide to teaching methods for teachers of grades 2-12); *Edna Hibel: Her Life and Her Art*, by Olga Cossi (ages 10-adult, biography).

How to Contact/Writers: Query. Submit outline/synopsis and 3 sample chapters. Looking for historical plays for grades 4-8. Reports on queries in 1-2 weeks "only if SASE provided"; mss in 3-6 months. Publishes a book 6-12 months after acceptance. Will consider simultaneous submissions "on American inventors and scientists."

Illustration: Works with 3 illustrators/year. "No preference in medium or style, but artist must be able to do portraits, as these are biographies." Illustrations only: Query with samples; provide resume, promotional literature and tearsheets to be kept on file. Reports in 4-6 weeks. Samples not returned; samples kept on file. Original artwork returned at job's completion "but not for two years."

Terms: Pays authors royalty of 5-10% based on wholesale price or outright purchase ($300-1,500). Offers $1,000 advance on book assignments only. Pays playwrights 10% on net sales only. No advance. Pays illustrators by the project (range: $100-1,500) or royalty of 5-10% based on wholesale price. Book catalog/ms guidelines available for #10 SAE with 64¢ postage.

Tips: Wants "neat, clean artwork, presented professionally." For writers, good cover letter, outline and sample chapters necessary. "Watch for grammatical errors. I prefer separate submissions from artists and authors. Carefully research and accurately illustrate art for histories and biographies in any medium. We are looking for biographies of women in sciences/computers; curriculum guides regarding Turn of the Century for grades 5-8; historical plays. Send query letter with résumé and list of published works, areas of special interest and expertise—in nonfiction only." Sees trend toward more nonfiction for use in classrooms to supplement or replace textbooks, as well as more emphasis on multi-racial books, women's history, peace, etc.

DISNEY PUBLISHING, Subsidiary of Walt Disney Co., 500 S. Buena Vista, Burbank CA 91521. Prefers not to share information.

- Disney Publishing ranks the 9th, based on net sales, of the top 15 children's publishers.

DISTINCTIVE PUBLISHING CORP., P.O. Box 17868, Plantation FL 33318-7868. (305)975-2413. Fax: (305)972-3949. Book publisher and independent book producer/packager. Editor: F. Knauf. Publishes 1-2 books/year. 95% of books by first-time authors.

Fiction: Picture books, young readers: adventure, animal, fantasy, multicultural, nature/environment and sports. Middle readers: animal, multicultural, nature/environment, religion, sports and suspense/mystery. Young adults/teens: nature/environment, religion, sports, suspense/mystery. "We will consider all submissions." Published *Ships of Children*, by Richard Taylor (middle-young adult, adventure); and *Daniel and the Ivory Princess*, written and illustrated by Kevin Martin.

Nonfiction: Picture books, young readers: animal, biography, careers, geography, history, social issues. "As with fiction we will consider all submissions."

How to Contact/Writers: Nonfiction: Submit complete ms. Reports on queries in 1-2 weeks; mss in 1-3 months. Publishes book 6-12 months after acceptance. Will consider simultaneous submissions and previously published work.

Illustration: Works with 3-5 illustrators/year. Reviews ms/illustration packages from artists. Submit complete package. Contact: Alan Erdlee, publisher. Illustrations only: Query with samples, résumé and promo sheet. Reports in 1 month. Original artwork is returned at job's completion.

Photography: Buys photos from freelancers. Buys stock and assigns work. Contact: Alan Erdlee, publisher. Type of photos used depends on project. Model/property release required; captions required. Interested in stock photos. Publishes photo concept books. Uses 4×6 glossy color prints, 2¼×2¼ transparencies. Photographer should query with samples; query with resume of credits; provide resume, business card, tearsheets to be kept on file.
Terms: Pays authors royalty of 6-15% based on wholesale. "Each project is different." Offers advances. Pays illustrators by the project (range: $100-1,000) or royalty of 3-10%. Photographers are paid by the project or per photo. Sends galleys to author; dummies to illustrators. Book catalog available for 9×12 SASE.
Tips: Best chance of selling to this market is with adventure and educational mss.

DORLING KINDERSLEY, INC., 95 Madison Ave., New York NY 10016. (212)213-4800. Book publisher. Associate Editor, Children's Books: C. Decaire. 100% of books from agented authors (fiction list only).

- Dorling Kindersley ranks 11th, based on net sales, of the top 15 children's publishers.

Fiction: Picture books: adventure, contemporary, folktales, history, multicultural, nature/environment. Multicultural needs include relationship stories/family stories. Does not want to see fiction with licensed characters. Average length: picture books—48 pages.
Nonfiction: Young readers: activity books, animal, arts/crafts, geography, history, nature/environment, science and sports. "We produce almost all nonfiction inhouse." Does not want to see "manuscripts imitating books we've already published, suggestions for fiction series, long fiction and alphabet books." Average length: young readers—32 pages. Published Look Closer series, Eyewitness Books and Eyewitness Explorers Guides.
How to Contact/Writers: Only interested in agented material. Fiction/Nonfiction: Submit agented ms. Reports on queries/mss in 4 months. Publishes a book about 18 months after acceptance. Will consider simultaneous submissions.
Illustration: Works with about 10 illustrators/year. Reviews ms/illustration packages from artists. Submit ms with dummy. Contact: C. Decaire, associate editor. Illustrations only: Query with samples; provide promo sheet and tearsheets. Reports only if immediately interested. Otherwise samples go in file. Samples returned with SASE (if requested).
Photography: Purchases photos from freelancers. Contact: Dirk Kaufman, designer. Works on assignment only. Photographers should submit cover letter and résumé.
Terms: Pays author royalty based on retail price. Pays illustrators by the project or royalty. Pays photographers by the project. Sends galleys to authors; dummies to illustrators. Book catalog available for 9×12 SAE and 3 first-class stamps; ms guidelines available for SASE; artist's guidelines not available.
Tips: A writer has the best chance of selling well-written picture book stories that work internationally. Also, innovative manuscripts that combine fiction and nonfiction. "See our published book, *Mr. Frog Went A-Courting*, by Gary Chalk."

DOWN EAST BOOKS, P.O. Box 679, Camden, ME 04843. (207)594-9544. Fax: (207)594-7215. Book publisher. Editor: Karin Womer. Publishes 1-2 young middle readers/year. 90% of books by first-time authors. All books pertain to Maine/New England region.
Fiction: All levels: adventure, animal, history, nature/environment. Published *Silas the Bookstore Cat*, by Karen Mather (young-middle readers, animal); and *Junior—A Little Loon Tale*, by John Hassett (middle readers, animal/conservation).
Nonfiction: All levels: animal, geography, nature/environment. Published *Wild Fox*, by Cherie Mason (Middle readers, animal/nature).
How to Contact/Writers: Fiction/Nonfiction: Query. Reports on queries/mss in 2 weeks to 2 months. Publishes a book 6-18 months after acceptance. Will consider simultaneous and previously published submissions.
Illustration: Works with 2-3 illustrators/year. Reviews ms/illustration packages from artists. Query. Contact: Karin Womer, editor. Illustrations only: Query with samples. Reports in 2 weeks to 2 months. Samples returned with SASE; samples filed sometimes. Original artwork returned at job's completion.
Terms: Pays authors royalty (varies widely). Pays illustrators by the project or by royalty (varies widely). Sends galleys to authors; dummies to illustrators. Book catalog available. Manuscript guidelines available for SASE.

***DUTTON CHILDREN'S BOOKS**, 375 Hudson St., New York NY 10014. (212)366-2600. Division of Penguin USA. Book publisher. Editor-in-Chief: Lucia Monfried. Art Associate: Julia Goodman. Publishes approximately 60 picture books/year; 4 young reader titles/year; 10 middle reader titles/year; 8 young adult titles/year. 10% of books by first-time authors.

- Dutton won both a Caldecott Honor Medal and a Boston Globe-Horn Book Honor Award for a picture book in 1995 for *Swamp Angel*, illustrated by Paul O. Zelinsky, written by Anne Issacs. See First Books for an interview with Dutton illustrator Shelley Jackson on her book *Great-Aunt Martha*.

Fiction: Picture books: adventure, animal, folktales, history, multicultural, nature/environment, poetry. Young readers: adventure, animal, contemporary, easy-to-read, fantasy, pop-up, suspense/mystery. Middle readers: adventure, animal, contemporary, fantasy, history, multicultural, nature/environment, suspense/mystery. Young adults: adventure, animal, anthology, contemporary, fantasy, history, multicultural, nature/environment, poetry, science fiction, suspense/mystery. Recently published *Isla*, by Arthur Dorrus, illustrated by Elisa Kleven (picture book); *The Bravest Thing*, by Donna Jo Napol, (novel); and *The Eye of the Pharaoh*, by Iain Smith (pop-up mystery).
Nonfiction: Picture books: animal, history, multicultural, nature/environment. Young readers: animal, history, multicultural, nature/environment. Middle readers: animal, biography, history, multicultural, nature/environment. Young adults: animal, biography, history, multicultural, nature/environment, social issues. Recently published *Chile Fever: A Celebration of Peppers*, by Elizabeth King (ages 7-10, photo essay); *Part of Me Died, Too: Stories of Creative Survival Among Bereaved Children and Teenagers*, by Virginia Lynn Fry (ages 10 and up).
How to Contact/Writers: Query. Reports on queries in 1 month; mss in 3 months. Publishes a book 12-18 months after acceptance. Will consider simultaneous submissions.
Illustration: Works with 40-60 illustrators/year. Reviews ms/illustration packages from artists. Query first. Illustrations only: Query with samples; send résumé, portfolio, slides—no original art please. Reports on art samples in 2 months. Original artwork returned at job's completion.
Photography: Purchases photos from freelancers. Assigns work. Wants "nature photography."
Terms: Pays authors royalties of 4-10% based on retail price. Book catalog, ms guidelines for SAE. Pays illustrators royalties of 2-10% based on retail price unless jacket illustration—then pays by flat fee. Photographers paid royalty per photo.
Tips: Writers: "We publish high-quality trade books and are interested in well-written manuscripts with fresh ideas and child appeal. Avoid topics that appear frequently. We have a complete publishing program. Though we publish mostly picture books, we are very interested in acquiring more novels for middle and young adult readers. We are also expanding our list to include more books for preschool-aged children. In nonfiction, we are looking for history, general biography, science and photo essays for all age groups." Illustrators: "We would like to see samples and portfolios from potential illustrators of picture books (full color), young novels (b&w) and jacket artists (full color)." Foresee "even more multicultural publishing, plus more books published in both Spanish and English."

E.M. PRESS, INC., P.O. Box 4057, Manassas VA 22110. (703)439-0304. Book publisher. Publisher/Editor: Beth Miller. Publishes 2 middle readers/year; 2 young adult titles/year. 50% of books by first-time authors.
Fiction: Middle readers: adventure, animal, contemporary. Young adults: fantasy, folktales, nature, religion, suspense/mystery, religion. Published *The Search For Archerland*, by H.R. Coursen (adventure, 12 and up); *Some Brief Cases of Inspector Alec Stuart of Scotland Yard*, by Archibald Wagner MD (mystery, 12 and up).
Nonfiction: Young adults: religion.
How to Contact/Writers: Fiction: Query. Submit outline/synopsis. Nonfiction: Query. Reports on ms/queries in 6 weeks. Publishes a book 18 months after acceptance. Will consider simultaneous submissions.

Always include a self-addressed, stamped envelope (SASE) with submissions within your own country. When sending material to other countries, include a self-addressed envelope (SAE) and International Reply Coupons (IRCs).

Illustration: Works with 1 children's illustrator/year. Ms/illustration packages should be submitted to Beth Miller, Publisher. Reports back in 1½ months. Samples returned with SASE. Samples kept on file. Original artwork returned at job's completion.
Terms: Pays authors 6-10% royalty on wholesale price. Ms illustrators paid by the project. Offers varied advances. Sends galleys to authors. Manuscript guidelines for SASE.

WM. B. EERDMANS PUBLISHING COMPANY, 255 Jefferson Ave. SE, Grand Rapids MI 49503. (616)459-4591. Book publisher. Children's Book Editor: Amy Eerdmans. Publishes 6 picture books/year; 4 young readers/year; 4 middle readers/year.
Fiction: All levels: fantasy, parables, problem novels, religion, retold Bible stories from a Christian perspective.
Nonfiction: All levels: biography, history, nature/environment, religion.
How to Contact/Writers: Fiction/Nonfiction: Query; submit complete ms. Reports on queries in 1-2 weeks; mss in 4-6 weeks.
Illustration: Reviews ms/illustration packages from artists. Reports on ms/art samples in 1 month. Illustrations only: Submit résumé, slides or color photocopies. Contact: Willem Mineur, art director. Original artwork returned at job's completion.
Terms: Pays authors in royalties of 5-10%. Pays illustrators royalty or permission fee. Sends galleys to authors; dummies to illustrators. Book catalog free on request; ms and/or artist's guidelines free on request.
Tips: "We're looking for fiction and nonfiction that project a positive spiritual message and imply Christian values. We are also looking for material that will help children explore their faith. Accept all genres."

ENSLOW PUBLISHERS INC., 44 Fadem Rd., Box 699, Springfield NJ 07081. Vice President: Brian D. Enslow. Estab. 1978. Publishes 30 middle reader titles/year; 30 young adult titles/year. 30% of books by first-time authors.
Nonfiction: Young readers, middle readers, young adults: activity books, animal, biography, careers, health, history, hobbies, nature/environment, sports. Average word length: middle readers-5,000; young adult-15,000. Published *Louis Armstrong*, by Patricia and Fredrick McKissack (grades 2-3, biography); *Lotteries: Who Wins, Who Loses?*, by Ann E. Weiss (grades 6-12, issues book).
How to Contact/Writers: Nonfiction: Query. Reports on queries/mss in 2 weeks. Publishes a book 18 months after acceptance. Will not consider simultaneous submissions.
Illustration: Submit résumé, business card or tearsheets to be kept on file.
Terms: Pays authors royalties or work purchased outright. Sends galleys to authors. Book catalog/ms guidelines available for $2.

***EVAN-MOOR EDUCATIONAL PUBLISHERS**, 18 Lower Ragsdale Dr., Monterey CA 93940-5746. (408)649-5901. Fax: (408)649-6256. Book publisher. Acquisitions Editor: Bob DeWeese. Production Director: Joy Evans. Publishes 30-50 books/year. 10-20% of books by first-time authors.

- Evan-Moor does not publish fiction.

Nonfiction: "Pre-K through 6th grade classroom activity books in all subjects. Thematic units, teaching resources and strategy books. Also books for home use by parents and their children." Average length 48 or 64 pages. Recently published *How to Make Books with Children, Science & Math*, written and illustrated by Joy Evans (teacher resource for grades 1-6); *The Ugly Duckling*, by Judith Gold and Carrie Mapes, illustrated by N.J. Taylor (literature theme unit for grades K-2); and *Math in the Kitchen*, by Laura Mackey, illustrated by Jo supancich (math-based theme unit for grade 1-3).
How to Contact/Writers: Nonfiction: Submit complete ms. Reports on queries in 3 weeks; mss in 4 months. Publishes a book 12-18 months after acceptance. Will consider simultaneous submissions if so noted.
Illustration: Works with 7-10 illustrators/year. Uses b&w artwork primarily. Illustrations only: Query with samples; send résumé, tearsheets. Contact: Joy Evans, production director. Reports only if interested. Samples returned with SASE. Originals not returned.
Terms: Work purchased outright from authors, "dependent solely on size of project and 'track record' of author." Pays illustrators by the project (range: varies). Sends galleys to authors. Book

catalog available for 9×12 SAE; ms guidelines available for SASE.
Tips: "Writers—know the supplemental education or parent market. Tell us how your project is unique and what consumer needs it meets. Illustrators, you need to be able to produce quickly, and be able to render realistic and charming children and animals."

FARRAR, STRAUS & GIROUX, 19 Union Square W., New York NY 10003. (212)741-6934. Book publisher. Children's Books Editor-in-Chief: Margaret Ferguson. Estab. 1946. Publishes 21 picture books/year; 6 middle reader titles/year; 5 young adult titles/year. 15% of books by first-time authors; 50% of books from agented writers.
Fiction: "Original and well-written material for all ages." Published *Tell Me Everything*, by Carolyn Coman (ages 12 up).
How to Contact/Writers: Fiction/Nonfiction: Query; submit outline/synopsis and sample chapters. Reports on queries in 6 weeks; mss in 12 weeks. Publishes a book 18 months after acceptance. Will consider simultaneous submissions.
Illustration: Reviews ms/illustration packages from artists. Submit ms with 1 example of final art, remainder roughs. Illustrations only: Query with tearsheets. Reports on art samples only if interested. Original artwork returned at job's completion.
Terms: "We offer an advance against royalties for both authors and illustrators." Sends galleys to authors; dummies to illustrators. Book catalog available for 6½×9½ SAE and 64¢ postage; ms guidelines for 1 first-class stamp.
Tips: "Study our catalog before submitting. We will see illustrator's portfolios by appointment."

FAWCETT JUNIPER, 201 E. 50 St., New York NY 10022. (212)751-2600. Imprint of Ballantine/DelRey/Fawcett Books. Book publisher. Editor-in-Chief/Vice President: Leona Nevler. Publishes 36 young adult titles/year.
Fiction: Middle readers: contemporary, romance, science fiction. Young adults: contemporary, fantasy, romance.
How to Contact/Writers: Fiction: Query.
Terms: Pays authors in royalties.

THE FEMINIST PRESS AT THE CITY UNIVERSITY OF NEW YORK, 311 E. 94th St., New York NY 10128. (212)360-5790. Book publisher. Children's Books: Kim Mallett. Publishes 1-2 middle reader, young reader and young adult books/year.
Fiction: Picture books and young readers: adventure, fantasy, folktales, history, humor, multicultural. Middle readers: adventure, fantasy, folktales, history, humor, multicultural, science fiction, suspense. Young adults: concept, contemporary, humor, multicultural, science fiction, sports, suspense/mystery.
Nonfiction: Picture books, young reader: history, multicultural. Middle reader: history, multicultural, science. Young adult: multicultural, science.
How to Contact/Writers: Fiction/Nonfiction: Query. Reports on queries/mss in 2-3 weeks. Publishes a book 1-2 years after acceptance.
Illustration: Works with 1-2 illustrators/year. Uses primarily b&w artwork. Reviews ms/illustration packages from artist. Submit query or ms with final art. Contact: Ann Mallett, assistant-to-the-publisher. Reports back in 1 month only if interested and only if SASE is included. Samples returned with SASE; samples kept on file. Original artwork returned at job's completion.
Terms: Pays authors 6-10% royalty on retail price. Offers advances (average amount: $100). Pays illustrators by the project or royalty; "depends on project." Sends galleys to authors. Book catalog and ms/artists' guidelines available for SASE.

FIESTA CITY PUBLISHERS, Box 5861, Santa Barbara CA 93150-5861. (805)733-1984. Book publisher. Editorial Contact: Ann Cooke. Publishes 1 middle reader/year; 1 young adult/year. 25% of books by first-time authors. Publishes books about cooking and music or a combination of the two.
Nonfiction: Young adult: cooking, music/dance, self-help. Average word length: 30,000. Does not want to see "cookbooks about healthy diets or books on rap music." Published *Kids Can Write Songs, Too!* (revised second printing), by Eddie Franck; *Bent-Twig*, by Frank E. Cooke, with some musical arrangements by Johnny Harris (a 3-act musical for young adolescents).
How to Contact/Writers: Query. Reports on queries in 2 weeks; on mss in 1 month. Publishes a book 1 year after acceptance. Will consider simultaneous submissions.

Illustration: Works with 1 illustrator/year. Will review ms/illustrations packages (query first). Contact: Frank E. Cooke, president. Illustrations only: Send résumé.
Terms: Pays authors royalty based on wholesale price.
Tips: "Write clearly and simply. Do not write 'down' to young adults (or children). Looking for self-help books on current subjects, original and unusual cookbooks, and books about music, or a combination of cooking and music."

***✤FIFTH HOUSE PUBLISHERS**, 620 Duchess St., Saskatoon, Saskatchewan 57L 5V6 Canada. Book publisher. Managing Editor: Charlene Dobmeier.
- This publisher no longer accepts unsolicited manuscripts.

Illustration: Works with 1-2 illustrators/year. Illustrations only: Query with samples. Reports in 2 months only if interested. Samples returned with SASE; samples filed.

✤FITZHENRY & WHITESIDE LTD., 195 Allstate Pkwy., Markham, Ontario L3R 4T8 Canada. (905)477-9700. Fax: (905)477-9179. Book publisher. Vice President: Robert W. Read. Publishes 2 picture books/year; 5 young readers/year; 5 middle readers/year; 5 young adult titles/year. 15% of books by first-time authors. Publishes mostly nonfiction—social studies, visual arts, biography, environment. Prefers Canadian subject or perspective.
Fiction: Picture books: folktales, history, multicultural, nature/environment and sports. Young readers: contemporary, folktales, health, history, multicultural, nature/environment and sports. Young readers: contemporary, folktales, health, history, multicultural, nature/environment and sports. Middle readers: adventure, contemporary, folktales, history, humor, multicultural, nature/environment and sports. Young adults: adventure, contemporary, folktales, history, multicultural, nature/environment, sports and suspense/mystery. Average word length: young readers—less than 2,000; middle readers—2,000-5,000; young adults—10,000-20,000.
Nonfiction: Picture books: arts/crafts, biography, history, multicultural, nature/environment, reference and sports. Young readers: arts/crafts, biography, geography, history, hobbies, multicultural, nature/environment, reference, religion and sports. Middle readers: arts/crafts, biography, careers, geography, history, hobbies, multicultural, nature/environment, reference, social issues and sports. Young adults: arts/crafts, biography, careers, geography, health, hi-lo, history, multicultural, music/dance, nature/environment, reference, social issues and sports. Average word length: young readers—500-1,000; middle readers—2,000-5,000; young adults—10,000-20,000. Recently published *Inuit of the North*, by Stan Garrod (ages 8-12, nonfiction native studies); *Ladybug Garden*, by Celia Godkin (ages 5-10, environment/nature); and *Wayne Gretzky*, by Fred McFadden (ages 8-12, sports biography).
How to Contact/Writers: Fiction: Submit outline/synopsis and 1 sample chapter. Nonfiction: Submit outline/synopsis. Reports in 3 months. Publishes a book 1 year after acceptance. Will consider simultaneous submissions.
Illustration: Works with 5-10 illustrators/year. Reviews ms/illustration packages from artist. Submit outline and sample illustration (copy). Illustrations only: Query with samples and promo sheet. Reports in 3 months. Samples returned with SASE; samples filed if no SASE.
Photography: Buys photos from freelancers. Buys stock and assigns work. Captions required. Uses b&w 8×10 prints; 35mm and 4×5 transparencies. Submit stock photo list and promo piece.
Terms: Pays authors royalty of 10%. Offers "modest" advances. Pays illustrators by the project and royalty. Pays photographers per photo. Sends galleys to authors; dummies to illustrators.
Tips: "We respond to quality."

***FORWARD MOVEMENT PUBLICATIONS**, 412 Sycamore St., Cincinnati OH 45202. (513)721-6659. Fax: (513)421-0315. E-mail: forward_movement@ecunet.org.
How to Contact/Writers: Fiction/Nonfiction: Query.
Terms: Pays authors honorarium. Pays illustrators by the project. Book catalog available for #10 SAE and 3 first-class stamps.
Tips: "Forward Movement is just beginning to explore publishing books for children and does not know its niche. We are an agency of the Episcopal Church. Suggest queries only—no manuscripts."

FRANKLIN WATTS, Sherman Turnpike, Danbury CT 06816. (203)797-3500. Subsidiary of Grolier Inc. Book publisher. Editorial Contact: E.R. Primm. 10% of books by first-time authors; 5% of books from agented writers.

Nonfiction: Young readers: activity books. Middle readers: activity books, animal, arts/crafts, biography, concept, cooking, geography, health, hi-lo, history, multicultural, music/dance, nature/environment, reference, religion, science, social issues, special needs, sports. Young adults: arts/crafts, biography, careers, concepts, geography, health, history, multicultural, music/dance, nature/environment, reference, religion, science, social issues, special needs, sports. Does not want to see fiction or poetry. Average word length: middle readers—5,000; young adult/teens—16,000-35,000.

How to Contact/Writers: Query. No mss. Include SASE. Reports on queries in 6-8 weeks.

Illustration: Works with 10-15 illustrators/year. Reviews ms/illustration packages from artist. Query with samples, résumé, promo sheet, client list. Contact: Vicki Fischman, art director. Reports back only if interested. Samples returned with SASE or filed. Original artwork returned at job's completion.

Photography: Purchases photos from freelancers. Contact photo editor. Buys stock and assigns work.

Terms: Pays authors royalties or work purchased outright. Illustrators paid by the project. Photographers paid per photo. Book catalog for 10×13 SASE.

Tips: Looks for children's nonfiction grades 5-8 or 9-12.

FREE SPIRIT PUBLISHING, 400 First Ave. N., Suite 616, Minneapolis MN 55401-1730. (612)338-2068. Fax: (612)337-5050. Book publisher. Publisher/President: Judy Galbraith. Publishes 1-2 young readers/year; 3-4 middle reader titles/year; 3-4 young adult titles/year. 80% of books by first-time authors. "Our books pertain to the education and psychological well being of young people."

- Free Spirit appeared on a 1995 Hot List® compiled by *Children's Book Insider*. This list of "10 Book and Magazine Publishers Most Receptive to New Writers" is updated every few months, and available to new and renewing subscribers. They no longer accept fiction submissions.

Nonfiction: All levels: health, multicultural, self-esteem, self help, social issues, special needs, psychology, education. Multicultural needs include: materials related to conflict resolution; getting along with others; accepting/tolerating/celebrating differences; respect for self and others. Special needs include: materials that relate specifically to special needs that affect school learning (i.e. learning disabilities, attention deficit disorder, hyperactivity). "We're not as interested in materials that address physical challenges (such as using a wheelchair or being visually impaired), or mental challenges (such as Down Syndrome)." Recently published *Psychology for Kids II: 40 Fun Experiments That Help You Learn About Others*, by Jonni Kircher (ages 12 and up); *Girls and Young Woman Inventing: Twenty True Stories about Inventors Plus How You Can Be One Yourself*, by Frances A. Karnes Ph.D. and Suzanne M. Bean, Ph.D. (ages 11 and up); and *Young Person's Guide to Becoming A Writer*, by Janet Grant (ages 12 and up).

How to Contact/Writers: Submit résumé, outline/synopsis and sample chapters. Reports on queries/mss in 3 months. Publishes a book 12-18 months after acceptance. Write or call for catalog and submission guidelines before sending submission.

Illustration: Works with 5 illustrators/year. Reviews ms/illustration packages from artist. Submit ms with 2-3 sample chapters. For freelance art and photography submissions, contact: Pat Scheunemann, Maclean & Tuminelly, 400 First Ave. N., Suite 626, Minneapolis MN 55401. "MacLean & Tuminelly is a firm that designs and produces our books."

Photography: Buys photos from freelancers.

Terms: Pays authors in royalties of 7-12% based on wholesale price. Offers advance payment of $500-$1,000. Pays illustrators by the project. Pays photographers by the project or per photo. Sends galleys to authors. Book catalog free on request; guidelines available for SASE.

Tips: Does not accept unsolicited artists' or photographers' samples. Wants to see "a book that helps kids help themselves, or that helps adults help kids help themselves; one that complements our list without duplicating current titles; one that is written in a direct, straightforward manner (no jargon, please); one that teaches without preaching or being condescending."

***■FREEDOM PUBLISHING COMPANY**, 400 W. Dundee Rd., #108, Buffalo Grove IL 60089. (708)465-0770. Fax: (708)520-7597. Book publisher. President: Jay Brown. Publishes 1-3 picture books/year; 1-3 young readers/year; 1-3 middle readers/year. 1-3 young adult titles/year. 25% of books by first-time authors; 25% subsidy published.

Fiction: Picture books and young readers: adventure, animal, health, humor. Middle readers: adventure, animal, health, humor, suspense/mystery. Young adults: adventure, contemporary, health, humor, suspense/mystery.

Nonfiction: Picture books, young readers, middle readers and young adults: health, how-to, self help, social issues. Average word length: picture books—1,000-2,000; young readers—2,000-5,000; middle readers—5,000-7,000; young adult/teens—7,000. Recently published *How Kids Make Friends...Secrets for Making Lots of Friends No Matter How Shy You Are*, by Lonnie Michelle (self-help book for ages 8 and up).

How to Contact/Writers: Fiction: Submit outline/synopsis and 1-2 sample chapters. Nonfiction: Submit outline/synopsis; submit outline/synopsis and 1-2 sample chapters. Reports on queries in 4-6 weeks; mss in 4-6 weeks. Publishes a book 6-8 months after acceptance. Materials returned with SASE.

Illustration: Works with 2-3 illustrators/year. Reviews ms/illustration packages from artists. Send ms with dummy. Contact: Jay Brown, president. Illustrations only: Query with samples; send promo sheet, client list, tearsheets. Contact: Jay Brown, president. Reports in 4-6 weeks. Samples returned with SASE. Originals not returned.

Terms: Pays authors royalty. Pays illustrators royalty based on wholesale price. Sends galleys to authors.

***FRIENDS UNITED PRESS**, 101 Quaker Hill Dr., Richmond IN 47355. (317)962-7573. Fax: (317)966-1293. Book publisher. Editor: Ardith Talbot. Publishes 1 middle reader/year; 1 young adult title/year. 90% of books by first-time authors.

Fiction: Young readers, middle readers and young adults: history, religion. Recently published *Luke's Summer Secret*, by Randall Wisehart, Jr. (historical fiction); *Stories for Jason*, by Mary Cromer (historical fiction); and *Betsy Ross, Quaker Rebel*, by Ethlyn Walkington (historical fiction for young adults).

Nonfiction: Young readers, middle readers and young adults: history, religion.

How to Contact/Writers: Fiction/Nonfiction: Submit outline/synopsis and complete ms. Reports on queries in 6 weeks; 12 months on mss. Publishes a book 1 year after acceptance. Will consider simultaneous, previously published work.

Illustration: Works with 1 illustrator/year. Reviews ms/illustration packages from artists. Query.

Terms: Pays authors royalty of 7½% based on wholesale price.

Tips: "Write or call before submitting materials."

FRIENDSHIP PRESS, 475 Riverside Dr., Room 860, New York NY 10115. (212)870-2497. National Council of Churches of Christ in the USA. Book publisher. Editorial Contact: Barbara Withers. Art Director: Paul Lansdale. Publishes 1-2 picture books/year; 1 young reader title/year; 1 middle reader title/year; 1 young adult title/year. 75% of books commissioned for set themes.

Fiction: All levels: multicultural, mission and religion. Average word length: young adults—20,000-40,000. Book catalog free on request. Published *Pearlmakers*, by Vilma May Fuentes (grades 1-6, stories about the Philippines); *Aki and the Banner of Names*, by Atsuko Gōda Lolling (grades 1-6, stories about Japan).

Nonfiction: All levels: activity books, geography, multicultural, social issues, mission and religion. Average word length: middle readers—10,000; young adults—10,000.

How to Contact/Writers: Fiction/Nonfiction: Query. Reports on queries in 1 month; mss in 6 months. Publishes a book 18 months after acceptance. Will consider simultaneous submissions. Ms guidelines free on request.

Illustration: Works with 1 illustrator/year. Reviews ms/illustration packages from artists. Submit 3 chapters of ms with 1 piece of final art. Illustrations only: Submit résumé and tearsheets. Contact: Paul Lansdale, art director. Reports only if interested. Original artwork returned at job's completion.

The asterisk before a listing indicates the listing is new in this edition.

Terms: Buys ms outright for $25-1,200. Pays illustrators by the project (range: $25-1,200). Sends galleys to authors; dummies to illustrators. Book catalog and ms guidelines free on request.
Tips: Seeking "a book that illustrates what life is like for children in other countries, especially Christian children, though not exclusively."

LAURA GERINGER BOOKS, 10 E. 53rd St., New York NY 10022. (212)207-7554. Fax: (212)207-7192. Imprint of HarperCollins Publishers. Editorial Director: Laura Geringer. Publishes 10-12 picture books/year; 2 middle readers/year; 2-4 young adult titles/year. 20% of books by first-time authors; 50% of books from agented authors.
Fiction: Picture books: adventure, animal, concept, contemporary, fantasy, folktales, history, nature/environment, poetry. Young readers: adventure, anthology, animal, contemporary, fantasy, folktales, health-related, history, humor, multicultural, poetry, sports, suspense/mystery. Middle readers, young adults: adventure, anthology, animal, contemporary, fantasy, folktales, health-related, history, nature/environment, poetry, problem novels, sports, suspense/mystery. Average word length: picture books—250-1,200. Published *Santa Calls*, by William Joyce (all ages, picture book); *The Borning Room*, by Paul Fleischman (ages 10 and up, middle grade); *The Tub People*, by Pam Conrad (preschool-3rd grade, picture book); and *What Hearts*, by Bruce Brooks (age 10-young adult).
How to Contact/Writers: Submit complete ms. Reports on queries in 2-4 weeks; mss in 3-4 months. Publishes a book 1½-3 years after acceptance. Will consider simultaneous submissions.
Illustration: Works with 20-25 illustrators/year. Reviews ms/illustration packages from artists. Submit complete package. Illustrations only: Query with samples; submit portfolio for review; provide résumé, business card, promotional literature or tearsheets to be kept on file. Contact: Laura Geringer or Harriett Barton, art director. Reports only if interested. SASE for return of samples; samples kept on file. Original artwork returned at job's completion.
Terms: Pays authors royalties of 5-6¼% (picture book) or 10-12½% (novel) based on retail price. Offers advances. Pays illustrators royalties of 5-6¼%. Sends galleys to authors; proofs to illustrators. Book catalog available for 9×11 SASE; ms/artist's guidelines available for SASE.
Tips: "Write about what you *know*. Don't try to guess our needs. And don't forget that children are more clever than we give them credit for!" Wants "artwork that isn't overly 'cutesy' with a strong sense of style and expression."

GIBBS SMITH, PUBLISHER, P.O. Box 667, Layton UT 84041. (801)544-9800. Imprint: Peregrine Smith Books. Book publisher. Editorial Director: Madge Baird. Publishes 6-8 books/year. 10% of books by first-time authors. 50% of books from agented authors.
Fiction: Picture books: multicultural, nature/environment, humor, western. Young readers: adventure, animal, folktales, history, humor, multicultural, nature/environment. Middle readers: adventure, animal, folktales, history, humor, multicultural, nature/environment. Average word length: picture books—1,000. Recently published *Under the Moon and Stars*, by Scott Emerson, illustrated by Howard Posa (ages 4-8, picture book); and *Once There Was a Bull . . . Frog*, by Rick Walton, illustrated by Greg Hally (ages 4-8, picture book).
Nonfiction: Picture books: activity, how-to, multicultural, nature/environment, western/cowboy. Young readers: activity, multicultural, nature/environment. Middle readers: activity, arts/crafts, cooking, history, how-to, multicultural, nature/environment. Average word length: picture books—up to 3,000.
How to Contact/Writers: Fiction/Nonfiction: Query or submit several chapters or complete ms. Reports on queries and mss in 6-8 weeks. Publishes a book 1-2 years after acceptance. Will consider simultaneous submissions. Ms returned with SASE.
Illustration: Works with 6-8 illustrators/year. Reviews ms/illustration packages from artists. Query. Submit ms with 3-5 pieces of final art. Contact: Theresa Desmond, associate editor. Illustrations only: Query with samples; provide résumé, promo sheet, slides (duplicate slides, not originals). Reports back only if interested. Samples not returned; samples filed. Original artwork returned at job's completion.
Terms: Pays authors royalty of 4-7½% based on wholesale price or work purchased outright ($500 minimum). Offers advances (average amount: $2,000). Pays illustrators by the project or royalty of 4-5% based on wholesale price. Sends galleys to authors; color proofs to illustrators. Book catalog available for 9×12 SAE and postage. Ms/artist's guidelines not available.

Tips: "We target ages 5-11." Wants "multi-dimensional products (book, tape, toy, etc.)."

GLOBE FEARON EDUCATIONAL PUBLISHER, 1 Lake St., Upper Saddle River NJ 07458. Imprint of Paramount Publishing. Book publisher. Production Director: Penny Gibson. Publishes 100 special education, young adult titles/year.
Fiction: Young adults: hi-lo, multicultural, special needs. Average word length: 10,000-15,000.
Nonfiction: Young adults: biography, careers, health, hi-lo, history, multicultural, nature/environment, science, special needs, textbooks.
How to Contact/Writers: Fiction/Nonfiction: Query "but, we don't respond to all queries." Reports on queries in 6 months; mss in 12-18 months.
Illustration: Works with 20 illustrators/year. "Will review samples/portfolio." Illustrations only: Query with samples, résumé, promo sheet, portfolio, slides, client list, tearsheets; arrange personal portfolio review. Contact: Penny Gibson, production director. Reports in 2 months. Samples returned with SASE. "We prefer to keep on file."
Photography: Buys photos from freelancers. Buys stock and assigns work. "We don't accept general submissions. We commission as needed." Model/property releases required. Uses wide

Artist Greg Hally sought to create "a feeling of fun and adventure with a western flair" when he illustrated Gibbs Smith, Publisher's* Once There Was a Bull . . . (frog), *by Rick Walton. Painting with acrylics on watercolor paper, Hally rendered a series of grainy, whimsical illustrations that lead the reader through a hapless bullfrog's search for his missing hop. Hally's work has appeared in national magazines and advertisements, and this was his first effort at children's book illustration.

range of color and b&w prints. Submit cover letter, résumé, published samples, slides, client list, stock photo list, portfolio, promo piece.
Terms: Work purchased outright ($2,500 minimum). Pays illustrators by the project. Pays photographers by the project. Sometimes sends galleys to authors.
Tips: "Be very sure the house you approach publishes the type of work you do. Make sure your work has solid, carefully crafted development with no dangling details."

DAVID R. GODINE, PUBLISHER, P.O. Box 9103, Lincoln MA 01773. (617)259-0700. Fax: (617)259-9198. Book publisher. Estab. 1970. Contact: Editorial Department. Publishes 3-4 picture books/year; 2 young reader titles/year; 3-4 middle reader titles/year. 10% of books by first-time authors; 50% of books from agented writers.

- This publisher is no longer considering unsolicited manuscripts of any type.

Fiction: Picture books: adventure, animal, contemporary, fantasy, folk tales, nature/environment, sports. Young readers: adventure, animal, easy-to-read, fantasy, folk or fairy tales, history, multicultural, sports. Middle readers: adventure, animal, fantasy, folk or fairy tales. history, humor, multicultural, nature/environment, poetry, sports. Young adults/teens: adventure, contemporary, history, humor, multicultural, sports. Multicultural needs include: primarily Judaica. Published *The Last Giants*, by François Place (award-winning illustrated fable); *No Effect*, by Daniel Hayes (YA fiction); and *Rotten Island*, by William Steig.
Nonfiction: Picture books, young readers: history. Middle readers, young adults/teens: Activity books, arts/crafts, biography, history, hobbies, multicultural, music, nature/environment. Multicultural needs include: primarily Judaica.
How to Contact/Writers: Query. Reports in 2 weeks. Publishes a book 2 years after acceptance.
Illustration: Review ms/illustration packages from artists. "Submit roughs and one piece of finished art plus either sample chapters for very long works or whole ms for short works." Illustrations only: "After query, submit slides, with one full-size blow-up of art." Reports on art samples in 2 weeks. Original artwork returned at job's completion. "Almost all of the children's books we accept for publication come to us with the author and illustrator already paired up. Therefore, we rarely use freelance illustrators."
Terms: Pays authors in royalties based on retail price. Number of illustrations used determines final payment for illustrators. Pay for separate authors and illustrators "differs with each collaboration." Illustrators paid by the project. Sends galleys to authors; dummies to illustrators.

GOLDEN BOOKS, 850 Third Ave., New York NY 10022. (212)753-8500. Imprint of Western Publishing Co. Co-Editorial Directors: Marilyn Salomon and Kenn Goin. Book publisher. 100% of books from agented authors.
Fiction: Board books, novelty books, picture books: "accepts a variety of age-appropriate subject matter." Middle readers: series lines.
Nonfiction: Picture books: history, nature/environment, sports. Young and middle readers: animals, education, history, nature/environment, sports.
How to Contact/Writers: "Material accepted only through agent."
Illustration: Sometimes reviews ms/illustration packages from artists. Query first. Illustrations only: Will review work for possible future assignments. Contact: Remo Cosentino and Sandra Forrest, art directors.
Terms: Pays authors outright and occasionally in royalties based on retail price.

GRAPEVINE PUBLICATIONS, INC., P.O. Box 2449, Corvallis OR 97339-2449. (503)754-0583. Fax: (503)754-6508. Book publisher. Managing Editor: Chris Coffin. Publishes 1 picture book/year; 1 young reader/year. 100% of books by first-time authors.
Fiction: Picture books, young readers, middle readers: all categories considered. Average length: picture books—16-32 pages; young readers—32 pages; middle readers—64 pages.
How to Contact/Writers: Submit complete ms. Reports on queries and mss in 6 weeks only if interested. "Due to volume received, we report *only* on material of interest." Publishes a book 1 year after acceptance. Will consider simultaneous and previously published submissions.
Illustration: Works with 1-2 illustrators/year. Reviews ms/illustration packages from artists. Submit ms with dummy. Contact: Chris Coffin. Illustrations only: Query with samples; provide tearsheets. Reports only if interested. Samples returned with SASE; samples filed.

INSIDER REPORT

Always, the Story Comes First

Chris Crutcher

Chris Crutcher loves to tell stories, and if his tales are enlightening to the reader, great. Otherwise, he is simply happy to entertain. He doesn't flinch at those who want to (and sometimes do) ban his books. "I love it," he says. He is flattered that *USA Today* puts him behind only Twain and Salinger as author of the most banned books in America. His books make people think and argue, and that's exactly what he wants. Whether the subject is sexual molestation (as in *Chinese Handcuffs*), free speech (as in *Staying Fat for Sarah Byrnes*), or the growing pains of adolescence, he hopes that his stories inspire readers to understand different viewpoints.

Author of eight novels (six for young adults for Greenwillow Books) and a screenplay, Crutcher has raised more than a few eyebrows by his streetwise tackling of controversial subjects. His stories, always told in first person to create "the feeling that the writer is talking to you," are often the target of school boards and community advocates.

Admittedly, the language of his characters is often "rough," and their lifestyles and attitudes a bit unorthodox, but rightly so, he claims. "I want to tell a story that's real. I have to include different perceptions of things" regardless of his own views. This is life, and he knows from experience how rough real life is.

Before his plunge into publishing, Crutcher worked as a child and family therapist in Spokane, Washington. Working in the mental health field for 12 years and spending a decade as director of an alternative school in Oakland, California, have given him first-hand knowledge of "the complexities of family dynamics." Although he now spends most of his time writing, he maintains his position as chairperson for the Spokane Child Protection Team.

Understandably, writing has been somewhat "therapeutic" for Crutcher. "It makes you decide how you feel because you have to know to write it down." He often gathers information from his therapy work for use in his novels. "If something happens, or I read something, I can add that current information (to the story) that day. I have changed stories." Particularly while working with domestic violence cases, he can "generalize" and use pieces of life in his fiction.

Although Crutcher's former work fits into his position of writer, his past literary experience is surprising. He read only one book (*To Kill A Mockingbird*) during his high school years. Yet while teaching in Oakland, he learned from friend and author Terry Davis as he wrote *Vision Quest*. "I got to watch the process from the inside," from writing and revising to the final editing.

Throughout this period, Crutcher's first novel was forming in his mind. During a four month hiatus between jobs, he followed Davis's lead and wrote *Running Loose*, a story which explores racism in the context of a high school football player's experience. A week later Crutcher had a book contract. He's been working with Greenwillow and its parent company William Morrow, ever since. Seven of his books have been named ALA Best Book for Young Adults.

Crutcher's advice to fledgling novelists stems from his experience in this market. Although billed as a writer of young adult novels, and sometimes even as a sports fiction writer (which couldn't be farther from the truth), Crutcher fights against categorization. Out of necessity, he defines himself as a writer of "coming of age" novels. "I seem to have gotten into a place that I didn't know existed," he says. He cautions other writers of "young adult" fiction that sales are "pretty much by word of mouth, school journals and magazines. Early on, you're not going to get into any bookstores. Serious adult lit is going to get in."

Crutcher, however, doesn't worry about marketing. He urges novice writers to start at the beginning—write a good story. "The better you're able to tell the truth and pull no punches, that's how you get into the passion of the book, the intimacy of the character." Don't get too caught up in how others will respond. "You want no constraints on yourself as a storyteller."

When the story is complete, every writer needs to go through it and edit "as an editor would." Laughing, he says, "They'd burn *Running Loose* the way it was originally written." He urges writers to "remember that words are more powerful on the page than they are spoken."

As school officials and church leaders argue and editors worry, Crutcher continues to write as he always has, with a love for storytelling and a "goal to make sense of the world." He takes his job quite seriously. "Storytelling is an important thing. When somebody says one of my stories 'changed my life,' he really means he can now see things differently." Put simply and with a chuckle, Crutcher's "job in life is checkin' things out, and maybe movin' them around a bit."

—*Jennifer Hogan-Redmond*

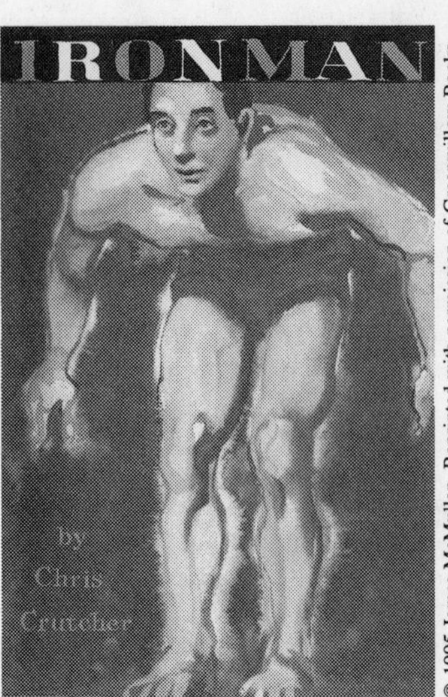

Through third-person narration and a young man's letters to radio talker Larry King, acclaimed author Chris Crutcher's* Ironman *chronicles the psychological and physical struggles of triathelete-in-training Bo Brewster. To keep from being expelled from high school, Bo is relegated to a before school anger management group. There he falls for Shelly, a future American Gladiator, who, along with others in the group of troubled teenagers, encourages him as he trains for competition. Bo proves his strength (in both muscle and character) to his father, his teacher, Larry and ultimately himself.

Terms: Pays authors royalty of 9% on wholesale price. Pays illustrators and photographers by the project. Sends galleys to authors; dummies to illustrators.
Tips: "Test books on kids other than those who know you. Match the 'look and feel' of text and illustrations to the subject and age level." Wants "early/middle reader fiction with polished writing and 'timeless' feel."

GREENHAVEN PRESS, 10911 Technology Place, San Diego CA 92127. (619)485-7424. Book publisher. Estab. 1970. Senior Editor: Bonnie Szumski. Publishes 40-50 young adult titles/year. 35% of books by first-time authors.
Nonfiction: Middle readers: biography, controversial topics, history, issues. Young adults: biography, history, nature/environment. Other titles "to fit our specific series." Average word length: young adults—15,000-25,000.
How to Contact/Writers: Query only. "We accept no unsolicited manuscripts. All writing is done on a work-for-hire basis."
Terms: Buys ms outright for $1,500-3,000. Offers advances. Sends galleys to authors. Book catalog available for 9×12 SAE and 65¢ postage.
Tips: "Get our guidelines first before submitting anything."

GREENWILLOW BOOKS, 1350 Avenue of the Americas, New York NY 10019. (212)261-6500. Imprint of William Morrow & Co. Book publisher. Editor-in-Chief: Susan Hirschman. Art Director: Ava Weiss. Publishes 50 picture books/year; 10 middle readers books/year; 10 young adult books/year.
Fiction: Will consider all levels of fiction; various categories.
How to Contact/Writers: Submit complete ms to editorial department "not specific editor." Do not call. Reports on mss in 10-12 weeks. Publishes a book 18-24 months after acceptance. Will consider simultaneous submissions.
Illustration: Reviews ms/illustration packages from artists.Illustrations only: Query with samples, résumé.
Terms: Pays authors royalty. Offers advances. Pays illustrators royalty or by the project. Sends galleys to authors. Book catalog available for 9×12 SAE with $2 postage; ms guidelines available for SASE.

GROSSET & DUNLAP, INC., 200 Madison Ave., New York NY 10016. (212)951-8700. Imprint of The Putnam & Grosset Group. Book publisher. Editor-in-chief: Judy Donnelly. Art Director: Ronnie Ann Herman. Publishes 80-90 titles/year: picture books; young readers; middle readers; young adult titles; board books; novelty books and easy chapter books. 5% of books by first-time authors; 50% of books from agented authors. Publishes fiction and nonfiction for mass market; novelty and board books.
Fiction: Picture books: animal, concept. Young readers: adventure, animal, concept, history, humor, nature/environment, sports. Most categories will be considered. "We publish series fiction, but not original novels in the young adult category." Sees too many trade picture books. Published *Snakes*, by Pat Demuth, illustrations by J. Moffatt (grades 1-3, All Aboard Reading); *Nina, Nina Ballerina*, by Jane O'Connor, illustrations by DyAnne DiSalvo-Ryan (preschool-grade 1, All Aboard Reading).
Nonfiction: Picture books: animal, concept, nature/environment, science. Young readers: activity books, animal, arts/crafts, biography, concept, history, sports. Recently published *Seeing Stars*, by Barbara Seiger, illustrated by Craig Callsbeek (ages 6-10, poster and stickers); *Zoom!*, written and illustrated by Margaret A. Hartelius (ages 4-8, paper airplane kit).
How to Contact/Writers: Fiction/Nonfiction: Query. Reports in 2-4 weeks on queries; 1-2 months on mss. Publishes book 1-2 years after acceptance. Will consider simultaneous submissions.
Illustrations: Works with 50 illustrators/year. Reviews ms/illustration packages from artists. Query. Illustrations only: Query with samples; provide résumé, promo sheet, portfolio, slides, tearsheets. "Portfolio drop-off on Wednesdays." Contact: Ronnie Ann Herman, art director. Reports only if interested. Original artwork returned at job's completion.
Photography: Buys photos from freelancers. Contact: Ronnie Ann Herman, art director. Buys stock. Uses photos of babies and toddlers, interactive children, animals—full color. Publishes photo concept books. Uses color prints; 35mm, 2¼×2¼, 4×5 and 8×10 transparencies. To

contact, photographers should query with samples, send unsolicited photos by mail, submit portfolio, provide promotional literature or tearsheets to be kept on file.
Terms: Pays authors royalty or by outright purchase. Offers advances. Pays illustrators by the project or by royalty. Photographers paid by the project or per photo. Book catalog available for 9×12 SASE. Ms guidelines available for SASE.
Tips: "We are interested in early chapter books and middle grade series ideas."

GRYPHON HOUSE, P.O. Box 207, Beltsville MD 20704-0207. (301)595-9500. Fax: (301)595-0051. E-mail: kcharner@gryphonhouse.com. Book publisher. Editor-in-Chief: Kathy Charner.
Nonfiction: Parent and teacher resource books. Recently published *500 Five Minute Games*, by Jackie Silberg; *Transition Time*, by Jean Feldman; *Never, EVER, Serve Sugary Snacks on Rainy Days*, by Shirley Raines; and *The Complete Learning Center Book*, by Rebecca Isbell.
How to Contact/Writers: Query. Submit outline/synopsis and 2 sample chapters. Reports on queries/mss in 3 months. Publishes a book 18 months after acceptance. Will consider simultaneous submissions, electronic submissions via disk or modem.
Illustration: Uses b&w artwork only. Reviews ms/illustration packages from artists. Submit query letter with table of contents, introduction and sample chapters. Illustrations only: Query with samples, promo sheet. Reports back in 2 months only if interested. Samples are filed. Original artwork returned at job's completion.
Photography: Buys photos from freelancers. Contact: Kathy Charner, editor-in-chief. Buys stock and assigns work. Submit cover letter, published samples, stock photo list.
Terms: Pays authors royalty based on retail price. Offers advances. Pays illustrators by the project. Pay photographers by the project or per photo. Sends galleys to authors. Book catalog and ms guidelines available for SASE.
Tips: "We are looking for books of creative, participatory learning experiences that have a common conceptual theme to tie them together. The books should be on subjects that teachers want to do on a daily basis in the classroom. If a book caters to a particular market in addition to teachers, that would be a plus."

***■GUMBS & THOMAS PUBLISHERS**, 142 W. 72nd St., Suite 9, New York NY 10023. (212)255-1506. Fax: (212)255-1843. Book publisher. President: V. Thomas. Executive Vice President: B. Gumbs. Publishes 4 young readers/year. 75% of books by first-time authors; 50% subsidy published. Primary themes include African-American, Caribbean history, fiction and how-to.
Fiction: Picture books, young readers, middle readers and young adults: contemporary, multicultural.
How to Contact/Writers: Fiction: Query; submit outline/synopsis and 2 sample chapters. Reports on queries in 3 months; mss in 6 months. Publishes a book 1 year after acceptance. Will consider previously published work.
Illustration: Works with 3 illustrators/year. Uses both b&w and color artwork. Reviews ms/illustration packages from authors. Query. Illustrations only: Send promo sheet. Reports only if interested. Samples not returned.
Terms: Pays authors royalty. Offers advances. Sends galleys to authors; dummies to illustrators.

***HACHAI PUBLISHING**, 156 Chester Ave., Brooklyn NY 11218. (718)633-0100. Fax: (718)633-0103. Book publisher. Submissions Editor: Deborah Leah Rosenfeld. Publishes 3 picture books/year; 3 young readers/year; 1 middle reader/year. 75% of books published by first-time authors. "All books have spiritual/religious themes, specifically traditional Jewish content. We're seeking books about morals and values; the Jewish experience in current and Biblical times; and Jewish observance, Sabbath and holidays."
Fiction: Picture books and young readers: contemporary, fantasy, history, religion. Middle readers: adventure, contemporary, problem novels, religion. Does not want to see animal stories, romance, problem novels depicting drug use or violence. Recently published *Shimmy the Youngest*, by Miriam Elias, illustrated by Aidel Baekman (ages 3-6, picture book).
Nonfiction: Recently published *My Jewish ABC's*, by Draizy Zelcer, illustrated by Patti Nemeroff (ages 3-6, picture book).
How to Contact/Wrtiers: Fiction/Nonfiction: Submit complete ms.
Illustration: Works with 4 illustrators/year. Uses color artwork only. Reviews ms/illustration packages from authors. Submit ms with 1 piece of final art. Contact: Devorah Leah Rosenfeld,

INSIDER REPORT

Attitude Is an Artist's Best Friend

Denise Fleming's pulp-painted illustrations are a lot like her personality—vibrant, bold, and sometimes humorous. An award-winning illustrator and author of six picture books, she is testimony that enthusiasm and determination are crucial to success in the children's book market.

Denise Fleming

Fleming's work was not always ripe with colorful, graphic images. "My old style was tight, controlled, very sweet . . . and I'm not any of those things," says the Toledo, Ohio, artist. She had been illustrating licensed characters (such as Care Bears) for novelty books through Random House when she discovered papermaking in 1989 at a local high school class. "It was just a fun thing to do with my sister in the evenings," she says. Yet, once she started experimenting with this medium, her brushes and pencils became dust collectors. "It was meant to be."

Pulp painting is derived from papermaking. First, Fleming buys cotton rag fiber that is recycled from the garment industry. The fiber is beaten to a fine pulp and suspended in water. She purchases the white fiber mixture (similar in consistency to mashed potatoes) in five-gallon buckets, then uses universal pigments to color the pulp, adding water to create a slurry mixture.

The second phase of the process begins with pouring the pulp onto a large screen. The water drains out, leaving only the damp pulp on the surface. Over this layer Fleming applies additional layers using a variety of stencils (which she designs and cuts from recyclable foam board). Creating the shapes and effects she wants often requires as many as 23 layers of pulp.

After the layering is complete, she flips the screen over and presses the pulp layers between cloth to create the paper. To completely dry each sheet, she also uses a vacuum table and places the paper in a drying press.

Despite this "very physical" and sometimes lengthy procedure, Fleming insists that "it's an easy process—it's kind of like magic." She enjoys the unpredictability of the medium, as well as the bright, strong color the blending of the fibers yields.

After nearly a year perfecting her pulp-painting technique, Fleming began presenting her portfolio to editors in New York City. On her first visit to the Big Apple to show her new technique, she attracted the attention of an editor at Henry Holt & Company. She has been working with the publisher ever since.

Fleming attributes her success not only to her distinctive style, but to her enthusiasm for her work. "I love what I do," she says. Before discovering pulp

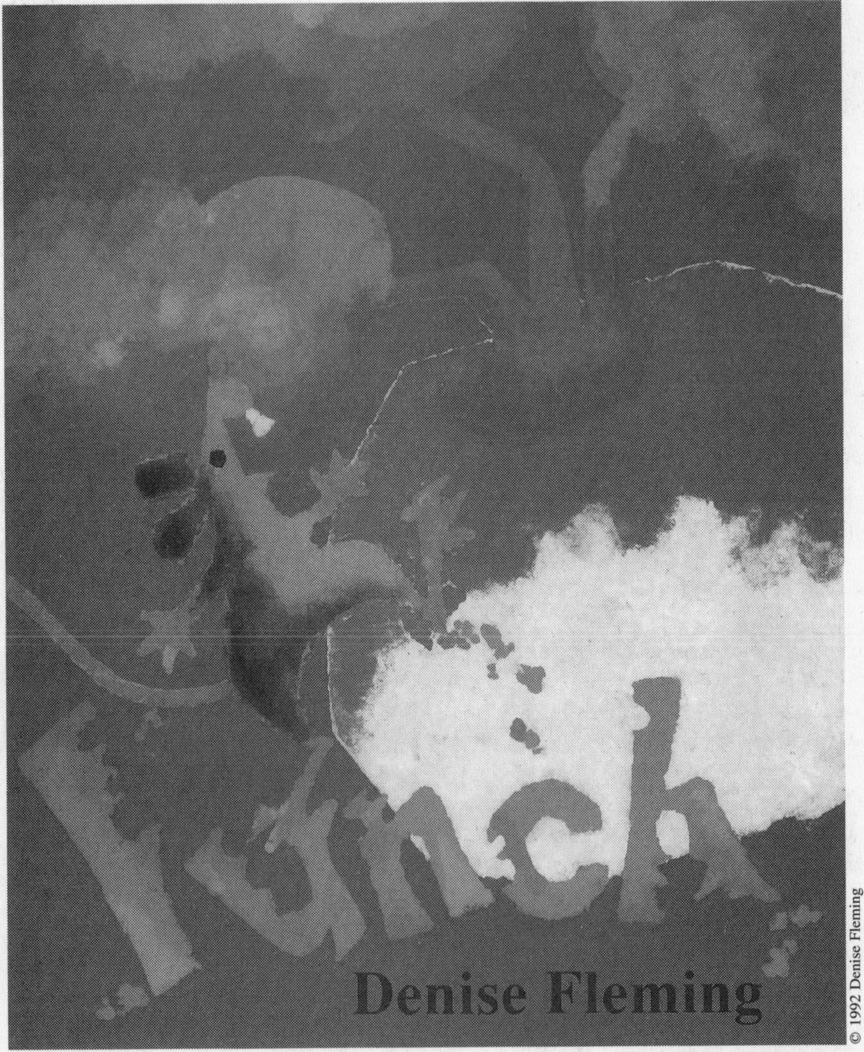

© 1992 Denise Fleming

A voracious little mouse gobbles his way through an array of colorful, healthful foods—from a crisp white turnip to a juicy pink watermelon (seeds and all)—in Denise Fleming's* Lunch. *The author/artist's unusual technique of creating illustrations in handmade paper yielded a fuzzy, toothy mouse and big, bold fruits and vegetables set off by a black and white tablecloth, giving young readers both a lesson in colors and a fun look at nutritious foods.

painting, "I was picking up work illustrating spark plugs. I hated it." Although she admits that "when you have a different style, more attention is paid to you," an illustrator "can definitely find work in a conventional style if you're good." The key is that your work "reflects who you are."

Because her work is so personal, Fleming pulls many of the images in her books from her life. *In the Tall, Tall Grass*, her first book using pulp painting, and *Where Once There Was a Wood*, her most recent publication, are based on long-ago adventures in the woods near her home with her young daughter.

In these and all of her books, she takes great pains to assure that her young readers experience each part of nature as if they're actually there with her. "I love little ones—they're very strong, bold little folks. I wanted the books to reflect that." Fleming does everything from manipulating the type to choosing full bleeds and double-page spreads so her readers can feel fully involved. "I want you to have a joyful feeling; I want you to have a sense of being there. I don't care if a raccoon looks exactly like a raccoon."

Although Fleming's books clearly emphasize images, she chooses her words just as carefully as her pigments. Referring to *In the Tall, Tall Grass* and *In a Small, Small Pond*, Fleming "wanted words to be part of the illustration. I wanted words that felt good in your mouth." She wants her books to be full feasts for the senses.

Fleming took the same careful yet enthusiastic approach when she tried to capture editors' interest in 1990. At first hesitant to approach New York publishers as an artist living and working in the Midwest, she put her fear aside and tackled the market with vigor.

Her most important asset was a carefully prepared portfolio filled with work she loves. She urges all illustrators to follow her lead. "Don't put in anything that you re not completely confident about . . . you don't want to make excuses." Secondly, "Don't put in anything you really don't want to do. What if you get a book project" doing this type of work? And finally, "Don't put in anything you can't do again," referring to those "happy accidents" all artists encounter.

When compiling this work, remember that your portfolio is a reflection of you, and you need to present yourself "as a professional, even if you've never done it before. Work that's dog-eared and dirty will make an editor wonder if you're really capable, if you can make deadlines."

Once her portfolio was complete, Fleming concentrated on procuring appointments with editors at New York publishing houses, always following proper business etiquette. A strict believer in observing such "social niceties," she stresses the importance of calling editors weeks ahead of your planned visits to arrange appointments to show your portfolio. Then, arrive on time and send thank-you letters after your visits.

Fleming offers a final piece of advice to novice illustrators: Ask for suggestions. Listen and consider an editor's tips, but be cautious about making changes. "Don't outright change everything." You must feel comfortable with your own work. "Develop a really strong faith in yourself." And always remember, "attitude is very important."

—Jennifer Hogan-Redmond

submissions editor. Illustrations only: Query with samples; arrange personal portfolio review. Samples returned with SASE.
Terms: Work purchased outright from authors for $1,000. Pays illustrators by the project (range: 2,000).

HARCOURT BRACE & CO., 525 B St., Suite 1900, San Diego CA 92101-4495. (619)699-6810. Children's Books Division which includes: Harcourt Brace Children's Books, Gulliver Books, Voyager Paperbacks, Odyssey Paperbacks, Jane Yolen Books, Browndeer Press, Red Wagon Books and Magic Carpet Books. Book publisher. Publishes 40-45 picture books/year; 15-20 middle reader titles/year; 8-12 young adult titles/year. 20% of books by first-time authors; 50% of books from agented writers.

• Harcourt Brace won a Caldecott Medal in 1995 for *Smoky Night*, illustrated by David Diaz, written by Eve Bunting. The staff of Harcourt Brace's children's book department is no longer accepting unsolicited manuscripts. Only query letters and manuscripts submitted by agents will be considered. They rank 13th, based on net sales, of the top 15 children's publishers.

Fiction: Picture books, young readers: animal, contemporary, fantasy, history. Middle readers, young adults: animal, contemporary, fantasy, history, problem novels, romance, science fiction, sports, spy/mystery/adventure. Average word length: picture books—"varies greatly"; middle readers—20,000-50,000; young adults—35,000-65,000.
Nonfiction: Picture books, young readers: animal, biography, history, hobbies, music/dance, nature/environment, religion, sports. Middle readers, young adults: animal, biography, education, history, hobbies, music/dance, nature/environment, religion, sports. Average word length: picture books—"varies greatly"; middle readers—20,000-50,000; young adults—35,000-65,000.
How to Contact/Writers: Only interested in agented material.
Illustration: Reviews ms/illustration packages from artists. "For picture book ms—complete ms acceptable. Longer books—outline and 2-4 sample chapters." Send several samples of art; no original art. Illustrations only: Submit résumé, tearsheets, color photocopies, color stats all accepted. "Please DO NOT send original artwork or transparencies. Include SASE for return, please." Reports on art samples in 6-10 weeks. Original artwork returned at job's completion.
Terms: Pays authors in royalties based on retail price. Pays illustrators by the project. Sends galleys to authors; dummies to illustrators. Book catalog available for 9×12 SASE; ms/artist's guidelines for business-size SASE.
Tips: "Become acquainted with Harcourt Brace's books in particular if you are interested in submitting proposals to us."

HARPERCOLLINS CHILDREN'S BOOKS, 10 E. 53rd St., New York NY 10022. (212)207-7044. Fax: (212)207-7192.

• HarperCollins won a Newbery Medal in 1995 for *Walk Two Moons*, by Sharon Creech. They rank 3rd, based on net sales, of the top 15 children's publishers. For submission information, see listing for Laura Geringer Books.

HARVEST HOUSE PUBLISHERS, 1075 Arrowsmith, Eugene OR 97402. (503)343-0123. Book publisher. Manuscript Coordinator: LaRae Weikert. Publishes 1-2 picture books/year; 2 young reader titles/year; 2 young adult titles/year. 2-5% of books by first-time authors. Books follow a Christian theme.

• Harvest House no longer accepts unsolicited children's manuscripts.

Illustration: Reviews ms/illustration packages from artists. Submit "3 chapters of ms with copies (do not send originals) of art and any approximate rough sketches. Illustrations only: Send résumé, tearsheets. Submit to production manager. Reports on art samples in 2 months.
Terms: Pays authors in royalties of 10-15%. Average advance payment: "negotiable." Pays illustrator: "Sometimes by project." Sends galleys to authors; sometimes sends dummies to illustrators. Book catalog, ms guidelines free on request.

HAYES SCHOOL PUBLISHING CO. INC., 321 Pennwood Ave., Wilkinsburg PA 15221. (412)371-2373. Fax: (412)371-6408. Estab. 1940. Produces folders, workbooks, stickers, certificates. Wants to see supplementary teaching aids for grades K-12. Interested in all subject areas. Will consider simultaneous and electronic submissions.

How to Contact/Writers: Query with description or complete ms. Reports in 3-4 weeks. SASE for return of submissions.
Terms: Work purchased outright. Purchases all rights.

THE HEARST BOOK GROUP, 1350 Avenue of the Americas, New York NY 10019.

- Hearst ranks 10th, based on net sales, of the top 15 children's publishers. For submissions information see the listing for Avon Books.

HENDRICK-LONG PUBLISHING COMPANY, P.O. Box 25123, Dallas TX 75225. Book publisher. Vice President: Joann Long. Publishes 1 picture book/year; 4 young reader titles/year; 4 middle reader titles/year. 20% of books by first-time authors.
Fiction: Middle readers: history books on Texas and the Southwest. No fantasy or poetry. Recently published *Baxter Badger's Home*, by Doris McClennan, illustrated by Vicki Diggs (young reader picture book); and *Race to Velasco*, by Paul Spellman (ages 9 and up).
Nonfiction: Middle, young adults: history books on Texas and the Southwest, biography, multicultural. Recently published *Camels for Uncle Sam*, by Diane Yancey (ages 9 and up); and *Brave Bessie: Flying Free*, by Lillian M. Fisher (ages 9 and up).
How to Contact/Writers: Only interested in agented material. Fiction/Nonfiction: Query with outline/synopsis and sample chapter. Reports on queries in 2 weeks; mss in 2 months. Publishes a book 18 months after acceptance. No simultaneous submissions. Include SASE.
Illustration: Works with 3-4 illustrators/year. Uses primarily b&w interior artwork; color covers only. Illustrations only: Query first. Submit résumé or promotional literature or photocopies or tearsheets—no original work sent unsolicited. Contact: Joann Long. Material kept on file. No reply sent.
Terms: Pays authors in royalty based on selling price. Advances vary. Pays illustrators by the project or royalty. Sends galleys to authors; dummies to illustrators. Ms guidelines for 1 first-class stamp and #10 SAE.
Tips "Material **must** pertain to Texas or the Southwest. Check all facts about historical figures and events in both fiction and nonfiction. Be accurate."

HERALD PRESS, 616 Walnut Ave., Scottdale PA 15683. (412)887-8500. Fax: (412)887-3111. Division of Mennonite Publishing House. Estab. 1908. Publishes 1 picture storybook/year; 1 young reader title/year; 2-3 middle reader titles/year; 1-2 young adult titles/year. Editorial Contact: S. David Garber. Art Director: Jim Butti. 20% of books by first-time authors; 3% of books from agented writers.
Fiction: Young readers, middle readers, young adults: contemporary, history, problem novels, religious, self-help, social concerns. Recently published *April Bluebird*, by Esther Bender; *Whispering Brook Farm*, by Carrie Baker. Does not want stories on fantasy, science fiction, war, drugs, cops and robbers.
Nonfiction: Young readers, middle readers, young adults: how-to, religious, self-help, social concerns. Published *Storytime Jamboree*, by Peter Dyck; and *We Knew Jesus*, by Marian Hostetler (both fiction and nonfiction collections).
How to Contact/Writers: Fiction/Nonfiction: "Send to Book Editor, the following: (1) a one-page summary of your book, (2) a one- or two-sentence summary of each chapter, (3) the first chapter and one other, (4) your statement of the significance of the book, (5) a description of your target audience, (6) a brief biographical sketch of yourself, and (7) SASE for return of the material. You may expect a reply in about a month. If your proposal appears to have potential for Herald Press, a finished manuscript will be requested. Herald Press depends on capable and dedicated authors to continue publishing high-quality Christian literature." Reports on queries in 1 month; mss in 2 months. Publishes a book 12 months after acceptance. Will consider simultaneous submissions but prefers not to.
Illustration: Works with 3 illustrators/year. Reviews ms/illustration packages from artists. Illustrations only: Query with samples. Send résumé, tearsheets and slides. Contact: Jim Butti, art director.
Photography: Purchases photos from freelancers. Contact: Debbie Cameron. Buys stock and assigns work.
Terms: Pays authors in royalties of 10-12% based on retail price. Pays for illustrators by the project (range: $220-600). Sends galleys to authors. Book catalog for 3 first-class stamps; ms guidelines free on request.

Tips: "We invite book proposals from Christian authors in the area of juvenile fiction. Our purpose is to publish books which are consistent with Scripture as interpreted in the Anabaptist/Mennonite tradition. Books that are honest in presentation, clear in thought, stimulating in content, appropriate in appearance, superior in printing and binding, and conducive to the spiritual growth and welfare of the reader."

***HIGHSMITH PRESS**, P.O. Box 800, Ft. Atkinson WI 53538. (414)563-9571. (414)563-4801. E-mail: hpress@highsmith.com. Imprint: Alleyside Press. Book publisher. Publisher: Donald Sager.
Nonfiction: "Nonfiction published by Highsmith Press is for teachers' use in the classroom." No picture books for young readers accepted. Publishes only activity books, reference, library skills, study skills. Average length: 48-120 pages. Recently published *Research to Write*, by Maity Schrecengost (study skills for ages 8-11); *An Alphabet of Books, Literature Based Activities for Schools and Libraries*, by Robin Davis (activity book for ages 3-7); and *World Guide to Historical Fiction for Young Adults*, by Lee Gordon (reference for ages 11-17).
How to Contact/Writers: Query; submit complete ms; submit outline/synopsis. Reports on queries in 1 month; mss in 2 months. Publishes a book 6 months after acceptance. Will consider simultaneous submissions.
Illustration: Illustrations only: Query with samples. Cotnact: Don Sager, publisher. Reports in 1 month. Samples returned with SASE. Original artwork returned at job's completion.
Photography: Buys stock. Model/property releases required. "We rarely use external submissions." Submit cover letter, published samples.
Terms: Pays authors royalty of 10-12% based on wholesale price. Offers advances. Sends galleys to authors. Book catalog available for 9 × 12 SAE and 2 first-class stamps; ms guidelines available for SASE.
Tips: "Look at our catalog to see what we publish. It's getting to be a tougher market, with more electronic versions, especially reference."

***HODDER CHILDREN'S BOOKS**, Hodder Headline PLC, 338 Euston Rd., London NW1 3BH England. (071)873-6000. Fax: (071)873-6229. Book publisher. Contact: Editorial Dept. Children's Art Dept. Publishes 12 picture books/year; 24 young readers/year; 50 middle readers; 6 young adult titles/year.
Fiction: Picture books, young readers and middle readers: adventure, animal, concept, contemporary, fantasy, humor, nature/environment and suspense/mystery. Young adults: adventure, contemporary, fantasy, humor, science fiction, suspense/mystery, horror. Average word length: picture books—1,000; read alones (6-8 years) 2,000-4,000; story books (7-9 years) 8,000-12,000; novels (8 and up) 20,000-50,000.
Nonfiction: Picture books: animal. Young readers: activity books, humor. Middle readers: activity books. Young adults: careers, health, self-help, social issues. Average word length: picture books—1,000; young readers—5,000; middle readers—15,000; young adults—20,000. Recently published *Just 17 Quiz Book*, by Anita Naik (ages 10-14, teen self help/fun); and *Addition and Subtraction*, by R. Whiteford and Jim Fitzsimmons (ages 5-7, infant home-learning).
How to Contact/Writers: Fiction: Submit outline/synopsis and 3 sample chapters. Reports on queries in 1 month; mss in 1 month. Publishes a book 12-18 months after acceptance. Will consider simultaneous submissions.
Illustration: Uses both b&w and color artwork. Reviews ms/illustration packages from authors. Submit ms with dummy. Contact: Children's Editor. Illustrations only: query with samples. Reports in 1 month. Samples returned with SASE; samples filed. Original artwork returned at job's completion.
Photography: Buys photos from freelancers. Contact: Children's Art Dept. Buys stock and assigns work. Submit cover letter.
Terms: Pays authors royalty or work purchased outright. Pays illustrators by the project or royalty. Pays photographers by the project. Sends galleys to authors. Ms guidelines available.
Tips: "Write from the heart. Don't patronize your reader. Do your research—read the finest writers around, see where the market is. We're looking for something original with a clear sense of the first reader."

HOLIDAY HOUSE INC., 425 Madison Ave., New York NY 10017. (212)688-0085. Fax: (212)421-6134. Book publisher. Vice President/Editor-in-Chief: Margery Cuyler. Associate Editor: Ashley Mason. Publishes 30 picture books/year; 3 young reader titles/year; 10 middle reader titles/year; 3 young adult titles/year. 20% of books by first-time authors; 10% from agented writers.

Fiction: For all levels: adventure, animal, contemporary, fantasy, history, humor, multicultural and religion. Recently published *I Am an Artichoke*, by Lucy Frank; *2×2=Boo*, by Loreen Leedy; and *Iron John*, retold by Eric A. Kimmel, illustrated by Trina Schart Hyman.

Nonfiction: Biography, concept, geography, history, religion, science and sports.

How to Contact/Writers: Reports on queries in 2 weeks; mss in 6-8 weeks.

Illustration: Works with 20 illustrators/year. Reviews ms/illustration packages from artists. Send ms with dummy. Contact: Ashley Mason, associate editor. Reports back in 6 weeks if interested. Samples returned or filed. Originals returned at job's completion.

Terms: Pays authors and illustrators royalty. Ms/artist's guidelines available for a SASE.

Tips: "Fewer books are being published. It will get even harder for first-timers to break in."

HENRY HOLT & CO., INC., 115 W. 18th St., New York NY 10011. (212)886-9200. Book publisher. Editor-in-Chief/Vice President/Associate Publisher: Brenda Bowen. Publishes 20-30 picture books/year; 60-80 young reader titles/year; 10 middle reader titles/year; 10 young adult titles/year. 5% of books by first-time authors; 40% of books from agented writers.

- Henry Holt ranks 15th, based on net sales, of the top 15 children's publishers.

How to Contact/Writers: Fiction/Nonfiction: Submit complete ms. Reports on queries/mss in 2 months. Publishes a book 12-18 months after acceptance. Will consider simultaneous submissions.

Illustration: Reviews ms/illustration packages from artists. Random samples OK. Illustrations only: Submit tearsheets, slides. Do *not* send originals. Reports on art samples only if interested. If accepted, original artwork returned at job's completion.

Terms: Pays authors/illustrators advance plus royalty based on retail price. Sends galleys to authors; dummies to illustrators.

HOMESTEAD PUBLISHING, Box 193, Moose WY 83012. Book publisher. Editor: Carl Schreier. Publishes 15 picture books/year; 2 young reader titles/year; 2 middle reader titles/year; 2 young adult titles/year. 30% of books by first-time authors; 1% of books from agented writers.

Fiction: Average word length: young readers—1,000; middle readers—5,000; young adults—5,000-150,000.

Nonfiction: Picture books, middle readers: animal (wildlife), biography, history, nature/environment. Young readers: nature/environment (wildlife). Young adults: history, nature/environment (wildlife). Average word length: young readers—1,000; middle readers—5,000; young adults—5,000-250,000.

How to Contact/Writers: Fiction/Nonfiction: Query; submit outline/synopsis and sample chapters. Reports on queries/mss in 1 month. Publishes a book 1 year after acceptance. Will consider simultaneous submissions.

Illustration: Prefers to see "watercolor, opaque, oil" illustrations. Reviews ms/illustration packages from artists."Query first with sample writing and art style." Illustrations only: Submit résumés, style samples. Reports on art samples in 1-2 months. Original artwork returned at job's completion with SASE.

Terms: Pays authors in royalties of 5-10% based on wholesale price. Work purchased outright "depending on project." Pays illustrators by the project (range: $50-10,000) or royalty of 3-10% based on wholesale price. Sends galleys to authors; dummies to illustrators.

***JOHN HONEA PUBLISHERS**, 1495 Alpharetta Hwy., Alpharetta GA 30201. Book publisher. Editor: John Honea. Publishes 6 picture books/year; 8 young readers/year; 6 middle readers/year; 7 young adult titles/year. 50% of books by first-time authors.

Fiction: Picture books, young readers: animal, contemporary, health, multicultural, nature/environment. Middle readers: adventure, contemporary, fantasy, humor, multicultural, nature/environment, religion, sports. Young adults/teens: adventure, contemporary, fantasy, health, multicultural, nature/environment, problem novels, religion, sports, suspense/mystery.

How to Contact/Writers: Include "a brief cover letter explaining why your book will sell" with submissions.

Terms: Offers advances. Pays illustrators royalty based on retail price. Pays photographers royalty based on retail price. Sends galleys to authors; dummies to illustrators.

HOUGHTON MIFFLIN CO., Children's Trade Books, 222 Berkeley St., Boston MA 02116 and 215 Park Ave. S., New York NY 10003. (617)351-5000. Book publisher. Publisher: Anita Silvey. Editor: Matilda Welter. Editors: Audrey Bryant, Margaret Raymo. Assistant Editor: Amy Thrall. Art Director: David Saylor. Averages 80 titles/year. Publishes hardcover originals and trade paperback reprints.

- Ticknor & Fields has merged with Houghton Mifflin and kept its Boston address. Houghton Mifflin ranks 12th, based on net sales, of the top 15 children's publishers. See First Books for interview with Houghton author Shelley Moore Thomas on her book *Putting the World to Sleep*.

Fiction: All levels: all categories except religion. "We do not rule out any theme, though we do not publish specifically religious material." Published *The Giver*, by Lois Lowry (novel); *Owl in Love*, by Patrice Kindl (ages 10 and up, novel); and *The Sweetest Fig*, by Chris Van Allsburg (all ages, picture book).

Nonfiction: Published *Grandfather's Journey*, by Allen Say (all ages picture book); and *Amish Home*, by Raymond Bial (ages 7-14, photo essay).

How to Contact/Writers: Fiction: Submit complete ms. Nonfiction: Submit outline/synopsis and sample chapters. Reports on queries in 2 weeks; on mss in 1-8 weeks.

Illustration: Works with 60 illustrators/year. Reviews ms/illustration packages from artists. Ms/illustration packages or illustrations only: Query with samples (colored photocopies are fine); provide tearsheets.

Terms: Pays standard royalty; offers advance. Illustrators paid by the project and royalty. Book catalog free with SASE.

***HUMANICS CHILDREN'S HOUSE**, Humanics Limited, 1482 Mecaslin St. NW, Atlanta GA 30309. (404)874-2176. Fax: (404)874-1976. Book publisher. Acquisitions: W. Arthur Bligh. Publishes 6 picture books/year. 50% of books by first-time authors. "Primary themes include self-esteem, and building the child's awareness of self and others through a multicultural, non-ethnocentric approach."

Fiction: Picture books and young readers: animal, concept, contemporary, fantasy, folktales, multicultural, nature/environment. Multicultural needs include stories dealing with bridging cultural gaps. Average length: picture books—32 pages; young readers—32 pages. Recently published *The Adventure of Paz in the Land of Numbers*, by Miriam Bowden (English and Spanish counting, picture book); *Planet of the Dinosaurs*, by Dr. Barbara Carr (adventure, picture book); and *Cambio Chameleon*, by Mauro Magellan (self-esteem, picture book), all for ages pre-K to grade 3.

Nonfiction: Picture books: activity books, animal, arts/crafts, multicultural, music/dance, nature/environment, self help, social issues. Young readers: activity books, animal, multicultural, music/dance, nature/environment, self help, social issues. Average length: activity books—160 pages; young readers—160 pages.

How to Contact/Writers: Fiction: Query. Will consider simultaneous submissions.

Illustration: Samples returned with SASE. Original artwork returned at job's completion.

Terms: "All pay is negotiable." Sends galleys to authors; dummies to illustrators. Book catalog available for 9×12 SAE and 2 first-class stamps; ms and art guidelines available for SASE.

Tips: "Please send query letters which detail your writing experience and goals, plus a product that is innovative and memorable."

HUNTER HOUSE PUBLISHERS, P.O.Box 2914, Alameda CA 94501-0914. Fax: (510)865-4295. Book publisher. Independent book producer/packager. Editor: Lisa Lee. Publishes 0-1 titles for teenage women/year. 50% of books by first-time authors; 5% of books from agented writers.

Nonfiction: Young adults: health, multicultural, self help (self esteem), social issues. "We emphasize that all our books try to take multicultural experiences and concerns into account. We would be interested in a social issues or self-help book on multicultural issues." Books are

***A bullet within a listing introduces special comments by the editor of* Children's Writer's & Illustrator's Market.**

INSIDER REPORT

Wegman's Career Develops into a Fairy 'Tail'

William Wegman

William Wegman remembers a time early in his career when he traveled through Europe carrying all his work in "three little 11 × 14 photo boxes." His entire body of work consisted of roughly 30 pieces and he was eager to show them off. "I'm the type of person who likes to say, 'See what I did,' " says Wegman. "Other artists are very protective. They only show a couple things and let them out slowly."

Times have changed. Wegman no longer needs to struggle for acclaim. He has become one of today's foremost photographers. In 1994, *American Photo* placed Wegman on a list of its top 100 photo industry professionals. He is a two-time winner of the Guggenheim Fellowship (1975 and 1986); he has exhibited in premier galleries, such as The Corcoran Gallery of Art in Washington DC, The Museum of Modern Art and the Whitney Museum of American Art in New York City; and, in recent years, he has played off the popularity of his anthropomorphic weimaraners to create numerous children's books, such as *Cinderella* and *Little Red Riding Hood* (both published by Hyperion Books for Children).

And, he has much more work to show. "Now I've done more things than any one person can look at. There are caves and walls of photos. I get that bloated feeling," says Wegman from his home in Maine.

For the rest of us, Wegman's bloated feeling is something to cherish. It means there is plenty of work to admire and analyze—from his early conceptual work of the 1960s when he floated Styrofoam commas down the Milwaukee River, to the kids' books and videos of today that showcase his weimaraners.

Since graduating from the Massachusetts College of Art in Boston in 1965, Wegman's work has continued to evolve. This is something newcomers should take to heart. Even though the majority of his videos and photos feature his four-legged models, Wegman has an ability to keep his subject matter fresh. "The later work is more seduced by how the dogs look—how beautiful they are, where they are looking, what they appear to be thinking," says Wegman. "In the old work, the dogs are more stoic. The dogs are there on the box, or in the box, looking left, looking right, doing really simple, very strong gestures."

His playful, comedic approach fits nicely with his more recent projects. Wegman says he began working on children's books when Hyperion asked him to recreate some fairy tales. "Once I got started I got kind of addicted to it. I like the process of having a photograph end up, not just in a gallery or in a museum

Renowned photographer William Wegman, famous for shots of his beloved weimaraners, transformed his dogs into the cast of **Little Red Riding Hood** ***for his version of the tale published by Hyperion. In this Polaroid Polacolor photo Wegman's costumed canine plays the title character.***

or on somebody's walls, but in another form."

Wegman re-told the fairy tales by dressing up the weimaraners as characters and placing them in intricate scenes. The cast included one of his favorite subjects, Fay Ray, who died in 1995. "As soon as I made Fay tall it seemed to make the characters more believable as mythological figures," he says. "When people dress up dogs and they're little, they look like beer ads. There's something demeaning about them. When I made Fay tall, and I put her up on something and put a dress over her, she became really quite profound looking. Then the anthropomorphic possibilities became really strong."

In creating the books, Wegman wanted to match the dogs' personalities with the characters they were playing. He also tried to influence the character of the dogs by the types of gowns they wore. "I noticed in one picture that Fay looked rather evil in her wig, so she became the stepmother to Cinderella. I noticed that Battina, no matter how I dressed her up, always looked sweet and forlorn. She became a good choice for Cinderella."

Along with the fairy tales, Wegman has produced fun and educational material for children, such as his books *ABC* and *1,2,3* (both by Hyperion). There also are videos for the home, such as *Alphabet Soup* and *Fay's Twelve Days of Christmas*; and any pre-schooler can tell you about Wegman's videos that appear on the TV show *Sesame Street*. His relationship with *Sesame Street* evolved after the show's producers sent him a book "the size of the Manhattan Yellow Pages" with concepts that he could tackle.

"It's fun to work on something that gets nursed along, like videos. You have to do voice-overs, music, editing, some set building, scriptwriting. So many parts to it involve so many people, and it just takes time. It's very operatic," he says.

Often, however, completing the opera is not as easy as it seems when looking at the finished product. Wegman's weimaraners are attentive to what he wants, but they are not trained. "In still photography it's easy. You can get a moment that's magical and it transcends what you're thinking about. In film work you have to think up new ways to get it to happen. If you want the dogs to look in four different directions, you can do it once, but the next time they're going to look directly at you. . . . To make Chundo (the Wolf) look mean, I had to go away from him about 100 feet so that he would squint to see me. When I approached him he would look kind and happy."

—Michael Willins

therapy/personal growth-oriented. Does *not* want to see books for young children; fiction; illustrated picture books; autobiography. Published *Turning Yourself Around: Self-Help Strategies for Troubled Teens*, by Kendall Johnson, Ph.D.; *Safe Dieting for Teens*, by Linda Ojeda, Ph.D.
How to Contact/Writers: Query; submit overview and chapter-by-chapter synopsis, sample chapters and statistics on your subject area, support organizations or networks and marketing ideas. "Testimonials from professionals or well-known authors are crucial." Reports on queries in 1 month; mss in 4 months. Publishes a book 18 months after acceptance. Will consider simultaneous submissions.
Photography: Purchases photos from freelancers. Contact: Paul Frindt. Buys stock images.
Terms: Pays authors royalty of 12% based on wholesale price. Pays illustrators by the project. Sends galleys to authors. Book catalog available for 9×12 SAE and 79¢ postage; ms guidelines for standard SAE and 1 first-class stamp.
Tips: Wants therapy/personal growth workbooks; teen books with solid, informative material. "We do few children's books. The ones we do are for a select, therapeutic audience. No fiction! Please, no fiction."

HUNTINGTON HOUSE PUBLISHERS, P.O. Box 53788, Lafayette LA 70505. (318)237-7049. Book publisher. Editor-in-Chief: Mark Anthony. Publishes 2 young readers/year. 100% of books by first-time authors. "All books have spiritual/religious themes."
Fiction: Picture books, young readers, middle readers, young adults: all subjects. Does not want to see romance, nature/environment, multicultural. Average word length: picture books—12-50; young readers—100-300; middle readers—4,000-15,000; young adults/teens—10,000-40,000. Published *Greatest Star of All*, by Greg Gulley and David Watts (ages 9-11, adventure/religion).
Nonfiction: Picture books: animal, religion. Young readers, middle readers, young adults/teens: biography, history, religion. No nature/environment, multicultural. Average word length: picture books—12-50; young readers—100-300; middle readers—4,000-15,000; young adult/teens—10,000-40,000. Published *To Grow By Storybook Readers*, by Marie Le Doux and Janet Friend (preschool to age 8, textbook) *High on Adventure*, by Steve Arrington (young adult).
How to Contact/Writers: Fiction/Nonfiction: Query. Submit outline/synopsis, table of contents and proposal letter. One or two sample chapters are optional. Send SASE. Reports on queries/mss in 2-3 months. Publishes a book 8 months after acceptance. Will consider simultaneous submissions.
Illustration: Works with 2 illustrators/year. Reviews ms/illustration packages from artists. Query; submit ms with dummy. Contact: Mark Anthony, editor-in-chief. Reports in 1 month. Illustrations only: Query with samples; send résumé and client list. Reports in 2-3 months. Samples returned with SASE; samples filed. Original artwork returned at job's completion.
Photography: Buys photos from freelancers. Contact: Managing Editor. Buys stock images. Model/property releases required. Submit cover letter and résumé to be kept on file.
Terms: Pays authors royalty of 10% based on wholesale price. Pays illustrators by the project (range: $50-250) or royalty of 10% based on wholesale price. Sends galleys to authors; dummies to illustrators. Book catalog available for #10 SAE and 2 first-class stamps; ms guidelines for SASE.

HYPERION BOOKS FOR CHILDREN, 114 Fifth Ave., New York NY 10011. (212)633-4400. Fax: (212)633-4833. An operating unit of Walt Disney Publishing Group, Inc. Book publisher. Vice President/Publisher: Liz Gordon. 30% of books by first-time authors. Publishes various categories.
Fiction: Picture books, young readers, middle readers, young adults: adventure, animal, anthology (short stories), contemporary, fantasy, folktales, history, humor, multicultural, poetry, science fiction, sports, suspense/mystery. Middle readers, young adults: problem novels, romance. Published *Rescue Josh McGuire*, by Ben Mikaelsen (ages 10-14, adventure).
Nonfiction: All trade subjects for all levels.
How to Contact/Writers: Only interested in agented material.
Illustration: Works with 100 illustrators/year. "Picture books are fully illustrated throughout. All others depend on individual project." Reviews ms/illustration packages from artists. Submit complete package. Illustrations only: Submit résumé, business card, promotional literature or tearsheets to be kept on file. Contact: Ellen Friedman, art director. Reports back only if interested. Original artwork returned at job's completion.

Photography: Contact: Ellen Friedman, art director. Works on assignment only. Publishes photo essays and photo concept books. Provide résumé, business card, promotional literature or tear sheets to be kept on file.
Terms: Pays authors royalty based on retail price. Offers advances. Pays illustrators and photographers royalty based on retail price or a flat fee. Sends galleys to authors; dummies to illustrators. Book catalog available for 9×12 SAE and 3 first-class stamps; ms guidelines available for SASE.

✤HYPERION PRESS LIMITED, 300 Wales Ave., Winnipeg, Manitoba R2M 2S9 Canada. (204)256-9204. Fax: (204)255-7845. Book Publisher. Editor: Dr. M. Tutiah. Publishes authentic based, retold folktales/legends for ages 4-12.
Fiction: Young readers, middle readers: folktales/legends. Published *A Sled Dog for Moshi*, by Jeanne Bushey, illustrated by Germaine Arnaktauyok; *The Hummingbirds' Gift*, by Stefan Czernecki and Timothy Rhodes, illustrated by Stefan Czernecki; and *Som See and the Magic Elephant* by Jamie Oliviero, illustrated by Jo'Anne Kelly (all ages 5-9, picture books).
How to Contact/Writers: Fiction: Query. Reports on mss in 3 months.
Illustration: Reviews ms/illustration packages from artists. Ms/illustration packages and illustration only: Query. Samples returned with SASE.
Terms: Pays authors royalty. Pays illustrators by the project. Sends galleys to authors; dummies to illustrators. Book catalog available for 8 1/2×11 SAE and $1.40 postage (Canadian).

IDEALS CHILDREN'S BOOKS, 1501 County Hospital Rd., Nashville TN 37218. Imprint of Hambleton-Hill Publishing Inc. Book publisher. Manuscript Contact: Katherine Myers. Art Contact: Leslie Anderson. Publishes 40-50 picture books/year; 5-8 young reader titles/year. 5-10% of books by first-time authors; 5-10% of books from agented writers.
Fiction: Picture books: concept and health. Picture books and young readers: adventure, animal, contemporary, fantasy, folktales, history, humor, multicultural, nature/environment, science fiction, sports, suspense/mystery. Average word length: picture books—200-1,200; young readers—1,200-2,400. Recently published *See the Ocean*, by Estelle Condra, illustrated by Linda Crockett, (ages 5 to 8); *I Wish I Was the Baby*, by D.J. Long, illustrated by Gary Johnson (ages 3 to 7).
Nonfiction: Picture books: concept and health. Picture books and young readers: activity books, animal, arts and crafts, cooking, history, multicultural, nature/environment, science, sports. Does not want "ABC" and counting books of a general nature. "Only interested in them if they relate to specific themes." Average word length: picture books—200-1,200; young readers—1,000-2,400. Recently published: *Why Did the Dinosaurs Disappear?* by Melvin and Ceilda Berger, illustrated by Susan Harrison (ages 5-9, early reader); *Lunchbox Love Notes*, illustrated by Gary Johnson (ages 4-10, novelty); and *Five Minute Art Ideas: Draw* (ages 4-up, activity).
How to Contact/Writers: Fiction/Nonfiction: Submit complete ms. Reports on queries/mss in 3-6 months. Publishes a book 18-24 months after acceptance. Must include SASE for response.
Illustration: Works with 15-20 illustrators/year. Uses color artwork only. No cartoons—tight or loose, but realistic watercolors, acrylics. Editorial reviews ms/illustration packages from artists. Submit ms with 1 color photocopy of final art and remainder roughs. Illustrations only: Submit résumé and tearsheets showing variety of styles. Reports on art samples only if interested. "No original artwork, please." Samples returned with SASE. Originals not returned.
Terms: "All terms vary according to individual projects and authors/artists." Book catalog, ms and art guidelines for 9×12 SASE and/12 first-class stamps.
Tips: "Trend is placing more value on nonfiction and packaging. We are not interested in young adult romances." Illustrators: "Be flexible in contract terms—and be able to show as much final artwork as possible." Work must have strong storyline with realistic characters. Shows little interest in anthropomorphism.

JALMAR PRESS, 2675 Skypark Dr., #204, Torrance CA 90505. (310)784-0016. Fax: (310)784-1379. Subsidiary of B.L. Winch and Associates. Book publisher. Estab. 1971. President: B.L. Winch. Publishing Assistant: Jeanne Iler. Publishes 3 picture books and young reader titles/year. 10% of books by first-time authors. Publishes self-esteem (curriculum content related), drug and alcohol abuse prevention, peaceful conflict resolution, stress management and whole brain learning.
Fiction: All levels: concept, self-esteem. Does not want to see "children's fiction books that have to do with cognitive learning (as opposed to affective learning) and autobiographical work."

Published *Hilde Knows: Someone Cries for the Children*, by Lisa Kent, illustrated by Mikki Machlen (child abuse); *Scooter's Tail of Terror: A Fable of Addiction and Hope*, by Larry Shles (ages 5-105). "All submissions must teach (by metaphor) in the areas listed above."
Nonfiction: All levels: activity books, concept, how-to, social issues, textbooks within areas specified above. Does not want to see autobiographical work. Published *Esteem Builders Program*, by Michele Berpa, illustrated by Bob Brochett (for school use—6 books, tapes, posters).
How to Contact/Writers: Fiction/Nonfiction: Submit complete ms. Reports on queries/mss in 1-6 months. Publishes a book 6-12 months after acceptance. Will consider simultaneous submissions.
Terms: Pays authors 7-12% royalty based on net receipts. Average advance "varies." Book catalog free on request.
Tips: Wants "thoroughly researched, tested, practical, activity-oriented, curriculum content and grade/level correlated books on self-esteem, peaceful conflict resolution, stress management, drug and alcohol abuse prevention and whole brain learning and books bridging self-esteem to various 'trouble' areas, such as 'at risk,' 'dropout prevention,' etc."

JEWISH LIGHTS PUBLISHING, P.O. Box 237, Woodstock VT 05091. (802)457-4000. A division of LongHill Partners, Inc. Book publisher. President: Stuart M. Matlins. Publishes 1 picture book/year; 1 young reader/year. 50% of books by first-time authors; 50% of books from agented authors. All books have spiritual/religious themes.
Fiction: Picture books, young readers, middle readers:: spirituality. "We are not interested in anything other than spirituality." Recently published: *In God's Name*, by Sandy Eisenberg Sasson, illustrated by Phoebe Stone (K-5); and *But God Remembered: Stories of Women from Creation to the Promised Land*, by Sandy Eisenberg Sasso, illustrated by Bethanne Andersen (ages 8 and up).
Nonfiction: Picture book, young readers, middle readers: activity books, spirituality. Published *God's Paintbrush*, by Rabbi Sandy Eisenberg Sasso and Annette Carroll Compton (K-4, spiritual). Recently published *When a Grandparent Dies: A Kid's Own Remembering Workbook for Dealing with Shiva and the Year Beyond*, by Nechama Liss-Levinson, Ph.D. (ages 7-11).
How to Contact/Writers: Fiction/Nonfiction: Query. Submit outline/synopsis. Reports on queries/mss in 3-4 months. Publishes a book 6 months after acceptance. Will consider simultaneous submissions and previously published work.
Illustration: Works with 2 illustrators/year. Reviews ms/illustration packages from artists. Query. Contact: Sandra Korinchak, assistant editor. Illustrations only: Query with samples; provide résumé. Reports in 1 month. Samples returned with SASE; samples filed.
Terms: Pays authors royalty of 10% of revenue received. Offers advances. Pays illustrators by the project or royalty. Pays photographers by the project. Sends galleys to authors; dummies to illustrators. Book catalog available for 6½×9½ SAE and 59¢ postage; ms guidelines available for SASE.
Tips: "Explain in your cover letter why you're submitting your project to *us* in particular. (Make sure you know what we publish.)"

JEWISH PUBLICATION SOCIETY, 1930 Chestnut St., Philadelphia PA 19103. (215)564-5925. Fax: (215)564-6640. Editor-in-Chief: Dr. Ellen Frankel. Children's Editor: Bruce Black. Book publisher. All work must have Jewish content.
Fiction: Picture books, young readers, middle readers and young adults: adventure, contemporary, folktales, history, mystery, problem novels, religion, romance, sports. Recently published *Blessings: Our Jewish Ceremonies*, by Melanie Hope Greenberg (ages 3-8, picture book); *K'tonton's Yom Kippur Kitten*, by Sadie Rose Weilerstein, illustrated by Joe Boddy.
Nonfiction: Picture books: biography, history, religion. Young readers, middle readers, young adults: biography, history, religion, sports. Recently published *Teddy Kollek: Builder of Jerusalem*, by Abraham Rabinovich (ages 10 and up, biography).
How to Contact/Writers: Fiction/Nonfiction: Query, submit outline/synopsis and sample chapters. Will consider simultaneous submissions (please advise). Reports on queries/mss in 6-8 weeks.
Illustration: Works with 3-4 illustrators/year. Will review ms/illustration packages. Query first or send 3 chapters of ms with 1 piece of final art, remainder roughs. Illustrations only: Query with photocopies; arrange a personal interview to show portfolio.

The simple, clean lines and contemporary look of illustrator Joe Boddy's work led him to be hand-picked to illustrate the Jewish Publication Society's K'tonton stories. **K'tonton's Yom Kippur Kitten,** ***by Sadie Rose Weilerstein, is one of a series of picture books about the mischievious, lovable Jewish Tom Thumb. In the cover art, K'tonton befriends the hungry young feline, who eventually leads him to experience the true meaning of Yom Kippur. The illustrations were rendered in pen & ink on illustration board.***

Terms: Pays authors and illustrators flat fees or royalties based on net. Reports back only if interested. Samples returned with SASE. Orginals returned at job's completion.
Tips: Writer/illustrator currently has best chance of selling picture books to this market.

BOB JONES UNIVERSITY PRESS/LIGHT LINE BOOKS, 1500 Wade Hampton Blvd. Greenville SC 29614. (803)242-5100, ext. 4315. Book publisher. Editor: Mrs. Gloria Repp. Publishes 4 young reader titles/year; 4 middle reader titles/year; 4 young adult titles/year. 50% of books by first-time authors.
Fiction: Young readers: adventure, animal, contemporary, easy-to-read, history, sports, spy/mystery. Middle readers: adventure, animal, contemporary, history, problem novels, sports, spy/mystery. Young adults/teens: adventure, contemporary, history, problem novels, sports, spy/mystery. Average word length: young readers—20,000; middle readers—30,000; young adult/teens—50,000. Published *The Treasure of Pelican Cove*, by Milly Howard (grades 2-4, adventure story); *Right Hand Man*, by Connie Williams (grades 5-8, contemporary).
Nonfiction: Young readers: animal, biography, nature/environment. Middle readers: animal, biography, history, nature/environment. Young adults/teens: biography, history, nature/environment. Average word length: young readers—20,000; middle readers—30,000; young adult/teens—50,000. Published *With Daring Faith*, by Becky Davis (grades 5-8, biography); *Morning Star of the Reformation*, by Andy Thomson (grades 9-12, biography).
How to Contact/Writers: Fiction: "Send the complete manuscript or the first five chapters and synopsis for these genres: Christian biography, modern realism, historical realism, regional realism and mystery/adventure. Query with a synopsis and five sample chapters for these genres: fantasy and science fiction (no extra-terrestrials). Do not send stories with magical elements. We do not publish these genres: romance, poetry and drama." Nonfiction: Query, submit complete manuscript or submit outline/synopsis and sample chapters. Reports on queries in 3 weeks; mss in 2 months. Publishes book "approximately one year" after acceptance. Will consider simultaneous and electronic submissions via IBM-compatible disk or modem.
Terms: Buys ms outright for $1,000-1,500. Book catalog and ms guidelines free on request.
Tips: "Write something fresh and unique to carry a theme of lasting value. We publish only books with high moral tone, preferably with evangelical Christian content. Stories should reflect the highest Christian standards of thought, feeling and action. The text should make no reference to drinking, smoking, profanity or minced oaths. Other unacceptable story elements include magic, unrelieved suspense, sensationalism and themes advocating secular attitudes of cynicism, rebellion or materialism."

JUST US BOOKS, INC., 356 Glenwood Ave., East Orange NJ 07017. (201)676-4345. Fax: (201)677-7570. Imprint of Afro-Bets Series. Book publisher; "for selected titles" book packager. Estab. 1988. Vice President/Publisher: Cheryl Willis Hudson. Publishes 4-6 picture books/year; "projected 6" young reader/middle reader titles/year. 33% of books by first-time authors. Looking for "books that reflect a genuinely authentic African or African-American experience. We try to work with authors and illustrators who are from the culture itself." Also publishes *Harambee*, a newspaper for young readers, 6 times during the school year. (Target age for *Harambee* is 10-13.)
Fiction: Middle readers: adventure, contemporary, easy-to-read, history, multicultural (African-American themes), romance, suspense/mystery. Average word length: "varies" per picture book; young reader—500-2,000; middle reader—5,000. Wants African-American themes. Gets too many traditional African folktales. Published *Land of the Four Winds*, by Veronica Freeman Ellis, illustrated by Sylvia Walker (ages 6-9, picture book).
Nonfiction: Middle readers, biography (African-American themes). Published *Book of Black Heroes Vol. 2: Great Women in the Struggle*, by Toyomi Igus.
How to Contact/Writers: Fiction/Nonfiction: Query or submit outline/synopsis for proposed title. Reports on queries/ms in 2 months "or as soon as possible." Publishes a book 12-18 months after acceptance. Will consider simultaneous submissions (with prior notice).
Illustration: Works with 10 illustrators/year. Reviews ms/illustration packages from artists ("but prefers to review them separately"). "Query first." Illustrations only: Query with samples; send résumé, promo sheet, slides, client list, tearsheets; arrange personal portfolio review. Reports in 2-3 weeks. Samples returned with SASE; samples filed. Original artwork returned at job's completion "depending on project."

INSIDER REPORT

Preparation and Perseverance Pay Off

Sharon Draper knows the children's book market, and from her 20 years of experience teaching English in Cincinnati Public Schools, she also knows kids—"what they read, what they won't read, what they hate to read." Her knowledge is power, and she has used it to write three books and obtain contracts for two books in progress. The road to success is open to writers who embrace hard work and follow the credo of Draper's career: research, prepare and persist.

Sharon Draper

Tears of a Tiger (Simon & Schuster, 1994), Draper's first book, has garnered numerous awards, including the 1995 Coretta Scott King Genesis Award for an outstanding new book. The tale of troubled teen Andy Jackson and his unsuccessful struggle with personal and social adversity was the catalyst that not only sparked Draper's writing career, but filled a niche in children's literature. Andy is black, and as Draper points out, there are very few African-American characters (especially boys) in children's literature. More importantly, Draper notices very few positive African-American characters in books for young readers. "For a black child in a young market (namely fourth-sixth grade), there is not a whole lot."

Draper's *Ziggy and the Black Dinosaurs* (1994), the first in a series of mysteries about a group of boys and their adventures, has been a strong seller for Just Us Books. She contributes some of the book's success to its positive African-American characters. "The book can be read with ease by fourth-graders. The characters happen to be African-Americans, but my books can be read and enjoyed by anybody. They're not just for black children."

Despite her access to children's literature and her early recognition of the market's needs, Draper spent six months outside the classroom searching for books by other writers before she approached a single publisher, perusing local libraries and bookstores in search of titles geared toward young adolescents and teens. She laughs as she remembers the hours she spent scouring shelves for titles. "I literally got thrown out of bookstores," she says.

Such extensive research and reading, together with lots of personal experience with kids, helped Draper develop an ability to capture the spirit and concerns of youth in her writing, whether it be for elementary or high-school-age children. "It doesn't matter how good somebody says a book is if a kid won't read it," she says. "You have to get their interest on the first page." For example, in the first chapter of *Tears of a Tiger*, Andy (the main character) and his best friend are in a gruesome car crash. Andy was driving drunk; his friend was killed. The topic is serious and very relevant to teens, and the accident description is an immediate attention-getter.

Remember that not all readers are alike. Writing for elementary school students and high schoolers is very different. "I think the elementary stuff is harder. You have to think like a ten-year-old. You need to simplify." Although writing for the teen market is somewhat easier, Draper stresses caution to any writer approaching this venue. "Teens live in a world that is very complicated. You have to be very careful as to what you say; what you write *will* influence them."

Even if your writing is wonderful, it may end up in an editor's wastebasket if you're not careful. Draper vehemently believes in preparing a flawless submission package, from query letter to manuscript, if you want your work to be recognized. "Presentation makes a difference. Even if your work is good, publishers will toss it if it looks like junk." Your manuscript should be "your very best work."

Draper used *Writer's Market* to zero in on specific publishers who might be interested in her work. After submitting to two dozen publishers, her persistence paid off—her twenty-fifth submission was accepted. "You have to be able to accept rejection," she says. She was accepting it so readily that she almost tossed the acceptance for *Tears of a Tiger* without even opening it, thinking it was just another returned submission.

Despite her success with publishers and kids, Draper hasn't become rich from her work, a point she emphasizes to all writers. Eventually the royalties from her books will reach her, but it takes time. "Don't quit your day job," she says. "Do not expect to go on 'Good Morning America.' Do not expect a book tour . . . it won't happen. Most of what I did, I did on my own."

And Draper keeps on writing and researching, and stays abreast of the market in which she has become so involved. Her explanation of her success? "A lot of it has to do with being pushy, and a lot has to do with being lucky."

—Jennifer Hogan-Redmond

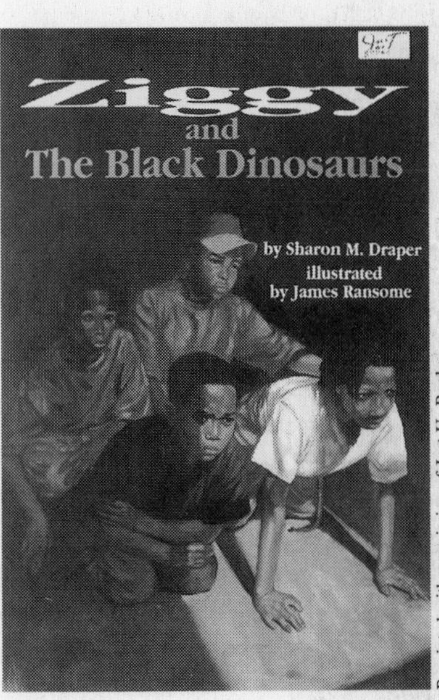

Rico, Jerome, Rashawn and title character Ziggy, the heroes in Sharon Draper's* Ziggy and the Black Dinosaurs *are depicted in this cover illustration by James Ransome. The four boys stumble upon a box of bones—and a mystery—while building their Black Dinosaurs' clubhouse during summer vacation. Draper's suspenseful tale has the boys uncovering clues as well as interesting historical information linked to the bones.

Photography: Purchases photos from freelancers. Buys stock and assigns work. Wants "African-American themes—kids age 10-13 in school, home and social situations for *Harambee* (newspaper)."
Terms: Pays authors royalty based on retail price or work purchased outright. Royalties based on retail price. Pays illustrators by the project or royalty based on retail price. Sends galleys to authors; dummies to illustrators. Book catalog for business-size SAE and 65¢ postage; ms/artist's guidelines for business-size SAE and 65¢ postage.
Tips: "Multicultural books are tops as far as trends go. There is a great need for diversity and authenticity here. They will continue to be in the forefront of children's book publishing until there is more balanced treatment on these themes industry wide." Writers: "Keep the subject matter fresh and lively. Avoid 'preachy' stories with stereotyped characters. Rely more on authentic stories with sensitive three-dimensional characters." Illustrators: "Submit 5-10 good, neat samples. Be willing to work with an art director for the type of illustration desired by a specific house and grow into larger projects."

KAR-BEN COPIES, INC., 6800 Tildenwood Lane, Rockville MD 20852. (301)984-8733. Fax: (301)881-9195. Book publisher. Estab. 1975. Vice President: Madeline Wikler. Publishes 5-10 picture books/year; 20% of books by first-time authors.
Fiction: Picture books: folktales, multicultural, *Must be* on a Jewish theme. Average word length: picture books—2,000. Published *Kingdom of Singing Birds*, by Miriam Aroner; *Northern Lights*, by Diana Cohen Conway; *Sammy Spider's First Hanukkah*, by Sylvia Rouss; and *Matzah Ball, A Passover Story*, by Mindy Avra Portnoy.
Nonfiction: Picture books, young readers: religion—Jewish interest. Average word length: picture books—2,000. Published *Jewish Holiday Games for Little Hands*, by Ruth Brinn; *Tell Me a Mitzvah*, by Danny Siegel; *My First Jewish Word Book*, by Roz Schanzer.
How to Contact/Writers: Fiction/nonfiction: Submit complete ms. Reports on queries/ms in 6 weeks. Publishes a book 1 year after acceptance. Will consider simultaneous submissions.
Illustration: Works with 6-10 illustrators/year. Prefers "4-color art to any medium that is scannable." Reviews ms/illustration packages from artists. Submit whole ms and sample of art (no originals). Illustrations only: Submit tearsheets, photocopies, promo sheet or anything representative that does *not* need to be returned. Enclose SASE for response. Reports on art samples in 4 weeks.
Terms: Pays authors in royalties of 6-8% based on net sales or work purchased outright (range: $500-2,000). Offers advance (average amount: $1,000). Pays illustrators royalty of 6-8% based on net sales or by the project (range: $500-3,000). Sends galleys to authors. Book catalog free on request. Ms guidelines for 9×12 SAE and 2 first-class stamps.
Tips: Looks for "books for young children with Jewish interest and content, modern, non-sexist, not didactic. Fiction or nonfiction with a *Jewish* theme—can be serious or humorous, life cycle, Bible story, or holiday-related."

KNOPF BOOKS FOR YOUNG READERS, 29th Floor, 201 E. 50th St., New York NY 10022. (212)751-2600. Random House, Inc. Book publisher. Estab. 1915. Publishing Director: Simon Boughton. Editor-in-Chief: Arthur Levine. Publisher, Apple Soup Books: Anne Schwartz. 90% of books published through agents.

- To learn more about Knopf Books, see Insider Report with Arthur Levine in the 1995 edition of *Children's Writer's & Illustrator's Market*.

Fiction: Upmarket picture books: adventure, animal, contemporary, fantasy, retellings of folktales, original stories. Young readers: adventure, animal, contemporary, nature/environment, science fiction, sports, suspense/mystery. Middle readers: adventure, animal, fantasy, nature/environment, science fiction, sports, suspense/mystery. Young adult: adventure, contemporary,

"Picture books" are for preschoolers to 8-year-olds; "Young readers" are for 5- to 8-year-olds; "Middle readers" are for 9- to 11-year-olds; and "Young adults" are for those ages 12 and up.

fantasy, science fiction—very selective; few being published currently.
Nonfiction: Picture books, young readers, middle readers: animal, biography, nature/environment, sports.
How to Contact/Writers: Fiction/Nonfiction: Submit through agent only. Publishes a book 12-18 months after acceptance. Will consider simultaneous submissions.
Illustration: Reviews ms/illustration packages from artists through agent only. Illustration only: Contact: Art Director.
Terms: Pays authors in royalties. Book catalog free on request.

***L&M PUBLISHING**, 1401 North Taft St., Suite 211, Arlington VA 22201. Phone/fax: (703)525-7379. Independent book producer/packager. Publisher: Mindy Schackman. Publishes 6 picture books/year. 100% of books by first-time authors. "For our books, stories must be about a child that could be male or female to facilitate personalization (our books are personalized for the children receiving them)."
Fiction: Picture books: adventure, animal, fantasy, health, history, multicultural, suspense/mystery. Does not want to see religion. Average word length: picture books—1,300-1,500.
How to Contact/Writers: Fiction: Submit complete ms. Reports on mss in 2-3 weeks. Publishes a book 4-6 months after acceptance. Will consider simultaneous submissions and electronic submissions via disk or modem.
Illustration: Works with 5 illustrators/year. Uses color artwork only. Reviews ms/illustration packages for authors. Contact: Mindy Schackman, publisher. Illustration only: Query with samples, résumé. Reports in 2-3 weeks. Samples returned with SASE; samples filed. Originals returned at job's completion.
Terms: Pays authors royalty of 5% based on retail price. Pays illustrators 5% royalty based on retail price. Book catalog available.

LAREDO PUBLISHING CO. INC., 8907 Wilshire Blvd., Beverly Hills CA 90211. (310)358-5288. Fax: (310)358-5282. Book publisher. Vice President: Raquel Benatar. Publishes 5 picture books/year; 15 young readers/year. 10% of books by first-time authors. Spanish language books only.
Fiction: Picture books: multicultural (Spanish). Young readers: adventure, animal, fantasy, folktales, health, multicultural (Spanish), poetry. Middle readers: adventure, animal, contemporary, fantasy, folktales, health, multicultural (Spanish), nature/environment, poetry. Published *Pregones*, by Alma Flor Ada (middle readers, personal experience in Spanish); *Pajaritos*, by Clarita Kohen (young readers, counting book in Spanish); *El Conejoyel Coyote*, by Clarita Kohen (young readers, folktale in Spanish).
Nonfiction: Published *Los Aztecas*, by Robert Nicholson (middle readers, history, culture and traditions of the Aztecs in Spanish); *Los Sioux*, by Robert Nicholson (middle readers; history, culture and traditions of the Sioux in Spanish); *La Antigua China*, by Robert Nicholson (middle readers; history, culture and traditions of the Chinese in Spanish).
How to Contact/Writers: Fiction: Submit complete ms. Reports on mss in 3 months. Publishes a book 1 year after acceptance. Will consider simultaneous submissions.
Illustration: Works with 20 illustrators/year. Uses color artwork only. Reviews ms/illustration packages from artists. Illustrations only: Query with samples, promo sheet. Reports in 2 months. Samples returned with SASE. Originals not returned.
Terms: Pays authors royalty of 5-7% based on wholesale price. Offers advances (varies). Pays illustrators by the project (range: $250-500). Sends galleys to authors; dummies to illustrators.
Tips: "We will only accept manuscripts in Spanish."

***LEADERSHIP PUBLISHERS, INC.**, Talented and Gifted Educ. P.O. Box 8358, Des Moines IA 50301. (515)278-4765. Fax: (515)270-8303. Book publisher.
Nonfiction: Middle readers and young adults: textbooks. Does not want to see material for enrichment programs for talented and gifted students. Recently published *What Do You Think: Opinions & Ideas*, by Sandy Achterbery (for ages 7-16); and *Readers' Theatre: Volume Three, Entrepreneurs* and *Incomplete Plays*, by Lois Roets.
How to Contact/Writers: Reports on queries in 1 week; mss in 1 month. Publishes a book 3-6 months after acceptance.

Terms: Pays authors royalty of 10% based on sales. Pays illustrators and photographers negotiated rate. Book catalog available for 8½×11 SAE and 2 first-class stamps. Ms guidelines available for SASE.
Tips: Leadership Publishers, Inc. publishes educational material for high-ability students. Study our catalog before submitting your manuscript or query and picture your book among our published titles. Will it fit?

LEE & LOW BOOKS, INC., 95 Madison Ave., New York NY 10016-7801. (212)779-4400. Book publisher. Editor-in-Chief: Elizabeth Szabla. Publishes 8-10 picture books/year. 50% of books by first-time authors.

- Lee & Low publishes only multicultural themes.

Fiction: Picture books: fiction or poetry that reflects the experiences of children of color, as well as children from countries/cultures outside the US. "We are not considering folktales or animal stories." Average word length: picture books—1,000-1,500 words. Recently published *Baseball Saved Us*, by Ken Mochizuki, illustrated by Dom Lee (ages 4-10, picture book); and *Giving Thanks: A Native American Good Morning Message* by Chief Jake Swamp, illustrated by Erwin Printup, Jr. (all ages, picture book).
Nonfiction: Picture books: biography and multicultural. Average word length: picture books—1,500. Recently published *Zora Hurston and the Chinaberry Tree*, by William Miller, illustrated by Cornelius Van Wright and Ying-Hwa Hu (ages 4-10, picture book).
How to Contact/Writers: Fiction/Nonfiction: Submit complete ms. Reports in 1-3 months. Publishes a book 12-24 months after acceptance. Will consider simultaneous submissions.
Illustration: Works with 8-10 illustrators/year. Uses color artwork only. Reviews ms/illustration packages from artists. Submit ms with dummy. Contact: Elizabeth Szabla, editor-in-chief. Illustrations only: Query with samples, résumé, promo sheet and tearsheets. Reports in 1-2 months. Samples returned with SASE; samples filed. Original artwork returned at job's completion.
Photography: Buys photos from freelancers. Works on assignment only. Model/property releases required. Submit cover letter, résumé, promo piece and book dummy.
Terms: Pays authors royalty based on retail price. Offers advances. Pays illustrators royalty based on retail price plus advance against royalty. Photographers paid royalty based on retail price plus advance against royalty. Sends galleys to authors; dummies to illustrators. Book catalog available for 9×12 SAE and 78¢ postage; ms and art guidelines available for SASE.
Tips: "We strongly urge writers to familiarize themselves with our list before submitting."

LERNER PUBLICATIONS CO., 241 First Ave. N., Minneapolis MN 55401. (612)332-3344. Fax: (612)332-7615. Book publisher. Editor: Jennifer Martin. Publishes 9 young readers/year; 62 middle readers/year; 5 young adults/year. 20% of books by first-time authors; 5% of books from agented writers. "Most books are nonfiction for children, grades 3-9."
Fiction: Middle readers: adventure, contemporary, hi-lo, multicultural, nature/environment, sports, suspense/mystery. Young adults: hi-lo, multicultural, nature/environment, problem novels, sports, suspense/mystery. "Especially interested in books with ethnic characters." Published the Kerry Hill Casecrackers series, by Joan Warnor and Peggy Nicholson (grades 4-7, mystery).
Nonfiction: Middle readers, young adults: animal, arts/crafts, biography, careers, concept, cooking, geography, health, hi-lo, history, hobbies, how-to, multicultural, music/dance, nature/environment, sports, science/math, social issues, self-help, special needs. Multicultural material must contain authentic details. Does not want to see textbooks, workbooks, song books, audiotapes, puzzles, plays, religious material, books for teachers or parents, picture or alphabet books. Average word length: young readers—3,000; middle readers—7,000; young adults—12,000. Published *J.M. Barrie: The Magic Behind Peter Pan*, by Brad Townsend (grades 5 and up, Lerner Biographies series); *Shagville O'Neal: Center of Attention*, by Brad Townsend (grades 4-9, Sports Achievers series).
How to Contact/Writers: Fiction: Submit outline/synopsis and sample chapters. Nonfiction: Query; submit outline/synopsis and sample chapters. Reports on queries in 3-4 weeks; mss in 3 months. Publishes a book 12-18 months after acceptance. Will consider simultaneous submissions.
Illustration: Works with 1-2 illustrators/year. "We tend to work only with local talent." Reviews ms/illustration packages from artists. Ms/illustration packages and illustrations only: Query with samples and résumé. Contact: Art Director. Samples kept on file.

Photography: Contact: Photo Research Department. Buys stock and assigns work. Model/property releases required. Publishes photo essays. Photographers should query with samples.
Terms: Pays authors royalty or work purchased outright. Pays illustrators by the project. Sends galleys to authors. Book catalog available for 9×12 SAE and $1.90 postage; ms guidelines for 4×9 SAE and 1 first-class stamp.
Tips: Wants "straightforward, well-written nonfiction for children in grades 3-9 backed by solid current research or scholarship. Before you send your manuscript to us, you might first take a look at the kinds of books that our company publishes. We specialize in publishing high-quality educational books for children from second grade through high school. Avoid sex stereotypes (e.g., strong, aggressive, unemotional males/weak, submissive, emotional females) in your writing, as well as sexist language." (See also Carolrhoda Books, Inc.)

LION BOOKS, PUBLISHER, 210 Nelson, Suite B, Scarsdale NY 10583. (914)725-2280. Imprint of Sayre Ross Co. Book publisher. Editorial contact: Harriet Ross. Publishes 5 middle readers/year; 10 young adults/year. 50-70% of books by first-time authors. Publishes books "with ethnic and minority accents for young adults, including a variety of craft titles dealing with African and Asian concepts."
Nonfiction: Activity, art/crafts, biography, history, hobbies, how-to, multicultural. Average word length: young adult—30,000-50,000.
How to Contact/Writers: Query, submit complete ms. Reports on queries in 3 weeks; ms in 2 months.
Illustration: Reports in 2 weeks.
Terms: Work purchased outright (range: $500-5,000). Average advance: $1,000-2,500. Illustrators paid $500-1,500. Sends galleys to author. Book catalog free on request.

LITTLE, BROWN AND COMPANY, 34 Beacon St., Boston MA 02108. (617)227-0730. Book publisher. Editor-in-Chief: Maria Modugno. Estab. 1837. Publishes 50% picture books/year; 50% young reader titles/year; 30% middle reader titles/year; 15% young adult titles/year.

- Little, Brown ranks 14th, based on net sales, of the top 15 children's publishers.

Fiction: Picture books: adventure, animal, contemporary, fantasy, folktales, history, humor, multicultural, nature/environment. Young readers: adventure, animal, contemporary, fantasy, history, humor, multicultural, nature/environment, science fiction, suspense/mystery. Middle readers: adventure, contemporary, fantasy, history, humor, multicultural, nature/environment, science fiction, suspense/mystery. Young adults: contemporary, health, humor, multicultural, nature/environment, suspense/mystery. Multicultural needs include "any material by, for and about minorities." No "rhyming texts, anthropomorphic animals that learn a lesson, alphabet and counting books, and stories based on an event rather than a character." Average word length: picture books—1,000; young readers—6,000; middle readers—15,000-25,000; young adults—20,000-40,000. Recently published *Fairy Wings*, by Lauren Mil (ages 4-8, picture book); *People of Corn*, by Mary-Joan Gerson (ages 4-8, picture book); *All Star Fever*, by Matt Christopher (ages 7-9, first chapter book); *On Winter's Wind*, by Patricia Hern (ages 8-12, middle reader).
Nonfiction: Picture books: animal, biography, concept, history, multicultural, nature/environment. Young readers: activity books, biography, multicultural. Middle readers: activity books, arts/crafts, biography, cooking, geography, history, multicultural. Young adults: multicultural, self-help, social issues. Average word length: picture books—2,000; young readers—4,000-6,000; middle readers—15,000-25,000; young adults—20,000-40,000. Recently published *Hearing Us Out*, by Roger Sutton (ages 12 and up, young adult); *The Great Midwest Flood*, by Carole G. Vogel (ages 8-12, picture book).
How to Contact/Writers: Submit through agent or, if previously published, submit with list of writing credits.
Illustration: Works with 40 illustrators/year. Illustrations only: Query art director with samples/slides; provide résumé, promo sheet or tearsheets to be kept on file. Reports on art samples in 6-8 weeks. Original artwork returned at job's completion.
Photography: Works on assignment only. Model/property releases required; captions required. Publishes photo essays and photo concept books. Uses 35mm transparencies. Photographers should provide résumé, promo sheets or tearsheets to be kept on file.
Terms: Pays authors royalties of 3-10% based on retail price. Offers advance (average amount: $2,000-10,000). Pays illustrators by the project (range: $1,500-5,000) or royalty of 3-10% based

on retail price. Photographers paid by the project, by royalty based on retail price. Sends galleys to authors; dummies to illustrators. Book catalog, manuscript/artist's guidelines for SASE.
Tips: "Publishers are cutting back their lists in response to a shrinking market and relying more on big names and known commodities. In order to break into the field these days, authors and illustrators research their competition and try to come up with something outstandingly different."

LODESTAR BOOKS, 375 Hudson St., New York NY 10014. (212)366-2627. Fax: (212)366-2011. E-mail: vbuckley@penguin.com. Affiliate of Dutton Children's Books, a division of Penguin Books, USA, Inc. Estab. 1980. Editorial Director: Virginia Buckley. Executive Editor: Rosemary Brosnan. Publishes 6 picture books/year; 6 middle readers/year; 7 young adults/year (20 books/year). 5-10% of books by first-time authors; 37% through agents.

- Lodestar is looking especially for material for a new Penguin imprint of titles for translation into Spanish: Penguin Ediciones.

Fiction: Picture books: adventure, animal, contemporary, folktales, history, humor, multicultural, nature/environment. Young readers: adventure, animal, contemporary, family humor, multicultural, nature/environment. Middle reader: adventure, animal, contemporary, folktales, humor, multicultural, nature/environment, suspense/mystery. Young adult: adventure, contemporary, history, humor, multicultural, nature/environment. Multicultural needs include "well-written books with good characterization. Prefer books by authors of same ethnic background as subject, but not absolutely necessary." No commercial picture books, science fiction or genre novels. Published *Toads and Diamonds*, retold and illustrated by Robert Bender (ages 4-8, picture book); *A Midnight Clear: Stories for the Christmas Season*, by Katherine Paterson (all ages, short stories); and *Like Sisters on the Homefront*, by Rita Williams-Garcia (ages 12 up, YA fiction).
Nonfiction: Picture books: activity books, animal, concept, geography, history, multicultural, nature/environment, science, social issues. Young reader: animal, concept, geography, history, multicultural, nature/environment, science, social issues, sports. Middle reader: animal, biography, careers, geography, history, multicultural, music/dance, nature/environment, science, social issues, sports. Young adult: history, multicultural, music/dance, nature/environment, social issues, sports. Multicultural needs include authentic, well-written books about African-American, Native American, Hispanic and Asian-American experiences. Also, books on Jewish themes. Published *Fiesta U.S.A.*, written and phtographed by George Ancona, English and Spanish editions (ages 8-10, photographic essay); *One Nation, Many Tribes*, by Kathleen Krull, photographs by David Hautzig (ages 8-12, A World of My Own series); and *For Home and Country* by Norman Bolotin and Angela Herb (Young Readers' History of the Civil War series).
How to Contact/Writers: Fiction: Submit synopsis and sample chapters or submit complete ms. Nonfiction: Query or submit synopsis and sample chapters. Reports on queries in 1 month; mss in 3 months. Publishes a book 7-8 months after acceptance. Will consider simultaneous submissions.
Illustration: Works with approximately 7-8 illustrators/year. Reviews ms/illustration packages from artists. Submit "manuscript and copies of art (no original art please)." Illustrations only: Query with samples; send portfolio or slides. Drop off portfolio for review. Reports back only if interested. Original art work returned at job's completion.
Photography: Buys photos from freelancers (infrequently).
Terms: Pays authors and illustrators royalties of 5-10% based on retail price. Pays illustrators by the project (range: $4,000-10,000—more for well-known artists) or royalty of 2-6% based on retail price. Pays photographers by the project (range: $800 for jacket-$6,000 for photo essay), per photo (range: $25-400 for jackets) or royalty of 5% (for photo essay). Sends galleys to author. Book catalog for SASE; manuscript guidelines for #10 SAE and 1 first-class stamp.
Tips: Wants "well-written books that show awareness of children's and young people's lives, feelings and problems; arouse imagination and are sensitive to children's needs. More books by African-American, Hispanic, Asian-American and Native American writers. More nonfiction early readers."

✱JAMES LORIMER & CO., 35 Britain St., Toronto, Ontario M5A 1R7 Canada. (416)362-4762. Book publisher. Publishing Assistant: Laura Ellis. Publishes 3 middle readers/year; 2 young adult titles/year. 20% of books by first-time authors. Uses Canadian authors only; wants realistic, contemporary material with Canadian settings.
Fiction: Middle readers: adventure, contemporary, hi-lo, multicultural, problem novels, sports and suspense/mystery. Young adults: contemporary, multicultural, problem novels and sports.

Canadian settings featuring characters from ethnic/racial/cultural minorities—prefers author from same background. Does not want to see fantasy, science fiction, verse, drama and short stories. Average word length: middle readers—18,000; young adults—20,000. Recently published *The Great Pebble Creek Bike Race*, by Kathy Stinson (ages 7-10, sport/adventure); *Gallop for Gold*, by Sharon Siamon (ages 7-10, adventure novel); *Curve Ball*, by John Danakas (ages 9-12, sport novel).
How to Contact/Writers: Submit outline/synopsis and 2 sample chapters. Reports on queries in 2 months; mss in 6 months. Publishes a book 8 months after acceptance.
Illustration: Works with 3 illustrators/year. Prefers realistic style.
Illustrations only: Submit promo sheet, photocopies OK. Reports only if interested. Samples returned with SASE; samples filed. Original artwork returned at job's completion.
Photography: Buys photos from freelancers. Contact: Laura Ellis, publishing assistant. Buys stock and assigns work. Uses color prints and 35mm transparencies. Submit letter.
Terms: Pays authors royalty of 6-10% based on retail price. Pays illustrators and photographers by the project. Sends galleys to authors. Ms and art guidelines available for SASE.
Tips: "Follow submission guidelines and research the market—read current kids' books, talk to kids." Wants realistic novels, set in Canada, dealing with social issues. Recent trends include hi-lo and multicultural.

LOTHROP, LEE & SHEPARD BOOKS, 1350 Avenue of the Americas, New York NY 10019. (212)261-6500. Division and imprint of William Morrow Co. Inc. Publishes 60 total titles/year. Prefers not to share information.

LUCAS/EVANS BOOKS INC., 407 Main St., Chatham NJ 07928. (201)635-5454. Executive Director: Barbara Lucas. Editor and Production Manager: Cassandra Conyers. Estab. 1984. Book packager specializing in children's books, preschool through high school age. Books prepared from inception to camera-ready mechanicals for all major publishers.
Fiction/Nonfiction: Particularly interested in series ideas, especially for middle grades and beginning readers. All subject categories except problem novels and textbooks considered. Published fiction titles: *Ghost Dog*, by Ellen Leroe (Hyperion); *Song for the Ancient Forest*, by Nancy Luenn (Atheneum); *Second-Grade Friends*, by Miriam Cohen (Scholastic). Published nonfiction titles: *They Had a Dream*/ Epoch Biography by Jules Archer (Viking), and *The Kids' Cookbook*, by West Village Nursery School (Outlet); *Science Source Books* (Facts on File series).
How to Contact/Writers: Query. Reports on queries in 2 months.
Illustration: Works with 15-20 illustrators/year. "Color photocopies of art welcome for our file."Illustrations only: Query with samples; provide résumé, promo sheet, slides, client list, tearsheets, arrange personal portfolio review.
Terms: Offers authors and illustrators royalty-based contracts with advances based on retail price. Work purchased outright.
Tips: Prefers experienced authors and artists but will consider unpublished work. "There seems to be an enormous demand for early chapter books, although we will continue our efforts to sell to publishers in all age groups and formats. We are interested in series since publishers look to packagers for producing time-consuming projects."

LUCENT BOOKS, P.O. Box 289011, San Diego CA 92128-9009. (619)485-7424. Sister Company to Greenhaven Press. Book publisher. Editor: Bonnie Szumski. 20% of books by first-time authors; 10% of books from agented writers.

- This publisher does not accept unsolicited manuscripts.

Nonfiction: Middle readers, young adults: education, health, topical history, nature/environment, sports, "any overviews of specific topics—i.e., political, social, cultural, economic, criminal, moral issues." No fiction. Average word length: 15,000-25,000. Published *The Persian Gulf War*, by Don Nardo (grades 6-12, history); *Photography*, by Brad Steffens (grades 5-8, history); and *Rainforests*, by Lois Warburton (grades 5-8, overview).
How to Contact/Writers: "Writers should query first; we do writing by assignment only. If you want to write for us, send SASE for guidelines."
Illustration: "We use photos, mostly." Uses primarily b&w artwork and prefers 7×9 format—4-color cover. Reviews ms/illustration packages from artists. Query first. Illustrations only: Query with samples; provide résumé, business card, promotional literature or tearsheets to be kept on file.

Terms: "Fee negotiated upon review of manuscript." Sends galleys to authors. Ms guidelines free on request.
Tips: "Books must be written at a 7th-8th-grade reading level. There's a growing market for quality nonfiction. Tentative topics: free speech, tobacco, alcohol, discrimination, immigration, poverty, the homeless in America, space weapons, drug abuse, terrorism, animal experimentation, endangered species, AIDS, pollution, gun control, etc. The above list is presented to give writers an example of the kinds of titles we are seeking. If you are interested in writing about a specific topic, please query us by mail before you begin writing to be sure we have not assigned a particular topic to another author. The author should strive for objectivity. There obviously will be many issues on which a position should be taken—e.g., discrimination, tobacco, alcoholism, etc. However, moralizing, self-righteous condemnations, maligning, lamenting, mocking, etc. should be avoided. Moreover, where a pro/con position is taken, contrasting viewpoints should be presented. Certain moral issues such as abortion and euthanasia, if dealt with at all, should be presented with strict objectivity."

LUCKY BOOKS, P.O. Box 1415, Winchester VA 22604. (540)662-3424. Book publisher. Co-Publishers: Mac S. Rutherford and Donna Rutherford. Publishes 1-2 picture books/year; 1-2 young readers/year. 90% of books by first-time authors.
Fiction: Picture books, young readers: adventure, animal, fantasy, nature/environment, poetry. Middle readers: animal, mystery, science fiction. No religion. Average word length: picture books—500-1,500; young readers—3,000-6,000. Published *Prince*, by Margery Van Susteren (8 and up, pet story); *Zonkey The Donkey*, by Virginia Athey, illustrated by Donna Rutherford (pre-school, poetic); *When the Zebras Came for Lunch*, by Barbara Van Curen (pre-school, fantasy). "We do not want to be limited by category. Quality of work is important to Lucky Books."
Nonfiction: Picture books: animal. Young readers: animal, arts/crafts, nature/environment. Middle readers: animal, arts/crafts, history, hobbies, sports. Not interested in how-to. Average word length: picture books—500-1,500.
How to Contact/Writers: Fiction/Nonfiction: Submit complete ms with SASE. Reports on mss in 4-6 months. Publishes a book 1-1½ years after acceptance (varies greatly).
Illustration: Works with 1-2 illustrators/year. Reviews ms/illustration packages from artists. Submit ms with 2-3 pieces of final art. Contact: Donna Rutherford, co-publisher. Illustrations only: Query with samples, résumé, slides. Reports back only if interested. Samples returned with SASE; samples filed.
Terms: Pays authors royalty of 3-6% based on wholesale or retail price. Pays illustrators by the project (range $500-1,000) or royalty of 1-3% based on wholesale or retail price.
Tips: Looking for "more artistic/fine art layouts with simple message (pre-school)."

***THE LUTTERWORTH PRESS**, Imprint of James Clarke & Co. Ltd., P.O. Box 60, Cambridge England CB12NT. (01223)350865. Fax: (01223)66951. Book publisher. Editorial Director. Mr. Cohn Lester.
Fiction: Picture books, young readers, middle readers and young adults: adventure, animal, folktales, health, history, nature/environment, religion.
Nonfiction: Picture books, young readers, middle readers and young adults: activity books, animal, arts/crafts, history, nature/environment, religion, science.
How to Contact/Writers: Fiction/Nonfiction: Submit outline/synopsis and 1 or 2 sample chapters. Reports on queries in 2 weeks; ms in 6 months.
Illustration: Reviews ms/illustration packages from authors. Submit ms with color or b&w copies of illustration. Contact: Mr. C. Lester, editorial director. Illustration only: Query with samples. Reports in 2-3 weeks. Samples returned with SASE; samples filed.
Photography: "Occasionally" buys photos from freelancers. Send résumé and samples. Contact: Mr. C. Lester, editorial director. Works on assignment only.
Terms: Pays authors royalty of 8%. Offers advances (average amount: $250). Book catalog available for SAE.

McCLANAHAN BOOK COMPANY, INC., 23 W. 26th St., New York NY 10010. (212)725-1515. Fax: (212)725-5911. Book publisher. CEO: Susan McClanahan. Editorial Director: Elise Donner. Creative Director: Dave Werner. Rights Director: Jessica Hewitt. Publishes 90 picture books/year. Publishes "affordable, high quality massmarket children's books, including activity books, workbooks and storybooks.

Fiction: Board story books.
How to Contact/Writers: Submit complete ms. Reports on queries in 1 month; mss in 3 months. Will consider simultaneous submissions.
Illustration: McClanahan Book Company is not accepting art submissions at this time.
Terms: Pays authors on work-for-hire basis (flat fee). Pays illustrators/photographers by the project.

MARGARET K. McELDERRY BOOKS, 1230 Sixth Ave., New York NY 10020. (212)702-7855. Fax: (212)605-3045. Imprint of Simon & Schuster Children's Publishing Division. Publisher: Margaret K. McElderry. Art Director: Ann Bobco. Publishes 10-12 picture books/year; 2-4 young reader titles/year; 8-10 middle reader titles/year; 5-7 young adult titles/year. 10% of books by first-time authors; 33% of books from agented writers.
Fiction: Young readers: adventure, contemporary, fantasy, history. Middle readers: adventure, contemporary, fantasy, mystery. Young adult: contemporary, fantasy, mystery, poetry. "Always interested in publishing picture books and beginning reader stories by people of color about cultures and people other than Caucasian American. We see too many rhymed picture book manuscripts which are not terribly original or special." Average word length: picture books—500; young readers—2,000; middle readers—10,000-20,000; young adults—45,000-50,000. Recently published *My Dad*, by Niki Daly; *Yolonda's Genius*, by Carol Fenner; and *Midget*, by Tim Bowler.
Nonfiction: Young readers, young adult teens, biography, history. Average word length: picture books—500-1,000; young readers—1,500-3,000; middle readers—10,000-20,000; young adults—30,000-45,000. Recently published *Hiawatha: Messenger of Peace*, by Dennis Fradin (ages 7-11); *To Hold This Ground: A Desperate Battle At Gettysburg*, by Susan Provost Beller (ages 10 and up); and *The Mystery of the Ancient Maya*, by Carolyn Meyer and Charles Gallenkamp (ages 12 and up).
How to Contact/Writers: Fiction/nonfiction: Submit query and/or complete ms. Reports on queries in 2-3 weeks; mss in 3-4 months. Publishes a book 18 months after acceptance. Will consider simultaneous submissions (only if indicated as such).
Illustration: Works with 20-30 illustrators/year. Review ms/illustration packages from artists. Query or submit ms (complete) and 2 or 3 copies of finished art. Illustrations only: Query with samples; provide, promo sheet or tearsheets; arrange personal portfolio review. Contact: Ann Bobco, art director. Reports on art samples in 2-3 months. Samples returned with SASE or samples filed. Original artwork returned at job's completion.
Terms: Pays authors royalty based on retail price. Pay illustrators by the project or royalty based on retail price. Pays photographers by the project. Sends galleys to authors; dummies to illustrators. Book catalog, ms guidelines free on request with 9×12 SASE.
Tips: Sees "more sales of beginning chapter books; more sales of poetry books; constant interest in books for the youngest baby market; more need for multicultural biographies and folktales."

MAGE PUBLISHERS INC., 1032 29th St. NW, Washington DC 20007. (202)342-1642. Book publisher. Editorial contact: A. Sepehri. Publishes 2-3 picture books/year.
Fiction: Contemporary/myth, Persian heritage. Average word length: 5,000.
Nonfiction: Persian heritage. Average word length: 5,000.
How to Contact/Writers: Fiction/Nonfiction: Query. Reports on queries/ms in 3 months. Will consider simultaneous submissions.
Illustration: Reviews ms/illustration packages from artists. Illustrations only: Submit résumé and slides. Reports in 3 months. Original artwork returned at job's completion.
Terms: Pays authors in royalties. Sends galleys to authors. Book catalog free on request.

MAGINATION PRESS, 19 Union Square West, New York NY 10003. (212)924-3344. Brunner/Mazel, Inc. Book publisher. Editor-in-Chief: Susan Kent Cakars. Publishes 2-6 picture books; and 0-1 middle reader and young adult title/year. Publishes "books dealing with the psycho/therapeutic treatment or resolution of children's serious problems—written by mental health professionals." Most books are by first-time authors.
Fiction: Picture books: mental health, special needs. Published *Gentle Willow: A Story for Children About Dying*, by Joyce C. Mills, Ph.D. (ages 4-8); *Sammy's Mommy Has Cancer*, by Sherry Kohlenberg (ages 4-8); *What About Me? When Brothers & Sisters Get Sick*, by Allan Peterkin, M.D. (ages 4-8).

Nonfiction: Middle readers: mental health, special needs. Published *Putting on the Brakes: Young People's Guide to Understanding Attention Deficit Hyperactivity Disorder (ADHD)*, by Patricia O. Quinn, M.D. and Judith M. Stern, M.A. (ages 8-13).
How to Contact/Writers: Fiction/Nonfiction: Submit complete ms. Reports on queries/mss: "up to 3 months (may be only days)." Publishes a book 1 year after acceptance. Will consider simultaneous submissions.
Illustration: Works with 3-6 illustrators/year. Reviews ms/illustration packages. Submit ms with dummy. Contact: Susan Kent Cakars, editor. Illustrations only: Query with samples. Reports only if interested. Samples returned with SASE; samples filed. Original artwork returned at job's completion.
Terms: Pays authors in royalties. Offers vary but low advance. Pays illustrators by the project. Book catalog and ms guidelines on request with SASE.

MARLOR PRESS, INC., 4304 Brigadoon Dr., St. Paul MN 55126. (612)484-4608. Fax: (612)490-1188. Book publisher. Editorial Director: Marlin Bree. Publishes 2 young readers/year. 100% of books by first-time authors.
Nonfiction: Young readers: activity books, arts/crafts. Middle readers: activity books. Recently published *Kid's Book to Welcome a New Baby*, by Barbara Collman, illustrated by Georgene Pomplin (ages 2-12, kid's activity book); and *Kid's Vacation Diary* (ages 6-12, diary and activity book for kids while traveling).
How to Contact/Writers: Query. Reports on queries in 6 weeks; mss in 2 months. Publishes a book 8-12 months after acceptance. Will consider simultaneous and previously published submissions.
Illustration: Works with 2 illustrators/year. Reviews ms/illustration packages from artists. Query. Contact: Marlin Bree, editorial director. Reports in 3 months. Samples returned with SASE. Originals returned at job's completion.
Terms: Pays authors 5-10% royalty based on wholesale price. Pays illustrators by the project (range: $150-400). Sends galleys to authors; dummies to illustrators. Book catalog available for #10 SAE and 2 first-class stamps. Ms guidelines available for SASE.

*■**MAYHAVEN**, 803 Buckthorn Circle, P.O. Box 557, Mahomet IL 61853. (217)586-4493. Fax: (217)586-6330. Book publisher, co-op publisher. Assistant Editor: Tonya Abbott. 50% of books by first-time authors; 50% co-op published.

- Mayhaven co-op publishes under its Wild Rose imprint; other titles are traditionally published.

Fiction: Picture books: adventure, fantasy, health, history, humor. Young adults/teens: adventure, animal, history, humor, nature/environment, suspense/mystery. Average word length: picture books—150-300; young adults/teens—50,000 (200 pages). Recently published: *Ebert Ein Swine Learns Line Dancing*, written and illustrated by Margaret Clem; and *The Peanut Butter Kid*, by Gertrude Stenesifer, illustrated by Denny Rogers.
Nonfiction: Picture books: activity books, animal, biography, geography, history, nature/environment, special needs. Young readers, middle readers: biography, geography, history, nature/environment. Young adults/teens: biography, geography, history, nature/environment, special needs. Recently published: *The Wellness Tree*, by Judy Cox, illustrated by Denny Rogers (for sick children, fiction that includes factual information). Average word length: picture books — 300; young adults/teens—50,000.
How to Contact/Writers: Fiction: Query; submit complete ms or outline/synopsis and 3 sample chapters. Nonfiction: Query; submit complete ms. Reports on queries in 3 months; mss in 3-6 months. Publishes a book 6-18 months after acceptance.
Illustration: Works with 3-5 illustrators/year. Reviews ms/illustration packages from artists. Send ms with dummy. Contact: Tonya Abbott, assistant editor. Illustrations only: query with samples. Contact: Tonya Abbott, assistant editor. Reports only if interested.
Photography: Buys photos from freelancers. Contact: Tonya Abbott, assistant editor. Works on assignment only. Model/property releases required. Uses 8×10 glossy b&w prints, 4×5 or 8×10 transparencies. Submit cover letter, résumé and published samples.
Terms: Pays authors royalty of 6-10% based on retail price, or co-op arrangement. Offers advances (average amount: $100). Pays illustrators by the project (range: $100-800) or royalty of 2-10% based on retail price. Pays photographers by the project (range: $50-250). Sends galleys

to authors; dummies to illustrators. Book catalog available for 6 × 9 SAE with 3 first-class stamps; ms and art guidelines available for SASE.
Tips: "Send one copy of best work. We hold illustrations for possible future assignments. Writers should submit full manuscript (one copy)."

MEADOWBROOK PRESS, 18318 Minnetonka Blvd., Deephaven MN 55391. (612)473-5400. Fax: (612)475-0736. Book publisher. Submissions Editor: Anita Newhead. Art Director: Amy Unger. Publishes 1-2 middle readers/year; 2-4 young readers/year. 20% of books by first-time authors; 10% of books from agented writers. Publishes children's activity books, gift books, humorous poetry anthologies and story anthologies.

- Meadowbrook appeared on a 1995 Hot List® compiled by *Children's Book Insider.* This list of "10 Book and Magazine Publishers Most Receptive to New Writers" is updated every few months, and available to new and renewing subscribers.

Fiction: Young readers and middle readers: anthology, folktales, humor, multicultural, poetry). "Poems representing people of color encouraged." Published *The New Adventures of Mother Goose*; *Girls to the Rescue*, (fairytale-style short stories featuring strong girls, for ages 8-12); and *A Bad Case of the Giggles* (all children's poetry anthologies).
Nonfiction: Young readers, middle readers: activity books, arts/crafts, hobbies, how-to, multicultural, self help. Multicultural needs include activity books representing traditions/cultures from all over the world, and especially fairy tale/folk tale stories with strong, multicultural heroines and diverse settings. "Books which include multicultural activities are encouraged." Average word length: varies. Recently published: *Kids' Party Games and Activities*, by Penny Warner; *Free Stuff for Kids* (activity book); and *Kids' Holiday Fun* (activity book).
How to Contact/Writers: Fiction/Nonfiction: Query, submit outline/synopsis and sample chapters or submit complete ms with SASE. Reports on queries/mss in 2-3 months. Publishes a book 1-2 years after acceptance. Send a business-sized SAE and 2 first-class stamps for free writer's guidelines and book catalog before submitting ideas. Will consider simultaneous submissions.
Illustration: Only interested in agented material. Works with 2-3 illustrators/year. Reviews ms/illustration packages from artists. Submit ms with 2-3 pieces of final art. Contact: Submissions editor. Illustrations only: Submit résumé, promo sheet and tearsheets. Contact: Amy Unger, art director. Reports back only if interested. Samples not returned; samples filed. Originals returned at job's completion.
Photography: Buys photos from freelancers. Buys stock and assigns work. Model/property releases required. Submit cover letter.
Terms: Pays authors in royalties of 5-7½% based on retail price. Offers average advance payment of $2,000-4,000. Pays for illustrators: $100-25,000; ¼-¾% of total royalties. Pays photographers per photo ($250). Book catalog available for 5 × 11 SASE and 2 first-class stamps; ms guidelines and artists guidelines available for SASE.
Tips: "Illustrators and writers should send away for our free catalog and guidelines before submitting their work to us. Also, illustrators should take a look at the books we publish to determine whether their style is consistent with what we are looking for. Writers should also note the style and content patterns of our books. For instance, our children's poetry anthologies contain primarily humorous, rhyming poems with a strong rhythm; therefore, we would not likely publish a free-verse and/or serious poem. I also recommend that writers, especially poets, have their work read by a critical, objective person before they submit anywhere. Also, please correspond with us by mail before telephoning with questions about your submission. We work with the printed word and will respond more effectively to your questions if we have something in front of us."

***MERIWETHER PUBLISHING LTD.**, 885 Elkton Dr., Colorado Springs CO 80907. Book publisher. Estab. 1969. Executive Editor: Arthur L. Zapel. Art Director: Tom Myers. "We do most of our artwork inhouse; we do not publish for the children's elementary market." 75% of books

The asterisk before a listing indicates the listing is new in this edition.

by first-time authors; 5% of books from agented writers. Publishes primarily how-to activity books for teens. Most books are related to theater arts or activities for church youth.

Fiction: Middle readers, young adults: anthology, contemporary, humor, religion. "We publish plays, not prose-fiction."

Nonfiction: Middle readers: activity books, religion. Young adults: activity books, how-to church activities, religion, drama/theater arts. Average length: 250 pages. Published *Directing for the Stage* by Terry John Converse; *Let's Play a Bible Game*, by Ed Dunlop, and *Acting Natural* by Peg Kehret.

How to Contact/Writers: Nonfiction: Query or submit outline/synopsis and sample chapters. Reports on queries in 3 weeks; mss in 6 weeks. Publishes a book 6-12 months after acceptance. Will consider simultaneous submissions.

Illustration: Works with 3 illustrators/year. Reviews ms/illustration packages from artists. Query first. Illustrations only: Query with samples; send résumé, promo sheet or tearsheets. Reports on art samples in 4 weeks.

Terms: Pays authors in royalties of 10% based on retail or wholesale price. Pays for illustrators by the project (range: $150-3,000); royalties based on retail or wholesale price. Sends galleys to authors. Book catalog for SAE and $2 postage; ms guidelines for SAE and 1 first-class stamp.

Tips: "We are currently interested in finding unique treatments for theater arts subjects: scene books, how-to books, monologs and short plays for teens."

JULIAN MESSNER, 250 James St., Morristown NJ 07960. Imprint of Silver Burdett Press, Simon & Schuster Education Group. Book Publisher. Editor: Adrianne Ruggiero. See Silver Burdett Press listing.

MILKWEED EDITIONS, 430 First Ave. North, Suite 400, Minneapolis MN 55401-1743. (612)332-3192. Book Publisher. Writers Contact: Children's Reader. Illustrators Contact: Art Director. Publishes 4 middle readers/year; 0-1 young adult titles/year. 25% of books by first-time authors. "Works must embody humane values and contribute to cultural understanding. There is no primary theme."

Fiction: Middle readers, young adults: adventure, animal, contemporary, fantasy, history, humor, multicultural, nature/environment, problem novels, science fiction, suspense/mystery. Does not want to see anthologies, folktales, health, hi-lo, poetry, religion, romance, sports. Average length: middle readers—110-350 pages; young adults—110-350 pages. Published *Gildaen*, by Emilie Buchwald (middle reader, fantasy); *I Am Lavina Cumming*, by Susan Lowell (middle reader, contemporary).

Nonfiction: Middle readers, young adults: biographies. Average length: middle readers—110-350 pages; young adults—110-350 pages. "We have not published any nonfiction as of yet."

How to Contact/Writers: Fiction/nonfiction: Query; submit complete manuscript. Reports on queries in 1 month, mss in 1-6 months. Publishes a book 1-12 months after acceptance. Will consider simultaneous submissions.

Illustration: Works with 3 illustrators/year. Reviews ms/illustration packages from artists. Query; submit manuscript with dummy. Illustrations only: Query with samples; provide resume, promo sheet, slides, tearsheets and client list. Samples filed or returned with SASE; samples filed. Originals returned at job's completion.

Terms: Pays authors royalty of 7½% based on retail price. Offers advance against royalties. Sends galleys to authors. Book catalog available for $1.50 to cover postage; ms guidelines available for SASE.

THE MILLBROOK PRESS, 2 Old New Milford Rd., Brookfield CT 06804. (203)740-2220. Book publisher. Manuscript Coordinator: Dottie Carlson. Art Director: Judie Mills. Publishes 20 picture books/year; 40 young readers/year; 50 middle readers/year; 10 young adult titles/year. 10% of books by first-time authors; 20% of books from agented authors. Publishes nonfiction, concept-oriented/educational books.

Nonfiction: All levels: activity books, animal, arts/crafts, biography, careers, concept, geography, health, history, hobbies, multicultural, music/dance, nature/environment, reference, social issues, sports, science. No fiction or poetry. Average word length: picture books—minimal; young readers—5,000; middle readers—10,000; young adult/teens—20,000. Published *Frog Counts to Ten*, by John Liebler (grades K-3, picture book); *The Scopes Trial: Defending the Right to Teach*,

Artist Jan Davey Ellis appropriately adopted an early American approach to illustrate the cover of The Millbrook Press's* A Quilt Block History of Pioneer Days, With Projects Kids Can Make*, by Mary Cobb. Through bold, colorful patterns and simple, direct illustrations the pioneers depicted their daily lives, special occasions and the natural world around them. Using tempra paints, Ellis recreated those designs—"Rock Road to Kansas," "Hole in the Barn," and "Log Cabin" among them—telling stories of life during the expansion westward. "Jan is not only a good illustrator but a good designer, and that's what this book called for," says Art Director Judy Mills, commenting on Ellis's ability to create imaginative borders. "She's very good with anything that requires flair."

by Arthur Blake (grades 4-6, history); *The U.S. Health Care Crisis*, by Victoria Sherrow (grades 7-up, contemporary issues).

How to Contact/Writers: Query. Submit outline/synopsis and 1 sample chapter. Reports on queries/mss in 1 month.

Illustration: Work with 20 illustrators/year. Reviews ms/illustration packages from artists. Query; submit 1 chapter of ms with 1 piece of final art. Illustrations only: Query with samples; provide résumé, business card, promotional literature or tearsheets to be kept on file. Contact: Judie Mills, art director. Reports back only if interested.

Photography: Buys photos from freelancers. Buys stock and assigns work.

Terms: Pays author royalty of 5-7½% based on wholesale price or work purchased outright. Offers advances. Pays illustrators by the project, royalty of 3-7% based on wholesale price. Sends galleys to authors. Book catalog for SAE; ms guidelines for SASE.

MISTY HILL PRESS, 5024 Turner Rd., Sebastopol CA 95472. (707)823-7437. Book publisher. Editor-in-Chief: Sally Karste. 100% of books by first-time authors.
Fiction: Middle readers, young adults: history. Published *Trails to Poosey*, by Olive Cooke (young adults, historical fiction).
Nonfiction: Middle readers, young adults: history.
How to Contact/Writers: Fiction/Nonfiction: Submit outline/synopsis and sample chapters. Reports on queries/ms in 2 weeks. Publishes a book 8 months after acceptance. Will consider simultaneous submissions.
Terms: Pays illustrators by the project. Sends galleys to authors.
Tips: Looking for "historical fiction: substantial research, good adventure or action against the historical setting."

***MONDO PUBLISHING**, One Plaza Rd., Greenvale NY 11548. (516)484-7812. Fax: (516)484-7813. Book publisher. Contact: Diane Snowball. Senior Editor: Louise May. Editor: Maureen Sullivan. Publishes 40 picture books/year. 20% of books by first-time authors. Publishes various categories.
Fiction: Picture books: adventure, animal, anthology, concept, contemporary, fantasy, folktales, history, humor, multicultural, nature/environment, science fiction, suspense/mystery. Young readers: adventure, animal, anthology, contemporary, fantasy, folktales, history, humor, multicultural, nature/environment, science fiction, sports, suspense/mystery. Recently published *Little Mouse's Trail Tale*, by JoAnn Vandine (3-7 year olds).
Nonfiction: Picture books: animal, arts/crafts, cooking, history, hobbies, how-to, multicultural, music/dance, nature/environment, science, social issues, sports. Young readers: animal, arts/crafts, biography, cooking, geography, history, hobbies, how-to, multicultural, music/dance, nature/environment, science, social issues, sports. Recently published *Exploring Land Habitats*, by Margaret Phinney (7-10 year-olds, environment).
How to Contact/Writers: Fiction/Nonfiction: Query, submit complete ms. Reports on queries in 1 month; mss in 3 months. Will consider simultaneous submissions and previously published work.
Illustration: Works with 30 illustrators/year. Uses color artwork only. Reviews ms/illustration packages from author. Submit ms with dummy. Contact: Diane Snowball, publisher. Illustration only: Query with samples, résumé, portfolio, arrange personal portfolio review. Reports in 1 month. Samples returned with SASE.
Photography: Buys photos from freelancers. Contact: Louise May, senior editor. Buys stock images. Uses mostly nature photos. Uses color prints; 35mm transparencies. Submit résumé.
Terms: Pays authors royalty of 4-10% based on wholesale/retail price. Offers advance of $500. Pays illustrators by the project (range: 3,000-8,000), royalty of 4-5% based on wholesale/retail price. Pays photographers by the project, per photo, royalty of 4-5% based on wholesale/retail price. Sends galleys to authors. Book catalog available for 9×12 SAE.

MOREHOUSE PUBLISHING CO., 871 Ethan Allen Hwy., Ridgefield CT 06877. (203)431-3927. Fax: (203)431-3964. Book publisher. Estab. 1884. Editor: Deborah Grahame-Smith. Publishes 4 picture books/year. 25% of books by first-time authors.
Fiction: Picture books: folktales, multicultural, religion. Young readers: adventure, folktales, humor, multicultural. Middle readers: folk tales, history, multicultural, poetry, religion. Young adults: contemporary, multicultural, mystery. Multicultural themes include "working together for the betterment of God's world." Does not want to see "anything other than traditional Christian values."
Nonfiction: Picture books: nature/environment, religion. Young readers: biography, nature/environment, religion. Middle readers: biography, religion, social issues. Young adults: biography, social issues.
How to Contact/Writers: Fiction/Nonfiction: Submit outline/synopsis and sample chapters to Deborah Grahame-Smith. Reports on queries in 4-6 weeks; mss in 3 months. Publishes a book 1 year after acceptance. "Agented ms are preferred."

Illustration: Works with 3 illustrators/year. Reviews ms/illustration packages from artists. Submit 3 chapters of ms with 1 piece of final art. Illustrations only: Submit résumé, tearsheets. Contact: Deborah Grahame-Smith, art director. Reports on art samples in 4-6 weeks. Original artwork returned at job's completion.
Photography: Buys photos from freelancers, Buys stock images. Uses photos of children/youth in everyday life experiences.
Terms: Pays authors royalty of 6-15% based on retail price and purchases more outright. Offers modest advance payment. Pay illustrators by the project. Sends galleys to authors. Book catalog free on request; send SASE ($1.25 postage).
Tips: Writers: "Prefer authors who can do their own illustrations. Be fresh, be fun, not pedantic, but let your work have a message." Illustrators: "Work hard to develop an original style." Looks for ms/illustration packages "with a religious or moral value while remaining fun and entertaining."

***MORGAN REYNOLDS PUBLISHING**, 803 S. Elam Ave., Greensboro NC 27403. (910)274-3704. Fax: (910)274-3705. Editor: John Riley. Book Publisher. Publishes 12 young adult titles/year. 50% of books by first-time authors.
Nonfiction: Middle readers, young adults/teens: biography, history, multicultural, social issues. Multicultural needs include Native American, African-American and Latino subjects. Average word length: middle readers—12,000-20,000; young adults/teens—20,000-35,000. Recently published: *Mr. Civil Rights: The Story of Thurgood Marshall*, by Nancy Whitelaw; *Smart Money: The Story of Bill Gates*, by Aaron Boyd; and *Boris Yeltsin: First President of Russia*, by Calvin Craig Miller.
How to Contact/Writers: Query; submit outline/synopsis with 3 sample chapters. Reports on queries in 1 month; mss in 2 months. Publishes a book 6 months after acceptance. Will consider simultaneous submissions or electronic submissions via disk (ASCII format).
Terms: Pays authors royalty of 8-12% based on wholesale price. Offers advances (average amount: $500). Sends galleys to authors. Book catalog available for business-size SAE with 1 first-class stamp; ms guidelines available for SASE.
Tips: "We are open to suggestions—if you have an idea that excites you send it along. We are mostly soliciting for our *World Writers* and *Champions of Freedom* series. Recent trends suggest that the field is open for younger, smaller companies. Writers, especially ones starting out, should search us out."

JOSHUA MORRIS PUBLISHING, 355 Riverside Ave., Westport CT 06880. (203)341-4300. Fax: (203)341-4385. Subsidiary of Reader's Digest, Inc. "We publish mostly early concept books and books for beginning readers. Most are in series of four titles and contain some kind of novelty element (i.e., lift the flap, die cut holes, book and soft toy, etc.). We publish 300-400 books per year." 5% of books by first-time Subisdiary of Reader's Digest, Inc. "We publish mostly early concept books and books for beginning readers. Most are in series of four titles and contain some kind of novelty element (i.e., lift the flap, die cut holes, book and soft toy, etc.). We publishs 300-400 books per year." 5% of books by first-time authors; 5% of books from agented authors; 90% of books published on commission (Book packaging).
Fiction: Picture books and young readers: activity books, adventure, animal, concept, nature/environment, reference, religion. Middle readers: animal, nature/environment, religion. Does not want to see poetry, short stories, science fiction. Average word length: picture books—300-400. Published *Whooo's There?*, by Lily Jones (ages 3-7, sound and light); *Ghostly Games*, by John Speirs, with additional text by Gill Speirs (ages 8-12, puzzle).
Nonfiction: Picture books, young readers and middle readers: activity books, animal, nature/environment, religion. Average word length: varies. Published *Alan Snow Complete Books (Dictionary, Atlas* and *Encyclopedia)*, by Alan Snow (ages 3-7, first reference); *Rain Forest Nature Search*, by Paul Sterry (ages 7-12, puzzle/activity).
How to Contact/Writers: Fiction/Nonfiction: Query. Nonfiction: Query. Reports on queries/mss in 3-4 months. Publishes a book 12-18 months after acceptance. Will consider simultaneous submissions and previously published work.
Illustration: Reviews ms/illustration packages from artists. Query. Illustrations only: Query with samples (nonreturnable). Provide résumé, promo sheet or tearsheets to be kept on file. Contact: Ira Teichberg art director. Reports back only if interested. Original artwork returned (only if requested).

Photography: Buys stock and assigns work. Contact: Ira Teichberg, art director. Uses photos of animals and children. Model/property releases required. Publishes photo concept books. Uses 4×6 glossy, color prints and 4×5 transparencies. Submit résumé, promo sheet or tearsheets to be kept on file.
Terms: Pays authors royalty or work purchased outright. Offers advances. Pays illustrators by the project or royalty. Photographers paid per photo.
Tips: Best bets with this market are "innovative concept and beginning readers, and books that have a novelty element."

MORROW JUNIOR BOOKS, 1350 Avenue of the Americas, New York NY 10019. Division of the Hearst Corporation. Does not accept unsolicited manuscripts.
Fiction: Recently published *The Book of Dragons*, by Michael Hague; and *Elsa in the Middle*, by Johanna Hurwitz.
Illustration: Reviews ms/illustration packages from artists. Reports in 4 months.
Photography: Purchases photos from freelancers.

JOHN MUIR PUBLICATIONS, INC., P.O. Box 613, Santa Fe NM 87504-0613. (505)982-4078. Book publisher. Editorial Contact: Steven Carey. Publishes 25 middle reader nonfiction picture books/year.
Nonfiction: Middle readers: animal, arts/crafts, biography, concept, hobbies, multicultural, nature/environment, science, social issues. Average word length: middle readers—12,000-15,000. Published *Kids' Explore Series* (5 titles), by different authors (middle readers); *Kids Explore America's Hispanic Heritage*, *Kids Explore America's African-American Heritage*, etc.
How to Contact/Writers: Query. Reports on queries/mss in 2 months. Publishes a book 8-12 months after acceptance. Will consider simultaneous submissions.
Illustration: Reviews ms/illustration packages. Query, outline and 1 chapter for illustration; 4 original finished pieces and roughs of ideas. Illustrations only: Submit résumé and samples of art that have been reproduced or samples of original art for style.
Photography: Purchases photos from freelancers. Buys stock images. Buys "travel, animal" photos.
Terms: Pays authors on work-for-hire basis, occasionally royalties. Some books are paid by flat fee for illustration or by the project. Book catalog free on request.
Tips: "We want nonfiction books for 8- to 12-year-old readers that can sell in bookstores as well as gift stores, libraries and classrooms."

NEW DISCOVERY BOOKS, 250 James St., Morristown NJ 07960. Imprint of Silver Burdett Press, Simon & Schuster Education Group. Book publisher. Editor: Debbie Biber. See Silver Burdett Press listing.

NORTHLAND PUBLISHING, P.O. Box 1389, Flagstaff AZ 86002-1389. (520)774-5251. Book publisher. Editor: Erin Murphy. Art Director: Trina Stahl. Publishes 6 picture books/year; 2 young readers/year. 75% of books by first-time authors. Primary theme is West and Southwest regionals, Native American folktales.

- Northland appeared on a 1995 Hot List® compiled by *Children's Book Insider*. This list of "10 Book and Magazine Publishers Most Receptive to New Writers" is updated every few months, and available to new and renewing subscribers.

Fiction: Picture books, young readers and middle readers: folktales, history, multicultural/bilingual. "Our Native American folktales are enjoyed by readers of all ages, child through adult." No religion, science fiction, anthology. Average word length: picture books—800; young readers—1,500; middle readers—20,000. Published *Grandmother Spider Brings the Sun*, by Geri Keams, illustrated by James Bernardin (ages 5 and up); *Carlos and the Cornfield*, by Jan Romero Stevens, illustrated by Jeanne Arnold (ages 5 and up); *Less Than Half, More Than Whole*, by Kathleen and Michael Lacapa, illustrated by Michael Lacapa (ages 5 and up).
Nonfiction: Picture books, young readers and middle readers: animal, multicultural, historical Average word length: picture books—800; young readers—1,500; middle readers—20,000.
How to Contact/Writers: Picture books/young readers: submit complete ms with cover letter. Middle readers: submit sample chapters with cover letter. Reports on queries in 4-6 weeks; mss in 10-12 months. "Acknowledgment sent immediately upon receipt." If ms and art are complete

at time of acceptance, publication usually takes 18 months. Will consider simultaneous submissions if labeled as such.

Illustration: Works with 6-8 illustrators/year. Uses color artwork only. Reviews ms/illustration packages from artists. Submit ms with samples; slides or color photocopies. Illustrations only: Query art director with samples, promo sheet, slides, tearsheets. Reports only if interested. Samples returned with SASE. Original artwork returned at job's completion.

Terms: Pays authors/illustrators royalty of 4-7% based on wholesale price. Offers advances. "This depends so much on quality of work and quantity needed." Ms guidelines available for SASE. Book catalog available for 9×12 with $1.47 postage.

Tips: Receptive to "Native American folktales (must be retold by a Native American author). Please research our company (look at our catalog) before submitting your work."

NORTHWORD PRESS, INC., P.O. Box 1360, Minocqua WI 54548. (715)356-7644. Managing Editor: Barbara Harold. Production Coordinator: Russ Kuepper. Publishes 10 picture books/year. 50% of books by first-time authors; 10% of books from agented authors. Publishes books pertaining to nature, wildlife and the environment. Also Native American topics.

Fiction: Picture books, young readers: animal, nature/environment. Does not want to see "anything without a strong nature/animal focus; no moralizing animal/nature stories (didactic)."

Nonfiction: Picture books, young readers: activity books, animal, nature/environment. Average word length: picture books—500-3,000; young readers—2,500-3,000. Recently published *Dolphins for Kids*, by Patricia Corrigan (ages 4-10, photo picture book); *Take Along Guides* (ages 8-12); *Secrets of the Forest*, by Muriel Steffy; and *My Little Book of Wood Ducks*, by Hope Irvin Marston, illustrated by Maria Magdalena Brown (ages 1-10).

How to Contact/Writers: Fiction: Query. Nonfiction: Query; submit outline/synopsis and 1 sample chapter. Reports on queries in 2 months; mss in 3 months. Publishes a book 9-12 months after acceptance. Will consider simultaneous submissions.

Illustration: Works with 1-3 illustrators/year. Reviews ms/illustration packages from artists. Query. Submit 1 chapter of ms with 3 pieces of final art. Illustrations only: Query with samples. Contact: Russ Kuepper, production coordinator. Reports back only if interested. Original artwork returned at job's completion.

Photography: Buys photos from freelancers. Contact: Larry Mishkar, photo editor. Uses nature and wildlife photos, full-color. Buys stock and assigns work. Model releases required. Publishes photo concept books. Uses color prints and 35mm transparencies. Query with samples. "Not responsible for damage to, or loss of, unsolicited materials."

Terms: Pays authors royalty based on wholesale price or work purchased outright. Offers negotiable advances. Pays illustrators by the project. Pays photographer by the project, per photo or royalty. Sends galleys to authors. Book catalog available for 9×12 SAE and 7 first-class stamps; ms guidelines available for SASE.

Tips: "The three key words are 'educational,' 'nature' and 'wildlife.' Beyond that, we're looking for fun, unusual and well-written manuscripts. We are expanding our children's line to include picture books that express a certain value or moral lesson related to nature."

THE OLIVER PRESS, INC., Charlotte Square, 5707 W. 36th St., Minneapolis MN 55416. Phone: (612)926-8981. Fax: (612)926-8965. Book publisher. Editor: Denise Sterling. Publishes 8 young adult titles/year. 10% of books by first-time authors. "We publish collective biographies of people who made an impact in one area of history, including science, government, archaeology, business and crime."

Nonfiction: Young adults: biography, geography and history. "Authors should only suggest ideas that fit into one of our existing series." Average word length: young adult—20,000 words. Recently published *Great Justices of the Supreme Court*, by Nathan Aaseng (ages 10 and up, collective biography); *Women Inventors and Their Discoveries*, by Ethlie Ann Vare and Greg Ptacek (ages 10 and up, collective biography); and *The World's Greatest Explorers*, by William Scheller (ages 10 and up, collective biography).

How to Contact/Writers: Nonfiction: Query. Submit outline/synopsis. Contact: Denise Sterling. Reports in 3 months. Publishes a book approximately 1 year after acceptance.

Illustration: Reviews mss illustration packages from artists. Query. Contact: Denise Sterling, editor. Reports in 3 months. Samples returned with SASE; samples kept on file. Originals returned at jobs completion.

Photography: Buys photos from freelancers. Contact: Denise Sterling, editor. Buys stock images. Looks primarily for photos of people in the news. Captions required. Uses 8×10 b&w prints. Submit cover letter, résumé and stock photo list.
Terms: Work purchased outright from authors for $1,000. Pays illustrators and photographers per photo (range: $20-50). Sends galleys to authors upon request. Book catalog available for SASE; ms and art guidelines available for SASE.
Tips: "Authors should read some of the books we have already published before sending a query to The Oliver Press. Authors should propose collective biographies for one of our existing series."

OPEN HAND PUBLISHING INC., P.O. Box 22048, Seattle WA 98122. (206)447-0597. Book publisher. Acquisitions Editor: Pat Andrus. Publishes 1-3 children's books/year. 50% of books by first-time authors. Multicultural books: African-American theme or bilingual.

- Open Hand is not currently accepting manuscripts, just queries.

Fiction: Picture books: folktales, history and African-American. Young readers and middle readers: history and African-American. Young adult/teens: African-American. Average length: picture books—32-64 pages; young readers—64 pages; middle readers—64 pages; young adult/teens—120 pages.
Nonfiction: All levels: history and African-American. Average length: picture books—32-64 pages; young readers—64 pages; middle readers—64 pages; young adult/teens: 64-120 pages.
How to Contact/Writers: Fiction/Nonfiction: Query. Reports on queries in 3 weeks; reports on mss in 5 weeks. Publishes a book 12-18 months after acceptance. Will consider simultaneous submissions.
Illustration: Reviews ms/illustration packages from artists. Query. Contact: P. Anna Johnson, publisher. Illustrations only: Query with samples. Reports in 3 weeks. Original artwork returned "depending on the book."
Terms: Pays authors royalty of 5-10% based on wholesale price. Offers advances. Pays illustrators by the project; commission for the work. Sends galleys to authors. Book catalog available for SAE and 2 first-class stamps; ms guidelines available for SAE and 1 first-class stamp.

✤ORCA BOOK PUBLISHERS, P.O. Box 5626 Station B, Victoria, British Columbia V8R 6S4 Canada. (604)380-1229. Fax: (604)380-1892. Book publisher. Children's Books Editor: Ann Featherstone. Publishes 8 picture books/year; 1-2 middle readers/year; 2-3 young adult titles/year. 25% of books by first time authors. "We only consider authors and illustrators who are Canadian or who live in Canada."
Fiction: Picture books: animals, contemporary, fairy tales, folktales, nature/environment. Middle readers: adventure, contemporary, history, nature/environment, problem novels, suspense/mystery. Young adults: adventures, contemporary, history, multicultural, nature/environment, problem novels, suspense/mystery. Average word length: picture books—500-2,000; middle readers—20,000-35,000; young adult—25,000-45,000. Published *The Magic Ear*, by Laura Lanston, illustrated by Victor Bosson (picture book, ages 5-8); and *The Moccasin Goalie*, written and illustrated by William Roy Brownridge (picture book, ages 4-8).
Nonfiction: Young readers, middle readers: history, nature/environment. Young adult: history. "We have enough whale stories to hold us for a while." Average word length: picture books—300-500; middle readers—2,000-3,000. Recently published *In the Company of Whales*, by Alexandra Morton, photos by Alexandra and Robin Morton (ages 8-12).
How to Contact/Writers: Fiction: Submit complete ms if picture book; submit outline/synopsis and 3 sample chapters. Nonfiction: Query with SASE. "All queries or unsolicited submissions should be accompanied by a SASE." Reports on queries in 3-6 weeks; mss in 1-3 months. Publishes book 12-18 months after acceptance.
Illustration: Works with 6-8 illustrators/year. Reviews ms/illustration packages from artists. Submit ms with 3-4 pieces of final art. "Reproductions only, no original art please." Illustrations only: Query with samples; provide résumé, slides. "We prefer to use local illustrators." Reports in 6-8 weeks. Samples returned with SASE; samples filed. Original artwork returned at job's completion if picture books.
Terms: Pays authors royalty of 5% for picture books, 10% for novels, based on retail price. Offers advances (average amount: $1,000). Pays illustrators royalty of 5% minimum based on retail price or advance on royalty of $1,000. Sends galleys to authors. Book catalog available for legal or 8½×11 manila SAE and 2 first-class stamps. Ms guidelines available for SASE. Art guidelines not available.

Tips: "American authors and illustrators should remember that the U.S. stamps on their reply envelopes cannot be posted in any country outside of the U.S."

ORCHARD BOOKS, 95 Madison Ave., New York NY 10016. (212)951-2600. Division and imprint of Grolier, Inc. Book publisher. President and Publisher: Neal Porter. "We publish between 60 and 70 books yearly including fiction, poetry, picture books, and some non-fiction." 10-25% of books by first-time authors.

- Orchard Books won several awards in 1995: a Newbery Honor Medal for *The Ear, the Eye and the Arm*, by Nancy Farmer; a Boston Globe-Horn Book Award for fiction for *Some of the Kinder Planets*, by Tim Wynne-Jones; and a Boston Globe-Horn Book Honor Award for fiction for *Earthshine*, by Theresa Nelson. To learn more about Orchard, see Insider Report with Rosanne Main in the 1995 edition of *Children's Writer's & Illustrator's Market*.

Fiction: All levels: animal, anthology, contemporary, fantasy, folktales, history, humor, multicultural, nature/environment, poetry, science fiction, sports, suspense/mystery. Does not want to see anthropomorphized animals. Recently published *The Barn*, by Avi; and *The Eagle Kite*, by Paula Fox (both novels).
Nonfiction: Picture books, young readers: animal, history, multicultural, nature/environment, science, social issues. "We publish nonfiction on a very selective basis."
How to Contact/Writers: Send mss to attention of Submissions Committee. Fiction: Submit entire ms. Nonfiction: Submit outline/synopsis and sample chapters. Reports on queries in 2 months; mss in 6 months. Average length of time between acceptance of a book-length ms and publication of work "depends on the editorial work necessary. If none, about 8 months or longer if schedule of books dictates."
Illustration: Works with 40 illustrators/year. Editorial Reviews ms/illustration packages from artists. "It is better to submit ms and illustration separately." Submit 3 chapters of ms with 1 piece of final art, remainder roughs. Illustrations only: Submit "tearsheets or photocopies or photostats of the work." Contact: Art Department. Reports on art samples in 1 month. Samples returned with SASE. Original artwork returned at job's completion. No disks or slides, please.
Terms: Pays authors in royalties "industry standard" based on retail price. Sends galleys to authors; dummies to illustrators. Book catalog free on request with 8½×11 SASE with 4 oz. postage.
Tips: "Read some of our books to determine first whether your manuscript is suited to our list."

OUR CHILD PRESS, 800 Maple Glen Lane, Wayne PA 19087-4797. (610)964-0606. Fax: (610)293-9038. Book publisher. President: Carol Hallenbeck. 90% of books by first-time authors.
Fiction/Nonfiction: All levels: adoption, multicultural, special needs. Word length: Open. Published *Don't Call Me Marda*, by Sheila Kelly Welch; *Is That Your Sister?* by Catherine and Sherry Burin; and *Oliver: A Story About Adoption*, by Lois Wichstrom.
How to Contact/Writers: Fiction/Nonfiction: Query or submit complete ms. Reports on queries/mss in 6 months. Publishes a book 6-12 months after acceptance.
Illustration: Works with 1 illustrator/year. Uses primarily b&w artwork. Reviews ms/illustration packages from artists. Ms/illustration packages and illustration only: Query first. Submit résumé, tearsheets and photocopies. Contact: Carol Hallenbeck, president. Reports on art samples in 2 months. Samples returned with SASE; samples kept on file. Original artwork returned at job's completion.
Terms: Pays authors in royalties of 5-10% based on wholesale price. Pays illustrators royalties of 5-10% based on wholesale price. Book catalog for business-size SAE and 52¢ postage.
Tips: Won't consider anything not related to adoption.

***OUR SUNDAY VISITOR, INC.**, 200 Noll Plaza, Huntington IN 46750. (219)356-8400. Fax: (219)356-8472. Book publisher. Acquisitions Editor: Jacquelyn M. Lindsey. Publishes primarily religious, educational, parenting, reference and biographies.

- Our Sunday Visitor, Inc., was not publishing children's books at the time of this printing. Contact the acquisitions editor for manuscript guidelines and a book catalog.

How to Contact/Writers: Nonfiction: Query, submit complete ms, or submit outline/synopsis, and 2-3 sample chapters. Reports on queries in 2 months; 3-4 months. Publishes a book 18-24 months after acceptance. Will consider simultaneous submissions, electronic submissions via disk or modem, previously published work.

Illustration: Reviews ms/illustration packages from artists. Contact: Jacquelyn Lindsey, acquisitions editor. Illustration only: Query with samples. Contact: Aquisitions Editor. Reports in 2 weeks. Original artwork returned at job's completion.
Photography: Buys photos from freelancers. Contact: Jacquelyn M. Murphy, acquisitions editor.
Terms: Pays authors bsed on retail price. Offers royalty. Sends galleys to authors; dummies to illustrators. Book catalog available for SAE; ms guidelines available for SASE.
Tips: "Stay in accordance with our guidelines."

RICHARD C. OWEN PUBLISHERS, INC., P.O. Box 585, Katonah NY 10536. (914)232-3903. Fax: (914)241-2873. Book publisher. Editor/Art Director: Janice Boland. Publishes 3-13 picture story books/year. 90% of books by first-time authors. Publishes "child focused, meaningful books about characters and situations with which five, six, and seven-year-old children can identify. We include multicultural stories that present minorities in a positive and natural way. Our stories show the diversity in America."
Fiction: Picture books for young readers: adventure, animal, contemporary, folktales, humor, multicultural, nature/environment, suspense/mystery. Does not want to see holiday, religious themes, moral teaching stories. No talking animals with personified human characteristics, jingles and rhymes, holiday stories, alphabet books, lists without plots, stories with nostalgic views of childhood, soft or sugar-coated tales. No stereotyping. Average word length: 40-100 words.
Nonfiction: Picture books for young readers: animals, geography, multicultural, music/dance, nature/environment, science. Multicultural needs include: "Good stories respectful of all heritages, races, cultural—African-American, Hispanic, American Indian." Wants lively stories. No "encyclopedic" type of information stories. Average word length: 40-100 words.
How to Contact/Writers: Fiction/Nonfiction: Submit complete ms. "*Must* request guidelines first with #10 SASE." Reports on mss in 1-4 months. Publishes a book 2-3 years after acceptance. Will consider simultaneous submissions.
Illustration: Works with 10 illustrators/year. Uses color artwork only. Reviews ms/illustration packages from artists. Send ms with dummy. Illustration only: Send color copies/reproductions or photos of art or provide tearsheets. Must request guidelines first. Reports in 1-4 months only if interested. Samples filed.
Photography: Buys photos from freelancers. Contact: Janice Boland, art director. Wants photos that are child oriented; not interested in portraits. "Natural, bright, crisp and colorful—of children and of subjects and compositions attractive to children." Sometimes interested in stock photos for special projects. Uses 35mm, $2\frac{1}{4} \times 2\frac{1}{4}$, color transparencies.
Terms: Pays authors royalties of 5% based on retail price. Offers no advances. Work purchased outright from illustrators (range: $1,000-2,500). Pays photographers by the project (variable) or per photo. Sends galleys to authors. Ms/artist guidelines available for SASE.
Tips: Seeking "stories (both fiction and nonfiction) that have charm, magic, impact and appeal; that children living in today's society will want to read and reread; books with strong storylines, child-appealing language, action and interesting, vivid characters. Write from your heart—for the ears and eyes and heart of your readers—use an economy of words."

***🍁PACIFIC EDUCATIONAL PRESS**, Faculty of Education, UBC, Vancouver British Columbia V6T 1Z4 Canada. (604)822-5385. Fax: (604)822-6603. Director: C.V. Edwards. Publishes 1 picture book/year; 2 middle readers/year; 1 young adult title/year. 20% of books by first-time authors.
Fiction: Picture books: folktales, history, multicultural, nature/environment. Middle readers: folktales, history, multicultural, nature/environment, science fiction. Young adults: contemporary, folktales, history, multicultural, nature/environment, science fiction. Average word length: picture books—2,500; middle readers—25,000. Recently published *A Sea Lion Called Salena*. by Dayle Gaetz (ages 8-11, novel with environmental theme); *Trapped by Coal*, Constance Horne (ages 8-11, novel with historical setting) and *The Suzie A*, by Alan Haig-Brown (ages 11 and up, novel with historical and multicultural setting of Japanese internment in WWII).
Nonfiction: Picture books: animal, arts/crafts, history, multicultural, music/dance, nature/environment, reference, science, social issues, textbooks. Young readers and middle readers: animal, arts/crafts, biography, cooking, history, multicultural, music/dance, nature/environment, reference, science, social issues, textbooks, native studies. Young adults: animal, arts/crafts, biography,

cooking, history, multicultural, music/dance, nature/environment, reference, science, social issues, textbooks. Average word length: picture books—2,500; middle readers—25,000; young adults—35,000. Recently published *Folk Rhymes from Around the World*, by Evelyn Neaman and Sally Davies (ages 7-9, collection of folk poems for children from 20 countries); and *It's Elementary! Investigating the Chemical World*, by Douglas Hayward and Gordon Bates, illustrated by Nyla Sunga (ages 11-15, collection of chemistry experiments and background information about science).

How to Contact: Fiction/Nonfiction: Query or submit complete ms. Reports on queries in 1 month; mss in 4 months. Publishes a book a year or so after acceptance, "depending on a large number of factors." Will consider electronic submissions via disk or modem.

Illustration: Works with 3-4 illustrators/year. Uses both b&w and color artwork. Reviews ms/illustration packages from authors. Submit ms with dummy. Contact: CV Edwards, director. Illustration only: Query with samples, résumé, tearsheets, color photocopies to keep on file. Reports in 4 months. Samples returned with SASE; samples filed, "but I'm not likely to even use an illustrator who won't send samples I can keep."

Photography: Buys photos from freelancers. Contact: C.V.G. Edwards, director. Sometimes buys stock and assigns work. Uses mostly photos of kids, West Coast flora and fauna. Submit cover letter, résumé, published samples, slides, client list, stock photo list.

Terms: Pays authors royalty of 10-12% based on wholesale price. Pays illustrators by the project or royalty of 5% based on wholesale price. Pays photographers by the project or per photo. Sends galleys to authors. Book catalog available for 9×12 SAE and IRC.

PACIFIC PRESS, P.O. Box 7000, Boise ID 83707. (208)465-2500. Fax: (208)465-2531. E-mail: 74617.3165@compuserve.com. Book publisher. Acquisitions Editor: Jerry D. Thomas. Publishes 2-4 young readers, 2-4 middle readers, 4-6 young adult titles/year. 5% of books by first-time authors. "Not currently looking for picture books." Seventh-day Adventist Christian publishing house which publishes books pertaining to religion, spiritual values (strong spiritual slant).

Fiction: Picture books, young readers: religion. Middle readers: adventure, animal, contemporary, religion, suspense/mystery. Young adults: adventure, animal, religion, suspense/mystery. "All books have spiritual/religious themes." Does not want to see fantasy or totally non-factual stories. "We prefer true stories that are written in fiction style." Average word length: picture books—500-1,000; young readers—6,000-7,000; middle readers—25,000-33,000; young adult/teens—33,000-75,000. Recently published *500 Degrees in the Shade*, by Andy Demsky (teens); the Detective Zack series, by Jerry D. Thomas (8-12); and A Child's Steps to Jesus series by Linda Porter Carlyle (ages 3-7).

Nonfiction: All levels: religion. "We publish very little nonfiction for children. All manuscripts must have a religious/spiritual/health theme." Average word length: picture books—500-1,000; young readers—6,000-7,000; middle readers—25,000-33,000; young adult/teens—33,000-80,000. Recently published *Just Like You and Me*, by Ginger Ketting (ages 3-6).

How to Contact/Writers: Fiction: Submit complete ms; submit outline/synopsis and 2 sample chapters. Nonfiction: Query; submit complete ms; submit outline/synopsis and 2 sample chapters. Reports on queries in 1 month; mss in 2 months. Publishes a book 6-12 months after acceptance. Will consider simultaneous submissions and electronic submissions via disk or modem.

Illustration: Works with 4-6 illustrators/year. Reviews ms/illustration packages from artists. Submit complete package. Illustrations only: Query with samples; submit portfolio for review. Contact: Randy Maxwell, advertising director. Reports in 2 weeks. Original artwork returned at job's completion.

Terms: Pays authors royalty of 6-16% based on wholesale price. Offers advances ($300-1,500). Pays illustrators by the project (range: $500-750); 6% royalty based on wholesale price. Sends

galleys to authors. Book catalog available for 9×12 SASE. Ms guidelines available for SASE.
Tips: "Character building stories with a strong spiritual emphasis have the best chance of being published by our press. Also, adventure, and mystery stories that incorporate spirituality and character building are especially welcome."

***🍁PACIFIC-RIM PUBLISHERS**, 130 E. 15th St., #302, Vancouver, British Columbia V5T 4L3 Canada. (604)872-7373. (604)872-2622. Book publisher and distributor. Contact: Naomi Wakan. Publishes 2-4 middle readers/year.
Fiction: Middle readers: folktales, multicutural. Multicultural needs include Pacific Rim and global subjects.
Nonfiction: Middle readers: activity books (with a link to social studies), multicultural (Pacific Rim countries), music/dance (Pacific Rim countries).
How to Contact/Writers: Fiction/Nonfiction: submit complete ms if under 50 pages. Reports on queries in 2 weeks; mss in 6 weeks. Publishes a book 1 year after acceptance.
Illustration: Uses primarily b&w artwork. Illustration only: b&w. "Send a few samples for our files. Nothing is returned. Don't send originals." Reports back only if interested.
Terms: Pays authors royalty based on retail price. Pays illustrators royalty based on retail price. Sends galleys to authors; dummies to illustrators. Book catalog available for $2, US; $3, Canadian.
Tips: "If you are not writing from the heart, please do not submit work."

PANDO PUBLICATIONS, 5396 Laurie Lane, Memphis, TN 38120. (901)682-8779. Book publisher. Estab. 1988. Owner: Andrew Bernstein. Publishes 2-6 middle readers/year; 2-6 young adults/year. 20% of books by first-time authors.
Fiction: Animal, concept, folktales, history, nature/environment. No poetry, science fiction, religion.
Nonfiction: Middle readers, young adults: activity books, animal, arts/crafts, biography, concept, cooking, geography, history, hobbies, how-to, multicultural, nature/environment, reference, science, social issues, special needs, sports. Average length: middle readers—175 pages; young adults—200 pages.
How to Contact/Writers: Fiction/Nonfiction: Query only. "All unsolicited manuscripts are destroyed. Please, no phone calls." Reports on queries in 6 months; on mss in 7 months. Publishes a book 1 year after acceptance. Will consider simultaneous submissions. "Prefers" electronic submissions via disk.
Illustration: Works with 2 illustrators/year. Editorial reviews all illustration packages from artists, and illustration-only submissions. Ms/illustrations: Query first. Illustrations only: Query with samples. Reports on art samples in 3 months. Original artwork returned at job's completion.
Terms: Pays authors royalty of 7-10%. Offers average advance payment of "⅓ royalty due on first run." Sends galleys to authors; dummies to illustrators. "Book descriptions available on request."
Tips: Writers: "Find an untapped market then write to fill the need." Illustrators: "Find an author with a good idea and writing ability. Develop the book with the author. Join a professional group to meet people—ABA, publishers' groups, as well as writers' groups and publishing auxiliary groups. Talk to printers." Looks for "how-to books, but will consider anything."

PAULINE (ST. PAUL) BOOKS AND MEDIA, (formerly St. Paul Books and Media), 50 St. Paul's Ave., Jamaica Plain MA 02130. (617)522-8911. Daughters of St. Paul. Book publisher. Estab. 1934. Editor: Sister Mary Mark, fsp. Design Director: Sister Helen Rita. Publishes 1-2 picture books/year; 1-2 young reader titles/year. 20% of books by first-time authors.
Fiction: All levels: moral values, religion. Average word length: picture books—150-300; young readers—1,500-5,000.
Nonfiction: All levels: biography (saints), devotionals, religion. Average word length: picture books—200; young readers—1,500-5,000; middle readers—10,000; young adults—20,000-50,000.
How to Contact/Writers: Fiction/Nonfiction: Submit outline/synopsis and sample chapters. Reports on queries in 3-8 weeks; on mss in 3 months. Publishes a book 2-3 years after acceptance. No simultaneous submissions.
Illustration: Works with 20 illustrators/year. Style/size of illustration "varies according to the title." Reviews ms/illustration packages from artists. "Submit outline first with art samples."

Illustrations only: Query with samples; send promo sheets or tearsheets. Reports on art samples in 3-8 weeks.
Photography: Buys photos from freelancers. Contact: Sister Helen Rita. Buys stock. Looking for children, animals—active interaction. Uses 4×5 or 8×10 b&w prints; 35mm or 4×5 transparencies.
Terms: Pays authors in royalties of 4-12% based on gross sales. Illustrations paid by the project. Photographers paid by the project, $15-200. Book catalog for 9×12 SAE and 5 first-class stamps. Manuscript guidelines for legal-size SAE and 1 first-class stamp.
Tips: "We are a Roman Catholic publishing house looking for devotional material for all ages (traditional and contemporary prayer-forms); obviously, material should be consonant with Catholic doctrine and spirituality!"

Freelance artist Christopher Fay's eye for detail made his work perfect for* Countdown to Christmas, Advent Thoughts, Prayers and Activities, *by Susan Heyboer O'Keefe. "The little details are what Fay notices, right down to the broken shoelace," says Paulist Press Book Editor Karen Scialabba. "The artist captures the reality and chaos of children." A current of gentle humor running throughout Fay's pen & ink illustrations complements the more serious tone of the book, which is a collection of daily scripture readings for Advent and the Christmas season, Scialabba says.

PAULIST PRESS, 997 Macarthur Blvd., Mahwah NJ 07430. (201)825-7300. Fax: (201)825-8345. Book publisher. Estab. 1865. Editor: Karen Scialabba. Publishes 9-11 picture books/year; 6-7 young reader titles/year; 3-4 middle reader titles/year. 85% of books by first-time authors; 15% of books from agented writers.
Fiction: Picture books: animal, concept, folktales, health, history, multicultural, nature/environment, religion, special needs. Young readers, middle readers: concept, contemporary, folktales, health, history, multicultural, nature/environment, religion, special needs. Young adults: anthology, concept, contemporary, history, multicultural, nature/environment, religion, special needs. Average length: picture books—24 pages; young readers—24-32 pages; middle readers—64 pages. Recently published *After the Funeral*, by Jane L. Winsch, illustrated by Pamela Keating; *Countdown to Christmas*, by Susan Heyboer O'Keefe, illustrated by Christopher Fay; and *It Takes Courage*, by Christine Schritt, illustrated by Jami Moffett.
Nonfiction: Picture books: activity books, animal, biography, concept, health, history multicultural, nature/environment, religion, social issues, special needs. Young readers: activity books, animal, arts/crafts biography, concept, health, history, multicultural, nature/environment, religion, social issues, special needs, textbooks. Middle readers: activity books, animal, biography, concept, health, history, multicultural, nature/environment, religion, self help, social issues, special needs, textbooks. Young adults: biography, careers, concept, health, history, multicultural, nature/environment, religion, self help, social issues, special needs, textbooks. Recently published *A Child's Bible, Old and New Testaments*, (The Old Testament rewritten for children, by Ann Edwards; The New Testament rewritten for children, by Shirley Steen ages 9-11); and *Iñigo*, by James Janda, illustrated by Christopher Fay.
How to Contact/Writers: Fiction/nonfiction: Submit complete ms. Reports on queries in 1-2 months; mss in 2-3 months. Publishes a book 12-16 months after acceptance.
Illustration: Works with 10-12 illustrators/year. Editorial reviews all varieties of ms/illustration packages from artists. Submit complete ms with 1 piece of final art, remainder roughs. Contact: Karen Scialabba, children's book editor. Illustrations only: Submit résumé, tearsheets. Reports

on art samples in 6 weeks. Original artwork returned at job's completion, "if requested by illustrator."

Photography: Buys photos from freelancers. Contact: Karen Scialabba. Works on assignment only. Uses inspirational photos.

Terms: Pays authors royalty of 8% based on retail price. Offers average advance payment of $450-$650. Pays illustrators by the project (range: $50-100) or royalty of 2-6% based on retail price. Factors used to determine final payment: color art, b&w, number of illustrations, complexity of work. Pay for separate authors and illustrators: Author paid by royalty rate; illustrator paid by flat fee, sometimes by royalty. Sends galleys to authors; dummies to illustrators.

Tips: Not interested in reviewing novels. Looking for "concept books for young readers that explore self-esteem, community involvement and care, social issues, families and spiritual development."

PEACHTREE PUBLISHERS, LTD., 494 Armour Circle NE, Atlanta GA 30324. (404)876-8761. Fax: (404)875-2578. Book publisher. Editorial: Helen Harriss.

Fiction: Picture books: adventure, animal, concept, history, nature/environment. Young readers: adventure, animal, concept, history, nature/environment, poetry. Middle readers: adventure, animal, history, nature/environment. Young adults: history, humor, nature/environment. Does not want to see science fiction, romance.

Nonfiction: Picture books: animal, history, nature/environment. Young readers, middle readers, young adults: animal, biography, history, nature/environment. Does not want to see sports, religion.

How to Contact/Writers: Fiction/Nonfiction: Submit complete manuscript. Reports on queries in 2-3 months; mss in 4 months. Publishes a book 1-1½ years after acceptance. Will consider simultaneous and previously published submissions.

Illustration: Works with 4 illustrators/year. Illustrations only: Query with samples, résumé, slides, color copies to keep on file. Reports back only if interested. Samples returned with SASE; samples filed.

Terms: Manuscript guidelines for SASE.

■**PEARTREE**, P.O. Box 14533, Clearwater FL 34629-4533. (813)531-4973. Book publisher. Owner: Barbara Birenbaum. Publishes 1-5 young readers/year; 1-5 middle readers/year. 50% of books by first-time authors; 50% subsidy publishes. "Publishes events (i.e. Liberty Centennial, Groundhog Day) and general stories with 'lessons,' no Christian themes."

Fiction: Books for readers/grades 2-6: adventure, animal, environment/nature, safety, contemporary, hi-lo, holidays, multicultural. Does not want to see material on religion, science fiction, suspense, sports (per se), anthology or folktales.

How to Contact/Writers: Query with SASE. Reports on queries in 2 weeks; mss in 3-6 months. Publishes book 9 months after acceptance. Will consider simultaneous submissions and previously published work.

Illustration: Works with 3 illustrators/year. Uses primarily b&w artwork with text. Reviews ms/illustration packages from artists. Query; then submit ms with dummy. Illustrations only: Query with samples and SASE. Samples returned with SASE; samples filed ("if we anticipate an interest").

Terms: Work purchased outright. Other methods of payment include profits from sales of books. Pays illustrators by the project (range—$10 per illustration to $200 per book). Sends galleys to authors.

Tips: "We will consider publishing and marketing books as subsidy when major houses reject titles. Be willing to get illustrations in books at minimum cost. Understand that small presses offer budding artists/writers chance to get in print and 'launch' careers on shoestring budgets."

***PEEL PRODUCTIONS**, P.O. Box 546, Columbus NC 28722. (704)894-8838. Fax: (704)894-8839. E-mail: peelbks@aol.com. Book publisher. Editor: S. Dubosque. Publishes 2-4 picture books/year. 25% of books by first-time authors.

Fiction: Peel Productions will not publish fiction for children until 1997.

Nonfiction: Young readers and middle readers: activity books (how to draw).

How to Contact/Writers: Fiction/Nonfiction: Submit outline/synopsis and 2 sample chapters. Reports on queries in 2-3 weeks; mss in 6 weeks. Publishes a book 1 year after acceptance. Will consider simultaneous submissions.

Terms: Pays authors royalty. Offers advances. Sends galleys to authors. Book catalog available for SAE and 2 first-class stamps. Ms guidelines available for SASE.

PELICAN PUBLISHING CO. INC., 1101 Monroe St., Gretna LA 70053. (504)368-1175. Book publisher. Estab. 1926. Editor: Nina Kooij. Production Manager: Cynthia Welch. Publishes 8 young readers/year; 6 middle reader titles/year. 5% of books from agented writers.
Fiction: Young readers: folktales, history, multicultural, religion. Middle readers: folktales, history, multicultural, religion. Multicultural needs include stories about Native Americans and African-Americans. Does not want animal stories, general Christmas stories, "day at school" or "accept yourself" stories. Average word length: "when printed" young readers—32 pages; middle readers—112 pages. Recently published *An Irish Night Before Christmas* by Sarah Kirwan Blazek, (ages 5-8), describes an Irish Christmas; *Little Freddie's Legacy*, by Kathryn Cocquyt, illustrated by Sylvia Corbett (novel about a horse running a famous race in Ireland) (ages 8-12).
Nonfiction: Young readers: biography, history, multicultural, music/dance, nature/environment, religion. Middle readers: biography, cooking, history, multicultural, music/dance, nature/environment, religion, sports. Published *Floridians All*, by George S. Fichter, illustrated by George Cardin (ages 8-12, collection of biographies on famous Florida figures).
How to Contact/Writers: Fiction/Nonfiction: Query. Reports on queries in 1 month; mss in 3 months. Publishes a book 12-18 months after acceptance.
Illustration: Works with 10 illustrators/year. Reviews ms/illustration packages from artists. Query first. Reports only if interested. Illustrations only: Query with samples (no originals). Contact: Nina Kooij, editor. Reports only if interested. Samples not returned; samples kept on file.
Terms: Pays authors in royalties; buys ms outright "rarely." Sends galleys to authors.
Tips: No anthropomorphic stories, pet stories (fiction or nonfiction), fantasy, poetry, science fiction or romance. Writers: "Be as original as possible. Develop characters that lend themselves to series and always be thinking of new and interesting situations for those series. Give your story a strong hook—something that will appeal to a well-defined audience. There is a lot of competition out there for general themes." Looks for: "writers whose stories have specific 'hooks' and audiences, and who actively promote their work."

***PENGUIN CHILDREN'S BOOKS**, 27 Wrights Lane, London W8 5T7 England. (071)416 3000. Imprints: Viking, Hamish Hamilton, Dutton, Puffin. Contact: Children's Reader or Children's Designer. Publishes varying number of picture books, young readers, middle readers and young adult titles/year. Percentage of books by first-time authors vary. Publishes various categories of fiction.
Fiction: Will consider all categories for all ages, preschool through teens. "We are interested in an original approach and good quality writing." Average word length: picture books—under 1,000; young readers—under 3,000; middle readers—under 7,000; young adults—up to 35,000.
How to Contact/Writers: Fiction: Submit outline/synopsis and 3 sample chapters. Reports on queries/mss in 1 month. Publishes a book 1 year after acceptance. Will consider simultaneous submissions.
Illustration: Works with varying number of illustrators/year. Uses both b&w and color artwork. Reviews ms/illustration packages from authors. Submit ms with 1 piece of final art. Contact: Children's Reader. Illustrations only: Query with samples. Reports only if interested. Samples returned with SASE; samples filed.
Tips: "Study the market by reading our hardback catalog. We're most interested in 'series' books."

PENGUIN USA, 375 Hudson St., New York NY 10014. (212)366-2000. See listings for Cobblehill, Dial Books for Young Readers, Dutton Children's Books and Puffin Books.

- Penguin USA ranks 7th, based on net sales, of the top 15 children's publishers.

***PERFECTION LEARNING CORPORATION**, Cover to Cover, 10520 New York, Des Moines IA 50322. (515)278-0133. Fax: (515)278-2245. E-mail: 74140.3526@compuserve.com. Book publisher, independent book producer/packager. Senior Editors: J. Cosson (K-6), M. James (6 and up). Art Director: Randy Messer. Publishes 10 middle readers/year; 10 young adult titles/year.

● Perfection Learning Corp. publishes all hi-lo children's books on a variety of subjects.
Fiction: Middle readers and young adults: hi-lo. Average word length: middle readers—10,000-30,000; young adults: 10,000-30,000. Recently published *When a Hero Dies*; and *Kimo and the Secret Waves*.
Nonfiction: Middle readers and young adults: biography, careers, geography, health, hi-lo, history, multicultural, nature/environment, science, social issues, sports. Does not want to see ABC books. Average word length: middle readers—10,000; young adults—10,000.
How to Contact/Writers: Fiction/Nonfiction: Submit complete ms. Reports on queries in 2 months; mss in 4 months. Publishes a book 18 months after acceptance.
Illustration: Works with 20 illustrators/year. Illustration only: Query with samples; send résumé, promo sheet, client list, tearsheets. Contact: Randy Messer, art director. Reports only if interested. Samples filed. Original artwork returned on a "case by case basis."
Photography: Buys photos from freelancers. Contact: Randy Messer, art director. Buys stock and assigns work. Uses children. Uses color or up to 8× b&w glossy prints; 2¼×2¼, 4×5 transparencies. Submit cover letter, client list, stock photo list, promo piece (color or b&w).
Terms: Pays authors "depending on going rate for industry." Offers advances, Pays illustrators by the project. Pays photographers by the project.
Tips: "Our materials are sold through schools for use in the classroom. Talk to a teacher about his/her needs."

PERSPECTIVES PRESS, P.O. Box 90318, Indianapolis IN 46290-0318. (317)872-3055. Book publisher. Estab. 1982. Publisher: Pat Johnston. Publishes 1-3 picture books/year; 1-3 young reader titles/year. 95% of books by first-time authors.
Fiction/Nonfiction: Picture books, young readers: adoption, foster care, donor insemination or surrogacy. Does not want young adult material. Published *Lucy's Feet*, by Stephanie Stein, illustrated by Kathryn A. Imler, *Two Birthdays for Beth* by Gay Lynn Cronin, illustrated Joanne Bowring and *Let Me Explain: A Story about Donor Insemination*, by Jane Schnitter, illustrated by Joanne Bowring.
How to Contact/Writers: Fiction/Nonfiction: Query or submit outline/synopsis and sample chapters. "No query necessary on subject appropriate picture books." Reports on queries in 2 weeks; mss in 6 weeks. Publishes a book 10-12 months after acceptance.
Illustration: Only interested in agented material. Works with 1-2 illustrators/year. Illustrations only: Submit promo sheet and client list. Reports in 2-6 weeks. Samples returned with SASE.
Terms: Pays authors royalties on a sliding scale based on net sales or by work purchased outright. Pays illustrators royalty or by the project. Sends galleys to authors; dummies to illustrators. Book catalog, ms guidelines available for #10 SAE and 2 first-class stamps.
Tips: "Do your homework! I'm amazed at the number of authors who don't bother to check that we have a very limited interest area and subsequently submit unsolicited material that is completely inappropriate for us. For children, we focus *exclusively* on issues of adoption and interim (foster) care plus families built by donor insemination or surrogacy; for adults we also include infertility issues."

PHILOMEL BOOKS, 200 Madison Ave., New York NY 10016. (212)951-8700. Imprint of The Putnam & Grosset Group. Book publisher. Editorial Director: Patricia Gauch. Associate Editor: Michael Green. Art Director: Cecilia Yung. Publishes 30 picture books/year; 5-10 young reader titles/year. 20% of books by first-time authors; 80% of books from agented writers.
Fiction: All levels: adventure, animal, fantasy, folktales, history, nature/environment, special needs, multicultural. Middle readers, young adults: problem novels. No concept picture books, mass-market "character" books, or series.
Nonfiction: All levels: arts/crafts, biography, history, multicultural, music/dance. "Creative nonfiction on any subject." Average length: "not to exceed 150 pages."
How to Contact/Writers: Fiction/Nonfiction: Query; submit outline/synopsis and sample chapters. Reports on queries in 4-6 weeks. Publishes a book 2 years after acceptance.
Illustration: Works with 20-25 illustrators/year. Reviews ms/illustration packages from artists. Query first. Illustrations only: Query with samples. Send resume, promo sheet, portfolio, slides, client list, tearsheets or arrange personal portfolio review. Reports on art samples in 2 months. Original artwork returned at job's completion.
Terms: Pays authors in royalties. Average advance payment "varies." Illustrators paid by advance and in royalties. Sends galleys to authors; dummies to illustrators. Book catalog, ms/artist's

To convey an atmosphere of mystery and intrigue, artist Michael A. Aspengren used black prisma colored pencil on coquille board in illustrating The Hidden Dagger, *by Margo Sorenson. One of Perfection Learning's new trade book series Cover-to-Cover, the novel is set in 17th-century England, where main character Walter witnesses a murder and sets out to prove the killer's identity. The finely stippled detail ''gives a good feel for the sense of wealth and space in the castle where the murder takes place,'' says Art Director Randy Messer.*

guidelines free on request with SASE (9×12 envelope for catalog).
Tips: Wants "unique fiction or nonfiction with a strong voice and lasting quality. Discover your own voice and own story—and persevere." Looks for "something unusual, original, well-written. Fine art. The genre (fantasy, contemporary, or historical fiction) is not so important as the story itself, and the spirited life the story allows its main character. We are also interested in receiving adolescent novels, particularly novels that contain regional spirit, such as a story about a young boy or girl written from a Southern, Southwestern or Northwestern perspective."

***THE PLACE IN THE WOODS**, Read, America! 3900 Glenwood Ave., Golden Valley MN 55422. (612)374-2120. Fax: (612)593-5593. Book publisher. Publisher/Editor: Roger Hammer. Publishes 2 middle readers/year; 2 young adult titles/year. 100% of books by first-time authors. Books feature primarily diversity/multicultural storyline and illustration.
Fiction: Picture books and young adults: adventure, multicultural, suspense/mystery. Young readers: adventure, animal, fantasy, folktales, hi-lo, humor, multicultural, sports, suspense/mystery. Middle readers: adventure, animal, fantasy, folktales, hi-lo, humor, multicultural, problem novels, sports, suspense/mystery. Average word length: young readers—no limits; middle readers—no limits.
Nonfiction: Picture books and young adults: history, multicultural, special needs. Young readers and middle readers: activity books, animal, hi-lo, history, hobbies, how-to, multicultural, self help, social issues, special needs. sports. Multicultural themes must avoid negative stereo types. Average word length: young readers—no limits; middle readers—no limits.
How to Contact/Writers: Fiction/Nonfiction: Submit complete ms. Reports on queries/mss in 1 week.
Illustration: Works with 2 illustrators/year. Uses primarily b&w artwork only. Reviews ms/illustration packages from authors. Query; submit ms with dummy. Contact: Roger Hammer, editor. Illustration only: Query with samples. Reports in 1 week. Samples with SASE. Original artwork not returned at job's completion. "We buy all rights."
Photography: Buys photos from freelancers. Contact: Roger Hammer, editor. Works on assignment only. Uses photos that appeal to children. Model/property releases required; captions required. Uses any b&w prints. Submit cover letter and samples.
Terms: Work purchased outright from authors ($10-250). Pays illustrators by the project (range: $10-250). Pays photographers by project (range $10-250). For all contracts, "initial payment repeated with each printing." Book available for #10 SAE and 1 first-class stamp; ms and art guidelines available for SASE.

PLANET DEXTER, One Jacob Way, Reading MA 01867. (617)944-3700. Imprint of Addison-Wesley Publishing Co. Book publisher. Contact: Editorial Department. Publishes 10-15 young readers, middle readers/year. 25% of books by first-time authors. Publishes nonfiction interactive books—mainly math and science. No fiction, poetry, whole language or early readers at all. "All of our products are 'book and thing' packages; all proposals should address the 'thing' that would accompany the book (e.g.: calculator, dice, cards). The 'thing' is an integral part of the product and not just a 'value-added item.' "
Nonfiction: Young readers, middle readers: hobbies, how-to, nature/environment, science, math. No curriculum-oriented or textbook-style manuscripts; no characters or narratives. Average word length: middle readers—15,000; young readers—10,000. Published *Planet Dexter's Calculator Mania* (comes with calculator); *Planet Dexter's Money Madness* (comes with real U.S. coins); and *The Card Zone* (comes with playing cards); and *Grossology*, by Sylvia Branzei (comes with magnifying glass).
How to Contact/Writers: Query. Submit outline/synopsis and 2 sample chapters with SASE. Reports in 8-12 weeks. Publishes a book 18 months after acceptance.
Illustration: Works with 1-2 illustrators/year. Uses color artwork only.
Terms: Pay authors royalty, or work purchased outright from authors. Offers advances. Pays illustrators/photographers by the project. Sends final ms to authors for review; dummies to illustrators. Ms guidelines available for SASE.
Tips: "The more thorough a proposal, the better. Include outline, competition analysis, marketing 'hooks,' etc. Children's publishing is as competitive as adult's, so preparation on the author's part is key. We want fun, hip, irreverent, educational titles—books that kids learn from without realizing it (we call it 'stealth learning')."

PLAYERS PRESS, INC., P.O. Box 1132, Studio City CA 91614. (818)789-4980. Book publisher. Estab. 1965. Vice President/Editorial: R. W. Gordon. Publishes 2-10 young readers dramatic plays and musicals/year; 2-10 middle readers dramatic plays and musicals/year; 4-20 young adults dramatic plays and musicals/year. 35% of books by first-time authors; 1% of books from agented writers.
Fiction: "We use all categories (young readers, middle readers, young adults) but only for dramatic plays and/or musicals. No novels or storybooks." Recently published *Tower of London*, a play by William Hezlep; and *Punch and Judy*, a play by William-Alan Landers.
Nonfiction: "Any children's nonfiction pertaining to the entertainment industry, performing arts and how-to for the theatrical arts only." Needs include and activity, arts/crafts, how-to, music/dance, reference and textbook. Published *Stagecrafter's Handbook*, by I.E. Claric; and *New Monologues for Readers Theatre*, by Steven Porter.
How to Contact/Writers: Fiction/Nonfiction: Submit plays or outline/synopsis and sample chapters of entertainment books. Reports on queries in 2-4 weeks; mss in 4 weeks-12months. Publishes a book 10 months after acceptance. No simultaneous submissions.
Illustration: Works with 1-4 illustrators/year. Use primarily b&w artwork. Illustrations only: Submit résumé, tearsheets. Reports on art samples only if interested. Samples returned with SASE; samples filed.
Terms: Pays authors in royalties of 6-12% based on wholesale price or by outright purchase. Pay illustrators by the project; royalties range from 2-5%. Sends galleys to authors; dummies to illustrators. Book catalog available for SASE.
Tips: Looks for "plays/musicals and books pertaining to the performing arts only."

POLYCHROME PUBLISHING CORPORATION, 4509 N. Francisco, Chicago IL 60625. (312)478-4455. Fax: (312)478-0786. Book publisher. Contact: Editorial Board. Publishes 2-4 picture books/year; 1-2 middle readers/year; and 1-2 young adult titles/year. 50% of books are by first-time authors. Books aimed at children of Asian ancestry in the United States.
Fiction: All levels: adventure, contemporary, history, multicultural, problem novels. Multicultural needs include Asian American children's experiences. Not interested in animal stories, fables, fairy tales, folk tales. Recently published *Nene and the Horrible Math Monster*, by Marie Villanueva; *Stella: On the Edge of Popularity*, by Lauren Lee.
Nonfiction: All levels: history, multicultural problem-solving. Multicultural needs include Asian-American themes.
How to Contact/Writers: Fiction/Nonfiction: Submit complete manuscript along with an author's bio regarding story background. Reports on queries in 3-4 months; mss in 4-6 months. Publishes a book 1-2 years after acceptance. Will consider simultaneous submissions.
Illustration: Works with 4 illustrators/year. Reviews ms/illustration packages from artists. Submit ms with bio of author re story background and photocopies of sample illustrations. Contact: Editorial Board. Illustrations only: Query with résumé and samples (can be photocopies) of drawings of multicultural children. Reports back only if interested. Samples returned with SASE; samples filed "only if under consideration for future work."
Terms: Pays authors royalty of 2-10% based on wholesale price. Work purchased outright ($25 minimum). Pays illustrators 2-10% royalty based on wholesale price. Sends galleys to authors; dummies to illustrators. Book catalog available for #10 SAE and 52¢. Manuscript guidelines available for SASE.
Tips: Wants "stories about experiences that will ring true with Asian Americans."

***PPI PUBLISHING**, P.O. Box 292239, Kettering OH 45429. (513)294-5057. Book publisher. Managing Editor: Shary Price. Publishes 30 books/year for grades 7-12. 80% of books by first-time authors; 20% subsidy published. All books are nonfiction, on "hot, contemporary topics."
Nonfiction: Middle readers: careers, health, nature/environment, self-help, social issues, contemporary. Young adults: careers, health, nature/environment, self help, social issues. Recently published *Suicide: Reason for Living*, *Gang Awareness* and *Communication, Commitment & Compromise: A Practical Guide for Teen, Parents & Teachers*.
How to Contact/Writers: Nonfiction: Query; submit outline/synopsis; submit outline/synopsis and 2 sample chapters. Publishes a book 6 months after acceptance. Will consider simultaneous submissions, electronic submissions, previously published work.

INSIDER REPORT

Fun, Irreverent Books Trick Kids Into Learning

"Our goal is to publish books that parents value and kids enjoy," says Liz Doyle, product development coordinator at Planet Dexter, the children's trade imprint of Addison-Wesley. Planet Dexter publishes nonfiction interactive books for young and middle readers called "book and thing" packages; each book comes with a toy that helps kids better understand the information presented to them. For instance, *Calculator Mania!* is accompanied by a working calculator; *Money Madness!* provides the young reader with real U.S. money to spend; and *Grossology* comes with a magnifying glass so kids can get a close-up look at some truly repulsive things.

Doyle refers to the type of learning Planet Dexter promotes as "stealth learning." "Kids think the book is cool and they're having fun, so they don't realize they're learning," she says. A writer needs to relate to kids on their level and convey a sense of fun—while at the same time providing an educational service. "We like manuscripts that are fun, hip, well-written and kid-oriented without being patronizing," Doyle says. Planet Dexter is not interested in fiction, poetry, textbook-like nonfiction or what Doyle calls "Martha Stewart books—those activity books that send kids (and their parents) around the house looking for lime Jell-O, empty toilet paper rolls and one purple go-go boot. We're looking for topics that are fun and educational and lend themselves to including a 'thing'." The 'thing' is an integral part of each book and not just an add-on incentive. "It's much better when the book is written with the 'thing' in mind," Doyle says. "We've rejected great books because there was no 'thing' we could attach."

Educational publishers like Planet Dexter are part of a children's nonfiction market that is growing along with the recent emphasis on home schooling and supplementing a child's public school education. In this age of video games, computers and cable television, nonfiction books must be different and unique to hold a kid's attention. Straightforward text is not enough, and Doyle sees increased need for the stimulation of other senses by including 'things' and dolls along with books. "Nonfiction books have become so much more fun and interactive, much more so than fiction. I'd like to see more interactive fiction and fiction-and-thing books."

Many of Planet Dexter's authors are first-timers, and the publisher seeks fresh voices to bring the stealth-learning concept to children in an entertaining, irreverent manner. When writing for an educational publisher, writers should remember that learning doesn't have to be dull. Doyle sees many manuscripts cross her desk that are too serious, and that come across as patronizing and boring to children. "Be clear and make it fun. We usually reject manuscripts for being too textbooky. Keep it light and put information in context of things kids understand and relate to. Listen to how kids talk. Read what they read, watch the TV and movies they like, and check out the toys they think are cool." Careful research helps a writer keep in touch with what today's kids are interested in—and what they want to

Nonfiction: Picture books: multicultural. Young readers: biography, history, multicultural. Middle readers and young adults: biography, history, multicultural, social issues, special needs. No hard science, series. Average word length: picture books—200-1,500; middle readers: 10,000-30,000; young adults: 30,000-50,000. Recently published *Freedom's Children*, by Ellen Levine; *Crazy Horse* by Judith St. George; and *You Want Women to Vote, Lizzie Stanton?*, by Jean Fritz.
How to Contact/Writers: Fiction/Nonfiction: Query; submit outline/synopsis and 3 sample chapters. Unsolicited picture book mss only. Reports on queries in 1 month; mss in 8-10 weeks. Publishes a book two years after acceptance. Will consider simultaneous submissions on queries only.
Illustration: Works with 40 illustrators/year. Reviews ms/illustration packages from artists. Ms/illustration packages and illustration only: Query. Reports in 6-8 weeks. Samples returned with SASE; samples filed. Original artwork returned at job's completion.
Terms: Pays authors royalty based on retail price. Pays illustrators by the project or royalty based on retail price. Sends galleys to authors. Books catalog and ms guidelines available for SASE.
Tips: "Study our catalogs and get a sense of the kind of books we publish, so that you know whether your project is likely to be right for us."

QUESTAR PUBLISHERS, INC., 305 W. Adams, P.O. Box 1720, Sisters OR 97759. (503)549-1144. Imprint: Gold 'n' Honey. Book publisher. Editorial Coordinator: Melody Carlson. Art Director: David Uttley. Publishes 3-5 picture books/year; 5-8 young readers/year; 1-2 middle readers/year; and 1-2 adult titles/year. 10% of books by first-time authors. Publishes spiritual/religious titles.
How to Contact/Writers: Questar Publishers was not accepting unsolicited mss at the time of publication.
Illustration: Works with 8-12 illustrators/year. Uses color artwork only. Reviews ms/illustration packages from artists. Query. Illustrations only: Query with samples, résumé, promo sheet. Reports back only if interested. Samples filed.
Photography: Buys photos from freelancers. Contact: David Uttley, art director. Buys stock and assigns work. Uses children, animals and nature photos. Model/property releases required; captions required. Uses 35mm, 2¼×2¼, 4×5 transparencies. Submit cover letter, résumé, published samples, color promo piece.
Terms: Pays royalty based on wholesale price. Pays illustrators by the project or royalty. Pays photographers by the project or per photo. Sends galleys to authors.

***🍁RAGWEED PRESS**, P.O. Box 2023, Charlottetown, Prince Edward Island C1A 7N7 Canada. (902)566-5750. Fax: (902)566-4473. Book publisher. Contact: Senior Editor or Designer. Publishes 2 picture books/year; 2 middle readers/year; 1 young adult title/year. 20% of books by first-time authors.
Fiction: Young readers: adventure, folktales, history, multicultural. Middle readers, young adults: adventure, anthology, contemporary, history, multicultural. Average word length: picture books—1,000-24 pages (full color illustration); middle readers: 96 pages; young adults: 256 pages. Recently published The Rosalie Series, including *Rosalie's Catastrophes* and *Rosalie's Big Dream*, by Ginette Anfousse, illustrated by Marisol Sarrazin (for ages 8-12); and *Next Teller, A Book of Canadian Storytelling*, colleted by Dan Yashinsky (for ages 12 and up).
How to Contact/Writers: Fiction: Query. Submit outline/synopsis and 2 sample chapters. Reports on queries/mss in 5-6 months. Publishes a book 6 months from final ms, "up to 2 years before editorial process is completed." Will consider simultaneous submissions.
Illustration: Works with 2-3 illustrators/year. Uses color artwork only. Reviews ms/illustration packages from artists. Query. Submit ms with 3-5 pieces of final art. Contact: Janet Riopelle, designer. Illustrations only: Query with samples. Contact: Janet Riopelle, designer. Reports only if interested. Samples returned with SASE; samples filed. Original artwork returned at job's completion.
Terms: Pays authors/illustrators royalty of 5-10% based on retail price. Sends galleys to authors; dummies to illustrators. Book catalog available for 9×12 SAE and 2 first-class stamps; ms and art guidelines available for SASE.
Tips: "Submit in writing—phone calls won't get results. We do look at everything we receive and make our decision based on our needs. Be patient."

Artist Marisol Sarrazin used oils to depict the exuberance of the title character in the cover art for* Rosalie's Big Dream*, by Ginette Anfousse. Sarrazin's illustration "captures the free-spirited, adventuresome character, and makes a very attractive piece of art that draws the reader to the book," says Louise Fleming, publisher. Fleming adds that children have responded "very positively" to the fun-filled cover art, rendered for the third in a five-book series of Rosalie adventures, written and illustrated by a mother-daughter team.

RANDOM HOUSE BOOKS FOR YOUNG READERS, 201 E. 50th St., New York NY 10022. (212)572-2600. Random House, Inc. Book publisher. Vice President/Publishing Director: Kate Klimo. Executive Editors: Jane Gerver and Linda Hayward. Vice President/Executive Art Director: Cathy Goldsmith. 100% of books published through agents; 2% of books by first-time authors.

- Random House now accepts agented material only. They rank 2nd, based on net sales, of the top 15 children's publishers.

Fiction: Picture books: animal, easy-to-read, history, sports. Young readers: adventure, animal, easy-to-read, history, sports, suspense/mystery. Middle readers: adventure, history, science, sports, suspense/mystery.

Nonfiction: Picture books: animal. Young readers: animal, biography, hobbies. Middle readers: biography, history, hobbies, sports.

How to Contact/Writers: Only interested in agented material.

Illustration: Reviews ms/illustration packages from artists through agent only.

Terms: Pays authors in royalties; sometimes buys mss outright. Sends galleys to authors. Book catalog free on request.

■**READ'N RUN BOOKS**, P.O. Box 294, Rhododendron OR 97049. (503)622-4798. Subsidiary of Crumb Elbow Publishing. Book publisher. Publisher: Michael P. Jones. Publishes 3 picture books/year; 5 young reader titles/year; 2 middle reader titles/year; 5 young adult titles/year. 50% of books by first-time authors; 8% of books from agented writers; 2% subsidy published.

Fiction: All levels: adventure, animal, concept, contemporary, fantasy, folktales, health, history, humor, multicultural, nature/environment, poetry, problem novels, sports. Picture books: anthology. Young readers: anthology, science fiction, suspense/mystery. Middle readers: suspense/mystery. Young adults: hi-lo, religion, romance, science fiction, suspense/mystery.

Nonfiction: All levels: animal, arts/crafts, biography, geography, health, history, hobbies, multicultural, music/dance, nature/environment, religion, science, sports. Picture books: activity books. Young readers: careers, self help, textbooks. Middle readers: activity books, concept. Young adults: hi-lo, religion, romance, science fiction, suspense/mystery.

How to Contact/Writers: Fiction/Nonfiction: Young readers: Animal, arts/crafts, biography, career, concept, geography, health, hi-lo, history, hobbies, how-to, multicultural, music/dance, nature/environment, reference, religion, science, self help, social issues, sports, textbooks. Middle readers: animal, arts/crafts, biography, careers, hi-lo, history, hobbies, multicultural, nature/environment, reference, science, social issues, textbooks. Young adults: animal, arts/crafts, biography, careers, cooking, hi-lo, history, hobbies, multicultural, nature/environment, reference, science, social issues, textbooks. Query. Reports on queries in 2 weeks; mss in 1 month. Publishes a book about 8 months to a year after acceptance depending on workload and previously committed projects. Will consider simultaneous submissions. "If samples and manuscripts are not accompanied by a SASE, we will not return, nor will we maintain them. We are overwhelmed by responses."

Illustration: Works with 50 illustrators/year. "Black & white, 8×10 or 5×7 illustrations. No color work for finished artwork, but color work is great to demonstrate the artist's talents." Reviews ms/illustration packages from artists. Query with entire ms and 5 pieces of the artwork. Reports on ms/art samples in 2 weeks. Illustrations only: Query with samples; provide portfolio, slides and tearsheets. Samples returned with SASE; samples filed if requested by artist. Original artwork returned at job's completion.

Photography: Purchases photos from freelancers. Contact: Michael P. Jones. Buys stock and assigns work. Looking for wildlife, history, nature. Model/property releases required; photo captions optional. Publishes photo essays and photo concept books. Uses 5×7 or 8×10 b&w prints; 4×5 or 35mm transparencies. Query with samples.

Terms: Pays in published copies only. Sends galleys to authors; dummies to illustrators. Book catalog available for $2. Ms/art guidelines available for 1 first-class stamp and #10 SAE.

Tips: "Don't give up. Be flexible and don't be afraid to try new things." Wants natural history and historical books. Sees trend toward "more computer-generated artwork. More environmental and multicultural books are being sought by schools and families."

***🍁REIDMORE BOOKS INC.**, 10109-106 St., 1200, Edmonton, Alberta TSJ 3L7 Canada. (403)424-4420. Fax: (403)441-9919. E-mail: reidmore@compusmart.ab.ca. Book publisher. Editor-in-chief: Leah-Ann Lymer. Publishes 4 textbooks/year (grades 2-12). 25% of books by first-time authors.

- Reidmore Books is not looking at fiction titles this year.

Nonfiction: Young readers: history. Middle readers, young adults/teens: geography, history, multicultural, nature/environment, science, textbooks. Does not want to see "material that is not directly tied to social studies, science or math curricula. No picture books, please." Recently published: *Canada: Its Land and People*, Second Edition, by Don Massey and Pat Shields, illustrated by Yu Chao (grades 5-6, geography textbook).

How to Contact/Writers: Nonfiction: Query, submit complete ms or submit outline/synopsis. Reports on queries in 1 month, mss in 2 months. Publishes a book 18 months after acceptance. Will consider simultaneous submissions.

Illustration: Works with 1 illustrator/year. Uses color artwork only. Illustration only: Query with samples. Contact: Leah-Ann Lymer, editor-in-chief. Samples returned with SASE; samples filed.

Photography: Buys photos from freelancers. Buys stock images. Uses "content-rich photos, often geography-related." Photo captions required. Uses color prints and 35mm transparencies. Submit cover letter.

Terms: Pays authors royalty. Pays illustrators by the project. Pays photographers by the project or per photo. Sends galleys to authors. Book catalog available for 9×12 SAE and 2 first-class stamps.

Tips: "Call first—it tends to speed up the process and saves everyone time, money and effort."

***RHACHE PUBLISHERS, LTD.**, 9 Orchard Dr., Gardiner NY 12525. (914)883-5884. Book publisher. Publisher: Richard H. Adin. Associate Publisher: Carolyn H. Edlund. Publishes 1-5 middle readers/year; 1-5 young adult titles/year. 90% of books by first-time authors. "We are looking for books for children eight and up. They need to be primarily nonfiction. By that, we mean the story line can be fiction (e.g., a mystery) but the story must teach and not too subtly why a 'clue' in the mystery can't be correct because it defies a natural law, with a good solid exploration of that natural law. We are not looking for stories of the 'Little Engine That Could' or the Peter Cottontail type."

Nonfiction: Middle readers and young adults: animal, arts/crafts, biography, careers, cooking, health, history, hobbies, how-to, music/dance, nature/environment, reference, science, self help, computer. Average word length: middle readers—50,000 (minimum); young adults—50,000 (minimum).

How to Contact/Writers: Nonfiction: Query. Submit outline/synopsis and 2-4 sample chapters. Reports on queries in 2-3 weeks; mss in 1 month. Anticipates publishing a book 4 months after acceptance.

Illustration: Uses both b&w and color artwork. Reviews ms/illustration packages from authors. Query. Submit ms with 4-5 pieces of final art. Contact: Carolyn Edlund, associate publisher. Illustrations only: Query with samples, résumé. Reports in 4-5 weeks. Samples returned with SASE. Originals not returned.

Photography: Buys photos from freelancers. Contact: Carolyn Edlund, associate publisher. Buys stock and assigns work. Model/property releases required; captions required. Uses 3×5, 4×5 glossy, color or b&w prints; or 35mm, 4×5 transparencies. Submit cover letter, résumé, samples.

Terms: Pays authors royalty of 10-17.5% based on wholesale price. Pays illustrators royalty of 5-10% based on wholesale price. Pays photographers per photo. Sends galleys to authors. Ms guidelines available for SASE.

RIZZOLI BOOKS FOR CHILDREN, 300 Park Ave. S., New York NY 10010. (212)387-3653. Fax: (212)387-3535. Book publisher. Senior Editor: M. Soares. Publishes 6-10 picture books/year; 2-3 middle readers/year; 2-3 young adult titles/year. 80% of books by first-time authors. Rizzoli Books seeks to introduce children to the world of fine art, architecture, literature and music through artbooks, picture books and biographies. The work of historic and contemporary figures is of interest, in addition to contemporary stories and folk tales.

• Rizzoli is currently not accepting unsolicited manuscripts.

Fiction: Young readers: adventure, anthology, contemporary, folktale, multicultural. Middle readers, young adults: adventure, anthology, contemporary, folktales, history, multicultural, poetry. Average word length: picture books—500-750; middle readers—2,500; and young readers—4,000.

Nonfiction: Young readers: biography, history, multicultural. Middle readers: arts/crafts, biography, cooking, history, multicultural, music/dance, nature/environment. Young adults: biography, cooking, history, multicultural. Multicultural needs include music, poetry, dance, biography. Average word length picture books 500-750; middle readers—2,500; young adults—4,000. Special needs include music, poetry, dance, biography. Average word length: picture books—500-750; middle readers—2,500; young adults—4,000.

How to Contact/Writers: Query.

Terms: Pays authors royalty of 3-10% based on wholesale price. Offers advances (average $2,000-3,000). Pays illustrators by the project (range: $2,000-4,000) or royalty of 3-10% based on wholesale price. Sends galleys to authors; dummies to illustrators. Ms and art guidelines available for SASE.

THE ROSEN PUBLISHING GROUP, 29 E. 21st St., New York NY 10010. (212)777-3017. Book publisher. Estab. 1950. Editorial Contact: Gina Strazzabosco. Publisher: Roger Rosen. Publishes 50 juvenile readers/year; 25 middle readers/year; 50 young adults/year. 35% of books by first-time authors; 3% of books from agented writers.

Nonfiction: Young adults: careers, hi-lo, multicultural, special needs, psychological self-help. No fiction. Average word length: middle readers—10,000; young adults—40,000. Published *Everything You Need to Know When a Parent is in Jail*, (hi-lo, young adult, The Need to Know Library); *The Value of Trust*, by Rita Milios (young adult, The Encyclopedia of Ethical Behavior); *Careers as an Animal Rights Activist*, by Shelly Field (young adult, The Career Series).

How to Contact/Writers: Submit outline/synopsis and sample chapters. Reports on queries/mss in 1-2 months. Publishes a book 9 months after acceptance.

Photography: Buys photos from freelancers. Contact: Roger Rosen. Works on assignment only.

Terms: Pays authors in royalties or work purchased outright. Book catalog free on request.

Tips: "Target your manuscript to a specific age group and reading level and write for established series published by the house you are approaching."

***ROYAL FIREWORKS**, First Ave., Unionville NY 10988. (914)726-3333. Fax: (914)726-3824. Book publisher. Editor: Charles Morgan. Publishes 50 middle readers; 50 young adult titles.

Publishes historical fiction, science fiction, mystery/adventure, growing up/peer pressure, overcoming handicapping situations.

Fiction: Middle readers and young adults: adventure, contemporary, history, problem novels, science fiction, suspense/mystery. "All reasonable word lengths accepted for age levels." Recently published *Death of Old Man Manson*, by D. Mull (grades 5-9, mystery); *Life in Caves*, by G. Cheney (grades 6-12, growing up theme); and *Beyond Yellow Star*, by I. Auerbacher (all ages, biography).

Nonfiction: Middle readers and young adult titles: biography, careers, hobbies, nature/environment, self help.

How to Contact/Writers: Fiction/Nonfiction: Query. Reports on queries in 2 weeks; mss in 3-4 weeks. Publishes a book within 1 year of acceptance.

Illustration: Works with 5-10 illustrators/year. Uses both b&w and color artwork. Reviews ms/illustration packages from authors. Query. Contact: Charles Morgan, editor. Illustration only: Query with samples. Reports only if interested. Samples returned with SASE; samples not filed. Originals not returned.

Photography: Buys photos from freelancers. Contact: Charles Morgan, editor. Works on assignment only. Needs "constantly differ."

ST. ANTHONY MESSENGER PRESS, 1615 Republic St., Cincinnati OH 45210. (513)241-5615. Fax: (513)241-0399. Book publisher. Managing Editor: Lisa Biedenbach. 25% of books by first-time authors. "All books nurture and enrich Catholic Christian life. We also look for books for parents and religious educators."

Nonfiction: Middle readers, young adults: religion. "We like all our resources to include anecdotes, examples, etc., that appeal to a wide, diverse audience." Does not want to see fiction, story books, picture books for preschoolers. Recently published *The Wind Harp and Other Angel Tales*, by Ethel Pochocki (middle to adult readers).

How to Contact/Writers: Query; submit outline/synopsis and sample chapters. Reports on queries in 2-4 weeks; mss in 4-6 weeks. Publishes a book 12-18 months after acceptance.

Illustration: Works with 2 illustrators/year. "We design all covers and do most illustrations in-house." Uses primarily b&w artwork. Reviews ms/illustration packages from artists. Query with samples, résumé. Contact: Mary Alfieri, art director. Reports on queries in 2-4 weeks. Samples returned with SASE; or samples filed.

Photography: Purchases photos from freelancers. Contact: Mary Alfieri, art director. Buys stock and assigns work.

Terms: Pays authors royalties of 10-12% based on net receipts. Offers average advance payment of $600. Pays illustrators by the project. Pays photographers by the project. Sends galleys to authors. Book catalog and ms guidelines free on request.

Tips: "Know our audience—Catholic. We seek popularly written manuscripts that include the best of current Catholic scholarship. Parents, especially baby boomers, want resources for teaching children about the Catholic faith for passing on values."

SASQUATCH BOOKS, 1008 Western Ave., #300, Seattle WA 98110. (206)467-4300. Fax: (206)467-4301. Book Publisher. Acquisitions Editor: Stephanie Irving. Art Director: Nancy Deahl. Publishes 2-3 picture books/year; and 2-3 young readers/year. 40% of books by first-time authors. "Most of our books have something to do with the greater Northwest (Northern California to Alaska) or the Pacific Rim. Most are nonfiction."

Fiction: Picture books, young readers: adventure, animal, folktales, multicultural, nature/environment, special needs. Multicultural needs include Native American, Pacific Rim, Black. "We've also published one book about a little hearing dog and would consider others for the physically or mentally challenged." Does not want to see science fiction, poetry or religion. Average word length: picture books—less than 200; young readers—300-500.

Nonfiction: Picture books, young readers: activity books, animal, arts/crafts, cooking, geography, how-to, multicultural, music/dance, nature/environment, special needs. Multicultural needs include Native American, Pacific Rim, Black. Average word length: picture books—less than 200; young readers—200-600. Recently published *Red Hot Peppers*, by Bob and Diane Boardman (ages 8 and up, jump rope book with tape and rope included); *Seya's Song*, by Ron Hirschi (ages 3 and up, Native American story that shows relationship of salmon to people and seasons); and *O is for Orca*, photographs by Art Wolfe, text by Andrea Helman (ages 3 and up, a Northwest alphabet book).

How to Contact/Writers: Fiction: Query; submit complete ms. Nonfiction: Query; submit outline/synopsis and 2 sample chapters. Include SASE. Reports on queries in 1 month; mss in 3 months. Publishes a book 1 year after acceptance. Will consider simultaneous submissions.
Illustration: Works with 3 illustrators/year. Reviews ms/illustration packages from artists. Send ms with dummy. Contact: Stephanie Irving, acquisitions editor. Illustrations only: Query with samples; provide resume, promo sheets and slides. Contact: Nancy Deahl, art director. Reports in 3 months. Samples returned with SASE; "good ones" filed. Original artwork returned at job's completion.
Photography: Buys photos from freelancers. Contact: Nancy Deahl, art director. Works on assignment only.
Terms: Pays authors royalty of 6-10% based on retail price (split with illustrator); negotiable. Offers advances (Average amount: $2,000.) Pays illustrators royalty of 6-10% based on retail price (split with author); negotiable. Pays photographers royalty of 6-10%; negotiable. Sends galleys to authors; dummies to illustrators. Book catalog available upon request; ms guidelines available for SASE.
Tips: "We concentrate on publishing material with some sort of Northwest regional perspective, but we are not limited by this focus."

***🍁■SCHOLASTIC CANADA LTD.**, 123 Newkirk Rd., Richmond Hill, Ontario L4C 3G5 Canada. (905)883-5300. Fax: (905)882-1648. Book publisher. Assistant Editor: Joanne Richter. Art Director: Yüksel Hassan. Publishes 6 picture books/year; 4 young readers/year; 6 middle readers/year; and 6 young adult titles/year. Co-publishes approximately 20 ms/year. 2% of books by first-time authors.
Fiction: Picture books: adventure, animal, contemporary, fantasy, folktales, humor, multicultural, nataure/environment, poetry. Young readers: adventure, animal, contemporary, fantasy, folktales, hi-lo, history, humor, multicultural, science fiction, sports, suspense/mystery. Middle readers: adventure, animal, contemporary, fantasy, folktales, history, humor, multicultural, nature/environment, problem novels, science fiction, sports, suspense/mystery. Young adults/teens: adventure, contemporary, fantasy, history, humor, multicultural, nature/environment, problem novels, science fiction, sports, suspense/mystery. "We do not have a multicultural program, but welcome characters from diverse ethnic backgrounds." Average word length: picture books—under 1,000; young readers—under 10,000; middle readers—25,000-40,000; young adults/teens—30,000-60,000. Recently published: *The Gypsy Princess*, written and illustrated by Phoebe Gilman (ages 5-8, picture book); *Mistaken Identity*, by Norah McClintock (ages 12-15); and *My Homework is in the Mail*, by Becky Citra (easy reader, ages 6-9).
Nonfiction: Young readers: activity books, animal, arts/crafts, biography, careers, cooking, geography, history, hobbies, how-to, music/dance, reference, science, sports. Middle readers, young adults/teens: activity books, arts/crafts, biography, careers, cooking, geography, history, hobbies, how-to, music/dance, reference, science, sports. Average word length: young readers—16,000-32,000; middle readers, young adult/teens—24,000-64,000. Recently published *Hockey Superstars*, by Paul Romanuh (ages 6-14, poster book); *Big Ben*, by L. Scanlan (ages 8-12, horses/biography); and *Take a Hike*, by S. McKay and D. MacLeod (ages 9-12, hiking).
How to Contact/Writers: Fiction: query; submit outline/synopsis and 2-3 sample chapters. Nonfiction: query. Reports on queries in 2-4 weeks; mss in 1-3 months. Publishes a book 1 year after acceptance.
Illustration: Works with 15 illustrators/year. Illustrations only: Query with samples; send résumé, promo sheets, client list, tearsheets. "No original work, please!" Contact: Yüksel Hassan, art director. Reports only if interested. Samples returned with SASE, samples filed "if we like them." Originals returned at job's completion.
Photography: Buys photos from freelancers. Buys stock and assigns work. Uses color prints, 35mm or 4×5 tranparencies. Submit cover letter, published samples, slides, client list, stock photo list, portfolio, color promo pieces.
Terms: Pays authors royalty of 8% based on retail price. Offers advances. Pays illustrators and photographers by the project ($1,500 minimum), royalty of 5% based on retail price. Sends galleys to authors. Book catalog available for 8½×11 SAE with 90¢ Canadian postage or IRC.

***SCHOLASTIC HARDCOVER**, 555 Broadway, New York NY 10012. (212)343-6100. Book publisher. Imprint of Scholastic Inc. Contact: Editorial Submissions. Publishes 37 picture books/

year; 28 young adult titles/year. 1% of books by first-time authors.

Fiction: Picture books: adventure, animal, concept, contemporary, fantasy, folktales, history, humor, multicultural, nature/environment, poetry. Young readers: adventure, anthology, contemporary, fantasy, folktales, history, humor, multicultural, nature/environment, poetry. Young adults: adventure, anthology, contemporary, fantasy, history, humor, multicultural, poetry. Multicultural needs include strong fictional or nonfictional themes featuring non-white characters and cultures. Does not want to see mainstream religious, bibliotherapeutic, adult. Average length: picture books—varies; young adults—150 pages. Recently published *Winter Poems*, by Barbara Rogasky and Trina Schart Hyman (ages 7 and up, picture book); and *The Glory Field*, by Walter Dean Myers (10 and up, young adult novel).

Nonfiction: Picture books: animal, biography, concept, history, multicultural, nature/environment. Young readers: biography, history, multicultural, nature/environment. Young adults: biography, history, multicultural. Multicultural needs "usually best handled on biography format." Average length: picture book—varies; young adults—150 pages. Recently published *Sense Suspense*, by Bruce McMillan (ages 4-7, photo-picture book); *Fur, Feathers, and Flippers: How Animals Live Where They Do*, by Patricia Lauber (ages 8-10, picture book); and the *Magic School Bus* series.

How to Contact/Writers: Fiction: "Due to large numbers of submissions, we are discouraging unsolicited submissions—send query (don't call!) only if you feel certain we publish the type of book you have written." Nonfiction: young adult titles: query; picture books: submit complete ms. Reports on queries/mss in 6 months. Publishes a book in 1-3 years after acceptance, "depending on chosen illustrator's schedule. Will not consider simultaneous submissions.

Illustrations: Works with 30 illustrators/year. Uses both b&w and color artwork. Reviews ms/illustration packages from authors. Submit ms with dummy. Contact: Editorial Submissions. Illustration only: Query with samples; send tearsheets. Reports only if interested. Samples returned with SASE. Original artwork returned at job's completion.

Photography: Buys photos from freelancers. Contact: Photo Research Dept. Buys stock and assigns work. Uses photos to accompany nonfiction. Model/property releases required; captions required. Submit cover letter, résumé, client list, stock photo list.

Terms: Pays authors by varying royalty (usually standard trade rates) or outright purchase (rarely). Offers variable advance. Pays illustrators by the project (range: varies) or standard royalty based on retail price. Pays photographers by the project or royalty. Sends galleys to authors.

Tips: "Read *currently* published children's books. Revise, rewrite, rework and find your own voice, style and subject. We're looking for something with a theme or style strong enough to overcome the fact that the author/illustrator is unknown in the market. Children's publishers are becoming more selective, looking for irresistable talent and fairly broad appeal, yet still very willing to take risks, just to keep the game interesting."

***SCHOLASTIC INC.**, 555 Broadway, New York NY 10012. (212)343-6100. See listings for Blue Sky Press and Scholastic Hardcover.

- Scholastic won several awards in 1995: a Boston Globe-Horn Book Honor Award for nonfiction for *The Great Fire*, by Jim Murphy; a Coretta Scott King Award for *Christmas in the Big House, Christmas in the Quarters*, by Patricia and Fred McKissack; and two King Honor Awards for *Black Diamond: The Story of the Negro Baseball League*, also by the McKissacks and *The Captive*, by Joyce Hansen. Scholastic does not currently accept unsolicited manuscripts. They rank 5th, based on net sales, of the top 15 children's publishers.

Illustration: Works with 50 illustrators/year. Does not review ms/illustration packages. Illustrations only: Send promo sheet and tearsheets. Contact: Claire Counihan, art director or Marijka Kostiw, associate art director. Reports back only if interested. Samples not returned. Original artwork returned at job's completion.

Terms: All contracts negotiated individually. Sends galleys to author; dummies to illustrators.

SCIENTIFIC AMERICAN BOOKS FOR YOUNG READERS, 131 Greenwood Dr., Masapequa NY 11758. (516)796-6113. Book publisher. Executive Editor: Marc Gave. Approximately 30 titles/year. 25% of books from agented authors. Publishes science, social science, math subjects.

Fiction: "We publish fiction with science or math content if there is real learning *and* entertainment value. In the picture book category are the *Mouse & Mole* books, by Doug Cushman and

The Rajah's Rice, by David Barry. Successful midgrade series include *Dinosaur Detective*, by B.B. Calhoun and *Mathnet Casebooks*, by David D. Connell and Jim Thurman."

Nonfiction: All levels: science, math, nature/ecology, health, anthropology, related biography. All material should have substance but must not resemble a textbook. All books are heavily illustrated. Recently published *One Small Square* series, by Donald M. Silver, illustrated by Patricia J. Wynne (ages 7-12, ecosystems); *Science Superstars* series (ages 8-12, biographies); *In the Air and Eveywhere*, by Jody Marshall, illustrated by Elizabeth McClelland (ages 8 and up, pop-up book of birds), *Incredible Edible Science*, by Tina Seelig (ages 9-14, cooking chemistry).

How to Contact/Writers: Fiction/Nonfiction: Query. Reports on queries in 1 month; reports on mss in 2 months. Will consider simultaneous submissions.

Illustration: Reviews ms/illustration packages from artists. Query. Illustrations only: Query with samples (reply only upon request); submit portfolio for review; provide tearsheets. Contact: Maria Epes, art director, children's books. Reports in 1 month.

Photography: Buys photos from freelancers. Contact: Maria Epes, art director, children's books. Uses scientific subjects. Model/property release required. May publish photo essays. Uses 35mm transparencies. Photographers should query with samples; submit portfolio for review; provide tearsheets.

Terms: Pays authors royalty based on net sales receipts. Offers advances. Pays illustrators by the project or royalty. Photographers paid by the project or per photo. Sends galleys to authors. Book catalog available. Ms and art guidelines available for SASE.

Tips: "Study the publishers' lists to find out who is publishing what. Don't send anything out to a publisher without finding out if the publisher is interested in receiving such material." Looking for "well-researched, well-written, thoughtful but lively books on a focused aspect of science, social science (anthropology, psychology—not politics, history), with lots of kid interest, for ages 4-14. Also now considering toddler material."

SILVER BURDETT PRESS, 250 James St., Morristown NJ 07960. Fax: (201)739-8000. Simon & Schuster Education Group. Imprints: Crestwood House, Dillon Press, Julian Messner, New Discovery. Book publisher. Editor: Dorothy Goeller. Publishes 40 young readers/year and 40 young titles/year. 1% of books by first-time authors.

- Silver Burdett Press currently is not accepting unsolicited manuscripts.

Fiction/Nonfiction: "Our list ranges from pre-school to young adult books, both fiction and nonfiction. This also includes Crestwood House which is a hi-lo nonfiction imprint." Considers all fiction and nonfiction categories. Recently published *Riddle by the River*, *The United States Holocaust Memorial Museum*, *The White Stallions* and *Insects*.

How to Contact/Writers: Only interested in agented material. Fiction/Nonfiction: Submit outline/synopsis and 1 sample chapter. Reports on queries in 6 months; mss in 12 months. Publishes a book 1 year after acceptance. Will consider simultaneous and electronic submissions via disk or modem.

Illustration: Only interested in agented material. Works with 40 illustrators/year. Reviews ms/illustration packages from artists. Submit ms with dummy. Contact: Dorothy Goeller, senior editor. Illustrations only: Submit résumé and portfolio. Reports only if interested. Samples returned with SASE.

Photography: Buys photos from freelancers. Contact: Debbie Biber, senior product editor. Buys stock and assigns work. Captions required. Uses color or b&w prints, ½-full page. Submit published samples and client list.

Terms: Pays authors royalty of 3-7½% based on wholesale or retail price or work purchased outright from authors, $5,000 minimum. Offers advances (average amount: $7,500). Pays illustrators by the project (range: $500-10,000) or royalty of 3-7½% based on wholesale or retail price. Sends galleys to authors; dummies to illustrators. Book catalog available for 9×11 SAE and $2.60 postage.

SILVER MOON PRESS, 126 Fifth Ave., New York NY 10011. (212)242-6499. Book publisher. Managing Editor: Eliza Booth. Publishes 2 picture books/year; 2 books for grades 1-3; 10 books for grades 4-6. 25% of books by first-time authors; 10% books from agented authors.

Fiction: All levels: historical and mystery. Average word length: varies. Recently published *The Conspiracy of the Secret Nine*, by Celia Bland (ages 10-12, historical fiction); and *Told Tales*, by Jo Sepha Sherman (ages 10-12, folktales).

Nonfiction: All levels. Recently published *Techno Lab*, by Robert Sheely (ages 8-12, science).
How to Contact/Writers: Fiction/Nonfiction: Query. Reports on queries in 2-4 weeks; mss in 1-2 months. Publishes a book 1-2 years after acceptance. Will consider simultaneous submissions, electronic submissions via disk or moden, previously published work.
Illustration: Reviews ms/illustration packages from artists. Query. Illustrations only: Query with samples, résumé, client list; arrange personal portfolio review. Reports only if interested. Samples returned with SASE. Original artwork returned at job's completion.
Photography: Buys photos from freelancers. Buys stock and assigns work. Uses archival, historical, sports photos. Captions required. Uses color, b&w prints; 35mm, 2¼×2¼, 4×5, 8×10 transparencies. Submit cover letter, résumé, published samples, client list, promo piece.
Terms: Pays authors royalty or work purchased outright. Pays illustrators by the project, royalty. Pays photographers by the project, per photo, royalty. Sends galleys to authors; dummies to illustrators. Book catalog available for SAE.

SIMON & SCHUSTER BOOKS FOR YOUNG READERS, 1230 Avenue of the Americas, New York NY 10022. (212)698-7200. Imprint of Simon & Schuster Children's Publishing Division. Vice President/Editorial Director: Stephanie Owens Lurie. Art Director: Lucille Chomowicz. Publishes 100 books/year.

- Simon & Schuster ranks 4th, based on net sales, of the top 15 children's publishers.

Fiction: Picture books: animal, contemporary, folktales, history, multicultural, poetry. young readers: Animal, adventure, contemporary, fantasy, folktales, history, humor, multicultural, poetry, mystery. Middle readers: adventure, animal, contemporary, fantasy, history, humor, multicultural, mystery. Young adults: contemporary, multicultural, poetry, suspense/mystery. Does not want to see picture books with anthropomorphic animals; didactic stories; problem novels. Recently published *Walter the Baker*, by Eric Carle; *Heart of a Jaguar*, by Marc Talbert (ages 12 and up, young adult novel); and *Angel's Gate*, by Gary Crew.
Nonfiction: Picture books, middle readers, young readers: animal, biography, history, multicultural, nature/environment, religion, science. Young adults: social issues. "We're looking for multicultural manuscripts that portray a variety of cultures honestly and sensitively."
How to Contact/Writers: Fiction: Submit complete ms to Editorial Director. Reports on queries/mss in 3 months. Publishes book 2-4 years after acceptance. Will consider simultaneous submissions.
Illustration: Works with 75 illustrators/year. Do not submit original artwork. Editorial reviews ms/illustration packages from artists. Submit entire ms, prints, slides or color photocopies of illustrations and dummy to Editorial Director. Illustrations only: Query with samples; provide promo sheet, tearsheets. Contact: Lucille Chomowicz, art director. Reports only if interested. Original artwork returned at job's completion.
Terms: Pays authors royalty (varies) based on retail price. Pays illustrators by the project or royalty (varies) based on retail price. Photographers paid royalty. Ms/artist's guidelines free on request.
Tips: "We're looking for picture books centered on a strong, fully-developed protagonist who grows or changes during the course of the story; YA novels that are challenging and psychologically complex; also imaginative and humorous middle fiction. And we want nonfiction that is as engaging as fiction."

SOUNDPRINTS, 165 Water St., P.O. Box 679, Norwalk CT 06856. (203)838-6009. Fax: (203)866-9944. Book publisher. Assistant Editor: Dana Rau. Publishes 12 picture books/year. 10% of books by first-time authors; 10% of books from agented authors. Subjects published include North American wildlife and habitats.
Fiction: Picture books, young readers: animal, nature/environment. No fantasy or anthropomorphic animals. Average word length: picture books—700. Recently published *Dolphin's First Day*, by Kathleen Weidner Zoehfeld, illustrated by Steven James Petruccio (grades PS-2, picture book); *Woodchuck at Blackberry Road*, by C. Drew Lamm, illustrated by Allen Davis (grades PS-2 picture book); and *Swan Flyway*, by Dana Limpert, illustrated by Jo-Ellen Bosson (grades K-3, picture book).
Nonfiction: Picture books, young readers: animal.
How to Contact/Writers: Query. Reports on queries/mss in 6-8 weeks. Publishing time "can vary from one to two years, depending on where it can fit in our publishing schedule." Will

consider simultaneous submissions. "Do NOT send manuscripts without reading our guidelines first."

Illustration: Works with 8-10 illustrators/year. Uses color artwork only. Illustrations are usually full bleed 2-page spreads. Reviews ms/illustration packages from artists "if subject matter is appropriate." Query. Contact: Dana Rau, assistant editor. Illustrations only: Query with samples; provide résumé, portfolio, promo sheet, slides. "If interest is generated, additional material will be requested." Reports in 1 month. Samples returned with SASE. Original artwork returned at job's completion.

Terms: Pays authors royalty or outright purchase. Offers advances. Pays illustrators by the project or royalty. Book catalog for 8¼×11 SAE and 98¢ postage; ms guidelines and artist guidelines for SASE. "It's best to request both guidelines and catalog. Both can be sent in self-addressed envelope at least 8½×11 with 98¢ postage."

Tips: Wants a book that "features North American wildlife and habitats with great accuracy while capturing the interest of the reader/listener through an entertaining storyline."

THE SPEECH BIN, INC., 1965 25th Ave., Vero Beach FL 32960. (407)770-0007. Fax: (407)770-0006. Book publisher. Senior Editor: Jan J. Binney. Publishes 10-12 books/year. 50% of books by first-time authors; less than 15% of books from agented writers. "Nearly all our books deal with treatment of children (as well as adults) who have communication disorders of speech or hearing or children who deal with family members who have such disorders (e.g., a grandparent with Alzheimer's disease or stroke)."

Fiction: Picture books: animal, easy-to-read, fantasy, health, special needs. Young readers, middle readers, young adult: health, special needs.

Nonfiction: Picture books, young readers, middle readers, young adults: activity books, health, textbooks, special needs. Published *Chatty Hats and Other Props*, by Denise Mantione; *Holiday Hoopla: Holiday Games for Language & Speech*, by Michele Rost; and *Speech Sports*, by Janet M. Shaw.

How to Contact/Writers: Fiction/Nonfiction: Query. Reports on queries in 4-6 weeks; mss in 2-3 months. Publishes a book 10-12 months after acceptance. "Will consider simultaneous submissions *only* if notified; too many authors fail to let us know if manuscript is simultaneously submitted to other publishers! We *strongly* prefer sole submissions."

Illustration: Works with 4-5 illustrators/year ("usually inhouse"). Reviews ms/illustration packages from artists. Ms/illustration packages and illustration only: "Query first!" Submit tearsheets (no original art). SASE required for reply or return of material. Original artwork returned at job's completion.

Photography: Photographers should contact Jan J. Binney, senior editor. Buys stock and assigns work. Looking for scenic shots. Model/property releases required. Uses glossy b&w prints, 35mm or 2¼×2¼ transparencies. Submit résumé, business card, promotional literature or tearsheets to be kept on file.

Terms: Pays authors in royalties based on selling price. Pay illustrators by the project. Photographers paid by the project or per photo. Sends galleys to authors. Book catalog for 4 first-class stamps and 9×12 SAE; ms guidelines for #10 SASE.

SRI RAMA PUBLISHING, Box 2550, Santa Cruz CA 95063. (408)426-5098. Book publisher. Estab. 1975. Secretary/Manager: Karuna K. Ault. Publishes 1 or fewer young reader titles/year.

Illustration: Illustrations used for fiction. Will review artwork for possible future assignments. Contact: James McElheron, graphic design director. Not reviewing at this time, however.

Terms: "We are a nonprofit organization. Proceeds from our sales support an orphanage in India, so we encourage donated labor, but each case is worked out individually." Pays illustrators $200-1,000. Sends galleys to authors; dummies to illustrators. Book catalog free on request.

Always include a self-addressed, stamped envelope (SASE) with submissions within your own country. When sending material to other countries, include a self-addressed envelope (SAE) and International Reply Coupons (IRCs).

STANDARD PUBLISHING, 8121 Hamilton Ave., Cincinnati OH 45231. (513)931-4050. Book publisher. Director: Mark Taylor. Children's Editor: Diane Stortz. Creative Director: Coleen Davis. Number and type of books vary yearly. Many projects are written inhouse. No juvenile or young adult novels. 25-40% of books by first-time authors; 1% of books from agented writers. Publishes well-written, upbeat books with a Christian perspective.
Fiction: Adventure, animal, contemporary, Bible stories. Average word length: board/picture books—400-1,000.
Nonfiction: Bible background, nature/environment, sports devotions. Average word length: 400-1,000.
How to Contact/Writers: Fiction/Nonfiction: Send complete ms except for longer works. Reports on queries/mss in 2 months. Publishes a book 18 months after acceptance. Will consider simultaneous and electronic submissions via disk or modem.
Illustration: Works with 6-10 new illustrators/year. Illustrations only: Submit cover letter and photocopies. Contact: Coleen Davis, creative director. Reports on art samples only if interested.
Terms: Pays authors royalties of 5-10% based on wholesale price or work purchased outright (range $250-1,000). Sends galleys to authors. Book catalog available for $2 and 8½×11 SAE; ms guidelines for letter-size SASE.
Tips: "We look for manuscripts that help draw children into a relationship with Jesus Christ; help children develop insights about what the Bible teaches; make reading an appealing and pleasurable activity."

STARBURST PUBLISHERS, P.O. Box 4123, Lancaster PA 17604. (717)293-0939. Editorial Director: Ellen Hake. Publishes 10-15 picture books/year. 60% of books by first-time authors; 25% of books from agented authors. "Only looking for Bible-related children's books."
Nonfiction: All levels: religion. Only interested in Bible related themes. Recently published *The Truth About Power Rangers*, by Phil Phillips.
How to Contact/Writers: Submit outline, 3 sample chapters, bio, photo and SASE. Reports on queries in 2-3 weeks; mss in 6-8 weeks. Publishes a book less than 1 year after acceptance. Will consider simultaneous submissions.
Illustration: Works with 2 illustrators/year. Reviews ms/illustration packages from artists. Query; submit ms with 3 pieces of final art. Contact: Ellen Hake, editorial director. Illustrations only: Query with samples; provide résumé. Reports on queries in 1 month. Cannot return samples. Original artwork returned at job's completion.
Terms: Pays authors royalty of 6-16% based on net price to retailer. Pays illustrators by the project ($100 minimum). Sends galleys to authors; dummies to illustrators. Book catalog available for 9×12 SAE and 5 first-class stamps; ms guidelines available for SASE.

STEMMER HOUSE PUBLISHERS, INC., 2627 Caves Rd., Owings Mills MD 21117. (410)363-3690. Fax: (410)363-8459. Book publisher. Estab. 1975. President: Barbara Holdridge. Publishes 1-3 picture books/year. "Sporadic" numbers of young reader, middle reader, young adult titles/year. 60% of books by first-time authors.
Fiction: Picture books, young readers: folktales, history, multicultural, nature/environment. Does not want to see anthropomorphic characters. Recently published *How Pleasant to Know Mr. Leon: Poems by Edward Leon*, illustrated by Bohdan Butenko; and *The Marvelous Maze*, by Maxine Rose Schur, illustrated by Robin DeWitt and Patricia DeWitt-Grush.
Nonfiction: Picture books: young readers: animal, arts/crafts, biography, multicultural, music/dance, nature/environment. Multicultural needs include Native American, African. Published *The Hawaiian Coral Reef Coloring Book*, by Katherine Orr; *The First Teddy Bear*, by Helen Kay, illustrations by Susan Kranz.
How to Contact/Writers: Fiction/Nonfiction: Query; submit outline/synopsis and sample chapters. Reports on queries/mss in 2 weeks. Publishes a book 18 months after acceptance. Will consider simultaneous submissions.
Illustration: Works with 2 illustrators/year. Uses color artwork only. Reviews ms/illustration packages from artists. Query first with several photocopied illustrations. Contact: Barbara Holdridge, president. Illustrations only: Submit tearsheets and/or slides (with SASE for return). Reports in 2 weeks. Samples returned with SASE; samples filed. Original artwork returned at job's completion.
Terms: Pays authors royalties of 4-15% based on wholesale price. Offers average advance payment of $300. Pays illustrators royalty of 4-5% based on wholesale price. Pays photographers

4-5% royalty. Sends galleys to authors. Book catalog and ms guidelines for 9×12 SASE.
Tips: Writers: "Simplicity, literary quality and originality are the keys." Wants to see ms/illustration packages.

STERLING PUBLISHING CO., INC., 387 Park Ave. S., New York NY 10016. (212)532-7160. Fax: (212)213-2495. Book publisher. Acquisitions Director: Sheila Anne Barry. Publishes 30 middle readers/year. 10% of books by first-time authors.
Nonfiction: Middle readers: activity books, animal, arts/crafts, geography, ghosts, hobbies, music, humor, true mystery, nature/environment, reference, science, sports, supernatural incidents. "Since our books are highly illustrated, word length is seldom the point. Most are 96-128 pages." Does not want to see fiction, poetry, story books or personal narratives. Recently published *Ballet Beginners*, by Marie-Laure Medova (ages 8 and up); *Magnet Science*, written and illustrated by Glen Vecchione (ages 9 and up); and *Great Card Tricks*, by Bob Longe, illustrated by Myron Miller (ages 9 and up, easy to follow instructions).
How to Contact/Writers: Reports on queries in 1-2 weeks; mss in 1-12 weeks. "If we are interested it may take longer." Publishes a book 6-18 months after acceptance. Will consider simultaneous submissions.
Illustration: Works with 10 illustrators/year. Reviews ms/illustration packages from artists. "Query first." Illustrations only: "Send sample photocopies of line drawings; also examples of some color work." Reports only if interested. Original artwork returned at job's completion "if possible, but usually held for future needs."
Terms: Pays authors in royalties of up to 10%; "standard terms, no sliding scale, varies according to edition." Usually pays illustrators flat fee/project. Sends galleys to authors. Ms guidelines for SASE.
Tips: Looks for "humor, hobbies, science books for middle-school children." Also, "mysterious occurrences, activities and fun and games books."

SUNBELT MEDIA, INC./EAKIN PRESS, P.O. Box 90159, Austin TX 78709. (512)288-1771. Fax: (512)288-1813. Book publisher. Estab. 1978. President: Ed Eakin. Publishes 1-2 picture books/year; 2-3 young readers/year; 9 middle readers/year; 2 young adult titles/year. 50% of books by first-time authors; 5% of books from agented writers.
Fiction: Picture books: animal. Middle readers, young adults: history, sports. Average word length: picture books—3,000; young readers—10,000; middle readers—15,000-20,000; young adults—20,000-30,000. "90% of our books relate to Texas and the Southwest."
Nonfiction: Picture books: animal. Middle readers and young adults: history, sports. Recently published *Sam and the Speaker's Chair*.
How to Contact/Writers: Fiction/Nonfiction: Query. Reports on queries in 2 weeks; mss in 6 weeks. Publishes a book 18 months after acceptance. Will consider simultaneous submissions.
Illustration: Reviews ms/illustration packages from artists.Query. Illustrations only: Submit tearsheets. Reports on art samples in 2 weeks.
Terms: Pays authors royalties of 10-15% based on net to publisher. Pays for separate authors and illustrators: "Usually share royalty." Pays illustrators royalty of 10-15% based on wholesale price. Sends galleys to authors. Book catalog, ms/artist's guidelines for $1.25 postage and SASE.
Tips: Writers: "Be sure all elements of manuscript are included—include bio of author or illustrator." Submit books relating to Texas only.

SUNDANCE PUBLISHING, 234 Taylor St., Littleton MA 01460. (508)486-9201. Book distributor and publisher of teacher resources.
Fiction: Picture books, young reader: folktales, multicultural.
Nonfiction: Picture books: activity books, biography, geography, multicultural, photo essays. Young readers, young adults: activity books, geography, multicultural (all groups, strong contemporary narratives). Middle readers: geography, multicultural. Multicultural needs include "all groups; strong, contemporary narratives." Average word length: picture books—300-500; young readers—1,500-4,000. Published *Regalia: Native American Dress & Dance*, by Russell Peters, photos by Richard Haynes (ages preschool-8, "Big Books").
How to Contact/Writers: Fiction: Query (for young readers and up); submit complete ms (for picture books). Nonfiction: Query. Reports on queries/ms in 6-8 weeks.
Illustration: Works with 10 illustrators/year. Reviews ms/illustration packages from artists. Query with samples. Contact: Susan A. Blair, executive editor. Reports in 6-8 weeks only if

interested. Samples returned with SASE; samples "sometimes" filed. Original artwork "usually" returned.

Photography: Buys photos from freelancers. Buys stock and assigns work. Uses series of multicultural subjects. Model/property releases required; captions required. Uses 4×5 transparencies. Photographers should submit cover letter, résumé, published samples, client list.

Terms: "Fees vary, depending on project."

Tips: "We're a school publisher. Only submit school material to us. We are interested in curriculum materials to accompany works of literature."

TAMBOURINE BOOKS, 1350 Sixth Ave., New York NY 10019. Imprint of William Morrow & Co. Inc. Book publisher. Editor-in-Chief: Paulette Kaufmann. Art Director: Golda Laurens. Publishes 20 picture books/year; 4 middle readers/year; 2 young adults/year.

Fiction/Nonfiction: No primary theme for fiction or nonfiction—publishes various categories.

How to Contact/Writers: Fiction/Nonfiction: Submit complete ms. Reports on mss in 1-3 months.

Illustration: Reviews ms/illustration packages from artists. Submit complete package. Illustrations only: Submit portfolio for review; provide résumé, business card, promotional literature or tearsheets to be kept on file. Original artwork returned at job's completion.

Terms: Pays authors royalty based on retail price. Offers advances. Pays illustrators royalty. Sends galleys to authors. Book catalog available for 9×12 SASE; ms guidelines available for SASE.

TEXAS CHRISTIAN UNIVERSITY PRESS, Box 30783, Fort Worth TX 76129. (817)921-7822. Fax: (817)921-7333. Book Publisher. Editorial Contact: Judy Alter. Art Director: Tracy Row. Publishes 1 young adult title/year. 75% of books by first-time authors. Only publishes historical works set in Texas.

Fiction: Young adults/teens: Texas history. Average word length: 35,000-50,000. Recently published *Whistle Punk*, by Alice Chapin and Kent Ross; *Cherub in Stone*, by Catherine Gonzalez; and *A House Divided*, by Marj Gurasich. Does not want to see picture books, inspirational fiction.

Nonfiction: Young adults/teens: Texas biography, Texas history. Average word length: 35,000-50,000.

How To Contact/Writers: Fiction/Nonfiction: Query. Reports on queries in 1 week; mss in 1 month. Publishes a book 1-2 years after acceptance.

Illustration: Works with 1 illustrator/year. Reviews ms/illustration packages from artists. Ms/illustration packages and illustration only: Query with samples. Contact: Tracy Row, art director. Reports back to artists within 1 week. Originals returned to artist at job's completion.

Terms: Pays in royalty of 10% based on net sales. Pays illustrators by the project. Book catalog free on request. Ms guidelines free on request.

Tips: Wants "well written, thoroughly researched historical fiction set in Texas. We are interested in fiction portraying various ethnicities."

✤THISTLEDOWN PRESS LTD., 633 Main St., Saskatoon, Saskatchewan S7H 0J8 Canada. (306)244-1722. Book publisher. Contact: Patrick O'Rourke. Publishes numerous middle reader and young adult titles/year. "Thistledown originates books by Canadian authors only, although we have co-published titles by authors outside Canada. We do not publish children's picture books."

Fiction: Middle readers: animal, folktales. Young adults: adventure, contemporary, folktales, humor, multicultural, suspense/mystery. Average word length: middle readers—35,000; young adults—40,000. Published *The Blue Jean Collection*, by various authors (young adult, short story anthology); *Fish House Secrets*, by Kathy Stinson (young adult); *The Mystery of the Missing Will*, by Jeni Mayer (middle reader, mystery series) and *Notes Across the Aisle*, edited by Peter Carver.

How to Contact/Writers: Submit outline/synopsis and sample chapters. Reports on queries in 3 weeks, mss in 3-6 months. Publishes a book about one year after acceptance. No simultaneous submissions.

Illustration: Works with 2-3 illustrators/year. Illustrations only: Query with samples, promo sheet, slides, tearsheets. Contact: A.M. Forrie, art director.

Terms: Authors' pay negotiaged. Pays illustrators by the project (range: $250-750). Sends galleys to authors. Book catalog free on request. Ms guidelines for #10 envelope and IRC.

***THOMSON LEARNING**, One Penn Plaza, 41st Floor, New York NY 10301. (212)594-8211. Fax: (212)594-8685. Book publisher. Publishes 20 young readers; 130 middle readers; 10 young adult titles.

Nonfiction: Young readers, middle readers and young adults: history and science.

- Thomson Learning is not accepting any manuscripts at this time. Please do not submit ms before querying.

***THORSON & ASSOCIATES**, P.O. Box 94135, Washington MI 48094. (810)781-0907. Editorial Director: Timothy D. Thorson. 60% of books by first time authors. All children's books are nonfiction and relate to architecture, history, archeology or technology.

Nonfiction: Young adults: history, nature/environment, reference, science. Recently published *The Seven Wonders of the Ancient World* (a large format illustrated book engineered to introduce young minds to architecture and archeology through an examination of 7 ancient masterpieces); and *The Backyard Wilderness* (a profusely illustrated guide which introduces school age children to science through the natural wonders that surround us every day).

How to Contact/Writers: Nonfiction: Query. Reports on queries/mss in 1 month. Publishes a book at least 18 months after acceptance. Will consider simultaneous submissions, electronic submissions via disk or modem, previously published work.

Illustration: Works with 2-3 illustrators/year. Uses both b&w and color artwork. Reviews ms/illustration packages from authors. Query. Contact: Timothy D. Thorson. Illustrations only: Query with samples; résumé; promo sheet. Reports in 1 month. Samples returned with SASE; samples filed. Original artwork returned at job's completion.

Photography: Buys photos from freelancers. Contact: Timothy D. Thorson. Buys stock and assigns work. Uses photos on aviation, automotive, architecture (ancient to modern). Model/property releases required; captions required. Submit cover letter, résumé.

Terms: Authors paid "competitive royalties." No advance offered. Photographer's pay negotiable. Ms and art guidelines available for SASE.

Tips: "We're looking for well-researched and illustrated nonfiction books with sales possibilities in the adult market. We are primarily a book producer."

TICKNOR & FIELDS, See Houghton Mifflin Co. listing.

***TILBURY HOUSE, PUBLISHERS**, 132 Water St., Gardiner ME 04345. (207)582-1899. Fax: (207)582-8227. Book publisher. Associate Publisher: Jennifer Elliott. Publishes 1-3 young readers/year.

Fiction: Young readers and middle readers: multicultural, nature/environment. Special needs include books that teach children about tolerance and how to honor diversity.

Nonfiction: Young readers and middle readers: multicultural, nature/environment. Recently published *Talking Walls* and *Who Belongs Here?* both by Margy Burns Knight, illustrated by Anne Sisley O'Brien (middle readers).

How to Contact/Writers: Fiction/Nonfiction: Submit outline/synopsis. Reports on queries/mss in 1 month. Publishes a book 1-2 years after acceptance. Will consider simultaneous submissions "with notification."

Illustration: Works with 1-2 illustrators/year. Illustrations only: Query with samples. Contact: J. Elliott, associate publisher. Reports in 1 month. Samples returned with SASE. Original artwork returned at job's completion.

Photography: Buys photos from freelancers. Contact: J. Elliott, associate publisher. Works on assignment only.

Terms: Pays authors royalty. Pays illustrators/photographers by the project; royalty. Sends galleys to authors. Book catalog available for 9×12 SAE and 78¢ postage.

Tips: "We are primarily interested in children's books that teach children about tolerance in a multicultural society and how to honor diversity. We are also interested in books that teach children about environmental issues."

***TIME-LIFE FOR CHILDREN**, Subsidiary of Time Life, Inc., 777 Duke St., Alexandria VA 22314. (703)838-5264. Fax: (703)838-7209. Book publisher. Contact: Mary Saxton. Senior Art Director: Sue White. "Contact in writing only—no calls!" Publishes 4 picture books/year; 8 young readers/year; and 6 middle readers/year.

Fiction: Picture books: animal, concept, health, nature/environment, religion. Young readers: animal, health, history, nature/environment, religion. Middle readers: adventure, fantasy, health, history, humor, nature/environment, sports, suspense/mystery. Young adults: adventure, history, sports, suspense/mystery. Does not want to see single titles—"only series concepts." Average word length: picture books—0-300; young readers—1,000-3,000.
Nonfiction: Picture books: animal, concept, nature/environment, religion, values. Young readers: animal, health, nature/environment, reference, religion, science, values. Middle readers: animal, geography, health, history, nature/environment, reference, science, sports. Young adults: geography, history, nature/environment, reference, science. Does not want to see single titles—"only series concepts." Average word length: picture books: 0-300; young readers: 1,000-3,000; middle readers: any; young adult titles: any. Recenly published *Why Do Roosters Crow?: First Questions and Answers About Farms*, by Jacqueline Ball, illustrated by Peter and Jim Kavanagh (ages 2-5, first reference book); *What Do You Hear?: A Book About Animal Sounds*, by Anne Miranda, illustrated by Jean Pidgeon (ages 1-3, concept book); *Simple Experiments* (ages 4-8, reference book).
How to Contact/Writers: Fiction/Nonfiction: Query, submit complete ms, submit outline/synopsis. Reports on queries in 2 weeks; mss in 3 weeks. Publishes a book 6 months after acceptance. Will consider simultaneous submissions, electronic submissions via disk, previously published work.
Illustration: Works with 10-20 illustrators/year. Uses both b&w and color artwork. Reviews ms/illustration packages from authors. Submit ms with dummy. Contact: Mary Saxton. Illustration only: Query with samples; tearsheets. Reports only if interested. Samples not returned; samples filed. Original artwork returned at job's completion.
Photography: Uses photos from freelancers. Contact: Jack Weiser, Director of Photography and research, Time-Life, Inc. Buys stock and assigns work. Model/property releases required; captions required. Uses 35mm transparencies.
Terms: Work purchased outright from authors. Pays illustrators by the project. "Important: We require authors to sign a release form before we review their work. Send SASE to receive form."
Tips: "We're looking for nonfiction educational books that can be published in continuity series."

TOR BOOKS, Forge, Orb, 175 Fifth Ave., New York NY 10010. Publisher, Children's and Young Adult Division: Kathleen Doherty. Children's, Young Adult Editor: Jonathan Schmidt. Educational Sales Coordinator: Nichole Rajana. Publishes 2-3 picture books/year; 5-10 young readers/year; 10-15 middle readers/year; 20-25 young adults/year.
Fiction: Young readers: humor, multicultural, nature. Middle readers, young adult titles: adventure, contemporary, history, humor, multicultural, nature/environment, problem, suspense/mystery. "We are interested and open to books which tell stories from a wider range of perspectives. We are interested in materials that deal with a wide range of issues." Average word length: picture books—5,000; young readers—10,000; middle readers—10,000; young adults—30,000-60,000. Published *The Furious Flycycle*, by Jan Wahl/Ted Erik (ages 6-12/children's, fully illustrated); *The Eyes of Kid Midas*, by Neal Shusterman (ages 10-16, young adult novel).
Nonfiction: Young readers, middle readers: activity books, geography, history, how-to, multicultural, nature/environment, science, social issues. Young adult: geography, history, multicultural, nature/environment, social issues. Does not want to see religion, cooking. Average word length: young readers—6-10,000; middle readers—10,000-15,000; young adults—40,000. Published *Strange Unsolved Mysteries*, by Phyllis Rabin Emert; *Stargazer's Guide* (to the Galaxy to the Galaxy), by Q.L. Peorce (ages 8-12, guide to constellations, illustrated).
How to Contact/Writers: Fiction/Nonfiction: Submit outline/synopsis and 3 sample chapters or complete ms. Reports on queries in 1 month; mss in 2-3 months.
Illustration: Works with 40 illustrators/year. Reviews ms/illustration packages from artists. Query with samples. Contact: Nichole Rajana or Jonathan Schmidt. Reports only if interested. Samples returned with SASE; samples kept on file.
Terms: Pays authors royalty. Offers advances. Pays illustrators by the project. Book catalog available for 9×12 SAE and 3 first-class stamps.
Tips: "Know the house your are submitting to, familiarize yourself with the types of books they are publishing. Get an agent. Allow him/her to direct you to publishers who are most appropriate. It saves time and effort."

***TREASURE CHEST BOOKS**, P.O. Box 5250, Tuscon AZ 85703. (520)623-9558. Fax: (520)624-5888. Book publisher. Publisher: Ross Humphreys. Publishes 2-4 picture books/year.
Fiction: Picture books: animal, contemporary, fantasy, folktales, history, humor, multicultural, nature/environment. Special needs include Southwestern US cultures. Average word length: picture books—1,200.
Nonfiction: Picture books: animal, multicultural, nature/environment. Special needs include Southwestern US cultures.
How to Contact/Writers: Fiction: Query. Submit complete ms. Reports on queries in 1 month; mss in 2 months. Publishes a book 1 year after acceptance. Will consider simultaneous submissions, electronic submissions via disk or modem, previously published work.
Illustration: Works with 2 illustrators/year. Reviews ms/illustration packages from artists. Send ms with dummy. Illustrations only: Query with samples. Reports in 2 months. Samples returned with SASE; samples filed. Original artwork returned at job's completion.
Photography: Buys photos from freelancers. Contact: Ross Humphreys. Buys stock and assigns work. Model/property releases required; captions required. Submit cover letter.
Terms: Pays authors royalty. Pays illustrators by the project, royalty. Pays photographers by the project, per photo, royalty. Sends galleys to authors; dummies to illustrators. Ms guidelines available for SASE.

TRICYCLE PRESS, P.O. Box 7123, Berkeley CA 94707. Acquisitions Editor: Nicole Geiger. Publishes 5 picture books/year; 1 young adult/year. 30% of books by first-time authors.
Fiction: Picture books: Concept, folktales, health, multicultural, nature/environment. Middle readers: Health, multicultural, nature/environment. Average word length: picture books-1,200. Recently published *Fairies from A to Z*, by Adrienne Keith and Wendy Wallin Malinow (ages 3 and up); and Amelia's Notebook, by Merissa Moss (ages 7-9, picture book).
Nonfiction: Picture books: Activity books, arts/crafts, concept, geography, health, how-to, nature/environment, science, self help, social issues. Young readers: Activity books, arts/crafts, health, how-to, nature/environment, science, self help, social issues. Middle readers: Activity books, health, nature/environment, science, self help. Young adults: Careers, concept, health, how-to, reference, self help, social issues. Recently published *Ask Me If I Care: Voices from an American High School*, Nancy Rubin (ages 14 and up); *More Mudpies: 101 Alternatives to Television*, by Nancy Blakey (ages 2-12, activity book); and *Pretend Soup and Other Real Recipes: A Cookbook for Preschoolers and Up*, by Mollie Katzen and Ann Henderson (ages 3-6, children's cookbook).
How to Contact/Writers: Fiction: Submit complete ms for picture books; submit outline/synopsis and 3 sample chapters for anything else. Nonfiction: Submit complete ms. Reports on queries/mss in 8-10 weeks. Publishes a book 1 year after acceptance. Will consider simultaneous submissions.
Illustration: Works with 6 illustrators/year. Reviews ms/illustration package from artists. Submit ms with dummy. Contact: Nicole Geiger, acquisitions editor. Illustrations only: Query with samples, promo sheet, tearsheets. Reports back only if interested. Samples returned with SASE; samples filed. Original artwork returned at job's completion unless work for hire.
Terms: Pays authors 15% royalty (but lower if illustrated ms) based on wholesale price. Offers advances. Pays illustrators by the project or royalty. Sends galleys to authors. Book catalog for 9×12 SAE and 98¢. Ms guidelines for SASE.
Tips: "We are looking for something a bit outside the mainstream and with lasting appeal (no one-shot-wonders). Lately we've noticed a sacrifice of quality writing for the sake of illustration."

TROLL ASSOCIATES, 100 Corporate Dr., Mahwah NJ 07430. Book publisher. Editor: Marian Frances.

- Troll Associates is not accepting unsolicited manuscripts at this time.

Illustration: Reviews ms/illustration packages from artists. Contact: Marian Frances, editor. Illustrations only: Query with samples; arrange a personal interview to show portfolio; provide résumé, promotional literature or tearsheets to be kept on file. Reports in 2-4 weeks.

TROPHY BOOKS, 10 E. 53rd St., New York NY 10022. Fax: (212)207-7915. Subsidiary of HarperCollins Children's Books Group. Book publisher. Publishes 6-9 chapter books/year, 25-30 middle grade titles/year, 30 reprint picture books/year, 25-30 young adult titles/year.

• Trophy is primarily a paperback reprint imprint. They do not publish original illustrated manuscripts.

TUDOR PUBLISHERS, INC., P.O. Box 38366, Greensboro NC 27438. Contact: Pam Cox. Publishes 1 middle readers/year; 2 young adults/year. 30% of books by first-time authors. Primarily publishes young adult novels and fiction.

Fiction: Young adults: adventure, contemporary, health, multicultural (African-American, Native American), problem novels, sports. Does not want to see romance. Word length varies. Recently published *Locked Out*, by Margaret Yang (young adult novel), and *The Sweet Revenge of Melissa Chavez*, by Neil Davidson (young adult novel).

Nonfiction: Middle readers, young adults: biography, health, history, multicultural (folklore, history), reference, self-help, social issues, sports. Average word length: middle readers—10,000-12,000; young adults—15,000-25,000. Recently published *Who's Who on the Moon; A Biographical Dictionary of Lunar Nomenclature*, by Elijah E. Cocks and Josiah C. Cocks (Reference).

How to Contact/Writers: Fiction: Submit outline/synopsis and 3 sample chapters. Nonfiction: Submit outline/synopsis and 1-3 sample chapters. Reports on queries in 4-6 weeks; mss in 1-2 months. Publishes a book 9-12 months after acceptance.

Illustration: Reviews ms/illustrations packages from artists. Query. Contact: Pam Cox, senior editor. Reports in 4-6 weeks. Samples returned with SASE; samples filed. Original artwork returned at job's completion.

Terms: Pays authors royalty of 8-10% based on wholesale price. Pays illustrators by the project (range: $100-350). Pays photographers by the project (range: $50-150). Offers "occasional modest advance." Sends galleys to authors. Book catalog available for #10 SAE and 1 first-class stamp.

TYNDALE HOUSE PUBLISHERS, INC., 351 Executive Dr., P.O. Box 80, Wheaton IL 60189. (708)668-8300. Book publisher. Children's editorial contact: Marilyn Dellorto. Children's illustration contact: Marlene Muddell. Publishes approximately 20 children's titles/year.

• Tyndale House no longer reviews unsolicited manuscripts.

Fiction: Middle readers: adventure, religion, suspense/mystery.

Nonfiction: Picture books: activity books, religion. Young readers: religion.

How to Contact/Writers: Fiction/Nonfiction: Query. Reports on queries in 6 weeks.

Illustration: Uses full-color for book covers, b&w or color spot illustrations for some nonfiction. Illustrations only: Query with photocopies (color or b&w) of samples, résumé.Contact: Marlene Muddell.

Photography: Buys photos from freelancers. Contact: Marlene Muddell. Works on assignment only.

Terms: Pay rates for authors and illustrators vary.

Tips: "All accepted manuscripts will appeal to Evangelical Christian children and parents."

UNIVERSITY CLASSICS, LTD. PUBLISHERS, One Bryan Rd., P.O. Box 2301, Athens OH 45701. (614)592-4543. Book publisher. President: Albert H. Shuster. Publishes 1 young readers/year; 1 middle readers/year; 1 young adult title/year. 50% of books by first-time authors.

• This publisher is "booked for the next 2 years" in children's fiction and nonfiction. Do not submit work (manuscripts or illustrations) to them at this time.

Fiction: Picture books: animal, concept, health, nature/environment. Young readers: concept, health, nature/environment, special needs. Middle readers: health, nature/environment, problem novels, special needs. Young adults: health, nature/environment, special needs. Average word length: young readers—1,200; middle readers—5,000. Published *Toodle D. Poodle*, by Katherine Oaha/Dorathyre Shuster (grades 4-6, ages 10-12); *The Day My Dad and I Got Mugged*, by Howard Goldsmith (grades 5-8, ages 12-15).

Nonfiction: Picture books: activity books, animal, arts/crafts, concept, health, nature/environment, self help, special needs. Young readers: activity books, animal, arts/crafts, concept, health, nature/environment, self help, special needs, textbooks. Middle readers, young adults: arts/crafts, concept, health, nature/environment, self help, special needs, textbooks. Average word length: young readers—1,200; middle readers—5,000. Published *Fitness and Nutrition: The Winning Combination*, by Jane Buch (ages 13-17, textbook); *The Way We Live: Practical Economics*, by John Shaw (ages 13-adult, textbook); *Ride Across America: An Environmental Commitment*, by Lucian Spataro (ages 13-17, trade).

Illustration: Works with 2 illustrators/year.
Terms: Pays authors royalty of 5-12% based on retail price. Pays illustrators by the project. Book catalog available for #10 SAE and 2 first-class stamps.
Tips: "Consumers are looking more for educational than fictional books, and this will continue."

VICTOR BOOKS, Scripture Press, 1825 College Ave., Wheaton IL 60187. (708)668-6000. Fax: (708)668-3806. Book publisher. Children's Editor: Liz Duckworth. Publishes 9 picture books/year; 6 middle readers/year. "No young readers at this point, but open to them." 20% of books by first-time authors; 10% of books from agented authors. All books are related to Christianity.
Fiction: Picture books: adventure, religion. Young readers: adventure, religion, suspense/mystery. Middle readers: adventure, history, religion, suspense/mystery. Does not want to see stories with "Christian" animals; no holiday legends. Recently published *Where's God?*, by Karen King (ages 4-7, picture book); *The Jesters' Quest*, by Sigmund Brouwer (ages 8-12, middle reader); and *Danger at Outlaw Creek*, by Jerry Jerman (ages 8-12, middle reader).
Nonfiction: Picture books, young readers: activity books with Christian themes. Middle readers: Science in a Christian context.
How to Contact/Writers: Fiction/Nonfiction: Submit complete ms for picture books. Submit outline/synopsis and 2 sample chapters for middle readers. Reports on queries in 2 months; mss in 3 months. Publishes a book 18 months after acceptance. Will consider simultaneous submissions.
Illustration: Works with 4 illustrators/year. Uses color artwork only. Reviews ms/illustration packages from artists. Submit complete package. Contact: Liz Duckworth, managing editor, children's books. Illustrations only: Submit portfolio for review; provide résumé, promotional literature or tearsheets to be kept on file. Contact: Paul Higdon, art director. Reports in 3 months. Samples returned with SASE. Original artowrk returned at job's completion.
Photography: Uses photos of children. Contact: Paul Higdon, art director. Model/property releases required. Buys stock images. Photographers should submit portfolio for review; provide résumé, promotional literature or tearsheets to be kept on file.
Terms: Pays authors royalty of 5-10% based on wholesale price, outright purchase $125-2,500. Offers advance "based on project." Pays illustrators by the project, royalty of 5% based on wholesale price. Photographers paid by the project, per photo. Sends galleys to authors. Book catalog available for 9×12 SAE and 2 first-class stamps. Ms guidelines available for SASE.
Tips: "In general children's books I see trends toward increasingly high quality. It's a crowded field, so each idea must be fresh and unique. Ask yourself, 'Does this book belong primarily on the shelf of a *Christian* bookstore?' That's how we distribute so your answer should reflect that."

VICTORY PUBLISHING, 3504 Oak Dr., Menlo Park CA 94025. (415)323-1650. Book publisher. Publisher: Yolanda Garcia. 95% of books by first-time authors. "All books pertain to instruction of elementary age children—specifically bilingual, Spanish/English."
Fiction: Picture books, young readers: multicultural, poetry. Middle readers: poetry. Does not want to see mystery, religion, fantasy, sports and short stories.
Nonfiction: Picture books, young readers: activity books, arts/crafts, cooking, how-to, science. No animals. Recently published *Spanish in a Taco Shell*, by Yolanda Garcia, illustrated by Veronica J. Garcia (learn Spanish language and Mexican cooking, for ages 8 to adult).
How to Contact/Writers: Fiction/Nonfiction: Query. Submit outline/synopsis and 2 sample chapters. "Must send SASE." Reports on queries in 2-3 weeks; mss in 1-2 months. "Must send SASE." Publishes a book 1 year after acceptance.
Illustration: Works with 1 illustrator/year. Reviews ms/illustration packages from artists. Query. Illustration only: Query with samples; provide résumé, promo sheet to be kept on file. Contact: Veronica Garcia, illustrator. Reports on queries in 3 weeks. Samples returned with SASE (if requested); samples filed. "Originals are purchased."

***A bullet within a listing introduces special comments by the editor of* Children's Writer's & Illustrator's Market.**

Terms: Work purchased outright from authors (average amount: $100-500). Pays illustrators by the project or set amount per illustration (range: $5-10) depending on complexity. Sends dummies to illustrators.
Tips: Wants "teacher resources for elementary school—bilingual Spanish/English activity books."

WALKER AND CO., 435 Hudson St., New York NY 10014. (212)727-8300. Division of Walker Publishing Co. Inc. Book publisher. Estab. 1959. Editorial Director: Emily Easton. Publishes 4-6 picture books/year; 10-15 middle readers/year; 15 young adult titles/year. 10-15% of books by first-time authors; 65% of books from agented writers.
Fiction: Picture books: animal, history, multicultural, special needs. Young readers: animal, contemporary, history, multicultural. Middle readers: animal, contemporary, history, multicultural, special needs. Young adults: history. Recently published *Miss Malarkey Doesn't Live in Room 10*, by J. Finchler (picture book); *Graveyard Girl*, by Anna Myers (young adult); and *Shin's Tricycle*, by T. Kodama (middle grade).
Nonfiction: Young readers: animals. Middle readers: animal, biography, health, history, multicultural, reference, social issues. Young adults: biography, careers, health, history, multicultural, reference, social issues, sports. Published *Pilgrim Voices*, by C. and R. Roop (picture book history); *Red-Tail Angels*, by P. and F. McKissack (young adult history). Multicultural needs include "contemporary, literary fiction and historical fiction written in an authentic voice. Also high interest nonfiction with trade appeal."
How to Contact/Writers: Fiction/nonfiction: Submit outline/synopsis and sample chapters. Reports on queries/mss in 2-3 months. Will consider simultaneous submissions.
Illustration: Works with 4-6 illustrators/year. Uses color artwork only. Editorial reviews ms/illustration packages from artists. Query or submit ms with 4-8 pieces of final art. Illustrations only: Tearsheets. Reports on art samples only if interested. Samples returned with SASE. Original artwork returned at job's completion.
Terms: Pays authors in royalties of 5-10% based on wholesale price "depends on contract." Offers average advance payment of $2,000-4,000. Pays illustrators by the project (range: $500-5,000); royalties from 50%. Sends galleys to authors. Book catalog available for 9×12 SASE; ms guidelines for SASE.
Tips: Writers: "Don't take rejections personally and try to consider them objectively. We receive more than 20 submissions a day. Can it be improved?" Illustrators: "Have a well-rounded portfolio with different styles." Does not want to see folktales, ABC books, genre fiction (mysteries, science fiction, fantasy).

***WARREN PUBLISHING HOUSE, INC.**, P.O. Box 2250, Everett WA 98203. (206)353-3100. Book publisher. Managing Editor: Kathleen Cubley. "All books are supplementary resources for early childhood educators and parents. We do not publish fiction."
Nonfiction: Picture books, young readers: activity books for teachers. Recently published *Busy Bee's Spring, Fun for Two's and Three's, Play and Learn with Rubber Stamps*, and *Bear Hugs for Transition Times*, all compiled by staff editors and written for adults who work with children aged 2-8.
How to Contact/Writers: Nonfiction: Query. Reports on queries in 3 months.
Illustration: Works with 8-10 illustrators/year. Uses both b&w and color artwork. Reviews ms/illustration packages from authors. Query with samples. Contact: Uma Kukathes, art director. Illustration only: Query with samples. Reports in 3 months. Samples returned with SASE; samples filed. Original artwork returned, "depending on contract."
Terms: Offers advance. Pays illustrators by the project (varies depending on type of project) or 5% royalty based on wholesale price. Book catalog available for 8½×11 SAE and 2 first-class stamps.

✤WEIGL EDUCATIONAL PUBLISHERS, 1902 11th St. SE., Calgary, Alberta T2G 3G2 Canada. (403)233-7747. Fax: (403)233-7769. Book publisher. Publisher: Linda Weigl.
Nonfiction: Young reader, middle reader, young adult: textbooks. Young reader, middle reader: careers, multicultural. Average length: young reader, middle reader, young adult—64 pages. Recently published *Career Connections Series II*, (middle readers); *Digging for Dinosaurs*, (young readers, middle readers); and *Introducing Japan*, (young readers, middle readers).

How to Contact/Writers: Nonfiction: Submit query and résumé. Reports on queries in 3 months; mss in 4 months. Publishes a book 2 years after acceptance. Will consider simultaneous submissions.
Illustration: Works with 1 illustrator/year. Uses color artwork only. Reviews ms/illustration packages from artists. Query first. Contact: A. Woodrow, project coordinator. Illustrations only: Query with samples. Reports back only if interested or when appropriate project comes in. Samples returned with SASE; samples filed. Original artwork returned at job's completion.
Photography: Buys photos from freelancers. Buys stock and assigns work. Wants political, juvenile, multicultural photos. Contact: A. Woodrow.
Terms: Pays authors royalty or work purchased outright. Pays illustrators/photographers by the project. Sends galleys to author; dummies to illustrator. Book catalog for SASE.
Tips: Looks for "a manuscript that answers a specific curriculum need, or can be applied to a curriculum topic with multiple applications (e.g. career education)."

DANIEL WEISS ASSOCIATES, INC., 11th Floor, 33 W. 17th St., New York NY 10011. (212)645-3865. Fax: (212)633-1236. Independent book producer/packager. Editorial Assistant: Sigrid Berg. Publishes 30 young readers/year; 40 middle readers/year; and 70 young adults/year. 25% of books by first-time authors. "We do mostly series!"
Fiction: Middle readers: sports. Young adults: fantasy, romance.
Nonfiction: Young adults: history.
How to Contact/Writers: Submit outline/synopsis and 2 sample chapters. Reports on queries in 1-2 months; mss in 2 months. Publishes a book 1 year after acceptance. Will consider simultaneous submissions.
Illustration: Works with 20 illustrators/year. Reviews ms/illustration packages from artists. Submit query. Contact: Michael Fitzgerald, editorial assistant. Illustrations only: Provide promo sheet. Contact: Paul Matarazzo, art director. Reports in 2 months. Samples returned with SASE. Original artwork returned at job's completion.
Terms: Pays authors royalty of 4%. Work purchased outright from authors, $1,000 minimum. Offers advances (average amount: $3,000). Pays illustrators by the project. Ms guidelines available if SASE sent.

WESTERN PUBLISHING CO., 850 Third Ave., New York, NY 10022. (212)753-8500. Fax (212)371-1091. See the listing for Golden Books.

- Western Publishing ranks 1st based on net sales, of the top 15 children's publishers.

WHITEBIRD BOOKS, 200 Madison Ave., New York NY 10016. An imprint of Putnam and Grosset Group. See G.P. Putnam's Sons.

ALBERT WHITMAN & COMPANY, 6340 Oakton St., Morton Grove IL 60053-2723. (708)581-0033. Book publisher. Editor-in-Chief: Kathleen Tucker. Publishes 30 books/year. 15% of books by first-time authors; 15% of books from agented authors. "We publish various categories, but we're mostly known for our concept books—books that deal with children's problems or concerns."

- Albert Whitman appeared on a 1995 Hot List® compiled by *Children's Book Insider*. This list of "10 Book and Magazine Publishers Most Receptive to New Writers" is updated every few months, and available to new and renewing subscribers.

Fiction: Picture books: adventure, animal, contemporary, fantasy, folktales, health, nature/environment. Young readers and middle readers: adventure, animal, contemporary, fantasy, folktales, health, history, multicultural, nature/environment, problem novels, special needs, sports, suspense/mystery. Does not want to see "religion-oriented, ABCs, pop-up, romance, counting or

"Picture books" are for preschoolers to 8-year-olds; "Young readers" are for 5- to 8-year-olds; "Middle readers" are for 9- to 11-year-olds; and "Young adults" are for those ages 12 and up.

any book that is supposed to be written in." Published *Nigntfall, Country Lake*, written and illustrated by David Cunningham; and *My Two Uncles*, written and illustrated by Judith Vigna.
Nonfiction: Picture books, young readers and middle readers: animal, careers, health, history, hobbies, multicultural, music/dance, nature/environment, special needs, sports. Does not want to see "religion, any books that have to be written in, biographies of living people." Recently published *Focus: Five Women Photographers*, by Sylvia Wolf; *Theodore Roosevelt Takes Charge*, by Nancy Whitelaw (ages 8 and up, middle readers).
How to Contact/Writers: Fiction/Nonfiction: Submit complete ms. Reports on queries in 4-6 weeks; mss in 2 months. Publishes a book 18 months after acceptance. Will consider simultaneous submissions "but let us know if it is one" and previously published work "if out of print."
Illustration: Uses more color art than b&w. Reviews ms/illustration packages from artists. Submit all chapters of ms with any pieces of final art. Contact: Editorial. Illustrations only: Query with samples. Send slides or tearsheets. Reports back in 2 months. Original artwork returned at job's completion.
Photography: Photographers should contact Editorial. Publishes books illustrated with photos but not stock photos—desires photos all taken for project. "Our books are for children and cover many topics; photos must be taken to match text. Books often show a child in a particular situation (e.g., a First Communion, a sister whose brother is born prematurely)." Photographers should query with samples; send unsolicited photos by mail.
Terms: Pays authors royalty. Offers advances. Pays illustrators royalty. Sends galleys to authors; dummies to illustrators. Book catalog available for 9×12 SAE and 5 first-class stamps. Ms guidelines available for SASE.
Tips: "In both picture books and nonfiction, we are seeking stories showing life in other cultures and the variety of multicultural life in the U.S. We also want fiction and nonfiction about mentally or physically challenged children—some recent topics have been AIDS, asthma, cerebral palsy."

***■WILD HONEY**, Ottenheimer Publishers, Inc., 10 Church Lane, Baltimore MD 21208. (410)484-2100. Fax: (410)486-6475. Publisher: Bea Jackson. Publishes 3-6 picture books/year. 25% of books by first-time authors; 75% subsidy published. "Titles are literary/art oriented.'
Fiction: Picture books and young readers: adventure, animal, anthology, concept, contemporary, fantasy, folktales, health, hi-lo, history, humor, multicultural, nature/environment, poetry.
Nonfiction: Picture books: geography, history, multicultural, music/dance.
How to Contact/Writers: Fiction/Nonfiction: Submit outline/synopsis and 1 sample chapter. Reports on queries in 1 month; mss 4 months. Publishes a book 1½ years after acceptance. Will consider simultaneous submissions, electronic submissions via disk.
Illustration: Works with 10 illustrators/year. Uses color artwork only. Reviews ms/illustration packages from authors. Submit ms with dummy. Contact: Betty Davies, assistant to publisher. Illustration only: Submit promo sheet, client list, tearsheets, "non-returnable." Reports in 1 month. Samples not returned; samples filed. Original artwork returned at job's completion.
Terms: Pays authors royalty of 3-8% based on wholesale price or work purchased outright from authors (range: $1,000-90,000). Offers advances (average amount: $5,000-$20,000). Pays illustrators by the project (range: $1,000-25,000) or royalty of 3-8% based on wholesale price. Sends galleys to author. Book catalog available for 8×10 SAE and 3 first-class stamps.

JOHN WILEY & SONS, INC., 605 Third Ave., New York NY 10158. (212)850-6206. Fax: (212)850-6095. Book publisher. Editor: Kate Bradford. Publishes 15 middle readers/year; 2 adult titles/year. 20% of books by first-time authors. Publishes educational, nonfiction primarily science, nature and activities.
Nonfiction: Middle readers: activity books, animal, arts/crafts, cooking, geography, health, hobbies, how-to, nature/environment, reference, science, self help. Young adults: activity books, arts/crafts, health, hobbies, how-to, nature/environment, reference, science, self help. Average word length middle readers—20,000-40,000. Published *Dinosaurs for Every Kid*, by Janice Van Cleave, (8-12, science activities); *Roller Coaster Science*, by Jim Wiese, (8-12, science activities); and *Earth-Friendly Toys*, by George Pfiffner, (8-12, crafts).
How to Contact/Writers: Query. Submit outline/synopsis and 2 sample chapters. Reports on queries in 1 month; mss in 3 months. Publishes a book 1 year after acceptance. Will consider simultaneous and previously published submissions.
Illustration: Works with 10 illustrators/year. Uses primarily black & white artwork. Reviews ms/illustration packages from artists. Query. Illustrations only: Query with samples, résumé,

client list. Reports back only if interested. Samples filed. Original artwork returned.
Terms: Pays authors royalty of 7% based on wholesale price. Offers advances. Pays illustrators by the project. Sends galleys to authors. Book catalog available for SAE.
Tips: "There's a glut of children's publishing in many areas. Horror fiction and merchandise seem to be the hottest areas. Electronic publishing for kids is coming on strong."

***WRS PUBLISHING**, WRS Group, Inc., P.O. Box 21207, Waco TX 76702-1207. (817)776-6461. Fax: (817)757-1454. E-mail: 75543.3041@compuserve.com. Book publisher. Editor-in-Chief: Thomas Spence. Publishes 1 picture book/year. 50% of books by first-time authors.
Fiction: Picture books and young readers: character-building, concept, health, multicultural. Middle readers and young adults: character-building, health, multicultural. Multicultural needs include bilingual books.
Nonfiction: Picture books: biography, character-building, concept, health, multicultural, self help, social issues. Young readers, middle readers and young adults: character-building, multicultural. Special needs include bilingual books. Recently published *Calor: A Story of Warmth for All Ages* (Spanish and English), by Juanita Alba, illustrated by Amado Peña (children's picture book); and *Orient: Hero Dog Guide of the Appalachian Trail*, by Tom McMahon, illustrated by Erin Mauterer (story for young readers and pre-readers).
How to Contact/Writers: Fiction/Nonfiction: Query; submit outline/synopsis. Reports on queries in 3 weeks; mss 1 month. Publishes a book 1 year after acceptance. Will consider simultaneous submissions, previously published work.
Illustration: Works with 1-2 illustrators/year. Reviews ms/illustration packages from artists. Query. Illustrations only: Query with samples; send résumé, promo sheet. Reports in 1 month. Samples returned with SASE; samples not filed. Original artwork returned at job's completion.
Photography: Buys photos from freelancers. Contact: Thomas Spence, editor-in-chief. Buys stock images. Model/property releases required; captions required. Uses color or b&w prints and 35mm, $2\frac{1}{4} \times 2\frac{1}{4}$, 4×5, 8×10 transparencies. Submit cover letter, résumé and promo piece.
Terms: Pays authors royalty of 15% based on wholesale price. Offers negotiable advance. Illustrator's and photographer's payment varies with project. Sends galleys to authors. Book catalog available for 9×12 SAE and $1.02 postage. Ms guidelines available for SASE.
Tips: "We look for well-written books on character-building, education and social issues."

JANE YOLEN BOOKS, 525 B St., Suite 1900, San Diego CA 92101-4455. See listing for Harcourt Brace & Co. for submissions information.

Book Publishers/'95-'96 changes

The following markets were included in the 1995 edition of *Children's Writer's & Illustrator's Market* but do not have listings in this edition. The majority did not respond to our request to update their listings. If a reason was given for exclusion, it appears in parentheses after the market's name.

ABC, All Books for Children
Aegina Press/University Editions
Andersen Press Limited
Aquila Communications Ltd.
Arcade Publishing (no longer does children's books)
Artists & Writers Guild Books (no longer publishing)
Blue Heron Publishing, Inc.
Bradbury Press
Bright Ring Publishing
Children's Library Press
China Books
Clear Light Publishers
Cool Kids Press
Crocodile Creek Press/European Toy Collection (per request)
Dimi Press
Eakin Press
Facts on File (unable to contact)
Falcon Press Publishing Co.
Harvest House Publishers
Hi-Time Publishing Corporation
Incentive Publications, Inc.
Kabel Publishers
Key Porter Books
Kruza Kaleidoscopix, Inc.
Look and See Publications
Magination Press
Metamorphous Press
Nar Publications (not accepting unsolicited mss)
Naturegraph Publisher, Inc.
Pavilion Books Ltd.
Pocahontas Press, Inc.
The Preservation Press
The Press of Macdonald & Reinecke
Prometheus Books
Pumpkin Press Publishing House
Rosebrier Publishing Co.
William H. Sadlier, Inc.
Scientific American Books for Young Readers (per request)
Seacoast Publications of New England
Harold Shaw Publishers
Shoestring Press
The Summit Publishing Group
Tab Books
Titan Books
Transworld Publishers Limited
University Editions, Inc.
Usborne Publishing Ltd.
W.W. Publications
Waterfront Books
Willowisp Press
Women's Press
Woodbine House
Zino Press Children's Book

Magazines

Children's magazines are a great place for unpublished writers and illustrators to break into the market. Eric Kimmel, now author of close to 40 children's books, started out writing for *Cricket Magazine* (see Telling Tales from Around the World: An Interview with Eric Kimmel, page 25), and does work for it even today. Illustrator Joan Holub finds that having tearsheets from magazines helps her get book assignments, and she continues to do magazine work along with book work. Illustrating for magazines, Holub says, lets you see your work in print quickly, and gives you practice dealing with editors and art directors. (See Insider Report with Holub on page 188.)

The number of juvenile magazines that writers, illustrators and photographers may approach is growing. There are now a couple hundred kids' magazines found in homes, libraries and classrooms, about 100 of which are listed in this section. Magazines devoted to licensed characters (such as Barney or Batman), or publications that serve as promotions for toys, movies or TV shows (primarily produced inhouse) aren't included. What you'll find are diverse magazines aimed at children of all ages and interests.

Some of the listings in this section are religious-oriented or special interest publications; others are general interest magazines. Though large circulation, ad-driven publications generally offer a better pay rate than religious or nonprofit magazines, smaller magazines are more open to reviewing the work of newcomers, and can provide an excellent source for clippings as you work your way toward more lucrative markets.

Something for every kid

Publishers have acknowledged that children—and their interests—are as varied as adults. In this section, for instance, you'll find magazines targeting boys (such as *Boys' Life* and *Boys' Quest*) and magazines targeting girls (like *Girls' Life* and *Seventeen*) just as you might find newsstand publications specifically for men or women.

Magazines for young people affiliated with almost every religious denomination are listed. You'll also notice specialized magazines devoted to certain sports, such as *Soccer Jr.* Publications addressing various world cultures like *Skipping Stones* and *Faces* supply readers with ethnically diverse stories and artwork. However, the need for multicultural material is also present in general interest magazines (many editors have indicated specific multicultural needs within their listings). If you're not a member of the group you're interested in writing about, thoroughly research your subject to insure authenticity. Better yet, pass your work by an expert on the culture before submitting it.

Another plus for the children's magazine industry is that teachers are using fact-based educational publications—such as those teaching history, math or science—as supplements in their classrooms. As a result, it's not unusual for children to want their own personal subscriptions after initially being exposed to the magazines at school.

Above all, children today are worldly and desire to know what's going on around them. More and more informational adult magazines (*TIME*, *Sports Illustrated* and *Consumer Reports* to name a few) are publishing versions for kids. Since magazines have the advantage of timeliness, they can relay information about current events or interests much more quickly than books—and at less cost. The average one-year subscription, in fact, is about the same as the cost of one hardcover picture book.

Matters of the market

It's not uncommon for juvenile magazines to purchase all rights to both stories and artwork. Though work for hire is generally frowned upon among freelancers, selling all rights may prove to be advantageous in the end. *Highlights for Children* buys all rights, as do all of the magazines published by the Children's Better Health Institute. Yet these magazines are very reputable, and any clips acquired through them will be valuable.

Classic subjects considered by magazines include stories and features about the alphabet, outer space, computers and animals (even dinosaurs). As with books, nonfiction features—especially photo features—are popular, and many magazines are devoting more room to such material. Sports stories, environmental issues, historical fiction, retold folktales, mysteries, science fiction and fantasy, and articles describing how things work are all marketable to children's magazines too.

Get on target

No matter what the trends in the magazine industry, writers and illustrators must know what appeals to today's youth and target their material appropriately. To insure that your work will interest young people—and editors—find out what kids are talking about. If unsure about the relevance of an article or story, read the material to children and see how they respond. By learning what appeals to today's kids, you may find yourself at the beginning of a trend instead of the end.

While it's important to know the current interests of children, you must also know the topics typically covered by different children's magazines. To help you match your work with the right publications, a Subject Index is included at the back of this book. This index lists both book and magazine publishers by the fiction and nonfiction subjects they're seeking.

New this year is a Photography Index listing all the children's magazines which use photos from freelancers. Use this in combination with the Subject Index, and you can quickly narrow your search of markets that suit your work. For instance, if you photograph sports, compare the Magazine list in the Photography Index with the lists under Sports in the Subject Index. Highlight the markets that appear on both lists, then read those listings to decide which are best for you.

Writers can use the Subject Index in conjunction with the Age-Level Index to narrow their list of markets. Targeting the correct age-group with your submission is an important consideration. The majority of rejection slips are sent because the writer has not targeted a manuscript to the correct age. Few magazines are aimed at children of all ages, so you must be certain your manuscript is written for the audience level of the particular magazine you're submitting to.

Study, study, study

To ensure you're targeting the right age level, study both the listings and the actual publications. Each magazine has a different editorial philosophy. Language usage also varies between periodicals, as does the length of feature articles and the use of artwork and photographs. Reading the magazines you're considering submitting to is the best way to determine if your material is appropriate. Also, because magazines targeted to specific age-groups have a natural turnover in readership every few years, old topics (with a new slant) can be recycled.

Since many kids' magazines sell subscriptions through direct mail or schools, you may not be able to find a particular publication at bookstores or newsstands. Check your local library, or send for copies of the magazines you're interested in. Most magazines in this section have sample copies available and will send them for a SASE or small fee.

It's important to carefully review the listings of markets you wish to target for their preferred method of receiving submissions. Some editors may wish to see an entire manuscript; others prefer a query letter and outline, especially for nonfiction articles (with which accompanying photographs are generally welcome). If you're an artist or photographer, review the listing for the types of samples the art director wants to see. Following a magazine's guidelines and sending only your best work improve your chances of having work accepted in a growing and competitive market.

AIM MAGAZINE, America's Intercultural Magazine, P.O. Box 20554, Chicago IL 60620. (312)874-6184. Articles Editor: Ruth Apilado. Fiction Editor: Mark Boone. Photo Editor: Betty Lewis. Quarterly magazine. Circ. 8,000. Readers are high school and college students, teachers, adults interested in helping, through the written word, to create a more equitable world. 15% of material aimed at juvenile audience.

- *AIM* appeared on a 1995 Hot List® compiled by *Children's Book Insider*. This list of "10 Book and Magazine Publishers Most Receptive to New Writers" is updated every few months, and available to new and renewing subscribers.

Fiction: Young adults: history, multicultural, "stories with social significance." Wants stories that teach children that people are more alike than they are different. Does not want to see religious fiction. Buys 20 mss/year. Average word length: 1,000-4,000. Byline given.

Nonfiction: Young adults: interview/profile, multicultural, "stuff with social significance." Does not want to see religious nonfiction. Buys 20 mss/year. Average word length: 500-2,000. Byline given.

How to Contact/Writers: Fiction: Send complete ms. Nonfiction: Query with published clips. Reports on queries/mss in 1 month. Will consider simultaneous submissions.

Illustration: Buys 20 illustrations/issue. Preferred theme: Overcoming social injustices through nonviolent means. Reviews ms/illustration packages from artists. Query first. Illustrations only: Query with tearsheets. Reports on art samples in 2 months. Original artwork returned at job's completion "if desired." Credit line given.

Photography: Wants "photos of activists who are trying to contribute to social improvement."

Terms: Pays on publication. Buys first North American serial rights. Pays $15-25 for stories/articles. Pays in contributor copies if copies are requested. Pays $5-25 for b&w cover illustration. Photographers paid by the project (range: $10-15). Sample copies for $4.

Tips: "We need material of social significance, stuff that will help promote racial harmony and peace and illustrate the stupidity of racism."

***AMERICAN CHEERLEADER**, Lifestyle Publications LLC, 350 W. 50th St., Suite 2AA, New York NY 10019. Phone/fax: (212)447-0148. Editor: Julie Davis. Bimonthly magazine. Estab. 1995. Circ. 125,000. Special interest teen magazine for kids who cheer.

Nonfiction: Young adults: careers, fashion, health, how-to, problem-solving, sports, cheerleading specific material. "We're looking for authors who know cheerleading." Buys 50 mss/year. Average word length: 200-1,000. Byline given.

How to Contact/Writers: Query with published clips. Reports on queries/mss in 3 months. Publishes ms 3 months after acceptance. Will consider electronic submission via disk or modem.

Illustration: Buys 6 illustrations/issue; 30-50 illustrations/year. Works on assignment only. Reviews ms/illustration packages from artists. Illustrations only: Query with samples; arrange portfolio review. Reports only if interested. Samples filed. Originals not returned at job's completion. Credit line given.

Photography: Buys photos from freelancers. Looking for cheerleading at different sports games, events, etc. Uses 35mm, 2¼×2¼ transparencies. Query with samples; provide résumé, business card, tearsheets to be kept on file. "After sending query, we'll set up an interview." Reports only if interested.

Terms: Pays on publication. Buy all rights for mss, artwork and photographs. Pays $100-1,000 for stories. Pays illustrators $50-200 for b&w inside, $100-300 for color inside. Pays photographers by the project $300-800; per photo (range: $25-100). Sample copies for $5.

Tips: "Authors: Absolutely must have cheerleading background. Photographers and illustrators must have teen magazine experience or high profile experience."

AMERICAN GIRL, Pleasant Company, P.O. Box 620986, Middleton WI 53562-0984. (608)836-4848. Fiction Editor: Harriet Brown. Editor-in-Chief: Judith Woodburn. Bimonthly magazine. Estab. 1992. Circ. 500,000. "For girls ages 8-12. We run fiction and nonfiction, historical and contemporary."
Fiction: Middle readers: contemporary, historical, multicultural, suspense/mystery, good fiction about anything. No preachy, moralistic tales or stories with animals as protagonists. Only a girl or girls as characters—no boys. Buys approximately 6 mss/year. Average word length: 1,000-2,500. Byline given.
Nonfiction: Any articles aimed at girls ages 8-12. Buys 3-10 mss/year. Average word length: 600. Byline sometimes given.
How to Contact/Writers: Fiction: Send complete ms. Nonfiction: Query with published clips. Reports on queries/mss in 6-12 weeks. Will consider simultaneous submissions.
Illustration: Works on assignment only.
Terms: Pays on acceptance. Buys first North American serial rights. Pays $500 minimum for stories; $300 minimum for articles. Sample copies for $3.95 and 9×12 SAE with $1.93 in postage (send to Editorial Department Assistant). Writer's guidelines free for SASE.
Tips: "Keep (stories and articles) simple but interesting. Kids are discriminating readers, too. They won't read a boring or pretentious story."

ASPCA ANIMAL WATCH, ASPCA, 424 E. 92nd St., New York NY 10128. (212)876-7700, ext. 4441. Fax: (212)534-8888. E-mail: aniberian@aol.com. Art Director: Amber Alliger. Quarterly magazine. Estab. 1951. Circ. 200,000. Focuses on animal issues. 15% of publication aimed at juvenile market.
Nonfiction: Animal, multicultural, nature/environment.
Illustration: Buys 4 illustrations/issue; 12 illustrations/year. Works on assignment only. Reviews ms/illustration packages from artists. Send ms with dummy. Illustrations only: Send color tearsheets, quality photocopies to hold on file. Reports back only if interested. Samples returned with SASE or kept on file. Originals returned upon job's completion. Credit line given.
Photography: Looking for animal care, animal abuse, and animal protection. Model/property releases required. Uses 8×10, glossy color/b&w prints; 35mm, 2¼×2¼ and 4×5 transparencies. Photographers should send stock list. Reports in 2 months.
Terms: Pays on publication. Buys one-time rights for artwork/photographs. Pays illustrators $100-150 for color cover; $100-125 for b&w, $100-200 for color inside. Photographers paid per photo (range: $50-100). Sample copies for 9×12 SASE with $2 postage. Writer's guidelines not available. Illustrator's/photo guidelines for SASE.
Tips: Trends include "more educational, more interactive" material. Children's section is "Eye on Animals." Not interested in realism. "Only cartoon or creative work needed."

***BABYBUG**, Carus Corporation, P.O. Box 300, Peru IL 61354. (815)224-6643. Editor: Paula Morrow. Art Director: Suzanne Beck. Published 9 times/year (every 6 weeks). Estab. 1994. "A listening and looking magazine for infants and toddlers ages 6 to 24 months. *Babybug* is 6 ¼×7, 24 pages long, printed in large type (26-point) on high-quality cardboard stock with rounded corners and no staples."
Fiction: Looking for very simple and concrete stories, 4-6 short sentences maximum.
Nonfiction: Must use very basic words and concepts, 10 words maximum.
Poetry: Maximum length 8 lines. Looking for rhythmic, rhyming poems.
How to Contact/Writers: "Please do not query first." Send complete ms with SASE. "Submissions without SASE will be discarded." Reports in 6-8 weeks.
Illustration: Uses color artwork only. Works on assignment only. Reviews ms/illustration packages from artists. "The manuscripts will be evaluated for quality of concept and text before the art is considered." Contact: Paula Morrow, editor. Illustrations only: Send tearsheets or photo prints/photocopies with SASE. "Submissions without SASE will be discarded." Reports in 12 weeks. Samples filed.
Terms: Pays on publication. Buys first rights with reprint option or (in some cases) all rights. Rates vary ($25 minimum).

Cheer-o-Scope

Leo (Jul. 23-Aug. 22): You're a natural performer and everyone's favorite cheerful person. So cheerleading is an extension of your true personality! It gives you a chance to dress up, display your talents and fire up the crowd. Competition and drill can challenge you to achieve even more.

Virgo (Aug. 23-Sept. 22): Fitness and keeping in shape are both important to you, and cheering provides a great workout. Accuracy and attention to detail are your strong points: You're willing to practice till all's perfect. A neat, pressed uniform and clean shoes just make you feel good about yourself.

What Are Your Cheer Strengths?

BY KAREN CHRISTINO

Your zodiac sign can clue you into many of your personal characteristics and may help you discover where you best fit in on the squad!

Libra (Sept. 23-Oct. 22): You simply enjoy being with people: Cheering provides fun times with friends and gives you plenty of opportunities to meet team players. The beauty and balance of cheer routines can highlight your artistic side, while dance moves bring out your natural poise.

Scorpio (Oct. 23-Nov. 21): You are passionate and intense and feel a great personal commitment to your squad and sports teams. Your great gusto and determination are infectious: Scorpio cheering can really encourage the team toward victory. You have the patience and commitment to succeed with difficult routines and gymnastics.

Sagittarius (Nov. 22-Dec. 21): You're extremely athletic and a bit of a daredevil, often the best jumper and tumbler around. Making noise is also a specialty, and your big, booming voice should be heard above all the rest. The thrills of travel and tough competition excite and animate you.

Capricorn (Dec. 22-Jan. 19): With a super attitude you can be the best all-around cheerleader. You're willing to work hard and are usually there for your teammates. Your dedication and organizational skills could take you straight to squad captain.

Aquarius (Jan. 20-Feb. 18): A team player at heart, you love being part of a squad and interfacing with the teams and fans. Sharing experiences and goals gives you a feeling of friendship and camaraderie. But you also remain an individualist and can invent original moves and routines—choreography may be your strongest suit.

Pisces (Feb. 19-Mar. 20): Your many creative talents should find excellent outlets in cheering. You'd be great at writing cheers or choreographing routines, coaching younger cheerleaders or even teaching those less experienced. A beloved member of the squad, you inspire others to feel good, even when your team loses.

Aries (Mar. 21-Apr. 19): Energized and enthusiastic, you love to be right in the thick of the action! Your competitive spirit makes you feel strong and alive when backing your team. A natural leader, you easily motivate others and make a great team captain.

Taurus (Apr. 20-May 20): Your athleticism and grace guarantee fluid movement and your clear speaking voice is easily heard. Squadmates appreciate your reliability, while you enjoy the regularity of cheerleading practice. You're strong and solid enough to support the whole pyramid—no matter what your size!

Gemini (May 21-Jun. 20): You're a real chatterbox who never stops talking, and cheerleading lets you keep on doing it! You are multitalented and revel in the opportunity to combine action, words and feelings. Cheering also allows you to meet new people and learn about the latest cheer trends.

Cancer (Jun. 21-Jul. 22): Although usually shy and reserved by nature, you can shine in the public spotlight. Cheering allows you to do just that, without pressure directly on you. You have a love of your school and want to do all you can to support the team and your community.

ILLUSTRATIONS BY LISA BLACKSHEAR

Artist Lisa Blackshear pulls together the distinctly different concepts of cheerleading and astrology with her bright, colorful illustrations for American Cheerleader magazine's "Cheer-O-Scope, What Are Your Cheer Strengths?," by Karen Christino. "Lisa uses color in a very high-impact way," says Editor Julie Davis of Blackshear's computer-created art. "She brings a fresh, light look to her illustrations." Combining the bright colors with action-oriented people and animals helped convey the message that "astrology is fun," Davis says.

Tips: "*Babybug* would like to reach as many children's authors and artists as possible for original contributions, but our standards are very high, and we will accept only top-quality material. Before attempting to write for *Babybug*, be sure to familiarize yourself with this age child." (See listings for *Cricket*, *Ladybug* and *Spider*.)

THE BLUFTON NEWS PUBLISHING AND PRINTING COMPANY, 103 N. Main St., Blufton OH 45817. See listings for *Boys' Quest* and *Hopscotch*.

BOY SCOUTS OF AMERICA, 1325 W. Walnut Lane, P.O. Box 152079, Irving TX 75015-2079. See listings for *Boys' Life* and *Exploring*.

BOYS' LIFE, Boy Scouts of America, 1325 W. Walnut Hill Lane, P.O. Box 152079, Irving TX 75015-2079. (214)580-2000. Managing Editor: J.D. Owen. Articles Editor: Michael Goldman. Fiction Editor: Shannon Lowry. Director of Design: Joseph P. Connolly. Art Director: Elizabeth Hardaway Morgan. Monthly magazine. Estab. 1911. Circ. 1,300,000. *Boys' Life* is "a general interest magazine for boys 8 to 18 who are members of the Cub Scouts, Boy Scouts or Explorers. A general interest magazine for all boys."
Fiction: Middle readers: adventure, animal, contemporary, fantasy, history, humor, problem-solving, science fiction, sports, spy/mystery. Does not want to see "talking animals and adult reminiscence." Buys 12 mss/year. Average word length: 1,000-1,500. Byline given.
Nonfiction: "Subject matter is broad. We cover everything from professional sports to American history to how to pack a canoe. A look at a current list of the BSA's more than 100 merit badge pamphlets gives an idea of the wide range of subjects possible. Even better, look at a year's worth of recent issues. Column headings are science, nature, earth, health, sports, space and aviation, cars, computers, entertainment, pets, history, music and others." Average word length: 500-1,500. Columns 300-750 words. Byline given.
How to Contact/Writers: Fiction: Send complete ms with SASE. Nonfiction: Query with SASE for response. Reports on queries/mss in 6-8 weeks.
Illustration: Buys 5-7 illustrations/issue; 23-50 illustrations/year. Works on assignment only. Reviews ms/illustration packages from artists. "Query first." Illustrations only: Send tearsheets. Reports on art samples only if interested. Original artwork returned at job's completion.
Terms: Buys first rights. Pays $750 and up for fiction; $400-1,500 for major articles; $150-400 for columns; $250-300 for how-to features.
Tips: "I strongly urge you to study at least a year's issues to better understand type of material published. Articles for *Boys' Life* must interest and entertain boys ages 8 to 18. Write for a boy you know who is 12. Our readers demand crisp, punchy writing in relatively short, straightforward sentences. The editors demand well-reported articles that demonstrate high standards of journalism. We follow *The New York Times* manual of style and usage. All submissions must be accompanied by SASE with adequate postage." (See listing for *Exploring*.)

***BOYS' QUEST**, The Blufton News Publishing and Printing Company, 103 N. Main St., Blufton OH 45817 (419)358-4610. Editor: Marilyn Edwards. Estab. 1995. A magazine of "hands-on adventure for boys of elementary school age."

- Editors of *Boys' Quest* encourage unsolicited articles, artwork and photo submissions. Send SASE for guidelines. See listing for *Hopscotch*.

BREAD FOR GOD'S CHILDREN, Bread Ministries, Inc., P.O. Box 1017, Arcadia FL 33821. (813)494-6214. Editor: Judith M. Gibbs. Monthly magazine. Estab. 1972. Circ. 10,000 (US and Canada). "*Bread* is designed as a teaching tool for Christian families." 85% of publication aimed at juvenile market.
Fiction: Young readers, middle readers, young adults/teens: adventure, contemporary, history, humorous, nature/environment, problem-solving, sports. Looks for "teaching stories that portray

The asterisk before a listing indicates the listing is new in this edition.

Christian lifestyles without preaching." Buys approximately 20 mss/year. Average word length: 900-1,500 (for teens); 600-900 (for young children). Byline given.
Nonfiction: Middle readers and young adult/teens: history, problem-solving, religion, sports, social issues. "We do not want anything detrimental of solid family values." Buys 3-4 mss/year. Average word length: 500-800. Byline given.
How to Contact/Writers: Fiction/nonfiction: Send complete ms. Reports on mss in 2 weeks-6 months "if considered for use." Will consider simultaneous submissions and previously published work.
Terms: Pays on publication. Pays $30-40 for stories; $10-20 for articles. Sample copies free for 9×12 SAE and 6 first-class stamps (for 3 copies).
Tips: "Know the readership . . . know the publisher's guidelines. Edit carefully for content and grammar."

***BRILLIANT STAR**, National Spiritual Assembly of the Bahá'ís of the United States, Bahá'í National Center, Wilmette IL 60091. Managing Editor and Art Director: Pepper Peterson Oldziey. Bimonthly magazine. Estab. 1968. Circ. 2,300. A magazine for Bahá'í children that emphasizes the history, teachings and beliefs of the Bahá'í faith. We look for "sensitivity to multi-racial, multi-cultural audience and a commitment to assisting children in understanding the oneness of the human family." 90% of material aimed at juvenile audience.
Fiction: Young readers, middle readers: contemporary, history, folktales, humorous, multicultural, nature/environment, problem solving, religious, sports, suspense/mystery All "should contain analogy or reference to spiritual principles of our faith." Does not want to see material related to traditional Christian holidays or to secular holidays such as Christmas, Easter or Halloween. Nothing that pontificates! Acquires 12-15 mss/year. Average word length: 250-500. Byline given.
Nonfiction: Young readers, middle readers: arts/crafts, biography, cooking, games/puzzles, geography, history, how-to, humorous, interview/profile, multicultural, nature/environment, problem-solving, religion, sports, travel. All "should contain analogy or reference to spiritual principles of our faith." Multicultural needs include material about interracial groups working together. Does not want to see crafts or activities specific to holidays. Accepts 12-15 mss/year. Average word length: 100-250. Byline given.
Poetry: Reviews poetry. Poems "should contain analogy or reference to spiritual principles of our faith." Word/line length open.
How to Contact/Writers: Fiction/nonfiction: Send complete ms. Reports in 2 months. Publishes ms 8-12 months after acceptance. Will consider simultaneous submissions and previously published work.
Illustration: Works on assignment only. "Illustrations for specific stories on assignment for art director." Reviews ms/illustration packages from artists. Illustrations only: Query; send résumé, promo sheet, tearsheets. Reports on art samples in 2 months. Original artwork returned at job's completion. Credit line given.
Terms: "*Brilliant Star* cannot purchase art or stories at this time." Provides 2 copies of issue in which work appears. Sample copy with 9×12 SAE and 5 oz. worth of postage; writer's/illustrator's/photo guidelines free with SASE.
Tips: Writers: "Know the age range and interests of your reader. Read the magazine before you submit. Express a willingness to adapt a story to the editor's needs. A story from real life is always more interesting than what you think children should read. Avoid morals. Any writer who is willing to learn and study the Bahá'í faith in order to write a story from Bahá'í history will be most welcome and encouraged." Illustrators: "Don't be too cute. Get past the one thing you like to draw best and be ready to expand your range. Art director is open to reviewing general submissions. Need artists who can illustrate diversity of peoples without stereotyping, and in a sensitive way that affirms the beauty of different racial characteristics."

CALLIOPE, World History for Young People, Cobblestone Publishing, Inc., 7 School St., Peterborough NH 03458. (603)924-7209. Managing Editor: Denise L. Babcock. Art Director: Ellen Klempner Beguin. Magazine published 5 times/year. "*Calliope* covers world history (East/West) and lively, original approaches to the subject are the primary concerns of the editors in choosing material."
Fiction: Middle readers and young adults: adventure, folktales, history, biographical fiction. Material must relate to forthcoming themes. Word length: up to 800.

Nonfiction: Middle readers and young adults: arts/crafts, biography, cooking, games/puzzles, history. Material must relate to forthcoming themes. Word length: 300-800.
Poetry: Maximum line length: 100. Wants "clear, objective imagery. Serious and light verse considered."
How to Contact/Writers: "A query must consist of the following to be considered (please use nonerasable paper): a brief cover letter stating subject and word length of the proposed article; a detailed one-page outline explaining the information to be presented in the article; an extensive bibliography of materials the author intends to use in preparing the article; a self-addressed stamped envelope. Writers new to *Calliope* should send a writing sample with query. If you would like to know if your query has been received, please also include a stamped postcard that requests acknowledgment of receipt. In all correspondence, please include your complete address as well as a telephone number where you can be reached. A writer may send as many queries for one issue as he or she wishes, but each query must have a separate cover letter, outline, bibliography and SASE. Telephone queries are not accepted. Handwritten queries will not be considered. Queries may be submitted at any time, but queries sent well in advance of deadline *may not be answered for several months*. Go-aheads requesting material proposed in queries are usually sent five months prior to publication date. Unused queries will be returned approximately three to four months prior to publication date."
Illustration: Illustrations only: Send tearsheets, photocopies. Original work returned upon job's completion (upon written request).
Photography: Buys photos from freelancers. Wants photos pertaining to any forthcoming themes. Uses b&w/color prints, 35 mm transparencies. Send unsolicited photos by mail (on speculation).
Terms: Buys all rights for mss and artwork. Pays 20-25¢/word for stories/articles. Pays on an individual basis for poetry, activities, games/puzzles. "Covers are assigned and paid on an individual basis." Pays photographers per photo ($15-100 for b&w; $25-100 for color). Sample copy for $3.95 and SAE with $1.05 postage. Writer's/illustrator's/photo guidelines for SASE. (See listings for *Cobblestone, The History Magazine for Young People; Faces, The Magazine About People*; and *Odyssey, Science That's Out of This World.*)

CARUS CORPORATION, P.O. Box 300, Peru IL 61354. See listings for *Babybug*, *Cricket*, *Ladybug* and *Spider.*

CHALLENGE, Brotherhood Commission, SBC, 1548 Poplar Ave., Memphis TN 38104. (901)272-2461. Articles Editor: Jeno Smith. Art Director: Roy White. Monthly magazine. Circ. 30,000. Magazine contains youth interests, sports, crafts, sports personalities, religious.
Nonfiction: Young men: career, geography, health, hobbies, how-to, humorous, multicultural, nature/environment, religion, science, social issues, sports, travel, youth issues. Looking for stories on sports heroes with Christian testimony. Buys 36 mss/year. Average word length: 700-900. Byline given.
How to Contact/Writers: Nonfiction: Send complete ms. Reports on queries/mss in 1 month. Will consider simultaneous submissions.
Photography: Purchases photography from freelancers. Wants b&w photos with youth appeal.
Terms: Pays on acceptance. Buys one-time and reprint rights. Pays $25-50 for articles. $5-20 for b&w, $10-35 for color inside. Photographers paid per photo (range: $5-100). Sample copies free for #10 SAE and 3 first-class stamps. Writer's/illustrator's guidelines for SAE and 1 first-class stamp.
Tips: "We prefer photo essays and articles about teenagers and teen activities, interests and issues (sports, nature, health, hobbies). Most open to new writers are features on sports figures 213ztwho offer good moral guidelines to youth, especially those with an effective Christian testimony. We appreciate articles that encourage Christ-like character."

The maple leaf before a listing indicates that the market is Canadian.

✦CHICKADEE MAGAZINE, Owl Communications, Suite 500, 179 John St., Toronto, Ontario M5T 3G5 Canada. Phone/fax: (416)971-5275. Editor-in-Chief: Nyla Ahmad. Managing Editor: Carolyn Meredith. Art Director: Tim Davin. Magazine published 10 times/year. Estab. 1979. Circ. 150,000. *Chickadee* is a "hands-on" publication designed to interest 3-8 year olds in science, nature and the world around them.

Fiction: Young readers: adventure, contemporary, fantasy, folktales, history, humorous, multicultural, problem-solving, science fiction, sports. Does not want to see religious, anthropomorphic animal, romance material, material that talks down to kids. Buys 8 mss/year. Average word length: 800-900. Byline given.

Nonfiction: Young readers: animal (facts/characteristics), arts/crafts, cooking, games/puzzles, interview/profile, travel. Does not want to see religious material. Buys 2-5 mss/year. Average word length: 20-200. Byline given.

Poetry: Limit submissions to 5 poems at a time.

How to Contact/Writers: Fiction/nonfiction: Send complete ms. SASE for answer and return of ms. Reports on mss in 2 months. Will consider simultaneous submissions. "We prefer to read complete manuscript on speculation."

Illustration: Buys 3-5 illustrations/issue; 40 illustrations/year. Preferred theme or style: realism/humor (but not cartoons). Works on assignment only. Illustration only: Send résumé, promo sheet, tearsheets. Reports on art samples only if interested. Credit line given.

Photography: Looking for animal (mammal, insect, reptile, fish, etc.) photos. Uses 35mm and 2¼×2¼ transparencies. Write to request photo package for $1 money order, attention Ekaterina Gitlin, researcher.

Terms: Pays on acceptance. Buys all rights for mss. Buys one-time rights for photos. Pays $25-210 for stories. Pays illustrators $100-650 for color inside, pays photographers per photo (range: $100-350). Sample copies for $4.50. Writer's guidelines free.

Tips: "Study the magazine carefully before submitting material. Fiction most open to freelancers. Kids should be main characters and should be treated with respect." (See listing for *OWL*.)

CHILD LIFE, Children's Better Health Institute, 1100 Waterway Blvd., P.O. Box 567, Indianapolis IN 46206. (317)636-8881. Editor: Lise Hoffman. Art Director: Rebecca Ray. Magazine published 8 times/year. Estab. 1921. Circ. 80,000. "Targeted toward kids ages 9-11, we are the nation's oldest, continuously published children's magazine. Help us celebrate our 75th anniversary year in 1996!" Focuses on health, sports, fitness, nutrition, safety, and general interests.

- To learn more about *Child Life* and other Children's Better Health Institute publications, see Insider Report with CBHI editor Steve Charles in the 1995 edition of *Children's Writer's & Illustrator's Market*.

Fiction: Middle readers: adventure, animal, contemporary, health, humorous, problem-solving, sports, suspense/mystery. "Health and fitness is an ongoing need." Buys 8-10 fiction mss/year. Maximum word length: 800. Byline given.

Nonfiction: Middle readers: animal, arts/crafts, biography, careers, cooking, games/puzzles, health, history, hobbies, how-to, humorous, interview/profile, nature/environment, problem solving, science, social issues, sports, travel. Buys 20-25 nonfiction mss/year. Maximum word length: 800. Byline given.

Poetry: Reviews poetry.

How to Contact/Writers: Fiction/nonfiction: Send complete ms. No queries please. Reports on mss in 3 months. Will not consider previously published material.

Illustration: Buys 8-10 illustrations/issue. Preferred theme: "Need realistic styles especially." Works on assignment only. Illustrations only: Send query, résumé and portfolio. Samples must be accompanied by SASE for response and/or return. Credit line given.

Photography: Purchases professional quality photos with accompanying ms only.

Terms: Pays on publication. Writers paid 10-12¢/word for stories/articles. Buys all rights. Pays illustrators $275/cover; $35-90 b&w inside; $70-155 color inside. For artwork, buys all rights. Pays photographers per photo (range: $25-30). Buys one-time rights for photographs. Writer's guidelines available for SASE.

Tips: "We need profiles of young athletes, aged 9-11, and their sports (825 words maximum) and short pieces on outdoor games/exercise (200 words maximum). Submit all material 8-10 months in advance. Examples: planned features on tennis, beach volleyball, surfing and Olympic sports. We have used adult profiles occasionally. Already covered golf, baseball, basketball, track, sailing, circus, tennis, beach volleyball, surfing and hockey. We also need lowfat recipes for mini-meals and healthful snacks for monthly feature. Avoid sugar, whole eggs (egg whites acceptable), red meat, chocolate (alas), and shortening (when possible). Test recipes before sending them! We do use dessert recipes, but not cakes, cookies, pies, etc., unless they meet above criteria." (See listings for *Children's Digest*, *Children's Playmate*, *Humpty Dumpty's Magazine*, *Jack and Jill*, *Turtle Magazine* and *U*S*Kids*.)

CHILDREN'S BETTER HEALTH INSTITUTE, 1100 Waterway Blvd., P.O. Box 567, Indianapolis IN 46206. See listings for *Child Life*, *Children's Digest*, *Children's Playmate*, *Humpty Dumpty's*, *Jack and Jill*, *Turtle* and *U*S* Kids*.

CHILDREN'S DIGEST, Children's Better Health Institute, 1100 Waterway Blvd., P.O. Box 567, Indianapolis IN 46206. (317)636-8881. Articles/Fiction Editor: Layne Cameron. Art Director: Mary Stropoli. Magazine published 8 times/year. Estab. 1950. Circ. 125,000. For preteens; approximately 33% of content is health-related.

- To learn more about *Children's Digest* and other Children's Better Health Institute publications, see Insider Report with CBHI editor Steve Charles in the 1995 edition of *Children's Writer's & Illustrator's Market.*

Fiction: Middle readers: adventure, animal, contemporary, fantasy, folktales, health, history, humorous, nature/environment, problem-solving, science fiction, sports, suspense/mystery. Buys 25 mss/year. Average word length: 500-1,500. Byline given.
Nonfiction: Middle readers: animal, arts/crafts, biography, cooking, education, games/puzzles, geography, health, history, hobbies, how-to, humorous, interview/profile, nature/environment, science, sports, travel. Buys 16-20 mss/year. Average word length: 500-1,200. Byline given.
Poetry: Maximum length: 20-25 lines.
How to Contact/Writers: Fiction/nonfiction: Send complete ms. Reports on mss in 10 weeks.
Illustration: Reviews ms/illustration packages from artists. Works on assignment only. Query first. Illustrations only: Send résumé and/or slides or tearsheets to illustrate work; query with samples. Reports on art samples in 8-10 weeks. Credit line given.
Photography: Purchases photos with accompanying ms only. Model/property releases required; captions required. Uses 35mm transparencies.
Terms: Pays on acceptance for illustrators, publication for writers. Buys all rights for mss and artwork; one-time rights for photos. Pays 12¢/word for accepted articles. Pays $275 for color cover illustration; $35-90 for b&w, $70-155 for color inside. Photographers paid per photo (range: $10-50). Sample copies for $1.25. Writer's/illustrator's guidelines for SAE and 1 first-class stamp. (See listings for *Child Life*, *Children's Playmate, Humpty Dumpty's Magazine*, *Jack and Jill, Turtle Magazine* and *U*S* Kids*.)

CHILDREN'S MINISTRIES, 6401 The Paseo, Kansas City MO 64131. See listings for *Discoveries* and *Power and Light*.

CHILDREN'S PLAYMATE, Children's Better Health Institute, 1100 Waterway Blvd., P.O Box 567, Indianapolis IN 46206. (317)636-8881. Editor: Terry Harshman. Art Director: Chuck Horsman. Magazine published 8 times/year. Estab. 1929. Circ. 115,000. For children between 6 and 8 years; approximately 33% of content is health-related.

- To learn more about *Children's Playmate* and other Children's Better Health Institute publications, see Insider Report with CBHI editor Steve Charles in the 1995 edition of *Children's Writer's & Illustrator's Market.*

Fiction: Young readers: animal, contemporary, fantasy, folktales, history, humorous, science fiction, sports, suspense/mystery/adventure. Buys 25 mss/year. Average word length: 200-700. Byline given.
Nonfiction: Young readers: animal, arts/crafts, biography, cooking, games/puzzles, health, history, how-to, humorous, sports, travel. Buys 16-20 mss/year. Average word length: 200-700. Byline given.
Poetry: Maximum length: 20-25 lines.
How to Contact/Writers: Fiction/nonfiction: Send complete ms. Reports on mss in 8-10 weeks.
Illustration: Works on assignment only. Reviews ms/illustration packages from artists. Query first.

Photography: Buys photos with accompanying ms only. Model/property releases required; captions required. Uses 35mm transparencies. Send completed ms with transparencies.
Terms: Pays on publication for illustrators and writers. Buys all rights for mss and artwork; one-time rights for photos. Pays 17¢/word for assigned articles. Pays $275 for color cover illustration; $35-90 for b&w inside; $70-155 for color inside. Pays photographers per photo (range: $10-75). Sample copy $1.25. Writer's/illustrator's guidelines for SASE. (See listings for *Child Life*, *Children's Digest*, *Humpty Dumpty's Magazine*, *Jack and Jill*, *Turtle Magazine* and *U*S* Kids*.)

CHOICES, The Magazine for Personal Development and Practical Living Skills, Scholastic Inc. 555 Broadway, New York NY 10012-3999. (212)343-6100. Editor: Lauren Tarshis. Art Director: Ellen Jacobs. Monthly magazine. Estab. 1986 as *Choices* (formerly called *Coed*). "We go to teenagers in home economics, health and living skills classes. All our material has curriculum ties: Personal Development, Family Life, Careers, Food & Nutrition, Consumer Power, Child Development, Communications, Health."
Nonfiction: Buys 10 mss/year. Word length varies. Byline given (except for short items).
How to Contact/Writers: Nonfiction: Query with published clips "We don't want unsolicited manuscripts." Reports on queries in 2 weeks.
Illustration: Works on assignment only. "All art is *assigned* to go with specific articles." Pays on acceptance. Sample copy for 9×12 SAE and 2 first-class stamps.
Tips: "*Read* the specific magazines. We receive unsolicited manuscripts and queries that do not in any way address the needs of our magazine. For example, we don't publish poetry, but we get unsolicited poetry in the mail. This is a teenage magazine, and we don't want articles that are of interest to parents and adults." (See listings for *Dynamath*, *Junior Scholastic*, *Scholastic Math Magazine* and *Superscience Blue*.)

***CLASS ACT**, Class Act, Inc., P.O. Box 802, Henderson KY 42420. Articles Editor: Susan Thurman. Monthly, September-May. Newsletter. Estab. 1993. Circ. 300. "We are looking for practical, ready-to-use ideas for the English/language arts classroom (grades 5-12)."
Nonfiction: Middle readers and young adults: games/puzzles. Does not want to see esoteric material; no master's theses; no poetry (except articles about how to write poetry). Buys 35 mss/year. Average word length: 200-4,000. Byline given.
How to Contact/Writers: Send complete ms. Reports in 10-12 months. Publishes ms 3-12 months after acceptance. Will consider simultaneous submissions. Must send SASE.
Terms: Pays on acceptance. Buys all rights. Sample copy for $3 and SASE.
Tips: "Writers need to realize teens often need humor in classroom assignments. In addition, we are looking for teacher-tested ideas that have already worked in the classroom. If sending puzzles, we usually need at least 20 entries per puzzle to fit our format."

COBBLESTONE, The History Magazine for Young People, Cobblestone Publishing, Inc., 7 School St., Peterborough NH 03458. (603)924-7209. Fax: (603)924-7380. Editor: Meg Chorlian. Art Director: Cat Pragoff. Magazine published 10 times/year. Circ. 38,000. "*Cobblestone* is theme-related. Writers should request editorial guidelines which explain procedure and list upcoming themes. Queries must relate to an upcoming theme. Fiction is not used often, although a good fiction piece offers welcome diversity. It is recommended that writers become familiar with the magazine (sample copies available)."
Fiction: Middle readers, young adults: history. "Authentic historical and biographical fiction, adventure, retold legends, etc., relating to the theme." Buys 6-10 mss/year. Average word length: 800. Byline given.
Nonfiction: Middle readers, young adults: activities, biography, games/puzzles (no word finds), history (world and American), interview/profile, science, travel. All articles must relate to the issue's theme. Buys 120 mss/year. Average word length: 800. Byline given.
Poetry: Up to 100 lines. "Clear, objective imagery. Serious and light verse considered." Pays on an individual basis. Must relate to theme.
How to Contact/Writers: Fiction/nonfiction: Query. "A query must consist of all of the following to be considered (please use nonerasable paper): a brief cover letter stating the subject and word length of the proposed article; a detailed one-page outline explaining the information to be presented in the article; an extensive bibliography of materials the author intends to use in preparing the article; a self-addressed stamped envelope. Writers new to *Cobblestone* should

send a writing sample with query. If you would like to know if your query has been received, please also include a stamped postcard that requests acknowledgment of receipt. In all correspondence, please include your complete address as well as a telephone number where you can be reached. A writer may send as many queries for one issue as he or she wishes, but each query must have a separate cover letter, outline, bibliography and SASE. Telephone queries are not accepted. Handwritten queries will not be considered. Queries may be submitted at any time, but queries sent well in advance of deadline *may not be answered for several months*. Go-aheads requesting material proposed in queries are usually sent five months prior to publication date. Reports on queries/mss in 2 weeks. Unused queries will be returned approximately three to four months prior to publication date."

Illustration: Buys 3 illustrations/issue; 27 illustrations/year. Preferred theme or style: Material that is simple, clear and accurate but not too juvenile. Sophisticated sources are a must. Works on assignment only. Reviews ms/illustration packages from artists. Query. Contact: Meg Chorlian. Illustrations only: Send photocopies, tearsheets, or other nonreturnable samples. Contact: Cat Pragoff, art director. "Illustrators should consult issues of *Cobblestone* to familiarize themselves with our needs." Reports on art samples in 2 weeks. Samples returned with SASE; samples not filed. Original artwork returned at job's completion (upon written request). Credit line given.

Photography: Contact: Meg Chorlian, editor. Photos must relate to upcoming themes. Send transparencies and/or color/b&w prints. Submit on speculation.

Terms: Pays on publication. Buys all rights to articles and artwork. Pays 20-25¢/word for articles/stories. Pays on an individual basis for poetry, activities, games/puzzles. Pays photographers per photo ($15-100 for b&w; $25-100 for color). Sample copy $3.95 with 7½×10½ SAE and 5 first-class stamps; writer's/illustrator's/photo guidelines free with SAE and 1 first-class stamp.

Tips: Writers: "Submit detailed queries which show attention to historical accuracy and which offer interesting and entertaining information. Be true to your own style. Study past issues to know what we look for. All feature articles, recipes, activities, fiction and supplemental nonfiction are freelance contributions." Illustrators: "Submit b&w samples, not too juvenile. Study past issues to know what we look for. The illustration we use is generally for stories, recipes and activities." (See listings for *Calliope, The World History Magazine for Young People*; *Faces, The Magazine About People*; and *Odyssey, Science That's Out of This World*.)

COBBLESTONE PUBLISHING, INC., 7 School St., Peterborough NH 03458. See listings for *Calliope*, *Cobblestone*, *Faces* and *Odyssey*.

COUNSELOR, Scripture Press Publications, Inc., P.O. Box 632, Glen Ellyn IL 60138. (708)668-6000. Articles/Fiction Editor: Janice K. Burton. Art Director: Blake Ebel. Newspaper distributed weekly; published quarterly. Estab. 1940. "Audience: children 8-12 years. Papers designed to present everyday living stories showing the difference Christ can make in a child's life. Must have a true Christian slant, not just a moral implication. Correlated with Scripture Press Sunday School curriculum."

Fiction: Middle readers: adventure, history, multicultural, nature/environment, problem-solving, sports (all with Christian context). "Actually, true stories preferred by far. I appreciate well-written fiction that shows knowledge of our product. I suggest people write for samples." Buys approximately 12 mss/year. Average word length: 300-500. Byline given.

Nonfiction: Middle readers: arts/crafts, biography, games/puzzles, history, interview/profile, nature/environment, problem-solving, religion, science, social issues, sports. Buys approximately 12 mss/year. Average word length: 900-1,100. Byline given.

How to Contact/Writers: Fiction/nonfiction: Send complete ms. Reports on mss in 8-10 weeks. Publishes ms 1-2 years after acceptance (we work a year in advance). Will consider previously published work.

Illustration: Buys 24-30 illustrations/year. Reviews ms/illustration packages from artists, but not often. Contact Blake Ebel for details.

Photography: Purchases photos from freelancers.

Terms: Pays on acceptance. Buys second (reprint) rights, one-time rights, or all rights for mss. Pays 7-10¢/word for stories or articles, depending on amount of editing required. Sample copies for #10 SAE and 1 first-class stamp. Writers/photo guidelines for SASE.

Tips: "Send copy that is as polished as possible. Indicate if story is true. Indicate rights offered. Stick to required word lengths. Include Social Security number on manuscript. Write for our tips for writers, sample copies and theme lists." (See listing for *Primary Days*, *Teen Power* and *Zelos*.)

***CRAYOLA KIDS**, Meredith Corporation, 1912 Grand Ave., Des Moines IA 50309-3379. Estab. 1994. Bimonthly magazine of crafts, games and stories for kids. Prefers not to share information.

CRICKET MAGAZINE, Carus Corporation, P.O. Box 300, Peru IL 61354. (815)224-6656. Articles/Fiction Editor-in-Chief: Marianne Carus. Editor: Deborah Vetter. Art Director: Ron McCutchan. Monthly magazine. Estab. 1973. Circ. 83,000. Children's literary magazine for ages 9-14.
Fiction: Middle readers, young adults: adventure, animal, contemporary, fantasy, folk and fairy tales, history, humorous, multicultural, nature/environment, science fiction, sports, suspense/mystery. Buys 180 mss/year. Maximum word length: 2,000. Byline given.
Nonfiction: Middle readers, young adults: animal, arts/crafts, biography, environment, experiments, games/puzzles, history, how-to, interview/profile, natural science, problem-solving, science and technology, space, sports, travel. Multicultural needs include articles on customs and cultures. Requests bibliography with submissions. Buys 180 mss/year. Average word length: 1,000. Byline given.
Poetry: Reviews poems, 1-page maximum length. Limit submissions to 5 poems or less.
How to Contact/Writers: Send complete ms. Do not query first. Reports on mss in 2-3 months. Does not like but will consider simultaneous submissions. SASE required for response.
Illustration: Buys 35 illustrations (14 separate commissions)/issue; 425 illustrations/year. Uses b&w and full-color work. Preferred theme or style: "strong realism; strong people, especially kids; good action illustration; no cartoons. All media, but prefer other than pencil." Reviews ms/illustration packages from artists "but reserves option to re-illustrate." Send complete ms with sample and query. Illustrations only: Provide tearsheets or good quality photocopies to be kept on file. SASE required for response/return of samples. Reports on art samples in 2 months. Original artwork returned at job's completion.
Photography: Purchases photos with accompanying ms only. Model/property releases required. Uses color transparencies, b&w glossy prints.
Terms: Pays on publication. Buys first publication rights in the English language. Buys first publication rights plus promotional rights for artwork. Pays up to 25¢/word for unsolicited articles; up to $3/line for poetry. Pays $750 for color cover; $75-150 for b&w, $150-250 for color inside. Pays $750 for color cover; $75-150 for b&w, $150-250 for color inside. Writer's/illustrator's guidelines for SASE.
Tips: Writers: "Read copies of back issues and current issues. Adhere to specified word limits. *Please* do not query." Illustrators: "Edit your samples. Send only your best work and be able to reproduce that quality in assignments. Put name and address on *all* samples. Know a publication before you submit—is your style appropriate?" (See listings for *Babybug*, *Ladybug* and *Spider*.)

CRUSADER, Calvinist Cadet Corps, P.O. Box 7259, Grand Rapids MI 49510. (616)241-5616. Editor: G. Richard Broene. Art Director: Robert DeJonge. Magazine published 7 times/year. Circ. 13,000. "Our magazine is for members of the Calvinist Cadet Corps—boys aged 9-14. Our purpose is to show how God is at work in their lives and in the world around them."
Fiction: Middle readers, young adults: Considers all categories but science fiction and romance. Wants to see more adventure, nature and sports. Buys 12 mss/year. Average word length: 800-1,500.
Nonfiction: Middle readers, young adults: considers all categories but fashion. Buys 6 mss/year. Average word length: 400-900.
How to Contact/Writers: Fiction/nonfiction: Send complete ms. Reports on queries/mss in 3-5 weeks. Will consider simultaneous submissions.
Illustration: Buys 1 illustration/issue; buys 6 illustrations/year. Works on assignment only. Reviews ms/illustration packages from artists. Reports in 3-5 weeks. Credit line given.
Photography: Buys photos from freelancers. Wants nature photos and photos of boys.
Terms: Pays on acceptance. Buys first North American serial rights; reprint rights. Pays $10-100 for stories/articles. Pays illustrators $50-200 for b&w cover or inside. Sample copy free with 9×12 SAE and 3 first-class stamps.
Tips: Publication is most open to fiction: write for a list of themes (available yearly in January). See trends in children's magazines in "hard line, real world, to the point and action" material.

CURRENT HEALTH I, The Beginning Guide to Health Education, 60 Revere Dr., Northbrook IL 60062-1563. (708)205-3000. Monthly (during school year September-May) magazine. "For classroom use by students, this magazine is curriculum-specific and requires experienced educators who can write clearly and well at fifth grade reading level."
Nonfiction: Middle readers: health, nature/environment. Buys 60-70 mss/year. Average word length: 1,000. "Credit given in staff box."
How to Contact/Writers: Nonfiction: Query with published clips and résumé. Publishes ms 6-7 months after acceptance.
Illustration: Works on assignments only. Query with samples. Samples returned with SASE; samples filed. Originals returned at job's completion. Credit line given.
Terms: Pays on publication. Buys all rights. Pays $100-150, "more for longer features." Writer's guidelines available for SASE.
Tips: Needs material about drug education, nutrition, fitness and exercise. Articles are assigned to freelance writers on specific topics.

CURRENT HEALTH 2, The Continuing Guide to Health Education, 60 Revere Dr., Northbrook IL 60062-1563. (708)205-3000. Monthly (during school year September-May). "For classroom use by students, this magazine is curriculum specific and requires experienced educators who can write clearly and well at a ninth grade reading level."
Nonfiction: Young adults/teens: health (psychology, disease, nutrition, first-aid and safety), health-related drugs, environment, problem solving, fitness and exercise. Buys 70-90 mss/year. Average word length: 1,000-2,500. Byline given.
How to Contact/Writers: Nonfiction: Query with published clips and résumé. Does not accept unsolicited mss. Reports on queries in 2 months. Publishes ms 6-7 months after acceptance.
Illustration: Buys 2-4 illustrations/issue; 20-40 illustrations/year. Works on assignment only. Query with samples, promo sheet, slides, tearsheets. Contact: Jill Sherman, suvervisor of art direction. Reports only if interested. Samples not returned; samples filed. Originals returned at job's completion. Credit line given.
Terms: Pays on publication. Buys all rights. Pays average $150 for assigned article, "more for longer features." Pays illustrators $200-300 for color cover; $50 for b&w inside; $75-125 for color inside. Sample copies for 9×12 SAE with 3 first-class stamps. Writer's guidelines available only if writers are given an assignment; photo guidelines for SASE.
Tips: Needs writers with background in drug education, first aid and safety.

DISCOVERIES, Children's Ministries, 6401 The Paseo, Kansas City MO 64131. (816)333-7000. Editor: Rebecca Raleigh. Executive Editor: Mark York. Weekly tabloid. *Discoveries* is a leisure reading piece for third and fourth graders. It is published weekly by WordAction Publishing. "The major purposes of *Discoveries* are to provide a leisure reading piece which will build Christian behavior and values and provide reinforcement for Biblical concepts taught in the Sunday School curriculum. The focus of the reinforcement will be life-related, with some historical appreciation. *Discoveries'* target audience is children ages 8-10 in grades three and four. The readability goal is third to fourth grade."
Fiction: Young readers, middle readers: adventure, contemporary, problem-solving, religious. "Fiction—stories should vividly portray definite Christian emphasis or character-building values, without being preachy. The setting, plot and action should be realistic." Average word length: 500-700. Byline given.
How to Contact/Writers: Fiction: Send complete ms. Reports on mss in 6-8 weeks.
Illustration: "*Discoveries* publishes a wide variety of artistic styles, i.e., cartoon, realistic, montage, etc., but whatever the style, artwork must appeal to 8-10 year old children. It should not simply be child-related from an adult viewpoint. All artwork for *Discoveries* is assigned on a work for hire basis. Samples of art may be sent for review. Illustrations only: send résumé, portfolio, client list, tearsheets. Reports back only if interested. Credit line given.
Terms: Pays "approximately one year before the date of issue." Buys multi-use rights. For illustration, buys all rights. Pays 5¢/word. Pays illustrators $75 for color cover. Contributor receives 4 complimentary copies of publication. Writer's/artist's guidelines free with #10 SAE.
Tips: "*Discoveries* is committed to reinforcement of the Biblical concepts taught in the Sunday School curriculum. Because of this, the themes needed are mainly as follows: faith in God, obedience to God, putting God first, choosing to please God, accepting Jesus as Savior, finding

God's will, choosing to do right, trusting God in hard times, prayer, trusting God to answer, importance of Bible memorization, appreciation of Bible as God's Word to man, Christians working together, showing kindness to others, witnessing." (See listing for *Power and Light*.)

DISNEY ADVENTURES, The Walt Disney Company, 114 Fifth Ave., New York NY 10011-9060. Fiction Editor: Suzanne Harper. Monthly Magazine. Estab. 1990. Circ. 1 million.
Fiction: Middle readers: adventure, contemporary, fantasy, humorous, science fiction, sports, suspense/mystery. Buys approximately 6-10 mss/year. Averge word length: 1,500-2,000. Byline given.
Nonfiction: Middle readers: animal, biography, games/puzzles, interview/profile, nature/environment and sports. Buys 100-150 mss/year. Average word length: 250-750. Byline given.
How to Contact/Writers: Fiction: Send complete ms. Nonfiction: Query with published clips. Reports in 1 month. Publishes ms 6-12 months after acceptance. Will consider simultaneous submissions and electronic submissions via disk or modem.
Illustration: Buys approximately 20 illustrations/issue; 250 illustrations/year. Works on assignment only. Reviews ms/illustration packages from artists. Illustrations only: Provide résumé, business card, promotional literature or tearsheets to be kept on file. Reports only if interested. Does not return original artwork.
Photography: Purchases photos separately. Model/property releases required; captions required. Send "anything but originals—everything sent is kept on file." Photographers should provide résumé, business card, promotional literature or tearsheets to be kept on file. Reports only if interested.
Terms: Pays on acceptance. Buys all rights. Purchases all rights for artwork, various rights for photographs. Pays $250-750 for assigned articles. Pays illustrators $50 and up. Photographers paid $100 minimum per project, or $25 minimum per photo. Sample copies: "Buy on newsstand or order copies by calling 1-800-435-0715." Writer's guidelines for SASE.

DOLPHIN LOG, The Cousteau Society, 870 Greenbrier Circle, Suite 402, Chesapeake VA 23320-2641. Editor: Elizabeth Foley. Bimonthly magazine for children ages 7-13. Circ. 80,000. Entirely nonfiction subject matter encompasses all areas of science, natural history, marine biology, ecology and the environment as they relate to our global water system. The philosophy of the magazine is to delight, instruct and instill an environmental ethic and understanding of the interconnectedness of living organisms, including people. Of special interest are articles on ocean- or water-related themes which develop reading and comprehension skills.
Nonfiction: Middle readers, young adult: animal, games/puzzles, geography, interview/profile, nature/environment, science, ocean. Multicultural needs include indigenous peoples, lifestyles of ancient people, etc. Does not want to see talking animals. No dark or religious themes. Buys 10 mss/year. Average word length: 500-700. Byline given.
How to Contact/Writers: Nonfiction: Query first. Reports on queries in 3 months; mss in 6 months.
Illustration: Buys 1 illustration/issue; buys 6 illustrations/year. Preferred theme: Biological illustration. Reviews ms/illustration packages from artists. Illustrations only: Query; send résumé, promo sheet, slides. Reports on art samples in 8 weeks only if interested. Credit line given to illustrators.
Photography: Wants "sharp, colorful pictures of sea creatures. The more unusual the creature, the better."
Terms: Pays on publication. Buys first North American serial rights; reprint rights. Pays $25-200 for articles. Pays $75-200/color photos. Sample copy $2.50 with 9×12 SAE and 3 first-class stamps. Writer's/illustrator's guidelines free with #10 SASE.
Tips: Writers: "Write simply and clearly and don't anthropomorphize." Illustrators: "Be scientifically accurate and don't anthropomorphize. Some background in biology is helpful, as our needs range from simple line drawings to scientific illustrations which must be researched for biological and technical accuracy."

DYNAMATH, Scholastic Inc., 555 Broadway, New York NY 10012-3999. (212)343-6432. Editor: Joe D'Agnese. Art Director: Pam Mitchell. Monthly magazine. Estab. 1981. Circ. 300,000. Purpose is "to make learning math fun, challenging and uncomplicated for young minds in a very complex world."

Nonfiction: All levels: animal, arts/crafts, cooking, fashion, games/puzzles, health, history, hobbies, how-to, humorous, math, multicultural, nature/environment, problem-solving, science, social issues, sports—all must relate to math and science topics.
How to Contact/Writers: Nonfiction: Query with published clips, send ms. Reports on queries in 1 month; mss in 6 weeks. Publishes ms 4 months after acceptance. Will consider simultaneous submissions.
Illustration: Buys 4 illustrations/issue. Illustration only: Query first; send résumé and tearsheets. Reports back on submissions only if interested. Originals returned to artist at job's completion. Credit line given.
Terms: Pays on acceptance. Buys all rights for mss, artwork, photographs. Pays $50-300 for stories. Pays artists $800-1,000 for color cover illustration; $100-800 for color inside illustration. Pays photographers $300-1,000 per project.
Tips: See listings for *Choices*, *Junior Scholastic*, *Scholastic Math Magazine* and *Superscience Blue*.

EXPLORING, Boy Scouts of America, 1325 W. Walnut Hill Lane, P.O. Box 152079, Irving TX 75015-2079. (214)580-2365. Executive Editor: Scott Daniels. Art Director: Joe Connally. Photo Editor: Brian Payne. Magazine published "4 times a year (January, April, June and November)." *Exploring* is a 20-page, 4-color magazine published for members of the Boy Scouts of America's Exploring program. These members are young men and women between the ages of 14-21. Interests include careers, computers, life skills (money management, parent/peer relationships, study habits), college, camping, hiking, canoeing.
Nonfiction: Young adults: interview/profile, problem-solving, travel. Buys 12 mss/year. Average word length: 600-1,200. Byline given.
How to Contact/Writers: Nonfiction: Query with published clips. Reports on queries/mss in 1 week.
Illustration: Buys 3 illustrations/issue; 12 illustrations/year. Works on assignment only. Illustration only: Reports on art samples in 2 weeks. Original artwork returned at job's completion.
Terms: Pays on acceptance. Buys first North American serial rights. Pays $300-500 for assigned/unsolicited articles. Pays $1,000 for color illustrated cover; $250-500 for b&w inside; $500-800 for color inside. Sample copy with 8½×11 SAE and 5 first-class stamps. Free writer's/illustrator's guidelines.
Tips: Looks for "short, crisp career profiles of 1,000 words with plenty of information to break out into graphics." (See listing for *Boys' Life*.)

FACES, The Magazine About People, Cobblestone Publishing, Inc., 7 School St., Peterborough NH 03458. (603)924-7209. Fax: (603)924-7380. Editor-in-Chief: Carolyn P. Yoder. Picture Editor: Francelle Carapetyan. Magazine published 9 times/year (September-May). Circ. 15,000. "Although *Faces* operates on a by-assignment basis, we welcome ideas/suggestions in outline form. All manuscripts are reviewed by the American Museum of Natural History in New York before being accepted. *Faces* is a theme-related magazine; writers should send for theme list before submitting ideas/queries."
Fiction: Middle readers: anthropology; young adults: contemporary, folktales, history, multicultural, religious. Does not want to see material that does not relate to a specific upcoming theme. Buys 9 mss/year. Maximum word length: 800. Byline given.
Nonfiction: Middle readers and young adults: anthropology, arts/crafts, games/puzzles, history, interview/profile, religious, travel. Does not want to see material not related to a specific upcoming theme. Buys 63 mss/year. Average word length: 300-800. Byline given.
How to Contact/Writers: Fiction/nonfiction: Query with published clips and 2-3 line biographical sketch. "Ideas should be submitted six to nine months prior to the publication date. Responses to ideas are usually sent approximately four months before the publication date."
Illustration: Buys 3 illustrations/issue; buys 27 illustrations/year. Preferred theme or style: Material that is meticulously researched (most articles are written by professional anthropologists); simple, direct style preferred, but not too juvenile. Works on assignment only. Roughs required. Reviews ms/illustration packages from artists. Illustrations only: Send samples of b&w work. "Illustrators should consult issues of *Faces* to familiarize themselves with our needs." Reports on art samples in 1-2 months. Original artwork returned at job's completion (upon written request).

Photography: Wants photos relating to forthcoming themes.
Terms: Pays on publication. Buys all rights for mss and artwork. Pays 20-25¢/word for articles/stories. Covers are assigned and paid on an individual basis. Pays photographers per photo ($15-100 for b&w; $25-100 for color). Sample copy $3.95 with 7½×10½ SAE and 5 first-class stamps. Writer's/illustrator's/photo guidelines free with SAE and 1 first-class stamp.
Tips: "Writers are encouraged to study past issues of the magazine to become familiar with our style and content. Writers with anthropological and/or travel experience are particularly encouraged; *Faces* is about world cultures. All feature articles, recipes and activities are freelance contributions." Illustrators: "Submit b&w samples, not too juvenile. Study past issues to know what we look for. The illustration we use is generally for retold legends, recipes and activities." (See listing for *Calliope, The World History Magazine for Young People*; *Cobblestone, The History Magazine for Young People*; and *Odyssey, Science That's Out of This World.*)

FALCON MAGAZINE, Falcon Press, 48 Last Chance Gulch, P.O. Box 1718, Helena MT 59624. (406)449-1335. Executive Editor: Kay Morton Ellerhoff. Editorial Director: Carolyn Zieg Cunningham. Design Editor: Bryan Knaff. Bimonthly magazine. Estab. 1993. Circ. 55,000. "A magazine for young conservationists."
Nonfiction: Middle readers: nature/environment, wildlife habitat and outdoor recreation. Average word length: 800 maximum. Byline given.
How to Contact/Writers: Fiction/nonfiction: Query. Reports in 2 months.
Illustration: Buys 6 illustrations/issue; 75 illustrations/year. Prefers work on assignment. Reviews ms/illustration packages from artists. Illustrations only: Query; send slides, tearsheets. Reports in 2 months. Samples returned with SASE; samples sometimes filed. Original work returned upon job's completion. Credit line given.
Photography: *Must* be submitted in 20-slide sheets and individual protectors, such as KYMAC. Looks for "children outdoors—camping, fishing, doing 'nature' projects." Model/property releases required. Photo captions required. Uses 35mm transparencies. To contact photographers should query with samples. Reports in 2 months.
Terms: Pays 30-60 days after publication. Buys one-time rights for mss. Purchases one-time rights for photographs. Pays $100 and up for full-length features. Additional payment for ms/illustration packages ($200). Pays illustrators variable rate for b&w inside; $250 color cover; $35-100 color inside. Photographers paid by the project ($50 minimum); per photo (range: $50-100). Sample copies for 8½×11 SAE. Writer's/illustrator's/photo guidelines for SASE.

***FAMILY FUN**, Disney Magazine Publishing, 244 Main St., Northampton MA 01060. (413)585-0444. Articles Editor: Susan Clare Ellis. Fiction Editor: Deanna F. Cook. Art Director: David Kendrick. Photo Editor: Mark Mantega. Monthly magazine. Estab. 1991. Circ. 700,000. "*Family Fun* is a magazine for parents of children ages 3 to 12. It covers all the great things families can do together: travel, educational projects, holiday celebrations, crafts and more." 5-10% of publication aimed at juvenile market.
Fiction: Buys 10-12 mss/year. Average word length: 500-750. Byline given.
How to Contact/Writers: Send complete ms. Reports on mss in 1-3 months. Will consider simultaneous submissions and previously published work.
Terms: Pays on acceptance. Pays $500 maximum for stories. Writer's guidelines free for SASE.
Tips: "We are a magazine for parents of children ages three to twelve and we cover all the great things families can do together. We deem an idea a good one when it is fun for the whole family, it is inexpensive, and it is not time consuming for a parent to plan. *Family Fun*'s style is upbeat and straightforward. Ours is not a child-rearing magazine—we do not give out advice about health, discipline, or other concerns in child development—so we do not consider queries on

those topics or quote psychologists or other experts. We rely primarily on our staff members and regular contributors for features and feature ideas, but we welcome freelance queries for a number of sections in the magazine. With each query or manuscript you send, please include a short cover letter and two or three relevant clips for our review."

FIELD & STREAM, Times Mirror Magazines, 2 Park Ave., New York NY 10016. (212)779-5000. Editor: Duncan Barnes. Designer: Daniel J. McClain. Estab. 1989. Circ. 2 million. "Field & Stream Jr.," a special 3- to 4-page section of *Field & Stream*, is designed to teach young sportsmen about hunting, fishing and related topics. "We publish straightforward how-to pieces, crafts and projects, puzzles, adventure stories, and fillers about hunting and fishing."
Nonfiction: Middle readers: animal, arts/crafts, biography, games/puzzles, how-to, interview/profile, nature/environment, hunting/fishing. "We are looking for articles that are related to hunting and/or fishing. We see too many articles not connected to these topics, and too many 'my first fishing trip' type stories." Buys 25 mss/year. Average word length: 25 to 500 (25 for fillers). Byline given.
How to Contact/Writers: Nonfiction: Query with published clips. Reports on queries/mss in 1 month. Publishes ms 3-12 months after acceptance. Will consider electronic submissions via disk or modem.
Illustration: Buys 5 illustrations/issue; 30 illustrations/year. Works on assignment only. Reviews ms/illustration packages from artists. Query. Illustrations only: Send résumé, promo sheet and portfolio. Samples returned with SASE; samples filed. Original work returned at job's completion. Credit line given.
Photography: Buys photos from freelancers. Uses 35mm transparencies. Query with samples. Reports in 1 month.
Terms: Pays on acceptance. Buys first North American serial rights for mss. Buys first North American serial rights for artwork and photographs. Pays $75-650 for articles. Additional payment for ms/illustration packages and for photos accompanying articles. Pays illustrators $300-800 for color inside. Pays photographers per photo ($450). Sample copies for $4. Writer's/photo guidelines for SASE.
Tips: "Study back issues of magazines to see what kinds of articles they use and what topics they cover. For 'Field & Stream Jr.,' we are looking for manuscripts that cover hunting and fishing and related topics, such as conservation, natural history and sporting ethics. Most photos or illustrations are requested by the editors in order to complement and illustrate stories. We also include writing by children."

***FLORIDA LEADER, for high school students**, Oxendine Publishing, Inc., P.O. Box 14081, Gainesville FL 32604-2081. (904)373-6907. Fax: (904)373-8120. E-mail: 75143.2043@compuserve.com. Articles Editor: Kay Quinn. Art Director: Jeff Riemersma. Quarterly magazine. Estab. 1992. Circ. 50,000. Audience includes ages 14-17. Aimed at the juvenile market.
Nonfiction: Young adult: careers, fashion, humorous, interview/profile, social issues, sports. Looking for "more advanced pieces on college preparation—academic skills, career exploration and general motivation for college." Buys 6-8 mss/year. Average word length: 800-1,000. 200-300 for columns.
How to Contact/Writers: Nonfiction: Query with published clips. Reports on queries in 3 weeks; mss in 2 weeks. Publishes ms 3-5 months after acceptance. Will consider simultaneous submissions, electronic submissions, previously published work.
Illustration: Buys 5 illustrations/issue; 20 illustrations/year. Uses color artwork only. Works on assignment only. Reviews ms/illustration packages from artists. Query. Contact: Jeff Riemersma, art director. Illustrations only: query with samples; send résumé, promo sheet, tearsheets. Contact: Jeff Riemersma, art director. Reports only if interested. Samples returned with SASE; samples filed. Originals returned at job's completion. Credit line given.
Photography: Buys photos from freelancers. Buys photos separately. Works on assignment only. Model/property release required. Uses color prints and 35mm, $2\frac{1}{4} \times 2\frac{1}{4}$, 4×5 transparencies. Query with samples. Reports only if interested.
Terms: Pays on publication. Buys first North American serial rights, reprint rights for mss. Buys first time rights for artwork; first time rights for photos. Pays $35-50 for articles. Pays first-time or less experienced writers or for shorter items with contribution copies or other premiums. Pays illustrators $50-75 for color inside. Pays photographers by the project (range: $150-300). Sample copies for $3.50. Writer's guidelines free for SASE.

Tips: "Review past issues for style and topics."

FOCUS ON THE FAMILY CLUBHOUSE; FOCUS ON THE FAMILY CLUBHOUSE JR., Focus on the Family, 8605 Explorer Dr., Colorado Springs CO 80920. (719)531-3400. Editors: Lisa Brock and Marianne Hering. Art Director: Timothy Jones. Monthly magazine. Estab. 1987. Combined circulation is 250,000. "*Focus on the Family Clubhouse* is a 16-page Christian magazine, published monthly, for children ages 8-12. Similarly, *Focus on the Family Clubhouse Jr.* is published for children ages 4-8. We want fresh, exciting literature that promotes biblical thinking, values and behavior in every area of life."
Fiction: Picture-oriented material and young readers: adventure, animal, contemporary, humorous, multicultural, religious. Middle readers: adventure, contemporary, humorous, multicultural, nature/environment, science fiction, sports. Multicultural needs include: "interesting, informative, accurate information about other cultures to teach children appreciation for the world around them." Buys approximately 6-10 mss/year. Average word length: *Clubhouse*, 500-1,400; *Clubhouse Jr.*, 250-1,100. Byline given on all fiction; not on puzzles.
Nonfiction: Picture-oriented material, young readers and middle readers: animal, arts/crafts, cooking, games/puzzles, hobbies, multicultural, nature/environment, science, sports. Middle readers: biography. Buys 3-5 mss/year. Average word length: 200-1,000. Byline given.
Poetry: Wants to see "humorous or biblical" poetry. Maximum length: 25 lines.
How to Contact/Writers: Fiction/nonfiction: send complete ms. Reports on queries/mss in 4-6 weeks. Publishes ms 4-6 months after acceptance.
Illustration: Buys 8 illustrations/issue. Uses color artwork only. Works on assignment only. Reviews ms/illustration packages from artists. Submit ms with rough sketches. Contact: Tim Jones, art director. Illustrations only: Query with samples, arrange portfolio review or send tearsheets. Contact: Tim Jones, art director. Reports in 2-3 months. Samples returned with SASE; samples kept on file. Original work returned at job's completion. Credit line given.
Photography: Buys photos from freelancers. Uses 35mm transparencies. Photographers should query with samples; provide résumé and promotional literature or tearsheets. Reports in 2 months.
Terms: Pays on acceptance. Buys first North American serial rights and reprint rights (occasionally) for mss. Buys first rights or reprint rights for artwork and photographs. Additional payment for ms/illustration packages. Pays writers $100-300 for stories; $100-150 for articles. Pays illustrators $400-700 for color cover; $200-700 for color inside. Pays photographers by the project or per photo. Sample copies for 9×12 SAE and 3 first-class stamps. Writer's/illustrators/photo guidelines for SASE.
Tips: "Test your writing on children. The best stories avoid moralizing or preachiness, and are not written *down* to children. They are the products of writers who share in the adventure with their readers, exploring the characters they have created without knowing for certain where the story will lead. And they are not always explicitly Christian, but are built upon a Christian foundation (and, at the very least, do not contradict biblical views or values)."

FOR SENIORS ONLY, Campus Communications, Inc., 339 N. Main St., New City NY 10956. (914)638-0333. Articles/Fiction Editor: Judi Oliff. Art Director: Randi Wendelkin. Semiannual magazine. Estab. 1971. Circ. 350,000. Publishes career-oriented articles for high school students, college-related articles, and feature articles on travel, etc.
Fiction: Young adults: health, humorous, sports, travel. Byline given.
Nonfiction: Young adults: careers, games/puzzles, health, how-to, humorous, interview/profile, social issues, sports, travel. Buys 4-6 mss/year. Average word length: 1,000-2,500. Byline given.
How to Contact/Writers: Fiction/nonfiction: Query; query with published clips; send complete ms. Publishes ms 2-4 months after acceptance. Will consider simultaneous submissions, electronic submissions via disk or modem and previously published work.
Illustration: Reviews ms/illustration packages from artists. Query; submit complete package with final art; submit ms with rough sketches. Illustrations only: Query; send slides. Reports back only if interested. Samples not returned; samples kept on file. Original work returned upon job's completion. Credit line given.
Photography: Model/property release required. Uses 5½×8½ and 4⅞×7⅜ color prints; 35mm and 8×10 transparencies. Query with samples; send unsolicited photos by mail. Reports back only if interested.
Terms: Pays on publication. Buys exclusive magazine rights. Payment is byline credit. Writer's/illustrator's/photo guidelines for SASE.

THE FRIEND MAGAZINE, The Church of Jesus Christ of Latter-day Saints, 50 E. North Temple, Salt Lake City UT 84150. (801)240-2210. Managing Editor: Vivian Paulsen. Art Director: Richard Brown. Monthly magazine. Estab. 1971. Circ. 350,000. Magazine for 3-11 year olds.
Fiction: Picture material, young readers, middle readers: adventure, animal, contemporary, folktales, history, humorous, problem-solving, religious, ethnic, sports, suspense/mystery. Does not want to see controversial issues, political, horror, fantasy. Average word length: 400-1,000. Byline given.
Nonfiction: Picture material, young readers, middle readers: animal, arts/crafts, biography, cooking, games/puzzles, history, how-to, humorous, problem-solving, religious, sports. Does not want to see controversial issues, political, horror, fantasy. Average word length: 400-1,000. Byline given.
Poetry: Reviews poetry. Maximum length: 20 lines.
How to Contact/Writers: Fiction/nonfiction: Send complete ms. Reports on mss in 2 months.
Illustration: Illustrations only: Query with samples; arrange personal interview to show portfolio; provide résumé and tearsheets for files.
Terms: Pays on acceptance. Buys all rights for mss. Pays 9-11¢/word for unsolicited articles. Contributors are encouraged to send for sample copy for $1.50, 9×11 envelope and $1 postage. Free writer's guidelines.
Tips: "*The Friend* is published by The Church of Jesus Christ of Latter-day Saints for boys and girls up to 12 years of age. All submissions are carefully read by the *Friend* staff, and those not accepted are returned within two months when a self-addressed, stamped envelope is enclosed. Submit seasonal material at least eight months in advance. Query letters and simultaneous submissions are not encouraged. Authors may request rights to have their work reprinted after their manuscript is published."

"Realistic and lively" is the way Editor Amy Ruth describes Mary Moye-Rowley's illustrations for "Jeremiah's Gift," a short story published in the magazine* The Goldfinch, Iowa History for Young People. *That blend of realism and action was "a perfect combination for a fictional story about events in Iowa history," Ruth says. Using pencil and pen & ink, Moye-Rowley captured movement in young Jeremiah, and minute detail in the background storefronts and patrons. A long-time contributor to the magazine, Moye-Rowley penned four other drawings to illustrate the story of a boy who learns that giving is really a gift for the giver.

***GIRLS' LIFE**, Monarch Avalon, 4517 Harford Rd. Baltimore MD 21214. (410)254-9200. Fax: (410)254-0991. Articles Editors: Michelle Silver and Kelly White. Art Director: Chun Kim. Bimonthy magazine. Estab. 1994. General interest magazine for girls, ages 7-14.
Nonfiction: Accepts articles on any subject except religion. Buys 25 mss/year. Word length varies. Byline given.

How to Contact/Writers: Nonfiction: Query with published clips. Send complete ms on spec only. Reports in 4 months. Publishes ms 3 months after acceptance. Will consider simultaneous submissions.
Illustration: Buys 40 illustrations/issue. Uses color artwork only. Works on assignment only. Reviews ms/illustration packages from artists. Send ms with dummy. Contact: Michelle Silver, senior editor. Illustration only: Query with samples; send tearsheets. Contact: Chun Kim, art director. Reports back only if interested. Samples filed. Credit line given.
Photography: Buys photos from freelancers. Uses 35mm transparencies. Provide samples. Reports back only if interested.
Terms: Pays on publication. Sample copies available for $2.95. Writer's guidelines for SASE.

THE GOLDFINCH, Iowa History for Young People, State Historical Society of Iowa, 402 Iowa Ave., Iowa City IA 52240. (319)335-3916. Fax: (319)335-3924. Editor: Amy Ruth. Quarterly magazine. Estab. 1975. Circ. 40,000. "The award-winning *Goldfinch* consists of 10-12 nonfiction articles, short fiction, poetry and activities per issue. Each magazine focuses on an aspect or theme of history that occurred in or affected Iowa."
Fiction: Middle readers: historical fiction only. "Study past issues for structure and content. Most manuscripts written inhouse." Average word length: 500-1,500. Byline given.
Nonfiction: Middle readers: arts/crafts, biography, games/puzzles, history, interview/profile, "all tied to an Iowa theme." Uses 20-30 mss/year. Average word length: 500-800. Byline given.
Poetry: Reviews poetry. No minimum or maximum word length; no maximum number of submissions. "All poetry must reflect an Iowa theme."
How to Contact/Writers: Fiction/nonfiction: Query with published clips. Reports on queries/mss in up to 2 months. Publishes ms 1 month-1 year after acceptance. Will consider electronic submissions via disk or modem.
Illustration: Buys 8 illustrations/issue; 32 illustrations/year. Works on assignment only. Prefers cartoon, line drawing. Illustrations only: Query with samples. Reports in up to 2 weeks. Samples returned with SASE.
Photography: Types of photos used vary with subject. Model/property releases required with submissions. Uses b&w prints; 35mm transparencies. Query with samples. Reports in 2-4 weeks.
Terms: Pays on publication. Buys all rights. Payment for mss is in copies at this time. Pays illustrators $10-150. Photographers paid per photo (range: $10-100). Sample copies for $4. Writer's/illustrator's/photo guidelines free for SASE.
Tips: "The editor researches the topics and determines the articles. Writers, most of whom live in Iowa, work from primary and secondary research materials to write pieces. The presentation is aimed at children 8-14. All submissions must relate to an upcoming Iowa theme. Please send SASE for our writer's guidelines and theme lists before submitting manuscripts."

GUIDE MAGAZINE, Review and Herald Publishing Association, 55 W. Oak Ridge Dr., Hagerstown MD 21740. (301)791-7000. Articles Editor: Carolyn Rathbun. Art Director: Bill Kirstein. Weekly magazine. Estab. 1953. Circ. 34,000. "Ours is a weekly Christian journal written for middle readers and young adults, presenting true stories relevant to the needs of today's young person, emphasizing positive aspects of Christian living."
Nonfiction: Middle readers, young adults: adventure, animal, biography, character-building, contemporary, games/puzzles, humorous, nature/environment, problem-solving, religious, social issues, sports, suspense/mystery. "We need true, or based on true, happenings, not merely true-to-life. Our stories and puzzles must have a spiritual emphasis." No violence. No articles. "We always need humorous adventure stories." Buys 300 mss/year. Average word length: 500-600 minimum, 1,000-1,200 maximum. Byline given.
How to Contact/Writers: Nonfiction: Send complete ms. Reports in 1-2 weeks. Will consider simultaneous submissions. "We can only pay half of the regular amount for simultaneous submissions." Reports on queries/mss in 1 week. Credit line given.
Terms: Pays on acceptance. Buys first North American serial rights; first rights; one-time rights; second serial (reprint rights); simultaneous rights. Pays 3-6¢/word for stories and articles. "Writer receives several complimentary copies of issue in which work appears." Sample copy free with 5×9 SAE and 2 first-class stamps. Writer's guidelines for SASE.
Tips: Children's magazines "want mystery, action, discovery, suspense and humor—no matter what the topic."

GUIDEPOSTS FOR KIDS, Guideposts, 16 E. 34th St., New York NY 10016. Fax: (219)926-3839. Editor: Mary Lou Carney. Articles Editor: Sailor Metts. Fiction Editor: Lurlene McDaniel. Art Director: Mike Lyons. Photo Editor: Wendy Martinick. Bimonthly magazine. Estab. 1990. Circ. 200,000. "*Guideposts for Kids* is published bimonthly by Guideposts for kids 7-12 years-old (emphasis on upper end of that age bracket). It is a Bible-based, direct mail magazine that is *fun* to read. It is *not* a Sunday school take-home paper or a miniature *Guideposts*."

Fiction: Middle readers: adventure, animal, contemporary, fantasy, folktales, historical, humorous, multicultural, nature/environment, problem-solving, religious, sports, suspense/mystery. Multicultural needs include: Kids in other cultures—school, sports, families. Does not want to see preachy fiction. "We want real stories about real kids doing real things—conflicts our readers will respect; resolutions our readers will accept. Problematic. Tight. Filled with realistic dialogue and sharp imagery. No stories about 'good' children always making the right decision. If present at all, adults are minor characters and *do not* solve kids' problems for them." Buys approximately 10 mss/year. Average word length: 500-1,300. Byline given.

Nonfiction: Middle readers: concept, current events, games/puzzles, hobbies, how-to, humorous, interview/profile, multicultural, nature/environment, problem-solving, profiles of kids, religious, science, seasonal, social issues, sports, travel. "Make nonfiction issue-oriented, controversial, thought-provoking. Something kids not only *need* to know, but *want* to know as well." Buys 10 mss/year. Average word length: 200-1,300. Byline usually given.

How to Contact/Writers: Fiction: Send complete ms. Nonfiction: Query. Reports on queries/mss in 4-6 weeks.

Illustration: Buys 7 illustrations/issue; 40 illustrations/year. Uses color artwork only. Works on assignment only. Reviews ms/illustration packages from artists. Send ms with dummy. Contact: Mike Lyons, art director. Illustration only: Query; send résumé, tearsheets. Reports in 4 months. Credit line given.

Photography: Looks for "spontaneous, *real* kids in action shots."

Terms: Pays on acceptance. Buys all rights for mss. Buys first rights for artwork. "Features range in payment from $250-400; fiction from $250-400. We pay higher rates for stories exceptionally well-written or well-researched. Regular contributors get bigger bucks, too." Additional payment for ms/illustration packages "but we prefer to acquire our own illustrations." Sample copies for $3.25. Writer's guidelines free for SASE.

Tips: "Make your manuscript good, relevant and playful. No preachy stories about Bible-toting children. *Guideposts for Kids* is not a beginner's market. Study our magazine. (Sure, you've heard that before—but it's *necessary*!) Neatness *does* count. So do creativity and professionalism. SASE essential."

HIGH ADVENTURE, Assemblies of God, 1445 Boonville Ave., Springfield MO 65802. (417)862-2781, Ext. 4181. Fax: (417)862-0416. Editor: Marshall Bruner. Quarterly magazine. Circ. 86,000. Estab. 1971. Magazine is designed to provide boys with worthwhile, enjoyable, leisure reading; to challenge them in narrative form to higher ideals and greater spiritual dedication; and to perpetuate the spirit of Royal Rangers through stories, ideas and illustrations. 75% of material aimed at juvenile audience.

Fiction: Buys 100 mss/year. Average word length: 1,000. Byline given.

Nonfiction: Articles: Christian living, devotional, Holy Spirit, salvation, self-help; biography; missionary stories; news items; testimonies, inspirational stories based on true-life experiences.

How to Contact/Writers: Fiction/nonfiction: Send complete ms. Reports on queries in 6-8 weeks. Will consider simultaneous submissions. Will review ms/illustration packages.

How to Contact/Illustrators: Ms/illustration packages: Send complete ms with final art. Illustrations only: "Most of our artwork is done in-house."

Terms: Pays on acceptance. Buys first and second rights. Pays 2-3¢/word for articles. Sample copy free with 9×12 SASE. Free writer's/illustrator's guidelines for SASE.

HIGHLIGHTS FOR CHILDREN, 803 Church St., Honesdale PA 18431. (717)253-1080. Manuscript Coordinator: Beth Troop. Art Director: Janet Moir. Monthly magazine. Estab. 1946. Circ. 2.8 million. "Our motto is 'Fun With a Purpose.' We are looking for quality fiction and nonfiction that appeals to children, encourages them to read, and reinforces positive values. All art is done on assignment."

Fiction: Picture-oriented material, young readers, middle readers: animal, contemporary, fantasy, folktales, history, humorous, multicultural, nature/environment, sports. Young readers, middle readers: adventure, problem-solving, science fiction. Multicultural needs include first person accounts of children from other cultures. Does not want to see war, crime, violence. "We see too many stories with overt morals." Would like to see more suspense/stories/articles with world culture settings, sports pieces, action/adventure. Buys 150 mss/year. Average word length: 400-800. Byline given.

Nonfiction: Picture-oriented material, young readers, middle readers: animal, arts/crafts, biography, games/puzzles, geography, health, history, humorous, nature/environment, science, sports. Young readers, middle readers: careers, foreign, geography, interview/profile, problem-solving, social issues. Multicultural needs include articles set in a country *about* the people of the country. "We have plenty of articles with Asian and Spanish settings. We also have plenty of holiday articles." Does not want to see trendy topics, fads, personalities who would not be good role models for children, guns, war, crime, violence. "We'd like to see more nonfiction for younger readers—maximum of 600 words. We still need older-reader material, too—600-900 words." Buys 75 mss/year. Maximum word length: 900. Byline given.

How to Contact/Writers: Send complete ms. Reports on queries/mss in 4-6 weeks.

Illustration: Buys 25-30 illustrations/issue. Preferred theme or style: Realistic, some stylization, cartoon style acceptable. Works on assignment only. Reviews ms/illustration packages from artists. Send ms and sample illustrations. Contact: Beth Troop, manuscript coordinator. Illustrations only: photocopies, promo sheet, tearsheets or slides. Résumé optional. Portfolio only if requested. Contact: Janet Moir, art director. Reports on art samples in 4-6 weeks. Samples returned with SASE; samples filed. Credit line given.

Terms: Pays on acceptance. Buys all rights for mss. Pays 14¢/word and up for unsolicited articles. Pays illustrators $1,000 for color cover; $25-200 for b&w, $100-500 for color inside. Writer's/illustrator's guidelines free on request.

Tips: "Know the magazine's style before submitting. Send for guidelines and sample issue if necessary." Writers: "At *Highlights* we're paying closer attention to acquiring more nonfiction for young readers than we have in the past." Illustrators: "Fresh, imaginative work encouraged. Flexibility in working relationships a plus. Illustrators presenting their work need not confine themselves to just children's illustrations as long as work can translate to our needs. We also use animal illustrations, real and imaginary. We need party plans, crafts and puzzles—any activity that will stimulate children mentally and creatively. We are always looking for imaginative cover subjects."

HOBSON'S CHOICE, P.O. Box 98, Ripley OH 45167. (513)392-4549. Editor: Susannah C. West. Bimonthly magazine. Estab. 1974. Circ. 2,000. "*Hobson's Choice* is a science fiction magazine which also publishes science and technology-related nonfiction along with stories. Although the magazine is not specifically aimed at children, we do number teenagers among our readers. Such readers are the type who might enjoy reading science fiction (both young adult and adult), attending science fiction conventions, using computers, and be interested in such things as astronomy, the space program, etc."

Fiction: Young adults: fantasy, science fiction. "I'm really not interested in seeing fiction other than science fiction and fantasy. Nor am I interested in horror and cyberpunk, although these can be considered subgenres of fantasy and science fiction. I also see too much hackneyed science fiction and fantasy." Buys 12-15 mss/year. Average word length 2,000-10,000.

Nonfiction: Young adults: how-to (science), interview/profile, science. Does not want to see crafts. Buys 8-10 mss/year. Average word length: 1,500-5,000. Byline given.

How to Contact/Writers: Fiction: Send complete ms. Nonfiction: Query first. Reports on queries/mss in 4 months maximum. ("After 4 months, author should feel free to withdraw ms from consideration.") Will consider submissions via disk (Macintosh MacWrite, WriteNow, IBM PC or compatible on 3½ disks).

Illustration: Buys 2-5 illustrations/issue; 20-30 illustrations/year. Uses b&w artwork only. Prefers to review "science fiction, fantasy or technical illustration." Reviews ms/illustration packages; reviews artwork for future assignments.

How to Contact/Illustrators: Ms/illustration packages: "Would like to see clips to keep on file (b&w only, preferably photocopies)." Illustrations only: Query with tearsheets to be kept on file. "If we have an assignment for an artist, we will contact him/her with the ms we want illustrated. We like to see roughs before giving the go-ahead for final artwork." Reports in 4 months "if requested and if request accompanied by SASE." Original artwork returned at job's completion, "sometimes, if requested. We prefer to retain originals, but a high-quality PMT or Velox is fine if artist wants to keep artwork." Credit line given.

Photography: Purchases photos with accompanying ms only. Uses b&w prints. Wants photos for nonfiction.

Terms: Pays 25% on acceptance, 75% on publication. Buys first North American serial rights for mss, artwork and photographs. Pays $20-100 for stories/articles. Pay illustrators $25-50 for b&w cover; $5-25 for b&w inside. Pays photographers per photo (range: $5-25). Sample copies for $2.75. Writer's/illustrator's guidelines free with business-size SAE and 1 first-class stamp. "Specify fiction or nonfiction guidelines, or both." Tip sheet package for $1.25 and business-size envelope with 1 first-class stamp (includes all guidelines and tips on writing science fiction and nonfiction).

Tips: Writers: "Read lots of children's writing in general, especially specific genre if you're writing a genre story (science fiction, romance, mystery, etc.). We list upcoming needs in our guidelines; writers can study these to get an idea of what we're looking for. We're always looking for nonfiction." Illustrators: "Study illustrations in back issues of magazines you're interested in illustrating for, and be able to work in a genre style if that's the type of magazine you want to publish your work. Everything is open to freelancers, as almost all our artwork is done out-of-house. (We occasionally use public domain illustrations, copyright-free illustrations and photographs.)"

HODGEPODGE, R.R.#1, Box 161, Ethan, SD 57334. Editors: Darla J. Lees, Betty Jayne. Bimonthly magazine. Estab. 1994. "Our main goal is to get kids reading! That's why our magazine is just what the title implies: it's a mish-mash. A collection of this and that. With hopefully, a little something for everyone. If we can get our audience (aged 4-8) reading, and loving it, they'll continue."

Fiction: Picture-oriented material, young readers: adventure, animal, fantasy, folktales, history, humorous, multicultural, nature/environment, sports, suspense/mystery. "We want to make kids aware of and curious about other cultures. We do not want heavy moralizing, cliché or overdone 'lessons.' If you can tell a fun story and get a point across discretely, fantastic! Otherwise, just have fun." Buys 55 mss/year. Average word length: 2,000. Byline given.

Poetry: Reviews poetry. Anything fun, interesting, enjoyable to read. Maximum length: 24 lines. Limit submissions to 10 poems.

How to Contact/Writers: Fiction: Send complete ms. Reports on queries in 2 weeks; 4-6 weeks on mss. Publishes ms 6-8 months after acceptance. Will consider simultaneous submissions, electronic submissions and previously published work.

Illustration: Buys 10 illustrations/issue; 60 illustrations/year. Uses b&w artwork only. "Pen & ink is best for us; 8½×11 or smaller; any style or theme." Reviews ms/illustration packages from artists. Submit ms with dummy. Illustrations only: Query with samples. Reports only if interested. Samples kept on file. Credit line given.

Terms: Pays on publication. Acquires one-time rights. "We are a new publication with a very limited budget. We pay in copies." Writer's guidelines free for SASE. Illustrator's/photo guidelines available for SASE.

Tips: "Children are smart. Don't talk down to them. Half of the reason so few children love to read is that there is so little out there that talks to them, not at them. Think like a child. Dig out your coloring books and crayons. Sit on the floor and color. Get into the swing of things. Relax, get silly, have fun. Then write a story you'd love to read. If you giggle at your story odds are a child will too. And those are our very favorites. Illustrators: Again, think like a child. Remember their perspective is different from ours. Get down on your knees for a while and view the world from their level. Draw from what you see there. *Hodgepodge* welcomes freelance work in all areas. In fact almost 90% of our magazine comes from freelancers. Our favorite stories by far are the ones that made us laugh out loud as we read them; the ones that stick with us for days afterwards. Write freely, submit professionally. We use illustrations from freelancers heavily throughout the magazine. Some of the portfolios have contained pieces that were accepted immediately, because they fit perfectly in a poem or story we were working on! In others we find the style of the the author and illustrator blend perfectly. Every author has the illustrator who will complement him perfectly. Just let your style be your own, and a mate will be found for you."

***HOLIDAYS & SEASONAL CELEBRATIONS**, Teaching & Learning Company, 1204 Buchanan, P.O. Box 10, Carthage IL 62321. (217)357-2591. Articles Editor: Donna Borst. Art

Director: Teresa Mathis. Quarterly magazine. Estab. 1995. Every submission must be seasonal or holiday-related. Materials need to be educational and consistent with grades K-3 development and curriculum.

Fiction: Young readers: animal, fantasy, health, multicultural, holiday-related. Buys 5 mss/year. Byline given.

Nonfiction: Picture-oriented: animal, arts/crafts, biography, cooking, games/puzzles, geography, health, how-to, math, multicultural, nature/environment, science. Young readers: animal, arts/crafts, biography, cooking, games/puzzles, geography, health, history, how-to, math, multicultural, nature/environment, problem-solving. "We need holiday and seasonally-related ideas from all cultures." Buys 150 mss/year. Byline given.

Poetry: Reviews holiday or seasonal poetry.

How to Contact/Writers: Fiction: Query. Nonfiction: Send complete ms. Reports on queries in 2 months; mss in 3 months. Publishes ms 4-12 months after acceptance. Will consider electronic submissions via disk or modem.

Illustration: Buys 80 illustrations/issue; 300 illustrations/year. Uses b&w and color artwork. Works on assignment only. "Prefers school settings with lots of children; b&w sketches at this time." Reviews ms/illustration packages from artists. Submit ms with rough sketches. Illustrations only: submit résumé, promo sheet, tearsheets, sketches of children. Reports in 2 months. Samples filed. Credit line sometimes given.

Photography: Buys photos from freelancers. Looking for photos of children. Model/property releases required. Uses 35mm transparencies. Send unsolicited photos by mail or submit portfolio for review. Reports in 2 months.

Terms: Pays on acceptance. Buys all rights. Pays $15-30 for stories; $10-100 for articles. Additional payment for ms/illustration packages. Pays illustrators $150-300 for color cover; $10-15 for b&w inside. Pays photographers per photo. Writer's/illustrator's guidelines for SASE.

Tips: "95% of our magazine is written by freelancers. Writers must know that this magazine goes to teachers for use in the classroom, grades pre-K through 3. Also 90% of our magazine is illustrated by freelancers. We need illustrators who can provide us with 'cute' kids grades pre-K through 3. Representation of ethnic children is a must."

THE HOME ALTAR, Meditations for Families with Children, Augsburg Fortress, 426 S. Fifth St., Box 1209, Minneapolis MN 55440. Articles/Fiction Editor: Carol A. Burk. Quarterly magazine. Circ. approximately 70,000. This is a booklet of daily devotions, used primarily by Lutheran families. Each day's reading focuses on a specific Bible passage. 98% of material aimed at juvenile audience.

Fiction: Young readers, middle readers: contemporary, folktales, problem-solving, religious. Buys 365 mss/year. Average word length: 125-170. Byline given.

Nonfiction: Young readers, middle readers: interview/profile, problem-solving, religious. Average word length: 125-170. Byline given.

How to Contact/Writers: Fiction/nonfiction: Query with published clips.

Illustration: Buys 100 illustrations/year. Works on assignment only.

How to Contact/Illustrators: Reports on art samples only if interested.

Terms: Pays on acceptance. Buys all rights. Pays $10 for assigned articles. Free writer's guidelines for 6×9 SAE and 98¢ postage.

HOPSCOTCH, The Magazine for Girls, The Bluffton News Publishing and Printing Company, 103 N. Main St., Bluffton OH 45817. (419)358-4610. Editor: Marilyn Edwards. Bimonthly magazine. Estab. 1989. Circ. 10,000. For girls from 6 to 12 years, featuring traditional subjects—pets, games, hobbies, nature, science, sports, etc.—with an emphasis on articles that show girls actively involved in unusual and/or worthwhile activities."

Always include a self-addressed, stamped envelope (SASE) with submissions within your own country. When sending material to other countries, include a self-addressed envelope (SAE) and International Reply Coupons (IRCs).

● *Hopscotch* appeared on a 1995 Hot List® compiled by *Children's Book Insider.* This list of "10 Book and Magazine Publishers Most Receptive to New Writers" is updated every few months, and available to new and renewing subscribers.

Fiction: Young readers and middle readers: adventure, animal, folktales, health, history, humorous, multicultural, nature/environment, problem-solving, sports, suspense/mystery. Does not want to see stories dealing with dating, sex, fashion, hard rock music. Buys 24 mss/year. Average word length: 300-700. Byline given.

Nonfiction: Young readers and middle readers: animal, arts/crafts, biography, careers, cooking, games/puzzles, health, history, hobbies, how-to, humorous, interview/profile, math, multicultural, nature/environment, problem-solving, science. Does not want to see pieces dealing with dating, sex, fashion, hard rock music. "Need more nonfiction with quality photos about a Hopscotch-age girl involved in a worthwhile activity." Buys 46 mss/year. Average word length: 400-700. Byline given.

Poetry: Reviews traditional, wholesome, humorous poems. Maximum word length: 300; maximum line length: 20. Will accept 6 submissions/author.

How to Contact/Writers: Fiction: Send complete ms. Nonfiction: Query, send complete ms. Reports on queries in 3 weeks; on mss in 2 months. Will consider simultaneous submissions.

Illustration: Buys 8-12 illustrations/issue; buys 50-60 illustrations/year. "Generally, the illustrations are assigned after we have purchased a piece (usually fiction). Occasionally, we will use a painting—in any given medium—for the cover, and these are usually seasonal." Uses b&w artwork only for inside; color for cover. Review ms/illustration packages from artists. Query first or send complete ms with final art. Illustrations only: Send résumé, portfolio, client list and tearsheets. Reports on art samples with SASE in 2 weeks. Original artwork returned at job's completion. Credit line given.

Photography: Purchases photos separately (cover only) and with accompanying ms only. Looking for photos to accompany article. Model/property releases required. Uses 5×7, b&w prints; 35mm transparencies. Black and white photos should go with ms. Should have girl or girls ages 6-12.

Terms: For manuscripts, pays a few months ahead of publication. For mss, artwork and photos, buys first North American serial rights; second serial (reprint rights). Pays $30-100 for stories/articles—5¢ word and $10/photo used ($5/photo if it is a slide). "We always send a copy of the issue to the writer or illustrator." Text and art are treated separately. Pays $100-150 for color cover; $5-15 for b&w inside. Photographers paid per photo (range: $5-15; $150 for color cover photo). Sample copy for $3. Writer's/illustrator's guidelines free for #10 SASE.

Tips: "Please look at our guidelines and our magazine . . . and remember, we use far more nonfiction than fiction. If decent photos accompany the piece, it stands an even better chance of being accepted. We believe it is the responsibility of the contributor to come up with photos. Please remember, our readers are 6-12 years—most are 7-10—and your text should reflect that. Many magazines try to entertain first and educate second. We try to do the reverse of that. Our magazine is more simplistic like a book, to be read from cover to cover." (See listing for *Boys' Quest.*)

HUMPTY DUMPTY'S MAGAZINE, Children's Better Health Institute, 1100 Waterway Blvd., P.O. Box 567, Indianapolis IN 46206. (317)636-8881. Fax: (317)684-8094. Editor: Sandy Grieshop. Art Director: Rebecca Ray. Magazine published 8 times/year—Jan/Feb; Mar; April/May; June; July/Aug; Sept; Oct/Nov; Dec. *HDM* is edited for children approximately ages 4-6. It includes fiction (easy-to-reads; read alouds; rhyming stories; rebus stories), nonfiction articles (some with photo illustrations), poems, crafts, recipes and puzzles. Much of the content encourages development of better health habits. "We especially need material promoting fitness."

● *Humpty Dumpty's* appeared on a 1995 Hot List® compiled by *Children's Book Insider.* This list of "10 Book and Magazine Publishers Most Receptive to New Writers" is updated every few months, and available to new and renewing subscribers. To learn more about *Humpty Dumpty's* and other Children's Better Health Institute publications, see Insider Report with CBHI editor Steve Charles in the 1995 edition of *Children's Writer's & Illustrator's Market.*

Fiction: Picture-oriented material: adventure, animal, humorous, multicultural, nature/environment, problem-solving, science fiction, sports, health-related. Does not want to see "bunny-rabbits-with-carrot-pies stories! Also, talking inanimate objects are very difficult to do well.

Beginners (and maybe everyone) should avoid these." Buys 35-50 mss/year. Maximum word length: 500. Byline given.

Nonfiction: Picture-oriented material: animal, arts/crafts, cooking, games, puzzles, hobbies, humorous, interview/profile, science, sports, health-related. Does not want to see long, boring, encyclopedia rehashes. "We're open to almost any subject (although most of our nonfiction has a health angle), but it must be presented creatively. Don't just string together some facts." Looks for a fresh approach. Buys 6-10 mss/year. Prefers very short nonfiction pieces—350 words maximum. Byline given.

How to Contact/Writers: Send complete ms. Nonfiction: Send complete ms with bibliography if applicable. "No queries, please!" Reports on mss in 3 months.

Illustration: Buys 13-16 illustrations/issue; 90-120 illustrations/year. Preferred theme or style: Realistic or cartoon. Works on assignment only. Illustrations only. Query with slides, printed pieces or photocopies. Contact: Rebecca Ray, art director. Samples are not returned; samples filed. Reports on art samples only if interested. Credit line given.

Terms: Writers: Pays on publication. Artists: Pays within 1-2 months. Buys all rights. "One-time book rights may be returned if author can provide name of interested book publisher and tentative date of publication." Pays up to 22¢/word for stories/articles; payment varies for poems and activities. 10 complimentary issues are provided to author with check. Pays $250 for color cover illustration; $35-90 per page b&w inside; $60-120 for 2-color inside; $70-155 for color inside. Sample copies for $1.25. Writer's/illustrator's guidelines free with SASE.

Tips: Writers: "Study current issues and guidelines. Observe, especially, word lengths and adhere to requirements. It's sometimes easier to break in with recipe or craft ideas, but submit what you do best. Don't send your first, second, or even third drafts. Polish your piece until it's as perfect as you can make it." Illustrators: "Please study the magazine before contacting us. Your art must have appeal to three- to seven-year-olds." (See listings for *Child Life, Children's Digest, Children's Playmate, Jack and Jill, Turtle Magazine* and *U*S* Kids*.)

HYPE HAIR, (formerly *2 Hype* and *Hype Hair*), Word Up Publication, 210 Route 4 East, Suite 401, Paramus NY 07652. (201)843-4004. Editor: Marcia Cole. Bimonthly magazine. Estab. 1990. Publishes articles about music (rap and R&B)—fashion, hair trends, health, grooming, entertainment—all dealing with music.

Nonfiction: Young adults: careers, fashion, games/puzzles, health, hobbies, how-to, interview/profile, problem-solving. Byline given.

How to Contact/Writers: Nonfiction: Query with published clips. Publishes ms 5 months after acceptance. Will consider electronic submissions via disk or modem.

Illustration: Buys 10 illustrations/issue. Illustrations should be done on 8½×11 paper. Works on assignment only. Reviews ms/illustration packages from artists. Submit complete package with final art. Illustrations only: Send promo sheet, portfolio, tearsheets. Reports back only if interested. Samples not filed. Original work returned upon job's completion. Credit line given.

Photography: Model/property releases and photo captions required. Uses b&w and color prints. Photographers should send unsolicited photos by mail. Reports back only if interested.

Terms: Pays on publication. Buys one-time rights to mss. Pays $75-100 for articles. Additional payment for ms/illustration packages. Pays illustrators $50-75. Photographers paid per photo (range $35-150). Writer's/illustrator's/photo guidelines free for SASE.

Tips: "Send fun ideas for people with short attention spans."

JACK AND JILL, Children's Better Health Institute, 1100 Waterway Blvd., P.O. Box 567, Indianapolis IN 46206. (317)636-8881. Editor: Daniel Lee. Art Director: Mary Stropoli. Magazine published 8 times/year. Estab. 1938. Circ. 360,000. "Write entertaining and imaginative stories *for* kids, not just *about* them. Writers should understand what is funny to kids, what's important to them, what excites them. Don't write from an adult 'kids are so cute' perspective. We're also looking for health and healthful lifestyle stories and articles, but don't be preachy."

- To learn more about *Jack and Jill* and other Children's Better Health Institute publications, see Insider Report with CBHI editor Steve Charles in the 1995 edition of *Children's Writer's & Illustrator's Market*.

Fiction: Young readers: animal, contemporary, fantasy, history, humorous, problem-solving. Middle readers: contemporary, humorous. Buys 30-35 mss/year. Average word length: 900. Byline given.

Nonfiction: Young readers: animal, history, how-to, humorous, interview/profile, problem-solving, travel. Buys 8-10 mss/year. Average word length: 1,000. Byline given.
Poetry: Reviews poetry.
How to Contact/Writers: Fiction/nonfiction: Send complete ms. Reports on mss in 3 months.
Terms: Pays on publication; minimum 10¢/word. Buys all rights.
Tips: See listings for *Child Life*, *Children's Digest*, *Children's Playmate*, *Humpty Dumpty's Magazine*, *Turtle Magazine* and *U*S* Kids*.

JUNIOR SCHOLASTIC, Scholastic Inc., 555 Broadway, New York NY 10012-3999. (212)343-6295. Articles Editor: Lee Baier. Art Director: Glenn Davis. Photo Editor: Donna Frankland Magazine published biweekly during school year. Estab. 1937. Circ. 585,000. Social studies and current events classroom magazine for students in grades 6-8.
Nonfiction: Middle readers, young adults: geography, history, interview/profile, multicultural, nature/environment, social issues, foreign countries. "We mainly buy stories on countries in the news, that include interviews and profiles of kids 11-14." Buys 20 mss/year. Average word length: 500-1,000. Byline given.
How to Contact/Writers: Nonfiction: Query with published clips. Reports on queries in 2 months; mss in 6 months. Publishes ms 2 months after acceptance.
Illustration: Buys 1 illustration/issue; 20 illustrations/year. Works on assignment only. Reviews ms/illustration packages from artists. Illustrations only: send portfolio. Reports back only if interested. Samples returned with SASE; samples filed. Credit line given.
Photography: Buys photos from freelancers. Wants "photos of young teens in foreign countries; teens relating to national issues." Uses b&w/color prints and 35mm transparencies. Query with samples. Reports back only if interested.
Terms: Pays on publication. Buys all rights. Pays $300-600 for articles. Additional payment for photos accompanying articles. Pays illustrators $800 for color cover; $600 for color inside. Sample copies for 9×11 SAE. Writers/photo guidelines for SASE.
Tips: See listings for *Choices*, *Dynamath*, *Scholastic Math Magazine* and *Superscience Blue*.

JUNIOR TRAILS, Gospel Publishing House, 1445 Boonville Ave., Springfield MO 65802. (417)862-2781. Articles/Fiction Editor: Sinda S. Zinn. Art Director: Leonard Bailey. Quarterly magazine. Circ. 70,000. *Junior Trails* is an 8-page take-home paper for fifth and sixth graders. "Our articles consist of fiction stories of a contemporary or historical nature. The stories have a moral slant to show how modern-day people can work out problems in acceptable ways, or give examples in history from which we can learn."
Fiction: Middle readers: adventure, animal, contemporary, history, humorous, multicultural, nature/environment, problem-solving, religious. Does not want to see science fiction, mythology, ghosts and witchcraft. Wants to see more stories about "kids struggling with a problem in Christian living and solving it through biblical principles." Also looking for stories of ethnic background. Buys 100 mss/year. Average word length: 800-1,500. Byline given.
Nonfiction: Middle readers: animal, history, how-to, problem-solving, religious. Buys 30 mss/year. Average word length: 300-800. Byline given.
Poetry: Wants to see poetry with a religious emphasis.
How to Contact/Writers: Fiction/nonfiction: Send complete ms. Reports on mss in 2-4 weeks. Will consider simultaneous submissions.
Illustration: Uses color artwork only. Illustrations only: provide résumé, promo sheet or tearsheets to be kept on file; or arrange personal interview to show portfolio. Query with samples. Contact: Sinda S. Zinn, editor. Samples not returned; samples not filed. Originals not returned at job's completion. Reports only if interested.
Photography: Uses 2¼×2¼ transparencies. To contact, photographers should query with samples; provide résumé, promo sheet or tearsheets to be kept on file. Wants photos of "children involved with activity or with other people."
Terms: Pays on acceptance. For mss, buys one-time rights. Buys all rights to artwork; one-time rights to photographs. Pays 4-5¢/word for articles/stories. Photographers paid per photo (range: $30-100). Sample copy free with 9×12 SASE and 2 first-class stamps; writer's guidelines for SASE.
Tips: "Make the characters and situations real. The story should unfold through their interaction and dialogue, not narration. Don't fill up space with unnecessary details. We are always in need

of good fiction stories." Looks for: "fiction that presents believable characters working out their problems according to Bible principles. Present Christianity in action without being preachy; articles with reader appeal, emphasizing some phase of Christian living, presented in a down-to-earth manner; biography or missionary material using fiction technique; historical, scientific or nature material with a spiritual lesson; fillers that are brief, purposeful, usually containing an anecdote, and always with a strong evangelical emphasis."

***KIDSOFT MAGAZINE**, 10275 N. De Anza Blvd., Cupertino CA 95014. (408)255-2424. Fax: (408)342-3500. Editor: Kelly Quiroz. Art Director: Colleen Stokes. Bimonthly magazine. Circ. 100,000. "*KidSoft* reports on computers and technology to kids ages 8-12. We print only nonfiction articles about what's new and 'cool' in cyberspace."

Nonfiction: Middle readers: computers, games/puzzles, how-to, interview/profile, science, technology. "We would like more articles on actual kids who are using computers to do new and exciting things." Buys 16 mss/year. Word length: 440 maximum. Byline given.

How to Contact/Writers: Query with published clips. Reports on queries in 1 month. Will consider electronic submission via disk or modem.

Illustration: Buys 10 illustrations/issue. Uses color artwork only. Illustration only: Query with samples; send résumé, promo sheet, tearsheets. Contact: Colleen Stokes, art director. Reports back only if interested. Samples returned with SASE; samples filed. Originals returned at job's completion. Credit line given.

Photography: Buys photos with accompanying ms only. Model/property release required; captions required. Uses 4×5 transparencies.

Terms: Pays on publication. Buys all rights. Payment varies. Additional payment for photos accompanying articles. Sample copies free for 9×12 SAE and $1.01 postage. Writer's guidelines for SASE.

Tips: "*KidSoft*'s mission is to help kids understand and use computers, and to inform them about new and interesting ways computers are being used today. We are therefore looking for 'wired' writers who can fuel us with articles about the cutting edge of technology. Although our subject matter is technical, our voice is very informal, like kids talking to kids. If your published work is in a more formal style, convince us in your query that you can write for our market. Be sure to send for our guidelines."

LADYBUG, The Magazine for Young Children, Carus Corporation, P.O. Box 300, Peru IL 61354. (815)224-6643. Editor-in-Chief: Marianne Carus. Editor: Paula Morrow. Art Director: Suzanne Beck. Monthly magazine. Estab. 1990. Circ. 135,000. Literary magazine for children 2-6, with stories, poems, activities, songs and picture stories.

Fiction: Picture-oriented material: adventure, animal, fantasy, folktales, humorous, multicultural, nature/environment, problem-solving, science fiction, sports, suspense/mystery. "Open to any easy fiction stories." Buys 50 mss/year. Average word length 300-850 words. Byline given.

Nonfiction: Picture-oriented material: activities, animal, arts/crafts, concept, cooking, humorous, math, nature/environment, problem-solving, science. Buys 35 mss/year.

Poetry: Reviews poems, 20-line maximum length; limit submissions to 5 poems. Uses lyrical, humorous, simple language.

How to Contact/Writers: Fiction/nonfiction: Send complete ms. Queries not accepted. Reports on mss in 3 months. Publishes ms up to 2 years after acceptance. Does not like, but will consider simultaneous submissions.

Illustration: Buys 12 illustrations/issue; 145 illustrations/year. Prefers "bright colors; all media, but use watercolor and acrylics most often; same size as magazine is preferred but not required." To be considered for future assignments: Submit promo sheet, slides, tearsheets, color and b&w photocopies. Reports on art samples in 3 months. Original artwork returned at job's completion.

Terms: Pays on publication for mss; after delivery of completed assignment for illustrators. For mss, buys first publication rights; second serial (reprint rights). Buys first publication rights plus promotional rights for artwork. Pays up to 25¢/word for prose; $3/line for poetry; $25 minimum for articles. Pays $750 for color (cover) illustration, $50-100 for b&w (inside) illustration, $250/page for color (inside). Sample copy for $4. Writer's/illustrator's guidelines free for SASE.

Tips: Writers: "Get to know several young children on an individual basis. Respect your audience. Wants less cute, condescending or 'preach-teachy' material. Less gratuitous anthropomorphism. More rich, evocative language, sense of joy or wonders. Set your manuscript aside for at

INSIDER REPORT

Vitalize Your Career with Magazine Work

Magazine assignments invigorate your day and can be a springboard to book contracts, says author/illustrator Joan Holub. The Seattle-based freelancer struggled to break into books until credits from *LadyBug* and *Scholastic* magazines paved the way. Today she values both markets. Book projects, with their long range deadlines, can mean waiting a year or so for the reward of seeing her work in print. Fast-paced magazine assignments bring vitality to her work, allowing her to wake each day to a new challenge.

Joan Holub

Yet unlike most of us who are jarred awake by blaring radios and buzzers, Holub wakes at her own pace, easing into her day before heading to her home studio around ten. "I'm a night person," says Holub, who often works until 8 p.m. depending on deadlines. "I could get up earlier, but I don't work as effectively early in the morning—so what's the point?"

Once at her drawing table, Holub grabs a brush and gets down to business tackling the day's assignments. Lost bunny rabbits, bemused pet snakes and turtles named Myrtle come to life in vibrant opaque watercolors. If the assignment calls for it, she happily switches gears to write poems and stories or to design lettering. Phone calls, fax machines and trips to the post office keep her in touch with art directors and editors in far-flung states.

"I don't think I would have landed my first book contract without tearsheets from magazines," says Holub. Before that, she had no published work so she submitted illustrations of fairy tales. Lack of response to her samples was puzzling until an art director provided a clue. "Your work is great," he sighed, "but if I see one more Little Red Riding Hood I'll run screaming out of the building!"

"Had I drawn a really funky Red Riding Hood, he might have reacted differently, but all my sample did was say 'Look, I can draw Red Riding Hood like everybody else!' "

Holub initially had better luck submitting to magazines. "They are easier to break into. There's plenty of work to go around, and the competition isn't as stiff because people overlook the market." In addition to *Children's Writer's & Illustrator's Market*, Holub finds leads in teachers' trade magazines, such as *Teaching K-8*, *Pre-K Today* and *Instructor*. She recommends joining The Society of Children's Book Writers and Illustrators. "The newsletter alone is worth the price of membership."

Keep your eyes peeled for new markets. "I spotted an issue of *Let's Find Out* at aerobics class, noted the art director's name, called her and got an assignment right away." Holub even surfs the Internet for leads, sharing ideas with freelancers on The Children's Writer's Chat every Tuesday night on America Online.

Submit illustrations, short stories or poems to children's magazines and see what happens. As long as you sell only first rights, you can always develop your ideas and submit to book publishers later. At first, take any assignment you can get. You'll learn to work with editors and art directors, meet deadlines and find out what works and what doesn't, says Holub. "Beginners often avoid vivid colors. They are sometimes too wary about applying areas of dark paint for contrast, not realizing that some color is lost in the printing process." Some knowledge is only gained through experience.

Though she has since worked with Western, Random House, Scholastic, and other major book publishers, Holub doesn't regard magazines as a mere stepping-stone to books. She continues magazine work because the market offers its own advantages. "There's an instant gratification not possible with books. You may wait a year before your book is published. In one month you can flip through a magazine and see your work—and that feels great."

You'll be freer to incorporate trends. "Book publishers usually avoid fads—so illustrating the latest sneakers or trendy hair clips may be out," she says, citing an illustration sent back to her for revisions because it showed a toddler sporting a stylish hairdo. "By the time the book's out a trend could be over. But magazines love to show new styles.

"People say 'I'd love to do what you do.' I can identify with them—I was a dreamer too. But success won't drop in your lap. If someone slams the door in your face, just try another door!" That kind of determination leads to success.

—Mary Cox

© 1993 Joan Holub

Joan Holub worked in watercolor to create this tenderhearted illustration accompanying "My Natural Mama," a poem in the January 1993 issue of* Ladybug *magazine. Holub also designed the "cookie dough" lettering for the poem's title. The work earned her a SCBWI Magazine Illustration Merit Honor Award.

least a month, then reread critically." Illustrators: "Include examples, where possible, of children, animals, and—most important—action and narrative (i.e., several scenes from a story, showing continuity and an ability to maintain interest). Keep in mind that people come in all colors, sizes, physical conditions. Be inclusive in creating characters." (See listings for *Babybug*, *Cricket* and *Spider.*)

LIGHTHOUSE, Lighthouse Publications, Box 1377, Auburn WA 98071-1377. Editor/Publisher: Tim Clinton. Quarterly magazine. Estab. 1986. Circ. 300. Magazine contains timeless stories and poetry for family reading. 25% of material aimed at juvenile audience.
Fiction: Young readers, middle readers, young adults: adventure, history, humorous, nature, problem-solving, sports, suspense/mystery (not murder). Young adults: romance. Does not want to see anything not "G-rated," any story with a message that is not subtly handled or stories without plots. Buys 36 mss/year. Average word length: 2,000. Byline given.
Poetry: Reviews poetry. Maximum line length: 50. Limit submissions to 5 poems.
How to Contact/Writers: Fiction: Send complete ms and SASE with sufficient postage for return of ms. Reports on mss in 3-4 months.
Terms: Pays on publication. Buys first North American serial rights; first rights. Pays $5-50. Sample copy for $3 (includes guidelines). Writer's guidelines free with regular SAE and 1 first-class stamp.
Tips: "All sections are open to freelance writers—just follow the guidelines and stay in the categories listed above. Try to think of a *new* plot (see so many stories on bullies, storms and haunted houses)."

LISTEN, Celebrating Positive Choices, 55 West Oak Ridge Dr., Hagerstown MD 21740. (301)791-7000, ext. 2535. Monthly magazine. Circ. 50,000. *Listen* offers positive alternatives to drug use for its teenage readers.
Fiction: Young adults: contemporary, health, humorous, nature/environment, problem solving activities, sports. Buys 12 mss/year. Average word length: 1,200-1,500. Byline given.
Nonfiction: Young adults: arts/crafts, hobbies, health, nature/environment, problem solving activities, sports. Wants to see more factual articles on drug abuse. Buys 50 mss/year. Average word length: 1,200-1,500. Byline given.
How to Contact/Writers: Fiction/nonfiction: Send complete ms. Reports on queries/mss in 2 months.
Illustration: Reviews ms/illustration packages from artists. Ms/illustration packages and illustration only:Query, send promo sheet and slides. Reports in 1 month. Credit line given.
Photography: Purchases photos from freelancers. Looks for "youth oriented—action (sports, outdoors), personality photos."
Terms: Pays on acceptance. Buys exclusive magazine rights for ms. Buys one-time rights for artwork and photographs. Pays $50-250 for stories/articles. Pays illustrators $150-300 for b&w cover; $250-600 for color cover; $75-150 for b&w inside; $100-300 for color inside. Pays photographers by the project (range: $200-500) or per photo (range: $50-500). Sample copy for $1 and SASE. Writer's guidelines free with SASE.
Tips: "*Listen* is a magazine for teenagers. It encourages development of good habits and high ideals of physical, social and mental health. It bases its editorial philosophy of primary drug prevention on total abstinence from alcohol and other drugs. Because it is used extensively in public high school classes, it does not accept articles and stories with overt religious emphasis. Four specific purposes guide the editors in selecting materials for *Listen*: (1) To portray a positive lifestyle and to foster skills and values that will help teenagers deal with contemporary problems, including smoking, drinking and using drugs. This is *Listen*'s primary purpose. (2) To offer positive alternatives to a lifestyle of drug use of any kind. (3) To present scientifically accurate information about the nature and effects of tobacco, alcohol and other drugs. (4) To report medical research, community programs and educational efforts which are solving problems connected with smoking, alcohol and other drugs. Articles should offer their readers activities that increase one's sense of self-worth through achievement and/or involvement in helping others. They are often categorized by three kinds of focus: (1) Hobbies; (2) Recreation; (3) Community Service."

MAGIC REALISM, Pyx Press, P.O. Box 922648, Sylmar CA 91392-2648. Editor: C. Darren Butler. Managing Editor: Julie Thomas. Associate Editor: Patricia Hatch. Associate Publisher:

Lisa S. Laurencot. Quarterly magazine. Estab. 1990. Circ. 1,000. "We publish magic, realism, exaggerated realism, literary fantasy; glib fantasy of the sort found in folktales, fables, myth." 10-20% of publication aimed at juvenile market.

Fiction: Middle readers and young adults: fantasy, folktales. Sees too much of wizards, witches, card readings, sword-and-sorcery, silly or precious tales of any sort, sleight-of-hand magicians. Especially needs short-shorts. Buys approximately 80 mss/year. Byline given.

Poetry: Reviews poetry. Length: prefers 3-30 lines. Limit submissions to 3-8 poems.

How to Contact/Writers: Fiction: send complete ms. Reports on queries in 1 month; mss in 3-6 months. Publishes ms 4 months-2 years after acceptance. "Simultaneous and previously published submissions are welcome if clearly labeled as such."

Illustration: Uses b&w or color covers; b&w inside. Reviews ms/illustration packages from artists. Query; submit complete package with final art or submit ms with rough sketches. Illustrations only: Query or send résumé and portfolio. Reports in 3 months. Samples returned with SASE. Original work returned at job's completion. Credit line given.

Photography: "We consider photos, but have received very few submissions." Model/property releases preferred. Photographers should query with samples and résumé of credits; submit portfolio for review.

Terms: Pays on acceptance. Buys first North American serial rights or one-time rights and reprint rights for ms, artwork and photographs; also buys worldwide Spanish language rights for Spanish edition published 1-2 years after English edition. Pays 4¢/word plus 3 copies for stories; 1 copy for poetry. Pays illustrators $50 for b&w or $100 for color cover; $3-10 for b&w inside. Photographers paid per photo (range: $3-10). Sample copies for $4.95 (back issue); $5.95 (current issue). Writer's guidelines for SASE.

Tips: "Only a fraction of the material we publish is for children. We rarely use anthropomorphic tales. Most material for children is related to folklore."

MY FRIEND, The Catholic Magazine for Kids, Pauline Books & Media, 50 St. Paul's Ave., Jamaica Plain, Boston MA 02130. (617)522-8911. Articles/Fiction Editor: Sister Anne Joan Flanagan, fsp. Art Director: Sister M. Joseph, fsp. Magazine published 10 times/year. Estab. 1979. Circ. 12,000. "*My Friend* is a magazine of inspiration and entertainment for a predominantly Catholic readership. We reach ages 6-12."

Fiction: Young readers, middle readers: adventure, animal, Christmas, contemporary, ethnic, fantasy, history, humorous, nature/environment, religious, science fiction, suspense/mystery, sports. Does not want to see poetry, animals as main characters in religious stories, stories whose basic thrust would be incompatible with Catholic values. Buys 50 mss/year. Average word length: 450-750. Byline given.

Nonfiction: Young readers: arts/crafts, games/puzzles, health, history, hobbies, humorous, problem-solving, religious. Middle readers: arts/crafts, games/puzzles, health, history, hobbies, how-to, humorous, interview/profile, media literacy, nature/environment, problem-solving, religion, science, sports. Does not want to see material that is not compatible with Catholic values; no "New Age" material. Buys 10 mss/year. Average word length: 450-750. Byline given.

How to Contact/Writers: Fiction/nonfiction: Send complete ms. Reports on queries in 1 month; mss in 1-2 months.

Illustration: Buys 8 illustrations/issue; buys 60-80 illustrations/year. Preferred theme or style: Realistic depictions of children, but open to variety! "We'd just like to hear from more illustrators who can do *humans*! (We see enough of funny cats, mice, etc.)" Looking for a "Bible stories" and comic book style artist, too. Reviews ms/illustration packages from artists. Send complete ms with copy of final art. Contact: Sister Anne Joan, managing editor. Illustrations only: Query with samples. Send résumé, promo sheet and tearsheets. Contact: Sister Anne Joan, managing editor. Reports only if interested. Original artwork returned at job's completion. Credit line given.

Photography: Wants photos of "children at play or alone; school scenes."

Terms: Pays on acceptance for mss. Buys first rights for mss; variable for artwork. Pays $35-100 for stories/articles. Pays illustrators $50-100/b&w (inside); $50-175/color (inside). Sample copy $2 with 9×12 SAE and 5 first-class stamps. Writer's guidelines free with SAE and 1 first-class stamp.

Tips: Writers: "Right now, we're especially looking for articles and activities on media literacy. We are not interested in poetry unless it is humorous. Fiction needs are *amply* provided for already." Illustrators: "Please contact us! For the most part, we need illustrations for fiction stories." In the future, sees children's magazines "getting more savvy, less sappy. Suspect that electronic media styles will penetrate a greater number of magazines for kids and adults alike; literary or intellectual publications would be less affected."

***THE MYTHIC CIRCLE**, Mythopoeic Society, P.O. Box 6707, Altadena CA 91001. Editors: Tina Cooper and Christine Lowentrout. Art Director: Lynn Maudlin. Magazine published three times annually. Circ. 150. Fantasy writer's workshop in print featuring reader comments in each issue. 5% of publication aimed at juvenile market.

How to Contact/Writers: Fiction: Send complete ms. Nonfiction: Query. SASE (IRC) for answer to query and return of ms. Reports on queries/mss in 2 months. Will consider photocopied and computer printout (dark dot matrix). "No simultaneous submissions."

Illustration: Buys 10 illustrations/issue; buys 30 illustrations/year. Preferred theme or style: fantasy, soft science fiction. Illustration only: Reports on art samples in 3-6 weeks. Original artwork returned at job's completion (only if postage paid).

Terms: Pays on publication. Buys one-time rights. Pays in contributor copies. Sample copy $6.50. Writer's guidelines free with SAE and 1 first-class stamp.

Tips: "We are a good outlet for a story that hasn't sold but 'should' have—good feedback and tips on improvement."

NATIONAL GEOGRAPHIC WORLD, National Geographic Society, 1145 17th St. NW, Washington DC 20036-4688. (202)857-7000.

- *World* does not accept unsolicited manuscripts.

NATURE FRIEND MAGAZINE, Pilgrim Publishers, 22777 State Road 119, Goshen IN 46526. (219)534-2245. Articles Editor: Stanley Brubaker. Monthly magazine. Estab. 1983. Circ. 9,000. Monthly magazine.

Nonfiction: Picture-oriented material, young readers, middle readers, young adults: animal, nature. Does not want to see evolutionary material. Buys 50-80 mss/year. Average word length: 350-1,500. Byline given.

How to Contact/Writers: Nonfiction: Send complete ms. Reports on mss in 1-4 months. Will consider simultaneous submissions.

Illustration: Works on assignment only.

Terms: Pays on publication. Buys one-time rights. Pays $15-75. Payment for illustrations: $15-80/b&w inside. Two sample copies for $5 with 7×10 SAE and 85¢ postage. Writer's/illustrator's guidelines for $2.50.

Tips: Looks for "main articles, puzzles and simple nature and science projects. Please examine samples and writer's guide before submitting."

NEW ERA MAGAZINE, Official Publication for Youth of the Church of Jesus Christ of Latter-Day Saints, 50 E. North Temple St., Salt Lake City UT 84150. (801)240-2951. Articles/Fiction Editor: Richard M. Romney. Art Director: B. Lee Shaw. Monthly magazine. Estab. 1971. Circ. 200,000. General interest religious publication for youth ages 12-18 who are members of The Church of Jesus Christ of Latter-Day Saints (Mormons).

Fiction: Young adults: contemporary, humorous, religious, romance, science fiction, sports. "All material must relate to Mormon point of view." Does not want to see "formula pieces, stories not sensitive to an LDS audience." Buys 20 mss/year. Average word length: 250-2,500. Byline given.

Nonfiction: Young adults: biography, games/puzzles, history, religion, social issues, travel, sports; "general interest articles by, about and for young Mormons. Would like more about Mormon youth worldwide." Does not want to see "formula pieces, articles not adapted to our specific voice and our audience." Buys 150-200 mss/year. Average word length: 250-2,000. Byline given.

The asterisk before a listing indicates the listing is new in this edition.

Poetry: Reviews poems, 30-line maximum. Limit submissions to 10 poems.
How to Contact/Writers: Fiction/nonfiction: Query. Reports on queries/mss in 2 months. Publishes ms 1 year or more after acceptance. Will consider electronic submissions via disk.
Illustration: Buys 5 illustrations/issue; 50-60 illustrations/year. "We buy only from our pool of illustrators. We use all styles and mediums." Works on assignment only. Illustrations only: Query with samples or to arrange portfolio review. Send résumé, promo sheet, slides and tearsheets. Samples returned with SASE; samples filed. Originals returned at job's completion. Reports only if interested. Original artwork returned at job's completion. Credit line given.
Terms: Pays on acceptance. For mss, buys first rights; right to publish again in other church usage (rights reassigned on written request). Buys all or one-time rights for artwork and photos. Pays $25-375 for stories; $25-350 for articles. Pays illustrators and photographers "by specific arrangements." Sample copies for $1. Writer's guidelines free for #10 SASE.
Tips: Open to "first-person and true-life experiences. Tell what happened in a conversational style. Teen magazines are becoming more brash and sassy. We shy away from the outlandish and trendy, but still need a contemporary look."

***NEW MOON: The Magazine For Girls & Their Dreams**, New Moon Publishing, Inc., P.O. Box 3620, Duluth MN 55803-3620. (218)728-5507. Fax: (218)728-0314. Articles Editor: Joe Kelly. Art Director: Nancy Gruver. Bimonthly magazine. Estab. 1992. Circ. 25,000. *New Moon* is for every girl who wants her voice heard and her dreams taken seriously. *New Moon* portrays strong female role models of all ages, backgrounds and cultures now and in the past. 100% of publication aimed at juvenile market.

- See Insider Report with Editor Joe Kelly in Young Writer's & Illustrator's Markets section.

Fiction: Middle readers, young adults: adventure, animal, contemporary, fantasy, folktales, health, history, humorous, multicultural, nature/environment, problem-solving, religious, romance, science fiction, sports, suspense/mystery. Buys 6 mss/year. Average word length: 300-900. Byline given.
Nonfiction: Middle readers, young adults: animal, arts/crafts, biography, careers, concept, cooking, fashion, games/puzzles, health, history, hobbies, humorous, interview/profile, math, multicultural, nature/environment, problem-solving, religion, science, social issues, sports, travel, stories about real girls. Does not want to see how-to stories. Wants more stories about real girls doing real things. Buys 6 mss/year. Average word length: 300-900. Byline given.
Poetry: Reviews poetry.
How to Contact/Writers: Fiction: send complete ms. Nonfiction: query with published clips. Reports on queries in 1 months; 2-3 months on mss. Will consider simultaneous submissions, electronic submissions via disk or modem, previously published work.
Illustration: Buys 6 illustrations/year from freelancers. Uses b&w artwork only. *New Moon* seeks small graphics, borders and other illustrations which are multicultural, whimsical and positively portray girls. Reviews ms/illustrations packages from artists. Query. Submit ms with rough sketches. Illustration only: Query; send résumé. Samples returned with SASE; samples filed. Reports only if interested. Originals returned at jobs completion. Credit line given.
Photography: Buys photos from freelancers. Model/property releases required; captions required. Uses color, b&w, glossy prints. Query with samples. Reports only if interested.
Terms: Pays on publication. Buys first rights, one-time rights, reprint rights for mss. Buys one-time rights, reprint rights, first rights for artwork and photographs. Pays 4-8¢/word for stories; 4-8¢/word for articles. Pays in contributor's copies. Additional payment for ms/illustration packages and for photos accompanying articles. Pays illustrators $200 for color cover. Samples copies for $6.50. Writer's/illustrator's/photo guidelines for SASE.
Tips: "Please refer to a copy of *New Moon* to understand the style and philosophy of the magazine. Writers and artists who comprehend our goals have the best chance of publication. We're looking for stories about real girls, women's careers, and articles for our Global Village feature on the lives of girls from other countries." Publishes writing/art/photos by children.

ODYSSEY, Science That's Out of This World, Cobblestone Publishing, Inc., 7 School St., Peterborough NH 03458. (603)924-7209. Editor: Elizabeth E. Lindstrom. Managing Editor: Denise L. Babcock. Art Director: Ann Dillon. Magazine published 10 times/year. Estab. 1979. Circ. 35,000. Magazine covers astronomy and space exploration for children ages 8-14. All material

must relate to the theme of a specific upcoming issue in order to be considered.
Fiction: Middle readers and young adults: adventure, folktales, history, biographical fiction. Does not want to see anything not theme-related. Average word length: 750 maximum.
Nonfiction: Middle readers and young adults: arts/crafts, biography, cooking, games/puzzles (no word finds), science (space). Don't send anything not theme-related. Average word length: 200-750, depending on section article is used in.
How to Contact/Writers: "A query must consist of all of the following to be considered (please use nonerasable paper): a brief cover letter stating the subject and word length of the proposed article; a detailed one-page outline explaining the information to be presented in the article; an extensive bibliography of materials the author intends to use in preparing the article; a SASE. Writers new to *Odyssey* should send a writing sample with query. If you would like to know if your query has been received, please also include a stamped postcard that requests acknowledgment of receipt. In all correspondence, please include your complete address as well as a telephone number where you can be reached. A writer may send as many queries for one issue as he or she wishes, but each query must have a separate cover letter, outline, bibliography, and SASE. Telephone queries are not accepted. Handwritten queries will not be considered. Queries may be submitted at any time, but queries sent well in advance of deadline *may not be answered for several months*. Go-aheads requesting material proposed in queries are usually sent five months prior to publication date. Unused queries will be returned approximately three to four months prior to publication date."
Illustration: Buys 3 illustrations/issue; 27 illustrations/year. Works on assignment only. Reviews ms/illustration packages from artists. Query. Contact: Beth Lindstrom, editor. Illustration only: Query with samples. Send tearsheets, photocopies. Contact: Ann Dillon, art director. Reports in 2 weeks. Samples returned with SASE; samples not filed. Original artwork returned upon job's completion (upon written request).
Photography: Wants photos pertaining to any of our forthcoming themes. Uses b&w and color prints; 35mm transparencies. Photographers should send unsolicited photos by mail on speculation.
Terms: Pays on publication. Buys all rights for mss and artwork. Pays 20-25¢/word for stories/articles. Covers are assigned and paid on an individual basis. Pays photographers per photo ($15-100 for b&w; $25-100 for color). Sample copy for $3.95 and SASE with $1.05 postage. Writer's/illustrator's/photo guidelines for SASE.
Tips: (See listings for *Calliope, The World History Magazine for Young People*; *Cobblestone, The History Magazine for Young People*; and *Faces, The Magazine About People*.)

ON COURSE, A Magazine for Teens, General Council of the Assemblies of God, 1445 Boonville Ave., Springfield MO 65802-1894. (417)862-2781. Fax: (417)866-1146. E-mail: oncourse@ag.org. Editor: Melinda Booze. Assistant Editor: Valorie Hurd. Quarterly magazine. Estab. 1991. Circ. 162,000. *On Course* is a religious quarterly for teens "to encourage Christian, biblical discipleship; to promote denominational post-secondary schools; to nurture loyalty to the denomination."
Fiction: Young adults: adventure, contemporary, history, humorous, religious, Christian discipleship, sports. Average word length: 1,000. Byline given.
Nonfiction: Young adults: careers, hobbies, humorous, interview/profile, religion, social issues, sports, college life, Christian discipleship.
How to Contact/Writers: Fiction/nonfiction: Send complete ms. Reports on mss in 2 months. Publishes ms 6-24 months after acceptance. Will consider simultaneous submissions, electronic submissions via disk or modem and previously published work.
Illustration: Buys 4 illustrations/issue; 16 illustrations/year. Uses color artwork only. Reviews ms/illustration packages from artists. Query. Contact: Melinda Booze, editor. Illustration only: Query with samples or send résumé, promo sheet, slides, client list and tearsheets. Contact Melinda Booze, editor. Reports in 2 months. Samples returned with SASE; samples filed. Originals not returned at job's completion. Credit line given.
Photography: Buys photos from freelancers. "Teen life, church life, college life; unposed; often used for illustrative purposes." Model/property releases required. Uses color glossy prints and 35mm or $2\frac{1}{4} \times 2\frac{1}{4}$ transparencies. Query with samples; send business card, promotional literature, tearsheets or catalog. Reports only if interested.

Terms: Pays on acceptance. Buys first or reprint rights for mss. Buys one-time rights for photographs. Pays 6¢/word for stories/articles. Pays illustrators and photographers "as negotiated." Sample copies free for 9×11 SAE. Writer's guidelines for SASE.
Tips: Also publishes writing by teens.

ON THE LINE, Mennonite Publishing House, 616 Walnut Ave., Scottdale PA 15683. (412)887-8500. Editor: Mary Clemens Meyer. Magazine published "monthly in weekly parts." Estab. 1970. Circ. 6,500.
Fiction: Young adults: contemporary, history, humorous, problem-solving, religious, sports and suspense/mystery. "No fantasy or fiction with animal characters." Buys 60 mss/year. Average word length: 1,000-1,800. Byline given.
Nonfiction: Middle readers, young adults: animal, arts/crafts, biography, cooking, games/puzzles, health, history, hobbies, how-to, humorous, nature/environment, problem-solving. Does not want to see articles written from an adult perspective. Average word length: 200-600. Byline given.
Poetry: Wants to see light verse, humorous poetry. Maximum length: 12 lines.
How to Contact/Writers: Fiction/nonfiction: Send complete ms. Reports on queries/mss in 1 month. Will consider simultaneous submissions.
Illustration: Buys 1-2 illustrations/issue; buys 52 illustrations/year. "Illustrations are done on assignment only, to accompany our stories and articles—our need for new artists is very limited." Illustrations only: "Prefer samples they do not want returned; these stay in our files." Reports on art samples only if interested. Original art work returned at job's completion.
Photography: Looking for photography showing ages 12-14, both sexes, good mix of races, wholesome fun. Uses 8×10 glossy b&w prints. Photographers should send unsolicited photos by mail.
Terms: Pays on acceptance. For mss buys one-time rights; second serial (reprint rights). Buys one-time rights for artwork and photos. Pays 2-5¢/word for assigned/unsolicited articles. Pays $25-50 for color inside illustration. Photographers are paid per photo, $25-50 (cover). Sample copy free with 7×10 SAE. Free writer's guidelines.
Tips: "We will be focusing on the 12-13 age-group of our age 10-14 audience. (Focus was somewhat younger before.)"

✤OWL COMMUNICATION, 179 John St., Suite 50, Toronto, Ontario M5T 3G5 Canada. See listings for *Chickadee* and *OWL*.

✤OWL MAGAZINE, The Discovery Magazine for Children, Owl Communication, 179 John St., Suite 50, Toronto, Ontario M5T 3G5 Canada. (416)868-6001. Editor: Nyla Ahmad. Art Director: Tim Davin. Magazine published 10 times/year. Circ. 160,000. "*OWL* helps children over eight discover and enjoy the world of science and nature. We look for articles that are fun to read, that inform from a child's perspective, and that motivate hands-on interaction. *OWL* explores the reader's many interests in the natural world in a scientific, but always entertaining, way."

- *OWL* appeared on a 1995 Hot List ® compiled by *Children's Book Insider*. This list of "10 Book and Magazine Publishers Most Receptive to New Writers" is updated every few months, and available to new and renewing subscribers.

Nonfiction: Middle readers, young adults: animal, biology, games/puzzles, high-tech, humor, interview/profile, travel. Especially interested in puzzles and game ideas: logic, math, visual puzzles. Does not want to see religious topics, anthropomorphizing. Buys 20 mss/year. Average word length: 1,500. Byline given.
How to Contact/Writers: Nonfiction: Query with published clips. Reports on queries in 4-6 weeks; mss in 6-8 weeks.

***A bullet within a listing introduces special comments by the editor of* Children's Writer's & Illustrator's Market.**

Illustration: Buys 3-5 illustrations/issue; 40-50 illustrations/year. Uses color artwork only. Preferred theme or style: lively, involving, fun, with emotional impact and appeal. "We use a range of styles." Works on assignment only. Illustrations only: Send tearsheets and slides. Reports on art samples only if interested. Original artwork returned at job's completion.
Photography: Looking for shots of animals and nature. "Label the photos." Uses 2¼×2¼ and 35mm transparencies. Photographers should query with samples.
Terms: Pays on acceptance. Buys first North American and world rights for mss, artwork and photos. Pays $200-500 (Canadian) for assigned/unsolicited articles. Pays up to $650 (Canadian) for illustrations. Photographers are paid per photo. Sample copies for $4.28. Free writer's guidelines.
Tips: Writers: "Talk to kids and find out what they're interested in; make sure your research is thorough and find good consultants who are doing up-to-the-minute research. Be sure to read the magazine carefully to become familiar with *OWL*'s style." (See listing for *Chickadee*.)

PKA'S ADVOCATE, (formerly *The Advocate*), PKA Publication, 301A Rolling Hills Park, Prattsville NY 12468. (518)299-3103. Articles/Fiction Editor: Remington Wright. Art Director/Photo Editor: CJ Karlie. Bimonthly tabloid. Estab. 1987. Circ. 12,000. "*PKA's Advocate* advocates good writers and quality writings. We publish art, fiction, photos and poetry. *PKA's Advocate*'s submitters are talented people of all ages who do not earn their livings as writers. We wish to promote the arts and to give those we publish the opportunity to be published through a for-profit means rather than in a not-for-profit way. We do this by selling advertising and offering reading entertainment."
Fiction: Middle readers and young adults/teens: adventure, animal, contemporary, fantasy, folktales, health, humorous, nature/environment, problem-solving, romance, science fiction, sports, suspense/mystery. Looks for "well written, entertaining work, whether fiction or nonfiction." Buys approximately 42 mss/year. Average word length: 1,500. Byline given. Wants to see more humorous material, nature/environment and romantic comedy.
Nonfiction: Middle readers and young adults/teens: animal, arts/crafts, biography, careers, concept, cooking, fashion, games/puzzles, geography, history, hobbies, how-to, humorous, interview/profile, nature/environment, problem-solving, science, social issues, sports, travel. Buys 10 mss/year. Average word length: 1,500. Byline given.
Poetry: Reviews poetry any length.
How to Contact/Writers: Fiction/nonfiction: send complete ms. Reports on queries in 4-6 weeks/mss in 6-8 weeks. Publishes ms 2-18 months after acceptance.
Illustration: Uses b&w artwork only. Uses cartoons. Reviews ms/illustration packages from artists. Submit a photo print (b&w or color), an excellent copy of work (no larger than 8×10) or original. Illustrations only: "Send previous unpublished art with SASE, please." Reports in 2 months. Samples return with SASE; samples not filed. Original work returned upon job's completion. Credit line given.
Photography: Buys photos from freelancers. Model/property releases required. Uses color and b&w prints. Send unsolicited photos by mail with SASE. Reports in 2 months. Wants nature, artistic and humorous photos.
Terms: Pays on publication. Acquires first rights for mss, artwork and photographs. Pays in copies or other premiums. Sample copies for $4. Writer's/illustrator/photo guidelines for SASE.
Tips: "Artists and photographers should keep in mind that we are a b&w paper."

POCKETS, Devotional Magazine for Children, The Upper Room, 1908 Grand, P.O. Box 189, Nashville TN 37202. (615)340-7333. Articles/Fiction Editor: Janet R. Knight. Art Director: Chris Schechner, Suite 207, 3100 Carlisle Plaza, Dallas TX 75204. Magazine published 11 times/year. Estab. 1981. Circ. 96,000. "Stories should help children 6 to 12 experience a Christian lifestyle that is not always a neatly wrapped moral package but is open to the continuing revelation of God's will."
Fiction: Picture-oriented, young readers, middle readers: contemporary, folktales, multicultural, nature/environment, problem-solving, religious. Does not want to see violence or talking animal stories. Buys 40-45 mss/year. Average word length: 800-1,600. Byline given.
Nonfiction: Picture-oriented, young readers, middle readers: cooking, games/puzzles, interview/profile, multicultural, nature/environment, problem-solving. Does not want to see how-to articles. "Our nonfiction reads like a story." Multicultural needs include: stories that feature children of

various racial/ethnic groups and do so in a way that is true to those depicted. Buys 10 mss/year. Average word length: 800-1,600. Byline given.

How to Contact/Writers: Fiction/nonfiction: Send complete ms. "Prefer not to deal with queries." Reports on mss in 2-4 weeks. Will consider simultaneous submissions.

Illustration: Buys 50 illustrations/issue. Preferred theme or style: varied; both 4-color and 2-color. Works on assignment only. Illustrations only: Send promo sheet, tearsheets and slides to Chris Schechner, Suite 207, 3100 Carlisle Plaza, Dallas TX 75204. "Include samples of both 2-color and 4-color, if you have them." Reports on art samples in 3 months. Samples returned with SASE. Original artwork returned at job's completion. Credit line given.

Photography: Purchases photography from freelancers. Buys photos with accompanying ms only.

Terms: Pays on acceptance. Buys first North American serial rights for mss; one-time rights for artwork and photos. Pays 12-15¢/word for stories/articles. Pays $500-600 for color cover illustration; $50-400 for color inside; $50-250 (2-color). Pays $25 for color transparencies accompanying articles; $500 for cover photos. Sample copy free with 8×10 SAE and 4 first-class stamps. Writer's/illustrator's guidelines free with SASE.

Tips: "Ask for our themes first. They are set yearly in the fall. Also, we are looking for articles about real children involved in environment, peace or similar activities. We have added a two-page story, about 600 words, for beginning readers. Become familiar with *Pockets* before submitting. So much of what we receive is not appropriate for our publication."

POWER AND LIGHT, Children's Ministries, 6401 The Paseo, Kansas City MO 64131. (816)333-7000. Editor: Beula Postlewait. Associate Editor: Melissa Hammer. Weekly story paper. "*Power and Light* is a leisure reading piece for fifth and sixth graders. It is published weekly by the Department of Children's Ministries of the Church of the Nazarene. The major purposes of *Power and Light* are to provide a leisure reading piece which will build Christian behavior and values; provide reinforcement for Biblical concepts taught in the Sunday School curriculum. The focus of the reinforcement will be life-related, with some historical appreciation. *Power and Light*'s target audience is children ages 11-12 in grades five and six."

Fiction: Middle readers: adventure, contemporary, multicultural, nature/environment, problem-solving, religious. "Avoid fantasy, science fiction, abnormally mature or precocious children, personification of animals. Also avoid extensive cultural or holiday references, especially those with a distinctly American frame of reference. Our paper has an international audience. We need stories involving multicultural preteens in realistic settings dealing with realistic problems with God's help." Average word length: 500-700. Byline given.

How to Contact/Writers: Send complete ms. Reports on queries in 1 month; mss in 2 months. Publishes ms 2 years after acceptance.

Illustration: *Power and Light* publishes a wide variety of artistic styles, i.e., cartoon, realistic, montage, etc., but whatever the style, artwork must appeal to 11-12 year old children. Illustrations only: Query; send résumé, promo sheet and portfolio. Reports back only if interested. Credit line given.

Photography: Buys "b&w archaeological/Biblical for inside use and color preteen/contemporary/action for cover use."

Terms: Pays on publication. "Payment is made approximately one year before the date of issue." Buys multiple use rights for mss. Purchases all rights for artwork and first/one-time rights for photographs. Pays 5¢/word for stories/articles. Pays illustrators $40 for b&w, $75 for color cover; $40 for b&w, $50-75 for color inside. Photographers paid per photo (range: $35-45; $200 maximum for cover color photo). Writer's/illustrator's guidelines for SASE.

Tips: "Themes and outcomes should conform to the theology and practices of the Church of the Nazarene, Evangelical Friends, Free Methodist, Wesleyan and other Bible-believing Evangelical churches." Looks for "bright, colorful illustrations; concise, short articles and stories." (See listing for *Discoveries*.)

PRIMARY DAYS, Scripture Press Publications, Inc., P.O. Box 632, Glen Ellyn IL 60138. (708)668-6000. Articles/Fiction Editor: Janice K. Burton. Art Director: Blake Ebel. Distributed weekly; published quarterly. Estab. 1935. "Our audience is children 6-8 years old." All materials attempt to show God's working in the lives of children. Must have a true Christian slant, not just a moral implication.

Fiction: Young readers: adventure, multicultural, nature/environment, problem-solving, religious, sports (Christian concepts only). Average word length: 300-350.
Nonfiction: Young readers: arts/crafts, biography, games/puzzles, history, interview/profile, multicultural, hobbies, how-to, nature/environment, problem-solving, religion, sports (all need Christian slant). Multicultural needs include: Stories that have their settings in other countries and deal with ethnic family situations. Average word length: 100-200.
How to Contact/Writers: Fiction/nonfiction: Send complete ms. Reports on mss in 8-10 weeks. Publishes ms 1-2 years after acceptance. "We work 1 year ahead." Will consider previously published work.
Illustration: Buys 24-30 illustrations/year. Contact: Blake Ebel, art director, for submission information. Credit line sometimes given.
Photography: Buys photos from freelancers.
Terms: Pays on acceptance. Buys all rights, one-time rights and second (reprint) rights for mss. Pays 7-10¢/word for stories/articles depending on amount of editing required. Sample copies for #10 SASE. Writer's/photo guidelines for SASE.
Tips: "I'm not interested in material that lacks any spiritual element. Stories/articles must be appropriate for a Sunday School take-home paper. Write for Tips to Writers, sample copies, theme lists. Include Social Security number on manuscript." (See listings for *Counselor, Teen Power* and *Zelos*.)

RACING FOR KIDS, Griggs Publishing Company Inc., P.O. Box 500, Concord NC 28026. (704)455-5111. Fax: (704)455-2227. Editor: Gary McCredie. Monthly magazine. Estab. 1990. Circ. 17,000. Publication caters to kids interested in racing.
Nonfiction: Young readers: auto racing, sports. Middle readers and young adults: sports (motor sports). Multicultural needs include: sensitivity to minorities in racing—women and African-Americans; with foreign drivers, tell a little about their home country. Buys 12-20 mss/year. Average word length: 400-1,200. Byline given.
How to Contact/Writers: Nonfiction: Query. Reports on queries in 2-4 weeks only if interested. Publishes ms 6-12 months after acceptance.
Illustration: Works on assignment only. Reviews ms/illustration packages from artists. Query. Contact: Gary McCredie, editor. Illustrations only: Query with samples and tearsheets. Contact: Bob Vlasich, art director. Reports in 2-4 weeks. Samples not returned. Originals returned at job's completion if requested. Credit line given.
Terms: Pays on publication. Buys exclusive magazine rights for mss. Pays $50-150 for stories, $50-150 for articles. Additional payment for photos that accompany article.
Tips: "Know the subject matter, study publication. All stories are racing-related. We like stories about NASCAR, NHRA and Monster Truck drivers."

R-A-D-A-R, Standard Publishing, 8121 Hamilton Ave., Cincinnati OH 45231. (513)931-4050. Editor: Elaina Meyers. Weekly magazine. Circ. 120,000. *R-A-D-A-R* is a weekly take-home paper for boys and girls who are in grades 3-6. "Our goal is to reach these children with the truth of God's Word, and to help them make it the guide of their lives. Many of our features, including our stories, now correlate with the Sunday school lesson themes. Send SASE for a quarterly theme list and sample copies of *R-A-D-A-R*. Keep in mind that others will be submitting stories for the same themes—this is not an assignment."
Fiction: Young readers and middle readers: adventure, animal, contemporary, history, humorous, nature/environment, problem-solving, religious, sports, suspense/mystery, travel. Does not want to see fantasy or science fiction. Buys 150 mss/year. Average word length: 400-1,000. Byline given.
Nonfiction: Young readers and middle readers: animal, health, hobbies, humorous, interview/profile, nature/environment, problem-solving, religious, science, sports, travel. Buys 50 mss/year. Average word length: 400-1,000. Byline given.
Poetry: Reviews poetry. Maximum length: 16 lines.
How to Contact/Writers: Fiction/nonfiction: Send complete ms. Reports on mss in 6-8 weeks. Will consider simultaneous submissions (but prefers not to).
Illustration: Buys 3 illustrations/issue; 156 illustrations/year. "Works on assignment only; there have been a few exceptions to this." Reviews ms/illustration packages from artists. Query with samples. Send résumé, promo sheet and tearsheets. Contact: Elaina Meyers, editor. Illustrations

only: Send résumé, tearsheets or promo sheets; samples of art can be photocopied. Reports in 1-2 weeks. Samples returned with SASE; samples filed. Originals not returned at job's completion. Credit line given.

Photography: Purchases photos from freelancers. Model/property releases required. Send résumé, business card, promotional literature or tearsheets to be kept on file.

Terms: Pays on acceptance. Buys first rights, one-time rights, second serial, first North American rights for mss. Purchases all rights for artwork. Pays 3-7¢/word for unsolicited articles (few are assigned). Contributor copies given "not as payment, but all contributors receive copies of their art/articles." Pays $125 for b&w (cover); $150 for color (cover); $40 for b&w (inside); $70-100 for color (inside). Photographers paid $125 maximum per photo. Sample copy and writer's guidelines free with 9⅜×4¼ SASE.

Tips: "Write about current topics, issues that elementary-age children are dealing with. Keep illustrations/photos current. Children are growing up much more quickly these days. This is seen in illustrations and stories. Times are changing and writers and illustrators should keep current with the times to be effective. Send a SASE for sample copies, guidelines, and theme sheet. Be familiar with the publication for which you wish to write." (See listing for *Straight*.)

RANGER RICK, National Wildlife Federation, 8925 Leesburg Pike, Vienna VA 22184. (703)790-4000. Editor: Gerald Bishop. Design Director: Donna Miller. Monthly magazine. Circ. 850,000. "Our audience ranges from ages six to twelve, though we aim the reading level of most material at nine-year-olds or fourth graders."

Fiction: Middle readers: animal (wildlife), fantasy, humorous, science fiction. Buys 4-6 mss/year. Average word length: 900. Byline given.

Nonfiction: Middle readers: animal (wildlife), conservation, outdoor adventure, humorous. Buys 20-30 mss/year. Average word length: 900. Byline given.

How to Contact/Writers: Fiction: Query with published clips; send complete ms. Nonfiction: Query with published clips. Reports on queries/mss in 6 weeks.

Illustration: Buys 6-8 illustrations/issue; 75-100 illustrations/year. Preferred theme: nature, wildlife. Works on assignment only. Illustrations only: Send résumé, tearsheets. Reports on art samples in 6 weeks. Original artwork returned at job's completion.

Terms: Pays on acceptance. Buys all rights (first North American serial rights negotiable). Pays up to $575 for full-length of best quality. For illustrations, buys one-time rights. Pays $250-1,000 for color (inside, per page) illustration. Sample copies for $2. Writer's guidelines free with SASE.

Tips: "Fiction and nonfiction articles may be written on any aspect of wildlife, nature, outdoor adventure and discovery, domestic animals with a 'wild' connection (such as domestic pigs and wild boars), science, conservation or related subjects. To find out what subjects have been covered recently, consult our annual indexes and the *Children's Magazine Guide*. These are available in many libraries. The National Wildlife Federation (NWF) discourages the keeping of wildlife as pets, so the keeping of such pets should not be featured in your copy. Avoid stereotyping of any group. For instance, girls can enjoy nature and the outdoors as much as boys can, and mothers can be just as knowledgeable as fathers. The only way you can write successfully for *Ranger Rick* is to know the kinds of subjects and approaches we like. And the only way you can do that is to read the magazine. Recent issues can be found in most libraries or are available from our office for $2 a copy."

***REACT MAGAZINE, The Magazine That Raises Voices**, Parade Publications, 711 Third Ave., New York NY 10017. Fax: (212)450-0978. Art Director: Paula Wood. Photo Editor: Nancy Iacoi. Weekly magazine. Estab. 1995. Circ. 4 million. 100% publication aimed at juvenile market.

Nonfiction: Young adult: animal, entertainment, games/puzzles, health, hobbies, interview/profile, nature/environment, news, science, social issues, sports. Average word length: 250-600. Byline sometimes given.

How to Contact/Writers: Query with published clips.

Illustration: Works on assignment only. Illustration only: arrange portfolio review. Contact: Paula Wood, art director. Credit sometimes given.

Photography: Query with résumé or credits.. Reports only if interested.

Terms: Pays on acceptance. Buys all rights for mss, artwork and photographs. Pays $250-2,000 for stories. Additional payment for photos accompanying articles. Pays photographers by the project. Writer's guidelines for SASE.

"Each character has a personality of his own," says Editor Elaina Meyers of the cover illustration of R-A-D-A-R, a Christian weekly. "The mood of the work is lively and happy." Artist Mary Bausman used prisma colored pencils on colored, pastel paper to create the whimsical animals and cartoon boy, Matt. In the story "Nothing but Trouble," by Lyn Jackson, young Matt learns a lesson about honesty when trying to buy a puppy from the neighborhood pet store. For initial contact, Bausman mailed portfolio samples to Standard Publishing's art department, and was given an assignment. "She turned in excellent quality work, and met her deadline," Meyers says. "I am very glad that Bausman sent her samples—I encourage other aspiring writers and illustrators to do the same."

SCHOLASTIC INC., 555 Broadway, New York NY 10012-3999. See listings for *Choices*, *Dynamath*, *Junior Scholastic*, *Scholastic Math Magazines* and *Superscience Blue*. Scholastic publishes 40 children's magazines. Contact them for more information.

SCHOLASTIC MATH MAGAZINE, Scholastic Inc., 555 Broadway, New York NY 10012-3999. (212)343-6100. Editor: Sarah Jane Brian. Senior Designer: Leah Bossio. Art Director: Joan

Michael. Magazine published 14 times/year, September-May. Estab. 1980. Circ. 230,000. "We are a math magazine for seventh, eighth and ninth grade classrooms. We present math in current, relevant, high-interest topics. Math skills we focus on include whole number, fraction and decimal computation, percentages, ratios, proportions, geometry."

Nonfiction: Young adults: animal, arts/crafts, careers, cooking, fashion, games/puzzles, geography, health, history, hobbies, how-to, humorous, interview/profile, math, multicultural, nature/environment, problem solving, science, social issues, sports, travel. No fiction. Does not want to see "anything dealing with *very* controversial issues—e.g., teenage pregnancy, etc." Buys 20 mss/year. Byline given.

How to Contact/Writers: Query. Reports on queries in 2 months. Will consider simultaneous submissions.

Illustration: Buys 4 illustrations/issue; 56 illustrations/year. Prefers to review "humorous, young adult sophistication" types of art. Works on assignment only. Reviews ms/illustration packages from artists. Query first. Illustrations only: Query with samples; submit portfolio for review. Reports back only if interested. Original artwork returned at job's completion.

Terms: Pays on publication. Buys all rights for mss. Pays $25 for puzzles and riddles; maximum of $350 for stories/articles. Photographers are paid by the project.

Tips: "For our magazine, stories dealing with math concepts and applications in the real world are sought." (See listings for *Choices*, *Dynamath*, *Junior Scholastic* and *Superscience Blue*.)

***SCHOOL MAGAZINE, (BLAST OFF!, COUNTDOWN, ORBIT, TOUCHDOWN)**, New South Wales Dept. of School Education, Private Bag 3, Ryde NSW 2112 Australia. (02)808-9683. Editor: Jonathan Shaw. 4 monthly magazines. Circ. 200,000. "*School Magazine* is a literary magazine that is issued to all N.S.W. primary public schools. Private schools and individuals subscribe for a small fee. We include stories, plays and poems." The 4 magazines issued each month are graded according to age level, 8-12 years.

Fiction: Young readers: animal, contemporary, fantasy, humorous. Middle readers: animal, contemporary, fantasy, humorous, problem solving, science fiction, suspense/mystery/adventure. Buys 30 mss/year. Average word length: 500-2,500. Byline given.

Poetry: Maximum length: 150 lines. Limit submissions to 10 poems.

How to Contact/Writers: Fiction: Send complete ms. Include SAE (IRC) for return of ms. Reports on queries in 2 weeks; on mss in 2 months. Publishes ms at least 6 months after acceptance.

Terms: Pays on acceptance. Buys first Australian serial rights. "Pays $137 per thousand words."

SCHOOL MATES, USCF's Magazine for Beginning Chess Players, United States Chess Federation, 186 Rt. 9W, New Windsor NY 12553. (914)562-8350. Fax: (914)561-CHES. Articles Editor: Brian Bugbee. Assistant Editor: Judy Levine. Art Director: Jami Anson. Bimonthly magazine. Estab. 1987. Circ. 30,000. Magazine for beginning chess players. Offers instructional articles, features on famous players, scholastic chess coverage, games, puzzles, occasional fiction, listing of chess tournaments.

Fiction: Young readers, middle readers, young adults: chess. Middle readers: humorous (chess-related). Average word length: 500-2,500 words.

Nonfiction: Young readers, middle readers, young adults: games/puzzles, chess. Middle readers, young adults: interview/profile (chess-related). "No *Mad Magazine* type humor. No sex, no drugs, no alcohol, no tobacco. No stereotypes. We want to see chess presented as a wholesome, non-nerdy activity that's fun for all. Good sportsmanship, fair play, and 'thinking ahead' are extremely desirable in chess articles. Also, celebrities who play chess."

Poetry: Infrequently published. Must be chess related.

How to Contact/Writers: Send complete ms. Reports on queries/mss in 5 weeks.

Illustration: Buys 10-25 illustrations/year. Prefers b&w and ink; cartoons OK. Illustration only: Query first. Reports back only if interested. Credit line sometimes given. "Typically, a cover is credited while an illustration inside gets only the artist's signature in the work itself."

Photography: Purchases photos from freelancers. Wants "action shots of chess games (at tournament competitions), well-done portraits of popular chess players."

Terms: Pays on publication. Buys one-time rights for mss, artwork and photos. For stories/articles, pays $20-100. Pays illustrators $50-75 for b&w cover; $20-50 for b&w inside. Pays photographers per photo (range: $25-75). Sample copies free for 9×12 SAE and 2 first-class stamps. Writer's guidelines free on request.

Tips: Writers: "Lively prose that grabs and sustains kids' attention is desirable. Don't talk down to kids or over their heads. Don't be overly 'cute.' " Illustration/photography: "Whimsical shots are often desirable."

SCIENCE WEEKLY, Science Weekly Inc., P.O. Box 70638, Chevy Chase MD 20813. (301)680-8804. Fax: (301)680-9240. Editor: Deborah Lazar. Magazine published 16 times/year. Estab. 1984. Circ. 250,000.

- *Science Weekly* uses freelance writers to develop and write an entire issue on a single science topic. Send résumé only, not submissions.

Nonfiction: Young readers, middle readers, (K-8th grade): science/math education, education, problem-solving. "Author must be within the greater DC, Virginia, Maryland area." Works on assignment only.
Terms: Pays on publication. Prefers people with education, science and children's writing background. *Send résumé.*

SCIENCELAND, To Nurture Scientific Thinking, Scienceland Inc., 501 Fifth Ave., #2108, New York NY 10017-6165. (212)490-2180. Fax: (212)490-2187. Editor/Art Director: Al Matano. Magazine published 8 times/year. Estab. 1977. Circ. 16,000. This is "a content reading picture-book for the preschool youngster being read to, the first-grader learning to read and for the second and third grader beginning to read independently."

- To learn more about *Scienceland*, see Insider Report with Al Matano in the 1995 edition of *Children's Writer's & Illustrator's Market.*

Nonfiction: Picture-oriented material, young readers: animal, art/crafts, biography, careers, cooking, education, games/puzzles, health, history, how-to, nature/environment, problem-solving. Does not want to see unillustrated material; All material must be illustrated in full color.
Poetry: Reviews poetry. Maximum length: 12 lines.
How to Contact/Writers: *Must* be picture or full-color illustrated stories.
Illustration: Uses color artwork only. Prefers to review "detailed, realistic, full color art. No abstracts or fantasy." Reviews captioned/illustration packages from artists. "Query first." Illustrations only: Send unsolicited art by mail; provide résumé, promotional literature or tearsheets to be kept on file. Reports back in 3-4 weeks. Exclusively contracted original artwork retained at our option for exhibits, etc. Others returned at job's completion.
Photography: Wants to see "physical and natural science photos with children in scenes whenever possible." Model/property release and photo captions required where applicable. Uses 35mm transparencies. Photographer should submit portfolio for review; provide résumé, promotional literature or tearsheets to be kept on file.
Terms: Pays on publication. Buys nonexclusive rights to artwork and photos. Payment for captioned/illustration packages: $50-500 and up. Payment for illustrations: $25-300 and up for color cover; $25-300 and up for color inside. Photographers paid by the project. Sample copy free with 9×12 SASE.
Tips: "Must be top notch illustrator or photographer. No amateurs."

SCRIPTURE PRESS INC., P.O. Box 632, Glen Ellyn IL 60138. See listings for *Counselor*, *Primary Days*, *Teen Power* and *Zelos*.

SEVENTEEN MAGAZINE, K-III Magazines, 850 Third Ave., New York NY 10022. (212)407-9700. Editor-in-Chief: Caroline Miller. Fiction Editor: Joe Bargmann. Senior Editor: Rory Evans. Art Director: Daniel Pfeffer. Monthly magazine. Estab. 1944. Circ. 1.95 million. "General interest magazine for teenage girls."
Fiction: Young adults: animal, contemporary, fantasy, folktales, health, history, humorous, religious, romance, science fiction, sports, spy/mystery/adventure. "We consider all good literary short fiction." Buys 12-20 mss/year. Average word length: 1,000-4,000. Byline given.
Nonfiction: Young adults: animal, fashion, careers, health, hobbies, how-to, humorous, interview/profile, multicultural, religion, social issues, sports. Buys 150 mss/year. Word length: Varies from 800-1,000 words for short features and monthly columns to 800-2,500 words for major articles. Byline given.
How to Contact/Writers: Fiction: Send complete ms. Nonfiction: Query with published clips or send complete ms. "Do not call." Reports on queries/mss in 1 month. Will consider simultaneous submissions.

Illustration: Uses 1 illustration per short story. Will review ms/illustration packages. Pays illustrators by the project. Writer's guidelines for business-size SASE.
Terms: Pays on acceptance. Writer's guidelines available for SASE.

SHARING THE VICTORY, Fellowship of Christian Athletes, 8701 Leeds, Kansas City MO 64129. (816)921-0909. Fax: (816)921-8755. Articles/Photo Editor: John Dodderidge. Art Director: Frank Grey. Monthly magazine. Estab. 1982. Circ. 55,000. "Purpose is to present to coaches and athletes, and all whom they influence, the challenge and adventure of receiving Jesus Christ as Savior and Lord."
Nonfiction: Young adults: interview/profile, sports. Buys 20-25 mss/year. Average word length: 400-900. Byline given.
Poetry: Reviews poetry. Maximum length: 50-75 words.
How to Contact/Writers: Nonfiction: Query with published clips. Reports in 3 weeks. Publishes ms 3 months after acceptance. Will consider simultaneous submissions, electronic submissions via disk or modem and previously published work.
Photography: Purchases photos separately. Looking for photos of sports action. Uses color, b&w prints and 35mm transparencies.
Terms: Pays on publication. Buys first rights and second serial (reprint) rights. Pays $50-250 for assigned and unsolicited articles. Photographers paid per photo (range: $50-300). Sample copies for 9×12 SASE and $1. Writer's/photo guidelines for SASE.
Tips: "Be specific—write short. Take quality photos that are usable." Wants interviews and features. Interested in colorful sports photos.

SHOFAR, 43 Northcote Dr., Melville NY 11747. (516)643-4598. Managing Editor: Gerald H. Grayson. Magazine published monthly October through May—double issues December/January and April/May. Circ. 17,000. For Jewish children ages 8-13.
Fiction: Middle readers: cartoons, contemporary, humorous, poetry, religious, sports. All material must be on a Jewish theme. Buys 10-20 mss/year. Average word length: 500-700. Byline given.
Nonfiction: Middle readers: history, humorous, interview/profile, puzzles, religious. Buys 10-20 mss/year. Average word length: 500-1,000. Byline given.
How to Contact/Writers: Fiction/nonfiction: Send complete ms (preferred) with SASE. Queries welcome. Publishes special holiday issues. Submit holiday theme pieces at least 4 months in advance. Reports on queries/mss in 1 month. Will consider simultaneous submissions.
Illustration: Buys 3-4 illustrations/issue; buys 15-20 illustrations/year. Works on assignment only. Reviews ms/illustration packages from artists. Query first. Illustrations only: Send tearsheets. Works on assignment only. Reports on art samples only if interested. Original artwork returned at job's completion.
Terms: Buys first North American serial rights or first serial rights for mss and artwork. Pays on publication. Pays 10¢/word plus 5 contributor's copies. Photos purchased with mss at additional fees. Pays $25-100/b&w cover illustration; $50-150/color (cover). Sample copy free with 9×12 SAE and 98¢ postage. Free writer's/illustrator's guidelines.

SKIPPING STONES, A Multicultural Children's Magazine, P.O. Box 3939, Eugene OR 97403. (503)342-4956. Articles/Photo Editor: Arun N. Toké. Fiction Editor: Amy Brandt. Quarterly magazine. Estab. 1988. Circ. 3,000. "*Skipping Stones* is a multicultural, nonprofit children's magazine designed to encourage cooperation, creativity and celebration of cultural and environmental richness. We encourage submissions by minorities and under-represented populations."
Fiction: Middle readers, young adult/teens: animal, contemporary, humorous. All levels: folktales, multicultural, nature/environment. Multicultural needs include: bilingual or multilingual pieces; use of words from other languages; settings in other cultures or multi-ethnic communities.
Nonfiction: All levels: animal, biography, cooking, games/puzzles, history, humorous, interview/profile, multicultural, nature/environment, problem-solving, religion and cultural celebrations, sports, travel, multicultural and environmental awareness. Does not want to see preaching or abusive language; no poems by authors over 18 years old; no suspense or romance stories for the sake of the same. Average word length: 500-750. Byline given.
How to Contact/Writers: Fiction: Query. Nonfiction: Send complete ms. Reports on queries in 2 months; mss in 4 months. Will consider simultaneous submissions; reviews artwork for future assignments. Please include your name on each page.

Illustration: Prefers b&w drawings especially by young adults. Will consider all illustration packages. Ms/illustration packages: Query; submit complete ms with final art; submit tearsheets. Reports back in 4 months. Original artwork returned at job's completion. Credit line given.
Photography: Black & white photos preferred, but color photos will be considered. Children 7-15, international, nature, celebration.
Terms: Pays on publication. Buys first or reprint rights for mss and artwork; reprint rights for photographs. Pays in copies for authors, photographers and illustrators; $50-75 for b&w cover. Sample copies for $4 with SAE and 4 first-class stamps. Writer's/illustrator's guidelines for 4×9 SASE.
Tips: Wants material "meant for children" with multicultural or environmental awareness theme. "Think, live and write as if you were a child. Let the 'inner child' within you speak out—naturally, uninhibited." Wants "material that gives insight on cultural celebrations, lifestyle, custom and tradition, glimpse of daily life in other countries and cultures. Photos, songs, artwork are most welcome if they illustrate/highlight the points. Translations are welcome if your submission is in a language other than English. In 1996, our themes will include homeless and street children, world religions and cultures, celebrations in various cultures, animals and plants, indigenous architecture, songs from various cultures, world in 2025 A.D., Native American culture, nutrition and foods from around the world, hospitality, sports and cooperative games."

SOCCER JR., The Soccer Magazine for Kids, Triplepoint Inc., 27 Unquowa Rd., Fairfield CT 06430. (203)259-5766. Articles/Fiction Editor: Priscilla Williams. Bimonthly magazine. Estab. 1992. Circ. 100,000. *Soccer Jr.* is for soccer players 8-16 years-old. It offers "instruction, inspiration and fun."
Fiction: Middle readers, young adults: sports (soccer). Does not want to see "cute," preachy or "moralizing" stories. Buys 3-4 mss/year. Average word length: 1,000-2,000. Byline given.
Nonfiction: Young readers, middle readers, young adults: games/puzzles—soccer-themed. Buys 10-12 mss/year.
How to Contact/Writers: Fiction/nonfiction: Send complete ms. Reports on mss in 2-3 months. Publishes ms 3-12 months after acceptance. Will consider simultaneous submissions.
Illustration: Uses color artwork only. Works on assignment only. Illustrations only: Send samples to be filed. Samples not returned. "We have a small pool of artists we work from, but look for new freelancers occasionally, and accept samples for consideration."
Terms: Pays on acceptance. Buys first rights for mss. Sample copies for 9×12 SAE and 5 first-class stamps.
Tips: "Read *Soccer Jr.* An astonishing number of manuscripts are submitted either by people who've never seen the publication or who send non-soccer-related material." The magazine also accepts stories written by children.

SPIDER, The Magazine for Children, Carus Corporation, P.O. Box 300, Peru IL 61354. Editor-in-Chief: Marianne Carus. Associate Editor: Christine Walske. Art Director: Ron McCutchan. Monthly magazine. Estab. 1994. Circ. 85,000. *Spider* publishes high-quality literature for beginning readers, primarily ages 6-9.
Fiction: Young readers: adventure, animal, contemporary, fantasy, folktales, history, humorous, multicultural, nature/environment, problem-solving, science fiction, sports, suspense/mystery. "Authentic, well-researched stories from all cultures are welcome. We would like to see more multicultural material. No didactic, religious, or violent stories, or anything that talks down to children." Average word length: 300-1,000. Byline given.
Nonfiction: Young readers: animal, arts/crafts, cooking, games/puzzles, geography, history, math, multicultural, nature/environment, problem-solving, science. "Well-researched articles on all cultures are welcome. Would like to see more games, puzzles and activities, especially ones adaptable to *Spider*'s takeout pages. No encyclopedic or overtly educational articles." Average word length: 300-800. Byline given.
Poetry: Serious, humorous, nonsense rhymes. Maximum length: 20 lines.
How to Contact/Writers: Fiction/nonfiction: Send complete ms. Reports on mss in 3 months. Publishes ms 1-2 years after acceptance. Will consider simultaneous submissions and previously published work.
Illustration: Buys 20 illustrations/issue; 240 illustrations/year. Uses color artwork only. "Any medium—preferably one that can wrap on a laser scanner—no larger than 20×24. We use more

realism than cartoon-style art." Works on assignment only. Reviews ms/illustration packages from artists. Submit ms with rough sketches. Illustrations only: Send promo sheet and tearsheets. Reports in 6 weeks. Samples returned with SASE; samples filed. Original work returned at job's completion. Credit line given.

Photography: Buys photos from freelancers. Buys photos with accompanying ms only. Model/property releases required; captions required. Uses 35mm or 2¼×2¼ transparencies. Send unsolicited photos by mail; provide résumé and tearsheets. Reports in 6 weeks.

Terms: Pays on publication for text; within 45 days from acceptance for art. Buys first, one-time or reprint rights for mss. Buys first and promotional rights for artwork; one-time rights for photographs. Pays 25¢/word for stories/articles. Authors also receive 2 complimentary copies of the issue in which work appears. Additional payment for ms/illustration packages and for photos accompanying articles. Pays illustrators $750 for color cover; $200-300 for color inside. Pays photographers per photo (range: $25-75). Sample copies for $4. Writer's/illustrator's guidelines for SASE.

Tips: "Writers: Read back issues before submitting." (See listings for *Babybug*, *Cricket*, and *Ladybug*.)

STANDARD PUBLISHING, 8121 Hamilton Ave., Cincinnati OH 45231. See listings for *R-A-D-A-R* and *Straight*.

STORY FRIENDS, Mennonite Publishing House, 616 Walnut Ave., Scottdale PA 15683. (412)887-5181. Fax: (412)887-3111. Editor: Rose Mary Stutzman. Art Director: Jim Butti. Magazine published monthly in weekly issues. Estab. 1905. Circ. 7,000. Story paper that reinforces Christian values for children ages 4-9.

Fiction: Young readers: contemporary, humorous, problem-solving, religious, relationships. Buys 45 mss/year. Average word length: 300-800. Byline given.

Nonfiction: Picture-oriented and young readers: interview/profile, nature/environment. Buys 10 mss/year. Average word length: 300-800. Byline given.

Poetry: "I like variety—some long story poems and some four-lines."

How to Contact/Writers: Fiction/nonfiction: Send complete ms. Reports on mss in 2-3 weeks. Will consider simultaneous submissions.

Illustration: Works on assignment only. Send tearsheets with SASE. Reports in 2 months. Credit line given.

Photography: Buys photos from freelancers. Wants photos of children ages 4-8.

Terms: Pays on acceptance. Buys one-time rights or reprint rights for mss and artwork. Pays 3-5¢/word for stories and articles. Pays $50 for color cover; $25 for b&w inside. Writer's guidelines free with SAE and 2 first-class stamps.

STRAIGHT, Standard Publishing, 8121 Hamilton Ave., Cincinnati OH 45231. (513)931-4050. Articles/Fiction Editor: Heather Wallace. Magazine published quarterly in weekly parts. Circ. 40,000. *Straight* is a magazine designed for today's Christian teenagers.

Fiction: Young adults: humorous, problem solving, religious, sports. Does not want to see science fiction, fantasy, historical. Buys 100-115 mss/year. Average word length: 1,100-1,500. Byline given.

Nonfiction: Young adults: humorous, interview/profile, problem-solving, religion. Does not want to see devotionals. Buys 24-30 mss/year. Average word length: 500-1,000. Byline given.

Poetry: Reviews poetry from teenagers only.

How to Contact/Writers: Fiction/nonfiction: Query or send complete ms. Reports on queries in 1-2 weeks; mss in 1-2 months. Will consider simultaneous submissions.

Illustration: Buys 40-45 illustrations/year. Uses color artwork only. Preferred theme or style: Realistic, cartoon (full-color only). Works on assignment only. Reviews ms/illustration packages from artists. Query first. Illustrations only: Submit promo sheets or tearsheets. Reports back only if interested. Credit line given.

Photography: Buys photos from freelancers. Looking for photos of contemporary, modestly-dressed teenagers. Model/property release required. Uses 5×7 or 8×10 b&w prints and 35mm transparencies. Photographer should send unsolicited photos by mail.

Terms: Pays on acceptance. Buys first rights and second serial (reprint rights) for mss. Buys full rights for artwork; one-time rights for photos. Pays 3-7¢ per word for stories/articles. Pays illustrators $150-300/color inside. Pays photographers per photo (range: $75-125). Sample copy free with business SASE. Writer's/illustrator's guidelines free with business SASE.

Tips: "The main characters should be contemporary teens who cope with modern-day problems using Christian principles. Stories should be uplifting, positive and character-building, but not preachy. Conflicts must be resolved realistically, with thought-provoking and honest endings. Accepted length is 1,100 to 1,500 words. Nonfiction is accepted. We use devotional pieces, articles on current issues from a Christian point of view and humor. Nonfiction pieces should concern topics of interest to teens, including school, family life, recreation, friends, part-time jobs, dating and music." (See listing for *R-A-D-A-R*.)

***STREET TIMES**, Outside In, 1236 SW Salmon, Portland OR 97205. Editor: Deborah Abela. Monthly newsletter. Estab. 1987. Circ. 800. Contains "resources, street life stories, poetry and art—designed as a pre-employment training tool for Portland street youth." 70% of publication aimed at juvenile market.

Fiction: Young adult: adventure, contemporary, fantasy, folktales, history, humorous, multicultural, problem-solving.

Nonfiction: Young adult: arts/crafts, careers, concepts, history, interview/profile, multicultural, problem-solving. Wants experiences of "other street youth or former street youth; difficulties of getting off the street."

Poetry: Reviews poetry.

How to Contact/Writers: Nonfiction: Send complete ms. Reports on queries/mss in 6 months. Will consider simultaneous submissions and previously published work.

Illustration: Buys 10 illustrations/year. Uses b&w artwork only. Illustrations only: query. Samples not returned; samples kept on file. Originals not returned.

Terms: Sample copies free for SASE.

STUDENT LEADERSHIP JOURNAL, InterVarsity Christian Fellowship, P.O. Box 7895, Madison WI 53707. (608)274-9001, ext. 425. Editor: Jeff Yourison. Quarterly magazine. Estab. 1988. Circ. 10,000.

Fiction: Young adults (collegiate): multicultural, religious. Multicultural themes include: Forming campus fellowships that reflect the ethnic makeup of the campus and demonstrating *reconciliation* beyond celebrating difference. "I see too much aimed at young teens. Our age group is 18-30 years old." Buys 4 mss/year. Average word length: 300-1,800. Byline given.

Nonfiction: Young adults: history, interview/profile, multicultural, nature/environment, religion, social issues. Multicultural themes include: Affirming the need for ethnic validation and reconciliation. "We don't affirm all lifestyles—therefore we are promoting multi-ethnicity but not full-orbed multiculturalism. We prefer articles on issues, leadership, spiritual growth, sexual healing, campus ministry, etc." Buys 6-8 mss/year. Average word length: 1,100-2,200. Byline given.

Poetry: Wants to see free verse; lots of good imagery. Maximum length: 18 lines. Limit submissions to 5 poems.

How to Contact/Writers: Fiction/nonfiction: Send complete ms. Reports on queries/mss in 6 months. Publishes ms 1-2 years after acceptance. Accepts IBM-compatible word processing files on diskettes.

Illustration: Buys 5 illustrations/issue; 20 illustrations/year. Uses b&w line art only. Prefers cartoon pen & ink 5×7 or 8×10 stand alone campus/religious humor. Illustrations only: Send promo sheet, portfolio and tearsheets. Reports only if interested. Samples not returned; samples kept on file. Original work returned at job's completion. Credit line given.

Photography: Looks for campus shots—all types: single faces, studying, thinking, "mood"—pairs and groups: praying, studying, talking, playing. 18-22 year old subjects or professor-types. Model/property release preferred. Uses color and b&w 5×7 glossy prints; 2¼×2¼, 4×5 or 35mm transparencies. Photographers should query with samples; send unsolicited photos by mail; provide business card, promotional literature or tearsheets. "Send photocopies I can keep. I'll call for the print." Reports only if interested.

Terms: Pays on acceptance for ms; on publication for photos and cartoons. Buys first North American serial rights, first rights and reprint rights for ms. Purchases first rights for artwork; one-time rights for photographs. Pays $50-75 for stories; $50-125 for articles; and contributor's copies. Pays illustrators $50-100 for b&w cover; $25-75 for b&w inside. Photographers paid per photo (range: $25-50). Sample copies for $3. Writer's/illustrator/photo guidelines for SASE.

Tips: "Please write and photograph according to the audience. Research the age group and the subculture. Older teens are really sensitive to tokenism and condescension toward their generation. They want to be treated as sophisticated even though they are frequently uninformed and hurting. To reach this audience requires credibility, vulnerability, transparency and confidence!"

SUPERSCIENCE BLUE, Scholastic Inc., 555 Broadway, New York NY 10012-3999. (212)343-6100. Editor: Kathy Burkett. Art Director: Susan Kass. Monthly (during school year) magazine. Estab. 1989. Circ. 375,000. "News and hands-on science for children in grades 4-6. Designed for use in a class setting; distributed by teacher. Articles make science fun and interesting for a broad audience of children. Issues are theme-based."

• *Superscience Blue* is not currently accepting submissions.

Nonfiction: Middle readers: animal, how-to (science experiments), nature/environment, problem-solving, science topics. Does not want to see "general nature stories. Our focus is science with a *news* or *hands-on* slant. To date we have never purchased an unsolicited manuscript. Instead, we assign articles based on clips—and sometimes queries." Average word length: 250-800. Byline sometimes given.

How to Contact/Writers: Nonfiction: Query with published clips. (Most freelance articles are assigned.)

Illustration: Buys 2-3 illustrations/issue; 10-12 illustrations/year. Works on assignment only. Illustrations only: Send résumé and tearsheets. Reports on art samples only if interested. Original artwork returned at job's completion.

Tips: Looks for "news articles and photo essays. Good journalism means always going to *primary* sources—interview scientists in the field, for example, and *quote* them for a more lively article." (See listings for *Choices*, *Dynamath*, *Junior Scholastic* and *Scholastic Math Magazine*.)

TEEN LIFE, (formerly *Hicall*), Gospel Publishing House, 1445 Boonville Ave., Springfield MO 65802-1894. (417)862-2781, ext. 4359. Fax: (417)862-6059. E-mail: tbicket@publishing.ag.org. Articles/Fiction Editor: Tammy Bicket. Art Director: Sonny Carder. Photo Editor: Carol Arnold. Quarterly newspaper (Sunday school take-home paper). Estab. 1920. Circ. 80,000. "Slant articles toward the 15- to 19-year-old teen. We are a Christian publication, so all articles should focus on the Christian's responses to life. Fiction should be realistic, not syrupy nor too graphic. Fiction should have a Christian slant also."

Fiction: Young adults: humorous, religious, sports (all with Christian slant). Also wants fiction based on true stories. Buys 50 mss/year. Average word length 700-1,500. Byline given.

Nonfiction: Young adults: humorous, interview/profile, religion, social issues, sports, "thoughtful treatment of contemporary issues (i.e., racism, preparing for the future); interviews with famous Christians who have noteworthy stories to tell. Buys 50 mss/year. "Looking for more articles and fewer stories." Average word length: 1,000. Byline given.

How to Contact/Writers: Fiction/nonfiction: Send complete ms. Do *not* send query letters. Reports on mss in 2-3 months. Will consider simultaneous submissions.

Illustration: Buys 50-200 illustrations/issue, 200 illustrations/year. Uses color artwork only. Prefers to review youth-oriented styles. Art director will assign freelance art. Works on assignment only. Reviews ms/illustration packages from artists. Send portfolio. "We are Mac literate." Contact: Sonny Carder, art director. Illustration only: arrange portfolio review or send promo sheet, slides, client list, tearsheets or on disk (Mac). Contact: Sonny Carder, art director. Illustrations and design: "We are interested in looking at portfolios consisting of illustration and design work that is teen-oriented." Reports in 3-4 weeks. Samples filed. Originals returned to artist at job's completion. Credit line given.

Photography: Buys photos from freelancers. Wants "teen photos that look spontaneous. Ethnic and urban photos urgently needed." Uses color prints, 35mm, $2\frac{1}{4} \times 2\frac{1}{4}$, 4×5 transparencies. Send unsolicited photos by mail.

Terms: Pays on acceptance. For mss, buys first North American serial rights, first rights, one-time rights, second serial (reprint rights), simultaneous rights. For artwork, buys one-time rights for cartoons; one-time rights for photos. Rights for illustrations negotiable. Pays $25 minimum for stories; $25-75 for articles. Pays illustration: $200-300 for color cover or inside. Pays $75-100/color cover photo; $35-45/b&w inside photo; $50-60/color inside photo. Sample copies free (2) with 6×9 SASE. Writer's/illustrator's/photo guidelines free with SASE.

Tips: "We want contemporary, real life articles, or fiction that has the same feel. Try to keep it teen-oriented—trendy, hip, interesting perspectives; current, topical situations that revolve around teens. We work on specific themes for each quarter, so interested writers should request current writers guidelines and topic list."

'TEEN MAGAZINE, Petersen Publishing Co., 6420 Wilshire Blvd., Los Angeles CA 90048-5515. (213)782-2950. Editor: Roxanne Camron. Managing/Fiction Editor: Amy Diamond. Art Director: Laurel Finnerty. Monthly magazine. Estab. 1957. Circ. 1,100,000. "We are a pure junior high and senior high female audience. *'TEEN* teens are upbeat and want to be informed."
Fiction: Young adults: contemporary, humorous, problem-solving, romance, suspense/mystery. Does not want to see "that which does not apply to our market—i.e., science fiction, history, religious, adult-oriented." Buys 12 mss/year. Length for fiction: 10-15 pages typewritten, double-spaced.
Nonfiction: Young adults: careers, cooking, health, multicultural, problem-solving, social issues, travel. Does not want to see adult-oriented, adult point of view." Buys 25 mss/year. Length for articles: 10-20 pages typewritten, double-spaced. Byline given.
How to Contact/Writers: Fiction/nonfiction: Query. Reports on queries in 3 weeks; mss in 3-4 weeks. Prefer submissions hard copy and disk.
Illustration: Buys 0-4 illustrations/issue. Uses various styles for variation. Uses a lot of b&w illustration. "Light, upbeat." Reviews ms/illustration packages from artists. "Query first." Illustrations only: "Want to see samples whether it be tearsheets, slides, finished pieces showing the style." Reports back only if interested. Credit line given.
Terms: Pays on acceptance. Buys all rights. Pays $100-400 for stories; $50-500 for articles. Pays $25-250/b&w inside; $100-400/color inside. Writer's/illustrator's guidelines free with SASE.
Tips: Illustrators: "Present professional finished work. Get familiar with magazine and send samples that would be compatible with the style of publication." There is a need for artwork with "fiction/specialty articles. Send samples or promotional materials on a regular basis."

TEEN POWER, Scripture Press Publications, Inc., P.O. Box 632, Glen Ellyn IL 60138. (708)668-6000. Editor: Amy J. Cox. Quarterly magazine. Estab. 1965. "*Teen Power* is an eight-page Sunday School take-home paper aimed at 11-16 year olds in a conservative Christian audience. Its primary objective is to help readers see how principles for Christian living can be applied to everyday life. We are looking for fresh, creative true stories, true-to-life, and nonfiction articles. All must show how God and the Bible are relevant in the lives of today's teens. All manuscripts must have a clear, spiritual emphasis or "take away value." We don't use stories which merely have a good moral. Be careful not to preach or talk down to kids. Also, be realistic. Dialogue should be natural. Resolutions should not be too easy or tacked on. We are a specialized market with a distinct niche, but we do rely heavily on freelance writers. We are open to any new writer who grasps the purpose of our publication."
Fiction: Young adults: adventure, contemporary, humorous, multicultural, problem-solving, religious, sports. Buys 75 mss/year. Average word length: 600-1,200. Byline given.
Nonfiction: Young adults: biography, games/puzzles, how-to, humorous, interview/profile, multicultural, problem-solving, religion, social issues, sports. Multicultural themes include: Christian teens in foreign countries, missions, missionary kids, ethnic Christian teens in US and Canada. Does not want to see "articles with no connection to Christian principles." Buys 75 mss/year. Average word length: 300-1,000. Byline given.
How To Contact/Writers: Fiction/nonfiction: Send complete ms. Reports on mss in 3-4 months. Publishes ms "at least one year" after acceptance. Will consider simultaneous submissions. Please include Social Security number on mss.
Illustration: Send résumé, promo sheet, tearsheets. Reports back only if interested. Credit line given.
Photography: Buys photos from freelancers. Looks for mood shots: teen fads and hang outs; sport and school activities shots.
Terms: Pays on acceptance. Buys one-time rights. Pays $25-120 for stories/articles. Negotiates illustrators' fees. Photographers paid per photo. Sample copies and writer's guidelines for #10 SAE and 1 first-class stamp.
Tips: "Take-home papers are a great 'break-in' point. Each weekly issue contains at least two freelance-written features. However, we are very specific about the type of material we are looking for. We want stories and articles to reinforce our Sunday School lessons and help our readers apply what they learned in Sunday School throughout the week. All submissions must

have a spiritual emphasis—not merely a moral lesson." (See listings for *Counselor*, *Primary Days* and *Zelos*.)

3-2-1 CONTACT, Children's Television Workshop, One Lincoln Plaza, New York NY 10023. (212)595-3456. Articles Editor: Curtis Slepian. Art Director: Gretchen Grace. Magazine published 10 times/year. Estab. 1979. Circ. 440,000. This is a science and technology magazine for 8-14 year olds. Features all areas of science and nature.
Fiction: "Our fiction piece is an on-going series called 'The Time Team.' It is written inhouse."
Nonfiction: Middle readers, young adults: animal, health, how-to, interview/profile, multicultural, nature/environment, science. Multicultural needs include: how kids live in other countries (with a science hook; profiles of minority scientists). Does not want to see religion, travel or history. "We see too many research reports on the life of a toad. We'd like to see more articles about scientists doing exciting work (in the field) with lots of quotes." Buys 20 mss/year. Average word length: 750-1,000. Byline given.
How to Contact/Writers: Nonfiction: Query with published clips. Reports on queries in 3 weeks.
Illustration: Buys 15 illustrations/issue; buys 150 illustrations/year. Works on assignment only. Illustrations only: Send tearsheets, portfolio. Reports on art samples only if interested. Original artwork returned at job's completion. Credit line given.
Photography: Buys photos from freelancers.
Terms: Pays on acceptance. Buys all rights for mss (negotiable). Buys one-time rights for photos unless on assignment. Pays $100-600 for assigned/unsolicited articles. Pays $500-1,000 for color cover illustration; $150-300 for b&w inside; $175-500 for color inside. Pays photographers per photo (range: $150-750). Sample copy for $1.75 and 8×14 SASE; writer's/illustrator's guidelines free with 8½×11 SASE.
Tips: Looks for "features. We do not want articles based on library research. We want on-the-spot interviews about what's happening in science now."

***TIME FOR KIDS**, 1271 Avenue of the Americas, 23rd Floor, New York NY 10020. (212)522-1212. Fax: (212)522-4799. E-mail: tfk@time.com. Managing Editor: Claudia Wallis. Art Director: Jason Lee. Photo Editor: Kimberlee Acquaro. Weekly magazine. Estab. 1995. Circ. 700,000. News magazine for kids in 4th-6th grades from the publishers of *TIME*.
Nonfiction: Middle readers: animal, arts/crafts, biography, careers, concept, cooking, fashion, geography, health, history, hobbies, how-to, humorous, interview/profile, math, multicultural, nature/environment, problem-solving, science, social studies, sports, travel. Average length: 100 lines. Byline sometimes given.
How to Contact/Writers: Query with published clips.
Illustration: Uses color artwork only. Works on assignment only.
Photography: Buys photos from freelancers. Wants general news photos. Model/property release required. Query with samples. Reports back only if interested.
Terms: Sample copies for 8×10 SAE with 2 first-class stamps.

TOGETHER TIME, WordAction Publications, 6401 The Paseo, Kansas City MO 64131. (816)333-7000. Fax: (816)333-4439. Contact: Lynda T. Boardman. Weekly magazine. Estab. 1981. Circ. 27,000. "*Together Time* is a story paper that correlates with the Sunday School Curriculum for 3- and 4-year-olds. Each paper contains a story, a poem, an activity, and an article directed to the parents."
Fiction: Picture-oriented material: religious. "We would like to see more realistic stories. We don't like them to seem staged. We also do not purchase stories that give life and feeling to inanimate objects." Buys 50 mss/year. Average word length: 100-150. Byline given.
Nonfiction: Picture-oriented material: arts/crafts.
Poetry: Reviews poetry. Maximum length: 8 lines. Limit submissions to 10 poems.
How to Contact/Writers: Fiction: Send complete ms. Reports on queries in 6-8 weeks; mss in 3 months. Publishes ms one year after acceptance.
Illustration: Buys 52 illustrations/year. "We do assignment only and like both realistic and cartoon. Must be age-appropriate." Works on assignment. Reviews ms/illustration packages from artists. Illustration only: Query with samples. Send résumé slides and tearsheets. Reports in 1 month. Sample returned with SASE. Credit line given.

Photography: Buys photos from freelancers. Looks for outdoor or indoor pictures of three- and four-year-old children. Uses color and b&w prints; 35mm transparencies. Query with samples. Reports in 1 month.
Terms: Pays on acceptance. Buys all rights for mss. Buys all rights for artwork; multi-use rights for photographs. Pays 5¢/word minimum for stories. "Writers receive payment and contributor copies." Pays illustrators $40 for b&w, $75 for color cover; $40 for b&w, $75 for color inside. Pays photographers per photo (range $30-75). Sample copies for #10. Writer's/illustrator's/photo guidelines for SASE.
Tips: "Make sure that the material you submit is geared to three- and four-year-old children. Request a theme list with the guidelines and try to submit things that apply." (See listing for *Wonder Time*.)

TOTALLY KIDS MAGAZINE, Peter Green Design/Fox Kids Network, 4219 W. Burbank Blvd., Burbank CA 91505. (818)953-2210. E-mail: bananadog@aol.com. Articles Editor: Scott Russell. Art Director: Debra Hintz. Quarterly magazine. Estab. 1990. Circ. 4 million. Features "fun and hip articles, games and activities for Fox Kids Club members ages 6-13, with special section for kids 2-6, promoting Fox Kids shows."
Fiction: Average word length: 200-500. Byline sometimes given. "No unsolicited fiction accepted."
Nonfiction: Picture-oriented material, young readers, middle readers: Any material tied in to a Fox Kids Network show or one of our other features (no religious material). Buys 20 mss/year. Average word length: 200-500.
How to Contact/Writers: Fiction/nonfiction: Query with published clips. Reports on queries/mss in 2 months. Publishes mss 2-6 months after acceptance. Will consider simultaneous submissions and electronic submissions via disk or modem.
Illustration: Buys 5 illustrations/issue. Uses color artwork only. Works on assignment only. Prefers "cartoon character work, must be *on model*." Reviews ms/illustration packages from artists. Query. Illustrations only: Send résumé, promo sheet, tearsheets. Reports only if interested. Samples returned with SASE; samples filed. Original work returned at job's completion. Credit line given.
Photography: Buys photos from freelancers. Uses a variety of subjects, depending on articles. Model/property release required. Uses color prints and 4×5 or 35mm transparencies. Query with résumé, business card, tearsheets. Reports only if interested.
Terms: Pays 30 days from acceptance. Buys all rights. Pays $100-400 for stories/articles. Additional payment for ms/illustration packages and for photos accompanying articles. Sample writer's guidelines for SASE.
Tips: "Practice. Read. Come up with some new and creative ideas. Our articles are almost always humorous. We try to give kids cutting edge information. All of our articles are tied into Fox Kids shows."

TOUCH, Calvinettes, Box 7259, Grand Rapids MI 49510. (616)241-5616. Managing Editor: Carol Smith. Art Director: Chris Cook. Monthly (with combined issues May/June, July/August) magazine. Circ. 16,000. "*Touch* is designed to help girls ages 9-14 see how God is at work in their lives and in the world around them."
Fiction: Middle readers, teens: animal, contemporary, history, humorous, problem-solving, religious, romance. Does not want to see unrealistic stories and those with trite, easy endings. Buys 40 mss/year. Average word length: 400-1,000. Byline given.
Nonfiction: Middle readers, teens: how-to, humorous, interview/profile, problem-solving, religious. Buys 5 mss/year. Average word length: 200-800. Byline given.
How to Contact/Writers: Send for biannual update for publication themes. Fiction/nonfiction: Send complete ms. Reports on mss in 2 months. Will consider simultaneous submissions.
Illustration: Buys 1-2 illustrations/issue; buys 10-15 illustrations/year. Prefers ms/illustration packages. Works on assignment only.
Terms: Pays on publication. Buys first North American serial rights, first rights, second serial (reprint rights) or simultaneous rights. Pays $20-50 for assigned articles; $5-30 for unsolicited articles. "We send complimentary copies in addition to pay." Pays $25-50 for color cover illustration; $15-25 for color inside illustration. Writer's guidelines free with SASE.
Tips: Writers: "The stories should be current, deal with adolescent problems and joys, and help girls see God at work in their lives through humor as well as problem-solving."

TURTLE MAGAZINE, For Preschool Kids, Children's Better Health Institute, 1100 Waterway Blvd., P.O. Box 567, Indianapolis IN 46206. (317)636-8881. Editor: Nancy S. Axelrad. Art Director: Bart Rivers. Monthly/bimonthly magazine published January/February, March, April/May, June, July/August, September, October/November, December. Circ. 550,000. *Turtle* uses read-aloud stories, especially suitable for bedtime or naptime reading. Also uses poems, simple science experiments, and health-related articles. All but 2 pages aimed at juvenile audience.

- To learn more about *Turtle Magazine* and other Children's Better Health Institute publications, see Insider Report with CBHI editor Steve Charles in the 1995 edition of *Children's Writer's & Illustrator's Market.*

Fiction: Picture-oriented material: adventure, animal, contemporary, fantasy, folktales, health-related, history, holiday themes, humorous, multicultural, nature/environment, problem-solving, sports, suspense/mystery. "Need very simple experiments illustrating basic science concepts. Also needs action rhymes to foster creative movement." Do not want stories about monsters or scary things. Avoid stories in which the characters indulge in unhealthy activities like eating junk food. Buys 50 mss/year. Average word length: 150-300. Byline given.

Nonfiction: Picture-oriented material: animal, arts/crafts, cooking, games/puzzles, geography, health, multicultural, nature/environment, science, sports. Buys 20 mss/year. Average word length: 150-300. Byline given.

How to Contact/Writers: Fiction/nonfiction: "Prefer complete manuscript to queries." Reports on mss in 8-10 weeks.

Illustration: Buys 20-25 illustrations/issue; 160-200 illustrations/year. Prefers "realistic and humorous illustration." Illustrations only: Send résumé, promo sheet, slides, tearsheets. Reports back only if interested. Credit line given.

Photography: Buys photos from freelancers with accompanying ms only.

Terms: Pays on publication. Buys all rights for mss/artwork; one-time rights for photographs. Pays up to 22¢/word for stories and articles (depending upon length and quality) and 10 complimentary copies. Pays $250 for color cover illustration, $30-70 for b&w inside; $65-140 for color inside; $20 for color slide inside. Sample copy $1.25. Writer's guidelines free with SASE.

Tips: "We're beginning to edit *Turtle* more for the very young preschooler, so we're looking for stories and articles that are written more simply than those we've used in the past. Our need for health-related material, especially features that encourage fitness, is ongoing. Health subjects must be age-appropriate. When writing about them, think creatively and lighten up! Fight the tendency to become boringly pedantic. Nobody—not even young kids—likes to be lectured. Always keep in mind that in order for a story or article to educate preschoolers, it first must be entertaining—warm and engaging, exciting, or genuinely funny. Understand that writing for *Turtle* is a difficult challenge. Study the magazine to see if your manuscript is right for *Turtle*. Magazines have distinct personalities which can't be understood by only reading market listings. Here the trend is toward leaner, lighter writing. There will be a growing need for interactive activities. Writers might want to consider developing an activity to accompany their concise manuscripts." (See listings for *Child Life*, *Children's Digest*, *Children's Playmate*, *Humpty Dumpty's Magazine*, *Jack and Jill* and *U*S*Kids*.)

U*S*KIDS, Children's Better Health Institute, 1100 Waterway Blvd., P.O. Box 567, Indianapolis IN 46206. (317)636-8881. Editor: Beth Struck. Art Director: Matthew Brinkman. Magazine published 8 times a year. Estab. 1987. Circ. 250,000.

- To learn more about U*S*Kids and other Children's Better Health Institute Publications, see Insider Report with CBHI editor Steve Charles in the 1995 edition of *Children's Writer's & Illustrator's Market.*

Fiction: Young readers and middle readers: adventure, animal, contemporary, health, history, humorous, multicultural, nature/environment, problem-solving, sports, suspense/mystery. "We see too many stories with no real story line. We'd like to see more mysteries and contemporary humor stories." Buys approximately 8-16 mss/year. Average word length: 500-800. Byline given.

Nonfiction: Young readers and middle readers: animal, arts/crafts, cooking, games/puzzles, health, history, hobbies, how-to, humorous, interview/profile, multicultural, nature/environment, science, social issues, sports, travel. Wants to see interviews with kids ages 5-10, who have done something unusual or different. Buys 30-40 mss/year. Average word length: 500-600. Byline given.

Poetry: Maximum length: 32 lines.
How to Contact/Writers: Fiction: Send complete ms. Nonfiction: Query. Reports on queries and mss in 1 month. Publishes ms 6 months after acceptance. Will consider simultaneous submissions, electronic submissions via disk or modem and previously published work.
Illustration: Buys 8 illustrations/issue; 70 illustrations/year. Color artwork only. Works on assignment only. Reviews ms/illustration packages from artists. Query. Illustrations only: Send résumé and tearsheets. Reports back only if interested. Samples returned with SASE; samples kept on file. Does not return originals. Credit line given.
Photography: Purchases photography from freelancers. Looking for photos that pertain to children ages 5-10. Model/property release required. Uses color and b&w prints; 35mm, 2¼×2¼, 4×5 and 8×10 transparencies. Photographers should provide résumé, business card, promotional literature or tearsheets to be kept on file. Reports back only if interested.
Terms: Pays on publication. Buys all rights for mss. Purchases all rights for artwork. Purchases one-time rights for photographs. Pays 10¢/word minimum. Additional payment for ms/illustration packages. Pays illustrators $140/page for color inside. Photographers paid by the project or per photo (negotiable). Sample copies for $2.50. Writer's/illustrator/photo guidelines for SASE.
Tips: "Write clearly and concisely without preaching or being obvious." (See listings for *Child Life*, *Children's Digest*, *Children's Playmate*, *Humpty Dumpty's Magazine*, *Jack and Jill* and *Turtle Magazine*.)

VENTURE, Christian Service Brigade, P.O. Box 150, Wheaton IL 60189. (708)665-0630. Articles/Fiction Editor: Deborah Christensen. Art Director: Robert Fine. Published 5 times a year. Estab. 1937. Circ. 19,000. The magazine is designed "to speak to the concerns of boys from a biblical perspective. To provide wholesome, entertaining reading for boys."
Fiction: Middle readers: adventure, humorous, religious. Does not want to see fantasy, romance, science fiction or anything without Christian emphasis. "We'd like to see more humor." Buys 5 mss/year. Average word length: 500-1,000. Byline given.
Nonfiction: Middle readers: animal, geography, hobbies, humorous, nature/environment, religion. Buys 5 mss/year. Average word length: 500-1,000. Byline given.
How to Contact/Writers: Fiction/nonfiction: Send complete ms. Don't send queries. Reports in 1-2 weeks. Will consider simultaneous submissions.
Illustration: Buys 3 illustrations/issue; 15 illustrations/year. Uses color artwork only. Works on assignment only. Reviews ms/illustration packages from artists. Send complete ms. Contact: Deborah Christensen (for mss); Robert Fine (for art). Illustrations only: Query with samples. Arrange portfolio review. Contact: Robert Fine, art director. Samples returned with SASE. Reports on art samples only if interested. Original artwork returned at job's completion. Credit line given.
Photography: Buys photos from freelancers. Wants photos of boys 8-11 years old.
Terms: Pays on publication for mss, artwork and photos. Buys first North American serial rights; first rights; second serial (reprint rights). Pays 5-10¢/word for stories/articles. Pays $75-125 for color cover illustration—usually photos only; $35-250 for color inside illustration (includes photos). "We're still figuring out payment because we've just started color with September/October 1994 issue." Sample copy $1.85 with 9×12 SAE and $1.01 postage. Writer's/illustrator's/photographer's guidelines free with SASE.
Tips: "Know kids and their language. Too many writers use the vernacular of their childhood instead of contemporary language. I've seen illustrations and stories become more wild and exciting. Kids like movement. Follow our guidelines. We won't even read manuscripts that don't."

WITH, The Magazine for Radical Christian Youth, Faith & Life Press, 722 Main, P.O. Box 347, Newton KS 67114. (316)283-5100. Editors: Eddy Hall, Carol Duerksen. Published 8 times a year. Circ. 5,600. Magazine published for teenagers, ages 15-18, in Mennonite, Brethren and Mennonite Brethren congregations. "We deal with issues affecting teens and try to help them make choices reflecting an Anabaptist-Mennonite faith."
Fiction: Young adults: adventure, contemporary, fantasy, folktales, health, humorous, multicultural, nature/environment, problem-solving, religious, science fiction, sports. Multicultural needs include: race relations, first-person stories featuring teens of ethnic minorities. "Would like to see more humor and parables/allegories." Buys 15 mss/year. Average word length: 1,000-2,000. Byline given.

Nonfiction: Young adults: first-person teen personal experience (as-told-to), humorous, multicultural, nature/environment, problem-solving, religion. Buys 15-20 mss/year. Average word length: 500-1,500. Byline given.
Poetry: Wants to see religious, humorous, nature. "Buys 5-6 poems/year." Maximum length: 50 lines.
How to Contact/Writers: Send complete ms. Query on first-person teen personal experience stories and how-to articles. (Detailed guidelines for first-person stories, how-tos, and fiction available for SASE.) Reports on queries in 1 month; mss in 6 weeks. Will consider simultaneous submissions.
Illustration: Buys 6-8 illustrations/issue; buys 50-60 illustrations/year. Uses b&w and 2-color artwork only. Preferred theme or style: candids/interracial. Reviews ms/illustration packages from artists. Query first. Illustrations only: Query with portfolio (photocopies only) or tearsheets. Reports only if interested. Original artwork returned at job's completion upon request. Credit line given.
Photography: Buys photos from freelancers. Looking for candid photos of teens (ages 15-18), especially ethnic minorities. Uses 8×10 b&w glossy prints. Photographers should send unsolicited photos by mail.
Terms: Pays on acceptance. For mss buys first rights, one-time rights; second serial (reprint rights). Buys one-time rights for artwork and photos. Pays 5¢/word for unpublished manuscripts; 3¢/word for reprints. Will pay more for assigned as-told-to stories. Pays $35-50 for b&w cover illustration; $25-40 for b&w inside illustration. Pays photographers per photo (range: $35-50, cover only). Sample copy for 9×12 SAE and $1.24 postage. Writer's/illustrator's guidelines free with SASE.
Tips: "We're hungry for stuff that makes teens laugh—fiction, nonfiction and cartoons. It doesn't have to be religious, but must be wholesome."

WORDACTION PUBLICATIONS, 6401 The Paseo, Kansas City MO 64131. See listings for *Together Time* and *Wonder Time*.

WONDER TIME, WordAction Publications, 6401 The Paseo, Kansas City MO 64131. (816)333-7000. Editor: Lois Perrigo. Weekly magazine. Circ. 45,000. "*Wonder Time* is a full-color story paper for first and second graders. It is designed to connect Sunday School learning with the daily living experiences and growth of the primary child. Since *Wonder Time*'s target audience is children ages six to eight, the readability goal is to encourage beginning readers to read for themselves. The major purposes of *Wonder Time* are to: Provide a life-related paper which will build Christian values and encourage ethical behavior and provide reinforcement for the biblical concepts taught in the WordAction Sunday School curriculum."
Fiction: Young readers: adventure, nature/environment, contemporary, problem-solving, religious. Buys 52 mss/year. Average word length: 300-400. Byline given.
Nonfiction: Young readers: social issues, problem solving, religious.
Poetry: Reviews religious poetry of 4-8 lines.
How to Contact/Writers: Fiction/nonfiction: Send complete ms. Reports on queries/mss in 6 weeks. Will consider simultaneous submissions.
Illustration: Buys 100 illustrations/year. Works on assignment only. Reviews ms/illustration packages from artists. Query. Contact: Lois Perrigo, *Wonder Time* editor. Illustrations only: Submit samples of work. Reports on art samples in 6 weeks. Samples returned with SASE; samples kept on file. Credit line given.
Terms: Pays on acceptance. Pays $25 per story for rights which allow the publisher to print the story multiple times in the same publication without repayment. Pays illustrators $40 for b&w cover or inside; $75 for color cover or inside. Photographers paid per photo (range: $25-75). Sends complimentary contributor's copies of publication. Sample copy and writer's/illustrator's guidelines with 9½×12 SAE and 2 first-class stamps.
Tips: "Basic themes reappear regularly. Please write for a theme list. Also be familiar with what *Wonder Time* is all about. Ask for guidelines, sample copies, theme list *before* submitting." (See listing for *Together Time*.)

***WRITER'S INTERNATIONAL FORUM**, (formerly *Writer's Open Forum*), Bristol Services International, P.O. Box 516, Tracyton WA 98393. Bimonthly magazine. Estab. 1990. Up to 25%

aimed at juvenile market. Some issues "Special Juniors Editions" include 100% material aimed at juvenile market.

Fiction: Young readers, middle readers and young adults: adventure, animal, contemporary, fantasy, folktales, humorous, nature/environment, problem-solving, science fiction, suspense/mystery. "No experimental formats; no picture books; no poetry. We see too many anthropomorphic characters. We would like to see more mysteries, problem-solving and adventures." Buys approximately 48-54 mss/year. Average word length: 400-2,000. Byline given.

How to Contact/Writers: Fiction: Reports on mss in 2 months. Publishes ms 4-6 months after acceptance.

Terms: Pays on acceptance. Buys first North American serial rights. Pays $5 minimum for stories. Sample copies for $3.50 standard edition; $5 for Juniors Edition.

Tips: "All the stories accepted for publication in *Writers' International Forum* are open to comments by our readers. Many of our readers write exclusively for children and/or are school teachers. The most often noted critique on our children's pieces is that writers fail to clearly write for a specific age group. Determine your audience's age, then write every word, description and action to that audience. Each issue includes lessons and tips on writing. Our 'Writer to Writer' column uses tips on the writing process and is our most open area; limit is 300 words and payment is one contributor copy."

YOUNG SALVATIONIST, The Salvation Army, 615 Slaters Lane, P.O. Box 269, Alexandria VA 22313. (703)684-5500. Monthly magazine. Estab. 1984. Circ. 50,000. "We accept material with clear Christian content written for high school age teenagers. *Young Salvationist* is published for teenage members of The Salvation Army, an evangelical part of the Christian Church."

Fiction: Young adults: multicultural, contemporary religious. Buys 12-20 mss/year. Average word length: 750-1,200. Byline given.

Nonfiction: Young adults: religious—health, interview/profile, multicultural, problem-solving, social issues. Buys 40-50 mss/year. Average word length: 750-1,200. Byline given.

Poetry: Reviews 16-20 line poetry dealing with a Christian theme. Send no more than 6 submissions.

How to Contact/Writers: Fiction/nonfiction: Query with published clips or send complete ms. Reports on queries/mss in 1 month. Will consider simultaneous submissions.

Illustrations: Buys 3-6 illustrations/issue; 20-30 illustrations/year. Reviews ms/illustration packages from artists. Send ms with art. Contact: Lisa Davis, production manager. Illustrations only: Query; send résumé, promo sheet, portfolio, tearsheets. Reports on artwork in 1 month (with SASE). Samples returned with SASE. Original artwork returned at job's completion "if requested." Credit line given.

Photography: Purchases photography from freelancers. Looking for teens in action.

Terms: Pays on acceptance. Buys first North American serial rights, first rights, one-time rights or second serial (reprint) rights for mss. Purchases one-time rights for artwork and photographs. For mss, pays 15¢/word; 10¢/word for reprints. Pays $100-150 color (cover) illustration; $50-100 b&w (inside) illustration; $100-150 color (inside) illustration. Sample copy for 9×12 SAE and 4 first-class stamps. Writer's/illustrator's guidelines free for #10 SASE.

Tips: "Ask for theme list/sample copy! Write 'up,' not down to teens. Aim at young *adults*, not children." Wants "less fiction, more 'journalistic' nonfiction."

YOUTH UPDATE, St. Anthony Messenger Press, 1615 Republic St., Cincinnati OH 45210. (513)241-5615. Articles Editor: Carol Ann Morrow. Art Director: June Pfaff. Monthly newsletter. Estab. 1982. Circ. 30,000. "Each issue focuses on one topic only. *Youth Update* addresses the faith and Christian life questions of young people and is designed to attract, instruct, guide and challenge its audience by applying the gospel to modern problems and situations. The students who read *Youth Update* vary in their religious education and reading ability. Write for average high school students. These students are 15-year-olds with a C+ average. Assume that they have paid attention to religious instruction and remember a little of what 'sister' said. Aim more toward 'table talk' than 'teacher talk.' "

Nonfiction: Young adults/teens: religion. Buys 12 mss/year. Average word length: 2,200-2,300. Byline given.

How to Contact/Writers: Nonfiction: Query. Reports on queries/mss in 6 weeks. Will consider computer printout and electronic submissions via disk.

Photography: Buys photos from freelancers. Uses photos of teens (high-school age) with attention to racial diversity and with emotion.
Terms: Pays on acceptance. Buys first North American serial rights for mss. Buys one-time rights for photographs. Pays $325-400 for articles. Pays photographers per photo ($40 minimum). Sample copy free with #10 SASE. Writer's guidelines free on request.
Tips: "Read the newsletter yourself—three issues at least. In the past, our publication has dealt with a variety of topics including: dating, Lent, teenage pregnancy, baptism, loneliness, violence, confirmation and the Bible. When writing, use the *New American Bible* as translation. Interested in church-related topics."

***ZELOS**, Scripture Press Publications Inc., P.O. Box 632, Glen Ellyn IL 60138. Quarterly spiral-bound Sunday School curriculum book. Estab. 1995. *Zelos* is a Christain lifestyle notebook which helps high school-aged students grow in their relationship with God. Each weekly section contains a calendar; a personal introduction to the topic of the week by author, speaker and youth leader Dewey Bertolini; daily journal activities; and one freelance-written feature which correlates with the weekly topic.
Fiction: Young adults: humorous, religious, slice-of-life vignettes. Buys 20 mss/year. Average word length: 400-1,000. Byline given.
Nonfiction: Young adult: humorous, interview/profile, religion, inspirational, personal experience. Buys 40 mss/year. Average word length: 400-1,000. Byline given.
Poetry: Reviews poetry. Wants free verse, light verse and traditional. Maximum length: 5-30 lines. Limit submissions to 3 poems.
How to Contact/Writers: Fiction/Nonfiction: Send complete ms. Reports on mss in 2-3 months. Publishes ms 12-18 months after acceptance. Will consider simultaneous submissions, previously published work.
Photography: Buys photos from freelancers. Model/property release required.
Terms: Pays on acceptance. Buys one-time rights for magazines. Pays $30-120 for stories and articles. Sample copies of articles free (#10 envelope stamped for 2 oz.); sample publication for $4.99.
Tips: "Whenever possible, we use true stories: personal experiences, 'as told tos,' profiles and interviews. Subjects can be everyday teens or celebrities with strong, Christian testimonies. We're looking for fresh, motivating, hard-hitting stories to challenge our readers. All material must have a clear, Christian perspective. We use some fiction—usually contemporary, true-to-life. Stories should be realistic. Resolutions should be natural and characters and subjects should not be too good to be true. *Zelos* is an exciting new product. We are looking for writers who will dig up interesting stories to challenge today's teens." (See listings for *Counselor*, *Primary Days* and *Teen Power*.)

Magazines/'95-'96 changes

The following markets were included in the 1995 edition of *Children's Writer's & Illustrator's Market* but do not have listings in this edition. The majority did not respond to our request to update their listings. If a reason was given for exclusion, it appears in parentheses after the market's name.

Appalachian Bride
Atalantik
Career World
Careers and Colleges
Clubhouse
FFA New Horizons
Freeway
Hob-Nob
International Gymnast
Keynoter
Kids Copy (ceased publication)
The Kiln
That Magazine for Christian Youth! (ceased publication)
Poem Train
The Single Parent
Teenage Christian Magazine

Audiovisual & Audiotape

As the business of kids' music and video continues to grow and mature, the different segments of children's media are beginning to blend. Children's record companies are producing work in videotape format. Production houses and book publishers alike are releasing story books in audio and video versions. Stores stock material for kids on both CD and CD-ROM.

After a 1991 surge in major record companies signing children's acts, many big labels realized that the market for kids' music was too unlike the one for adults, and they just weren't equipped to promote their children's acts. The labels proceeded to drop all but a few artists in favor of TV and product tie-ins with a built-in fan base. Although there may not be a great demand for performers these days, there is still a need for good, original songs for children's acts. And while video still dominates the children's market, children's audio (both music and story tapes) still enjoys steady sales, and sales of CD-ROM titles are beginning to make their mark on the market.

Just as in the children's book industry, the use of licensed characters in children's multimedia is booming. The top titles of the past year have been dominated by Disney's characters from *The Lion King*, Barney the dinosaur, and the Mighty Morphin Power Rangers.

And though the market is flooded with these character-driven products, this may help, not hinder, the sales of other audio and video titles. Stocking hundreds of items on store shelves featuring the Lion King, for example, brings consumers into the stores who will ultimately buy other audio and video products.

Several years ago, the Children's Entertainment Association (CEA), with a mission "to raise awareness of children's entertainment within the industry and among the general public," was founded by children's entertainment attorney Howard Leib, organizer of the annual Kids' Entertainment Seminar, which will hold its fourth annual meeting in the summer of 1996 in New York City. Leib is forming regional chapters of CEA around the country with membership including children's artists and writers, record-label and video executives, independent producers and managers. (The Children's Entertainment Association can be contacted through Leib at 75 Rockefeller Plaza, Suite 327, New York NY 10019. Fax: (212)275-3835. E-mail: askcea@aol.com.)

In an effort to promote work not tied to television shows and movies, the Coalition for Quality Children's Video has waged a campaign to increase awareness of titles driven neither by film nor TV characters. This nonprofit organization, based in Santa Fe, New Mexico, publishes Kids First!, a list of endorsed children's videos.

The children's sections of video stores have been well-stocked with titles in recent years, but record stores are just beginning to devote more space to kids' music. Children's music has also been getting more radio airtime. And *Billboard* magazine reports "Many kids' songwriters are finding a burgeoning market for their music in CD-ROMs."

With a lot happening in the world of children's entertainment, there are growing opportunities for a great many talents. In the Audiovisual Markets and Audiotape Markets sections that follow, you'll find record companies, book publishers, museums, video production houses and more. Many of the companies listed work with a variety of projects and may need anything from songs and short stories to illustration and clay animation.

To keep up on the dynamic world of children's entertainment, read "Child's Play," Moira McCormick's *Billboard* magazine column, as well as *Publishers Weekly*, which often covers and reviews audio and video in its children's section. Industry publications such as *Variety* and *Hollywood Reporter* may also offer useful information on kids' video. And entertainment magazines such as *Entertainment Weekly* are beginning to review CD-ROMs for kids.

Audiovisual Markets

The production houses listed here don't produce just video cassettes. Many also create filmstrips, slide sets, multimedia productions—even television shows. These studios and production houses are in need of illustration, video graphics, special effects, and a variety of animation techniques, including stop motion, cell, clay and computer animation. They also need the work of writers for everything from animation scripts to educational filmstrips, but be aware that audiovisual media rely more on the "visual" to tell the story.

Also note that technology in the world of video production is advancing. Many companies are producing CD-ROM and interactive titles for kids, and computer imaging is more and more becoming the norm in kids' video, so it's important that illustrators stay up-to-date on emerging techniques.

AERIAL IMAGE VIDEO SERVICES, 137 W. 19th St., New York NY 10011. (212)229-1930. Fax: (212)229-1929. President: John Stapsy. Estab. 1979. Type of company: Video production and post production, and audio production, post production, and computer-based program production. Uses videotapes and audio. (For list of recent productions consult the Random House catalog of children's videos.)
Children's Writing: Does not accept unsolicited material. Submissions returned with proper SASE. Reports in "days."
Illustration/Animation: Does not accept unsolicited material. Hires illustrators for computer and hand animation, storyboarding, live action and comprehensives. Types of animation produced: cel animation, clay animation, stop motion, special effects, 3-D, computer animation, video graphics, motion control and live action. To submit, send cover letter, résumé and demo tape. Art samples returned with proper SASE. Reports in "weeks." Pays "per project."
Tips: When reviewing a portfolio/samples, looks for "application to a project, general talent and interests based on examples."

BRIDGESTONE MULTIMEDIA GROUP, 300 North McKerny Ave., Chandler AZ 85226-2618. (800)622-3770. Fax: (602)940-8924. Estab. 1986. Video management and distribution, software publisher. Audience: Family, children. Produces multimedia productions. Recent children's productions: "Everyone Is Special," written by Tony Salerno (self-esteem video for ages 3-10); "Christmas Past," written by various (comedy clips video for family).
Illustration: Submit demo tape (VHS). Guidelines/catalog free on request.

BROADCAST QUALITY, INC., 5701 Sunset Dr., #316, South Miami FL 33143. (305)665-5416. President: Diana Udel. Estab. 1978. Video production and post production house. Produces videotapes. Children's productions: "It's Ours to Save—Biscayne National Park," written by Jack Moss, produced by Diana Udel/BQI, Betacam SP/1″ Master, (Environmental awareness for grades 4-7); "The Wildlife Show at Parrot Jungle," written by Amy Smith, produced by BQI, Betacam SP/1″ Master, (Hands on to Florida's Wildlife for K-8th grade). Uses 2-5 freelance writers/year; purchases various projects/year.
Tips: "Send a résumé and demo reel. Seeks variety, knowledge of subject and audience."

CENTRE COMMUNICATIONS, 1800 30th St., Suite #207, Boulder CO 80301. (303)444-1166. Contact: Deborah O'Grady. Estab. 1975. Production and distribution company. Audience: schools, libraries and television. Produces films and videotapes. Recent children's productions: "Violence: Dealing with Anger," (educational video for ages 10-12); "A Norman Rockwell

Christmas Story"; and "Pepper and All the Legs," written by Dick Gackenbach (children's story videos for ages 4-8). Uses 2-3 freelance writers/year; purchases 5-6 writing projects/year.
Children's Writing: Needs: educational material, documentaries and live action. "We only commission work or distribute finished products." Reports back only if interested. Buys material outright. Guidelines free on request.

CLEARVUE/eav, 6465 N. Avondale, Chicago IL 60631. (312)775-9433. Editor/Producer: Mary Watanabe. Estab. 1969. Type of company: production and distribution house. Audience: educational pre-school through high school. Uses filmstrips, slide sets, CD-ROM, videodiscs, videotapes. 50% of illustrating/animating is by freelancers.
Children's Writing: "At this time we are only accepting for review *finished* video projects that we will consider for distribution." Query with résumé. Reports back only if interested. Pays 5-10% royalty.
Illustration/Animation: Hires illustrators for computer animation of company-owned filmstrips. Send cover letter, résumé, demo tape (VHS). Reports in 2 weeks only if interested. Video samples returned. Guidelines/catalog free. Pay: "open."
Tips: "Programs must be designed for educational market—not home or retail. We are looking for good animators with equipment to scan in our filmstrips and animate the characters and action according to prepared directions that allow for artistic variations."

COUNTDOWN PRODUCTIONS, INC., P.O. Box 190537, Dallas TX 75219. Phone/fax: (214)321-3233. President: Thomas C. Crocker. Estab. 1986. Video Production. Audience: Children. Produces videotapes. Children's productions: "Mr. Donut and the Donut Factory," (Christian/morality video for ages 3-12); and "I've Got a Dream—Chuck E. Cheese," (love between siblings video for ages 4-12). Uses 5-6 freelance writers/year; buys 2 writing projects/year. Uses 5-6 artists/year; buys 10-12 art projects/year.
Children's Writing: Query with synopsis, résumé. Submissions cannot be returned; submissions filed. Reports only if interested. Buys material outright.
Illustration: Hires illustrators for computer/video, animation, storyboarding, live action. Types of animation produced: cel animation, clay animation, stop motion, computer animation, video graphics, live action. Submit cover letter, demo tape (VHS). Art samples not returned; art samples filed. Reports only if interested. Pays $45-85/hour for storyboarding/comp work; $50-100/hour for animation work.
Tips: "Have a ready-for-TV concept, developed characters and story line. Sequels or 13 weeks of material assist in the sale process."

EDUCATIONAL VIDEO NETWORK, 1401 19th St., Huntsville TX 77340. (409)295-5767. Production Manager: Brian Kastar. Estab. 1954. Production house. Audience: educational (school). Uses videotapes. 20% of writing by freelancers; 20% of illustrating/animating is by freelancers. Recent children's productions: "Gods and Heroes of Greece and Rome," written by Mary Lee Nolan (mythology/literature video for junior high-college); and "Cut the Fat from Your Diet," written and illustrated by Christina Vuckovic (nutrition video for junior high-college). Uses 1-2 freelance artists/year; buys 2-3 art projects/year.
Children's Writing: Needs: "Curriculum-oriented educational material" for junior high through college audiences. Query. Submissions returned with proper SASE. Reports in 1 month. Guidelines/catalog free. Pays writers royalties of 6-10% or buys material outright.
Illustration/Animation: Hires illustrators for animation. Types of animation produced: video graphics, limited computer animation. To submit, send cover letter and VHS demo tape. Art

samples returned with proper SASE. Reports in 1 month. Guidelines/catalog free. Pays $10-30/cel for animation work.

Tips: "Materials should fill a curriculum need for junior high to college. We seldom assign projects to freelancers. We want to be approached by people who know a particular subject and who have a plan for getting that information across to students. Programs should feature professional production techniques and involve the viewers in the message."

FILM CLASSIC EXCHANGE, 143 Hickory Hill Circle, Osterville MA 02655. (508)428-7198. President: J.H. Aikman. Estab. 1916. Distribution/production house. Audience: Pre-school through college. Produces films, videotapes. Recent children's productions: "The Good Deed," written by William P. Pounder, illustrated by Karen Losaq (film on family values aimed at preschool); "Willie McDuff's Big Day," written and illustrated by Joe Fleming (anti-drug film aimed at ages 12 and up). Uses 6 freelance writers and artists/year. Purchases 6 writing and 6 art projects/year.

Children's Writing: Needs: Preschool. Subjects include: Anti-drug. Query with synopsis or submit completed script. Submissions are returned with proper SASE. Reports back only if interested. Buys material outright.

Illustration/Animation: Hires illustrators for cel/video animation, storyboarding, character development, live action, comprehensives, pencil testing. Types of animation produced: cel animation, clay animation, stop motion, special effects, computer animation, video graphics, motion control, live action. To submit, send cover letter, résumé, demo tape (VHS), color print samples. Art samples returned with proper SASE. Reports back only if interested.

Tips: "Keep sending updated résumés/samples of work."

FILMS FOR CHRIST, INC., (aka, "Eden Productions"), 2628 W. Birchwood Circle, Mesa AZ 85202. (602)894-1300. Fax: (602)894-8406. Executive Director: Paul S. Taylor. Estab. 1961. Producer/distributor of films, videos and books. Audience: Christian families and church audiences. Produces multimedia productions, films, videotapes, books. Recent children's productions: "The Great Dinosaur Mystery," written by Paul S. Taylor, illustrated by Charles Zilch, Gary Webb, Paul S. Taylor (documentary on creation vs. evolution, 7-adult); and "The Great Dinosaur Mystery and the Bible," written by Paul S. Taylor, illustrated by C. Zilch, G. Webb, T. Tennant, J. Chong, P.S. Taylor (creation vs. evolution book, 7-adult). Uses 0-1 freelancer/year. Uses 1-2 artists/year; buys 3-8 art projects/year.

Children's Writing: Needs: documentaries (ages 5-8, 9-12, adult). Subjects include: creation vs. evolution. Query with synopsis; submit résumé. Submissions cannot be returned; submissions filed. Reports only if interested. Catalog free on request. Pays royalty or buys material outright.

Illustration: Hires illustrators for animation, live action, detailed renderings. Types of animation produced: cel animation, special effects, computer animation, video graphics. Submit cover letter, résumé, demo tape if available (VHS), color print samples. Art samples are filed if interested. Reports only if interested. Catalog is free on request. Rates negotiable, based on anticipated marketability of each project.

Tips: "As a nonprofit, evangelical ministry, we are most interested in developing working relationships with artists and illustrators who are anxious to use their gifts and talents to help propagate the life-changing truths of the Bible."

FINE ART PRODUCTIONS, 67 Maple St., Newburgh NY 12550. (914)561-5866. Director: Richie Suraci. Estab. 1989. "We cover every aspect of the film, video, publishing and entertainment industry." Audience: All viewers. Uses filmstrips, films, slide sets, videotapes, multimedia productions, any format needed. Children's productions: "1991 Great Hudson River Revival," illustrated by various artists (35mm film and print on environment, clearwater sailing ship); and "Wheel and Rock to Woodstock Bike Tour," written and illustrated by various artists (film, print, video on exercise, health, music and volunteerism). Percent of freelance illustrators/animators used varies.

Children's Writing: Query with synopsis, or submit synopsis/outline, completed script, résumé. Submissions are filed, or returned with proper SASE. Reports in 1 month if interested. Pay is negotiated.

Illustration/Animation: Hires illustrators for animation, storyboarding, character development, live action, comprehensives, pencil testing. Types of animation produced: cel animation, clay animation, stop motion, special effects, computer animation, video graphics, motion control, live action. To submit, send cover letter, résumé, demo tape (VHS or ¾"), b&w print samples, color print samples, tearsheets, business card. Art samples are filed, or returned with proper SASE. Reports in 1 month if interested. Guidelines/catalog for SASE. Pay is negotiated.

***GOOD FRIENDS FILM PRODUCTIONS, INC.**, 7365 Main St., #186, Stratford CT 06497. Phone/fax: (203)380-2906. E-mail: jackrush@aol.com. Executive Director: Jack Rushen. Estab. 1993. Production house. Audience: K-12th grade—different projects for different age groups. Produces films and videotapes. Recent children's productions: *Not Worth It*, written by Rushen, (anti-drug PSA for junior high); and *Second Wind*, written by Terry Keyes (child sexual abuse video for high school). Uses 3-4 freelance writers/year; buys 3-4 writing projects/year.
Children's Writing: Subjects include: anti drug/violence, teen suicide prevention, fairy tales (K-3). Query with synopsis. Submissions returned with SASE; submissions filed. Reports in 4-6 weeks. Guidelines/catalog is: for SASE. Pay varies depending on project.
Tips: "Scripts must be real, warm, with humor. Short (½-hour) scripts with a message (not preachy) to kids. Stories about compassion and respect for those who are different are a plus! Use humor! Then slip in a message. This is often a hard pill to swallow. So we get them to laugh, and when their mouth is open—drop it in!!"

I.N.I. ENTERTAINMENT GROUP, INC., 11845 W. Olympic Blvd., Suite 700, Los Angeles CA 90064. (310)479-6755. Fax: (310)479-3475. Chairman of the Board/CEO: Irv Holender. President: Michael Ricci. Estab. 1985. Producer/International Distributor. Audience: children of all ages. Uses films. Children's productions: "The Adventures of Oliver Twist," screenplay written by Fernando Ruiz (updated version of the Dickens tale for ages 4-12); "Alice Through the Looking Glass," screenplay written by James Brewer (updated and upbeat version of Carroll's book for ages 4-12). 100% of writing is by freelancers; 100% of illustrating/animating is by freelancers.
Children's Writing: Needs: animation scripts. "Anything from fantasy to fable." To submit, query with synopsis. Submit synopsis/outline, completed script, résumé. Submissions returned with proper SASE. Reports back only if interested. Pay varies.
Illustration/Animation: Type of animation produced: computer animation. To submit, send cover letter, résumé, demo tape (VHS), color print samples, business card. Art samples are filed, returned with proper SASE or not returned. Reports back only if interested.
Tips: "We are gearing to work with fairytales or classic stories. We look for concise retelling of older narratives with slight modifications in the storyline, while at the same time introducing children to stories that they would not necessarily be familiar with. We are currently in production doing "International Family Classics, Part II." We don't hire illustrators for animation. We hire the studio. The illustrators that we hire are used to create the advertising art."

KIDVIDZ: Special Interest Video for Children, 618 Centre St., Newton MA 02158. (617)965-3345. Fax: (617)965-3640. Partner: Jane Murphy. Estab. 1987. Home video publisher. Audience: pre-school and primary-age children, 2-12 years. Produces videotapes. Children's productions: "Let's Get a Move On! A Kid's Video Guide to a Family Move" (VHS video, a family move, 4-12 year olds); "Squiggles Dots & Lines, A Kid's Video Guide to Art & Creativity" (art video on creativity for 5-12 year olds). Uses 2 freelance writers/year. Uses 3 freelance artists/year. Submissions filed.
Tips: "Submit material strong on dialogue using a child-centered approach. Be able to write shooting scripts."

KJD TELEPRODUCTIONS, 30 Whyte Dr., Voorhees NJ 08043. (609)751-3500. Fax: (609)751-7729. President: Larry Scott. Creative Director: Kim Davis. Estab. 1989. Location production services (Betacam SP) plus interformat edit and computer animation. Audience: industrial and broadcast. Uses slide sets, multimedia productions, videotapes. Children's productions: "Kids-

The asterisk before a listing indicates the listing is new in this edition.

tuff," written by Barbara Daye, illustrated by Larry Scott (educational vignettes for ages 6-16). 10% of writing is by freelancers; 25% of animating/illustrating by freelancers.
Children's Writing: Needs: animation. To submit, query. Submissions are filed. Reports in 2 weeks. Pays royalty or buys material outright.
Illustration/Animation: Hires illustrators for animation. Types of animation produced: computer animation. To submit, send cover letter, résumé, demo tape (VHS or ¾″), b&w print samples, tearsheets, business card. Art samples are filed. Reports in 2 weeks. Pay varies.

NATIONAL GALLERY OF ART, Education Dept., Washington DC 20565. (202)737-4215. Fax: (202)789-2681. Head, Dept. of Teacher and School Programs: Anne Henderson. Estab. 1941. Museum. Audience: teachers and students. Uses film strips; slide sets, videotapes, laser disk reproductions. Children's productions: "The Magic Picture Frame," written by Maura Clarkin (reproductions of paintings for NGA Museum Guide for ages 7-10). 50% of writing is by freelancers.
Children's Writing: Needs: educational material for all levels. Subjects include knowledge of art-making and art history. To submit, send résumé. Submissions are filed. Reports back only if interested. Guidelines/catalog not available. Buys material outright.

NEW & UNIQUE VIDEOS, 2336 Sumac Dr., San Diego CA 92105. (619)282-6126. Fax: (619)283-8264. Acquisitions Managers: Candy Love, Mark Schulze. Estab. 1985. Video production and distribution services. "Audience varies with each title." Uses films and videotapes. Children's productions: "Battle at Durango: The First-Ever World Mountain Bike Championships," written by Patricia Mooney, produced by Mark Schulze (VHS video mountain bike race documentary for 12 and over); "John Howard's Lessons in Cycling," written by John Howard, direction and camera by Mark Schulze (VHS video on cycling for 12 and over). 50% of writing is by freelancers; 85% of illustrating/animating is by freelancers.
Children's Writing: Needs: Completed and packaged videotape productions (45 minutes to one hour in length) whose intended audiences may range from 1 and older. "Any subject matter focusing on a special interest that can be considered 'new and unique.' " Query. Submissions are returned with proper SASE. Reports in 2-3 weeks. Payment negotiable.
Illustration/Animation: Hires illustrators for film or video animation. Types of animation produced: computer animation and video graphics. To submit, send cover letter. Art samples returned with proper SASE. Reports back in 2-3 weeks. Payment negotiable.
Tips: "As more and more video players appear in homes across the world, and as the interest in special interest videos climbs, the demand for more original productions is rising meteorically."

OLIVE JAR ANIMATION, 35 Soldiers Field Place, Boston MA 02135. (617)783-9500. Fax: (617)783-9544. Executive Producer: Matthew Charde. Estab. 1984. Animation studio. Audience: all ages. Uses films, videotapes. 75% of writing is by freelancers; 75% of illustrating/animating is by freelancers.
Illustration/Animation: Hires illustrators for animation (all types), storyboarding, pencil testing, design, ink paint, sculpture, illustration. Types of animation produced: cel and clay animation, stop motion, special effects. To submit, send cover letter, résumé, demo tape, b&w print samples, color print samples, tearsheets, business card. Art samples are filed. Reports back only if interested. Pays flat rate according to job.
Tips: Looks for "someone who is really good at a particular style or direction as well as people who work in a variety of mediums. Attitude is as important as talent. The ability to work with others is very important."

RARE MEDIA WELL DONE, (formerly Michael Sand Inc.), 1110 Washington St., Boston MA 02124. (617)296-7000. Fax: (617)566-7001. E-mail: m.sand@aol.com. President: Michael Sand. Estab. 1964. Museum planning consultants. Audience: museum visitors. Produces multimedia productions, films, videotapes and interactive video disks. Children's productions: "The Water Course," written by Kathy Suter, illustrated by Valentin Sahleanu (interactive touch-screen exhibit); and "Transformations Exhibit," written by Michael Sand, illustrated by Frank Constantine (multimedia exhibit renderings on art evaluation for 8-year-olds). Uses 4 freelance writers/year; buys 12 writing projects/year. Uses 8 freelance artists/year; buys 30 art projects/year.
Children's Writing: Needs: animation scripts, educational material, documentaries (ages 5-8, 9-11, 12 and older). Subjects include: history, science, art. To submit, query with synopsis,

completed script, résumé, samples. Submissions are returned with proper SASE; submissions sometimes filed. Reports in 1 month. Guidelines/catalog not available. Buys material outright (pay varies).

Illustration: Hires illustrators for computer-based animation, storyboarding, character development, comprehensives, pencil testing, exhibit renderings, models, 3-D illustration. Type of animation produced: cel animation, stop motion, special effects, computer animation, video graphics, motion control, live action. Submit cover letter, résumé, demo tape (VHS), b&w print samples, color print samples, tearsheets, slides, promo sheet. Samples somtetimes filed. Reports in 1 month if interested. Guidelines/catalog not available. Pays minimum $25/hour.

Tips: "Submit one or more examples of your most imaginative work. Kids expect cute. We prefer authentic themes, pertinent to their lives."

SEA STUDIOS, INC., 810 Cannery Row, Monterey CA 93940. (408)649-5152. Fax: (408)649-1380. Office Manager: Melissa Lewington. Estab. 1985. Natural history video production company. Audience: general. Uses multimedia productions, videotapes. 50% of writing is by freelancers; 50% of illustrating/animating is by freelancers.

Children's Writing: Needs: educational material—target age dependent on project. Send résumé (no phone calls, please). Submissions returned with proper SASE. Reports back only if interested. Pay negotiable.

Illustration/Animation: Send cover letter, résumé (no phone calls please). Art samples returned with proper SASE. Reports back only if interested.

SHADOW PLAY RECORDS & VIDEO, P.O. Box 180476, Austin TX 78718. (512)345-4664. Fax: (512)345-9734. President: Peter J. Markham. Estab. 1984. Children's music publisher. Audience: families with children ages 3-10. Uses videotapes. Children's productions: "Joe's First Video," written by Joe Scruggs, illustrated by various artists (VHS children's music videos for preschool-10 years). 5% of writing is by freelancers; 100% of illustrating/animating by freelancers.

Children's Writing: Needs: poems or lyrics for children's songs. To submit, send query. "No unsolicited submissions accepted!" Submissions returned with proper SASE. Reports in 6 weeks. Pays royalty or buys material outright.

Illustration/Animation: Hires illustrators for animation, storyboarding, live action, pencil testing. Types of animation produced: cel animation, clay animation, stop motion, special effects, computer animation, video graphics, live action. To submit, send cover letter, résumé, demo tape (VHS), color print samples, business card. Art samples returned with proper SASE. Reports in 6 weeks. Pay varies by project and ability of artist.

SISU HOME ENTERTAINMENT, 18 W. 27th St., 10th Floor, New York NY 10001. (212)779-1559. Fax: (212)779-7118. President: Haim Scheinger. Estab. 1988. Video and audio manufacturers (production, distribution). Audience: Children (educational videos and entertainment videos). Uses videotapes and audio. Children's productions: "Lovely Butterfly—Chanuka," written by IETV (Israel Educational TV), illustrated by IETV (Jewish holiday-program for ages 2-5). 25% of writing is by freelancers.

Children's Writing: Needs: publicity writing—all ages. To submit, arrange interview.

Illustration/Animation: Types of animation produced: clay animation, video graphics illustrations for video box covers. To submit, send résumé. Art samples filed. Reports back only if interested.

TREEHAUS COMMUNICATIONS, INC., 906 W. Loveland Ave., P.O. Box 249, Loveland OH 45140. (513)683-5716. President: Gerard A. Pottebaum. Estab. 1968. Production house. Audience: preschool through adults. Produces film strips, multimedia productions, videotapes. Children's production: "Seeds of Self-Esteem" series, written by Dr. Robert Brooks, Jane Ward and Gerard A. Pottebaum, includes 2 books for teachers, 4 in-service teacher training videos and 27 posters for children from primary grades through junior high school, distributed by American Guidance Service, Inc. 30% of writing is by freelancers; 30% of illustrating/animating is by freelancers.

Children's Writing: Needs: educational material/documentaries, for all ages. Subjects include: "social studies, religious education, documentaries on all subjects, but primarily about people

who live ordinary lives in extraordinary ways." Query with synopsis. Submissions returned with proper SASE. Reports in 1 month. Guidelines/catalog for SASE. Pays writers in accordance with Writer's Guild standards.
Tips: Illustrators/animators: "Be informed about movements and needs in education, multicultural sensitivity." Looks for "social values, originality, competency in subject, global awareness."

***VIDEO AIDED INSTRUCTION, INC.**, 182 Village Rd., Roslyn Heights NY 11577. (516)621-6176. Fax: (516)484-8785. E-mail: usatest@aol.com. Contact: Peter Lanzer, President. Estab. 1983. Video publisher. Audience: grade 6 through adult. Uses videotapes. Recent children's productions: "GED" series (5 tapes) written by Peter Lanzer, M.B.A. and Karl Weber, M.A. (High School Equivalency Test—high school to adult); and "SAT" series (6 tapes) written by Karl Weber, M.A. and Dr. Harold Shane (high school).
Children's Writing: Needs: educational material for all age levels on all school subjects. Query. Submissions are filed. Reports in 1 month. Guidelines/catalog free on request. Pays royalty; buys material outright.
Illustration/Animation: Types of animation produced: video graphic, live action. Guidelines/catalog free on request.
Tips: "If you have an academic subject you can teach, call us!"

***BILL WADSWORTH PRODUCTIONS**, 1913 W. 37th St., Austin TX 78731-6012. (512)452-4243. Fax: (512)206-0606. E-mail: bw@bwp.com. Producer/Director: Bill Wadsworth. Estab. 1978. Production/animation company. Audience: youth/adult. Produces films, multimedia productions, videotapes. Recent children's productions: "Tailypo," written by Bill Wadsworth (live action folktale for elementary-aged children) and "Porfirio Salinas," Bill Wadsworth (live action biography for ages 12-adult). Uses 1 freelance writer/year.

- Bill Wadsworth Productions is looking only for illustrators at this time.

Illustration: Hires illustrators for animation, storyboarding, character development, comprehensives, rotoscope. Types of animation produced: computer animation, video graphics, rotoscope. Send cover letter, résumé. Samples not returned; art samples not filed. Reports only if interested. Pay scale provided on request.

Audiotape Markets

Among these listings you'll find companies with a range of offerings. Several listings, such as Dercum Audio and High-Top Productions, publish exclusively story tapes. More often, however, the companies listed publish and produce music as well as stories. In either case, these companies provide opportunities for songwriters and writers to showcase their work on tape or compact disk.

Among the record companies listed you'll find both large producers and distributors, like Peter Pan Industries and smaller independent studios such as Passing Parade Music (new to this edition). For more information about the children's entertainment industry, see the Audiovisual & Audiotape introduction on page 216.

ALISO CREEK PRODUCTIONS, INC., P.O. Box 8174, Van Nuys CA 91409. (818)787-3203. President: William Williams. Record company, book publisher. Estab. 1987.
Music: Releases 2 LPs-cassettes; 2 CDs/year. Records 20 children's songs/year. Works with composers, lyricists, team collaborators. For songs recorded pays musicians/artists on record contract and songwriters on royalty contract. Write first and obtain permission to submit material.

Always include a self-addressed, stamped envelope (SASE) with submissions within your own country. When sending material to other countries, include a self-addressed envelope (SAE) and International Reply Coupons (IRCs).

Submit 3-5 songs with lyric sheets on demo cassette. SASE/IRC for return of submission. Reports in 3 weeks. Recorded songs: "Brontosaurus Stomp," by Bob Menn and William Williams, recorded on Aliso Creek Records label (dixieland music for ages 3-8); "What Make a Car Go, Dad?," by Bob Menn and William Williams, recorded on Aliso Creek Records label (Gilbert & Sullivan-type music for ages 3-8).
Music Tips: "We're looking for music in a variety of styles that doesn't talk down to children or isn't preachy, but does convey positive values or educate."
Stories: Publishes 2 book/cassette packages/year; 2 cassettes/CDs/year. 100% of stories are fiction. Will consider all types of fiction, but story and songs must be related. "We publish musical plays on cassette aimed at ages 3-8." Will consider all types of nonfiction aimed at ages 3-8. Authors are paid negotiable royalty based on retail price; work purchased outright. Submit both cassette tape and ms. Reports on queries in 3 weeks. Catalog is free for #10 SASE. Published: *Take a Trip with Me*, by Bob Menn and William Williams, narrated by Kevin Birkbeck and Katy Morkri (ages 3-8); *Move!*, by Bob Men and William Williams, narrated by Katy Morkri (ages 3-8, a family adjusts to moving to a different city).
Story Tips: "We publish song and story cassettes with an illustrated lyric book so we need writers and illustrators to create a unified product."

AMERICAN MELODY, P.O. Box 270, Guilford CT 06437. (203)457-0881. Fax: (203)457-2085. President: Phil Rosenthal. Music publisher, record company (American Melody), recording studio, book publisher. Estab. 1985.
Music: Releases 4 LPs/year. Member of BMI. Publishes 20 and records 30 children's songs/year. Works with composers, lyricists, team collaborators. For music published pays standard royalty of 50%; for songs recorded, pays musicians/artists on record contract, musicians on salary for inhouse studio work, and songwriters on royalty contract. Call first and obtain permission to submit material. Submit demo cassette with lyric sheet. Submissions returned with SASE. Reports in 1 month. Recorded songs: "The Bremen Town Song," by Max Showalter and Peter Walker, recorded by Max Showalter on American Melody label (folk music for ages 2-10); "My Little Dog and Me," by Phil Rosenthal, recorded by Phil Rosenthal on American Melody label (bluegrass music for ages 1-8); and "I Can't Wait for Spring," by Sarah Pirtle, recorded by Linda Schrade and Dave Kiphuth on American Melody label (folk for ages 3-10).
Music Tips: "Submit as nice a demo as possible, with understandable lyrics."

AUDIO-FORUM, 96 Broad St., Guilford CT 06437. (203)453-9794 or (800)243-1234. Fax: (203)453-9774. Publicity & Reviews: Nancy Grant. Estab. 1972.
Stories: "We publish children's educational materials on audio and video cassettes on the following subjects: foreign languages, music, English as a second language, history, math, reading, grammar, spelling, touch typing, astronomy and games." Recently published story tapes: *Winko Teddy Bear: Flash cards with cassette in French, German, and Spanish* (ages 5-12 language teaching program). Free children's catalog available.

BARRON'S EDUCATIONAL SERIES, 250 Wireless Blvd., Hauppauge NY 11788. (516)434-3311. Fax: (516)434-3723. Managing Editor/Director of Acquisitions: Grace Freedson. Book publisher. Estab. 1940.
Stories: Publishes 1 book/cassette package/year. 100% of stories are fiction. For fiction, will consider foreign language. Pays authors royalty. Query. Catalog free for SAE. Ms guidelines free for SASE. Recently recorded story tapes: *Un, Deux, Trois—My First French Rhymes*, by Opal Dunn, illustrated by Patricia Aggs (ages 4-8 foreign language).

BRENTWOOD MUSIC, INC., One Maryland Farms, Suite 200, Brentwood TN 37027. (615)373-3950. Fax: (615)373-8612. Creative Director: Dale Mathews. Music publisher, book publisher, record company, children's video. Estab. 1980.
Music: Releases 40 cassettes/year; 24-30 CDs/year. Member of ASCAP, BMI and SESAC. Publishes 60-120 children's songs/year. Works with composers. Pays standard royalty of 50% of net receipts for music published. Submit demo cassette tape by mail; unsolicited submissions OK; 2 songs and lyric sheet or lead sheet. "No music can be returned unless you include a self-addressed, stamped envelope. Do not send stamps or postage only. If you want it back, send an *envelope* big enough to hold all material with the *proper* postage affixed. No exceptions." Reports

in 3-6 months. Recently recorded songs: "Once Upon an Orchestra," by Don and Lorie Marsh on Designer Music label (orchestral story—like "Peter & The Wolf," ages 3-7); "It's A Cocka-doodle Day," by Janet McMahan-Wilson, Tom McBryde, Mary Jordan on Brentwood Kids Co. label (sing along for ages 2-7).
Stories: Will consider fictional animal, fantasy or adventure aimed at preschool through 3rd or 4th grades. Author's pay is negotiable, depending on project. Query. Reports in 3 months. Recently recorded story tapes: *The Leap Year Frog*, by Freddy Richardson, narrated by Mother Goose (ages 2-6, birthday); *How the Donkey Got His Tail*, by Freddy Richardson, narrated by Mother Goose (ages 2-6, birthday).
Tips: "Songs and stories with a Christian or Bible theme fill more of our product development needs than other topics or themes."

***BRIGHT IDEAS PRODUCTIONS**, 31220 La Baya Dr., West Lake Village CA 91362. (818)707-7127. Fax: (818)707-0889. President: Lisa Marie Nelson. Music publisher, book publisher, record company (Bright Ideas Productions), interactive media. Estab. 1990.
Music: Releases 1 LP/cassette/year; 1 CD/year. Member of ASCAP. Publishes and records 14 children's songs/year. Works with composers, lyricists and team collaborators. For music published, pays usually on a per-project basis. Write for permission to submit material. Submit demo cassette with 3 songs and lyric sheet. Submissions returned with SASE. Recently recorded songs: "Go For It," by Nelson/Shur, recorded by Andre Garner on Bright Ideas (rock for elementary school ages); and "Club Crocodile," by Nelson/Shur, recorded by Curt Skinner on Bright Ideas (pop for elementary school ages).
Tips: Write first and ask permission to submit.

BROADCAST PRODUCTION GROUP, 1901 S. Bascom Ave., Campbell CA 95008. (408)559-6300. Fax: (408)559-6382. Creative Director: Kevin Sullivan. Video and film production and multimedia group. Estab. 1986.
Music: Hires staff writers for children's music. Works with composers and/or lyricists, team collaborators. "Our projects are on a single-purchase basis." Pays per project for songs recorded. Submit demo tape by mail; unsolicited submissions okay. Submit demo cassette, résumé and videocassette if available. Not necessary to include lyric or lead sheets. Reports in 3 weeks.

CENTER FOR THE QUEEN OF PEACE, 3350 Highway 6, Suite 412, Houston TX 77478. Music publisher, book/video publisher and record company. Record labels include Cosmotone Records, Cosmotone Music. Estab. 1984.

● Does not review material at this time.

Music: Releases 1 single, 1 12-inch single and 1 LP/year. Member of ASCAP. Works with team collaborators. For music published, pays negotiable royalty; for songs recorded, pays musicians on salary for inhouse studio work, songwriters on royalty contract.

CHILDREN'S MEDIA PRODUCTIONS, P.O. Box 40400, Pasadena CA 91114. (818)797-5462. Fax: (818)797-7524. President: C. Ray Carlson. Video publisher. Estab. 1983.
Music: Works with composers and/or lyricists. For songs recorded, pays musicians/artists on record contract. Write for permission to submit material.
Tips: "We use only original music and songs for videos. We serve markets worldwide and must often record songs in foreign languages. So avoid anything provincially *American*. Parents choose videos that will '*teach* for a lifetime' (our motto) rather than entertain for a few hours. State concisely what the 'message' is in your concept and why you think parents will be interested in it. How will it satisfy new FCC regulations concerning 'educational content?' We like ethnic and/or multi-racial stories and illustrations."

***A bullet within a listing introduces special comments by the editor of* Children's Writer's & Illustrator's Market.**

***CHOO CHOO RECORDS**, 13119 Garden Land Rd., Los Angeles CA 90049. (310)472-4211. Fax: (310)472-3436. Director: Richard Perlmutter. Music publisher, record company (Choo Choo Records). Estab. 1992.

Music: Releases 3-5 LPs-cassettes/year; 3-5 CDs/year. Member of ASCAP and BMI. Publishes 10-20 and records 50 songs/year. Works with composers and lyricists. For music published, pay varies; for songs recorded, pays musicians/artists on record contract, songwriters on royalty contract (percentage royalty paid: statutory rate or less). Submit demo tape by mail; unsolicited submissions OK. Submit demo cassette with 3-10 songs. Cannot return material. Reports in 2-4 weeks. Recently recorded songs: "When The Cat's Away," by Will Ryan, recorded by Victoria Jackson on Choo Choo Records (swing music for ages 2-10); and "Don't Fence Me In," by Cole Porter, recorded by Nickel Creek Band on Choo Choo Records (country western swing for ages 2-10).

***CREATIVE NETWORK CO.**, P.O. Box 2818, Newport Beach CA 92659. (714)494-0181. Fax: (714)494-0982. Consultant: J. Nicoletti. Record company (Global Village Records & CDs), consultant. Estab. 1976.

Music: Releases 4 singles/year; 4 12-inch singles/year; 4 LPs-cassettes/year; 10 CDs/year. Member of ASCAP. Publishes 10 children's songs/year; records 4 children's songs/year. Works with composers, lyricists and team collaborators. For music published, pays standard royalty of 50%. Submit demo tape by mail; unsolicited submissions OK. Submit demo cassette with 2-6 songs and lyric sheet. "Make clear, understandable demos." Submissions returned with SASE. Reports in 2 weeks. Recently recorded "On Time," by Carson Wittle, recorded by Big Boy on Global Village Records (for young adults ages 10-14); and "Toy World," written and recorded by Sean Wok on Globe Village Records (for children ages 4-9).

Stories: Publishes 3 book/cassette packages/year. For fiction, will consider all types (ages 5 and up). For nonfiction, will consider all types (ages 10 and up). Pays authors 25-50% royalties. "All types of royalties are negotiable." Submit outline/synopsis and sample chapters. Reports on queries/mss in 3 weeks. Recently recorded story tapes: *Another World*, by Coperteen, narrated by Eliza Lorenz (ages 10-16, family life and situations); and *Be Here Now*, by Royal Blue, narrated by Wanda Goldberg (ages 6 and up, getting along with others).

DERCUM AUDIO, P.O. Box 1425, West Chester PA 19380. (610)889-2410. Fax: (610)889-2412. Contact: Amy Lewis. Audio book producer. Estab. 1985.

Stories: For fiction, will consider fantasy, spy, mystery, etc. for production of unabridged audio books, particularly fantasy, mystery, science fiction, etc. in a narrative form. Recently produced story tapes: *Culpepper Adventure Series* (6 books), by Gary Paulsen, narrated by Bill Fantini (ages 8-14, mystery/adventure). Pays authors 10% maximum royalties based on wholesale price. Offers $500 average advance. Query. Submit outline/synopsis and sample chapters. Reports on queries/mss in 2-3 months.

DOVE AUDIO, Suite 203 N. Cañon Dr., Beverly Hills CA 90210. (310)273-7722. Fax: (310)273-0365. Customer Service Supervisor: Karrie Komaru. Audio book publisher. Estab. 1985.

Stories: Publishes approximately 100/year (audio, books and multimedia). 50% of stories are fiction; 50% nonfiction. Submit through agent only. Reports in 2 weeks. Catalog is free on request. Recently recorded story tapes include *Enchanted Tales*, narrated by Audrey Hepburn (ages 5 and up); *Rap, Rap, Rapunzel*, narrated by Patti Austin (ages 3 and up).

DUTTON CHILDREN'S BOOKS, 375 Hudson St., New York NY 10014. (212)366-2600. Fax: (212)366-2011. President and Publisher: Christopher Franceschelli. Book publisher.

Stories: Publishes 3 book/cassette packages/year. Publishes fiction and nonfiction. Will consider animal and fantasy. Story tapes aimed at ages 2-10. Authors are paid 5-12% royalties based on retail price; outright purchase of $2,000-20,000; royalty inclusive. Average advance $3,000. Submit outline/synopsis and sample chapters through agent. Reports on queries in 3 weeks; on mss in 6 months. Catalog is available for 8×11 SAE and 8 first-class stamps. Ms guidelines available for #10 SASE. Children's story tapes include *Noah's Ark*, narrated by James Earl Jones.

Tips: "Do not call publisher. Get an agent. Celebrity readers sell."

ROY EATON MUSIC INC., 595 Main St., Roosevelt Island NY 10044. (212)980-9046. Fax: (212)980-9068. President: Roy Eaton. Music publisher, TV and radio music production company. Estab. 1982.
Music: Member of BMI. Hires staff writers for children's TV commercial music only. Works with composers, lyricists, team collaborators. For music published, pays standard royalty of 50%. Write or call for permission to submit material. Submit demo cassette with lyric sheet.
Tips: "Primarily interested in commericals for children."

***EMERALD RECORDS**, 159 Village Green Dr., Nashville TN 37217. (615)361-7902. President: Cliff Ayers. Music publisher, record company (Emerald, American Sound). Estab. 1951.
Music: Releases 7 singles/year; 20 LPs-cassettes/year; 12 CDs/year. Member of ASCAP. Publishes 20 children's songs/year; records 10 children's songs/year. Works with composers, lyricists and team collaborators. For music published, pays standard royalty of 50%; for songs recorded, pays musicians/artists on royalty contract. Submit demo tape by mail; unsolicited submissions OK. Submit demo cassette with 2 songs and lyric sheet. Cannot return submissions. Reports in 2 weeks. Recently recorded "Birds of a Feather," by Miss Marti, recorded by Cathy Lemmon on Emerald Records (for ages 4-7) and "All God's Children," written and recorded by M. Jeffries on Emerald Records (ages 3-6).
Music Tips: "Keep the lyrics simple."
Stories: 70% of stories are fiction; 30% nonfiction. For fiction, will consider animal, fantasy (ages 2-7). For nonfiction, will consider animal and sports (ages 3-7). Pays authors royalty (no set rate). Submit both cassette tape and ms. Reports on queries in 2 weeks. Ms guidelines free for SASE.

FINE ART PRODUCTIONS, 67 Maple St., Newburgh NY 12550. (914)561-5866. Contact: Richie Suraci. Music publisher, record company, book publisher. Estab. 1989.
Music: Member of ASCAP and BMI. Publishes and records 1-2 children's songs/year. Hires staff writers for children's music. Works with composers, lyricists, team collaborators. For music published, pays standard royalty of 50% or other amount; for songs recorded, pays musicians/artists on record contract, musicians on salary for inhouse studio work, songwriters on varying royalty contract. Submit ½" demo tape by mail; unsolicited submissions OK. Submit demo cassette. Not neccessary to include lyric or lead sheets. Submissions returned with SASE. Reports in 3-4 months.
Stories: Publishes 1 book/cassette package and 1 audio tape/year. 50% of stories are fiction; 50% nonfiction. Will consider all genres for all age groups. Authors are paid varying royalty on wholesale or retail price. Submit both cassette tape and ms. Reports in 3-4 months. Catalog is not available. Ms guidelines free with SASE.

***FIREWORKS MUSIC**, 400 S. Green St., #310, Chicago IL 60607. (312)666-4676. Fax: (312)666-4666. CEO: Keith Hooper. Music publisher, record company (Fireworks Music Records), studio and live performance tours. Estab. 1980.
Music: Releases 1-2 singles/year; 1-2 LPs-cassettes/year; 2-3 CDs/year. Member of BMI. Publishes and records 1 children's song/year. Works with composers, lyricists and team collaborators. For music published, pays standard royalty of 50%. Submit demo tape by mail; unsolicited submissions OK. Submit demo cassette with 3-5 songs, lyric or lead sheet. Cannot return material. Reports in 2 months.
Stories: Publishes 1 CD package/year. For fiction, will consider animal and educational stories (ages 3-15). Work purchased outright.

HIGH WINDY AUDIO, 260 Lambeth Walk, Fairview NC 28730. (704)628-1728. Fax: (704)628-4435. Owner: Virginia Callaway. Record company.

- High Windy Audio is currently not accepting material.

Music: Releases 2 LPs-cassettes/year; 2 CDs/year. Member of BMI, AFTRA. Records 12 children's songs/year. Works with storytellers, musicians. Pays musicians/artists on record contract plus one time studio work.
Stories: Publishes 2 CDs/year. 100% of stories are fiction. Will consider animal, fantasy, history, scary, sports, spy/mystery/adventure. Authors are paid royalty based on retail price. Query. Reports on queries in 3 weeks. Catalog free on request. Submission guidelines not available. Re-

cently recorded story tapes: *Hairyman*, narrated by David Holt (ages 4-adult, folktale); *The Boy Who Loved Frogs*, narrated by Jaay O'Callahan (ages 4-adult, animal story).
Tips: "Call first."

HIGH-TOP PRODUCTIONS, 6290 Sunset Blvd., #925, Hollywood CA 90028. (213)957-5600. Fax: (213)957-3153. Publisher: Donald Allen. Audio book publisher. Estab. 1990.
Stories: Publishes 35 book/cassette packages/year. 25% of stories are fiction; 75% nonfiction. For fiction/nonfiction, will consider sports (ages 5-14). Pays authors 10% royalty. Offers $300 average advance. Submit complete ms, both cassette tape and ms. Reports on queries/mss in 6 weeks. Catalog free on request. Ms guidelines free for SASE. Recently recorded story tapes: *Willie's Last at Bat*, by Sussian Koulor and narrated by Sussian Koulor (ages 8-14, sports).
Tips: "We like sports themes for our children's stories. The book should have a specific moral with a very good story base."

LISTENING LIBRARY, INC., One Park Ave., Old Greenwich CT 06870. (203)637-3616. Fax: (203)698-1998. Contact: Editorial Review Committee. Spoken word recording company.
Stories: Buys material outright. Submit completed script. SASE/IRC for return of submission. Reports in 2 months. Recorded books: *A Wrinkle in Time*, by Madeleine L'Engle (ages 9-12); and *Superfudge*, by Judy Blume (ages 5-12).
Tips: "We primarily produce works that are already published. However, we occasionally find that an audio project will arise out of original material submitted to us."

MEDICINE SHOW MUSIC, INC., 19 Beech Court, Fishkill NY 12524. Phone/fax: (914)896-9359. President: Karan Bunin. Estab. 1991.
Music: Member of BMI. Publishes and records 12 children's songs/year. Does various projects requiring music. Hires staff writers for children's music. Works with composers and/or lyricists, team collaborators. Pay varies with projects. Submit demo tape by mail; unsolicited submissions OK. Submit demo cassette (videocassette if available), press kits. Include lyric sheet. Cannot return material. Recently recorded songs: *Skating On The Moon*, by Karan Bunin and Jeff Waxman, recorded by Karan & The Musical Medicine Show on 200M Express/BMG Kidz (children's music for ages preschool-adult); *Coming To Your Town*, by Karan Bunin, recorded by Karan & The Musical Medicine Show on 200M Express/BMG Kidz (Children's music for ages preschool-adults).
Tips: Send tapes with information about project and intentions (goals). Follow up with phone call 2 weeks after sending.

MELODY HOUSE, INC., 819 NW 92nd St., Oklahoma City OK 73114. (405)840-3383. Fax: (405)840-3384. President: Stephen Fite. Record company. Estab. 1972.
Music: Releases 6 LPs/year. Records 72 children's songs/year. Works with composers, lyricists, team collaborators. For songs recorded pays musicians on salary for inhouse studio work or standard mechanical royalty per song; pay songwriters on royalty contract (10%). Submit demo tape by mail; unsolicited submissions OK. Submit demo cassette (5 songs or more) with lyric and lead sheets. SASE/IRC for return of submission. Reports in 2 months if interested. Recently recorded songs: "Bop 'Til You Drop," written and recorded by Mr. Al on Melody House label (technopop for ages 3-9); "Sleighbells Jingling," written and recorded by Fred Koch on Melody House label (children's folk for ages 3-8).
Tips: "The music and the lyrics should reach out and grab the child's attention. Children are much more sophisticated in their listening than their parents were at the same age. Children's music is definitely taking on the characteristics of the pop market with the sounds and even the hype in some cases. Even some of the messages are now touching on issues such as divorce/separation, the environment and social consciousness, both in the U.S. and the world."

MUSIC FOR LITTLE PEOPLE, P.O. Box 1460, Redway CA 95560. (707)923-3991. Fax: (707)923-3241. Contact: Dixie Hamilton. Record company.
Music: Releases 6-12 cassettes/year; 6-12 CDs/year. Records 40 children's songs/year. Works with composers and/or lyricists, team collaborators. Pays musicians/artists on record contract. Write for permission to submit material. Cannot return material. Reports in 2-6 months. Recently recorded songs: "Water from Another Time," by John McCutcheon, recorded by Scott Petito

(folk for ages 3-8); "Three Little Birds," by Bob Marley, recorded at Banquet Studios—Santa Rosa on Music for Little People (reggae, ages 3-8).
Stories: Publishes 2-6 book/cassette packages/year. 100% nonfiction. For nonfiction, considers cultural and musical history; biography (ages 3-8). Work purchased outright, $500 minimum. Query. Reports on queries in 2-6 months. Catalog is free on request—call (800)727-2233. Submission guidelines not available.

✤OAK STREET MUSIC, 1067 Sherwin Rd., Winnipeg, Manitoba R3H 0T8 Canada. (204)694-3101. Fax: (204)697-0903. Contact: Lynn Burshtein. Record company. Estab. 1987.
Music: Releases 8 LPs-cassettes/year; 8 CDs/year. Member of SOCAN and PROCAN. Publishes and records 10 children's songs/year. Works with team collaborators. Pays standard royalty of 50% for music published; for songs recorded pays musicians/artists on record contract; songwriters on royalty contract. Submit demo tape by mail; unsolicited submissions OK. Include demo cassette (VHS videocassette if available); 3-5 songs, lead sheets. "We do not return demos." Reports on submissions in 3 months. Recently recorded songs: "The Mosquito Song," written by Al Simmons/Ken Whiteley, recorded by Al Simmons on Oak Street Music (family country, for 8 and up); and "Don't Make Me Sing Along," written by Lisa Lambert, recorded by Al Simmons on Oak Street Music (family/children's, for 4 and up).
Tips: "Listen to our music for an idea of what we need or choose a specific artist like Fred Penner to write music for. Send us original material—music that would sound fresh in the market. Get an idea of the type of music each label is partial to, and come up with new ideas."

***OMNI 2000 INC.**, 413 Cooper St., Camden NJ 08102. (609)963-6400. Fax: (609)964-3291. President: Michael Nise. Music publisher, book publisher (audio books), record company. Record labels include Power Up Records. Estab. 1995. Member of BMI. Works with composers, lyricists and team collaborators. For music published, pays standard royalty of 50%; for songs recorded, pays musicians/artists on record contract, musicians on salary for inhouse studio work. "Include SASE for artist's release form. Completion is required prior to (or with) submission." Submit demo cassette with 3 songs. "Make sure product is protected and you have our release signed and returned." Reports within 3 months.
Stories: For fiction and nonfiction submissions, will consider all formats (ages 2-11 and 12-17). Pays authors negotiable royalty; or outright purchase to be negotiated. Submit cassette tape of story. Reports on queries in approximately 3 months.

***PASSING PARADE MUSIC**, P.O. Box 872, West Covina CA 91790. Owner/Operator: Kelly D. Lammers. Music publisher. Estab. 1972.
Music: Member of ASCAP. Publishes 3-6 children's songs/year. Works with composers, lyricists, team collaborators. For music published, pays standard royalty of 50%. Submit demo tape by mail; unsolicited submissions OK. Submit demo cassette with maximum of 3 songs and lyric sheet. SASE/IRC for return of submission. Reports in 4-6 weeks. Published songs: *Let Me Be a Kid for Just Awhile*, by K. Lammers and D. Lammers, recorded by The Neighborhood Kids (anti-drug children's song for ages 6-15); *The Happy Song*, by Jim Pash, recorded by Jim Pash and The Neighborhood Kids (instrumental music for kids of all ages).
Tips: "We would like all children's material to have a positive and uplifting theme or message."

PETER PAN INDUSTRIES, 88 St. Francis St., Newark NJ 07105. (201)344-4214. Fax: (201)344-0465. Vice President of Sales: Shelly Rudin. Music publisher, record company. Record labels include Parade Video, Compose Music, Peter Pan Industries and PPI Entertainment Group. Estab. 1927.

- To learn more about Peter Pan, see Insider Report with Joseph Porrello in the 1995 edition of *Children's Writer's & Illustrator's Market*.

Music: Releases 20 singles/year; 45 CDs/year. Member of ASCAP and BMI. Publishes 50 children's songs/year; records 80-90 songs/year. Works with composers, lyricists, team collaborators. For music published pays standard royalty of 50%; for songs recorded pays musicians/artists on record contract, songwriters on royalty contract. Submit a 15 IPS reel-to-reel demo tape or VHS videocassette by mail—unsolicited submissions OK. SASE (or SAE and IRCs) for return of submissions. Reports in 4-6 weeks.
Stories: Publishes 12 book/cassette packages/year. 90% of stories are fiction; 10% nonfiction. Will consider all genres of fiction and nonfiction aimed at 6-month to 9-year-olds. Authors are

paid in royalties based on wholesale price. Query. Reports on queries in 4-6 weeks. Book catalog, ms guidelines free on request.

Tips: "Tough business but rewarding. Lullabies are very popular."

***PINE POINT RECORD CO.**, P.O. Box 901, Windham ME 04062. (207)892-7175. Fax: (207)892-6593. E-mail: 73651.2511@compuserve.com. Vice President: Roy Clark. Music publisher, record company. Record labels include Pine Point Records. Estab. 1985.

Music: Releases 1 LP-cassette/year; 2 CDs/year. Member of ASCAP. Publishes 10 and records 14 children's songs/year. Works with composers, lyricists and team collaborators. For music published, pays standard royalty of 50%; for songs recorded, pays songwriters on royalty contract (statutory). Submit demo cassette with 4-6 songs and lyric sheet. Submissions returned with SASE. Reports in 2 months. Catalog free on request. Recently recorded songs: "Popcorn," written and recorded by Rick Charette, on Pine Point Records (ages 3-11 years), and "Holiday Portrait," by PD, recorded by Winham Chamber Singers on Pine Point Records (Christmas, ages 10-adult).

Music Tips: "Send clean demos with as little orchestration as possible. Simple raw accompaniment is best (guitar or piano or similar)."

Stories: Catalog free on request.

PRAKKEN PUBLICATIONS, INC., 275 Metty Dr., Suite 1, P.O. Box 8623, Ann Arbor MI 48103. (313)769-1211. Fax: (313)769-8383. Publisher: George Kennedy. Magazine publisher. Estab. 1934.

Stories: Publishes 4-5 books/videos/year. 100% nonfiction. Will consider any genre of nonfiction (ages 3-8). Authors are paid 10% royalty based on net sales. Other payment negotiable. Advance not standard practice but possibly negotiable. Submit outline/synopsis and sample chapters. Reports on queries in 2 weeks; mss in 6 weeks if return requested and SASE enclosed. Catalog free on request. Submission free with SASE.

Tips: "We are presently a publisher of magazines and books for educators. We now seriously seek to expand into such areas as children's books and products other than print media."

RHYTHMS PRODUCTIONS/TOM THUMB MUSIC, P.O. Box 34485, Los Angeles CA 90034-0485. President: R.S. White. Multimedia production, cassette and book packagers. Record label, Tom Thumb—Rhythms Productions. Estab. 1955.

Music: Member of ASCAP. Works with composers and lyricists. For songs recorded pays musicians/artists on record contract, songwriters on royalty contract. Submit a cassette demo tape or VHS videotape by mail—unsolicited submissions OK. Requirements: "We accept musical stories. Must be produced in demo form, and must have educational content or be educationally oriented." Reports in 2 months. Recorded songs: *Adventures of Professor Whatzit & Carmine Cat*, by Dan Brown and Bruce Crook (6 book and cassette packages); and *First Reader's Kit* (multimedia learning program); all on Tom Thumb label.

***RODELL RECORDS, INC.**, P.O. Box 93457, Hollywood CA 90093. (714)434-7730. Fax: (714)434-7756. President: Adam Rodell. Music publisher, record company. Record labels include Rodell Records, Inc. Estab. 1989.

Music: Releases 25-50 singles/year; 5 CDs/year. Member of BMI and ASCAP. Publishes and records 1-3 children's songs/year. Works with composers, lyricists and team collaborators. For music published, pays standard royalty of 50%. Submit demo tape by mail; unsolicited submissions OK. Submit cassette, VHS videocassette, DAT or CD with 1-3 songs and lyric sheet. Reports in 1 month.

Tips: "If we like what we hear, we'll talk! Be patient!"

SATURN, A division of Rock Dog Records, P.O. Box 3687, Hollywood CA 90028. (213)661-0259. Fax: (310)641-5074. VP A&R: Gerry North. Record company. Estab. 1987.

The asterisk before a listing indicates the listing is new in this edition.

Stories: Publishes 2 book/cassettes and 2 cassette/CDs/year. 99% of stories are fiction; 1% nonfiction. For fiction, will consider fantasy, adventure, mystery, animal (ages 3-5). Payment negotiable. Query. "No phone calls please." Reports on queries in 1 month. Recently published songs: "Four Eyed Freddie" and "The Green Grickled Monster," both recorded by Saturn Studio (children's stories).
Tips: "Send typed script. If you want a reply or your materials returned, be sure to include SASE."

CHARLES SEGAL MUSIC, 16 Grace Rd., Newton MA 02159. (617)969-6196. Fax: (617)969-6114. Contact: Charles Segal. Music publisher and record company. Record labels include Spin Record. Estab. 1980.
Music: Publishes 24 children's songs/year. Works with composers and/or lyricists, team collaborators. For music published, pays standard royalty of 50%; for songs recorded, pays musicians/artists on record contract. Submit demo tape by mail; unsolicited submissions OK. Submit demo cassette if available with 1-3 songs and lyric or lead sheets. Reports in 6-7 weeks. Recorded songs: "Animal Concert," by Colleen Hay, recorded by Concert Kids on CBS label (sing along for ages 4-13); "Everyday Things," recorded by Charles Segal on MFP label (kids pop music for ages 6-15).
Music Tips: "Must be of educational value, entertaining easy listening. The lyrics should not be focused on sex, killing, etc.
Stories: Publishes 6 book/cassette packages/year. 50% of stories are fiction; 50% nonfiction. Will consider all genres aimed at ages 6-15. For nonfiction, considers all aimed at ages 6-15. Authors are paid royalty. Submit complete ms or submit both cassette tape and ms. Reports on queries in 6 weeks; mss in 2 months.
Story Tips: "I always look for the experienced writer who knows where he's going and not beating around the bush; in other words, has a definite message—a simple, good storyline."

SOUNDPRINTS, 165 Water St., P.O. Box 679, Norwalk CT 06856. (203)838-6009. Assistant Editor: Dana Rau. Book publisher. Estab. 1988.
Stories: Publishes 6-7 book/cassette packages/year. Almost 100% of stories are fiction. Will consider realistic animal stories for preschool-3rd grade. Query with SASE. Reports on queries in 2 weeks; mss in 1 month. Catalog for SASE. Ms guidelines free with SASE. Published and recorded story tapes: *Jackrabbit and the Prairie Fire*, by Susan Saunders, narrated by Peter Thomas (black-tailed jackrabbit on the Great Plains for preschool-3rd grade); *Seasons of a Red Fox*, by Susan Saunders, narrated by Peter Thomas (the first year in the life of a red fox for preschool-3rd grade).
Tips: "Stories should be realistic and not anthropomorphic. But they should not be dry nonfiction. We are looking for well-crafted storylines."

TWIN SISTERS PRODUCTIONS, INC., 1340 Home Ave., Suite D, Akron OH 44310. (216)633-8900. Fax: (216)633-8988. President: Kim Thompson. CEO: Karen Hilderbrand. Music publisher, record company. Estab. 1987.
Music: Releases 12 singles/year; 12 LPs-cassettes/year. Publishes and records 120 children's songs/year. Works with composers and teams collaborators. Pays musicians on salary for inhouse studio work. Call first and obtain permission to submit material. Submit demo cassette with lyric sheet and VHS videocassette. Not necessary to include lyric or lead sheets. List past history of successes. SASE/IRC for return of submission. Reports in 1 month. Recently recorded songs: "Did You Know That Monkeys Like to Swing?," by Kim Thompson and Karen Hilderbrand, recorded by Greg Fortson on the Twin Sisters Productions label (children's music for ages 2-7); "The Tiger's Loose," by Kim Thompson and Karen Hilderbrand, recorded by Greg Fortson on the Twin Sisters Productions label (children's music for ages 2-7).
Tips: "Send a professional-sounding recording, labelled with all information—name, phone number, etc. Children's music is starting to be widely recognized in mainstream music. Independent labels are major contributors."

WATCHESGRO MUSIC PUBLISHING CO., Watch Us Climb, ASCAP. 9208 Spruce Mountain Way, Las Vegas NV 89134-6024. (702)363-8506. President: Eddie Lee Carr. Music publisher, record company. Record labels include Interstate 40 Records, Tracker Records. Estab. 1970.

Music: Releases 12 singles/year; 5 12-inch singles/year; 1 LP/year; 1 CD/year. Member of BMI. Publishes 15 and records 4 children's songs/year. Works with composers, lyricists. For music published, pays standard royalty of 50%; for songs recorded, pays musicians/artists on record contract, musicians on salary for inhouse studio work. Write or call first and obtain permission to submit a cassette tape. Does not return unsolicited material. Reports in 1 week.

WE LIKE KIDS!, produced by KTOO-FM, 360 Egan Dr., Juneau AK 99801. (907)586-1670. Fax: (907)586-3612. Producer: Jeff Brown. Producer of nationwide children's radio show.
Music: Releases 50 programs/year. Member of Children's Music Network; National Storytelling Association. Submit demo tape by mail; unsolicited submissions OK. Submit demo cassette, vinyl, CD.
Music Tips: "The best advice we could give to anyone submitting songs for possible airplay is to make certain that you give your best performance and record it in the best way possible. A mix of well-honed songwriting skills, an awareness of a variety of international musical styles, and the advent of home studios have all added up to a delightful abundance of quality songs and stories for children."
Stories: "Our show is based on themes most of the time. Send us your *recorded* stories. We play an average of one story per show, *all* from pre-recorded cassettes, LPs and CDs. Please do not send us *written* stories. Many storytellers have discovered We Like Kids! as a way of sharing their stories with a nationwide audience."

Audiovisual & Audiotape changes/'95-'96

The following markets were included in the 1995 edition of *Children's Writer's & Illustrator's Market* but do not have listings in this edition. The majority did not respond to our request to update their listings.

AIMS Media
Artichoke Productions
Art Audio Publishing Company/Tight Hi-Fi Soul Music
Bennu Productions
Bridger Productions, Inc.
The Christian Science Publishing Society
Credence Cassettes
Dimension Films
Gordon Music Co./Paris Records
Home, Inc.
JEF Films
Kensington Falls Animation
KKDS-AM 1060—The Imagination Station
Mama-T Artists/The Folktellers
MarshMedia
Tom Nicholson Assoc., Inc.
Northwest Imaging & FX
NTC Publishing Group
Porter Versfelt & Associates Television Productions
Productions Diadem Inc.
Smarty Pants Audio, Inc
Stemmer House Publishers
Teeter-Tot Records
TVN—The Video Network
Upstream Productions
WUVT-FM; Hickory Dickory Dock Show
WXPN-FM; Kid's Corner

Scriptwriter's Markets

Any play for kids, whether an original script or a classical adaptation, must captivate its audience. One way to enthrall a group of youngsters is to use plenty of rhythm, repetition and effective dramatic action. Also make sure the dialogue is realistic, relate the play directly to the experience of the audience, and include an element of surprise. Avoid using subplots, which lengthen a play. (Most plays for children average less than an hour.)

"Fourth wall" plays, or plays where actors perform as if they are unaware of the audience, are still the standard in this field. But interactive plays which involve the audience are gaining popularity.

Since many theater groups have limited budgets, scripts containing elaborate staging and costumes might not meet their needs. Touring theaters also want simple sets that can be easily transported. Many touring productions are plays consisting of three to six actors. More characters than available actors might be in your play, so think about how the roles can be doubled up.

Plays using adult roles *and* plays with children's roles are needed by the markets in this section. Note the percentage of plays produced for adult roles, and the percentage for children's roles. Above all, study the types of plays a theater company wants. Most mention specific plays recently produced or published. Some may also supply additional information or catalogs upon request.

Finally, payment for playwrights is usually in royalties, outright payments or a combination of both. The pay scale isn't quite as high as screenplay rates, but playwrights *do* benefit by getting to see their work performed live.

A.D. PLAYERS, 2710 W. Alabama, Houston TX 77098. (713)526-2721. Estab. 1967. Produces 4-5 children's plays/year in new Children's Theatre Series; 1-2 musical/year. Produces children's plays for professional productions. 99-100% of plays/musicals written for adult roles; 0-1% for juvenile roles. "Cast must utilize no more than four actors. Need minimal, portable sets for proscenium or arena stage with no fly space and no wing space." Recently produced plays: *The Selfish Giant*, by Dr. Gillette Elvgren Jr. (a story of a child's sacrificial love, for ages 5-12); and *The Lion, the Witch and the Wardrobe*, dramatized by le Clanche du Rand, story by C.S. Lewis (Lewis's classic story of love, faith, courage and giving, for ages 5-14). Does not want to see large cast or set requirements or New Age themes. Will consider simultaneous submissions and previously performed work. Submission method: Query with synopsis, character breakdown and set description; no tapes until requested. Reports in 6-12 months. Buys some residual rights. Pay negotiated. Submissions returned with SASE.

- A.D. Players has received the Dove family approval stamp; an award from the Columbia International Film & Video Festival; and a Silver Angel Award.

Tips: "Children's musicals tend to be large in casting requirements. For those theaters with smaller production capabilities, this can be a liability for a script. Try to keep it small and simple, especially if writing for theaters where adults are performing for children. We are interested in material that reflects family values, emphasizes the importance of responsibility in making choices, encourages faith in God and projects the joy and fun of telling a story."

AMERICAN STAGE, P.O. Box 1560, St. Petersburg FL 33731. (813)823-1600. Artistic Director: Lisa Powers. Estab. 1977. Produces 3 children's plays/year. Produces children's plays for professional children's theater program, mainstage, school tour, performing arts halls. Limited by budget and performance venue. Subject matter: classics and original work for children (ages K-12) and

families. Recently produced plays: *Beauty and the Beast*, by Philip Hall and Lee Ahlin (grades K-6); and *The Jungle Books*, adapted by Victorian Holloway, music by Lee Ahlin (Kipling's classic tale of Mowgli the Mancub, and his life being raised in the Jungle, for grades K-6). Does not want to see plays that look down on children. Approach must be that of the child or fictional beings or animals. Will consider simultaneous submissions, electronic submissions via disk or modem and previously performed work. Submissions method: Query with synopsis, character breakdown and set description. Reports in 6 months. Purchases "professional rights." Pays writers in royalties (6-8%); $25-35/performance. SASE for return of submission.
Tips: Sees a move in plays toward basic human values, relationships and multicultural communities.

ARTREACH TOURING THEATRE, 3074 Madison Rd., Cincinnati OH 45209. (513)871-2300. Fax: (513)871-2501. Artistic Director: Kathryn Schultz Miller. Estab. 1976. "ArtReach has cast requirement of 3—2 men and 1 woman. Sets must look big but fit in large van." Professional theater. Produced plays: *Young Cherokee*, by Kathryn Schultz Miller (history and culture of early Cherokee tribe as seen through the eyes of a young brave, for primary students and family audiences); and *The Trail of Tears*, by Kathryn Schultz Miller (a companion play to *Young Cherokee* depicting story of Cherokee removal and unjust destruction of their culture, for intermediate through adult audiences). Does not want to see musicals, holiday plays, TV type scripts (about drugs, child abuse etc.) or fractured fairy tales. Will consider simultaneous submissions and previously performed work. Submission method: Query with synopsis, character breakdown and set description. Reports in 10 days to 6 weeks. Author retains rights. Pays writers in royalties. SASE for return of submission.
Tips: "Type script in professional form found in *Writer's Digest Book of Manuscript Formats*. Do not submit plays that are less than 45 pages long. Look to history, culture or literature as resources."

BAKER'S PLAYS, 100 Chauncy St., Boston MA 02111. (617)482-1280. Fax: (617)482-7613. Associate Editor: Raymond Pape. Estab. 1845. Publishes 10-20 children's plays/year; 2 musicals/year. 80% of plays/musicals written for adult roles; 20% for juvenile roles. Subject matter: full lengths for family audience and full lengths and one act plays for teens." Submission method: Submit complete ms, score and tape of songs. Reports in 3-8 months. Obtains worldwide rights. Pays writers in royalties (amount varies).
Tips: "Know the audience you're writing for before you submit your play anywhere. 90% of the plays we reject are not written for our market."

BIRMINGHAM CHILDREN'S THEATRE, P.O. Box 1362, Birmingham AL 35201. (205)324-0470. Executive Director: Charlotte Lane Dominick. Estab. 1947. Produces 8-10 children's plays/year; some children's musicals/year. "BCT is an adult professional theater performing for youth and family audiences September-May." 99% of plays/musicals written for adult roles; 1% for juvenile roles. "Our 'Wee Folks' Series is limited to four cast members and should be written with preschool-grade 2 in mind. We prefer interactive plays for this age group. We commission plays for our 'Wee Folks' Series (preschool-grade 1), our Children's Series (K-6) and our Young Adult (6-12)." Recently produced plays: *The Little Red Hen*, by Patricia Muse (classic story retold in interactive format for children in preschool through grade 1; 4 actors) and *Rapunzel*, by Randy Marsh (classic story told with a twist for children in grades K-6; 6 actors). Does not want plays which have references to witches, spells, incantations, evil magic or devils. No adult language. Will consider musicals, interactive theater for Wee Folks Series. Prefer mainstage limited to 4-7 cast members. Submission method: Query first, query with synopsis, character breakdown and set description. Reports in 4 months. Buys negotiable rights. Submissions returned with SASE.

***A bullet within a listing introduces special comments by the editor of* Children's Writer's & Illustrator's Market.**

Magazines: Uses 25 short stories (less than 4,000 words), plays; 8 nonfiction essays (less than 3,000 words); 10 pieces of poetry; letters to the editor; editorials; reviews of previously published works; and reviews of books, music, movies per issue. Published authors receive 3 contributor's copies and payment. Also, a discount is offered for additional copies of the issue. Submit up to 3 titles at one time. Will only accept typewritten mss. "All rejected manuscripts receive an editor's constructive critical comment in the margin." Reports in 10 weeks.
Artwork/Photography: Publishes artwork and photography by young adults, grades 6-12. Looks for b&w line drawings, cartoons, color art for cover. Published artists receive 3 contributor's copies plus payment. A discount is offered for additional copies. Send unmatted original artwork. Reports in 10 weeks.
Tips: "All manuscripts and artwork must be accompanied by a completed copy of *Merlyn's Pen* official cover sheet for submissions. Call to request cover sheet."

***NATION MAGAZINE**, 5998 Taylor Rd., Painesville OH 44077-9157. (216)254-4410. E-mail: repsisk@aol.com. Magazine. Published monthly except July and December. "*Nation* focuses on individuals who are involved or interested in pen-pals and correspondence. The age range is between 13 and 25. All submissions pertaining to the individual's life are accepted, with only token alterations made in the text. *Nation*'s purpose is to act as an economic substitute, where young adults may build friendships and maintain old acquaintances (from the small press community) in an altruistic environment of loving and dynamic youth." Writers must be between the ages of 10 and 25 years and provide a written statement entitling use of the work in *Nation*. Non-vulgar writing style required. Submissions must be no longer than 1,400 words. Writer's guidelines available on request.
Magazines: Uses 20 letters or essays probing the authors' lives (250-1,400 words). Pays "only in gratitude." Submit mss to Peter Kowalke, editor. Submit complete ms, complete letter of introduction. Will accept typewritten and legibly handwritten mss. Reports in 1 month.
Artwork/Photography: Publishes artwork and photography by children. Accepts most pen & ink sketches, no larger than 4×6. Must be "artsy." Photographs should be no larger than 4×6, depicting young adults engaged in their lives. Submit only flat artwork (no bending or folding). Submit art and photographs to Peter Kowalke, editor. Include SASE. Reports in 1 month.
Tips: "Practice what you love and watch the pros. Be yourself!"

***NEW MOON: The Magazine For Girls & Their Dreams**, New Moon Publishing, Inc., P.O. Box 3620, Duluth MN 55803-3620. (218)728-5507. Fax: (218)728-0314. E-mail: newmoon@newmoon.duluth.mn.us. Magazine. Published bimonthly. "*New Moon: The Magazine For Girls & Their Dreams* is an international magazine for every girl who wants her voice heard and her dreams taken seriously. With its editorial board of girls ages 8-14 and girl contributors from all over the world, *New Moon* celebrates girls, explores the passage from girl to woman, and builds healthy resistance to gender inequities. The *New Moon* girl is true to herself and *New Moon* is a tool for her to use as she develops and pursues her unique path in life, moving confidently out into the world. We usually publish work by girls age 8-14. Please include SASE." Reports in 2 months.
Magazine: 75% of magazine written by young people. Uses 4 fiction mss (300-900 words); 12 nonfiction mss (300-900 words) per year. Submit to Tya Ward and Barbara Stretchberry, associate managing editors. Submit query, complete mss for fiction and nonfiction. Will accept typewritten, legibly handwritten mss and disc (IBM compatible). "We do not return unsolicited material."
Artwork/Photography: Publishes artwork and photography by children. Looks for cover and inside illustrations. Pay negotiated. Submit art and photographs to Tya Ward or Barbara Stretchberry, associate managing editors. "We do not return unsolicited material." Reports in 2 months.
Tips: "Read *New Moon* to completely understand our needs."

***RASPBERRY PUBLICATIONS INC.**, P.O. Box 925, Westerville OH 43086-6925. (800)759-7171. Fax: (614)899-6147. Book publisher. Publishes 6-10 books/year by children. "We believe what children write has value and children like to read what other children write." Purpose in publishing books by children: to provide opportunities for young authors to be published and motivate all children to write. Books must be written and illustrated by children from grades K-12.
Books: Publishes all genres of fiction; nonfiction should have educational value. Pays royalties, but no advances. Contact: Curt Jenkins, publisher. Submit complete ms for fiction and nonfiction.

INSIDER REPORT

Magazine Offers Forum for Girls' Ideas

Youth and inexperience can work to the advantage of freelance writers hoping for publication in *New Moon: The Magazine For Girls & Their Dreams*.

While the publication includes freelance work from adults, most copy in the award-winning magazine is written by girls for girls. The work is also reviewed and edited by an editorial board comprised of 25 young women ages 8 to 14, which directs *New Moon*'s layout and printing, says Managing Editor Joe Kelly.

Joe Kelly

"To me, the message of that is if we give children something to do and get out of their way, they do exceptionally well," Kelly says. "We don't empower them—they've already got power."

New Moon was launched in 1993, because Kelly and his wife Nancy Gruver found a dearth of good resources for their twin daughters, then 11. They decided to co-publish *New Moon* as a forum for girls' thoughts and ideas, helping them make the passage through adolescence without suffering an erosion of their self-esteem. Step one was turning loose the first Girls Editorial Board, which developed the magazine's format.

As an alternative to its slick, image-packed competitors, *New Moon* has no advertising. Each issue revolves around a theme—from environmentalism to teddy bears—and dishes up a bimonthly fare of biographies and profiles of women leaders. The magazine also includes profiles of real girls, poetry, fiction, and features on such subjects as children's suffrage and support groups for kids whose parents have cancer.

"*New Moon* is more literary," Kelly says. "By that I mean it's not four-color, not hyper-flashy—a lot of kids' magazines are trying to look like MTV. *New Moon* is more reliant on the words."

Its words have caught the attention of both critics and readers: "The tools the magazine provides are connections with other girls, focusing on what they think and do, and not necessarily on how they look," wrote a critic from *The New York Times*. Says a *Chicago Tribune* writer: "*New Moon* is designed to help girls discover what they can be, instead of what society tells them they should be."

After three years, *New Moon* collected national awards from the Educational Press Association, Parent's Choice Foundation, Feminist Majority Foundation, Center for Women Policy Studies and the *Utne Reader*. The magazine also helped sponsor a delegation of girls to the United Nations' Fourth World Conference on Women in Beijing last year.

About half of each 48-page issue is written by girls. Contributors write for regular departments; profiles and personal experience articles; and poetry and other short features. "We like the kids' voice, even if it's not super polished."

Specifically, *New Moon* needs profiles of living girls from a wide range of backgrounds and cultures. Says Kelly, "We are always interested in girls who have accomplished remarkable things, but we're also interested in ordinary girls who are doing things that don't draw national attention." The board is also looking for personal experience stories and compelling opinion pieces, Kelly says. What the magazine doesn't need is more fiction from adult writers for children.

Kelly cautions adults submitting to magazines like *New Moon* to steer clear of the trap of writing down to the readers. "Say it straight," he says. "We're interested in female-focused pieces. If it's fiction, the protagonist should be female, and make the story happen. For nonfiction profiles, the more quotes the better. They are the vehicle that lets the person come through."

Submissions from adult and young writers are all considered by the Girls Editorial Board. At twice-monthly meetings, the board divides and reviews the hundreds of letters and dozens of submissions that come in weekly from around the country, and as far away as Europe, Australia, Asia and Africa.

"It functions very much like any other publication," Kelly says. "But in a sense (the girls) are more discerning in terms of choosing what girls that age want to read, because they are girls that age. They also have very keen condescension-detection devices . . . they don't like to be talked down to or written down to."

Whether budding writers want to contribute to *New Moon* or other publications for young people, Kelly recommends writers follow some basic instructions to strengthen their writing: "Read the publication you're submitting to. Edit yourself mercilessly. Write in the active voice, and write about what you know—a person you've interviewed, or an event you've gone to. That's what's going to work."

—Anne Bowling

New Moon *is looking for art and photography submissions, in addition to writing, from both young and adult contributors. The 7 × 9 wrap-around format typically features full bleeds, such as this January/February 1995 cover, illustrated in ink, gouache and acrylics by Alison Aune, an artist and teacher from Amherst, Massachusetts. For specific guidelines, artists can check out the July/August 1995 issue of* New Moon *for a call for cover art submissions including a sample cover template.*

Will accept typewritten, legibly handwritten and computer-printed mss. Include SASE. Reports in 3 months.

Tips: "Be original and creative. Make sure you have solid beginning, middle and end. The 'conflict' should have a child as the main character, and should be resolved by the child without help from adults in the story. We are looking for good mysteries for our 'Raspberry Crime Files' series."

SHOFAR MAGAZINE, 43 Northcote Dr., Melville NY 11747. (516)643-4598. Managing Editor: Gerald H. Grayson. Magazine published 6 times/school year. Audience consists of American Jewish children age 9-13.

Magazines: 10-20% of magazine written by young people. Uses fiction/nonfiction (500-750 words), Kids Page items (50-150 words). Submit mss to Gerald Grayson, managing editor. Submit complete ms. Will accept typewritten, legibly handwritten mss and computer disk (Mac only). SASE. Reports in 1-2 months.

Artwork/Photography: Publishes artwork and photography by children. Pays "by the piece, depending on size and quantity." Submit original with SASE. Reports in 1-2 months.

***SHOW AND TELL MAGAZINE**, 93 Medford St., Malden MA 02148. (617)321-3649. Fax: (617)321-3649. Magazine. Published monthly. "Show and Tell was established to publish creative, classic fiction authored by writers ages 14-100. *Show and Tell*'s audience is primarily readers/writers ages 18-70—well-read, open minded, creative readers." Purpose in publishing works by young people: "To show that children are just as creative and competent in writing fiction as adults. To give them a chance early in their lives and provide a fruitful outlet in a crazy, busy world. I am only interested in originality and proof that they had no help (significant) from an adult." Writer's guidelines available on request.

Magazines: 2% of magazine written by young people (because of infrequent submissions only!). Uses 1 fiction story of any genre except horror (up to 2,000 words) per issue. Pays $5/story. Submit mss to Donna Clark, editor or Thomas Conger, associate editor (2830 S. 2750 East, Salt Lake City, Utah 84109). Submit complete mss for fiction. Will accept typewritten and legibly handwritten mss. Include SASE. Reports in 1 month.

Artwork: Publishes artwork "if a child writer submits, with his or her submission, an illustration related to the story. I will do a simple photocopied paste-up of it near the story." Pays $5. Submit artwork as clean as possible, on a separate sheet of white paper, signed and labeled. Submit art to Donna Clark, senior editor. Include SASE. Reports in 1 month.

Tips: "Just send in your best and neatest work. Both the senior editor and associate editor are parents, and we love and respect children. Our own children write and we honor that with enthusiasm."

SKIPPING STONES, Multicultural Children's Quarterly, P.O. Box 3939, Eugene OR 97403. (503)342-4956. Articles/Fiction Editor: Arun N. Toké. Quarterly magazine. Estab. 1988. Circulation 3,000. "*Skipping Stones* is a multicultural, nonprofit, children's magazine to encourage cooperation, creativity and celebration of cultural and environmental richness. It offers itself as a creative forum for communication among children from different lands and backgrounds. We prefer work by children up to 17-18 year olds. International, minorities and underrepresented populations receive priority, multilingual submissions encouraged."

- *Skipping Stones* is winner of the 1995 Golden Shoestring Award of the Educational Press Association of America. Their theme for 1996 is "Envisioning the World in the Year 2025."

Magazines: 50% written by children. Uses 5-10 fiction short stories and plays (500-750 words); 5-10 nonfiction articles, interviews, letters, history, descriptions of celebrations (500-750 words); 15-20 poems, jokes, riddles, proverbs (250 words or less) per issue. Pays in contributor's copies.

***A bullet within a listing introduces special comments by the editor of* Children's Writer's & Illustrator's Market.**

Submit mss to Arun Toké, editor. Query for nonfiction; submit complete ms for fiction or other work; teacher may submit; parents can also submit their contributions. Submissions should include "cover letter with name, age, address, school, cultural background, inspiration for piece, dreams for future . . . " Will accept typewritten, legibly handwritten and computer/word processor mss. Include SASE. Responds in 3 months. Accepts simultaneous submissions.

Artwork/Photography: Publishes artwork and photography for children. Will review all varieties of ms/illustration packages. Wants comics, cartoons, b&w photos, paintings, drawings (preferably, ink & pen or pencil), 8 × 10, color photos OK. Subjects include children, people, celebrations, nature, ecology, multicultural. Pays in contributor's copies.

Terms: "*Skipping Stones* is a labor of love. No cash payment. You'll receive 1-4 copies (depending on the length of your contribution and illustrations." Reports back to artists in 3 months. Sample copy for $4 and 8½ × 11 SAE with 4 first-class stamps.

Tips: "Let the 'inner child' within you speak out—naturally, uninhibited." Wants "material that gives insight on cultural celebrations, lifestyle, custom and tradition, glimpse of daily life in other countries and cultures. Photos, songs, artwork are most welcome if they illustrate/highlight the points. Upcoming features: kids take on the world, cooperative games and sports, religions and cultures from around the world, death and loss, Spanish-English bilingual issue, Native American cultures, street children, songs and foods from around the world, resource conservation and sustainable lifestyles, indigenous architecture, family, women and young girls in various cultures, celebrations, etc."

SKYLARK, 2200 169th St., Hammond IN 46323. (219)989-2262. Editor: Pamela Hunter. Young Writers' Editor: Shirley Jo Moritz. Annual magazine. Circ. 650-1,000. 15% of material written by juvenile authors. Presently accepting material *by* children. "*Skylark* wishes to provide a vehicle for creative writing of all kinds, especially by writers ages five through eighteen, who live in the Illinois/Indiana area and who have not ordinarily been provided with such an outlet. Children need a place to see their work published alongside that of adults." Proof of originality is required from parents or teachers for all authors. Writer's guidelines available upon request.

Magazines: 15% of magazine written by young people. In previous issues, *Skylark* has published mysteries, fantasy, humor, good narrative fiction stories (400-1,000 words), personal essays, brief character sketches, nonfiction stories (400-650 words), poetry (no more than 16 lines). Does not want to see material that is obviously religious or sexual. Pays in contributor's copies. Submit ms to young writers' editor. Submit complete ms. Prefers typewritten ms. Must include SASE for response or return of material. Reports in 4 months. Byline given.

Artwork/Photography: Publishes artwork and photographs by children. Looks for "photos of animals, landscapes and sports, and for artwork to go along with text." Pays in contributor's copies. All artwork and photos must be b&w, 8½ × 11, unlined paper. Do not use pencil and no copyrighted characters. Markers are advised for best reproduction. Include name and address on the back of each piece. Package properly to avoid damage. Submit artwork/photos to Pamela Hunter, editor-in-chief. Include SASE. Reports in 5 months.

Tips: "Follow your feelings, be as original as you can and don't be afraid to be different. Some of our children or perhaps their teachers and parents don't understand that a SASE must accompany the submission in order to get a response or reply."

SNAKE RIVER REFLECTIONS, 1863 Bitterroot Dr., Twin Falls ID 83301. (208)734-0746. E-mail: wjan@aol.com. Newsletter. Publishes 10 times/year (not published in October or December). Proof of originality required with submissions. Guidelines available on request.

Magazines: 5% of magazine's poems written by children. Uses poetry (30 lines maximum). Pays in copies only. Submit mss to William White, editor. Submit complete ms. Will accept typewritten and legibly handwritten mss. #10 SASE. Reports in 1 month.

THE SOW'S EAR POETRY REVIEW, 19535 Pleasant View Dr., Abingdon VA 24211-6827. (703)628-2651. Magazine published quarterly. "Our editorial philosophy is to serve contemporary literature by publishing the best poetry we can find. Our audience includes serious poets throughout the US. We publish school-aged poets in most issues to encourage young writers and to show our older audience that able young poets are writing. We request young poets to furnish age, grade, school and list of any previous publication." Writer's guidelines available for SASE.

Magazines: 3% of magazine written by children. Uses 2-3 poems (1 page) per issue. Pays 1 copy. Submit complete ms. Will accept typewritten, legibly handwritten mss. SASE. Reports in 6 months.
Artwork/Photography: Publishes artwork and photographs by children "very rarely." "Prefer b&w line drawings or photographs. Any subject or size that may be easily reduced or enlarged." Pays 1 copy. Submit artwork to Mary Calhoun, graphics editor. SASE. Reports in 4 months.

SPRING TIDES, 824 Stillwood Dr., Savannah GA 31419. (912)925-8800. Annual magazine. Audience consists of children 5-12 years old. Purpose in publishing works by young people: To encourage writing. Requirements to be met before work is published: must be 5-12 years old. Writers guidelines available on request.
Magazines: 100% of magazine written by young people. Uses 5-6 fiction stories (1,200 words maximum), autobiographical experiences (1,200 words maximum), 15-20 poems (20 lines maximum) per issue. Writers are not paid. Submit complete ms or teacher may submit. Will accept typewritten mss. SASE.
Artwork: Publishes artwork by children. "We have so far used only local children's artwork because of the complications of keeping and returning pieces."

STONE SOUP, The Magazine by Young Writers and Artists, Children's Art Foundation, P.O. Box 83, Santa Cruz CA 95063. (408)426-5557. Articles/Fiction Editor, Art Director: Ms. Gerry Mandel. Magazine published 5 times/year. Circ. 20,000. "We publish fiction, poetry and artwork by children through age 13. Our preference is for work based on personal experiences and close observation of the world." Purpose in publishing works by young people: to encourage children to read and to express themselves through writing and art. Writer's guidelines available upon request.
Magazines: Uses animal, contemporary, fantasy, history, problem-solving, science fiction, sports, spy/mystery/adventure fiction stories. Uses 5-10 fiction stories (100-2,500 words), 5-10 nonfiction stories (100-2,500 words), 2-4 poems per issue. Does not want to see classroom assignments and formula writing. Buys 65 mss/year. Byline given. Pays on acceptance. Buys all rights. Pays $10 each for stories and poems, $15 for book reviews. Contributors also receive 2 copies. Sample copy $2. Free writer's guidelines. "We don't publish straight nonfiction, but we do publish stories based on real events and experiences." Send complete ms. Will accept typewritten and legibly handwritten mss. Include SASE. Reports in 1 month.
Artwork/Photography: Publishes any type, size or color artwork/photos by children. Pays $8 for b&w illustrations. Contributors receive 2 copies. Sample copy $2. Free illustrator's guidelines. Send originals if possible. Include SASE. Reports in 1 month. Original artwork returned at job's completion. All artwork must be by children through age 13.

***STONEFLOWER LITERARY JOURNAL**, 326 Lands End, Rockport TX 78382-9770. Magazine. Published annually. "We publish quality fiction and poetry with a section for children to age 16, which includes pen & ink and pencil drawings and b&w photography. Ours is a general reading audience with literary taste for good writing." Purpose in publishing works by young people: to encourage good writing and art among youth and to provide an outlet for their creative efforts. Submissions will be reviewed according to age group (i.e., work submitted by a child of 10 will only be compared to works by other children in his/her general age group and not to works by 16-year-olds, for example). If possible, manuscripts should be typewritten. However, handwritten or printed submissions will be considered if legibly written. "We consider: poems to 25 lines; stories to 1,000 words; and pen & ink or pencil drawings. To teachers: if you organize a school project of submissions and want the mss or artwork returned, one SASE large enough to hold all mss or artwork is acceptable. All submissions should have the name, address, age, school attending, and grade clearly written on the top of all mss and on the back of art work. Submit a separate biographical page. The student's name should appear in the upper left corner of the 'bio.' Hobbies, participation in other school programs and activities, prior publications or honors, favorite pastimes, plans for the future, etc., should be included in the bio." Writer's guidelines available for SASE.
Magazine: 10% of magazine written by young people. Averages 2 fiction stories/issue (1,000 words), 5-10 poems/issue (25 lines). Pays $5/short story; $2/poem; $5/artwork or photo. Submit mss to Brenda Davidson-Shaddox, editor. Submit complete fiction mss, poetry and art/photos.

May submit as class project: fiction, poetry and art/photos. Will accept typewritten and legibly handwritten mss. Include SASE. Reports in up to 3 months.
Artwork/Photography: Publishes pen & ink and pencil artwork and b&w photography. Looks for any subject except pornography. Pen & ink and pencil drawings (or top quality copies); 8½×11, no larger. Black & white photos. Pays $5/item. Submit to Brenda Davidson-Shaddox, editor. Include SASE. Reports in up to 3 months.
Tips: "Submit quality work, clean and neat, shorter writing gets preference but only if of high standard. Keep copies of all submissions. We cannot be responsible for losses. Pay attention to guidelines and always include SASE. Send bio according to guidelines."

STRAIGHT, Standard Publishing, 8121 Hamilton Ave., Cincinnati OH 45231. (513)931-4050. Magazine published weekly. Estab. 1951. Magazine includes fiction pieces and articles for Christian teens 13-19 years old to inform, encourage and uplift them. Purpose in publishing works by young people: to provide them with an opportunity to express themselves. Children must submit their birth dates and Social Security numbers (if they have one). Writer's guidelines available on request, "included in regular guidelines."
Magazines: 15% of magazine written by children. Uses fiction (500-1,000 words), personal experience pieces (500-700 words), poetry (approximately 1 poem per issue). Pays flat fee for poetry; 5¢/word for stories/articles. Submit mss to Carla J. Crane, editor. Submit complete ms. Will accept typewritten and computer printout mss. Reports in 1-2 months.

TEXAS HISTORIAN, Texas State Historical Association, 2/306 Sid Richardson Hall, University Station, Austin TX 78712. (512)471-1525. Articles Editor: David De Boe. Magazine published 4 times a year in February, May, September and November. "The *Texas Historian* is the official publication of the Junior Historians of Texas. Articles accepted for publication must be written by members of the Junior Historians of Texas."
Magazines: Uses history articles aimed at young adults (about 2,500 words). Does not accept unsolicited mss.

***TEXAS YOUNG WRITERS' NEWSLETTER**, P.O. Box 942, Adkins TX 78101-0942. E-mail: tywn1@aol.com. Newsletter. Published bimonthly during school year, monthly during summer. Our audience is young writers 12-19, their teachers and their parents. Purpose in publishing works by young people: to give them an opportunity to publish their work in a reputable publication along with other talented young writers, and to show them that they can be published authors. Children must be 12-19 years old. "We do send a form for them to sign after their work is accepted that states that their work is original." Writer's guidelines available on request.
Magazines: 50% of magazine written by young people. Uses 1 fiction story (400-800 words) or 1 opinionated essay, personal experience, etc. (400-800 words), 2 poems (maximum 30 lines) per issue. "Very experienced young writers may submit articles discussing the art and business of writing; relate experience in cover letter." Pays 5 copies for stories, essays and articles; two copies for poetry. Submit mss to Susan Currie, editor. Submit fiction, nonfiction, poetry mss on disk, over e-mail. Will accept typewritten ms. Include SASE. Reports in 3 weeks.
Artwork: "Does not currently publish artwork by children, but we may in future! Write for current information."
Tips: "Be persistent and careful in your submissions! Keep trying until you've published. We also need articles on the art and business of writing from adults. Send SASE for guidelines. We appreciate cover letters!"

THUMBPRINTS, 928 Gibbs St., Caro MI 48723. (517)673-6653. Newsletter. Published monthly. "Our newsletter is designed to be of interest to writers and allow writers a place to obtain a byline." Purpose in publishing works by children: to encourage them to seek publication. Statement of originality required. Writer's guidelines available on request, "same guidelines as for adults."
Newsletters: Percentage of newsletter written by children "varies from month to month." Pays in copies. Submit ms to Janet Ihle, editor. Submit complete ms or have teacher submit. Will accept typewritten and computer printout mss. Reports in 6-8 weeks.
Artwork: Publishes artwork by children. Looks for art that expresses our monthly theme. Pays in copies. Send pencil or ink line drawings no larger than 3×4. Submit artwork to Janet Ihle, editor. SASE. Reports in 3 months.

Tips: "We look forward to well written articles and poems by children. It's encouraging to all writers when children write and are published."

TURTLE MAGAZINE, Children's Better Health Institute, 1100 Waterway Blvd., P.O. Box 567, Indianapolis IN 46206. (317)636-8881. Magazine. "*Turtle* is a health-related magazine geared toward children from ages 2-5." Purpose in publishing works by young people: "We enjoy giving children the opportunity to exercise their creativity." Publishes artwork or pictures that children ages 2-5 have drawn or colored all by themselves. Writer's guidelines available on request.
Artwork: Publishes artwork by children. There is no payment for children's artwork. All artwork must have the child's name, age and complete address on it. Submit artwork to Nancy Axelrad, editor. "No artwork can be returned."

***TWISTED TEEN PUBLISHING CO.**, 5998 Taylor Rd., Painesville OH 44077-9157. (216)254-4410. E-mail: repsisk@aol.com. Book, magazine, newsletter. Publishes at least 3 times/year. Audience consists mostly of teens, although intended for the whole spectrum of readers. Purpose in publishing works by young people: to foster young talent and provide a distributor to all who choose assistance. "A signed statement certifying originality of work and rights granted to Twisted Teen for publication." Writer's guidelines available on request.
Books: Publishes all types of fiction; all types of nonfiction; all types of poetry, comic books. Length: 28,000-47,600 words for fiction; 28,000-47,600 words for nonfiction; 10-1,000 words or 3-70 lines for poetry; 28,000-47,600 words for other. Pays percentage of profits. Submit to Peter Kowalke, president. Query for fiction, nonfiction and poetry; submit complete mss for comic book scripts. Will accept typewritten and legibly handwritten mss. Include SASE. Reports in 2 months.
Artwork: Publishes artwork and photography by children. Open to inclusion of artwork or photographs provided by author of a Twisted Teen book. Please do not bend or fold art or photography submissions. Submit to Peter Kowalke, president. Include SASE. Reports in 2 months.
Tips: "Practice what you love. Work, live, think nothing but your art. Writers and artists of all natures should contact Twisted Teen Publishing Co. to be entered in our database. If a project arises, we can then contact them for work. *Or* children may come to us with publishing ideas, most of which we will publish."

TYKETOON YOUNG AUTHOR PUBLISHING COMPANY, 7417 Douglas Lane, Fort Worth TX 76180. (817)581-2876. Picture Books. Publishes 8 books/year by children only. "We only want picture books written and illustrated by elementary and middle school students (6-14 year-olds). Our audience should be the same age readers as the author and above. Purpose in publishing works by young people: "1) Provide incentives to write; 2) Publish books that are models of good writing and illustrating; 3) Publish teaching tools and guides, making teaching picture book writing easy." Must be ages 6-14. Writer's/illustrator's guidelines available for SASE.

- To learn more about Tyketoon, see Insider Report with Marty Kusmierski in the 1995 edition of *Children's Writer's & Illustrator's Market.*

Books: Publishes all types of fiction and nonfiction. Publishes poetry in book format with illustrations—one author's collection of poetry or a collaboration from two or more authors (same age level). Word length: under 5,000. Pays scholarship check. Submit mss to Ms. Marty Kusmierski, publisher. Submit complete ms with SASE to receive a personal critique of the work. Will accept typewritten and legibly handwritten mss or any readable format. Reports in 3 months.

VIRGINIA WRITING, Longwood College, 201 High St., Farmville VA 23909. (804)395-2160. Magazine published twice yearly. "*Virginia Writing* publishes prose, poetry, fiction, nonfiction, art, photography, music and drama from Virginia high school students and teachers. The purpose of the journal is to publish 'promise.' The children must be attending a Virginia high school, preferably in no less than 9th grade (though some work has been accepted from 8th graders). Originality is strongly encouraged. The guidelines are in the front of our magazine or available with SASE." No profanity or racism accepted.

- *Virginia Writing* is the recipient of 12 national awards, including eight Distinguished Achievement Awards for Excellence in Educational Journalism and the Golden Lamp Honor Award as one of the top four educational magazines in the U.S. and Canada.

Magazines: 85% of magazine written by children. Uses approximately 5 fiction and nonfiction short stories, 56 poems and prose pieces per issue. Submit mss to Billy C. Clark, founder and editor. Submit complete ms. Will accept typewritten mss. Reports as soon as possible, "but must include SASE to receive a reply in the event ms is not accepted."
Artwork: Publishes artwork by children. Considers all types of artwork, including that done on computer. Color slides of artwork are acceptable. All original work is returned upon publication in a non-bendable, well protected package. Submit artwork to Billy C. Clark. Reports as soon as possible.
Tips: "All works should be submitted with a cover letter describing student's age, grade and high school currently attending."

WHOLE NOTES, P.O. Box 1374, Las Cruces NM 88004. (505)382-7446. Magazine published twice yearly. "We look for original, fresh perceptions in poems that demonstrate skill in using language effectively, with carefully chosen images, clear ideas and fresh perceptions. Our audience (general) loves poetry. We try to recognize excellence in creative writing by children as a way to encourage and promote imaginative thinking." Writer's guidelines available for SASE.
Magazines: Every fourth issue is 100% by children. Writers should be 21 years old or younger. Uses 30 poems/issue (length open). Pays complimentary copy. Submit mss to Nancy Peters Hastings, editor. Submit complete ms. "No multiple submissions, please." Will accept typewritten and legibly handwritten mss. SASE. Reports in 3 weeks.
Artwork/Photography: Publishes artwork and photographs by children. Looks for b&w line drawings which can easily be reproduced; b&w photos. Pays complimentary copy. Send clear photocopies. Submit artwork to Nancy Peters Hastings, editor. SASE. Reports in 3 weeks.
Tips: Sample issue is $3. "We welcome translations."

WOMBAT: A Journal of Young People's Writing and Art, 365 Ashton Dr., Athens GA 30606. (706)549-4875. Published 4 times a year. "Illiteracy in a free society is an unnecessary danger which can and must be remedied. *Wombat*, by being available to young people and their parents and teachers, is one small incentive for young people to put forth the effort to learn to read and write (and draw) better, to communicate better, to comprehend better and—hopefully—consequently, to someday possess greater discernment, judgment and wisdom as a result." Purpose in publishing works by young people: to serve as an incentive, to encourage them to work hard at their reading, writing and—yes—drawing/art skills, to reward their efforts. Writers must be ages 6-16, from any geographic region and include a statement that work is original.

- According to its publisher, "*Wombat* is, unfortunately, on 'hold' probably throughout this entire school year; therefore, we are asking people to query as to when/if we will resume publication, before subscribing or submitting works to *Wombat* right now."

Magazines: 95% of magazine written by children. Have one 2-4 page "Guest Adult Article" in most issues/when available (submitted). Uses poetry; any fiction (3,000 words maximum; shorter preferred) but avoid extreme violence, religion or explicit sex; any nonfiction of interest to 6-16 year olds (3,000-4,000 words); cartoons, puzzles and solutions, jokes, games and solutions. Pays in copies and frameable certificates. Submit mss to Jacquelin Howe, publisher. Submit complete ms. Teacher can submit; parents, librarians, students can submit. Will accept typewritten, legibly handwritten, computer printout mss. Responds in 1-2 weeks with SASE; up to 1 year with seasonal or holiday works (past season or holiday). Written work is not returned. SASE permits *Wombat* to notify sender of receipt of work.
Artwork: Publishes artwork by children. Looks for works on paper, not canvas. Photocopies OK if clear and/or reworked for clarity and strong line definition by the artist. Pays in copies and frameable certificates. Submit artwork to Jacquelin Howe, publisher. "Artwork, only, will be returned if requested and accompanied by appropriate sized envelope, stamped with sufficient postage."

WORD DANCE, Playful Productions, Inc., 59 Pavilions Dr., Manchester CT 06040. (203)648-2388. Magazine. Published quarterly. "We're a magazine of creative writing and art that is for *and* by children in kindergarten through grade 8."
Magazines: Uses adventure, fantasy, humorous, etc. (fiction); travel stories, poems and stories based on real life experiences (nonfiction). Publishes 250 total pieces of writing/year; maximum length: 3 pages. Submit mss to Stuart Ungar, articles editor. Sample copy $3. Free writer's guidelines and submissions form. SASE. Reports in 6-8 months.

INSIDER REPORT

Good Writing Reaps Rewards for Teens

Writes of Passage is an unusual literary journal created for purely altruistic purposes. Published solely to encourage writers, this biannual magazine is more than a collection of poems, short stories and personal essays. The writing is poignant and the topics universal—embarrassment, apprehension, love and loss, even death. The writers are remarkably skilled and unabashedly frank. But what distinguishes them is their age—they are teenagers.

Wendy Mass

WP is the brainchild of Wendy Mass, also editor of children's books at Readers Digest Young Families, and longtime friend Laura Hoffman, now the journal's president/publisher. After completing her master's degree in creative writing and spending a few years in the publishing business, Mass noticed a lack of material in the teenage literary market. At the same time, more teens were expressing an interest in writing. "Creative writing programs are really hot in the schools right now," Mass says.

The response to the first issue of *Writes of Passage* two years ago was "overwhelming," says Mass. Although there are other magazines that publish work by teens, "there's nothing that looks like a literary journal." More important, *WP* provides the opportunity for young writers (ages 12-18) to tackle any topic. From the outset, "we decided that we weren't going to censor," she says. In fact, the philosophy behind *Writes of Passage* is clearly stated in the journal's promotional material: "It may make your parents cringe and your teacher blush, but your best friend will understand."

Mass and Hoffman are "out there to give kids the confidence to keep writing." Although they frequently wade through stacks of submissions, most of them poems, they promise that "if you've written something really good, it's going to get published. If we get something great, we'll get it in. . . . We'll make room." Many of the submissions to *WP* are part of school projects, and they try to publish at least one piece from each group.

What catches their eye? "Something that's different, that makes you think, even if it's a little amateurish . . . something special." Mass notes that short stories are scarce, and she'd like to see more of them. As an incentive, each issue includes a new chapter of a novel in progress. Writers are encouraged to continue the story—no restrictions apply—and submit their manuscripts for consideration. She will consider personal essays if they're "from the heart."

Mass's belief in encouraging young writers is so strong that she and Hoffman developed Writes of Passage USA, Inc., as a nonprofit educational organization. "We want to expand, have a bigger print run, and we'd like to give the journals out for free," says Mass. *WP* is in some bookstores, and many teachers, schools and teenagers subscribe.

To those novice writers who welcome the opportunity *Writes of Passage* provides, Mass offers some simple advice: "Let your guard down and write from the heart. . . . A writer is someone who writes every day." Keep a journal, and "read, read, read!" Also, check out the competition.

Her words echo those of Hayley R. Mitchell, a poet and editor whose guest column on getting published appears in the second issue of *WP*. She writes, "Check out the journal section in some of the better bookstores in your area and read the magazines that publish work by writers in your age-group. Take a trip to your public library. In the reference section you'll hopefully find current editions of *Novel & Short Story Writer's Market* and *Poet's Market*." Check the indexes for journals that publish work by young adults.

Also, computer services like America Online provide reference material and contact with other writers. Check out the writing "rooms" where you can network with freelance writers.

When you're ready to submit your piece, make sure your full name, phone number and address appear on everything, from the envelope to each page of the manuscript. Also, send a SASE to ensure a response. You may collect many rejection letters before receiving an acceptance, but if your research is thorough and your writing is first-class, your persistence will reap rewards.

The introduction of the premiere issue of *Writes of Passage* sums up Mass's and Hoffman's thoughts on writing. "We race against time, make it, take it, save it and waste it, but however hard we might try, we can never stop it. But there is one thing writers can do—CAPTURE it." Don't waste time waiting for your twenty-first birthday. If you want to write, do it. If your writing is good, it'll get published.

—*Jennifer Hogan-Redmond*

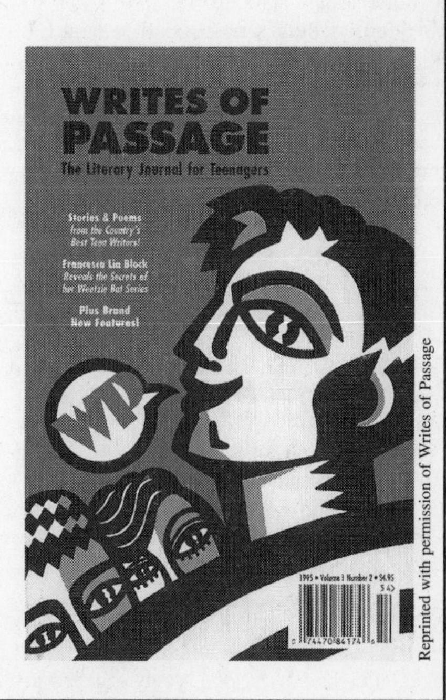

Reprinted with permission of Writes of Passage

Writes of Passage, The Literary Journal for Teens *showcases poems and stories by high-school-age writers from around the country, and includes a section of bios on the young contributors. This sophomore edition features a glossy cover and added inside design elements, as well as new features.*

Artwork: Illustrations accepted from young people in kindergarten through grade 8. Accepts illustrations of specific stories or poems and other general artwork. Must be high contrast. Query. Submit complete package with final art to Melissa Shapiro, art director. SASE. Reports in 6-8 months.

***THE WRITE NEWS, Newsletter of the Young Writers Club**, P.O. Box 5504, Coralville IA 52241. E-mail: kidsclubs@aol.com. Newsletter. Published 6 times/year. *The Write News* caters to members of the Young Writers Club (kids ages 7 to 13). The newsletter provides a forum where these aspiring writers can learn about writing and publishing, enter writing contests, and learn from other young writers. Purpose in publishing works by young people: "We are dedicated to guiding and encouraging young writers—the best way to do this is by letting them try their wings in an environment that is safe and supportive. By publishing the work of young writers we are showing them that they have the skills and know-how to grow into adult writers." To be eligible for publication in *The Write News* a child must be between the ages of 7 and 13 and must also be a member of the Young Writers Club. (Membership includes club ID card, membership certificate, club pencil and subscription to *The Write News*. Membership dues are $12.95 per year.) "Guidelines" appear in each issue of *The Write News* as calls for submissions and contest rules, etc.
Magazines: Usually 40% of magazine written by young people. "We welcome all types of manuscripts." Submit mss to *The Write News*. Will accept typewritten and legibly handwritten mss. "We encourage kids to send in photos of themselves when submitting their work. School photos are preferred." Include SASE (is you want ms back).
Tips: "Your voice is as important as those of adults. Use it to write stories, songs, poems, etc. about the things that are important to you. Once you've written something you're proud of, try to get it published. Ask your parents or teachers for help. And don't get discouraged if you're not successful. Some writers take years to get published!"

WRITER'S INTERNATIONAL FORUM, (formerly *Writer's Open Forum*), P.O. Box 516, Tracyton WA 98393. Magazine published bimonthly. Purpose in publishing works by young people: to promote an understanding of tight and clean traditional short story writing; this basis will serve young writers well as they and their writing matures. Our international readership offers a wide scope of opinions and helpful tips. Guidelines available on request; same as for adults, however. Please state age in cover letter.
Magazines: Publishes Special Juniors Edition at least once per year, featuring all stories and essays written either *by* children (50% of the issue) or *for* children. Also prints 1 or 2 stories (15% of issues) in each standard issue written by children. Uses up to 12 fiction short stories, any genre (400-2,000 words); 4 essays (under 1,200 words) per issue. Pays $5 minimum on acceptance. Submit mss to Sandra E. Haven, editorial director. Submit complete ms with cover letter stating author's age. Will accept typewritten mss. Please send SASE for full guidelines *before* submitting. Reports in 2 months.

THE WRITERS' SLATE, The Writing Conference, Inc., P.O. Box 664, Ottawa KS 66067. (913)242-0407. Magazine. Publishes 3 issues/year. *The Writers' Slate* accepts original poetry and prose from students enrolled in Kindergarten-12th grade. The audience is students, teachers and librarians. Purpose in publishing works by young people: to give students the opportunity to publish and to give students the opportunity *to read* quality literature written by other students. Writer's guidelines available on request.
Magazines: 90% of magazine written by young people. Uses 10-15 fiction, 1-2 nonfiction, 10-15 other mss per issue. Submit mss to Dr. F. Todd Goodson, editor, Dept. of English, East Carolina University, Greenville NC 27858-4353. Submit complete ms. Will accept typewritten mss. Reports in 1 month. Include SASE with ms if reply is desired.
Artwork: Publishes artwork by young people. Bold, b&w, student artwork may accompany a piece of writing. Submit to Dr. F. Todd Goodson, editor. Reports in 1 month.

WRITES OF PASSAGE, 817 Broadway, 6th Floor, New York NY 10003. (212)473-7564. Journal. Publishes 2 issues/year by children (spring/summer and fall/winter). "Our philosophy: 'It may make your parents cringe, your teacher blush, but your best friend will understand.' " Purpose in publishing works by young people: to give teenagers across the country a chance to express

themselves through creative writing. Writers must be 12-18 years old, work must be original, short biography should be included.
Magazines: Uses short stories (up to 4 double-spaced pages) and poetry. Pays in two copies. Will accept typewritten and legibly handwritten mss. SASE. Reports in 2 months. Sample copies available for $6. Writer's guidelines for SASE.
Tips: "We began *Writes of Passage* to encourage teenage reading and writing as fun and desirable forms of expression and to establish an open dialogue between teenagers in every state. Our selection process does not censor topics and presents submissions according to the authors' intentions. It gives teens an opportunity to expand on what they have learned in reading and writing classes in school by opening up a world of writing in which they can be free. As a result, submissions often reveal a surprising candidness on the part of the authors, including topics such as love, fear, struggle and death and they expose the diverse backgrounds of contributors."

WRITING!, 60 Revere Drive, Northbrook IL 60062. (708)205-3000. Magazine published monthly September-May. Purpose in publishing work by young people: "to teach students to write and write well; grades 6-12. *Writing!* prints well-written, creative, and original writing by students to inspire other students. Should indicate age, address, school and teacher with submission. No formal guidelines; but letter is sent if request received."
Magazines: Small percentage of magazine written by children. Uses 1-10 mss/issue. No pay for student writing. Submit mss to Carol Elliott, editor. Submit complete ms; include student's age, address, school and teacher with submission; either child or child's teacher may submit. Prefers typewritten mss. Include SASE.

YOUNG VOICES MAGAZINE, P.O. Box 2321, Olympia WA 98507. (360)357-4683. E-mail: scharak@aol.com. Magazine published bimonthly. "*Young Voices* is by elementary and high school students for people interested in their work." Purpose in publishing work by young people: to provide a forum for their creative work. "Home schooled writers *definitely* welcome, too." Writer's guidelines available on request with SASE.
Magazines: Uses 20 fiction stories, 5 reviews, 5 essays and 5 poems per issue (lengths vary). Pays $3-5 on acceptance (more depending on the length and quality of the writing). Submit mss to Steve Charak. Query first. Will accept typewritten and legibly handwritten mss. SASE. Reports in 2 months.
Artwork/Photography: Publishes artwork and photography by children. "Prefer work that will show up in black and white; anything but tanks and horses." Pays $3-5 on acceptance. Submit artwork to Steve Charak. Include SASE. Reports in 2 months.

Young Writer's & Illustrator's/'95-'96 changes

The following markets were included in the 1995 edition of *Children's Writer's & Illustrator's Market* but do not have listings in this edition. The majority did not respond to our request to update their listings. If a reason was given for exclusion, it appears in parentheses after the market's name.

KidsArt (per request)
Kopper Bear Press
The Magazine for Christian
Youth! (ceased publication)
National Geographic World
The Pikestaff Forum
Poem Train
Voices of Youth

Contests & Awards

Publication is not the only way to get your work recognized. Contests can also be viable vehicles to gain recognition in the industry. Placing in a contest or winning an award validates the time spent writing and illustrating. Even for those who don't place, many competitions offer the chance to obtain valuable feedback from judges and other established writers or artists.

Not all of the contests here are strictly for professionals. Many are designed for "amateurs" who have not yet been published. And many of the contests in this section are open to students (some of them exclusively). Young writers and illustrators will find all contests open to students marked with a double dagger (‡). Young writers can find additional contests in *Market Guide for Young Writers*, by Kathy Henderson (Betterway Books).

When considering contests, be sure to study guidelines and requirements. Regard entry deadlines as gospel and note whether manuscripts and artwork should be previously published or unpublished. Also, be aware that awards vary. While one contest may award a significant monetary amount, another may award a certificate or medal instead.

Note that some contests require nominations. For published authors and illustrators, competitions provide an excellent way to promote one's work. If your book is eligible for a contest or award, have the appropriate people at your publishing company nominate or enter your work for consideration. Then make sure enough copies of your book are sent to contest judges and others who must see it.

To select potential contests for your work, read through the listings that interest you, then send for more information about the types of written or illustrated material considered and other important details such as who retains the rights to prize-winning material. If you are interested in knowing who has received certain awards in the past, check your local library or bookstores. Many bookstores have special sections for books which are Caldecott and Newbery Award winners.

‡AIM Magazine Short Story Contest, P.O. Box 20554, Chicago IL 60620. (312)874-6184. Contest Directors: Ruth Apilado, Mark Boone. Annual contest. Estab. 1983. Purpose of contest: "We solicit stories with social significance. Youngsters can be made aware of social problems through the written word and hopefully they will try solving them." Unpublished submissions only. Deadline for entries: August 15. SASE for contest rules and entry forms. SASE for return of work. No entry fee. Awards $100. Judging by editors. Contest open to everyone. Winning entry published in fall issue of *AIM*. Subscription rate $10/year. Single copy $4.

***‡🍁ALCUIN CITATION AWARD**, The Alcuin Society, P.O. Box 3216, Vancouver, British Columbia V6B 3X8 Canada. Phone/fax: (604)888-9049. Secretary: Doreen E. Eddy. Annual award. Estab. 1983. Purpose of contest: Alcuin Citations are awarded annually for excellence in Canadian book design. Previously published submissions only, "in the year prior to the Awards Invitation to enter; i.e. 1995 awards went to books published in 1994." Submissions made by the author, publishers and designers. Deadline for entries: March 15. SASE. Entry fee is $10. Awards certificate. Judging by professionals and those experienced in the field of book design. Requirements for entrants: Winners are selected from books designed and published in Canada.

Awards are presented annually at the Annual General Meeting of the Alcuin Society held in late May or early June each year.

‡AMERICA & ME ESSAY CONTEST, Farm Bureau Insurance, Box 30400, 7373 W. Saginaw, Lansing MI 48909. (517)323-7000. Contest Coordinator: Lisa Fedewa. Annual contest. Estab. 1968. Purpose of the contest: to give Michigan 8th graders the opportunity to express their thoughts/feelings on America and their roles in America. Unpublished submissions only. Deadline for entries: mid-November. SASE for contest rules and entry forms. "We have a school mailing list. Any school located in Michigan is eligible to participate." Entries not returned. No entry fee. Awards savings bonds and plaques for state top ten ($500-1,000), certificates and plaques for top 3 winners from each school. Judging by home office employee volunteers. Requirements for entrants: "Participants must work through their schools or our agents' sponsoring schools. No individual submissions will be accepted. Top ten essays and excerpts from other essays are published in booklet form following the contest. State capital/schools receive copies."

***AMERICAS AWARD**, Consortium of Latin American Studies Programs (CLASP), CLASP Committee on K-12 Outreach, % Center for Latin America, University of Wisconsin-Milwaukee, P.O. Box 413, Milwaukee WI 53201. (414)229-5986. Fax: (414)229-2879. E-mail address: cla@csd.uwm.edu. Chairperson: Julie Kline. Annual award. Estab. 1993. Purpose of contest: "The award is given in recognition of a recent U.S. published work of fiction, poetry or folklore (from picture books to works for young adults) in English or Spanish which authentically and engagingly presents the experience of individuals in Latin America or the Caribbean, or of Latinos in the United States. By combining both and linking the "Americas," our intent is to go beyond geographic borders, as well as multicultural-international boundaries, focusing instead upon cultural heritages within the hemisphere." Previously published submissions only. Submissions open to anyone with an interest in the theme of the award. Must be published previous calendar year. Deadline for entries: January 15. SASE for contest rules and entry forms. Awards $200 cash prize, plaque and a formal presentation tentatively scheduled at the Library of Congress, Washington DC. Judging by a review committee consisting of individuals in teaching, library work, outreach and children's literature specialists.

‡AMHA LITERARY CONTEST, American Morgan Horse Association Youth, P.O. Box 960, Shelburne VT 05482. (802)985-4944. Contest Director: Erica Richard. Annual contest. The contest includes categories for both poetry and essays. The 1994 theme was "Olympic Size Morgan Dreams." Entrants should write to receive the 1995 entry form and theme. Unpublished submissions only. Submissions made by author. Deadline for entries: December 1. SASE for contest rules and entry forms. No entry fee. Awards $50 cash and ribbons to up to 5th place. "Winning entry will be published in *AMHA News and Morgan Sales Network*, a monthly publication."

‡AMHA MORGAN ART CONTEST, American Morgan Horse Association, Box 960, Shelburne VT 05482. (802)985-4944. Promotional Recognition Coordinator: Susan Bell. Annual contest. The art contest consists of three categories: Morgan art (pencil sketches, oils, water colors, paintbrush), Morgan cartoons, Morgan specialty pieces (sculptures, carvings). Unpublished submissions only. Deadline for entries: December 1. Contest rules and entry forms available for SASE. Entries not returned. Entry fee is $2. Awards $50 first prize in 3 divisions (for adults) and AMHA gift certificates to top 5 places (for children). Judging by *The Morgan Horse* magazine staff. "All work submitted becomes property of The American Morgan Horse Association. Selected works may be used for promotional purposes by the AMHA." Requirements for entrants: "We consider all work submitted." Works displayed at the annual convention and the AMHA headquarters; published in *AMAHA News* and *Morgan Sales Network*. The contest divisions consist of Junior (to age 17), Senior (18 and over) and Professional (commercial artists). Each art piece must have its own application form and its own entry fee. Matting is optional.

The maple leaf before a listing indicates that the market is Canadian.

***HANS CHRISTIAN ANDERSEN AWARD**, IBBY International Board on Books for Young People, Nonnenweg 12, Postfach, CH-4003 Switzerland. (004161)272 29 17. Fax: (004161)272 27 57. Award offered every 2 years. Purpose of award: A Hans Christian Andersen Medal shall be awarded every 2 years by the International Board on Books for Young People (IBBY) to an author and to an illustrator, living at the time of the nomination, who by the outstanding value of their work are judged to have made a lasting contribution to literature for children and young people. The complete works of the author and of the illustrator will be taken into consideration in awarding the medal, which will be accompanied by a diploma. Previously published submissions only. Submissions are nominated by national sections of IBBY in good standing. Contact the secretariat of IBBY for contest rules and entry forms. The Hans Christian Andersen Award, named after Denmark's famous storyteller, is the highest international recognition given to an author and an illustrator of children's books. The Author's Award has been given since 1956, the Illustrator's Award since 1966. The Andersen Award is often called the "Little Nobel Prize." Her Majesty Queen Margrethe of Denmark is the Patron of the Hans Christian Andersen Awards. At the discretion of the jury the distinction "Highly Commended" may also be awarded. The Hans Christian Andersen Jury judges the books submitted for medals according to literary and artistic criteria.

‡ARTS RECOGNITION AND TALENT SEARCH (ARTS), National Foundation for Advancement in the Arts, 800 Brickell Ave., Suite 500, Miami FL 33131. (305)377-1140. Fax: (305)377-1149. Contact: Sherry Thompson. Open to students/high school seniors or 17- and 18-year-olds. Annual award. Estab. 1981. "Created to recognize and reward outstanding accomplishment in dance, music, jazz, theater, photography, visual arts and/or writing. Arts Recognition and Talent Search (ARTS) is an innovative national program of the National Foundation for Advancement in the Arts (NFAA). Established in 1981, ARTS touches the lives of gifted young people across the country, providing financial support, scholarships and goal-oriented artistic, educational and career opportunities. Each year, from a pool of 5,000-7,500 applicants, an average of 250 ARTS awardees are chosen for NFAA support by panels of distinguished artists and educators. Each ARTS applicant, generally a high school senior, 17-18 years of age, has special talent in music, jazz, dance, theater, visual arts, photography or creative writing." Submissions made by the student. Deadline for entries: June 1 and October 1 (late). SASE for award rules and entry forms. Entry fee is $25/35 (late). Fee waivers available based on need. Awards $100-3,000—unrestricted cash grants. Judging by a panel of authors and educators recognized in the field. Rights to submitted/winning material: NFAA/ARTS retains the right to duplicate work in an anthology or in Foundation literature unless otherwise specified by the artist. Requirements for entrants: Artists must be high school seniors or, if not enrolled in high school, must be 17 or 18 years old. Applicants must be US citizens or residents, unless applying in jazz. Works will be published in an anthology distributed during ARTS Week, the final adjudication phase which takes place in Miami.

‡BAKER'S PLAYS HIGH SCHOOL PLAYWRITING CONTEST, Baker's Plays, 100 Chauncy St., Boston MA 02111. (617)482-1280. Contest Director: Raymond Pape. Annual contest. Estab. 1990. Purpose of the contest: to acknowledge playwrights at the high school level and to insure the future of American theater. Unpublished submissions only. Deadline for entries: January 31 each year. Notification: May. SASE for contest rules and entry forms. No entry fee. Awards $500 to the first place playwright and Baker's Plays will publish the play; $250 to the second place playwright with an honorable mention; and $100 to the third place playwright with an honorable mention in the series. Judged anonymously. Open to any high school student. Teachers must not submit student's work. The first place playwright will have his/her play published in an acting edition the September following the contest. The work will be described in the Baker's Plays Catalogue, which is distributed to 50,000 prospective producing organizations. Plays must be accompanied by the signature of a sponsoring high school drama or English teacher, and it is recommended that the play receive a production or a public reading prior to the submission. Please include a SASE.

MARGARET BARTLE ANNUAL PLAYWRITING AWARD, Community Children's Theatre of Kansas City, 8021 E. 129th Terrace, Grandview MO 64030. (816)761-5775. Chairperson: Blanche Sellens. Annual contest. Estab. 1947. "Community Children's Theatre of Kansas City,

Inc. was organized in 1947 to provide live theater for elementary aged children. We are now recognized as being one of the country's largest organizations providing this type of service." Unpublished submissions only. Deadline for entries: end of January. SASE for award rules and entry forms. SASE for return of entries. No entry fee. Awards $500. Judging by a committee of 5. "CCT reserves the right for one of the units to produce the prize winning play for two years. The plays are performed before students in elementary schools. Although our 5- to 12-year-old audiences are sophisticated, gratuitous violence, mature love stories, or slang are not appropriate—cursing is *not acceptable*. In addition to original ideas, subjects that usually provide good plays are legends, folklore, historical incidents, biographies and adaptations of children's classics."

BAY AREA BOOK REVIEWER'S ASSOCIATION (BABRA), %Chandler & Sharp, 11A Commercial Blvd., Novato CA 94949. (415)883-2353. Fax: (415)883-4280. Contact: Jonathan Sharp. Annual award for outstanding book in children's literature, open to Bay Area authors, northern California from Fresno north. Annual award. Estab. 1981. "BABRA presents annual awards to Bay Area (northern California) authors annually in fiction, nonfiction, poetry and children's literature. Purpose is to encourage Bay Area writers and stimulate interest in books and reading." Previously published submissions only. Must be published the calendar year prior to spring awards ceremony. Submissions nominated by publishers; author or agent could also nominate published work. Deadline for entries: December. No entry forms. Send 3 copies of the book to Jonathan Sharp. No entry fee. Awards $100 honorarium and award certificate. Judging by voting members of the Bay Area Book Reviewer's Association. Books that reach the "finals" (usually 3-5 per category) displayed at annual award ceremonies (spring). Nominated books are displayed and sold at BABRA's annual awards ceremonies, in the spring of each year.

JOHN AND PATRICIA BEATTY AWARD, California Library Association, 717 K. Street Suite 300, Sacramento CA 95814. (916)447-8541. Executive Director: Mary Sue Ferrell. Annual award. Estab. 1987. Purpose of award: "The purpose of the John and Patricia Beatty Award is to encourage the writing of quality children's books highlighting California, its culture, heritage and/or future." Previously published submissions only. Submissions made by the author, author's agent or review copies sent by publisher. The award is given to the author of a children's book published the preceding year. Deadline for entries: Submissions may be made January-December. Contact CLA Executive Director who will liaison with Beatty Award Committee. Awards cash prize of $500 and an engraved plaque. Judging by a 5-member selection committee appointed by the president of the California Library Association. Requirements for entrants: "Any children's or young adult book set in California and published in the U.S. during the calendar year preceding the presentation of the award is eligible for consideration. This includes works of fiction as well as nonfiction for children and young people of all ages. Reprints and compilations are not eligible. The California setting must be depicted authentically and must serve as an integral focus for the book." Winning selection is announced through press release during National Library Week in April. Author is presented with award at annual California Library Association Conference in November.

THE IRMA S. AND JAMES H. BLACK BOOK AWARD, Bank Street College of Education, 610 W. 112th St., New York NY 10025. (212)222-6700. Fax: (212)875-4752. E-mail: lindag@bnk1.bnkst.edu. Contact: Linda Greengrass. Annual award. Estab. 1972. Purpose of award: "The award is given each spring for a book for young children, published in the previous year, for excellence of both text and illustrations." Entries must have been published during the previous calendar year (between January '95 and December '95 for 1995 award). Deadline for entries: January 1. "Publishers submit books to us by sending them here to me at the Bank Street library. Authors may ask their publishers to submit their books. Out of these, three to five books are chosen by a committee of older children and children's literature professionals. These books are

The double dagger before a listing indicates the contest or organization is open to students.

then presented to children in selected second, third and fourth grade classes here and at a few other cooperating schools on the East Coast. These children are the final judges who pick the actual award. A scroll (one each for the author and illustrator, if they're different) with the recipient's name and a gold seal designed by Maurice Sendak are awarded in May."

WALDO M. AND GRACE C. BONDERMAN/IUPUI YOUTH THEATRE PLAYWRITING COMPETITION AND SYMPOSIUM, Indiana University-Purdue University at Indianapolis, 525 N. Blackford St., Indianapolis IN 46202. (317)274-2095. Fax: (317)278-1025. E-mail: wmccrear @indycms.iupui.edu. Director: Dorothy Webb. Entries should be submitted to W. Mark McCreary, Literary Manager. Contest every two years; next competition will be 1996. Estab. 1983. Purpose of the contest: "to encourage writers to create artistic scripts for young audiences. It provides a forum through which each playwright receives constructive criticism of his/her work and, where selected, writers participate in script development with the help of professional dramaturgs, directors and actors." Unpublished submissions only. Submissions made by author. Deadline for entries: September 1, 1996. SASE for contest rules and entry forms. No entry fee. "Awards will be presented to the top ten finalists. Four cash awards of $1,000 each will be received by the top four playwrights whose scripts will be given developmental work culminating in polished readings showcased at the symposium held on the IUPUI campus. This symposium is always held opposite years of the competition. Major publishers of scripts for young audiences, directors, producers, critics and teachers attend this symposium and provide useful reactions to the plays. If a winner is unable to be involved in preparation of the reading and to attend the showcase of his/her work, the prize will not be awarded. Remaining finalists will receive certificates." Judging by professional directors, dramaturgs, publishers, university professors. Write for guidelines and entry form.

✤BOOK OF THE YEAR FOR CHILDREN, Canadian Library Association, 200 Elgin St., Suite 620, Ottawa, Ontario K2P 1L5 Canada. (613)232-9625. Contact: Chairperson, Canadian Association of Children's Librarians. Annual award. Estab. 1947. "The main purpose of the award is to encourage writing and publishing in Canada of good books for children up to and including age 14. If, in any year, no book is deemed to be of award calibre, the award shall not be made that year. To merit consideration, the book must have been published in Canada and its author must be a Canadian citizen or a permanent resident of Canada." Previously published submissions only; must be published between January 1 and December 1 of the previous year. Deadline for entries: January 1. SASE for award rules. Entries not returned. No entry fee. Awards a medal. Judging by committee of members of the Canadian Association of Children's Librarians. Requirements for entrants: Contest open only to Canadian authors or residents of Canada. Winning books are on display at CLA headquarters.

BOOK PUBLISHERS OF TEXAS, Children's/Young People's Award, The Texas Institute of Letters, %TCU Press, P.O. Box 30783, Ft. Worth TX 76129. (817)921-7822. Contact: Judy Alter. Send to above address for list of judges to whom entries should be submitted. Annual award. Purpose of the award: "to recognize notable achievement by a Texas writer of books for children or young people or by a writer whose work deals with a Texas subject. The award goes to the author of the winning book, a work published during the calendar year before the award is given. Judges list available each October. Deadline is first postally operative day of January." Previously published submissions only. SASE for award rules and entry forms. No entry fee. Awards $250. Judging by a panel of 3 judges selected by the TIL Council. Requirements for entrants: The writer must have lived in Texas for 2 consecutive years at some time, or the work must have a Texas theme.

THE BOSTON GLOBE-HORN BOOK AWARDS, The Boston Globe & The Horn Book, Inc., The Horn Book, 11 Beacon St., Suite 1000, Boston MA 02108. (617)227-1555. Award Director: Stephanie Loer. Writing Contact: Stephanie Loer, children's book editor for *The Boston Globe*, 298 North St., Medfield MA 02052. Annual award. Estab. 1967. "Awards are for picture books, nonfiction and fiction. Up to two honor books may be chosen for each category." Books must be published between June 1, 1995 and May 30, 1996. Deadline for entries: May 15. "Publishers usually submit books. Award winners receive $500 and silver engraved bowl, honor book winners receive a silver plate." Judging by 3 judges involved in children's book field who are chosen by the editor-in-chief for The Horn Book, Inc. (*The Horn Book Magazine* and the *Horn Book Guide*) and Stephanie Loer, children's book editor for *The Boston Globe*. "*The Horn Book Magazine* publishes speeches given at awards ceremonies. The book must have been published in the U.S. The awards are given at the fall conference of the New England Library Association."

‡ANN ARLYS BOWLER POETRY CONTEST, *Read* Magazine, 245 Long Hill Rd., Middletown CT 06457. (203)638-2406. Contest Director: Kate Davis. Annual contest. Estab. 1988. Purpose of contest: to reward young-adult poets (grades 4-12). Unpublished submissions only. Submissions made by the author or nominated by a person or group of people. Must include signature of teacher, parent or guardian, and student. Deadline for entries: December 22. SASE for contest rules and entry forms. No entry fee. Awards 6 winners $100 each, medal of honor, letter of recognition from the U.S. Poet Laureate and publication. Semifinalists receive $50 each. Judging by *Read* editorial staff. "Entrant understands that prize will include publication, but sometimes pieces are published in other issues." Requirements for entrants: the material must be original. Winning entries will be published in the April issue of *Read* (all-student issue).

BUCKEYE CHILDREN'S BOOK AWARD, State Library of Ohio, 65 S. Front St., Columbus OH 43215-4163. (614)644-7061. Nancy Short, Chairperson. Correspondence should be sent to Floyd C. Dickman at the above address. Award every two years. Estab. 1981. Purpose of the award: "The Buckeye Children's Book Award Program was designed to encourage children to read literature critically, to promote teacher and librarian involvement in children's literature programs, and to commend authors of such literature, as well as to promote the use of libraries. Awards are presented in the following three categories: grades K-2, grades 3-5 and grades 6-8." Previously published submissions only. Deadline for entries: February 1. "The nominees are submitted by this date during the even year and the votes are submitted by this date during the odd year. This award is nominated and voted upon by children in Ohio. It is based upon criteria established in our bylaws. The winning authors are awarded a special plaque honoring them at a banquet given by one of the sponsoring organizations. The BCBA Board oversees the tallying of the votes and announces the winners in March of the voting year in a special news release and in a number of national journals. The book must have been written by an author, a citizen of the United States and originally copyrighted in the U.S. within the last three years preceding the nomination year. The award-winning books are displayed in a historical display housed at the Columbus Metropolitan Library in Columbus, Ohio."

BYLINE MAGAZINE CONTESTS, P.O. Box 130596, Edmond OK 73013. Contest Director: Marcia Preston. Purpose of contest: *ByLine* runs 4 contests a month on many topics. Past topics include first chapter of a novel, children's fiction, children's poem, nonfiction for children, personal essay, greeting card verse, valentine or love poem, etc. Send SASE for contest flier with topic list. Unpublished submissions only. Submissions made by the author. "We do not publish the contests' winning entries, just the names of the winners." SASE for contest rules and entry forms. Entry fee is $3-4. Awards cash prizes for first, second and third place. Amounts vary. Judging by qualified writers or editors. List of winners will appear in magazine.

RANDOLPH CALDECOTT MEDAL, Association for Library Service to Children, Division of the American Library Association, 50 E. Huron, Chicago IL 60611. (312)280-2163. Executive Director ALSC: Susan Roman. Annual award. Estab. 1938. Purpose of the award: to honor the artist of the most distinguished picture book for children published in the US (Illustrator must be US citizen or resident.) Must be published year preceding award. Deadline for entries: December. SASE for award rules and entry forms. Entries not returned. No entry fee. "Medal given at ALA Annual Conference during the Newbery/Caldecott Banquet."

‡CALIFORNIA YOUNG PLAYWRIGHTS CONTEST, Playwrights Project, Suite 215, 1450 Frazee Rd., San Diego CA 92108. (619)298-9242. Director: Deborah Salzer. Open to Californians under age 19. Annual contest. Estab. 1985. "Our organization, and the contest, is designed to nurture promising young writers. We hope to develop playwrights and audiences for live theater. We also teach playwriting." Submissions required to be unpublished and not produced professionally. Submissions made by the author. Deadline for entries: April 1. SASE for contest rules and entry form. No entry fee. Award is professional productions of 3-5 short plays each year, participation of the writers in the entire production process, with a royalty award of $100 per play. Judging by professionals in the theater community, a committee of 5-7; changes somewhat each year. Works performed "in San Diego at the Cassius Carter Centre Stage of the Old Globe Theatre. Writers submitting scripts of 10 or more pages receive a detailed script evaluation letter."

***‡♣CANADIAN AUTHORS ASSOCIATION STUDENTS' CREATIVE WRITING CONTEST**, 27 Doxsee Ave. N., Campbellford, Ontario K0L 1L0 Canada. (705)653-0323. Fax: (705)653-0593. Contact: Bernice Lever-Farrar. Entrants must be enrolled in secondary schools, colleges or universities and must be Canadian residents or Canadian citizens living abroad. Entries must be typed on one side of letter-sized white paper, and not published previously except in a student class anthology, student newspaper or student yearbook. Entries will not be returned. Entry fees: $5 per short story of 2,000 words or less; $5 per article of 2,000 words or less; $5 for 2 to 3 poems of not more than 30 lines each. Awards: $500 for best story; $500 for best article; $500 for best poem. Four Honourable Mentions in each category. All 15 winners will receive *Canadian Author* magazine for 1 year. First-place winners will be published in *Canadian Author*. Entry forms will be in the winter and spring issues of *Canadian Author*; deadline March 1996.

***REBECCA CAUDILL YOUNG READERS' BOOK AWARD**, Illinois Reading Council, Illinois School Library Media Association, Illinois Association of Teachers of English, P.O. Box 871, Arlington Heights IL 60006-0871. (708)420-6406. Fax: (708)420-3242. Award Director Jackie Plourde. Annual award. Estab. 1988. Purpose of contest: to award the Children's Choice Award for grades 4-8 in Illinois. Submissions nominated by a person or group of people. Must be published within the last 5 years. Awards honorarium, plaque. Judging by children, grades 4-8.

‡♣CHICKADEE COVER CONTEST, *Chickadee Magazine*, Owl Communications, Suite 500, 179 John St., Toronto, Ontario M5T 3G5 Canada. (416)971-5275. Contest Director: Mitch Butler, Chirp Editor. Annual contest. There is a different theme published each year. Announcement published each October issue. No entry fee. Winning drawing published on cover of February issue. Judging by staff of *Chickadee*. Requirements for entrants: Must be 3- to 9-year-old readers.

‡♣CHICKADEE'S GARDEN EVENT, *Chickadee Magazine*, Owl Communications, Suite 500, 179 John St., Toronto, Ontario M5T 3G5 Canada. (416)971-5275. Contest Director: Mitch Butler, Chirp Editor. Annual. *Chickadee* readers are asked "to grow a favorite fruit or vegetable (anything as long as you can eat it) and submit a photo or drawing of you and your plant, and tell us why you chose the plant you did, and who helped you to care for it. Include experiences and humorous adventures along the way." Unpublished submissions only. Contest is announced in May issue. Deadline for entries: September. Results published in January issue. Judging by staff of *Chickadee*. Requirements for entrants: Must be 3-9 year-old readers.

CHILDREN'S BOOK AWARD, Sponsored by Federation of Children's Book Groups, 30 Senneleys Park Rd., Northfield Birmingham B31 1AL England. (0121)427-4860. Fax: (0121)643-6411. Coordinator: Jenny Blanch. Purpose of the award: "The C.B.A. is an annual prize for the best children's book of the year judged by the children themselves." Categories: (I) picture books, (II) short novels, (III) longer novels. Estab. 1980. Previously unpublished submissions only. Deadline for entries: December 31. SASE for rules and entry forms. Entries not returned. Awards "a magnificent silver and oak trophy worth over $6,000 and a portfolio of children's work." Silver dishes to each category winner. Judging by children. Requirements for entrants: Work must be fiction and published during the current year (poetry is ineligible). Work will be published in current "Pick of the Year" publication.

CHILDREN'S WRITER WRITING CONTESTS, 95 Long Ridge Rd., West Redding CT 06896. (203)792-8600. Contest offered every 4 months by *Children's Writer*, the monthly newsletter of

The asterisk before a listing indicates the listing is new in this edition.

writing and publishing trends. Purpose of award: To promote higher quality children's literature. "Each contest has its own theme. Our last three were: (1) A humorous story for ages 8 to 12, 900 words; (2) A historical article for ages 8 to 12, 750 words; (3) A science fiction story for ages 7-10, 750 words. Any original unpublished piece, not accepted by any publisher at the time of submission, is eligible." Submissions made by the author. Deadline for entries: last Friday in February, June and October. "We charge a $10 entry fee for nonsubscribers only, which is applicable against a subscription to *Children's Writer*." Awards 1st place—$100 or $1,000, a certificate and publication in *Children's Writer*; 2nd place—$50 or $500, and certificate; 3rd-5th places—$25 or $250 and certificates. One or two contests each year with the higher cash prizes also include $100 prizes plus certificates for 6th-12th places. To obtain the rules and theme for the current contest send a SASE to *Children's Writer* at the above address. Put "Contest Request" in the lower left of your envelope. Judging by a panel of 5 selected from the staff of the Institute of Children's Literature. "We acquire First North American Serial Rights (to print the winner in *Children's Writer*), after which all rights revert to author." Open to any writer. Entries are judged on age targeting, originality, quality of writing and, for nonfiction, how well the information is conveyed and accuracy. "Submit clear photocopies only, not originals; submission will *not* be returned. Manuscripts should be typed double-spaced. No pieces containing violence or derogatory, racist or sexist language or situations will be accepted, at the sole discretion of the judges."

***✤MR. CHRISTIE'S BOOK AWARD® PROGRAM**, Christie Brown & Co., Division of Nabisco Ltd., 2150 Lakeshore Blvd., Toronto, Ontario M8V 1A3 Canada. (416)503-6050. Fax: (416)503-6010. Coordinator: Marlene Yustin. Competition is open to Canadian citizens, landed imigrants or books published in Canada in 1995. Estab. 1990. Purpose of award: to honor Canadian authors and illustrators of good English/French Canadian published children's books. Contest includes three categories: Best Book for 7 and under; 8-11; and 12 and up. Submissions are made by the author, made by the author's agent, publishers. Deadline for entries: January 31. SASE for contest rules and entry forms. No entry fee. Awards a total of $45,000. Judging by a panel consisting of people in the literary/teaching community across Canada. Requirements for entrants: must be published children's literature in English or French.

THE CHRISTOPHER AWARD, The Christophers, 12 E. 48th St., New York NY 10017. (212)759-4050. Christopher Awards Coordinators: Peggy Flanagan and Virginia Armstrong. Annual award. Estab. 1969 (for young people; books for adults honored since 1949). "The award is given to works, published in the calendar year for which the award is given, that 'have achieved artistic excellence, affirming the highest values of the human spirit.' They must also enjoy a reasonable degree of popular acceptance." Previously published submissions only; must be published between January 1 and December 31. "Books should be submitted all year. Two copies should be sent to Peggy Flanagan, 12 E. 48th St., New York NY 10017 and two copies to Virginia Armstrong, 22 Forest Ave., Old Tappan NJ 07675." Entries not returned. No entry fee. Awards a bronze medallion. Books are judged by both reading specialists and young people. Requirements for entrants: "only published works are eligible and must be submitted during the calendar year in which they are first published."

***COLORADO BOOK AWARDS**, Colorado Center for the Book, 1301 Arapahoe St., Suite 3, Golden CO 80401. (303)273-5933. Fax: (303)273-5935. Award Director: Suzan Moore. Award open to adults. Annual award. Estab. 1993. Previously published submissions only. Submissions are made by the author, author's agent, nominated by a person or group of people. Deadline for entries: December 31. SASE for contest rules and entry forms. Entry fee is $30. Awards $500 and plaque. Judging by a panel of literary agents, booksellers and librarians.

CHRISTOPHER COLUMBUS SCREENPLAY DISCOVERY AWARDS, Christopher Columbus Society of the Creative Arts, #600, 433 N. Camden Dr., Beverly Hills CA 90210. (310)288-1988. Award Director: Mr. Carlos Abreu. Annual and monthly awards. Estab. 1990. Purpose of award: to discover new screenplay writers. Unpublished submissions only. Submissions are made by the author or author's agent. Deadline for entries: December 1st and monthly (last day of month). Entry fee is $45. Awards: (1) Feedback—development process with industry experts; (2) Financial rewards—option moneys up to $10,000; (3) Access to key decision makers. Judging by entertainment industry experts, producers and executives.

‡CRICKET LEAGUE, *Cricket*, 315 Fifth St., Peru IL 61354. (815)224-6643. Fax: (815)224-6675. Address entries to: Cricket League. Monthly. Estab. 1973. "The purpose of Cricket League contests is to encourage creativity and give children an opportunity to express themselves in writing, drawing, painting or photography. There is a contest each month. Possible categories include story, poetry, art or photography. Each contest relates to a *specific theme* described on each *Cricket* issue's Cricket League page. Signature verifying originality, age and address of entrant required. Entries which do not relate to the current month's theme cannot be considered." Unpublished submissions only. Deadline for entries: the 25th of each month. Cricket League rules, contest themes, and submission deadline information can be found in the current issue of *Cricket*. "We prefer that children who enter the contests subscribe to the magazine, or that they read *Cricket* in their school or library." No entry fee. Awards certificate suitable for framing and children's books or art/writing supplies. Judging by *Cricket* editors. Obtains right to print prize-winning entries in magazine. Refer to contest rules in current *Cricket* issue. Winning entries are published on the Cricket League pages in the *Cricket* magazine 3 months subsequent to the issue in which the contest was announced.

MARGUERITE DE ANGELI PRIZE, Bantam Doubleday Dell Books for Young Readers, 1540 Broadway, New York NY 10036. Estab. 1992. Annual award. Purpose of award: to encourage the writing of fiction for children that examines the diversity of the American experience, either contemporary or historical, in the same spirit as the works of Marguerite de Angeli; to encourage unpublished writers in the field of middle grade fiction. Unpublished submissions only. Submissions made by author or author's agent. Entries should be postmarked between March 31st and June 30th. SASE for award rules. No entry fee. Awards a $1,500 cash prize plus a hardcover and paperback book contract with a $3,500 advance against a royalty to be negotiated. Judging by Bantam Doubleday Dell Books for Young Readers editorial staff. Open to US and Canadian writers who have not previously published a novel for middle-grade readers (ages 7-10). Works published in an upcoming Bantam Doubleday Dell Books for Young Readers list.

DELACORTE PRESS PRIZE FOR A FIRST YOUNG ADULT NOVEL, Delacorte Press, Books for Young Readers Department, 1540 Broadway, New York NY 10036. (212)354-6500. Fax: (212)782-9452. Annual award. Estab. 1982. Purpose of award: to encourage the writing of contemporary young adult fiction. Previously unpublished submissions only. Mss sent to Delacorte Press may not be submitted to other publishers while under consideration for the prize. "Entries must be submitted between Labor Day and New Year's Day. The real deadline is a December 31 postmark. Early entries are appreciated." SASE for award rules. No entry fee. Awards a $1,500 cash prize and a $6,000 advance against royalties on a hardcover and paperback book contract. Judged by the editors of the Books for Young Readers Deptartment of Delacorte Press. Rights acquired "only if the entry wins or is awarded an Honorable Mention." Requirements for entrants: The writer must be American or Canadian and must *not* have previously published a young adult novel but may have published anything else.

***MARGARET A. EDWARDS AWARDS**, Office of Young Adult Services, The New York Public Library, 455 Fifth Ave., New York NY 10016. Award Director: Marilee Foglesong. Annual award. Purpose of award: "ALA's Young Adult Library Services Association (YALSA), on behalf of librarians who work with young adults in all types of libraries, will give recognition to those authors whose book or books have provided young adults with a window through which they can view their world and which will help them to grow and to understand themselves and their role in society." Previously published submissions only. Submissions are nominated by a person or group of people. Must be published five years before date of award. SASE for award rules and entry forms. No entry fee. Judging by members of the Young Adult Library Services Association. "The award will be given annually to an author whose book or books, over a period of time, have been accepted by young adults as an authentic voice that continues to illuminate their experiences and emotions, giving insight into their lives. The book or books should enable them to understand themselves, the world in which they live, and their relationship with others and with society. The book or books must be in print at the time of the nomination."

***‡JOAN FASSLER MEMORIAL BOOK AWARD**, Association for the Care of Children's Health, 7910 Woodmont Ave., Suite 300, Bethesda MD 20814. (301)654-6549. Fax: (301)986-

4553. Membership Manager: Trish McClean. Competition open to adults and children. Annual award. Estab. 1989. Previously published submissions only. Submissions made by the author, author's agent. Must be published between 1994 and 1995. SASE for award rules and entry forms. No entry fee. Award $1,000 honorarium, plaque. Judging by multidisciplinary committee of ACCH members. Requirements for entrants: open to any writer. Display and book signing opportunities at annual conference June 9-12, 1996 in Albuquerque, New Mexico.

***‡FAULKNER PRIZES FOR FICTION**, The Pirate's Alley Faulkner Society, Inc., 632 Pirate's Alley, New Orleans LA 70116. (504)586-1609. Fax: (504)522-9725. Award Director: Joseph J. DeSalvo, Jr. Open to adult and students. Annual award. Estab. 1991. Purpose of award: to encourage literacy in the English language. Novel (more than 50,000 words); Novella (less than 50,000 words) Short Story (less than 15,000 words); Short story by a high school student (less than 10,000 words). Short story by high school student open to Louisiana students only. Submissions are made by the author. Deadline for entries: April 1. SASE for award rules and entry forms. Entry fee is $35 (novel); $30 (novella); $25 (short story); $10 (high school). Awards: $7,500 novel; $2,500 novella; $1,500 short story; $1,000 high school ($750 to student, $250 to sponsoring teacher). Judging by some 50 volunteer readers who provide a first reading. The second reading is done by still another group of qualified volunteers. The final reading and selection of winners by noted authors. The competition is only open to those residing in the United States.

***FLICKER TALE CHILDREN'S BOOK AWARD**, North Dakota Library Association, 515 N. Fifth St., Bismarck ND 58501. (701)222-6410. Fax: (701)221-6854. Award Director: Verna LaBounty, P.O. Box 145, Kindred ND 58051. Estab. 1979. Purpose of award: to give children across the state of North Dakota a chance to vote for their book of choice from a nominated list of 10: 5 in the picture book category; 5 in the juvenile category. Also, to promote awareness of quality literature for children. Previously published submissions only. Submissions nominated by a person or group of people. Awards a plaque from North Dakota Library Association and banquet dinner. Judging by children in North Dakota.

***FOCAL AWARD**, Friends of the Children's Literature Department (FOCAL), 630 W. Fifth St., Los Angeles CA 90071. (213)228-7252. Fax: (213)228-7259. Award Director: Edith McGovern. Competition is open to adults. Annual award. Estab. 1979. Purpose of award: the FOCAL Award is presented to an author and/or illustrator for a creative work which enriches a child's appreciation for and knowledge of California. Previously published submissions only. Submissions are made by author. Deadline for entries: September. SASE for award rules and entry forms. No entry fee. Awards: award luncheon; handmade puppet representing the main character. Judging by a committee of FOCAL members. The books may be fiction or nonfiction, and shall be judged on the following qualities: literary and/or artistic merit, interest/readability, universality and California enrichment content. Books shall be assigned points for each of the above qualities. The work receiving the highest number of points shall be declared the FOCAL Award winner. Winning works will be exhibited in the Children's Literature Department of the Los Angeles Public Library, 630 W. Fifth St., Los Angeles CA 90071.

***‡FOSTER CITY INTERNATIONAL WRITER'S CONTEST**, Foster City Arts & Culture Committee, 650 Shell Blvd., Foster City CA 94404. (415)345-5731. Contest Director: Clarke N. Simm. Open to all ages. Annual contest. Estab. 1975. Unpublished submissions only. Submissions made by the author. Deadline for entries: November 1, 1996. SASE for contest rules and entry forms. Entry fee is $10. Awards $250 cash award for first place; second through fourth place receives certificate of merit. Judging by Peninsula Press Club. Categories include: best fiction (not more than 3,000 words), best nonfiction (not more than 3,000 words), best humor (prose not more than 3,000 words), best story for children (not more than 2,000 words) and best poem (not to exceed two pages). Entries must be typed, double-spaced on white 8½×11 paper, pages with numbers at the top right corner. Your name should not appear on any page. Attach 3×5 typed card with your name, address, phone number, manuscript title and category. Enter in one or multiple categories. No illustrated manuscripts. For each entry include a non-refundable entry fee check for $10.

‡4-H ESSAY CONTEST, American Beekeeping Federation, Inc., P.O. Box 1038, Jesup GA 31545. (912)427-8447. Contest Director: Troy H. Fore. Annual contest. Purpose of contest: to recognize the best original (750-1,000 words) story on honey bees. 1996 essay topic: "How Honey Bees Ensure Our Food Supply." The object is to explore the role honey bees play, through their pollination of crops, in ensuring a plentiful, varied and inexpensive food supply for Americans. Unpublished submissions only. Deadline for entries: before March 1. No entry fee. Awards 1st place: $250; 2nd place: $100; 3rd place: $50. Judging by American Beekeeping Federation's Essay Committee. "All national entries become the property of the American Beekeeping Federation, Inc., and may be published or used as it sees fit. No essay will be returned. Essayists *should not* forward essays directly to the American Beekeeping Federation office. Each state 4-H office is responsible for selecting the state's winner and should set its deadline so state judging can be completed at the state level in time for the winning state essay to be mailed to the ABF office before March 1, 1996. Each state winner receives a book on honey bees, beekeeping or honey. The National Winner will announced by May 1, 1996." Requirements for entrants: Contest is open to active 4-H Club members only.

DON FREEMAN MEMORIAL GRANT-IN-AID, Society of Children's Book Writers and Illustrators, 22736 Vanowen St., Suite 106, West Hills CA 91307. (818)888-8760. Estab. 1974. Purpose of award: to "enable picture book artists to further their understanding, training and work in the picture book genre." Applications and prepared materials will be accepted between January 15 and February 15. Grant awarded and announced on June 15. SASE for award rules and entry forms. SASE for return of entries. No entry fee. Annually awards one grant of $1,000 and one runner-up grant of $500. "The grant-in-aid is available to both full and associate members of the SCBWI who, as artists, seriously intend to make picture books their chief contribution to the field of children's literature."

🍁AMELIA FRANCES HOWARD GIBBON AWARD FOR ILLUSTRATION, Canadian Library Association, Suite 602, 200 Elgin St., Ottawa, Ontario K2P 1L5 Canada. (613)232-9625. Contact: Chairperson, Canadian Association of Children's Librarians. Annual award. Estab. 1971. Purpose of award: "to honor excellence in the illustration of children's book(s) in Canada. To merit consideration the book must have been published in Canada and its illustrator must be a Canadian citizen or a permanent resident of Canada." Previously published submissions only; must be published between January 1 and December 31 of the previous year. Deadline for entries: January 1. SASE for award rules. Entries not returned. No entry fee. Awards a medal. Judging by selection committee of members of Canadian Association of Children's Librarians. Requirements for entrants: illustrator must be Canadian or Canadian resident. Winning books are on display at CLA Headquarters.

GOLD MEDALLION BOOK AWARDS, Evangelical Christian Publishers Association, Suite 101, 3225 S. Hardy Dr., Tempe AZ 85282. (602)966-3998. Fax: (602)966-1944. President: Doug Ross. Annual award. Estab. 1978. Categories include Preschool Children's Books, Elementary Children's Books, Youth Books. "All entries must be evangelical in nature and cannot be contrary to ECPA's Statement of Faith (stated in official rules)." Deadlines for entries: December 1. SASE for award rules and entry form. "The work must be submitted by the publisher." Entry fee is $250 for nonmembers. Awards a Gold Medallion plaque.

GOLDEN KITE AWARDS, Society of Children's Book Writers and Illustrators, 22736 Vanowen St., Suite 106, West Hills CA 91307. (818)888-8760. Coordinator: Sue Alexander. Annual award. Estab. 1973. "The works chosen will be those that the judges feel exhibit excellence in writing, and in the case of the picture-illustrated books—in illustration, and genuinely appeal to the interests and concerns of children. For the fiction and nonfiction awards, original works and single-author collections of stories or poems of which at least half are new and never before published in book form are eligible—anthologies and translations are not. For the picture-illustration awards, the art or photographs must be original works (the texts—which may be fiction or nonfiction—may be original, public domain or previously published). Deadline for entries: December 15. SASE for award rules. Self-addressed mailing label for return of entries. No entry fee. Awards statuettes and plaques. The panel of judges will consist of two children's book authors, a children's book artist or photographer (who may or may not be an author), a children's book editor and a librarian." Requirements for entrants: "must be a member of SCBWI." Winning books will be displayed at national conference in August. Books to be entered, as well as further inquiries, should be submitted to: The Society of Children's Book Writers and Illustrators, above address.

‡HIGHLIGHTS FOR CHILDREN FICTION CONTEST, 803 Church St., Honesdale PA 18431. (717)253-1080. Mss should be addressed to Fiction Contest. Editor: Kent L. Brown Jr. Annual contest. Estab. 1980. Purpose of the contest: to stimulate interest in writing for children and reward and recognize excellence. Unpublished submissions only. Deadline for entries: February 28; entries accepted after January 1 only. SASE for contest rules and return of entries. No entry fee. Awards 3 prizes of $1,000 each in cash and a pewter bowl (or, at the winner's election, attendance at the Highlights Foundation Writers Workshop at Chautauqua). Judging by *Highlights*' editors. Winning pieces are purchased for the cash prize of $1,000 and published in *Highlights*; semifinalists go to out-of-house judges (educators, editors, writers, etc.). Requirements for entrants: open to any writer; student writers must be 16 or older. Winners announced in June. "The 1996 contest is for stories about children in today's world. Length up to 900 words. Stories for beginning readers should not exceed 500 words. Stories should be consistent with *Highlights*' editorial requirements. No violence, crime or derogatory humor."

‡✤HOOT AWARDS, WRITING CONTEST, PHOTO CONTEST, POETRY CONTEST, COVER CONTEST, *Owl Magazine*, 179 John St., Suite 500, Toronto, Ontario M5T 3G5 Canada. (416)971-5275. Annual contest. Purpose of awards: "to encourage children to contribute and participate in the magazine. The Hoot Awards recognize excellence in an individual or group effort to help the environment." Unpublished submissions only. Deadlines change yearly. Prizes/awards "change every year. Often we give books as prizes." Winning entries published in the magazine. Judging by art and editorial staff. Entries become the property of Owl Communications. "The contests and awards are open to children up to 14 years of age."

***IBBY HONOUR LIST**, International Board on Books for Young People, Nonnerweg 12, Postfach CH-4003 Basel, Switzerland. (004161)272-2917. Fax: (004161)272-2757. Competition open to adults. Biennial award. The IBBY Honour List is a selection of outstanding recently published books honoring writers, illustrators, and translators from IBBY member countries. Important considerations in selecting the Honour List titles are that the books chosen be representative of the best in children's literature from each country, and that the books are recommended as suitable for publication throughout the world, thus furthering the IBBY objective of encouraging international understanding through children's literature. The selection of IBBY Honour List books has resulted in greater international awareness and recognition of these titles by book publishers and has considerably increased the number of translations and foreign editions of quality children's books. Previously published submissions only. Submissions are by IBBY National sections in good standing. The books are shown in 5 parallel traveling exhibitions before they are kept as permanent deposits in some of the world's leading children's book institutions. The accompanying catalogue presenting the Honour List books, their authors, illustrators and translators, is distributed throughout the world. The Honour List diplomas are presented to the recipients at the IBBY Congresses.

***‡INTERNATIONAL WRITING & PHOTOGRAPHY CONTEST**, Quill and Scroll Society, School of Journalism & Mass Communication, The University of Iowa, Iowa City IA 52242-1528. (319)335-5795. Fax: (319)335-5210. Executive Director: Richard Johns. Open to students. Annual contest. Estab. 1940. Purpose of contest: to reward excellence in newspaper writing and photography for students in grades 9 through 12. Previously published submissions only. Submissions made by the author, journalism teacher/newspaper adviser. Deadline for entries: February 5. SASE for contest rules and entry forms. Entry fee is $2 per category. Awards Gold Key; Sweepstakes Award in each category; Smith Corona Electric Typewriter to sweepstakes winner and opportunity to apply for journalism scholarship. Judging by professionals in the media. Most of the top winners will be published in *Quill & Scroll* magazine.

IOWA TEEN AWARD, Iowa Educational Media Association, 306 E. H Ave., Grundy Center IA 50638. (319)824-6788. Contest Director: Don Osterhaus. Annual award. Estab. 1983. Previously published submissions only. Purpose of award: to allow students to read high quality literature and to have the opportunity to select their favorite from this list. Must have been published "in last 3-4 years." Deadline for entries: April 1995 for '96-'97 competition. SASE for award rules/entry forms. No entry fee. "Media specialists, teachers and students nominate possible entries." Awards an inscribed brass apple. Judging by Iowa students in grades 6-9. Requirements: Work must be of recent publication, so copies can be ordered for media center collections. Reviews of submitted books must be available for the nominating committee. Works displayed "at participating classrooms, media centers, public libraries and local bookstores in Iowa."

‡ISLAND LITERARY AWARDS, Prince Edward Island Council of the Arts, P.O. Box 2234, Charlottetown, Prince Edward C1A 8B9 Canada. Fax: (902)368-4418. Annual award. Estab. 1988. Purpose of awards: to provide Island writers with the opportunity to enter work in one or more of these categories: poetry, short adult fiction, children's literature, feature article, playwriting and creative writing by Island youth. Unpublished submissions only (except for Feature Article Award). Submissions made by the author. Deadline for entries: February 15. SASE for contest rules and entry forms. Entry fee is $6. Awards range from $100-500 in adult categories; $25-75 for youth contest. Judging by Canadian writers chosen each year by the literary awards committee. Requirements for entrants: "The competitions are open to individuals who have been residents on Prince Edward Island at least six of the last twelve months. Authors of one or more books published within the last five years are not eligible to enter the genre(s) in which they have published."

***‡IYC ETHICS WRITING CONTEST**, *It's Your Choice Magazine*, P.O. Box 7135, Richmond VA 23221. Contact: Editor. Annual contest. Estab. 1993. Purpose of contest: to arouse interest in ethics and encourage discussion of ethical ideas. "All articles/stories must be related to ethics/morality issues in an essential way. Tacking on a couple of statements abouts ethics/morality to a story you have already written will not do. We regard ethics as the scientific study of the rightness or wrongness of human behavior in any context, which opens the field to a wide variety of articles. You might write about the larger social issues such as abortion, murder, capital punishment, war, greed; or about personal actions such as your son's hiding his report card because he got an F." Unpublished submissions only. Submissions made by the author. Deadline monthly. School districts may submit at any time (elementary, junior and senior high in separate batches) but only once in any calendar year. Monthly prizes: elementary, $25; junior high, $50; high school, $100. Winning entries are automatically entered in regional and national contests for larger prizes and awards ceremonies. Submissions from school age children should be submitted by school officials: vastly greater prize opportunities. SASE for contest rules and entry forms. Entry fee is $2 for purchase of mss registration form. Judging by editor. Right to publish entry in a collection of winning mss without further pay is required.

***EZRA JACK KEATS/KERLAN COLLECTION MEMORIAL FELLOWSHIP**, University of Minnesota, 109 Walter Library, 117 Pleasant St. SE, Minneapolis MN 55455. (612)624-4576. Fax: (612)625-5525. Competition open to adults. Offered annually. Deadline for entries: first Monday in May. Send request with SASE, including 52¢ postage. The Ezra Jack Keats/Kerlan Collection Memorial Fellowship from the Ezra Jack Keats Foundation will provide $1,500 to a "talented writer and/or illustrator of children's books who wishes to use the Kerlan Collection for the furtherance of his or her artistic development. Special consideration will be given to someone who would find it difficult to finance the visit to the Kerlan Collection." The fellowship winner will receive transnportation and per diem. Judging by the Kerlan Award Committee—3 representatives from the University of Minnesota faculty, one representative from the Kerlan Collection, one from the Kerlan Friends, and one from the Minnesota Library Association.

‡KENTUCKY STATE POETRY SOCIETY ANNUAL CONTEST, Kentucky State Poetry Society, % *Pegasus* editor Miriam L. Woolfolk, 3289 Hunting Hills Dr., Lexington KY 40515. (606)271-4662. Annual contest. Estab. 1966. Unpublished poems only. Deadline for entries: June 30. SASE for contest rules and entry forms. Categories are free for students; Grand Prix, $5; all others $1. Offers more than 30 categories and awards certificates of merit and cash prizes from $1 to $100. Sponsors pick judges. Contest open to all. "One-time printing rights acquired for publication of first prize winner in the Prize Poems Issue of *Pegasus*, our annual journal. All other winners will be displayed at our October annual awards banquet."

KERLAN AWARD, University of Minnesota, 109 Walter Library, 117 Pleasant St. SE, Minneapolis MN 55455. (612)624-4576. Curator: Karen Nelson Hoyle. Annual award. Estab. 1975. "Given in recognition of singular attainments in the creation of children's literature and in appreciation for generous donation of unique resources to the Kerlan Collection." Previously published submissions only. Deadline for entries: November 1. Anyone can send nominations for the award, directed to the Kerlan Collection. No materials are submitted other than the person's name. Requirements for entrants: open to all who are nominated. Anyone can submit names. "For serious consideration, entrant must be a published author and/or illustrator of children's books (including young adult fiction) and have donated original materials to the Kerlan Collection."

CORETTA SCOTT KING AWARD, Coretta Scott King Task Force, Social Responsibility Round Table, American Library Association, 50 E. Huron St., Chicago IL 60611. "The Coretta Scott King Award is an annual award for a book (one for test and one for illustration) that conveys the spirit of brotherhood espoused by M.L. King, Jr.—and also speaks to the Black experience—for young people. There is an award jury that judges the books—reviewing over the year—and making a decision in January. A copy of an entry must be sent to each juror. Acquire jury list from SRRT office in Chicago."

JANUSZ KORCZAK AWARDS, Joseph H. and Belle R. Braun Center for Holocaust Studies, Anti-Defamation League, 823 United Nations Plaza, New York NY 10017. (212)490-2525. Fax: (212)867-0779. Award Director: Mark Edelman. Award usually offered every 2 years. Estab. 1980. Purpose of award: "The award honors books about children which best exemplify Janusz Korczak's principles of selflessness and human dignity." Previously published submissions only; for 1997, books must have been published in 1995 or 1996. SASE for award rules and entry forms. No entry fee. Awards $1,000 cash and plaque (first prize); plaque (honorable mention). Judging by an interdisciplinary committee of leading scholars, editors, literary critics and educators. Requirements for entrants: Books must meet entry requirements and must be published in English. No entries are returned. They become the property of the Braun Center. Press release will announce winners.

‡ELIAS LIEBERMAN STUDENT POETRY AWARD, Poetry Society of America, 15 Gramercy Park, New York NY 10003. (212)254-9628. Fax: (212)673-2352. Award Director: Elise Paschen. Annual award. Purpose of award: Award is for the best unpublished poem by a high or preparatory school student (grades 9-12) from the US and its territories. Unpublished submissions only. Deadline for entries: December 22. SASE for award rules and entry forms. Entries not returned. Entry fee is $10. "High schools can send an unlimited number of submissions with one entry per individual student. Fee is $1 for individual entries." Award: $100. Judging by a professional poet. Requirements for entrants: Award open to all high school and preparatory students from the US and its territories. School attended, as well as name and address, should be noted. PSA submission guidelines must be followed. These are printed in our fall calendar, and are readily available if those interested send us a SASE. Line limit: none. "The award-winning poem will be included in a sheaf of poems that will be part of the program at the award ceremony and sent to all PSA members."

***‡LONGMEADOW JOURNAL LITERARY COMPETITION**, % Rita and Robert Morton, 6750 N. Longmeadow, Lincolnwood IL 60646. (312)726-9789. Fax: (312)726-9772. Contest Director: Rita and Robert Morton. Competition open to students (anyone age 10-19). Held annually and published every two years. Estab. 1986. Purpose of contest: to encourage the young to write. Submissions are made by the author, made by the author's agent, nominated by a person or group of people, by teachers, librarians or parents. Deadline for entries: May 31. SASE. No entry fee. Awards first place, $175; second place, $100; and five prizes of $50. Judging by Rita Morton, Robert Morton and Laurie Levy. Works are published every two years and are distributed to teachers and librarians and interested parties at no charge.

MAGAZINE MERIT AWARDS, Society of Children's Book Writers and Illustrators, 22736 Vanowen St., Suite 106, West Hills CA 91307. (818)888-8760. Award Coordinator: Dorothy Leon. Annual award. Estab. 1988. "Purpose of the award: "To recognize outstanding original magazine work for young people published during that year and having been written or illustrated by members of SCBWI." Previously published submissions only. Entries must be submitted between January 31 and December 15 of the year of publication. For brochure (rules) write Award Coordinator. No entry fee. Must be a SCBWI member. Awards plaques and honor certificates for each of the 3 categories (fiction, nonfiction, illustration). Judging by a magazine editor and two "full" SCBWI members. "All magazine work for young people by an SCBWI member—writer, artist or photographer—is eligible during the year of original publication. In the case of co-authored work, both authors must be SCBWI members. Members must submit their own work." Requirements for entrants: 4 copies each of the published work and proof of publication (may be contents page) showing the name of the magazine and the date of issue. The SCBWI is a professional organization of writers and illustrators and others interested in children's literature. Membership is open to the general public at large.

***‡THE MAGIC-REALISM-MAGAZINE SHORT-FICTION AWARD**, Pyx Press, P.O. Box 922648, Sylmar CA 91392-2648. Award Director: C. Darren Butler. Award open to adults and students. Annual award. Estab. 1994. Previously published submissions only. Submissions made by the author, made by the author's agent, nominated by a person or group of people. Must be published between January 1, 1995 and December 31, 1995. Deadline for entries: February 15, 1996. SASE for award rules and entry forms. Awards publication in chapbook form and $25 cash to author and original publisher. Judging by Pyx Press for 1996.

***‡MAJESTIC BOOKS WRITING CONTEST**, Majestic Books, P.O. Box 19097, Johnston RI 02919-0097. Contest Director: Cindy MacDonald. Open to students. Annual contest. Estab. 1992. Purpose of contest: to encourage students to write to the best of their ability and to be proud of their work. Unpublished submissions only. Submissions made by the author or teacher. Deadline for entries: second Friday in October. No entry fee, however, we do ask for a large self-addressed envelope (9 × 12) for our reply and certificate. Winners are published in an anthology. All entrants receive a certificate acknowledging their efforts. Judging by a panel of published writers. One-time publishing rights to submitted material required or purchased. Our contest is open to all students, age 6-17 in Rhode Island. *Anthology* comes off the press in December and a presentation ceremony is held for all winning students. Students must include their age, grade, school and statement of authenticity signed by the writer and a parent or teacher. Entries must be neat and will not be returned.

✤VICKY METCALF BODY OF WORK AWARD, Canadian Authors Association, 27 Doxsee Ave. N., Campbellford, Ontario K0L 1L0 Canada. (705)653-0323. Fax: (705)653-0593. Contact: Awards Chair. Annual award. Estab. 1963. Purpose: to honor a body of work inspirational to Canadian youth. Deadline for entries: December 31. SASE for award rules and entry forms. Entries not returned. No entry fee. Awards $10,000 and certificate. Judging by panel of CAA-appointed judges including past winners. "The prizes are given solely to stimulate writing for children by Canadian writers," said Mrs. Metcalf when she established the award. "We must encourage the writing of material for Canadian children without setting any restricting formulas."

✤VICKY METCALF SHORT STORY AWARD, Canadian Authors Association, 27 Doxsee Ave. N., Campbellford, Ontario K0L 1L0 Canada. (705)653-0323. Fax: (705)653-0593. Contact: Awards Chair. Annual award. Estab. 1979. Purpose: to honor writing by a Canadian inspirational to Canadian youth. Previously published submissions only; must be published between January 1 and December 31. Deadline for entries: December 31. SASE for contest/award rules and entry forms. Entries not returned. No entry fee. Awards $3,000 to Canadian author and $1,000 to editor responsible for publishing winning story if published in a Canadian periodical or anthology. Judging by CAA-selected panel including past winners.

The double dagger before a listing indicates the contest or organization is open to students.

‡MICHIGAN STUDENT FILM & VIDEO FESTIVAL, Detroit Area Film and Television, Harrison High School, 29995 W. 12 Mile Rd., Farmington Hills MI 48334. (810)489-3491. Contest Director: Margaret Culver. Open to students in grades K-12; *entrants must be Michigan residents*. Annual contest. Estab. 1968. Film entries must be VHS video or film that has been transferred to video; categories for video entries are teleplay, commercials, music, documentary, series, artistic, general entertainment, sports, news, editing, unedited, drug awareness (public service announcement), instructional and animation. Submissions may be made by the student or teacher. Deadline for entries is February 19, 1996. Contest rules and entry form available with SASE. Entry fee is $10. Prizes include certificates and medals for all entries; prizes for Best of Show award range from cameras to scholarships. Judging is done by professionals in media, education and production of film and video. The festival reserves the right to use the material for educational or promotional purposes. Work will be shown at the Detroit Film Theater, Detroit Institute of Arts.

MILKWEED PRIZE FOR CHILDREN'S LITERATURE, Milkweed Editions, 430 First Ave. N., Suite 400, Minneapolis MN 55401-1473. (612)332-6192. Award Director: Emilie Buchwald, publisher/editor. Annual award. Estab. 1993. Purpose of the award: to encourage writers to turn their attention to readers in the 8-12 age group. Unpublished submissions only "in book form." Must send SASE for award guidelines. The prize is awarded to the best work for children ages 8-12 that Milkweed agrees to publish in a calendar year by a writer not published by Milkweed before. The prize consists of $2,000 cash over and above any advance or royalties agreed to at the time of acceptance. Winners are announced in April of each year. "Submissions must follow our usual children's guidelines."

***‡MISSISSIPPI VALLEY POETRY CONTEST**, North American Literary Escadrille, P.O. Box 3188, Rock Island IL 61204. (309)788-8041. Director: Sue Katz. Annual contest. Estab. 1971. Purpose of contest: "To provide children, students, adults, senior citizens, ethnic groups and teachers the opportunity to express themselves in verse and poetry on a regional and national scale." Categories for adults, senior citizens, high school, junior high and elementary students include The Mississippi Valley, jazz, religious, humorous, rhyming, ethnic, haiku, history. Unpublished submissions only. Deadline for entries: April 1, 1996. SASE for contest rules. Entry fee of $3 student, $5 adult will cover up to 5 poems submitted. Awards cash from $50-175. Open to any student or adult poet, writer or teacher. "Prizes are presented during a special awards night at the Butterworth Center, a grand old mansion in Moline, Illinois. Winning poems are read by professional readers, and event is widely publicized. Those not present are notified by mail and prizes forwarded. Contest is nonprofit and registered as such in the state of Illinois."

‡MARY MOLLOY FELLOWSHIP IN CHILDREN'S WORKING FICTION, The Heekin Group Foundation, P.O. Box 209, Middlebury VT 05753. (802)388-8651. Children's Literature Division Director: Deirdre M. Heekin. Annual award. Estab. 1994. (The Heekin Group Foundation was established in 1992.) In order to foster the development of the literary arts, the Mary Molloy Fellowship for Children's Working Fiction is awarded each year to the beginning career writer whose work exhibits literary merit, perception, and is rich in imagination. Unpublished submissions only. Submissions made by the author. Deadline for entries: December 1. SASE for award rules and entry forms. Entry fee is $20. Submission requires the first 35-50 pages of a ms. Manuscripts should be a children's novel in progress and geared toward the 8-12 age group. Awards $2,000. Judging by a children's literature publisher. The competition is open to all beginning career writers who have not yet been published in children's fiction for middle readers (8-12 years old). "For further information regarding our other fiction and nonfiction fellowships, please contact our headquarters: The Heekin Group, 68860 Goodrich Rd., Foundation Sisters, OR 97759."

✤THE NATIONAL CHAPTER OF CANADA IODE VIOLET DOWNEY BOOK AWARD, 40 Orchard View Blvd., Suite 254, Toronto, Ontario M5R 1B9 Canada. (416)487-4416. Award Director: Marty Dalton. Annual award. Estab. 1985. Purpose of the award: to honor the best children's English language book by a Canadian published in Canada for ages 5-13, over 500 words. Fairy tales, anthologies and books adapted from another source are not eligible. Previously published submissions only. Books must have been published in Canada between February 1 and January 31. Submissions made by author, author's agent; anyone may submit. Must have been published during previous calendar year. Deadline for entries: January 31. SASE for award rules and entry forms. No entry fee. Awards $3,000 for the year 1996 for books published in 1995. Judging by a panel of 6, 4 IODE members and 2 professionals.

NATIONAL JEWISH BOOK AWARD FOR CHILDREN'S LITERATURE, Jewish Book Council Inc., 15 E. 26th St., New York NY 10010. (212)532-4949. Awards Coordinator: Carolyn Starman Hesse. Annual award. Estab. 1950. Previously published submissions only; must be published in 1994 for 1995 award. Deadline for entries: September 15, 1996. SASE for award rules and entry forms. Entries not returned. Entry fee is $75/title; $100 if listed in 2 categories. Awards $750. Judging by 3 authorities in the field. Requirements for entrants: Jewish children's books, published only for ages 8-14. Books will be displayed at the awards ceremony in NYC during Jewish Book Month, November 6—December 6, 1996.

NATIONAL JEWISH BOOK AWARD FOR PICTURE BOOKS, (Marcia & Louis Posner Award), Jewish Book Council, 15 E. 26th St., New York NY 10010. (212)532-4949. Awards Coordinator: Carolyn Starman Hesse. Annual award. Estab. 1980. Previously published submissions only; must be published the year prior to the awards ceremony—October 1, 1995 to September 30, 1996 for 1996 award. Deadline for entries: September 15, 1996. SASE for award rules and entry forms. Entries not returned. No entry fee. Awards $750. Judging by 3 authorities in the field. Requirements for entrants: subject must be of Jewish content, but not necessily religious published. Works displayed at the awards ceremony.

NATIONAL WRITERS ASSOCIATION ARTICLE/ESSAY CONTEST, 1450 S. Havana, Suite 424, Aurora CO 80012. (303)751-7844. Executive Director: Sandy Whelchel. Annual contest. Estab. 1971. Purpose of contest: "to encourage writers in this creative form and to recognize those who excel in nonfiction writing." Submissions made by author. Deadline for entries: December 31. SASE for contest rules and entry forms. Entry fee is $15. Awards three cash prizes; choice of books; Honorable Mention Certificate. "Two people read each entry; third party picks three top winners from top five." Top 3 winners are published in an anthology published by National Writers Association, if winners agree to this. Judging sheets sent if entry accompanied by SASE.

NATIONAL WRITERS ASSOCIATION NOVEL WRITING CONTEST, 1450 S. Havana, Suite 424, Aurora CO 80012. (303)751-7844. Executive Director: Sandy Whelchel. Annual contest. Estab. 1971. Purpose of contest: "to encourage writers in this creative form and to recognize those who excel in novel writing." Submissions made by the author. Deadline for entries: April 1. SASE for contest rules and entry forms. Entry fee is $35. Awards top 3, cash prizes; 4 to 10, choice of books; 10 to 20, Honorable Mention Certificates. Judging: "two people read the manuscripts; a third party picks the three top winners from the top 5. We display our members' published books in our offices." Judging sheets available for SASE.

NATIONAL WRITERS ASSOCIATION SHORT STORY CONTEST, 1450 Havana St., Suite 424, Aurora CO 80012. (303)751-7844. Executive Director: Sandy Whelchel. Annual contest. Estab. 1971. Purpose of contest: "To encourage writers in this creative form and to recognize those who excel in fiction writing." Submissions made by the author. Deadline for entries: July 1. SASE for contest rules and entry forms. Entry fee is $15. Awards 3 cash prizes, choice of books and certificates for Honorable Mentions. Judging by "two people read each entry; third person picks top three winners." Judging sheet copies available for SASE. Top three winners are published in an anthology published by National Writers Association, if winners agree to this.

‡THE NATIONAL WRITTEN & ILLUSTRATED BY . . . AWARDS CONTEST FOR STUDENTS, Landmark Editions, Inc., 1402 Kansas Ave., Kansas City MO 64127. (816)241-4919. Fax: (816)483-3755. Contest Director: Teresa Melton. Annual awards contest with 3 published winners. Estab. 1986. Purpose of the contest: to encourage and celebrate the creative efforts of students. There are 3 age categories (ages 6-9, 10-13 and 14-19). Unpublished submissions only.

Deadline for entries: May 1. For a free copy of the contest rules, send a self-addressed, business-sized envelope, stamped with 64¢ postage. "Need to send a self-addressed, sufficiently stamped (at least $3 postage), book mailer with book entry for its return. All entries which do not win are mailed back in November or December of each contest year." Entry fee is $1. Awards publication of book. Judging by national panel of educators, editors, illustrators, authors and school librarians. "Each student winner receives a publishing contract allowing Landmark to publish the book. Copyright is in student's name and student receives royalties on sale of book. Books must be in proper contest format and submitted with entry form signed by a teacher or librarian. Students may develop their illustrations in any medium of their choice, as long as the illustrations remain two-dimensional and flat to the surface of the paper." Winners are notified by phone by October 15 of each contest year. By September of the following year, all winners' books are published—after several months of pre-production work on the books by the students and the editorial and artistic staff of Landmark editions. Works are published in Kansas City, Missouri for distribution nationally and internationally.

‡THE NENE AWARD, Hawaii State Library, 478 S. King St., Honolulu HI 96813. (808)586-3510. Estab. 1964. "The Nene Award was designed to help the children of Hawaii become acquainted with the best contemporary writers of fiction, become aware of the qualities that make a good book and choose the best rather than the mediocre." Previously published submissions only. Books must have been copyrighted not more than 6 years prior to presentation of award. Work is nominated. Awards Koa plaque. Judging by the children of Hawaii in grades 4-6. Requirements for entrants: books must be fiction, written by a living author, copyrighted not more than 6 years ago and suitable for children in grades 4, 5 and 6. Current and past winners are displayed in all participating school and public libraries.

‡NEW ERA WRITING, ART, PHOTOGRAPHY & MUSIC CONTEST, The Church of Jesus Christ of Latter-day Saints, 50 E. North Temple, Salt Lake City UT 84150. (801)240-2951. Fax: (801)240-5997. Managing Editor: Richard M. Romney. Annual contest. Estab. 1971. Purpose of the contest: to feature the creative abilities of young Latter-day Saints. Unpublished submissions only. Submissions made by the author. Deadline for entries: January 6. SASE for contest rules and entry forms. No entry fee. Awards partial scholarships to LDS colleges, cash prizes. Judging by *New Era* magazine editorial and design staffs. All rights acquired; reassigned to author upon written request. Requirements for entrants: must be an active member of the LDS Church, ages 12-23. Winning entries published in each August's issue.

JOHN NEWBERY MEDAL, Association for Library Service to Children, Division of the American Library Association, 50 E. Huron, Chicago IL 60611. (312)280-2163. Executive Director, ALSC: Susan Roman. Annual award. Estab. 1922. Purpose of award: to recognize the most distinguished contribution to American children's literature published in the US. Previously published submissions only; must be published prior to year award is given. Deadline for entries: December. SASE for award rules and entry forms. Entries not returned. No entry fee. Medal awarded at Caldecott/Newbery banquet during annual conference. Judging by Newbery Committee.

THE NOMA AWARD FOR PUBLISHING IN AFRICA, Kodansha Ltd., % Hans Zell Associates, 11 Richmond Rd., P.O. Box 56, Oxford 0X1 2SJ England. (0765)511428. Fax: 44-1865311534. Secretary of the Managing Committee: Hans M. Zell. Annual award. Estab. 1979. Purpose of award: to encourage publications of works by African writers and scholars in Africa, instead of abroad, as is still too often the case at present. Books in the following categories are eligible: scholarly or academic, books for children, literature and creative writing, including fiction, drama and poetry. Previously published submissions only. 1996 award given for book published in 1995. Deadline for entries: end of February 1996. Submissions must be made through publishers. Conditions of entry and submission forms are available from the secretariat. Entries not returned. No entry fee. Awards $5,000. Judging by the Managing Committee (jury): African scholars and book experts and representatives of the international book community. Chairman: Walter Bgoya. Requirements for entrants: Author must be African, and book must be published in Africa. "Winning titles are displayed at appropriate international book events."

‡NORTH AMERICAN INTERNATIONAL AUTO SHOW SHORT STORY HIGH SCHOOL POSTER CONTEST, Detroit Auto Dealers Association, 1800 W. Big Beaver Rd., Troy MI 48084-3531. (810)643-0250. Public Relations/Writing: Heidi Knickerbocker. Public Relations/Art: Jackie McConnell. Annual contest. Submissions made by the author and illustrator. Deadline for entries: October 21. "We are still trying to improve the contest and are still debating the dates every year." SASE for contest rules and entry forms. No entry fee. Five winners of the short story contest will each receive $500. Entries will be judged by an independent panel comprised of knowledgeable persons engaged in the literary field in some capacity. Entrants must be Michigan residents, including high school students enrolled in grades 9-12. Junior high school students in 9th grade are also eligible. Winners of the High School Poster Contest will receive $1,000, first place; $500, second; $250, third. Entries will be judged by an independent panel of recognized representatives of the art community. Entrants must be Michigan high school students enrolled in grades 9-12. Junior high students in 9th grade are also eligible. Winners will be announced during the North American International Auto Show in January and may be published in the *Auto Show Program* at the sole discretion of the D.A.D.A.

OHIOANA AWARD FOR CHILDREN'S LITERATURE, Ohioana Library Association, 65 S. Front St., Room 1105, Columbus OH 43215. (614)466-3831. Fax: (614)728-6974. Award Director: Linda R. Hengst. Open to adults. Annual award. Purpose of award: "to provide recognition for an Ohio author of children's literature." Submissions are made by the author, made by the author's agent, nominated by a person or group of people. Deadline for entries: December 31, 1996. SASE for award rules and entry forms. No entry fee. Awards approximately $1,000. Judging by a committee of 3-5 individuals familiar with children's literature, teachers, librarians, etc. "The recipient must have been born in Ohio, or lived in Ohio for a minimum of five years; the recipient must have established a distinguished publishing record of books for children and young people; the author's body of work has made, and continues to make, a significant contribution to the literature for young people; through the recipient's work as a writer, teacher, administrator, or through community service, interest in children's literature has been encouraged and children have become involved with reading. Also, it is desirable for the recipient to be present at Ohioana Day to receive to award. Only authors are considered at this time, for this award—illustrators are elegible for other Ohioana Awards."

‡OKLAHOMA BOOK AWARDS, Oklahoma Center for the Book, 200 NE 18th, Oklahoma City OK 73105. (405)521-2502. Fax: (405)525-7804. Award Director: Tracy Alford. Annual award . Estab. 1989. Purpose of award: "to honor Oklahoma writers and books about our state." Previously published submissions only. Submissions made by the author, author's agent, or entered by a person or group of people, including the publisher. Must be published during the calendar year preceding the award. Deadline for entries: January. SASE for award rules and entry forms. No entry fee. Awards a medal—no cash prize. Judging by a panel of 5 people for each category—a librarian, a working writer in the genre, editors, etc. Requirements for entrants: author must be an Oklahoma native, resident, former resident or have written a book with Oklahoma theme. Book will be displayed at banquet at the Cowboy Hall of Fame in Oklahoma City.

ORBIS PICTUS AWARD FOR OUTSTANDING NONFICTION FOR CHILDREN, National Council of Teachers of English, 1111 W. Kenyon Rd., Urbana IL 61801-1096. (217)328-3870, ext. 268. Chair, NCTE Committee on the Orbis Pictus Award for Outstanding Nonfiction for Children: Evelyn Freeman, The Ohio State University at Newark, Newark Ohio. Annual award. Estab. 1989. Purpose of award: to honor outstanding nonfiction works for children. Previously published submissions only. Submissions made by author, author's agent, by a person or group of people. Must be published January 1-December 31 of contest year. Deadline for entries: December 31. Call for award information. No entry fee. Awards a plaque given at the NCTE Elementary Section Luncheon at the NCTE Annual Convention in November. Judging by a committee.

***THE ORIGINAL ART**, Society of Illustrators, 128 E. 63rd St., New York NY 10021. (212)838-2560. Fax: (212)838-2561. Open to adults. Annual contest. Estab. 1981. Purpose of contest: to celebrate the fine art of children's book illustration. Previously published submissions only. Deadline for entries: July 20. SASE for contest rules and entry forms. Entry fee is $15/book.

Tips: "We would like our commissioned scripts to teach as well as entertain. Keep in mind the age groups (defined by each series) that our audience is composed of. Send submissions to the attention of Charlotte Dominick, executive director."

BOARSHEAD: MICHIGAN PUBLIC THEATER, 425 S. Grand Ave., Lansing MI 48933. (517)484-7800. Fax: (517)484-2564. Artistic Director: John Peakes. Director of Education: Page Tufford. Estab. 1966. Produces 3 children's plays/year. Produces children's plays for professional production. Majority of plays written for adult roles. Prefers 6 characters or less for touring productions, 6 characters for mainstage productions; one unit set, simple costumes. Recently produced plays: *The Lion, the Witch & the Wardrobe*, written by Joseph Robinette (fantasy for ages 6-12); *Step on a Crack*, written by Susan Zeder (family play for ages 6-12). Does not want to see musicals. Will consider previously performed work. Submission method: Query with synopsis, character breakdown and set description. Send "Attention: Educational Director." Include 10 pages of representative dialogue. Reports in 2 weeks on queries; 4 months on submissions. Pays writers $15-25/performance. Submissions returned with SASE. If no SASE, send self-addressed stamped post card for reply.

***CALIFORNIA THEATRE CENTER**, P.O. Box 2007, Sunnyvale CA 94087. (408)245-2978. Artistic Director: Gayle Cornelison. Estab. 1975. Produces 15 children's plays and 3 musicals for professional productions. 75% of plays/musicals written for adult roles; 20% for juvenile roles. Prefers material suitable for professional tours and repertory performance; one-hour time limit, limited technical facilities. Recently produced *Jungle Book*, adapted by Will Huddleston (Kipling's classic for ages 4th grade-up); *Heidi*, by Gayle Cornelison (classic for ages K-up). Does not want to see arcane, artsy, cute material. Will consider previously performed work. Query with synopsis, character breakdown and set description. Reports in 4 months. Rights negotiable. Pays writers royalties; pays $35-50/performance. Submissions returned with SASE.
Tips: "We sell to schools, so the title and material must appeal to teachers who look for things familiar to them. We look for good themes, universality. Avoid the cute."

CHILDREN'S STORY SCRIPTS, Baymax Productions, 2219 W. Olive Ave., Suite 130, Burbank CA 91506. (818)563-6105. Fax: (818)563-2968. Editor: Deedra Bebout. Estab. 1990. Produces 3-10 children's scripts/year. "Except for small movements and occasionally standing up, children remain seated in Readers Theatre fashion." Publishes scripts sold to schools, camps, churches, scouts, hotels, cruise lines, etc.; wherever there's a program to teach or entertain children. "All roles read by children except K-2 scripts, where kids have easy lines, leader helps read the narration. Prefer multiple cast members, no props or sets." Subject matter: scripts on all subjects. Targeted age range—K-8th grade, 5-13 years old. Recently published plays: *Dave's Unhappy Teeth*, by Helen Ksypka (about caring for one's teeth for grades K, 1, 2); *Families Are For Finding*, by Ellen B. Jackson (about perceptions of nontraditional families for grades 4-8). No stories that preach a point, stories about catastrophic disease or other terribly heavy topics, theatrical scripts with no narrative prose to move the story along, or stories that have only one speaking character. Will consider simultaneous submissions and previously performed work (if rights are available). Submission method: Submit complete ms. Reports in 2 weeks. Purchases all rights; authors retain copyrights. "We add support material and copyright the whole package." Pays writers in royalties (10-15% on sliding scale, based on number of copies sold). SASE for reply and return of submission.
Tips: "We're only looking for stories related to classsroom studies—educational topics with a freshness to them. Our scripts mix prose narration with character dialogue—we do not publish traditional, all-dialogue plays." Writer's guidelines packet available for business-sized SASE with 2 first-class stamps. Guidelines explain what Children's Story Scripts are, give 4-page examples from 2 different scripts, give list of suggested topics for scripts.

THE CHILDREN'S THEATRE COMPANY, 2400 Third Ave. S., Minneapolis MN 55404. (612)874-0500. Fax: (612)874-8119. Artistic Director: Jon Cranney. Estab. 1965. Produces 7 children's plays/year; 1-3 children's musicals/year. Produces children's plays for professional, not-for-profit productions. 60% of plays/musicals written for adult roles; 40% for juvenile roles in all productions. Recently produced plays: *Amazing Grace*, by Shay Youngblood; and *East of the Sun and West of the Moon*, by Tina Howe. Does not want to see plays written for child performers only. Will consider simultaneous submissions and previously performed work. **Only interested in agented material.** Submission method: Submit complete ms and score (if a musical). Reports in 2-6 months. Rights negotiable. Pays writers in royalties (2%). Submissions returned with SASE.

Tips: "The Children's Theatre Company rarely (if ever) produces unsolicited manuscripts; we continue a long tradition of producing new works commissioned to meet the needs of our audience and catering to the artistic goals of a specific season. Though the odds of us producing submitted plays are very slim, we always enjoy the opportunity to become acquainted with the work of a variety of artists, particularly those who focus on young audiences."

CIRCA '21 DINNER THEATRE, P.O. Box 3784, Rock Island IL 61204-3784. (309)786-2667. Producer: Dennis Hitchcock. Estab. 1977. Produces 3 children's plays or musicals/year. Produces children's plays for professional productions. 95% of plays/musicals written for adult roles; 5% written for juvenile roles. "Prefer a cast of 4-8—no larger than ten. Plays are produced on mainstage sets." Recently produced plays: *Tortoise & The Hare*, by Mark Pence (for ages 4-8), *Christmas Carol*, by Phillip Wm. McKinley (for age 8 and up). Submission method: Reports in 3 months. Payment negotiable.

Tips: Send complete script with audiotape of music.

I.E. CLARK, PUBLISHER, P.O. Box 246, Schulenburg TX 78956. (409)743-3232. Fax: (409)743-4765. Estab. 1956. Publishes 3 children's plays/year; 1 or 2 children's musicals/year. Medium to large casts preferred. Publishes plays for all ages. Published plays: *Wind of a Thousand Tales*, by John Glore (story about a young girl who doesn't believe in fairy tales, for ages 5-12); *Rock'n'Roll Santa*, by R. Eugene Jackson (Santa's reindeer form a rock band, for ages 4-16). Does not want to see plays that have not been produced. Will consider simultaneous submissions and previously performed work. Submission method: Submit complete ms and audio or video tape. Reports in 4-8 months. Pays writers in negotiable royalties. SASE for return of submission.

Tips: "We publish only high-quality literary works."

COMMUNITY CHILDREN'S THEATRE OF KANSAS CITY INC., 8021 E. 129th Terrace, Grandview MO 64030. (816)761-5775. Contact: Blanche Sellens. Estab. 1951. Produces 5 children's plays/year. Prefers casts of between 6-8, performed by women only. Produces children's plays for amateur productions for ages K-6. Produced play: *Red Versus the Wolf*, by Judy Wolferman, (musical, for K-6 audience). Submission method: Query first then submit complete ms. Reports in a matter of months. "Winning script is performed by one of the units for two years."

Tips: "Write for guidelines and details for The Margaret Bartle Annual Playwriting Award."

CONTEMPORARY DRAMA SERVICE, Division of Meriwether Publishing Ltd., 885 Elkton Dr., Colorado Springs CO 80907. (719)594-4422. Fax: (719)594-9916. Editor: Arthur Zapel. Estab. 1979. Publishes 45 children's plays/year; 6-8 children's musicals/year. 15% of plays/musicals written for adult roles; 85% for juvenile roles. Recently published plays: *Children of the Holocaust*, by Robert Mauro; *After the Game*, by Chip Healy (a self-esteem play); and *Three Wishes*, by Ted Sod and Suzanne Grant (about teenage parenthood for teens). "We do not publish plays for elementary level except for church plays for Christmas and Easter. All of our secular plays are for teens or college level." Does not want to see "full-length, 3-act plays (unless they have production history) or plays with dirty language." Will consider simultaneous submissions or previously performed work. Submission method: Query with synopsis, character breakdown and set description; "query first if a musical." Reports in 1 month. Purchases first rights. Pays writers royalty (10%) or buys material outright for $100-1,000. SASE for return of submission.

Tips: "Send for our writer's guidelines. Prevention plays are becoming more popular—topics such as teenage pregnancy, drugs, vandalism, etc."

THE COTERIE, 2450 Grand, Kansas City MO 64108. Phone/fax: (816)474-6785. Artistic Director: Jeff Church. Estab. 1979. Produces 7 children's plays/year; 1 children's musical/year. "Prefer casts of between five-seven, no larger than 15." Produces children's plays for professional productions. 80% of plays/musicals written for adult roles; 20% for juvenile roles. "We produce original plays, musicals and literary adaptations for ages five through adult." Produced plays: *Amelia Lives*, by Laura Annawyn Shamas (one-woman show on Amelia Earhart, for 6th grade

through adult); *Dinosaurus*, by Ed Mast and Lenore Bensinger (Mobil Oil workers discover cavern of dinosaurs, for ages 5 through adult). "We do *not* want to see 'camp' adaptations of fairytales." Submission method: Query with synopsis, sample scene, character breakdown and set description. Reports in 8-10 months. Rights purchased "negotiable." Pays writers in royalties per play of approximately $1,000-1,500. SASE for return of submission.
Tips: "We're interested in adaptations of classic literature with small casts, simple staging requirements; also multicultural topics and biography plays of Latin and African-American figures. There is a need for non-condescending material for younger age groups (5-8) and for middle school (ages 9-13)."

CREEDE REPERTORY THEATRE, P.O. Box 269, Creede CO 81130. (719)658-2541. Fax: (719)658-2343. Artistic Director: Richard Baxter. Estab. 1966. Produces 1 children's play/year; 1 musical/year. Limited to 4-6 cast members and must be able to tour. Produces children's plays for summer theater, school or professional productions. 100% of plays/musicals written for adult roles. Publishes plays for ages K-12. Recently produced plays: *Coyote Tales*, by Daniel Kramer and Company (Native American Coyote legend, for grades K-6); and *The Two of Us*, by Michael Frayn (contemporary relationship story, for ages 12-adult). Will consider simultaneous submissions and previously performed work. Submission method: Query first, submit complete ms and score, or query with synopsis, character breakdown and set description. Reports in 1 year. Pays writers in royalties (5%); pays $15-30 per performance.
Tips: Sees trends in "non-sexist, non-traditional casting and Native American/Hispanic American interest. No fairy tales unless non-traditional."

DRAMATIC PUBLISHING, INC., 311 Washington St., Woodstock IL 60098. (815)338-7170. Fax: (815)338-8981. Estab. 1885. Publishes 5-8 children's plays/year; 4-6 children's musicals. Recently published: *Song for the Navigator*, by Michael Cowell (integrating cultural heritage with "modern" life, for ages 8-14); and *A Woman Called Truth*, by Sandra Fenichel Asher (life and times of Sojourner Truth, includes some period music, for ages 11-18). Submission method: Submit complete ms/score and cassette/video tape (if a musical); include SASE if materials are to be returned. Reports in 4-6 months. Pays writers in royalties.

- Dramatic Publishing's plays have won several awards recently. Both *A Women Called Truth* and *Song for the Navigator* won A.A.T.E. Distinguished Play Award for 1994. *A Play About the Mothers of Plaza de Mayo*, by Alisa Palmer, won the Canadian Children's Award for Best New Play.

Tips: "Scripts should be from ½ to 1½ hours long, and not didactic or condescending. Original plays dealing with hopes, joys and fears of today's children are preferred to adaptations of old classics."

***EL CENTRO SU TEATRO**, 4725 High, Denver CO 80216. (303)296-0219. Fax: (303)296-4614. Artistic Director: Anthony J. Garcia. Estab. 1971. Produces 6 children's plays/year. "We are interested in plays by Chicanos or Latinos that speak to that experience. We do not produce standard musicals. We are a culturally specific company." Recently produced *Joaquim's Christmas*, by Anthony J. Garcia (children's Christmas play for ages 7-15); and *The Dragonslayer*, by Silviana Woods (young boy's relationship with grandfather for ages 7-15). Does not want to see "cutesy stuff." Will consider simultaneous submissions and previously performed work. Submissions method: query with synopsis, character breakdown and set description. Reports in 6 months. Buys regional rights. Pays writers per performance: $35 1st night, $25 subsequent. Submissions returned with SASE.
Tips: "People should write within their realm of experience but yet push their own boundaries. Writers should approach social issues within the human experience of their character."

ELDRIDGE PUBLISHING CO. INC., P.O. Box 1595, Venice FL 34284. (941)496-4679. Fax: (941)493-9680. Editor: Nancy Vorhis. Estab. 1906. Publishes approximately 30 children's plays/year (5 for elementary; 20 for junior and senior high); 2-3 high school musicals/year. Prefers simple staging; flexible cast size. "We publish for junior and high school, community theater and children's theater (adults performing for children), all genres." Recently published plays: *Hollywood Hillbillies*, by Tim Kelly (comedy about country folks who strike it rich, for high school community theater audiences); and *Theatre for a Small Planet*, by Jules Tasca (3 plays

for children from different countries, for elementary and up). Does not want to see adult material with strong language or sexual context. Will consider simultaneous submissions ("please let us know, however") and previously performed work. Submission method: Submit complete ms, score and tape of songs (if a musical). Reports in 2 months. Purchases all dramatic rights. Pays writers royalties of 50%; 10% copy sales; buys material outright for $200-500.
Tips: "We're always on the lookout for comedies which provide a lot of fun for our customers. But other more serious topics which concern teens, as well as intriguing mysteries, and children's theater programs are of interest to us as well. We know there are many new talented playwrights out there and we look forward to reading their fresh scripts."

ENCORE PERFORMANCE PUBLISHING, P.O. Box 692, Orem UT 84059. (801)225-0605. Estab. 1978. Publishes 10-20 children's plays/year; 8-15 children's musicals/year. Prefers equal male/female ratio if possible. Adaptations for K-12 and older. 60% of plays written for adult roles; 40% for juvenile roles. Recently published plays: *Scars & Stripes*, by Thomas Cadwaleder Jones (about racial harmony for ages 11-20); *We've Got Something to Say (Algo Tenemos Que Decirles)*, by Sheila Revear (English/Hispanic monologues for teens 11-19). Will only consider previously performed work. Looking for issue plays and unusual fairy tale adaptations. Submission method: Query first with synopsis, character breakdown, set description and production history. Reports in 1 month. Purchases all publication and production rights. Author retains copyright. Pays writers in royalties (50%). SASE for return of submission.
Tips: "Give us issue and substance, be controversial without offense. Use a laser printer! Don't send an old manuscript. Make yours look the most professional."

***FIRST STAGE MILWAUKEE**, 929 N. Water St., Milwaukee WI 53202. (414)273-7121. Fax: (414)273-5595. E-mail: 73531.2315@compuserve.com. Artistic Director: Rob Goodman. Estab. 1986. Produces 7 children's plays/year; 1 children's musical/year. Produces children's plays for professional productions. 75% of plays/musicals written for adult roles; 25% for juvenile roles. Recently produced plays: *Dinosaur*, by James DeVita (mother/daughter relationship for ages 7-12); and *Caddie Woodlawn*, by Susan Hunter (about a girl growing up). Does not want to see whole mss. Will consider simultaneous submissions, electronic submissions via disk or modem, previously performed work. Submission method: Query with synopsis, character breakdown and set description. Reports in months. Pays royalty. Submissions returned with SASE.

FLORIDA STUDIO THEATRE, 1241 N. Palm Ave., Sarasota FL 34236. (813)366-9017. Artistic Director: Richard Hopkins. Estab. 1980. Produces 3 children's plays/year; 1-3 children's musicals/year. Produces children's plays for professional productions. 50% of plays/musicals written for adult roles; 50% for juvenile roles. "Prefer small cast plays that use imagination more than heavy scenery." Will consider simultaneous submissions and previously performed work. Submission method: Query with synopsis, character breakdown and set description. Reports in 3 months. Rights negotiable. Pay negotiable. Submissions returned with SASE.
Tips: "Children are a tremendously sophisticated audience. The material should respect this."

THE FOOTHILL THEATRE COMPANY, P.O. Box 1812, Nevada City CA 95959. (916)265-9320. Artistic Director: Philip Charles Sneed. Estab. 1977. Produces 0-2 children's plays/year; 0-2 children's musicals/year. Professional nonprofit theater. 95% of plays/musicals written for adult roles; 5% for juvenile roles. "Small is better, but will consider anything." Produced *The Golden Grotto*, by Cleve Haubold/James Alfred Hitt (fantasy about a frog prince, comedy for all ages); *The Best Christmas Pageant Ever*, by Barbara Robinson (family Christmas comedy, for all ages). Does not want to see traditional fairy tales. Will consider simultaneous submissions and previously performed work. Submission method: Query with synopsis, character breakdown and set description. Reports in 6 months. Buys negotiable rights. Payment method varies. Submissions returned with SASE.

The asterisk before a listing indicates the listing is new in this edition.

Tips: "Trends in children's theater include cultural diversity, real life issues (drug use, AIDS, etc.), mythological themes with contemporary resonance. Don't talk down to or underestimate children."

THE FREELANCE PRESS, P.O. Box 548, Dover MA 02030. (508)785-1260. Managing Editor: Narcissa Campion. Estab. 1979. Produces 3 musicals and/or plays/year. Casts are comprised of young people, ages 8-15, and number 25-30. "We publish original musicals on contemporary topics for children and adaptations of children's classics (e.g., Rip Van Winkle)." Published plays: *The Tortoise and the Hare* (based on story of same name, for ages 8-12); *Monopoly*, (3 young people walk through board game, for ages 11-15). No plays for adult performers. Will consider simultaneous submissions and previously performed work. Submission method: Submit complete ms and score with SASE. Reports in 3 months. Pays writers 10% royalties. SASE for return of submission.

THE GREAT AMERICAN CHILDREN'S THEATRE COMPANY, P.O. Box 92123, Milwaukee WI 53202. (414)276-4230. Fax: (414)276-2214. Executive Producer: Teri Solomon Mitze. Estab. 1975. Produces 2 children's plays/year. Produces children's plays for professional productions; 100% written for adult roles. Produced plays: *The Secret Garden*, by Brett Reynolds (children's classic, for grades K-8); *Charlie & the Chocolate Factory*, by Richard R. George (children's classic, for grades K-8). Will consider previously performed work. Submission method: Query with synopsis, character breakdown and set description. Reports in weeks. Rights and payment negotiable.

THE GROWING STAGE THEATRE, P.O. Box 132, Chester NJ 07930. (908)879-4946. Executive Director: Stephen L. Fredericks. Estab. 1982. Produces 8 children's plays/year; 3 children's musicals/year. "We have a 5-person professional company that works with our community performers." 60% of plays/musicals written for adult roles; 40% for juvenile roles. Produced: *Aladdin*, by Perry Arthur Kroeger, (adaptation from classic tale, for K-8th grade); and *The Pied Piper of Hamelin, AZ*, by Stephen L. Fredericks and Perry Arthur Kroeger (adaptation of classic poem, K-6th grades). Plays for young audiences only. Will consider previously performed work. Submission method: Query with synopsis, character breakdown and set description. Reports in 1 month. "Contracts are developed individually." Pays $25-75/performance. Submissions returned with SASE.

Tips: "There's an overabundance on issue-oriented plays. Creativity, quality, the standards we place on theater aimed at adults should not be reduced in preparing a script for young people. We, together, are forming the audience of tomorrow. Don't repel young people by making the theater another resource for the infomercial—nurture, challenge and inspire them."

***IMAGICATION LTD.**, 42 E. Gay St., Suite 710, Columbus OH 43207. (614)221-0022. Fax: (614)224-5881. E-mail: fngrassoc@aol.com. Artistic Director: Jeffrey J. Fanger. Estab. 1994. Produces 4 children's plays/year. 99% of plays/musicals written for juvenile roles. Subject matter: children stories (for ages 5-12). Recently produced audio dramas: *The Reluctant Dragon*, based on Kenneth Grahame's work (ages 5-10); *Legends of Pocahontas' People* (5 Indian myths for ages 5-12). Will consider simultaneous submissions, electronic submissions via disk or modem, previously performed work. Submission method: query first, query with synopsis, character breakdown and set description. Reports in 3 months. Buys copyright or audio rights. Buys material outright. Submissions returned with SASE.

INDIANA REPERTORY THEATRE, 140 W. Washington, Indianapolis IN 46204. (317)635-5277. Artistic Director: Libby Appel. Estab. 1971. Produces 3 children's plays/year. Produces children's plays for professional productions. 100% of plays written for adult roles. Limit 8 in cast, 75 minute running time. Recently produced plays: *Tales from the Arabian Nights*, by Michael Dixon; *Red Badge of Courage*, adaptation by Thomas Olson. Does not want to see preschool and K-4 material. Will consider previously performed work. Submission method: Query with synopsis, character breakdown and set description to Janet Allen, Association. Artistic Director. Reports in 6 months. Pays writers negotiable royalty (6%) or commission fee. Submissions returned with SASE.

JEWISH ENSEMBLE THEATRE, 6600 W. Maple Rd., West Bloomfield MI 48322. (810)788-2900. Fax: (810)661-3680. Artistic Director: Evelyn Orbach. Estab. 1989. Produces 2-3 children's plays/year. Produces children's plays for professional productions. Prefers small casts and unit set. Recently produced play: *Generations*, by Eden Cooper Sage and Marshall Zweig (about inter-generational conflicts for middle and high school audience).
Tips: "Plays are toured to various schools and youth organizations."

THE MUNY FIRST STAGE, (formerly The Muny Student Theatre), 634 N. Grand, Suite 118, St. Louis MO 63103. (314)652-5213. Fax: (314)533-3345. Executive Artistic Director: Christopher Limber. Estab. 1979. Produces 5 children's plays/year; 1 or 2 children's musicals/year. "We produce a touring and mainstage season September-May and offer extensive theater classes throughout the entire year." 100% of plays/musicals written for adult roles; 40% for juvenile roles. Prefers cast of 4 or 5 equity actors, for touring productions; no limit for mainstage productions. "Tour sets are limited in size." Produced plays: *Meet Willie*, adapted by Chris Limber (introduction to Shakespeare for 4th grade-adult); *On The Rays of The Sun* by Patton Hasegawa (about African heros and heroines for 1st grade-adult). Will consider simultaneous submissions and previously performed work. Submission method: Query with synopsis, character breakdown and set description. Reports in 3 months. Rights negotiable.
Tips: "We emphasize diverse ethnic casting and multicultural material. Tour shows should fit into the school curriculum. The Muny First Stage's mission is to introduce theater to young people, to encourage creative learning and to develop future theater audiences. The company is now one of the most comprehensive theater education programs in Missouri. Each year the company reaches more than 100,000 students through its resident touring company, professional storytellers, mainstage productions and theater classes. As film and television become more sophisticated, we're seeing a focus on theatricality, imaginative use of the live theater medium; use of young actors in major roles; opera for young performers; strong adaptations of classics which highlight contemporary issues."

THE NEW CONSERVATORY THEATRE CENTER, 25 Van Ness Ave., San Francisco CA 94102. (415)861-4914. Fax: (415)861-6988. Executive Director: Ed Decker. Estab. 1981. Produces 6-10 children's plays/year; 1-2 children's musicals/year. Limited budget. Produces children's plays as part of "a professional theater arts training program for youths ages 4-19 during the school year and two summer sessions. The New Conservatory also produces educational plays for its touring company." 100% written for juvenile roles. "We do not want to see any preachy or didactic material." Submission method: Query with synopsis, character breakdown and set description, or submit complete ms and score. Reports in 3 months. Rights purchased negotiable. Pays writers in royalties. SASE for return of submission.
Tips: Sees trend in: "addressing socially relevant issues for young people and their families."

NEW PLAYS INCORPORATED, P.O. Box 5074, Charlottesville VA 22905. (804)979-2777. Publisher: Patricia Whitton. Estab. 1964. Publishes 4 plays/year; 1 or 2 children's musicals/year. Publishes "generally material for kindergarten through junior high." Recently published: *Sitting in a Tree*, by Lou Furman (child's response to divorce for ages 7-12); and *3 Girls & Clorox*, by Belinda Acosta (relationships in middle school). Does not want to see "adaptations of titles I already have. No unproduced plays; no junior high improvisations." Will consider simultaneous submissions and previously performed work. Submissions method: Submit complete ms and score. Reports in 2 months. Purchases exclusive rights to sell acting scripts. Pays writers in royalties (50% of production royalties; 10% of script sales). SASE for return of submission.

NEW YORK STATE THEATRE INSTITUTE, 155 River St., Troy NY 12180. (518)274-3200. Fax: (518)274-3815. Artistic Director: Patricia B. Snyder. Estab. 1976. Produces 1-2 children's plays/year; 1-2 children's musicals/year. Produces family plays for professional theater. 90% of plays/musicals are written for adult roles; 10% for juvenile roles. Does not want to see plays for children only. Produced plays: *The Secret Garden*, adapted by Thomas W. Olson (for all ages); *To Kill a Mockingbird*, adapted by Christopher Sergel (for grade 8 and up). Will consider simultaneous submissions and previously performed work. Submission method: Query with synopsis, character breakdown and set description; submit complete ms and tape of songs (if a musical). Reports in 2-3 months on submissions; 1 month for queries. SASE for return of submission.

Tips: Writers should be mindful of "audience *sophistication*. We do not wish to see material that is childish. Writers should submit work that is respectful of young people's intelligence and perception—work that is appropriate for families, but that is also challenging and provocative."

OMAHA THEATER COMPANY FOR YOUNG PEOPLE, (formerly Emmy Gifford Children's Theater), 201 Farnam St., Omaha NE 68102. (402)345-4852. Artistic Director: James Larson. Estab. 1949. Produces 9 children's plays/year; 1 children's musical/year. Produces children's plays for professional productions. 100% of plays/musicals written for adult roles. Need plays with small casts, no fly space necessary. Produced plays: *Pippi Longstocking*; *Bye Bye Birdie*. Does not want to see adult plays. Will consider simultaneous submissions, electronic submissions via disk or modem, or previously performed work. Submission method: Query first. Reports in 6 months. Pays writers in royalties (6%). Submissions returned with SASE.

THE OPEN EYE THEATER, (formerly The Open Eye: New Stagings), P.O. Box 204, Denver NY 12421. Phone/fax: (607)326-4986. Artistic Director: Amie Brockway. Estab. 1972 (theater). Produces plays for a family audience. Most productions are with music, but are not musicals. "Casts are usually limited to six performers because of economic reasons. Technical requirements are kept to a minimum for touring purposes." Produces professional productions using members of Actor's Equity Association. Most plays/musicals written for adult roles. Produced plays: *The Wise Men of Chelm*, by Sandra Fenichel Asher (weaving of several Jewish folk tales, for ages 8 through adult); *Freedom is My Middle Name*, by Lee Hunkins (unsung African-American heroes, for ages 8 through adult). "No videos or cassettes. Letter of inquiry only." Will consider previously performed work. Rights agreement negotiated with author. Pays writers one time fee or royalty negotiated with publisher. SASE for return of submission.
Tips: "We are seeing a trend toward plays that are appropriate for a family audience and that address today's multicultural concerns."

PIONEER DRAMA SERVICE, P.O. Box 4267, Englewood CO 80155. (303)779-4035. Fax: (303)779-4315. Producer: Steven Fendrich. Estab. 1960. Publishes 7 children's plays/year; 7 children's musicals/year. Subject matter: Publishes plays for ages 9-high school. Recently published plays/musicals: *Kilroy Was Here*, by Tim Kelly and Bill Francoeur (musical salute to the G.I. Joes and Jills of 1940's for all ages); and *Great Expectations*, by David Coons and Karen Coons (adapted from Dicken's Classic novel, for ages high school and up). Wants to see "script, scores, tapes, pics and reviews." Will consider simultaneous submissions, CAD electronic submissions via disk or modem, previously performed work. Submission method: Query with synopsis, character breakdown and set description. Submit complete ms and score (if a musical). Contact: Lynne Zborowski, assistant editor. Reports in 3 months. Purchases all rights. Pays writers in royalties (10% on sales, 50% royalties on productions); or buys material outright for $200-1,000.

PLAYERS PRESS, INC., P.O. Box 1132, Studio City CA 91614-0132. (818)789-4980. Vice President: R. W. Gordon. Estab. 1965. Publishes 5-50 children's plays/year; varying children's musicals/year. Subject matter: "We publish for all age groups." Published plays: *Tall Betsy and the Cracker Barrel Tales*, by Jacque Wheeler (children's musical based on folktales, for grades 3-7); and *Try a Little Shakespeare* (Shakespearean play modernized, for grades 4-7). Considers previously performed work only. Submission method: Query with synopsis, character breakdown and set description; include #10 SASE with query. Reports on query in 2-4 weeks; submissions in 3-12 months. Purchases stage, screen, TV rights. Payment varies; work purchased possibly outright upon written request. Submissions returned with SASE.
Tips: "Entertainment quality is on the upswing and needs to be directed at the world, no longer just the U.S. Please submit with two #10 SASEs plus ms-size SASE. Please do not call."

THE PLAYHOUSE JR., 222 Craft Ave., Pittsburgh PA 15213. (412)621-4445. Fax: (412)687-3606. Managing Producer: Daniel Vinski. Estab. 1949. Produces 5 children's plays/year; 1 children's musical/year. Produces children's plays for semi-professional production with a college theater department. 100% of plays/musicals written for adult roles. Produced plays: *The Three Musketeers*, by Bruce Hurlbut (adaptation of Dumas's classic, for age 3-middle school); *Jack and the Beantree*, by Paul Laurakas (musical, Appalachian adaptation of the fairytale, for grades

K-4). Does not want to see "strong social problem plays." Will consider simultaneous submissions or previously produced work. Submission method: Query with synopsis, character breakdown and set description (first drafts); submit complete ms and score (if a musical). Reports in 6 weeks. Purchases performance rights; negotiable. Pays writers commission/royalty. SASE for return of submission.

Tips: Looks for "clearly developed plot lines, imaginative use of the space, rather than realistic interiors. Plays should stimulate the imaginations of the director/producer, casts, designers and, ultimately, the audiences."

PLAYS FOR YOUNG AUDIENCES, P.O. Box 4267, Englewood CO 80155. (303)779-4035. Fax: (303)779-4315. Producer: Steven Fendrich. Estab. 1989. Publishes 7 children's plays/year; 7 children's musicals/year. Subject matter: Publishes plays for preschool-12th grade audience. Recently produced musicals: "OZ!," by Tim Kelly and Bill Francoeur (new musical version of classic for ages preschool-adult); and "Legend of Pocahontas," by Vera Morris (ages 6- junior high). Wants to see "script, score, tape, pictures and reviews." Will consider simultaneous submissions, electronic submissions via disk or modem, previously performed work. Submission method: Query with synopsis, character breakdown and set description; submit complete ms and score (if a musical). Contact: Lynne Zborowski, assistant editor. Reports in 3 months. Purchases all rights. Pays writers in royalties (10% in sales, 50% on productions).

PLAYS, THE DRAMA MAGAZINE FOR YOUNG PEOPLE, 120 Boylston St., Boston MA 02116-4615. (617)423-3157. Managing Editor: Elizabeth Preston. Estab. 1941. Publishes 70-75 children's plays/year. "Props and staging should not be overly elaborate or costly. Our plays are performed by children in school from lower elementary grades through junior-senior high." 100% of plays written for juvenile roles. Subject matter: Audience is lower grades through junior/senior high. Recently published plays: *The Tutankhamun Murder Case*, by John Murray (murder mystery for for junior-senior high); and *Bunny Rabid*, by Steven Pricone (comedy explaining the food chain for middle grades). Send nothing downbeat—no plays about drugs, sex or other 'heavy' topics." Submission methods: Query first on adaptations of folk tales and classics; otherwise submit complete ms. Reports in 2-4 weeks. Purchases all rights. Pay rates vary. Guidelines available; send SASE. Sample copy $3.50.

Tips: "Above all, plays must be entertaining for young people with plenty of action, fast-paced dialogue and a satisfying conclusion. Any message imparted should be secondary to the entertainment value. No sex, drugs, violence, alcohol."

SEATTLE CHILDREN'S THEATRE, P.O. Box 9640, Seattle WA 98109. Literary Manager and Dramaturg: Deborah Frockt. Estab. 1975. Produces 6 full-length children's plays/year; 1 full-length children's musical/year. Produces children's plays for professional productions (September-June). 95% of plays/musicals written for adult roles; 5% for juvenile roles. "We generally use adult actors even for juvenile roles." Prefers no turntable, no traps. Produced *The Rememberer*, adapted by Steven Dietz (Native American girl struggles to maintain her cultural legacy when she is forced to attend boarding school in 1912, for ages 8 and up); *Afternoon of the Elves*, adapted by Y. York, book by Janet Taylor Lisle (friendship, imagination, getting to know those you think are different, for 8 and up). Does not want to see anything that condescends to young people—anything overly broad in style. Will consider simultaneous submissions and previously performed work. Submission method: Query with synopsis, maximum 10 sample pages of dialogue, résumé or bio. Reports in 3-6 months on synopsis; 6-12 months on mss. Rights vary. Payment method varies. Submissions returned with SASE.

Tips: "Please *do not* send unsolicited manuscripts. We welcome queries by all populations and encourage queries by women and minorities. We prefer sophisticated material (our weekend performances have an audience that is half adults). All shows SCT produces are multiracially cast."

STAGE ONE: THE LOUISVILLE CHILDREN'S THEATRE, 425 W. Market, Louisville KY 40202. (502)589-5946. Fax: (502)589-5779. Call for e-mail address. Producing Director: Moses Goldberg. Estab. 1946. Produces 8-10 children's plays/year; 1-4 children's musicals/year. Stage One is an Equity company producing children's plays for professional productions. 100% of plays/musicals written for adult roles. "Sometimes we do use students in selected productions."

Recently produced plays: *Young Black Beauty*, by Aurand Haivip (about a colt growing up for ages 6-12); and *John Lennon & Me*, by Cherie Bennett (about cystic fibrosis; peer acceptance for ages 11-17). Does not want to see "camp or condescension." Will consider simultaneous submissions, electronic submissions via disk or modem and previously performed work. Submission method: Submit complete ms, score and tape of songs (if a musical); include the author's résumé if desired. Reports in 3-4 months. Pays writers in royalties (5-6%) or $25-75/performance.
Tips: Looking for "stageworthy and respectful dramatizations of the classic tales of childhood, both ancient and modern; plays relevant to the lives of young people and their families; and plays directly related to the school curriculum."

TADA!, 120 W. 28th St., New York NY 10001. (212)627-1732. Fax: (212)243-6736. Artistic Director: Janine Nina Trevens. Estab. 1984. Produces 3-4 staged readings of children's plays and musicals/year; 2-3 children's musicals/year. "All actors are children, ages 6-17." Produces children's plays for professional, year-round theater. 100% of plays/musicals written for juvenile roles. Recently produced musicals: *Sleepover*, book by Philip Freedman, music and lyrics by James Beloff (story of girls' sleep-over party crashed by boys, ages 3-adult); and *The History Mystery*, book by Janine Nina Trevens and lyrics by Margaret Rose, music by Eric Rockwell (kids travel back in time and meet Martin Luther King, Jr., the Wright Brothers, and Ben Franklin when they were children. They also learn of the women's struggle to get the vote, Declaration of Independence and World War II, ages 4-adult). Does not want to see fairy tales or material that talks down to children. Submission method: Query with synopsis, character breakdown and set description; submit complete ms, score and tape of songs (if a musical). Reports in 6 months "or in February following the January deadline for our playwriting competition." Rights purchased "depend on the piece." Pays writers in royalties of 1-6% or pays commissioning fee. SASE for return of submissions.
Tips: "For plays for our Staged Reading Contest, submit between September and January. We're looking for plays with current topics that specific age ranges can identify with, with a small cast of children and one or two adults. Our company is multi-racial and city-oriented. We are not interested in fairy tales. We like to produce material that kids relate to and that touches their lives today."

THEATRE FOR YOUNG AMERICA, 4881 Johnson Dr., Mission KS 66205. (913)831-2131. Artistic Director: Gene Mackey. Estab. 1974. Produces 7 children's plays/year; 3-5 children's musicals/year. "We use a small cast (4-7), open thrust stage." Theatre for Young America is a professional equity company. 90% of plays/musicals written for adult roles; 10% for juvenile roles. Produced plays: *The Wizard of Oz*, by Jim Eiler and Jeanne Bargy (for ages 6 and up); *A Partridge in a Pear Tree*, by Lowell Swortzell (deals with the 12 days of Christmas, for ages 6 and up); *Three Billy Goats Gruff*, by Gene Mackey and Molly Jessup (Norwegian folk tales, for ages 6 and up). Submission method: Query with synopsis, character breakdown and set description. Will consider simultaneous submissions and previously performed work. Reports in 2 months. Purchases production rights, tour rights in local area. Pays writers in royalties or $10-50/performance.
Tips: Looking for "cross-cultural material that respects the intelligence, sensitivity and taste of the child audience."

THEATREWORKS/USA, 890 Broadway, New York NY 10003. (212)677-5959. Fax: (212)353-1632. Associate Artistic Director: Barbara Pasternack. Estab. 1960. Produces 3-4 children's plays and 8 children's musicals/year. Cast of 5 or 6 actors. Play should be 1 hour long, tourable. Professional children's theatre comprised of adult equity actors. 100% of musicals are written

for adult roles. Produced plays: *Curious George*, book and lyrics by Thomas Toce, music by Tim Brown (adaptation, for grades K-3); *Little Women*, by Allan Knee, incidental music by Kim Olen and Alison Hubbard (adaptation, for grades 4-8). No fractured, typical "kiddy theater" fairy tales or shows written strictly to teach or illustrate. Will consider previously performed work. Submission method: Query first with synopsis, character breakdown and set description. Reports in 6 months. Pays writers royalties of 6%. SASE for return of submission.
Tips: "Plays should be not only entertaining, but 'about something.' They should touch the heart and the mind. They should not condescend to children."

WEST COAST ENSEMBLE, 6760 Lexington Ave., Los Angeles CA 90038. (213)871-8673. Artistic Director: Les Hanson. Estab. 1982. Produces 1 children's play/year or 1 children's musical/year. "We operate under an Equity Theatre for Young Audiences contract or under the Los Angeles 99-seat Theatre Plan." 90% of plays/musicals written for adult roles; 10% for juvenile roles. Prefers simple sets; casts of no more than 8. There are no limits on style or subject matter. Will consider simultaneous submissions (no more than 2) and previously performed work. Submission method: Submit complete ms and score (if a musical). Purchases exclusive rights to perform play/musical in Southern California. Pays writers $25-50 per performance. Submissions returned with SASE.

THE YOUNG COMPANY, P.O. Box 225, Milford NH 03055. (603)889-2330. Producing Director: Daniel Henderson. Estab. 1984. Produces 4-6 children's plays/year; 1-2 children's musicals/year. "Scripts should not be longer than an hour, small cast preferred; very small production budgets, so use imagination." The Young Company is a professional training program associated with American Stage Festival, a professional theater. Produced plays/musicals: *Dancing on the Ceiling*, by Austin Tichenor (adaptation of Kafka's *Metamorphosis*, for ages 7 and up); *High Pressure Zone*, music by Andrew Howard, book and lyrics by Austin Tichenor (musical about addictive behavior, for middle school and older audience); *The First Olympics*, by Eve Muson and Austin Tichenor (deals with mythology/Olympic origins, for 6 year old through adult audience). Prefers adaptations with name recognition to young audiences. Does not want to see condescending material. Submission method: Query with synopsis, character breakdown and sample score. Purchases first production credit rights on all future materials. Pays small fee and housing for rehearsals.
Tips: Looks for "concise and legible presentation, songs that further dramatic action. Develop material with strong marketing possibilities. See your work in front of an audience and be prepared to change it if your audience doesn't 'get it.' Don't condescend to your audience. Tell them a *story*."

Scriptwriter's Markets/'95-'96 changes

The following markets were in the 1995 edition of *Children's Writer's & Illustrator's Market* but do not have listings in this edition. Most did not respond to our request to update their listings.

Art Extensions Theater
Samuel French, Inc.
Honolulu Theatre for Youth
St. Louis Black Repertory Co.
Santa Monica Group Theatre

Special Markets

Walk into any children's-only bookstore—or even the children's department of any book superstore—and you'll find a variety of ancillary products. In fact, posters, coloring books, activity books, stickers, greeting cards, giftwrap, puzzles and games may all have spaces on bookstore shelves, in addition to their usual places in department stores, card shops and toy stores. The reason is simple: Booksellers have discovered such sidelines are valuable.

First, these products act as bait to lure customers who might not visit the bookstore if it only carried books. Prominently displayed sidelines increase the visual appeal and enhance the image of a bookstore. Second, booksellers like selling sidelines because they offer a higher margin of profit than books, making them a good source of supplemental revenue. Bookstore owners are especially interested in products which are book-related or education-oriented.

This section features special markets that produce, among other items, greeting cards, comic books, games and puzzles for children and use the services of freelancers. Because these markets create a potpourri of products, their needs vary greatly. Carefully read through the listings to determine desired subjects and methods of submission. If more specific guidelines are available from companies, write to request them. As in other areas of the children's market, remember the materials created must not only appeal to children but also to the adults who will buy them.

ALEF JUDAICA, 8440 Warner Dr., Culver City CA 90232. (310)202-0024. Owner: Guy Orner. Greeting card and paper products company. Publishes Judaica card line, gift wrap and party goods. Publishes greeting cards (Hanukkah card line), books and novelties (Hanukkah party goods).
Writing: Needs freelance writing for children's greeting cards and books. Makes 50 writing assignments/year. To contact, send cover letter and writing samples. Reports only if interested. For greeting cards, pays flat fee of $100-200. For other writing, pays by the project (range: $1,000-5,000). Pays on publication. Purchases all rights and exclusive product rights. Credit line given.
Illustration: Needs freelance illustration for children's greeting cards and party goods. Makes about 50 illustration assignments/year. To contact, send published samples, photocopies and portfolio. Reports only if interested. Keeps materials on file. For children's greeting cards, pays flat fee of $100-200. For other artwork, payment "depends on how complicated the project is." Pays on publication. Buys all rights, exclusive product rights. Credit line sometimes given.
Tips: 25% of products are made for kids or have kids' themes. Seasonal material should be submitted 1 year in advance.

***ALLPORT EDITIONS**, 6323 SW 60th Ave., Portland OR 97221. (503)223-7268. Art Director: Victoria Allport. Estab. 1980. Publishes greeting cards with line specifically for the children's market. Publishes greeting cards (These Days Kids).
Writing: Needs freelance writing for children's greeting cards. Makes 3 writing assignments/month. For greeting cards, accepts both rhymed and unrhymed verse ideas. Looks for greeting card writing which addresses birthday themes. To contact, send cover letter and writing samples. Reports in 1 month. Materials returned with SASE. Pays on publication. Buys exclusive product rights; negotiable. Credit line sometimes given.
Illustration: Needs freelance illustration for children's greeting cards. Makes 75 illustration assignments/month. Prefers animals, florals, still life, humorous. Uses color artwork only. To contact send color photocopies or slides. To query with specific ideas, write to request disclosure

form first. Reports in 1 month. Materials returned with SASE, keeps materials on file. For greeting cards, pays flat fee of $150, royalty of 5% for life of card. Pays on publication. Buys exclusive product rights; negotiable. Credit line given. Artist's guidelines available for SASE.
Tips: "Submit seasonal material six months in advance."

ARISTOPLAY, LTD., P.O. Box 7529, Ann Arbor MI 48107. (313)995-4353. Fax: (313)995-4611. E-mail: aristo@chamber.ann-arbor.mi.vs. Product Development Director: Lorraine Hopping Egan. Art Director: Jack Thompson. Estab. 1979. Produces educational board games and card decks, activity kits—all educational subjects.
Illustration: Needs freelance illustration and graphic designers (including art directors) for games and card decks. Makes 2-4 illustration assignments/year. To contact, send cover letter, résumé, published samples or color photocopies. Reports back in 1 month if interested. For artwork, pays by the project, $500-5,000. Pays on acceptance (½-sketch, ½-final). Buys all rights. Credit line given.
Photography: Buys photography from freelancers. Wants realistic, factual photos.
Tips: 100% of products are made for kids or have kids themes. "Creating board games requires a lot of back and forth in terms of design, illustration, editorial and child testing; the more flexible you are, the better. Also, factual accuracy is important." Target age group 4-14. "We are an educational game company. Writers and illustrators working for us must be willing to research the subject and period of focus."

A/V CONCEPTS CORP., 30 Montauk Blvd., Oakdale NY 11769. (516)567-7227. Fax: (516)567-8745. Editor: Laura Solimene. President: Philip Solimene. Estab. 1969. "We are an educational publisher. We publish books for the K-12 market—primarily language arts and math and reading."
Writing: Needs freelance writing for classic workbooks only: adaptations from fine literature. Makes 5-10 assignments/year. To contact, send cover letter and writing samples and SASE. Reports in 3 weeks. For writing assignments, pays by the project ($700-1,000). Pays on publication. Buys all rights.
Illustration: Needs freelance illustration for classic literature adaptations, fine art, some cartoons, super heroes. Makes 15-20 illustration assignments/year. Needs "super hero-like characters in four-color and b&w." To contact, send cover letter and photocopies. Reports back in 3 weeks. For artwork, pays by the project (range: $200-1,000). Pays on publication. Buys all rights.
Tips: 20% of products are made for kids or have kid themes. Submit seasonal material 4 months in advance. "We're getting into CD-ROM development."

THE AVALON HILL GAME CO., 4517 Harford Rd., Baltimore MD 21214. (410)254-9200. Fax: (410)254-0991. President: Jack Dott. Editor: A. Eric Dott. Art Director: Chris Kim. Estab. 1958. Produces comic books (*Tales from the Floating Vagabone*), magazine for girls ages 7-14 and an extensive line of games.
Writing: Makes 6 writing assignments/month; 36/year. To contact send cover letter, résumé, client list, writing samples. Reports back only if interested. Pays on publication. Buys all rights. Credit line sometimes given.
Illustration: Makes 2-3 illustration assignments/month; 30/year. Prefers styles pertaining to general interest topics for girls. To contact send cover letter, résumé, published samples, portfolio. Reports in 1 month. Pays on acceptance. Buys all rights. Credit line sometimes given.

THE BEISTLE COMPANY, P.O. Box 10, Shippensburg PA 17257. (717)532-2131. Product Manager: C. Michelle Luhrs-Wiest. Art Director: Brad Clever. Estab. 1900. Paper products company. Produces decorations and party goods, bulletin board aides, posters—baby, baptism, birthday, holidays, educational.
Illustration: Needs freelance illustration for decorations, party goods, educational aides. Makes 20 illustration assignments/year. Prefers fanciful style, cute 4- to 5-color illustration in gouache.

The asterisk before a listing indicates the listing is new in this edition.

To contact, send cover letter, résumé, client list, promo piece. To query with specific ideas, phone or write. Reports only if interested. Materials returned with SASE; materials filed. Pays by the project (range: $300-400 or by contractual agreement; price varies according to type of project). Pays on acceptance. Buys all rights. Artist's guidelines available for SASE.
Photography: Buys photography from freelancers. Buys stock and assigns work. Buys 10-15 stock images/year. Makes 30-50 assignments/year. Uses 35mm, 2¼×2¼, 4×5 transparencies. To contact, send cover letter, résumé, slides, client list, promo piece. Reports only if interested. Materials returned if accompanied with SASE; materials filed. Pays on acceptance. Buys first rights. Credit line sometimes given—depends on project. Guidelines available for SASE.
Tips: 50% of products are made for kids' or have kids themes. Submit seasonal material 6-8 months in advance.

RUSS BERRIE & COMPANY, INC., 111 Bauer Dr., Oakland NJ 07436. (201)337-9000. Director, Greeting Cards: Angelica Urra. Estab. 1963. Greeting card and paper products company. Manufactures "all kinds of paper products and impulse gifts—photo frames, mugs, buttons, baby gift products, cards, plaques, plush, ceramics, toys, bibs, booties, etc."
Writing: Needs freelance writing for children's books, booklets, greeting cards and other children's products (T-shirts, buttons, bookmarks, stickers, diaries, address books, plaques, perpetual (undated) calendars). "We seek material for children's books with strong story lines and characters that can effectively stand alone as plush, dolls, toys, ceramics, etc. We also seek short, short stories or character sketches revolving around a character (plush or toy) that you have developed. The short, short story would then be used on a two to four page small hang tag for the item itself, rather than as a separate book. Educatational or environmental themes are welcome, but please, no preaching . . . an engaging story is most important." Makes 10-50 writing assignments/month. Tired of children's greeting card writing which talks down to kids. To contact, send writing samples. Reports in 2-3 months. Materials returned with SASE; files materials "if we think there may be interest later." For greeting cards, pays flat fee of $50-100 per piece of copy. For books, plaques and other writing, pays more, depending on the project. Pays on acceptance. Buys all rights or exclusive product rights. Writer's guidelines for SASE.
Illustration: Needs freelance illustration for children's greeting cards and other children's products. Makes 10-50 illustration assignments/month. Artwork should be "contemporary, eye catching, colorful—professional. Because we also do products for parents and parents-to-be, we seek both juvenile *and* adult looks in products about children." To contact, send client list, published samples, photocopies, slides and/or promo piece. To query with specific ideas, send tight roughs. Reports in 2 months. Returns material with SASE; files material "if future interest is anticipated." For greeting cards, pays flat fee of $250-500. Pays on acceptance. Buys all rights or exclusive product rights. Credit line sometimes given. Artist's guidelines for SASE.
Photography: Buys photography from freelancers. Buys stock and assigns work. Buys 100 stock images/year. Makes 100 assignments/year. Photos should be "humorous with animals or children; unusual, eye catching, interesting, contemporary—not too arty." Uses b&w prints; 35mm, 2¼×2¼, 4×5 and 8×10 transparencies. To contact, send slides, client list, published samples, promo piece, portfolio, prints. Reports in 2 months. Materials returned with SASE; files photos "if there will be future interest." Pays per photo or by the project. Pays on acceptance. Buys all rights or exclusive product rights. Credit line sometimes given. Photographer's guidelines for SASE.
Tips: "One third of our products are made for kids or have kids' themes. Seasonal material should be submitted 18 months in advance. We're using more freelance illustrators and freelance writers who can submit a concept rather than single piece of writing. We are upbeat, with a large, diverse baby/children's line. Send all material to greeting card director—if it is for another product it will be passed along to the appropriate department."

BURGOYNE INC., 2030 E. Byberry Rd., Philadelphia PA 19116. (215)677-8000. Art Studio Manager: Mary Beth Burgoyne. Creative Director: Jeanna Lane. Estab. 1907. Greeting card company. Publisher of Christmas and everyday cards.
Illustration: Interested in illustrations for greeting cards. To contact, send cover letter. To query with specific ideas, send slides, published samples. Reports in 2 months. Materials filed. Pays on acceptance. Buys greeting card US and worldwide rights. Credit line sometimes given. Artist's guidelines for SASE.

Tips: "We are looking for new traditional Christmas artwork with a detailed children's book look. We are also looking for juvenile birthday and all-occasion artwork year round."

***CAVU**, 2990 E. Northern Ave., Suite D100, Phoenix AZ 85028. (602)867-8787. Fax: (602)867-1414. Owner: Phil Lockard. Estab. 1986. Greeting card and clothing company. Publishes greeting cards and manufactures clothing.
Illustration: Needs freelance illustration for children's greeting cards. Makes 6 illustration assignments/month. Uses both color and b&w artwork. To contact, send cover letter, photocopies and promo pieces. To query with specific ideas, submit idea in rough format. Reports in 1 week. Materials returned with SASE; materials filed. For greeting cards, pays flat fee of $300. For other artwork, pays by the hour, $300 minimum per job. Pays on publication. Buys first rights, all rights. Credit line given.
Tips: 20% of products are made for kids or have kids themes. Submit seasonal material 6 months in advance.

CONTEMPORARY DESIGNS, 213 Main St., Gilbert IA 50105. (515)232-5188. Fax: (515)232-3380. Editor and Art Director: Sallie Abelson. Estab. 1977.

- Contemporary Designs wants greeting cards for campers and Jewish markets only. Puzzles, games and coloring books should be Judaic.

Writing/Illustration: Publishes greeting cards, coloring books and puzzles and games. "Greeting cards should be funny—for children who go to camp." 25% of material is written by freelancers; 20% illustrated by freelancers. Buys 50 freelance projects/year; receives 150 submissions/year. Materials returned with SASE. Reports in 1 month. Pays $40 for greeting cards. Pays on acceptance. Buys all rights on accepted material; negotiable amount for coloring books and puzzles. Writer's/illustrator's guidelines for SASE.
Tips: Submit seasonal material 1 year in advance.

CREATE-A-CRAFT, P.O. Box 330008, Fort Worth TX 76163-0008. Contact: Editor. Estab. 1967. Produces greeting cards, giftwrap, games, calendars, posters, stationery and paper tableware products for all ages.
Illustration: Works with 3 freelance artists/year. Buys 3-5 designs/illustrations/year. Prefers artists with experience in cartooning. Works on assignment only. Buys freelance designs/illustrations mainly for greetings cards and T-shirts. Also uses freelance artists for calligraphy, P-O-P displays, paste-up and mechanicals. Considers pen & ink, watercolor, acrylics and colored pencil. Prefers humorous and "cartoons that will appeal to families. Must be cute, appealing, etc. No religious, sexual implications or off-beat humor." Produces material for all holidays and seasons. Contact only through artist's agent. Some samples are filed; samples not filed are not returned. Reports only if interested. Write for appointment to show portfolio of original/final art, final reproduction/product, slides, tearsheets, color and b&w. Original artwork is not returned. "Payment depends upon the assignment, amount of work involved, production costs, etc. involved in the project." Buys all rights. For guidelines and sample cards, send $2.50 and #10 SASE.
Tips: Submit 6 months in advance. "Demonstrate an ability to follow directions exactly. Too many submit artwork that has no relationship to what we produce. No phone calls accepted."

***CREATIF LICENSING CORP.**, 31 Old Town Crossing, Mt. Kisco NY 10549. (914)241-6211. Estab. 1975. Gift industry licensing agency. Publishes greeting cards, comic books, puzzles, posters, calendars, fabrics, home furnishings, all gifts.
Illustration: Needs freelance illustration for children's greeting cards, all gift and home furnishings. Uses both color and b&w artwork. To contact, send cover letter, résumé, client list, published samples, photocopies, portfolio, promo piece and SASE. Reports in 1 month. Materials returned with SASE; materials filed. For greeting cards, pays royalty and advance. For other artwork,

***A bullet within a listing introduces special comments by the editor of* Children's Writer's & Illustrator's Market.**

pays royalty and advance. Pays on acceptance or publication. Buys reprint rights. Artist's guidelines available for SASE.

DESIGN DESIGN INC., P.O. Box 2266, Grand Rapids MI 49501. (616)774-2448. President: Don Kallil. Creative Director: Tom Vituj. Estab. 1986. Greeting card company.
Writing: Needs freelance writing for children's greeting cards. For greeting cards, prefers both rhymed and unrhymed verse ideas. To contact, send cover letter and writing samples. Reports in 3 weeks. Materials returned with SASE; materials not filed. For greeting cards, pays flat fee. Buys all rights or exclusive product rights; negotiable. No credit line given. Writer's guidelines for SASE.
Illustration: Needs freelance illustration for children's greeting cards, notecards, wrapping paper. Makes 30 illustration assignments/month. Uses color artwork only. To contact, send cover letter, published samples, color or b&w photocopies color or b&w promo pieces or portfolio. Reports in 3 weeks. Returns materials with SASE. Pays by the project or royalty. Buys all rights or exclusive product rights; negotiable. Artist's guidelines available for SASE.
Photography: Purchases photography from freelancers. Buys stock and assigns work. Uses 4×5 transparencies or high quality 35mm slides. To contact, send cover letter with slides, stock photo list, published samples and promo piece. Reports in 3 weeks. Materials returned with SASE; materials not filed. Pays per photo or royalties. Pays on usage. Buys all rights or exclusive product rights; negotiable. Photographer's guidelines for SASE.

***EPI GROUP LIMITED**, 250 Pequot Ave., Southport CT 06490. (203)255-1112. Vice President: Merryl Lambert. Estab. 1989. Paper products company. Publishes puzzles, activity kits, nature kits, games, books and plush toys, posters for nature and educational markers.
Writing: Needs freelance writing for children's books. Makes "hundreds of" freelance writing assignments/year. To contact, send cover letter and writing samples. To query with specific ideas, submit overview with sample. Reports back only if interested. Materials returned with SASE; materials filed. Pays on acceptance. Buys all rights; negotiable. Credit line given.
Illustration: Needs freelance illustration for books/activity kits. Makes "hundreds of" illustration assignments/year. Prefers animal/nature illustrations for packaging, posters, activity books, games, etc. Uses both b&w and color artwork. To contact, send photocopies and promo pieces. To query with specific ideas, submit samples with overview. Reports only if interested. Materials returned with SASE; materials filed. Pays on acceptance. Buys all rights; negotiable. Credit line given.
Photography: Buys stock and assigns work. Buys stock infrequently. Makes "hundreds of" assignments/year. Uses 4×5 prints. To contact, send promo piece. Reports only if interested. Returns material with SASE; materials filed. Pays on acceptance. Buys all rights; negotiable. Credit line given.
Tips: "80% of our products are made for children or have children's themes. Submit seasonal material six months in advance."

***EVERYTHING GONZO!**, P.O. Box 1322, Roslyn Heights NY 11577. (516)623-9477. Fax: (516)546-5535. Owner: H.J. Fleischer. Toy designer and manufacturer. Designs, licenses, manufactures toys, gifts and related products. Manufactures novelties (educational, impulse, creative), puzzles, games; publishes booklets.
Illustration: Needs freelance illustration for toys. Makes 5 illustration assignments/year. Uses both color and b&w artwork. To contact, send cover letter, résumé, published samples, portfolio, photocopies, promo pieces. To query with specific ideas, write to request disclosure form first. Reports only if interested. Materials returned with SASE; materials filed. For other artwork, pays by the hour($10); negotiable royalty. Pays on acceptance. Credit line sometimes given.
Photography: Buys photography from freelancers. Works on assignment only. Uses transparencies. To contact, send cover letter, published samples, portfolio, promo piece. Reports only if interested. Materials returned; materials filed. Pays on acceptance. Credit line sometimes given.
Tips: 100% of products are made for kids or have kids' themes. Submit seasonal material 6 months in advence.

FAX-PAX USA, INC., 37 Jerome Ave., Bloomfield CT 06002. (203)242-3333. Fax: (203)242-7102. Editor: Stacey L. Savin. Estab. 1990. Buys 1 freelance project/year. Publishes educational picture cards. Needs include US history, natural history.

Writing/Illustration: Buys all rights. Pays on publication. Cannot return material.
Tips: "Well-written, interesting U.S. and natural history sells best."

FOTOFOLIO/ARTPOST, 536 Broadway, New York NY 10012. (212)226-0923. Editorial Director: Ron Schick. Estab. 1976. Greeting card company. Also publishes fine art and photographic postcards, notecards, posters, calendars. New children's line.
Illustration: Needs freelance illustration for children's greeting cards, calendars and coloring books. To contact, send cover letter, published samples, photocopies, slides, promo piece. Reports back only if interested. Returns materials with SASE. Buys materials not filed. Rights negotiable. Credit line given. Artist's guidelines not available.
Photography: Buys photography from freelancers. Buys stock. To contact, send cover letter, slides, stock photo list, published samples and promo piece. Reports back only if interested. Returns material with SASE. Pays on usage. Rights negotiable. Credit line given. Photographer's guidelines not available.

***FREEDOM GREETING CARD CO. INC.**, 75 West St., Walpole MA 02081. (508)668-1224. Freelance Coordinator: Laura Rodman. Estab. 1969. Specializes in traditional cards. Publishes greeting cards (Freedom).
Writing: Needs freelance writing for children's greeting cards. Makes 100s of writing assignments/month. For greeting cards, accepts both rhymed and unrhymed verse ideas. To contact, send writing samples. Reports in 2 weeks. Materials returned with SASE; materials not filed. Pays on acceptance.
Illustration: Needs freelance illustration for children's greeting cards. Makes 100s of writing assignments/month. To contact, send samples—either published or copies. Reports in 2 weeks. Materials returned with SASE. Pays on acceptance.
Photography: Buys photography from freelancers. Buys stock. Uses 35mm, 2¼×2¼, 4×5, 8×10. To contact, send published samples. Reports in 2 weeks. Materials returned with SASE. Pay is negotiable.
Tips: 20% of products are made for kids or have kids' theme. Submit seasonal material 18 months in advance.

GALISON BOOKS, 36 W. 44th St., Suite 910, New York NY 10036. (212)354-8840. Estab. 1978. Paper products company. Publishes museum-quality gift products, including notecards, journals, address books and jigsaw puzzles. Publishes children's greeting cards and puzzles.
Illustration: Needs freelance illustration for adults and children's greeting cards, jigsaw puzzles. Makes 30 illustration assignments/year. Uses color artwork only. To contact, send cover letter, published samples and color promo piece. Reports back only if interested. Returns materials with SASE; materials filed. Pays flat fee. Pays on publication. Credit line given. Artist's guidelines not available.
Photography: Buys photography from freelancers. Buys stock. Uses 4×5 or larger transparencies. To contact, send cover letter, stock photo list, published samples and color promo piece. Reports back only if interested. Returns materials with SASE; materials filed. Pays flat fee. Pays on publication. Credit line given. Photographer's guidelines available for SASE.
Tips: 10% of products are made for kids or have kids' themes. Seasonal material should be submitted 1 year in advance.

***GALLERY GRAPHICS, INC.**, 227 Main St., P.O. Box 502, Noel MO 64854. (417)475-6191. Fax: (417)475-6494. Marketing Director: Terri Galvin. Estab. 1979. Greeting card, paper products company. Specializes in Victorian products including prints, cards, calendars, stationery, magnets, framed items, books, flue covers. "We market toward all age groups." Publishes reproductions of children's books from the 1800s.
Illustration: Needs freelance illustration for children's greeting cards, other children's products. Makes 2 illustration assignments/year. Prefers children, angels, animals in any medium. Uses color artwork only. To contact, send cover letter, published samples, photocopies (prefer color), promo pieces. Reports in 4-6 weeks. "We'll return materials at our cost." Materials not filed. "I'll usually make copies." For greeting cards, pays flat fee of $100-700, or royalty of 5-7% for life of card. Pays on sales. Buys exclusive product rights. Credit line sometimes given.
Tips: 70% of products are made for kids or have kids' theme. Submit seasonal material 1 year in advance. "We're currently looking for an artist to do infants and toddlers as angels, which

would interest adults also. We've mostly done reproductions of Victorian art and most are of children. We have used several artists to do artwork which fits in with the reproductions. We want to do a lot more, but haven't found any good artists."

***C.R. GIBSON CO.**, 32 Knight St., Norwalk CT 06856. (203)847-4543. Fax: (203)841-1165. Managing Editor: Eileen D'Andrea. Freelance Coordinator: Harriet Richards. Estab. 1870. Paper products company. Produces baby record books, wedding record books, photo albums, scrapbooks, kitchen products, stationery, gift wrap, paper tableware, greeting cards and gift books. Publishing greeting cards, gift wrap.
Illustration: Needs freelance illustration for children's greeting cards, gift wrap, baby products. Makes 400 illustration assignments/year. "Generally we sell our products to the better markets including department stores, gift shops and stationery stores. Our primary consumers are women for themselves or men. Masculine products and designs make up less than 10% of the line. Our designs are fashionable without being avant garde, always in good taste. A few tips about making unsolicited submissions: try to be aware of current design themes and colors. Regional designs should be avoided. Most of our designs are subject-oriented and not abstract prints or designs. We are always looking for freelance art with a fresh approach." Uses color artwork only. To contact, send slides, color photocopies, color promo pieces. To query with specific ideas, write to request disclosure form first. Reports in 4-6 weeks. Materials returned with SASE; materials filed. For greeting cards, pays flat fee of $175-300. For other artwork, pays by the project (negotiable). Pays on acceptance. Buys one-time rights. Credit line sometimes given. Artist's guidelines available for SASE.
Tips: 25% of products are made for kids or have kids' themes. Submit seasonal material 1 year in advance for Christmas. "Before we can review any artwork we require artists to sign a submission agreement. We ask you to please send it along with any submissions, as we will not review anything without this signed form. No computer art—we're looking for the very traditional and conservative."

GREAT AMERICAN PUZZLE FACTORY, INC., 16 S. Main St. S., Norwalk CT 06854. (203)838-4240. Fax: (203)838-2065. Art Director: Anne Mulligan. Estab. 1976. Produces puzzles.
Illustration: Needs freelance illustration for puzzles. Makes over 100 freelance assignments/year. To contact, send cover letter, color photocopies and color promo pieces (no slides) with SASE. Reports in 2 months. Artists guidelines available for SASE. Rights purchased vary. Buys all rights to puzzles. Pays on publication. Pay varies.
Photography: Needs local cityscapes for regional puzzles.
Tips: Wants "whimsical, fantasy" material. Targets ages 4-12 and adult. "No slides. Send color copies (3-4) for style. Looking for whimsical, fantasy and nature themes with a bright, contemporary style. Not too washy or cute."

GREAT SEVEN, INC., 3870 Del Amo Blvd., Unit 503, Torrance CA 90503. (310)371-4555. Vice President: Ronald Chen. Estab. 1984. Paper products company. Publishes educational and fun stickers for children and teenager markets.
Illustration: Needs freelance illustration for children's fun stickers. Makes 120 illustration assignments/year. Wants "kid themes." To contact, send published samples and b&w photocopies. To query with specific ideas, write to request disclosure form first. Reports back only if interested. Returns material with SASE; materials filed. Pays on acceptance. Buys all rights. No credit line given. Artist's guidelines not available.
Tips: 100% of products are made for kids or have kids' themes. Seasonal material should be submitted 10 months in advance.

HANDPRINT SIGNATURE, INC., P.O. Box 22682, Portland OR 97269. (503)295-1925. Fax: (503)295-3673. President: Paula Carlson. Greeting card company. "Manufacturer of greeting cards especially designed for kids to send. Each card to be 'signed' with a child's handprint or footprint."
Illustration: Needs freelance illustration for children's greeting cards. "All art must tie in with general theme of Handprint Signature—cards for kids to send. Pure colors." To contact, send cover letter, résumé, published samples and acknowledgement that he/she has seen and under-

stands Handprint Signature card line. Reports in 1 month. Returns materials with SASE. For greeting cards, pays $200/image or 4% royalty for national/life of card. Pays on publication. Credit line given. Artist's guidelines available.
Tips: 100% of products are made for kids or have kids' themes. "Even though an artist's work must tie in with other artists already published, the design and presentation must stand out as his or her own unique interpretation. The card design and the text should be harmonious and always conscious that even though the parent (adult) is buying the card, the card is from a child. The cards are viewed as gifts and are primarily marketed in toy and gift stores. It is a bigger market than stationery/children's cards."

INTERCONTINENTAL GREETINGS LTD., 176 Madison Ave., New York NY 10016. (212)683-5830. Contact: Robin Lipner. Estab. 1964. 100% of material freelance written and illustrated. Produces greeting cards, scholastic products (notebooks, pencil cases), novelties (gift bags, mugs), tin gift boxes, shower and bedding curtains.
Writing: "Greeting card (style) artwork in series of three or more. We use very little writing except for humor." Makes 4 writing assignments/year. To contact, send cover letter, résumé, client list and writing samples with SASE. Reports in 4-6 weeks. Pays advance of $20-100 and royalty of 20% for life. Pays on publication. Purchases exclusive product rights. Credit line sometimes given.
Illustration: Needs children's greeting cards, notebook cover, photo albums, gift products. Makes 15 illustration assignments/month. Prefers primarily greeting card subjects, suitable for gift industry. To contact, send cover letter, résumé, client list, published samples, photocopies, slides and promo piece with SASE. Reports in 4-6 weeks. For greeting cards pays advance of $75 against 20% royalty for life. For other artwork pays 20% royalty for life. Pays on publication. Buys exclusive product rights. Credit line sometimes given.
Tips: Target group for juvenile cards: ages 1-10. Illustrators: "Use clean colors, not muddy or dark."

***INTERNATIONAL PLAYTHINGS, INC.**, 120 Riverdale Rd., Riverdale NJ 07457. (201)831-1400. Fax: (201)831-8643. Product Manager: Cyndee Dalton. Estab. 1968. Toy/game company. Distributes and markets children's toys, games and puzzles in specialty toy markets.
Illustration: Needs freelance illustration for children's puzzles and games. Makes 20-30 illustration assignments/year. Prefers fine-quality, original illustration for children's puzzles. Uses color artwork only. To contact, send published samples, slides, portfolio, or color photocopies or promo pieces. Write to request disclosure form first. Reports in 1 month only if interested. Materials filed. For artwork, pays by the project (range: $1,000-5,000). Pays on publication. Buys one-time rights, negotiable.
Tips: 100% of products are made for kids or have kids' themes.

JILLSON & ROBERTS GIFTWRAP, INC., 5 Watson Ave., Irvine CA 92718. (714)859-8781. Art Director: Josh Neufeld. Estab. 1973. Paper products company. Makes giftwrap/giftbags.
Illustration: Needs freelance illustration for children's giftwrap. Makes 6-12 illustration assignments/year. Wants children/baby/juvenile themes. To contact, send cover letter. Reports in 1 month. Returns material with SASE; materials filed. For wrap and bag designs, pays flat fee of $250. Pays on publication. Rights negotiable. No credit line given. Artist's guidelines for SASE.
Tips: 20% of products are made for kids or have kids' themes. Seasonal material should be submitted up to 1 month in advance. "We produce two lines of giftwrap per year: one everyday line and one Christmas line. The closing date for everyday is June 30th and Christmas is September 15."

THE LANG COMPANIES, 514 Wells St., Delafield WI 53018. (414)646-5555. Art Director: Andrew Lang. Estab. 1982. Greeting card and paper product company. Publishes greeting cards (Lang Graphics, Main Street Press, R.A. Lang Card Company, rubber stamps, calendars, stickers.
Writing: Needs freelance writing for children's greeting cards, story books. For greeting cards, prefers both rhymed and unrhymed verse ideas. Other needs for freelance writing include books. To contact, send cover letter, résumé, client list, writing samples. To query with specific ideas write to request disclosure form first. Reports back in 1 month. Materials returned; materials filed. Pays on publication. Rights negotiable. Credit line sometimes given.

Illustration: Needs freelance illustration for children's greeting cards. To contact, send cover letter, résumé, client list, published samples, color photocopies. To query with specific ideas write to request disclosure form first. Reports back in 1 month. Materials returned; materials filed. Pays on publication. Rights negotiable. Credit line sometimes given.
Photography: Buys photography from freelancers. Buys stock and assigns work. Uses 4×5 transparencies. To contact, send cover letter, résumé, client list, published samples. Reports back in 1 month. Materials returned; materials filed. Pays on usage. Rights negotiable. Credit line sometimes given.

LOVE GREETING CARD CO. INC., 1717 Opa-Locka Blvd., Opa-Locka FL 33054. (305)685-5683. Editor: Norman Drittel. Estab. 1980. Greeting card, paper products and children's book company. Publishes greeting cards (Muffy 'N' Pebbles), posters, small books.
Writing: Needs freelance writing for children's greeting cards. Makes 2 writing assignments/month; 12/year. Prefers rhymed verse ideas. To contact, send writing samples. To query with specific ideas, contact Norman Drittel. Reports in 2 months. Materials returned with SASE; materials filed. For greeting cards, pays flat fee of $50-100. Pays on acceptance. Buys one-time rights, reprint rights; negotiable. Credit line given. Writer's guidelines available for SASE.
Illustration: Needs freelance illustration for children's greeting cards, book material. Makes 2 illustration assignments/month; 12/year. Prefers 8-10 page books. Uses color artwork only. To contact, send published samples, portfolio. Reports in months. Materials returned with SASE; materials filed. For greeting cards, pays flat fee of $100-250. For other artwork, pays by the project (range: $500-2,500). Pays on acceptance. Rights negotiable. Credit line given. Artist's guidelines available for SASE.
Photography: Buys photography from freelancers. Buys stock and assigns work. Buys 20 stock images/year. Makes 5 assignments/year. Wants children, any subject. Uses color prints; 8×10 transparencies. To contact, send slides, portfolio. Reports in 2 months. Materials returned with SASE; materials filed. Pays per photo (range for $100-150) for b&w/color. Pays on acceptance. Rights negotiable. Credit line given. Guidelines available for SASE.
Tips: 20% of produces are made for kids or have kids' themes. Submit seasonal material 6 months in advance.

MARCEL SCHURMAN COMPANY, 2500 N. Watney Way, Fairfield CA 94533. Editor: Meg Schutte. Creative Director: Diana Ruhl. Greeting card company. Publishes greeting cards, gift wrap, stationery, bags, journals and note cards.
Writing: Needs freelance writing for children's greeting cards. Makes 2-3 writing assignments/month; 50/year. For greeting cards, prefers unrhymed verse ideas. To query with specific ideas, write to request disclosure form first. Reports in 6 weeks. Materials returned with SASE; sometimes files material. For greeting cards, pays flat fee of $75-125 on acceptance. Writer's guidelines available for SASE.
Illustration: Needs freelance illustration for children's greeting cards. Makes 60 illustration assignments/month; 800/year. Uses color artwork only. To contact, send color photocopies. To query with specific ideas, send letter with or without samples. Reports in 1 month. Materials returned if accompanied by SASE; materials filed. For greeting cards pays advance of $300 against 5% royalty for 3 years. Pays "when final art is approved." Credit line sometimes given. Artist's guidelines available for SASE.
Photography: Buys photography from freelancers. Buys stock and assign work. Uses 4×5 transparencies. To contact, send slides. Reports in 1 month. Materials returned with SASE. Materials returned; materials filed. Pays advance of $250 and 5% royalties. Pays "when final art is approved." Buys exclusive product rights, worldwide, 3-year period. Credit line sometimes given. Guidelines for SASE.
Tips: 20% of products are made for kids or have kids' themes. Submit seasonal ideas 6-8 months in advance.

P.S. GREETINGS/FANTUS PAPER PRODUCTS, 5060 N. Kimberly Ave., Chicago IL 60630. (312)725-9308. Art Director: Bill Barnes. Greeting card company. Publishes boxed and individual counter cards. Publishes greeting cards (Kards for Kids—counter; Kids Kards—boxed; Christmas).
Writing: Needs freelance writing for children's greeting cards. Makes 1-10 writing assignments/year. Looks for writing which is "appropriate for kids to give to relatives." To contact, send

writing samples. Reports in 6 months. Material returned only if accompanied with SASE; materials filed. For greeting cards, pays flat fee. Pays on acceptance. Buys all rights. Credit line sometimes given. Writer's guidelines for SASE.

Illustration: Needs freelance illustration for children's greeting cards. Makes 50-100 illustration assignments/year. "Open to all mediums, all themes—use your creativity!" To contact, send published samples (up to 20 samples of any nature) and photocopies. Reports in 6 months. Returns materials with SASE; materials filed. For greeting cards, pays flat fee. Pays on acceptance. Buys all rights. Credit line sometimes given. Artist's guidelines for SASE.

Photography: Buys photography from freelancers. Buys stock. Buys 10-20 stock images/year. Wants florals, animals, seasonal (Christmas, Easter, valentines, etc.). Uses transparencies (any size). To contact, send slides. Reports in 6 months. Materials returned with SASE; materials filed. Pays on acceptance. Buys all rights. Credit line sometimes given. Photographer's guidelines for SASE.

Tips: "Only 7% of products are made for kids or have kids' themes, so it needs to be great stuff!" Seasonal material should be submitted 6 months in advance. "We are open to all creative ideas—generally not fads, however. All mediums are considered equally. We have a great need for 'cute' Christmas subjects."

PEACEABLE KINGDOM PRESS, 707B Heinz Ave., Berkeley CA 94710. (510)644-9801. Fax: (510)644-9805. Art Director: Olivia Hurd. Estab. 1983. Produces posters and greeting cards. Uses images from classic children's books.

Illustration: Needs freelance illustration for children's greeting cards and posters. Makes 5 illustration assignments/month; 60/year. To contact, send cover letter and color photocopies. Reports in 3 weeks. Pays on publication with advance. Pays 5-10% of wholesale for greeting cards. Buys rights to distribution worldwide.

Tips: "We only choose from illustrations that are from published children's book illustrators, or commissioned art by established children's book illustrators. Submit seasonal posters and greeting cards six months in advance."

***POCKETS OF LEARNING LTD.**, 31-G Union Ave., Sudbury MA 01776. (800)635-2994. Fax: (800)370-1580. Product Manager: Kyra Silva. Estab. 1989. Educational soft toy company. Specializes in design, import and distribution of high-quality educational cloth toys and gifts. Manufactures educational soft sculptures, wallhangings, travel bags.

Illustration: Needs freelance illustration for educational cloth toys. Makes 7 illustration assignments/year. We introduce 20-30 new products per year, including cloth books, travel bags, soft sculpture and wallhangings. Uses both color and b&w artwork. To contact, send cover letter, slides, photocopies. To query with specific ideas, write to request disclosure form first. Reports in 3-4 weeks. Pays on acceptance. Buys all rights. Credit line sometimes given.

Tips: 100% of products are made for kids or have kids' themes. "We accept new product ideas year 'round."

POPSHOTS, 19 Newtown Turnpike, Westport CT 06880. (203)454-9700. Founder: Paul Zalon. Estab. 1976. Greeting card and paper products company. Publishes greeting cards (Popshots, high end pop-up cards).

Illustration: Needs freelance illustration for children's greeting cards. Makes 4 illustration assignments/month; 60/year.

PRATT & AUSTIN CO., P.O. Box 587, Holyoke MA 01041. (413)532-1491. Product Development: Lorilee Costello. Estab. 1934. Paper products company. Targets women ages 16-60: stationery, tablets, envelopes, calendars, children's craft items. Produces calendars, paper dolls, paper airplanes, mobiles, etc.

Illustration: Needs freelance illustration for paper airplanes, crafts, paper dolls, calendars, storage boxes. Makes 2-4 illustration assignments/month; 30-40/year.

The asterisk before a listing indicates the listing is new in this edition.

PUZZLING POSTCARD CO., 79-815 Horseshoe Lane, La Quinta CA 92253. (619)347-1179. Fax: (619)347-4354. President: Tom Judge. Estab. 1991. Greeting card company, puzzle card producer. Produces Puzzling Postcard™, jigsaw puzzle greeting card. Publishes greeting cards, puzzles.
Illustration: Needs freelance illustration for greeting cards. Makes 12-24 illustration assignments/year. Uses color artwork only. To contact, send cover letter, client list, published samples, color photocopies. To query with specific ideas, call to discuss. Reports only if interested. Materials returned with SASE; materials filed. For greeting cards, pays flat fee of $100-200, advance of $50 against negotiable royalty for negotiable period. Pays on publication. Buys negotiable rights.
Photography: Buys photography from freelancers. Buys stock images. To contact, send cover letter, stock photo list, published samples. Reports only if interested. Materials returned with SASE; materials filed. Pays on usage. Buys negotiable rights.
Tips: 30% of products are made for kids or have kids' themes. Submit seasonal material 9 months in advance.

RECO INTERNATIONAL CORP., 138-150 Haven Ave., Pt. Washington NY 11050. (516)767-2400. President: Heio W. Reich. Estab. 1967. Collector's plate producer.
Illustration: Needs freelance illustration for collector's plates—children's subjects mainly, but also western, Indian, flowers, animals, fantasy and mystical. Makes 60-100 assignments/year. Uses color artwork only. To contact, send portfolio. Submit specific ideas. Reports in 6 weeks. Materials returned with SASE; materials filed. For greeting cards, pays flat fee and royalty. For other artwork, pays royalty and advance. Pays on acceptance. Buys exclusive product rights. Artist's guidelines available for SASE after review of portfolio.
Tips: 60% of products are made for kids or have kids' themes. Submit seasonal material 6-10 months in advance (although rarely uses seasonal work).

RED FARM STUDIO, 1135 Roosevelt Ave., P.O. Box 347, Pawtucket RI 02862. (401)728-9300. Contact: Production Coordinator. Estab. 1949. Greeting card company. Publishes coloring books and paintables.
Illustration: Needs freelance illustration for children's traditional subject greeting cards, coloring books and paintables. Makes 1 illustration assignments/month; 6-12/year. Prefers "watercolor, realistic styles yet cute." For first contact, request art guidelines with SASE. Reports in 2-4 weeks. Returns materials with SASE. Appropriate materials are kept on file. "We work on assignment using ink line work (coloring books) or pencil renderings (paintables)." For full color painting pays flat fee of $200-275. For b&w artwork, pays flat fee of $150-175 per page for color books and paintables. Pays on acceptance. Buys all rights. No credit line given but artist may sign artwork. Artist's guidelines for SASE.
Tips: 20% of products are made for kids or have kids' themes. Majority of freelance assignments made during January-May/yearly. "Research companies before sending submissions to determine whether your styles are compatible."

***REFLECTIVE IMAGES**, 42 Digital Dr. #10, Novato CA 94949. (415)883-5815. Fax: (415)883-8215. Owner: Kristin Greg. Estab. 1969. Screen-painted sportswear company. Produces T-shirts and sweats for zoos, animal parks, trains and ski resorts.
Illustration: Needs freelance illustration for children's T-shirts. Makes 10 illustration assignments/year. Prefers realistic and whimsical animals. Uses b&w artwork only. To contact, send cover letter, photocopies, promo pieces. "Call to discuss current needs." Reports back only if interested. Materials returned with SASE. Pays by the project (range: $50-200). Pays on acceptance. Buys all rights. Credit line sometimes given.
Tips: 60% of products are made for kids or have kids' themes. Submit seasonal material 6 months in advance.

***SCANDECOR INC.**, 430 Pike Rd., Southampton PA 18966. (215)355-2410. Product Manager: Lauren H. Karp. Poster publisher. Publishes posters for the children's market.
Writing: Needs freelance writing for posters. Makes 10 writing assignments/year. For posters, prefers rhymed verse ideas. To contact, send writing samples. To query with specific ideas, send SASE. Reports in 1 month. Materials returned with SASE. For poster assignments, pays flat fee

of $50. Pays on publication. Rights negotiable. Credit line given. Writer's guidelines available for SASE.

Illustration: Needs freelance illustration for children's posters. Makes 15 illustration assignments/year. Prefers poster art in children's themes. Uses color artwork only. To contact, send color photocopies, color promo piece. To query with specific ideas, send SASE. Reports in 1 month. Materials returned with SASE; materials filed. For poster artwork, pays flat fee of $300. Pays on publication. Rights negotiable. Credit line given. Artist's guidelines available for SASE.

Photography: Buys photography from freelancers. Buys stock and assigns work. Buys 100 stock images/year. Makes 10 assignments/year. Wants animals, children, children and animals, humor. Uses color and b&w prints; 35mm, 2¼×2¼, 4×5, 8×10 transparencies. To contact, send stock photo list, promo piece, model-released duplicate slides. Reports in 1 month. Materials returned; materials filed. Pays per photo ($300). Pays on usage. Rights negotiable. Credit line given. Guidelines available for SASE.

Tips: 90% of products are made for kids or have kids' themes. We don't use seasonal material. "Please look at the types/quality of photography/illustration being used for published products. We are working with more freelancers now than ever."

SHULSINGER SALES, INC., 50 Washington St., Brooklyn NY 11201. (718)852-0042. Art Director: Daniel Deutsch. Estab. 1950. Greeting card and paper products company. "We are a Judaica company, distributing products such as greeting cards, books, paperware, puzzles, games, novelty items—all with a Jewish theme." Publishes greeting cards, novelties, coloring books and puzzles.

Writing: Looks for greeting card writing which can be sent by children to adults and sent by adults to children (of all ages). To contact, send cover letter. To query with specific ideas, write to request disclosure form first. Reports in 2 weeks. Materials returned with SASE; materials filed. For greeting cards, pays flat fee (this includes artwork). Pays on acceptance. Buys exclusive product rights.

Illustration: Needs freelance illustration for children's greeting cards, books, novelties, games. Makes 10-20 illustration assignments/year. "The only requirement is a Jewish theme." To contact, send cover letter and photocopies, color if possible. To query with specific ideas, write to request disclosure form first. Reports in 2 weeks. Returns materials with SASE; materials filed. For children's greeting cards, pays flat fee (this includes writing). For other artwork, pays by the project. Pays on acceptance. Buys exclusive product rights. Credit line sometimes given. Artist's guidelines not available.

Tips: 40% of products are made for kids or have kids' themes. Seasonal material should be submitted 6 months in advance.

***SMART ART, INC.**, P.O. Box 661, Chatham NJ 07928. (201)635-1690. President: Barb Hauck-Mah. Estab. 1992. Greeting card company. Publishes photo-insert cards for card, gift and photo shops.

Illustration: Needs freelance illustration for photo-insert cards. Makes 1-2 illustration assignments/month; 20/year. Uses color artwork only. To contact, send color photocopies. To query with specific ideas, write to request confidentiality form. Reports in 1-2 months. Materials returned with SASE; materials not filed. For greeting cards, pays annual royalties for life of card or 5 years. Pays on publication. Credit line given. Artist's guidelines available for SASE.

Tips: About 15% of products are made for kids or have kids' themes. Submit seasonal material 6-8 months in advance. "Smart Art is looking for 'border design' artwork rendered in pen & ink with watercolors, or in cut/torn paper. We are interested in artists who can create interesting abstract textures as well as representational designs. Smart Art contributes part of its profits to organizations dedicated to improving the health and education of our nation's children."

TALICOR, INC., 190 Gentry St., Pomona CA 91767. (909)593-5877. President: Lew Herndon. Estab. 1971. Game manufacturer. Publishes games (adult and children's).

Illustration: Needs freelance illustration for games. Makes 14 illustration assignments/year. To contact, send promo piece. Reports only if interested. Materials returned with SASE; materials filed. For artwork, pays by the hour or by the project or negotiable royalty. Pays on acceptance. Buys negotiable rights.

Photography: Buys photography from freelancers. Buys stock and assigns work. Buys 6 stock images/year. Makes 6 assignments/year. Uses 4×5 transparencies. To contact, send color promo

piece. Reports only if interested. Materials returned with SASE; materials filed. Pays per photo, by the hour, by the day or by the project (negotiable rates). Pays on acceptance. Buys negotiable rights.
Tips: 80% of products are made for kids or have kids' themes. Submit seasonal material 6 months in advance.

***TEDCO, INC.**, 498 S. Washington St., Hagerstown IN 47346. (317)489-4527. Fax: (317)489-5752. Sales Director: Jane Shadle. Estab. 1982. Toy manufacturer. Produces educational toys; The Original Gyroscope, Gyros Gyroscope, prisms, magnet kits and science kits. Manufactures novelties, games, gyroscopes, prisms.
Writing: To contact, send cover letter, résumé, writing samples. Materials returned with SASE; materials filed.
Tips: 100% of products are made for kids or have kids' themes. "We have never hired a freelance writer. We would be interested in learning more about available talent."

WARNER PRESS, P.O. Box 2499, Anderson IN 46018. Fax: (317)649-3664. Product Editor: Robin Fogle. Art Department Manager: Roger Hoffman. Photo Editor: Millie Corzine. Estab. 1880. Publishes children's greeting cards, coloring and activity books and posters, all religious-oriented. "Need fun, up-to-date stories for coloring books, with religious emphasis. Also considering activity books for Sunday school classroom use."
Writing: Needs freelance writing for children's greeting cards, coloring and activity books. To contact, request guidelines first. Contact: Robin Fogle, Production Editor. Reports in 4-6 weeks. For greeting cards, pays flat fee (range: $20-30). Pays on acceptance. Buys all rights. Credit line sometimes given. Writer's guidelines for SASE.
Illustration: Needs freelance illustration for children's greeting cards, coloring and activity books. Wants religious, cute illustrations. Makes 6 illustration assignments/month; 72/year. To contact, send published samples, photocopies and promo pieces (all nonreturnable). Contact: Roger Hoffman, creative manager. Reports in 2 weeks "if we are interested." For greeting cards, pays flat fee (range: $250-350). Pays on acceptance. Buys all rights. Credit line given. Guidelines available for SASE.
Photography: Buys photography from freelancers. Church bulletin covers, calendars and other products. Contact: Millie Corzine, photo editor. Guidelines available for SASE.
Tips: Write for guidelines before submitting. Send seasonal material 6 months in advance. Looking for "high-quality art in bright colors illustrated on flexible material for scanning. Meeting deadlines is very important for children's illustrations. We publish simple styles. Unsolicited material that does not follow guidelines will not be reviewed."

Special Markets/'95-'96 changes

The following markets were in the 1995 edition of *Children's Writer's & Illustrator's Market* but do not have listings in this edition. The majority did not respond to our request to update their listings.

American Arts & Graphics, Inc.
BePuzzled/Lombard Marketing, Inc.
English Cards, Ltd.
Ephemera Buttons
European Toy Collection
Fantagraphic Books, Inc.
First Ideas, Inc.
The Gift Wrap Company
Kingdom Puzzles
Magic Moments Greeting Cards
Mayfair Games
Frances Meyer, Inc.
National Poly Consumer Products
Painted Hearts & Friends
Palm Press, Inc.
Peacock Papers, Inc.
Plum Graphics
Portal Publications, Ltd.
Rubber Stampede
The Straight Edge, Inc.
Sunrise Publications, Inc.

Young Writer's & Illustrator's Markets

The listings in this section are special because they seek work from talented young people. Some are magazines exclusively for children. Others are adult magazines with special sections featuring the work of younger writers and illustrators. And a few, such as Majestic Books, are publishers seeking children's stories and artwork.

Just like markets for adults, markets for children expect writers to be familiar with their editorial needs *before* submitting. And the best way to discover a publication's needs is to read several issues. You will easily find some magazines, such as *American Girl* and *Stone Soup*, on newsstands or in libraries, but many juvenile magazines, particularly small or literary publications, are primarily distributed through schools, churches or home subscriptions, and may be difficult to locate. If you can't find copies of publications that interest you, write to the editors and see if sample copies are available (and at what cost). Most editors will gladly supply sample copies for a small fee.

It is also important to send a self-addressed, stamped envelope (SASE)—with proper postage affixed—with each submission. This way, if the market is not interested in your work, it will be sent back to you. If you do not send a SASE with your submission, chances are you will not get your work returned. Make sure to read Guide to Submitting Your Work on page 13 for more information about proper submission procedures.

If your material is rejected the first time you send it out, rest assured you are not the only one this has happened to. Many of our best known writers and artists were turned down at the beginning of their careers more times than they can count. The key to becoming published lies in persistence as well as talent. Keep sending out stories and artwork as you continue to improve your craft. Someday, an editor may decide your work is just what she needs.

To locate competitions and workshops open to young writers and illustrators, turn to Contests & Awards and Conferences & Workshops. Listings in these sections which are designated by a double dagger (‡) are open to students (sometimes exclusively). Additional opportunities for writers can also be found in the *Market Guide for Young Writers* by Kathy Henderson (Writer's Digest Books). High-school-aged writers can get advice from Wendy Mass, an editor of *Writes of Passage, The Literary Journal for Teenagers* on page 276. And aspiring young female writers can learn about *New Moon*, a publication written by girls for girls, on page 268.

THE ACORN, 1530 Seventh St., Rock Island IL 61201. (309)788-3980. Newsletter. Estab. 1989. Audience consists of "kindergarten-12th grade students, parents, teachers and other adults." Purpose in publishing works for children: to expose children's manuscripts to others and provide a format for those who might not have one. Children must be K-12 (put grade on manuscripts). Guidelines available for SASE.

Magazines: 100% of magazine written by children. Uses 6 fiction pieces (500 words), 20 pieces of poetry (32 lines). No payment; purchase of a copy isn't necessary to be printed. Sample copy $2. Subscription $10 for 4 issues. Submit mss to Betty Mowery, editor. Send complete ms. Will accept typewritten, legibly handwritten and/or computer printout. Include SASE. Reports in 1 week.

Artwork: Publishes artwork by children. Looks for "all types; size 4×5. Use black ink in artwork." No payment. Submit artwork either with manuscript or separately to Betty Mowery. Include SASE. Reports in 1 week.

Tips: "My biggest problem is not having names on the manuscripts. If the manuscript gets separated from the cover letter, there is no way to know whom to respond to. Always put name and address on manuscripts, and if you want your material returned enclose a SASE."

AMERICAN GIRL, 8400 Fairway Place, Middleton WI 53562. (608)836-4848. Bimonthly magazine. Audience consists of girls ages 8-12 who are joyful about being girls. Young writers must be 8-12 years old. Writer's guidelines available with #10 SASE.
Magazines: 5% of magazine written by young people. "A few pages of each issue are set aside for children and feature articles that answer questions or requests that have appeared in a previous issue of *American Girl*." Pays in copies. Submit to Harriet Brown, editor. Will accept legibly handwritten ms. Include SASE. Reports in 2 months.

THE APPRENTICE WRITER, % Gary Fincke, Susquehanna University, Selinsgrove PA 17870. (717)372-4164. Fax: (717)372-4310. Magazine. Published annually. "Writing by high school students and for high school students." Purpose in publishing works by young people: to provide quality writing by students which can be read for pleasure and serve as a text for high school classrooms. Work is primarily from eastern and northeastern states, but will consider work from other areas of US. Students must be in grades 9-12. Writer's guidelines available for SASE.
Magazines: Uses 15 short stories (prefers under 5,000 words); 15 nonfiction personal essays (prefers under 5,000 words); 60 poems (no word limit) per issue. Pays in copies to writers and their schools. Submit mss to Gary Fincke, editor. Submit complete ms. Will accept typewritten mss. Include SASE. Submit ms by March 15. Responds by May of each year.
Artwork/Photography: Publishes artwork and photography by children. Looks for b&w. Pays in copies to artists and their schools. Submit originals or high quality copies. Submit art and photographs to Gary Fincke, editor. Include SASE. Submit artwork by March 15. Responds by May of each year.

BEYOND WORDS PUBLISHING, INC., 4443 NE Airport Rd., Hillsboro OR 97124. (503)693-8700. Book publisher. Director of Children's Department: Michelle Roehm. Publishes 3-4 books by children per year. Looks for "books that encourage creativity and an appreciation of nature in children." Wants to "encourage children to write, create, dream and believe that it is possible

"The style is clean and the lines good," says Editor Betty Mowery of the cover illustration for* The Acorn *(March, 1995). Rendered by 12-year-old Rita-Marie McFadden of Austin, Texas, the drawing "captured the look of the wolf—giving it a very proud look, but not fierce," Mowery said.* The Acorn *was established in 1989 to provide a publishing outlet for young writers, poets and artists in kindergarten through twelfth grade. One hundred percent of each publication is contributed by children.

to be published. The books must be unique, be of national interest and the child must be personable and promotable."
Books: Publishes stories and joke books.

BOODLE, P.O. Box 1049, Portland IN 47371. (219)726-8141. Magazine published quarterly. "Each quarterly issue offers children a special invitation to read stories and poems written by others. Children can learn from the ideas in these stories and the techniques of sharing ideas in picures and written form. Audience is ages 6-12. We hope that publishing children's writing will enhance the self-esteem of the authors and motivate other children to try expressing themselves in this form." Submission requirements: "We ask that authors include grade when written, current grade, name of school, and a statement from parent or teacher that the work is original."
Magazines: 100% of magazine written by children. Uses 12 short stories (100-500 words), 1 usually animal nonfiction piece (100-500 words), 30 poems (50-500 words), 2 puzzles and mazes (50-500 words) per issue. Pays 2 copies of issue. Submit mss to Mavis Catalfio, editor. Submit complete ms. Will accept typewritten and legibly handwritten mss. Include SASE.
Artwork: Wants "mazes, cartoons, drawings of animals or seasons or sports which will likely match a story or poem we publish." Pays 2 copies of issue. "Drawings should be done in black ink or marker." Submit artwork to Mavis Catalfio, editor. Reports in 2 months.
Tips: Submit seasonal materials at least a year in advance. "We love humor and offbeat stories. We seldom publish sad or depressing stories about death or serious illness."

BOYS' LIFE, 1325 W. Walnut Hill Lane, P.O. Box 152079, Irving TX 75015-2079. (214)580-2366. Magazine published monthly. Audience consists of children ages 7-17. *Boys' Life* is published by the Boy Scouts of America to make available to children ages 7-17 the highest caliber of fiction and nonfiction, to stimulate an interest in good reading and to promote the principles of Scouting. Writer's guidelines available for SASE.
Magazines: Small percentage of magazine written by young people under 18. Uses hobby and collecting tips for "Hobby Hows" and "Collecting" columns. Pays $10/tip. Uses jokes for "Think & Grin" column. Pays choice of $2 or copy of *Scout Handbook* or *Scout Fieldbook*/joke accepted. Several times/year uses personal stories (500 words maximum) for "Readers' Page." Pays $25. Submit mss to column. Submit complete ms. Will accept typewritten and legibly handwritten mss for consideration. Reports in 6-8 weeks. For nonfiction mss, query first. Submit ms to Mike Goldman, articles editor. All fiction mss should be double-spaced and typed copy, 1,000-1,500 words. Pays $750 and up for accepted stories. Story categories: humor, mystery, science fiction, adventure. Send one copy of story plus cover letter. Submit to Shannon Lowry, associate editor. Include SASE.
Tips: Study one year's worth of recent magazines before submitting.

✤CHICKADEE MAGAZINE, 179 John, Suite 500, Toronto, Ontario M5T 3G5 Canada. (416)868-6001. Magazine published 10 times/year. "*Chickadee* is for children ages 3-8. Its purpose is to entertain and educate children about science, nature and the world around them. We publish children's drawings to give readers the chance to express themselves. Drawings must relate the topics that are given in the 'Chirp' section of each issue."
Artwork: Publishes artwork by children. No payment given. Mail submissions with name, age and return address for thank you note. Submit to Mitch Butler, Chirp Editor. Reports in 4 months.

CHILD LIFE, Children's Better Health Institute, 1100 Waterway Blvd., P.O. Box 567, Indianapolis IN 46206. (317)636-8881. Magazine. Published 8 times/year. "Targeted toward kids ages 9-11, we are the nation's oldest continuously published children's magazine." Focuses on health, sports, fitness, nutrition, safety and general interest.

Always include a self-addressed, stamped envelope (SASE) with submissions within your own country. When sending material to other countries, include a self-addressed envelope (SAE) and International Reply Coupons (IRCs).

Magazines: "Publishes jokes, riddles, poems and original stories (250 words maximum) by children." Kids should include name, address, phone number (for office use) and school photo. "No mass duplicated, multiple submissions." Submit complete mss for fiction and nonfiction written by adults.

CHILDREN'S DIGEST, Children's Better Health Institute, 1100 Waterway Blvd., P.O. Box 567, Indianapolis IN 46206. (317)636-8881. Fax: (317)684-8094. Magazine. Published 8 times/year. Audience consists of preteens. Purpose in publishing works by children: to encourage children to express themselves through writing. Submissions must focus on health-related theme. Requires proof of originality before publishing stories. Writer's guidelines available on request.
Magazines: 10% of magazine written by children. Uses 1 fiction story (under 500 words), 6-10 poems, 10-15 jokes/riddles per issue. "There is no payment for manuscripts submitted by readers." Submit mss to *Children's Digest*, Layne Cameron, editor. Submit complete ms. Will accept typewritten, legibly handwritten and computer printout mss. "We don't respond unless the material will be published. Sorry, no materials can be returned."
Tips: "Submit jokes, poems, young author stories, and Weird World responses to me, Layne Cameron. I read every letter that comes to my magazine. We do not pay for children's submissions. We also don't encourage children to try to compete with professional writers. For best results, submit items to the columns listed above."

CHILDREN'S PLAYMATE, Children's Better Health Institute, 1100 Waterway Blvd., P.O. Box 567, Indianapolis IN 46206. (317)636-8881. Magazine. Estab. 1928. Audience consists of children between 6 and 8 years of age. Emphasizes health, fitness, safety, good nutrition, and *good* humorous fiction for beginning readers. Writer's guidelines available on request with SASE.
Artwork: Publishes artwork by children. "Prefers black line drawings on white paper. No payment for children's artwork published." No material can be returned. Submit artwork to *Children's Playmate*, Chuck Horsman, art director.

✦THE CLAREMONT REVIEW, 4980 Wesley Rd., Victoria, British Columbia Canada V8Y 1Y9. (604)658-5221. Magazine. Publishes 2 books/year by children. Publishes poetry and fiction with literary value by students aged 13-19 anywhere in North America. Purpose in publishing work by young people: to provide a literary venue.
Magazines: Uses 8-10 fiction stories (200-2,500 words), 25-35 poems. Pays in copies. Submit mss to editors. Submit complete ms. Will accept typewritten mss. SASE. Reports in 1 month.
Artwork: Publishes artwork by children. Looks for b&w copies of imaginative art. Pays in copies. Send picture for review. Negative may be requested. Submit art and photographs to editors. SASE. Reports in 1 month.

CLUBHOUSE, P.O. Box 15, Berrien Springs MI 49103. (616)471-9009. Director of Publications: Elaine Trumbo. Magazine. Estab. 1949. Published monthly. Occasionally publishes items by kids. "Audience consists of kids ages 9-14; philosophy is God loves kids, kids are neat people." Purpose in publishing works by young people: to give encouragement and demonstration of talent. Children must be ages 9-14; must include parent's note verifying originality.
Magazines: Uses adventure, historical, everyday life experience (fiction/nonfiction-1,200 words); health-related short articles; poetry (4-24 lines of "mostly mood pieces and humor"). Pays in prizes for children, money for adult authors. Query. Will accept typewritten, legibly handwritten and computer printout mss. "Will not be returned without SASE." Reports in 6 weeks.
Artwork: Publishes artwork by children. Looks for all types of artwork—white paper, black pen. Pays in prizes for kids. Send b&w art to Elaine Trumbo, editor. "Won't be returned without SASE."
Tips: "All items submitted by kids are held in a file and used when possible. We normally suggest they do not ask for return of the item."

CREATIVE KIDS, P.O. Box 8813, Waco TX 76714. (800)998-2208. Editor: Libby Lindsey. Magazine published 6 times/year. Estab. 1979. "All material is by children, for children." Purpose in publishing works by children: "to create a product that provides children with an authentic experience and to offer an opportunity for children to see their work in print. *Creative Kids* contains the best stories, poetry, opinion, artwork, games and photography by kids ages 8-14." Writers ages 8-14 must have statement by teacher or parent verifying originality. Writer's guidelines available on request with SASE.

Magazines: Uses "about 6" fiction stories (200-750 words); "about 6" nonfiction stories (200-750 words); poetry, plays, ideas to share 200-750 words/issue. Pays in "free magazine." Submit mss to submissions editor. Will accept typewritten mss. Include SASE. Reports in 1 month.

Artwork/Photography: Publishes artwork and photos by children. Looks for "any kind of drawing, cartoon, or painting." Pays "free magazine." Send original or a photo of the work to submissions editor. No photocopies. Include SASE. Reports in 1 month.

Tips: "*Creative Kids* is a magazine by kids, for kids. The work represents children's ideas, questions, fears, concerns and pleasures. The material never contains racist, sexist or violent expression. The purpose is to provide children with an authentic experience. A person may submit one piece of work per envelope. Each piece must be labeled with the student's name, birth date, grade, school, home address and school address. Include a photograph, if possible. Recent school pictures are best. Material submitted to *Creative Kids* must not be under consideration by any other publication. Items should be carefully prepared, proofread and double checked (perhaps also by a parent or teacher). All activities requiring solutions must be accompanied by the correct answers. Young writers and artists should always write for guidelines and then follow them. It is very frustrating to receive submissions that are not complete."

CREATIVE WITH WORDS, Thematic anthologies, Creative with Words Publications, P.O. Box 223226, Carmel CA 93922. Editor: Brigitta Geltrich. Publishes 6 anthologies/year. Estab. 1975. "We publish the creative writing of children." Audience consists of children, schools, libraries, adults, reading programs. Purpose in publishing works by children: to offer them an opportunity to get started in publishing. "Work must be of quality, original, unedited, and not published before; age must be given (up to 19 years old)." SASE must be enclosed with all correspondence and mss. Writer's guidelines and theme list available on request.

Books: Considers all categories except those dealing with death, violence, pornography and overly religious. Uses fairy tales, folklore items (1,000 words) and poetry (not to exceed 20 lines, 46 characters across). Published *Impossible Loves*, *Animals*, *Colors, the spectrum of the Rainbow* and *Mankind* (all children and adults). Pays 20% discount on each copy of publication in which fiction or poetry by children appears. Submit mss to Brigitta Geltrich, editor. Query; child, teacher or parent can submit; however, teacher and/or parents must verify originality of writing. Will accept typewritten and/or legibly handwritten mss. SASE. Reports in 1-2 months after deadline of any theme.

Artwork/Photography: Publishes artwork, photos and computer artwork by children (language art work). Pays 20% discount on every copy of publication in which work by children appears. Submit artwork to Brigitta Geltrich, editor.

Tips: "Enjoy the English language, life and the world around you. Look at everything from a different perspective. Be less descriptive and use words wisely."

FREE SPIRIT PUBLISHING INC., 400 First Ave. N., Suite 616, Minneapolis MN 55401-1730. (612)338-2068. Fax: (612)337-5050. Publishes 15-20 books/year. "We specialize in SELF-HELP FOR KIDS®. Our main interests include the development of self-esteem, self-awareness, creative thinking and problem-solving abilities, assertiveness, and making a difference in the world. We do not publish fiction or poetry. Children have a lot to share with each other. They also can reach and teach each other in ways adults cannot. "We accept submissions from young people ages 14 and older. Plese send a letter from a parent/guardian/leader verifying originality." Request catalog and "student guidelines" before submitting work..

Books: Publishes psychology, self-help, how-to, education. Pays advance and royalties. Submit mss to M.E. Salzmann, editorial assistant. Send query. Will accept typewritten mss. SASE. Reports in 3-4 months.

Tips: "Always ask publisher for guidelines before submitting your work to them. *Make sure* that your submission includes *your name and address*. Don't count on publishers keeping your envelope with your return address on it; whoever opens the mail will probably throw it away."

***THE FUDGE CAKE**, P.O. Box 197, Citrus Heights CA 95611-0197. Magazine. Published bimonthly. Audience consists of children and young adults, grandparents, teachers, parents, etc.

Purpose in publishing works by young people: to provide a showcase for young writers age 6-17. "We value the work of today's children. They have a lot to say and we feel they need an outlet to express themselves." To qualify for publication, children must be age 6-17; submit copies of original work; and include SASE. Writer's guidelines available on request. Sample copy for $3.

Magazines: Uses 2-3 pieces of fiction (all types—no erotica) (250-500 words), 15-20 poems (30 lines or less). Pays 1 copy of issue work appears in. Submit mss to Jancarl Campi, editor. Submit complete ms. Will accept typewritten form and legible handwritten mss. Include SASE. Reports in 1 month.

Tips: "Don't be afraid to use the pen—write and rewrite, then send it in. We often critique or comment on rejected manuscripts."

FUTURIFIC, INC., Foundation for Optimism, Futurific, 305 Madison Ave., Suite 10B, New York NY 10165. Publisher: B. Szent-Miklosy. (212)297-0502. Magazine published monthly. Audience consists of people interested in an accurate report of what is ahead. "We do not discriminate by age. We look for the visionary in all people. They must write what will be. No advice or 'maybe.' We've had 19 years of accurate forecasting." Sample copy for $5 postage and handling. Writer's guidelines available on request with SASE.

Magazines: Submit mss to B. Szent-Miklosy, publisher. Will accept typewritten, legibly handwritten, computer printout, 5.25 or 3.5 inch WordPerfect diskette mss.

Artwork: Publishes artwork by children. Looks for "what the future will look like." Pay is negotiable. Send b&w drawings or photos. Submit artwork to B. Szent-Miklosy, publisher.

THE GOLDFINCH, 402 Iowa Ave., Iowa City IA 52240. (319)335-3916. Fax: (319)335-3935. Magazine published quarterly. Audience is 4th-8th graders. "Magazine supports creative work by children: research, art, writing. *The Goldfinch* puts the fun back into history. We publish young Iowans' work to show them that they and their creative efforts are an important part of Iowa history." Submitted work must go with the historical theme of each issue.

Magazines: 10-20% written by children. Uses at least 1 nonfiction essay, poem, story/issue (500 words). Pays complimentary copies. Submit mss with SASE to Amy Ruth, editor. Submit complete ms. Will accept typewritten, legibly handwritten, computer disk (Apple) mss. Reports in 1 month.

Artwork/Photography: Publishes artwork/photographs by children. Art and photos must be b&w. Pays complimentary copies. Query first with SASE to Amy Ruth.

Tips: "We make the subject of Iowa history come alive through short features, games/puzzles/activities, fiction and cool historical photographs."

HIGH SCHOOL WRITER, P.O. Box 718, Grand Rapids MN 55744. (218)326-8025. Magazine published monthly during the school year. "The *High School Writer* is a magazine written *by* students *for* students. All submissions must exceed contemporary standards of decency." Purpose in publishing works by young people: "To provide a real audience for student writers—and text for study." Submissions by junior high and middle school students accepted for our junior edition. Senior high students' works are accepted for our senior high edition. Students attending schools that subscribe to our publication are eligible to submit their work." Writer's guidelines available on request.

Magazines: Uses fiction, nonfiction (2,000 words maximum) and poetry. Submit mss to Roxanne Kain, editor. Submit complete ms (teacher must submit). Will accept typewritten, computer-generated (good quality) mss.

Tips: "Submissions should not be sent without first obtaining a copy of our guidelines. Also, submissions will not be considered unless student's school subscribes."

HIGHLIGHTS FOR CHILDREN, 803 Church St., Honesdale PA 18431. (717)253-1080. Magazine. Published monthly. "We strive to provide wholesome, stimulating, entertaining material

The asterisk before a listing indicates the listing is new in this edition.

that will encourage children to read. Our audience is children ages 2-12." Purpose in publishing works by young people: to encourage children's creative expression. Age limit to submit is 15.
Magazines: 15-20% of magazine written by children. Uses 4-6 fiction stories (50-150 words)/year; 15-20 poems (4-12 lines) per issue. Also uses jokes, riddles, tongue twisters. Features which occur occasionally: "What Are Your Favorite Books?" (8-10/year), Recipes (8-10/year), "Science Letters" (15-20/year). Special features which invite children's submissions on a specific topic: "Tell the Story" (15-20/year), "You're the Reporter" (8-10/year), "Your Ideas, Please" (8-10/year), "Endings to Unfinished Stories" (8-10/year). Pays in copies. Submit complete mss to the editor. Will accept typewritten, legibly handwritten and computer printout mss. Reports in 3-6 weeks.
Artwork: Publishes artwork by children. No payment given. No cartoon or comic book characters. No commercial products. Submit b&w or color artwork for "Our Own Pages." Features include "Creatures Nobody Has Ever Seen" (5-8/year) and "Illustration Job" (18-20/year). Reports in 3-6 weeks.

HOW ON EARTH!, Youth supporting compassionate, ecologically sound living, P.O. Box 339, Oxford PA 19363-0339. (717)529-8638. Fax: (717)529-3000. E-mail: howonearth@aol.com. Magazine. Published quarterly. Youth audience. "Through providing a voice for youth, *How on Earth!* honors youth visions and expressions in creating and exploring options for compassionate, ecologically-sound living. *HOE!* acknowledges the interconnectedness of animal, environmental, human rights, peace and other social change issues and explores these relationships through the thoughts and feelings of youth." Must be ages 13-24 and work must be original. Articles well-referenced. "Please send SASE with 1 first-class stamp for submission guidelines."
Magazines: 95% of magazine written by youth. Uses 1-2 creative writing stories, 2-5 research or informative articles, 4-5 poems per issue. Submit mss to Sally Clinton, coordinator. Query for articles. Will accept typewritten and legibly handwritten mss or 3.5″ disk (Macintosh). Include SASE "only if they want it returned." Reports in 2 months.
Artwork/Photography: Publishes artwork and photographs taken by youth. "We accept material depicting nature, animals, ecology, social justice, activism, vegetarian food and anything concerning issues related to these topics. Full color art or photos accepted for cover. Cartoons welcome as well. Pen & ink or dark pencil only." No pay: "All volunteer at this point." Submit artwork and photos to Sally Clinton, coordinator. Include SASE "only if they want it returned." Reports in 2 months.

INK BLOT, 901 Day Rd., Saginaw MI 48609. Newsletter. Published monthly. "I want young writers to do their best work, learn proper form and have their work shared with others. We put our newsletter in libraries, hospitals, waiting rooms and copies to contributors." Purpose in publishing works by young people: to give children an outlet for publishing their talents; to have them write using their imagination and creativity and to share them with others. Accepts manuscripts from all ages. If student, please include age, grade and school name. Only print original works from contributors. Material is accepted from across the United States and Canada. Typewritten preferred—handwritten *neatly* OK.
Magazines: Sample copy and guidelines available for $1 (check made out to M. Larkin, editor) and include SASE. Maximum length 500 words (stories). "Must fit on one side of typewritten page."
Artwork: Publishes artwork by children. Wants small 3×3 b&w ink drawings only; especially drawings that accompany poetry and short stories. No derogatory or obscene pictures accepted. Pays in copies. Submit art to Margaret Larkin, editor, or Vicki Larkin, assistant editor. Include SASE. Reports in 3 months.

INTERRACE/BIRACIAL CHILD, P.O. Box 12048, Atlanta GA 30355. Fax: (404)364-9965. Magazine. "Our audience is primarily interracial couples, families and multiracial people." *Interrace/Biracial Child* is intended to "portray a positive view of multiracial, multicultural children."
Magazines: 5% of magazine written by young people. Uses fiction (750-1,500 words), nonfiction (600-1,500 words), poetry. Pays $25-75 for articles. Submit mss to Candy Mills, editor. Submit complete mss for fiction and nonfiction. Will accept typewritten, legibly handwritten, Mac disk mss. Contact: Candy Mills, editor. Include SASE. Reports in 1-6 months.
Artwork/Photography: Publishes artwork (high quality) and photography by and of children. Pays $10-25. Submit art and photographs to Candy Mills, editor. SASE. Reports in 1-6 months.

Tips: "Manuscripts, artwork, photographs, etc. should have an intercultural, interethnic or interracial theme."

IOWA WOMAN, P.O. Box 680, Iowa City IA 52244. (319)351-2068. E-mail: rbailey@blue.weeg.uiowa.edu. Published quarterly. "We publish quality fiction, essays, interviews, poetry, book reviews and feature articles for women everywhere. We welcome submissions by girls and young women to encourage them to communicate and share their creative work. If work is by children, we prefer it not be rewritten by an adult. We welcome drawings and visual art, too. Guidelines available for SASE.
Magazines: Less than 1% of magazine written by young people (we hardly ever get submissions). Pays $5/published page and 2 copies of issue. Submit complete mss. Mss must be typewritten (diskette if accepted). Include SASE. Reports in 6 weeks-3 months.
Artwork/Photography: Publishes artwork and photography by children. Looks for "specific illustrations for fiction and essays we've accepted; illustration by child for her own written work." Pays $15 for illustration per story, any genre (b&w only). No payment for photos accompanying a ms. "Ask to be on artist list or send photocopy samples." Include SASE. Submit art and photographs to Editor. Include SASE. Reports in 3 weeks.

***KIDS' BYLINE**, P.O. Box 1838, Frederick MD 21702. (301)695-5963. Fax: (301)845-7959. Magazine. Published bimonthly. "We don't like to edit. We prefer that material published represent the original work of the writer, not exist as the framework for an 'improved' piece. Work of students, grades 4-12, is published based on merit, not potential. Our magazine provides a forum for students to share and read the writing of their peers, and serves as an adjunct to the classroom. Readers range from grade one up to grandparents. We publish students in grades 4-12, and will consider work from younger individuals. We publish from any geographic region, even other countries. We rely on the individual's integrity for originality."
Magazines: 100% of publication written by children. Pays in copies, or on rare occasions pays for assigned article. Submit mss to Gwen McEntire, managing editor. Submit query for proposals on assigned articles—these would mostly be interviews; submit complete ms for all other writing. Will accept typewritten and legibly handwritten mss. Include SASE. Reports in 2-3 months.
Artwork/Photography: Publishes artwork and photography by students. Looks for b&w photos of just about any subject. Quality must be great to be considered. Pays in copies. Preferably in b&w high quality and unfolded. Submit art and photographs to Gwen McEntire, managing editor. Include SASE. Reports in 2-3 months.
Tips: "Our Student Advisory Board of six high school students reviews material and helps with selection and publication. If you're having fun, or care about what you're writing, our readers will too. No graphic violence. Stories should be short, due to the length of the magazine. Write about what you care about and think of creative ways of expression. We don't want factual reports of historic events, etc." Guidelines are available for a SASE and sample copies are available for $3/issue. Subscriptions cost $15/year (6 issues).

***KIDS' WORLD, The Magazine That's All Kids!**, 1300 Kicker Rd., Tuscaloosa AL 35404. (205)553-2284. E-mail: d.kopasks_me@genie.com. Magazine. Published 4 times a year. Audience consists of young children through teens. "I'm creating a fun magazine for kids to read and a good place for young writers to get a start." Purpose in publishing works by young people: "So that my magazine will be unique—edited by a kid, for kids, by kids (all kids!). Authors must be under 17—no horror." Writer's guidelines available on request.
Magazines: 100% of magazine written by young people. Uses 4-10 short stories; 1-2 essays about favorite things, etc.; 4-10 poems and art. Pays one free copy per ms or artwork. Submit mss to Morgan Kopaska-Merkel, editor. Submit complete mss. Will accept typewritten and legibly handwritten mss. Include SASE. Reports in 2-4 weeks.
Artwork/Photography: Publishes artwork and photography by children. Looks for "children/babies and things of interest to them (food, toys, animals . . .)." Must be b&w in pen. Pays one free copy per artwork. Send the artwork, plus a note and SASE. Include SASE. Reports in 2-4 weeks.
Tips: "Have an adult check spelling, punctuation and grammar."

THE LOUISVILLE REVIEW—CHILDREN'S CORNER, Dept. of English, University of Louisville, 315 Bingham Humanities, Louisville KY 40292. (502)852-6801. Semiannual magazine.

"We are a contemporary literary journal." Purpose in publishing works by young people: to encourage children to write with fresh images and striking metaphors. Not interested in the "cute" moral lesson or highly rhymed and metered verse. "We believe there are children writers who are as good as adult writers and therefore deserve to be published along with adult writers." Must supply SASE and permission slip from parent stating that work is original and giving permission to publish if accepted. Only accepts typewritten mss.
Magazines: 10-20% of magazine written by children. Uses 10-25 pages of fiction, essays and poetry, any length. Pays in copies. Submit mss to Children's Corner. Submit complete ms. Will accept typewritten mss. Include SASE. Deadline December 31. Reports by March.

THE MCGUFFEY WRITER, 5128 Westgate Dr., Oxford OH 45056. Fax: (513)523-5565. E-mail: jchurch@hcnet.muohio.edu. Magazine published 3 times per year. "We publish poems and stories by children that compel the editors to read them to the end because of extraordinary originality of content or facility with language given the age of the child author." Purpose in publishing works by children: to reward by recognition those who strive to create in words and/or drawings and to motivate other children to try to meet a standard set in a sense by their peers. Requirements: be in grades K-12, no geographic restriction, originality must be attested to by adult parent or teacher. Writer's guidelines available on request.
Magazines: 100% of magazine written by young people. Uses 3-5 fiction short stories (599 or fewer words), 0-3 nonfiction stories (500 or fewer words), 5-10 poems (30 lines or less). "We do not publish trite, violent, teen 'romance' or gloom and doom selections. We look for fresh, original writing on topics students know well." Pays 2 copies. Submit mss to Susan Kammeraad-Campbell, submissions editor. Submit complete ms. "Send copy—we do not return submissions." Will accept typewritten form and legible handwriting. Include SASE. Responds in 3 months to those who are published.
Artwork/Photography: Publishes black & white illustrations to fit 7½×8 page—any theme. Pays 2 contributor copies. Submit art and photographs to Linda Sheppard, art editor. Responds in 3 months.
Tips: "Trust your own voice—know that what you think and feel is of value and worth sharing with others. When you write about what you know, it's emotional knowledge, not necessarily autobiography."

***MAJESTIC BOOKS**, P.O. Box 19097-CW, Johnston RI 02919. Book publisher. Publishes 3 books/year. "Majestic Books is a small press which was formed to give children an outlet for their work. We publish softcover bound anthologies of fictional stories by children, for children and adults who enjoy the work of children." Purpose in publishing work by young people: "Our hope is that our publication will spark a child's interest in writing and give children talented in writing encouragement to continue." All children age 8 through 18 have a chance of being published with us as long as they state their age when submitting work. Writer's guidelines available on request. SASE required.
Books: Publishes short stories. Length: 2,000 words or less for fiction. Pays complimentary copy, occasionally pays small flat fee. Submit mss to Cindy MacDonald, publisher. Submit complete mss for fiction or poetry. Will accept typewritten and legibly handwritten mss. Include SASE. Reports in 3 weeks (slightly longer in summer).
Tips: "Use your imagination to create the best fictional story you can and then send it to us. We need to know your age when you submit work so we can judge your talent accordingly. We love stories that leave the reader thinking long after they have read the last word."

MERLYN'S PEN: The National Magazine of Student Writing, P.O. Box 1058, East Greenwich RI 02818. (800)247-2027. Fax: (401)885-5222. Magazine. Published every 2 months during the school year, September-May. "By publishing student writing, *Merlyn's Pen* seeks to broaden and reward the young author's interest in writing. Strengthen the self-confidence of beginning writers, and promote among all students a positive attitude toward literature. We publish a Senior Edition (grades 9-12) and a Middle School Edition (grades 6-9) including 150 manuscripts annually by students in grades 6-12. The entire magazine is dedicated to young adults' writing. Our audience is classrooms, libraries and students from grades 6-12." Writers must be in grades 6-12 and must send a completed *Merlyn's Pen* cover sheet with each submission. When a student is accepted, he/she, a parent and a teacher must sign a statement of originality.

Judging by 7 professional artists and editors. Works will be displayed at the Society of Illustrators Museum of American Illustration in New York City October-November annually. Medals awarded.

HELEN KEATING OTT AWARD FOR OUTSTANDING CONTRIBUTION TO CHILDREN'S LITERATURE, Church and Synagogue Library Association, P.O. Box 19357, Portland OR 97280. (503)244-6919. Fax: (503)977-3734. Chair of Committee: Lillian Koppin. Annual award. Estab. 1980. "This award is given to a person or organization that has made a significant contribution to promoting high moral and ethical values through children's literature." Deadline for entries: March 1. "Recipient is honored in July during the conference." Awards certificate of recognition and a conference package consisting of registration, meals and housing and a complementary 1 year membership. "A nomination for an award may be made by anyone. It should include the name, address and telephone number of the nominee plus the church or synagogue relationship where appropriate. Nominations of an organization should include the name of a contact person. A detailed description of the reasons for the nomination should be given, accompanied by documentary evidence of accomplishment. The person(s) making the nomination should give his/her name, address and telephone number and a brief explanation of his/her knowledge of the nominee's accomplishments. Elements of creativity and innovation will be given high priority by the judges."

PEN/NORMA KLEIN AWARD FOR CHILDREN'S FICTION, PEN American Center, 568 Broadway, New York NY 10012. (212)334-1660. Awarded in odd-numbered years. Estab. 1990. "In memory of the late PEN member and distinguished children's book author Norma Klein, the award honors new authors whose books demonstrate the adventuresome and innovative spirit that characterizes the best children's literature and Norma Klein's own work." Previously published submissions only. "Candidates may not nominate themselves. We welcome all nominations from authors and editors of children's books." Deadline for entries: December 15, 1996. Awards $3,000 which will be given in May. Judging by a panel of 3 distinguished children's book authors. Nominations open to authors of books for elementary school to young adult readers. "It is strongly recommended that the nominator describe in some detail the literary character of the candidate's work and how it promises to enrich American literature for children."

PLEASE TOUCH MUSEUM BOOK AWARD, Please Touch Museum, 210 N. 21st St., Philadelphia PA 19103. (215)963-0667. Director of Education and Research: Marzy Sykes, Ph.D. Annual award. Estab. 1985. Purpose of the award: "to recognize and encourage the publication of books for young children by American authors that are of the highest quality and will aid them in enjoying the process of learning through books. Awarded to two picture books that are particularly imaginative and effective in exploring a concept or concepts, one for children age three and younger, and one for children ages four-seven." Previously published submissions only. "To be eligible for consideration a book must: (1) Explore and clarify an idea for young children. This could include the concept of numbers, colors, shapes, sizes, senses, feelings, etc. There is no limitation as to format. (2) Be distinguished in both text and illustration. (3) Be published within the last year by an American publisher. (4) Be written by an American author and/or illustrator." Deadline for entries: March 15 (submissions may be made throughout the year). SASE for award rules and entry forms. No entry fee. Judging by selected jury of children's literature experts, librarians and early childhood educators. Education store purchases books for selling at Book Award Celebration Day and throughout the year. Receptions and autographing sessions held in bookstores, the main branch of the Philadelphia Free Library and the Please Touch Museum.

POCKETS MAGAZINE FICTION CONTEST, The Upper Room, P.O. Box 189, Nashville TN 37202-0189. (615)340-7333. Fax: (615)340-7006. Associate Editor: Lynn Gilliam. Annual contest. Estab. 1990. Purpose of contest: "to discover new freelance writers for our magazine and to encourage freelance writers to become familiar with the needs of our magazine." Unpublished submissions only. Submissions made by the author. Deadline for entries: August 15. SASE for contest rules and entry forms. No entry fee. Awards $1,000 and publication. Judging by *Pocket*'s editors and 3 other editors of other Upper Room publications. Winner and runners-up are published in the magazine.

EDGAR ALLAN POE AWARD, Mystery Writers of America, Inc., 17 E. 47th St., 6th Floor, New York NY 10017. (212)888-8171. Executive Director: Priscilla Ridgway. Annual award. Estab. 1945. Purpose of the award: to honor authors of distinguished works in the mystery field. Previously published submissions only. Submissions made by the author, author's agent; "normally by the publisher." Work must be published/produced the year of the contest. Deadline for entries: December 1 "except for works only available in the month of December." SASE for award rules and entry forms. No entry fee. Awards ceramic bust of "Edgar" for winner; scrolls for all nominees. Judging by professional members of Mystery Writers of America (writers). Nominee press release sent after first Wednesday in February. Winner announced at the Edgar Banquet, held in late April.

‡✤THE PRISM AWARDS, The Kids Netword, 1235 Williams Park, 68532, Brampton, Ontario L6S 4S0 Canada. (905)451-1725. Fax: (908)451-2035. Award Manager: Sylvia Chirco. Annual award. Estab. 1989. Purpose of the award: Children have an opportunity to submit mss for review. Winners are chosen based on originality of ideas and self-expression. Unpublished submissions only. Deadline for entries: January 26, 1996. SASE for award rules and entry forms. Entry fee is $2. Award consists of $500 cash and editorial training and possible publication. Judging by more than 40 independent judges. Requirements for entrants: a Native Indian, Canadian or landed immigrant in Canada, ages 7-14; story must be written solely by the submitter. No less than 4 pages, no more than 16 pages. Copyright to winning ms acquired by The Kids Netword upon winning.

‡PUBLISH-A-BOOK CONTEST, Raintree Steck/Vaughn Publishers. Send written entries to: PAB Contest, P.O. Box 27010, Austin TX 78755. (800)531-5015. Annual contest. Estab. 1984. Purpose of the contest: to stimulate 2nd- to 6th-graders to write outstanding stories for other children. Unpublished submissions only. Word limits: grades 4-6, 700-900 words; grades 2-3, 300-500 words. Deadline for entries: January 31. SASE for contest rules. Stories must be written on a given theme—for 1996 contest: "Mysteries." "Entries must be sponsored by a teacher or librarian." Entries not returned. No entry fee. Grand prizes: 5 winning entries are professionally illustrated and published in hardcover editions by Raintree. Each winner will receive a $500 advance against an author royalty contract and 10 free copies of the published book. The sponsor named on each of these entries will receive 20 free books from the Raintree catalog. Honorable mentions: each of the 20 honorable mention writers will receive $25. The sponsor named on each of these entries will receive 10 free books from the Raintree Steck-Vaughn catalog. Judging by an editorial team. Contract issued for Grand Prize winners. Payment and royalties paid. Requirements for entrants: Contest is open only to 2nd-6th graders enrolled in a school program in the United States or Canada. Books will be displayed and sold in the United States and foreign markets. Displays at educational association meetings, book fairs. For information contact Elaine Johnston, (512)795-3230, Fax (512)795-3676.

‡QUILL AND SCROLL INTERNATIONAL WRITING/PHOTO CONTEST, *Quill and Scroll*, School of Journalism, University of Iowa, Iowa City IA 52242. (319)335-5795. Contest Director: Richard Johns. Annual contest. Previously published submissions only. Submissions made by the author or school newspaper adviser. Must be published February 6, 1995 to February 4, 1996. Deadline for entries: February 5. SASE for contest rules and entry forms. Entry fee is $2/entry. Awards engraved plaque to junior high level sweepstakes winners. Each high school sweepstakes winner receives electric typewriter. Judging by various judges. *Quill and Scroll* acquires the right to publish submitted material in the magazine if it is chosen as a winning entry. Requirements for entrants: must be students in grades 6-9 for junior high school division; 9-12 for high school division.

‡READ WRITING & ART AWARDS, *Read* Magazine, 245 Long Hill Rd., Middletown CT 06457. (203)638-2406. Contest Director: Kate Davis. Annual award. Estab. 1978. Purpose of

The maple leaf before a listing indicates that the market is Canadian.

award: to reward excellence in writing and art in the categories of fiction, essay and art. Unpublished submissions only. Submissions made by the author or nominated by a person or group of people. Must include signature of teacher, parent or guardian and student. Deadline for entries: December 15. SASE for contest/award rules and entry forms. No entry fee. Awards first prize ($100), second prize ($75), third prize ($50). Prizes are given in each category, plus publication of first place winners. Judging by *Read* editorial staff. "Entrant understands that prize will include publication, but sometimes pieces are published in other issues. A story may be bought later." Work must be original. Art can be in color or b&w. Published in April issue of *Read* (all-student issue).

‡ANNA DAVIDSON ROSENBERG AWARD FOR POEMS ON THE JEWISH EXPERIENCE, Judah L. Magnes Museum, 2911 Russell St., Berkeley CA 94705. (510)849-2710. Poetry Award Director: Paula Friedman. Annual award. Estab. 1986-87. Purpose of the award: to encourage poetry in English on the Jewish experience (writer does not need to be Jewish). Previously unpublished submissions only. Deadline for entries: August 31. SASE for award rules and entry forms by July 31. SASE for list of winners. Awards $100-first prize, $50-second prize, $25-third prize; honorable mention certificates; $25 Youth Commendation (poets under 19) Emerging Poet Award. Judging by committee of 3 well-published poets with editing/teaching experience. There will be a reading of top award winners in December at Magnes Museum. Prospective anthology of winning entries. "We request permission to use in potential anthologies." Write for entry form and guidelines *first*; entries must follow guidelines and be accompanied by entry form. *Please do not phone.*

CARL SANDBURG LITERARY ARTS AWARDS, Friends of the Chicago Public Library, Harold Washington Library Center, 400 S. State St., Chicago IL 60605. (312)747-4907. Annual award. Categories: fiction, nonfiction, poetry, children's literature. Published submissions only; must be published between June 1 and May 31 (the following year). Deadline for entries: August 1. SASE for award rules. Entries not returned. No entry fee. Awards medal and $1,000 prize. Judging by authors, reviewers, book buyers, librarians. Requirements for entrants: native born Chicagoan or presently residing in the 6 county metropolitan area. Two copies must be submitted by August 1. All entries become the property of the Friends.

‡THE SCHOLASTIC ART AWARDS, The Alliance for Young Artists & Writers, 555 Broadway, New York NY 10012-3999. (212)343-6493. Director: Susan Ebersole. Annual award. Estab. 1927. Purpose of awards: encouragement and recognition of student achievement in the visual arts. "There are 15 categories: painting, drawing, computer graphics, video, film and animation, 2-D design, 3-D design, mixed media, printmaking, fiber arts and textile design, sculpture, ceramics, jewelry and metalsmithing, photography. Seniors only may submit art and photography portfolios. Awards consist of cash awards, scholarships and prizes. Unpublished submissions only. Some areas have sponsors who conduct a regional preliminary judging and exhibition." SASE for award rules and entry forms. Entry fees and deadlines vary depending on region in which a student lives. Judging by art educators, artists, photographers and art administrators. All publication rights are given to The Alliance (for 2 years). Requirements for entrants: Students must be in grades 7-12. National winners work on exhibition during the summer. Write to above address for more information.

‡SCHOLASTIC WRITING AWARDS, The Alliance for Young Artists & Writers, 555 Broadway, New York NY 10012. (212)343-6493. Director: Susan Ebersole. Annual award. Estab. 1923. Purpose of award: encouragement and recognition of young writers. Open to students in grades 7-12. Group I (grades 7, 8, 9). Group II (grades 10,11,12). There are 7 categories: short story, short short story, essay/nonfiction/persuasive writing, dramatic script, poetry, humor and science fiction. Seniors only may submit portfolios representing their best group of writing. Awards consist of cash awards, scholarships and prizes. Selected works will be published in *Scholastic* magazines. Unpublished submissions only. Entires must be postmarked by January except those from central Pennsylvania and Hains County, TX. Deadlines are indicated on entry forms. All publication rights are given to The Alliance for 2 years. Send SASE for guidelines and entry forms.

‡SEVENTEEN FICTION CONTEST, 9th Floor, 850 Third Ave., New York NY 10022. Fiction Editor: Joe Bargmann. Annual contest. Estab. 1945. Fax: (212)935-4236. E-mail: thespin@aol.com. Unpublished submissions only. Deadline for entries: April 30. SASE for contest rules and entry forms; contest rules also published in November issue of *Seventeen*. Entries not returned. No entry fee. Awards cash prize and possible publication in *Seventeen*. Judging by "inhouse panel of editors, external readers." If first prize, acquires first North American rights for piece to be published. Requirements for entrants: "Our annual fiction contest is open to anyone between the ages of 13 and 21 who submits on or before April 30. Submit only original fiction that has not been published in any form other than in school publications. Stories should be between 1,500 and 3,000 words in length (6-12 pages). All manuscripts must be typed double-spaced on a single side of paper. Submit as many original stories as you like, but each story must include your full name, address, birth date and signature in the top right-hand corner of the first page. Your signature on submission will constitute your acceptance of the contest rules."

‡SHUBERT FENDRICH MEMORIAL PLAYWRIGHTING CONTEST, Pioneer Drama Service, Inc., P.O. Box 4267, Englewood CO 80155-4267. Director: Steven Fendrich. Annual contest. Estab. 1990. Purpose of contest: "to encourage the development of quality theatrical material for educational and family theater." Previously unpublished submissions only. Deadline for entries: March 1. SASE for contest rules and entry forms. No entry fee. Awards $1,000 royalty advance and publication. Judging by editors. All rights acquired with acceptance of contract for publication. Restrictions for entrants: Any writers currently published by Pioneer Drama Service are not eligible.

‡SKIPPING STONES HONOR AWARDS, *Skipping Stones*, P.O. Box 3939, Eugene OR 97403. (503)342-4956. Annual award. Purpose of contest: "to recognize youth under age 16 for their contributions to multicultural awareness, nature and ecology, social issues, peace and nonviolence. Also to promote creativity, self-esteem and writing skills, and to promote and recognize important work being done by youth organizations." Submissions made by the author. For 1996, the theme is "Envisioning the world in the year 2025 AD." Deadline for entries: June 25, 1996. SASE for contest rules and entry forms. Entries must include certificate of originality by parents and/or teachers, and background information on the author written by the author. Entry fee is $3. Judging by *Skipping Stones*' staff. "Ten awards are given in three categories: (1) Compositions—(essays, poems, short stories, songs, travelogues, etc.) should be typed (double-spaced) or neatly handwritten. Fiction or nonfiction should be limited to 750 words; poems to 30 lines. Non-English writings are also welcome. (2) Artwork—(drawings, cartoons, paintings or photo essays with captions) should have the artist's name, age and address on the back of each page. Send the originals with SASE. Black & white photos are especially welcome. (3) Youth Organizations—Tell us how your club or group works to: (a) preserve the nature and ecology in your area, (b) enhance the quality of life for low-income, minority or disabled, or (c) improve racial or cultural harmony in your school or community. Use the same format as for compositions." The 1996 winners will be published in Vol. 8, #4 (September-October 1996) issue of *Skipping Stones*.

KAY SNOW WRITERS' CONTEST, Williamette Writers, 9045 SW Barbur Blvd. #5A, Portland OR 97219. (503)452-1592. Contest Director: Leona Grieve. Annual contest. Purpose of contest: "to encourage beginning and established writers to continue the craft." Unpublished, original submissions only. Submissions made by the author or author's agent. Deadline for entries: July 30. SASE for contest rules and entry forms. Entry fee is $10, Williamette Writers' members;, $15, nonmembers; $5, student writer. Awards cash prize of $200 per category (fiction, nonfiction, juvenile, poetry, script writing). "Judges are anonymous."

***SOUTHWEST BOOK AWARD**, Border Regional Library Association (BRLA), El Paso Public Library, 501 N. Oregon St., El Paso TX 79901. (915)543-5441. Fax: (915)543-5410. Estab. 1970. Purpose of contest: to recognize Southwestern books and authors. Any publisher having one or more items that meet the criteria is invited to submit a review copy of each for consideration. Nominations submitted by individuals are also welcome. Previously published submissions only. Submissions are made by publishers and individuals. Deadline for entries: September 30. SASE for contest rules and entry forms. No entry fee. Awards certificate. Gives about 12 awards/year for fiction, poetry and nonfiction; usually one or two are for children's books. Judging by BRLA members. Entries must be about the Southwest (defined as West Texas, New Mexico); appearing in book or audiovisual format for the first time; of high quality, both in the context of the current year's entries and in the existing body of Southwestern literature. Works will be displayed at a February banquet.

GEORGE G. STONE CENTER FOR CHILDREN'S BOOKS RECOGNITION OF MERIT AWARD, George G. Stone Center for Children's Books, The Claremont Graduate School, 131 E. 10th St., Claremont CA 91711-6188. (909)607-3670. Fax: (909)621-8390. Award Director: Doty Hale. Annual award. Estab. 1965. Purpose of the award: to recognize an author or illustrator of a children's book or a body of work exhibiting the "power to please and expand the awareness of children and teachers as they have shared the book in their classrooms." Previously published submissions only. SASE for award rules and entry forms. Entries not returned. No entry fee. Awards a scroll. Judging by a committee of teachers, professors of children's literature and librarians. Requirements for entrants: "Nominations are made by students, teachers, professors and librarians. Award made at annual Claremont Reading Conference in spring (March)."

JOAN G. SUGARMAN CHILDREN'S BOOK AWARD, Washington Independent Writers Legal and Educational Fund, Inc., #220, 733 15th St. NW, Washington DC 20005. (202)347-4973. Director: Isolde Chapin. Open to residents of D.C., Maryland, Virginia. Award offered every 2 years. Next awards presented in 1998 for publications done in 1996-1997. Estab. 1987. Purpose of award: to recognize excellence in children's literature, ages 1-15. Previously published submissions only. Submissions made by the author or author's agent or by publishers. Must be published in the 2 years preceeding award year. Deadline for entries: January 31. SASE for award rules and entry forms. No entry fee. Awards $1,000. Judging by selected experts in children's books. Requirements for entrants: publication of material; residence in DC, Maryland or Virginia. No picture books. Works displayed at reception for award winners and become part of the Sugarman Collection at The George Washington University.

***SUGARMAN FAMILY AWARD FOR JEWISH CHILDREN'S LITERATURE**, District of Columbia Jewish Community Center, 1836 Jefferson Place NW, Washington DC 20036. (202)775-1765. Fax: (202)331-7667. Award director: Marcia F. Goldberg. Open to adults. Annual award. Estab. 1994. Purpose of contest: to enrich all children's appreciation of Jewish culture and to inspire writers and illustrators for children. Previously published submissions only. Submissions are made by the author, made by the author's agent. Must be published January-December of year previous to award year. Deadline for entries published in 1995: December 31. SASE for award rules and entry forms. Entry fee is $25. Awards at least $750. Judging by a panel of 3 judges—a librarian, a children's bookstore owner and a reviewer of books. Requirements for entrants: must have lived or worked in Washington DC, or Connecticut, Florida, Illinois, Maine, Maryland, Massachusetts, New Jersey, Pennsylvania, Rhode Island, Virginia or West Virginia. Work displayed at the DC Jewish Community Center Library after March.

SYDNEY TAYLOR BOOK AWARD, Association of Jewish Libraries, %National Foundation of Jewish Culture, 330 Seventh Ave., 21st Floor, New York NY 10001. Chairman: Julie A. Moss. Annual awards. Estab. 1973. Purpose of the award: "to recognize books of quality in the field of Judaic books for children in two categories: picture books for young children and older children's books." Previously published submissions only. Submissions made by publisher only. Must be published January-December of the year being judged. Deadline for entries: January 31. No entry fee. Awards plaque and $1,000 total monies in each category. Judging by a committee of 6 librarians. Requirements for entrants: "Subject matter must be of Judaic content."

SYDNEY TAYLOR MANUSCRIPT COMPETITION, Association of Jewish Libraries, 1327 Wyntercreek Lane, Dunwoody GA 30338. (401)274-1117. Director: Paula Sandfelder. Annual contest. Estab. 1985. Purpose of the contest: "This competition is for unpublished writers of fiction. Material should be for readers ages 8-11, with universal appeal that will serve to deepen the understanding of Judaism for all children, revealing positive aspects of Jewish life." Unpublished submissions only. Deadline for entries: January 15. SASE for contest rules and entry forms. No entry fee. Awards $1,000. Judging by qualified judges from within the Association of

Jewish Libraries. Requirements for entrants: must be an unpublished fiction writer. "AJL assumes no responsibility for publication, but hopes this cash incentive will serve to encourage new writers of children's stories with Jewish themes for all children."

‡VEGETARIAN ESSAY CONTEST, The Vegetarian Resource Group, P.O. Box 1463, Baltimore MD 21203. (410)366-VEGE. Address to Vegetarian Essay Contest. Annual contest. Estab. 1985. Unpublished submissions only. Deadline for entries: May 1 of each year. SASE for contest rules and entry forms. No entry fee. Awards $50 savings bond. Judging by awards committee. Acquires rights for The Vegetarian Resource Group to reprint essays. Requirements for entrants: age 18 and under. Winning works may be published in *Vegetarian Journal*, instructional materials for students. "Submit 2-3 page essay on any aspect of vegetarianism, which is the abstinence of meat, fish and fowl. Entrants can base paper on interviewing, research or personal opinion. Need not be vegetarian to enter."

‡VERY SPECIAL ARTS YOUNG PLAYWRIGHTS PROGRAM, Very Special Arts, Education Office, The John F. Kennedy Center for the Performing Arts, Washington DC 20566. (202)628-2800 or 1-800-933-8721. National Programs Coordinator: Elena Widder. Annual contest. Estab. 1984. "All scripts must address or incorporate some aspect of disability." Unpublished submissions only. Deadline for entries: April 15. Write to Young Playwrights Coordinator for contest rules and entry forms. No entries returned. No entry fee. Judging by Artists Selection Committee. Entrants must be students age 12-18. "Script will be selected for production at The John F. Kennedy Center for the Performing Arts, Washington DC. The winning play is presented each October."

‡VIDEO VOYAGES CONTEST, Weekly Reader Corporation, 245 Long Hill Rd., P.O. Box 2791, Middletown CT 06457. (203)638-2400. Co-sponsor: Panasonic Company. Contest Director: Lois Lewis. Annual contest. Estab. 1991. Purpose of contest: to reward original videos made by elementary and upper grade students. Unpublished original student videos only. Submissions made by teams or classes of students. Deadline for entry: March 15. Write or call contest director for rules and entry forms. No entry fee. Prizes: Panasonic video equipment, including televisions, VCRs and camcorders. "All video equipment prizes are courtesy of Panasonic Company. All prizes are awarded to the winners' schools." Judging by staff members from Weekly Reader Corp. and Panasonic Company. All entries become the property of Weekly Reader Corp. and none will be returned. Requirements for entrants: open to students in grades 4-12. Each entry form must be signed by the supervising teacher(s).

VIRGINIA LIBRARY ASSOCIATION/JEFFERSON CUP, Virginia Library Association, 669 S. Washington St., Alexandria VA 22314. Award Director changes year to year. Annual award. Estab. 1983. Purpose of award: to honor a distinguished biography, historical fiction, or American history book for young people, thereby promoting reading about America's past, and encouraging writing of U.S. history, biography and historical fiction. Previously published submissions only. Must be published in the year prior to selection. SASE for contest rules and entry forms. Judging by committee. The book must be about U.S. history or an American person, 1492 to present, or fiction that highlights the U.S. past; author must reside in the U.S. The book must be published especially for young people.

‡THE STELLA WADE CHILDREN'S STORY AWARD, *Amelia* Magazine, 329 E St., Bakersfield CA 93304. (805)323-4064. Editor: Frederick A. Raborg, Jr. Annual award. Estab. 1988. Purpose of award: "With decrease in the number of religious and secular magazines for young people, the juvenile story and poetry must be preserved and enhanced." Unpublished submissions only. Deadline for entries: August 15. SASE for award rules. Entry fee is $5 per adult entry; there is no fee for entries submitted by young people under the age of 17, but such entry must be signed by parent, guardian or teacher to verify originality. Awards $125 plus publication. Judging by editorial staff. Previous winners include Maxine Kumin and Sharon E. Martin. "We use First North American serial rights only for the winning manuscript." Contest is open to all interested. If illustrator wishes to enter only an illustration without a story, the entry fee remains the same. Illustrations will also be considered for cover publication. Restrictions of mediums for illustrators: Submitted photos should be no smaller than 5×7; illustrations (drawn) may be in any medium. "Winning entry will be published in the most appropriate issue of either *Amelia*, *Cicada* or *SPSM&H*—subject matter would determine such. Submit clean, accurate copy."

‡WE ARE WRITERS, TOO!, Creative With Words Publications, P.O. Box 223226, Carmel CA 93922. Contest Director: Brigitta Geltrich. Annual contest. Estab. 1975. Unpublished submissions only. Deadline for entries: June 30. SASE for contest rules and entry forms. SASE for return of entries "if not winning poem." No entry fee. Awards publication in an anthology. Judging by selected guest editors and educators. Contest open to children only (up to and including 19 years old). Writer should request contest rules. SASE with all correspondence. Age of child must be stated and manuscript must be verified of its authenticity. Creative With Words Publications publishes anthologies on various themes throughout the year to which young writers may also submit. Request theme list, include SASE.

WELLSPRING SHORT FICTION CONTEST, 770g Tonkawa Rd., Long Lake MN 55356. (612)471-9259. Managing Editor: Chy Anne. Contest held twice a year. Estab. 1989. Purpose of contest: To support and encourage writers. Submissions are made by the author. Deadline for entries: January 1 and July 1 (entries received after deadline will be judged for subsequent issue). SASE for contest rules and entry forms. Entry fee $10 per entry (no limit on number of entries per writer). No foreign checks, currency or postage. Awards $100, 1st place; $75, 2nd place; $25, 3rd place. Winning entries published in *Wellspring* magazine. "To enter our next contest, submit one double-spaced, typed entry, 2,000 words maximum. Stick to word limit. Entries judged on intriguing, well-crafted work."

‡PAUL A. WITTY OUTSTANDING LITERATURE AWARD, International Reading Association, Special Interest Group, Reading for Gifted and Creative Learning, School of Education, P.O. Box 32925, Fort Worth TX 76129. (817)921-7660. Award Director: Dr. Cathy Collins Block. Annual award. Estab. 1979. Categories of entries: poetry/prose at elementary, junior high and senior high levels. Unpublished submissions only. Deadline for entries: February 1. SASE for award rules and entry forms. SASE for return of entries. No entry fee. Awards $25 and plaque, also certificates of merit. Judging by 2 committees for screening and awarding. Works will be published in Reading Association publications. "The elementary students' entries must be legible and may not exceed 1,000 words. Secondary students' prose entries should be typed and may exceed 1,000 words if necessary. At both elementary and secondary levels, if poetry is entered, a set of five poems must be submitted. All entries and requests for applications must include a self-addressed, stamped envelope."

PAUL A. WITTY SHORT STORY AWARD, International Reading Association, P.O. Box 8139, 800 Barksdale Rd., Newark DE 19714-8139. (302)731-1600. Annual award. Estab. 1986. Purpose of award: The entry must be an original short story appearing in a young children's periodical that regularly publishes short stories for children. (These would be periodicals generally aimed at readers to about age 12.) The short story should serve as a reading and literary standard by which readers can measure other writing and should encourage young readers to read by providing them with enjoyable and profitable reading. Deadline for entries: The entry must have been published for the first time in the eligibility year; the short story must be submitted during the calendar year of publication. Anyone wishing to nominate a short story should send it to the designated Paul A. Witty Short Award Subcommittee Chair by November 1. Deadline for completed entries to the subcommittee chair is December 1. Both fiction and nonfiction writing are eligible; each will be rated according to characteristics that are appropriate for the genre. Interested authors should send inquiry to Debra Gail Herrera, 111 East Conner, Eastland TX 76448. Award is $1,000 and recognition at the annual IRA Convention.

ALICE LOUISE WOOD OHIOANA AWARD FOR CHILDREN'S LITERATURE, Ohioana Library Association, 65 S. Front St., Suite 1105, Columbus OH 43215. (614)466-3831. Fax: (614)728-6974. Director: Linda R. Hengst. Annual award. Estab. 1991. Purpose of award: "to recognize an Ohio author whose body of work has made, and continues to make, a significant contribution to literature for children or young adults." SASE for award rules and entry forms. Gives monetary award (amount may vary). Requirements for entrants: "must have been born in Ohio, or lived in Ohio for a minimum of five years; established a distinguished publishing record of books for children and young people; body of work has made, and continues to make, a significant contribution to the literature for young people; through whose work as a writer, teacher, administrator, or through community service, interest in children's literature has been encouraged and children have become involved with reading."

***CARTER G. WOODSON BOOK AWARD**, National Council for the Social Studies, 3501 Newark St. NW, Washington DC 20016. (202)966-7840. Fax: (202)966-2061. E-mail: information@ncss.org Staff Competition Coordinator: Rose-Kathryn Young Chaisson. Annual award. Purpose of contest: to recognize books relating to ethnic minorities and authors of such books. NCSS established the Carter G. Woodson Book Awards for the most distinguished social science books appropriate for young readers which depict ethnicity in the United States. This award is intended to "encourage the writing, publishing, and dissemination of outstanding social studies books for young readers which treat topics related to ethnic minorities and race relations sensitively and accurately." Submissions must be previously published. Submissions generally made by publishers "because copies of the book must be supplied to each member of the committee and copies of winning books must be provided to NCSS headquarters." Eligible books must be published in the year preceding the year in which award is given, i.e., 1995 for 1996 award. Books must be received by members of the committee by February 1. Rules, criteria and requirements are available for SASE. No entry fee. Award consists of: an announcement published in NCSS periodicals and forwarded to national and Council affiliated media. The publisher and author receive written notification of the committee decision. Reviews of award recipients and outstanding merit book are published in the NCSS official journal, *Social Education*. The award is presented at the NCSS Annual Conference in November during the awards luncheon. Judging by committee of social studies educators (teachers, curriculum supervisors and specialists, college/university professors, teacher educators—with a specific interest in multicultural education and the use of literature in social studies instruction) appointed from the NCSS membership at large.

WORK-IN-PROGRESS GRANTS, Society of Children's Book Writers and Illustrators, 22736 Vanowen St., Suite 106, West Hills CA 91307. (818)888-8760. Annual award. "The SCBWI Work-in-Progress Grants have been established to assist children's book writers in the completion of a specific project." Five categories: (1) General Work-in-Progress Grant. (2) Grant for a Contemporary Novel for Young People. (3) Nonfiction Research Grant. (4) Grant for a work whose author has never had a book published. (5) Grant for a picture book writer. Requests for applications may be made beginning October 1. Completed applications accepted February 1-May 1 of each year. SASE for applications for grants. In any year, an applicant may apply for any of the grants except the one awarded for a work whose author has never had a book published. (The recipient of this grant will be chosen from entries in all categories.) Five grants of $1,000 will be awarded annually. Runner-up grants of $500 (one in each category) will also be awarded. "The grants are available to both full and associate members of the SCBWI. They are not available for projects on which there are already contracts." Previous recipients not eligible to apply.

‡WRITER'S EXCHANGE POETRY CONTEST, R.S.V.P. Press, Box 394, Society Hill SC 29593. (803)378-4556. Contest Director: Gene Boone. Quarterly contest. Estab. 1985. Purpose of the contest: to promote friendly competition among poets of all ages and backgrounds, giving these poets a chance to be published and win an award. Submissions are made by the author. Continuous deadline; entries are placed in the contest closest to date received. SASE for contest rules and entry forms. Entry fee is $1 per poem. Awards 50% of contest proceeds, usually $35-100 varying slightly in each quarterly contest due to changes in response. Judging by Gene Boone or a guest judge such as a widely published poet or another small press editor. "From the entries received, we reserve the right to publish the winning poems in an issue of *Writer's Exchange*, a literary newsletter. The contest is open to any poet. Poems on any subject/theme, any style, to 24 lines, may be entered. Poems should be typed, single-spaced, with the poet's name in the upper left corner."

‡WRITER'S INTERNATIONAL FORUM CONTESTS, *Writer's International Forum*, P.O. Box 516, Tracyton WA 98393. Contest Director: Sandra E. Haven. Estab. 1991. Purpose of contest: to inspire excellence in the traditional short story format. "We like identifiable characters, strong storylines, and crisp, fresh endings. We particularly like helping new writers, writers changing genres and young writers." Unpublished submissions only. Submissions made by the author. Deadlines, fees, and cash award prizes vary per contest. SASE for dates of each upcoming contest, contest rules and entry forms. Entry fee waived for subscribers. Judging by *Writer's International Forum* staff. "We reserve the right to publish cash award winners." Please state genre of story and age of intended audience (as "ages 9-11") in cover letter. Contest winners announced and first place published in issue following each contest. Word count restrictions vary with each contest. Some contests require following a theme or other stipulation. Please request guidelines for contest you want to enter.

‡WRITING CONFERENCE WRITING CONTESTS, The Writing Conference, Inc., P.O. Box 664, Ottawa KS 66067. (913)242-0407. Contest Director: John H. Bushman. Annual contest. Estab. 1988. Purpose of contest: to further writing by students with awards for narration, exposition and poetry at the elementary, middle school and high school levels. Unpublished submissions only. Submissions made by the author or teacher. Deadline for entries: January 6. SASE for contest rules and entry form. No entry fee. Awards plaque and publication of winning entry in *The Writers' Slate*, March issue. Judging by a panel of teachers. Requirements for entrants: must be enrolled in school—K-12th grade.

‡YEARBOOK EXCELLENCE CONTEST, *Quill and Scroll*, School of Journalism, University of Iowa, Iowa City IA 52242. (319)335-5795. Executive Director: Richard Johns. Annual contest. Estab. 1987. Previously published submissions only. Submissions made by the author or school yearbook adviser. Must be published between November 1, 1994 and November 1, 1995. Deadline for entries: November 1. SASE for contest rules and entry form. Entry fee is $2 per entry. Awards National Gold Key; sweepstakes winners receive plaque; seniors eligible for scholarships. Judging by various judges. Winning entries may be published in *Quill and Scroll* magazine.

✤YOUNG ADULT CANADIAN BOOK AWARD, The Canadian Library Association, 602-200 Elgin St., Ottawa, Ontario K2P 1L5 Canada. (613)232-9625. Fax: (613)563-9895. Contact: Committee Chair. Annual award. Estab. 1981. Purpose of award: "to recognize the author of an outstanding English-language Canadian book which appeals to young adults between the ages of 13 and 18 that was published the preceding calendar year. Information is available for anyone requesting. We approach publishers, also send news releases to various journals, i.e. *Quill & Quire*." Entries are not returned. No entry fee. Awards a leather-bound book. Requirement for entrants: must be a work of fiction (novel or short stories), the title must be a Canadian publication in either hardcover or paperback, and the author must be a Canadian citizen or landed immigrant. Award given at the Canadian Library Association Conference.

YOUNG READER'S CHOICE AWARD, Pacific Northwest Library Association, Box 352930, University of Washington, Graduate School of Library and Information Science, Seattle WA 98195-2930. (206)543-1897. Secretary: Carol Doll. Award Director: named annually. Annual award for published authors. Estab. 1940. Purpose of award: "to promote reading as an enjoyable activity and to provide children an opportunity to endorse a book they consider an excellent story." Previously published submissions only; must be published 3 years before award year. Deadline for entries: February 1. SASE for award rules and entry forms. No entry fee. Awards a silver medal, struck in Idaho silver. "Children vote for their favorite (books) from a list of titles nominated by librarians, teachers, students and other interested persons."

Contests & Awards/'95'-96 changes

The following listings were included in the 1995 edition of *Children's Writer's & Illustrator's Market* but do not have listings in this edition. The majority did not respond to our request to update their listings. If a reason was given for exclusion, it appears in parentheses after the listing's name.

Jane Addams Children's Book Award
The Amy Writing Awards
Byline Magazine Student Page
California Writers' Conference Awards
Canada Council Governor General's Literary Awards
The Commonwealth Club's Book Awards Contest
Drexel Citation
Carolyn W. Field Award
Dorothy Canfield Fisher Children's Book Award
Florida State Writing Competition
Indian Paintbrush Book Award
Iowa Children's Choice Award
The Ezra Jack Keats New Writer Award
Landers Theatre Children's Playwriting Award (defunct)
Manningham Poetry Trust Student Contests
The Milner Award
Minnesota Book Awards
National Peace Essay Contest
PEN Center USA West Literary Award for Children's Literature
The Ayn Rand Institute's Anthem Essay Contest
The Ayn Rand Institute's Fountainhead Essay Contest
Reading Round Table Award
Science Writing Award in Physics and Astronomy
Charlie May Simon Book Award
Society of Midland Authors Awards
VFW Voice of Democracy
Washington Post/Children's Book Guild Award for Nonfiction
Western Heritage Awards
Laura Ingalls Wilder Award
The Anna Zornio Memorial Children's Theatre Playwriting Award

Resources

Clubs & Organizations

Children's writers and illustrators can benefit from contacts made through organizations such as the ones listed in this section. Professional organizations provide writers and artists with numerous educational, business and legal services. Many of these services come in the form of newsletters, workshops or seminars that provide tips about how to be better writers or artists, as well as what types of business records to keep, health and life insurance coverage to carry and competitions to consider.

An added benefit of belonging to an organization is the opportunity to network with those who have similar interests, creating a support system to help you through tight creative and financial periods. As in any business, knowing the right people can often help your career, and important contacts can be made through your peers. Membership in a writer's or artist's group also shows publishers you're serious about your craft. While this provides no guarantee your work will be published, it offers an added dimension of credibility and professionalism.

Some of the organizations listed here welcome anyone with an interest, while others are only open to professionals. Still others, such as the Society of Children's Book Writers & Illustrators (SCBWI), have varying levels of membership. SCBWI offers associate membership to those with no publishing credits, while those who have had work for children published receive full membership. Many national organizations such as SCBWI also have regional chapters throughout the country. Feel free to write or call for more information regarding any group that sounds interesting. Be sure to inquire about local chapters, membership qualifications, and services offered.

AMERICAN SOCIETY OF JOURNALISTS AND AUTHORS, 1501 Broadway, New York NY 10036. (212)997-0947. Fax: (212)768-7414. E-mail: 75227.1650@compuserve.com. Executive Director: Alexandra Owens. Qualifications for membership: "Need to be a professional nonfiction writer published 8-10 times in general circulation publications." Membership cost: Initiation fee—$100; annual dues—$165. Group sponsors national conferences; monthly workshops in New York City. Workshops/conferences open to nonmembers. Publishes a newsletter for members that provides confidential information for nonfiction writers.

‡ARIZONA AUTHORS ASSOCIATION, 3509 E. Shea Blvd., #117, Phoenix AZ 85028-3339. (602)867-9001. President: Iva Martin. Purpose of organization: to offer professional, educational and social opportunities to writers and authors and serve as a network. Membership cost: $40/year professional and associate; $50/year affiliate; $25/year student. Different levels of membership include: Professional—published writers; Associate—writers working toward publication; Affili-

The double dagger before a listing indicates the contest or organization is open to students.

ate—professionals in publishing industry; Student—full-time students. Holds monthly educational workshops; contact office for current calendar. Publishes newsletter providing information useful to writers (markets, book reviews, calendar of meetings and events) and news about members. Non-member subscription $25/year. Sponsors Annual Literary Contest. Awards include total of $1,000 in prizes in several categories. Contest open to nonmembers.

‡ASSITEJ/USA, % Jolly Sue Baker, 2707 E. Union, Seattle WA 98122. (206)392-2147. Fax: (206)392-2069. Editor, *TYA Today*: Cyndi Pock. Purpose of organization: To service theaters focused on productions for young audiences. Also serves as US Center for International Association of Theatre for Children and Young People. Membership cost: $100 for organizations with budgets below $250,000; $200 for organizations with budgets of $250,000-$999,000; $300 for organizatons with budgets over $1 million; $50 annually/individual; $25 students and retirees; $65 for foreign organizations or individuals outside the US; $30 for library rate. Different levels of membership include: organizations, individuals, students, retirees, corresponding, libraries. Sponsors workshops or conferences. Publishes newsletter that focuses on information on field in US and abroad.

THE AUTHORS RESOURCE CENTER, 4725 E. Sunrise Dr., #219, Tucson AZ 85718. (602)325-4733. Executive Director: Martha R. Gore. Purpose of organization: To help writers understand the business and professional realities of the publishing world. Also operates literary agency (opened March 1, 1984) that markets members' books to publishers (interested only in authentic multicultural books). Qualifications for membership: serious interest in writing. Membership cost: $60 per year for aspiring and published members. The *Tarc Report* includes information about markets, resources, legal matters, writers workshops, reference sources, announcement of members' new books, reviews and other news important to members. Subscription included in membership fee.

CALIFORNIA WRITERS' CLUB, 1090 Cambridge St., Novato CA 94947-4963. (510)841-1217. Secretary: Dorothy V. Benson. Purpose of organization: "We are a nonprofit professional organization open to writers to provide writing and market information and to promote fellowship among writers." Qualifications for membership: "Publication for active members; expected publication in five years for associate members." Membership cost: entry fee $20; annual dues $35. (Entry fee is paid once.) Workshops/conferences: "Biennial summer conference, June 23-25, 1995, at Asilomar, Pacific Grove, CA; other conferences are held by local branches as they see fit." Conferences open to nonmembers. "Newsletter, which goes out to all CWC members and to newspapers and libraries, publishes the monthly meetings upcoming in the eight branches, plus the achievements of members, and market and contest opportunities." Sponsors contests. CWC's "major contest is every two years, and prizes are cash in each of five categories."

🍁CANADIAN AUTHORS ASSOCIATION, 27 Doxsee Ave. N., Campbellford, Ontario K0L 1L0 Canada. (705)653-0323. Fax: (705)653-0593. Contact: Administrator. Purpose of organization: to help "emerging" writers and provide assistance to professional writers. Membership is divided into two categories for individuals: Member (voting)—Persons engaged in writing in any genre who have produced a sufficient body of work; Associate (non-voting)—Persons interested in writing who have not yet produced sufficient material to qualify for full membership, or those who, though not writers, have a sincere interest in Canadian literature. Persons interested in learning to write may join the Association for one year. Membership cost: $123.05 includes GST for members, associates and introductory rate. Life membership is $963, which also includes GST. Workshops/conferences: Annual Conference, June 15-22 (approx.) at the University of Manitoba in Winnipeg, Manitoba. "The conference draws writers, editors and publishers together in a congenial atmosphere providing seminars, workshops, panel discussions, readings by award-winning authors, and many social events." Open to nonmembers. Publishes a newsletter for members. Also publishes a quarterly journal and a bienniel writer's guide available to nonmembers; latest edition 1992. "The Association created a major literary award program in 1975 to honor writing that achieves literary excellence without sacrificing popular appeal. The awards are in four categories—fiction, (for a full-length novel); nonfiction (excluding works of an instructional nature); poetry (for a volume of the works of one poet); and drama (for a single play published or staged). The awards consist of a handsome silver medal and $5,000 in cash; they are funded by Harlequin Enterprises, the Toronto-based international publisher." Contest open to non-members. Also contests for writing by students and for young readers; sponsors Air Canada Awards.

✤CANADIAN SOCIETY OF CHILDREN'S AUTHORS, ILLUSTRATORS AND PERFORMERS, (CANSCAIP), 35 Spadina Rd., Toronto, Ontario M5R 2S9 Canada. (416)515-1559. Secretary: Nancy Prasad. Purpose of organization: development of Canadian children's culture and support for authors, illustrators and performers working in this field. Qualifications for membership: Members—professionals who have been published (not self-published) or have paid public performances/records/tapes to their credit. Friends—share interest in field of children's culture. Membership cost: $60 (members dues), $25 (friends dues), $30 (institution dues). Sponsors workshops/conferences. Publishes newsletter: includes profiles of members; news round-up of members' activities countrywide; market news; news on awards, grants, etc; columns related to professional concerns.

***CAROLINA PLAYWRIGHTS CENTER**, P.O. Box 1705, Pinehurst NC 28374. (910)295-6896. Fax: (910)295-1203. Executive Director: Mrs. Shirley W. Farrar. The mission of the Carolina Playwrights Center, Inc. is to cultivate playwrights, develop plays, build audiences for new plays, and assure the future of live theater by investing in playwrights. The Center's programs and productions begin after Labor Day and run through June 30. Services to playwrights are available year-round. Playwrights must be dues paying members or invited guest playwrights to participate in the productions, programs, services and special projects at the center. Member playwrights must be native or current residents of North or South Carolina. There is no residency requirement for guest playwrights. Membership cost: $100. CPC produces an Annual Playwrights Festival. Publishes a newsletter linking the state's playwriting community by keeping the playwrights and playwriting groups informed about personal progress, production opportunities, grants, contests, and other items of interest to playwrights. The newsletter is published in February, May, August, November.

‡LEWIS CARROLL SOCIETY OF NORTH AMERICA, 617 Rockford Rd., Silver Spring MD 20902. (301)593-7077. Secretary: M. Schaefer. "We are an organization of Carroll admirers of all ages and interests and a center for Carroll studies." Qualifications for membership: "An interest in Lewis Carroll and a simple love for Alice (or even the Snark)." Membership cost: $20/year. There is also a contributing membership of $50. Publishes a newsletter.

THE CHILDREN'S BOOK COUNCIL, INC., 568 Broadway, New York NY 10012. (212)966-1990. Purpose of organization: "A nonprofit trade association of children's and young adult publishers, CBC promotes the enjoyment of books for children and young adults, and works with national and international organizations to that end. The CBC has sponsored National Children's Book Week since 1945." Qualifications for membership: US trade publishers of children's and young adult books are eligible for membership. Membership cost: "Individuals wishing to receive mailings from the CBC (our semi-annual newsletter, *CBC Features*, and our materials brochures) may be placed on our mailing list for a one-time-only fee of $60. Publishers wishing to join should contact the CBC for dues information." Sponsors workshops and seminars. Publishes a newsletter with articles about children's books and publishing, and listings of free or inexpensive materials available from member publishers. Sells reading encouragement graphics and informational materials suitable for libraries, teachers, booksellers, parents, and others working with children.

***✤FEDERATION OF BC WRITERS**, Main P.O. Box 2206, Vancouver, British Columbia V6B 3W2. (604)683-2057. Fax: (604)683-8269. E-mail: fedbcwrt@pinc.com. Manager: Corey Van't Haaff. Purpose of organization: with more than 600 members, we serve the needs of all writers

The maple leaf before a listing indicates that the market is Canadian.

with a newsletter, readings, workshops, assistance with grievances, and 2 annual literary competitions. Qualifications for membership: open to established and emerging writers of all genres. Membership cost: $50 Regular, $25 for those with a limited income who would be unable to join at $50. Publishes a quarterly newsletter featuring information on markets, awards, tips on getting published, many articles, features, interviews and computer programs for writers. Sponsors 2 contests: one for Canadian writers (with prizes of $500, $350 and $75) and one for emerging British Columbia writers.

***‡LITERARY MANAGERS AND DRAMATURGS OF THE AMERICAS**, Box 355, CASTA, CUNY Grad Center, 33 W. 42nd St., New York NY 10036. (212)642-2657. Fax: (212)642-1977. LMDA is a not-for-profit service organization for the professions of literary management and dramaturgy. Student Membership: $20/year. Open to students in dramaturgy, performing arts and literature programs, or related disciplines. Proof of student status required. Includes national conference, New Dramaturg activities, local symposia, job phone and select membership meetings. Active Membership: $45/year. Open to full-time and part-time professionals working in the fields of literary management and dramaturgy. All privileges and services including voting rights and eligibility for office. Associate Membership: $35/year. Open to all performing arts professionals and academics, as well as others interested in the field. Includes national conference, local symposia and select membership meetings. Institutional Membership: $100/year. Open to theaters, universities, and other organizations. Includes all privileges and services except voting rights and eligibility for office. Publishes a newsletter featuring articles on literary management, dramaturgy, LMDA program updates and other articles of interest.

THE NATIONAL LEAGUE OF AMERICAN PEN WOMEN, 1300 17th St. N.W., Washington D.C. 20036-1973. (202)785-1997. Fax: (202)785-1997. National President: Dr. Frances "Fran" T. Carter. Purpose of organization: to promote professional work in art, letters and music since 1897. Qualifications for membership: An applicant must show "proof of sale" in each chosen category—art, letters and music. Membership cost: $40 ($10 processing fee and $30 National dues); Annual fees—$25. Different levels of membership include: Active, Associate, International Affiliate, Members-at-Large, Honorary Members (in one or more of the following classifications: Art, Letters, and Music). Holds workshops/conferences. Publishes magazine 6 times a year titled *The Pen Woman*. Member and nonmember subscription $18 per year. Sponsors various contests in areas of Art, Letters and Music. Awards made at Biennial Convention. Also, contests in Art, Letters and Music involving Mature Women. Awards include cash prizes—up to $1,000. Specialized contest open to nonmembers.

NATIONAL WRITERS ASSOCIATION, 1450 S. Havana, Suite 424, Aurora CO 80012. (303)751-7844. Executive Director: Sandy Whelchel. Purpose of organization: association for freelance writers. Qualifications for membership: associate membership—must be serious about writing; professional membership—must be published and paid writer (cite credentials). Membership cost: $50-associate; $60-professional. Sponsors workshops/conferences: TV/screenwriting workshops, NWA Annual Conferences, Literary Clearinghouse, editing and critiquing services, local chapters, National Writer's School. Open to non-members. Publishes industry news of interest to freelance writers; how-to articles; market information; member news and networking opportunities. Nonmember subscription $18. Sponsors poetry contest; short story contest; article contest; novel contest. Awards cash for top three winners; books and/or certificates for other winners; honorable mention certificate places 11-20. Contests open to nonmembers.

NATIONAL WRITERS UNION, 873 Broadway, Suite 203, New York NY 10003. (212)254-0279. Office Manager: Ron Johnson. Purpose of organization: Advocacy for freelance writers. Qualifications for membership: "Membership in the NWU is open to all qualified writers, and no one shall be barred or in any manner prejudiced within the Union on account of race, age, sex, sexual preference, disability, national origin, religion or ideology. You are eligible for membership if you have published a book, a play, three articles, five poems, one short story or an equivalent amount of newsletter, publicity, technical, commercial, government or institutional copy. You are also eligible for membership if you have written an equal amount of unpublished material and you are actively writing and attempting to publish your work." Membership cost: annual writing income under $5,000—$75/year; annual writing income $5,000-25,000—$125/

year; annual writing income over $25,000—$170/year. National union newsletter quarterly, issues related to freelance writing and to union organization. Non-member subscription: $15.

PEN AMERICAN CENTER, 568 Broadway, New York NY 10012. (212)334-1660. Fax: (212)334-2181. Purpose of organization: "To foster understanding among men and women of letters in all countries. International PEN is the only worldwide organization of writers and the chief voice of the literary community. Members of PEN work for freedom of expression wherever it has been endangered." Qualifications for membership: "The standard qualification for a writer to join PEN is that he or she must have published, in the United States, two or more books of a literary character, or one book generally acclaimed to be of exceptional distinction. Editors who have demonstrated commitment to excellence in their profession (generally construed as five years' service in book editing), translators who have published at least two book-length literary translations, and playwrights whose works have been professionally produced, are eligible for membership. An application form is available upon request from PEN Headquarters in New York. Candidates for membership should be nominated by two current members of PEN. Inquiries about membership should be directed to the PEN Membership Committee. Friends of PEN is also open to writers who may not yet meet the general PEN membership requirements. PEN sponsors more than fifty public events at PEN Headquarters in New York, and at the branch offices in Boston, Chicago, New Orleans, San Francisco and Portland, Oregon. They include tributes by contemporary writers to classic American writers, dialogues with visiting foreign writers, symposia that bring public attention to problems of censorship and that address current issues of writing in the United States, and readings that introduce beginning writers to the public. PEN's wide variety of literary programming reflects current literary interests and provides informal occasions for writers to meet each other and to welcome those with an interest in literature. Events are all open to the public and are usually free of charge. The Children's Book Authors' Committee sponsors regular public events focusing on the art of writing for children and young adults and on the diversity of literature for juvenile readers. The PEN/Norma Klein Award was established in 1991 to honor an emerging children's book author. National union newsletter covers PEN activities, features interviews with international literary figures, transcripts of PEN literary symposia, reports on issues vital to the literary community. All PEN publications are available by mail order directly from PEN American Center. Individuals must enclose check or money order with their order. Subscription: $8 for 4 issues; sample issue $2. Pamphlets and brochures all free upon request. Sponsors several competitions per year. Monetary awards range from $700-7,500.

***PLAYMARKET**, P.O. Box 9767, Te Aro Wellington New Zealand. (64)4 3828462. Fax: (64)4 3828461. Executive Officer: John McDavitt. Script Advisor: Susan Wilson. Purpose of organization: funded by the Arts Council of New Zealand, Playmarket serves as New Zealand's script advisory service and playwrights agency. Playmarket offers script assessment, development and agency services to help New Zealand playwrights secure professional production for their plays. Playmarket also assists with negotiations for film and television, radio and publishing. Holds workshops/conferences. Publishes *Playmarket Directory of New Zealand Plays and Playwrights*. Nonmember subscription $10/year. Assists with the Bruce Mason Award: "Sunday Star Bruce Mason Award for Playwright at Beginning of Career." Award includes $5,000 annually. Contest open to nonmembers.

PUPPETEERS OF AMERICA, INC., #5 Cricklewood Path, Pasadena CA 91107. (818)797-5748. Membership Officer: Gayle Schluter. Purpose of organization: to promote the art of puppetry. Qualifications for membership: interest in the art form. Membership cost: single adult, $35; junior member, $20; retiree, $35 ($25 after member for 5 years); group or family, $55; couple, $45. Membership includes a bimonthly newsletter. Sponsors workshops/conferences. Publishes newsletter. *The Puppetry Journal* provides news about puppeteers, puppet theatres, exhibitions, touring companies, technical tips, new products, new books, films, television, and events sponsored by the Chartered Guilds in each of the eight P of A regions. Subscription: $30.

SCIENCE-FICTION AND FANTASY WRITERS OF AMERICA, INC., 5 Winding Brook Dr., #1B, Guilderland NY 12084. (518)869-5361. Executive Secretary: Peter Dennis Pautz. Purpose of organization: to encourage public interest in science fiction literature and provide organization format for writers/editors/artists within the genre. Qualifications for membership: at least one professional sale or other professional involvement within the field. Membership cost: annual active dues—$50; affiliate—$35; one-time installation fee of $10; dues year begins July 1. Different levels of membership include: active—requires three professional short stories or one novel published; affiliate—requires one professional sale or professional involvement. Workshops/conferences: annual awards banquet, usually in April or May. Open to nonmembers. Publishes newsletter. Nonmember subscription: $15 in US. Sponsors SFWA Nebula® Awards for best published science fiction in the categories of novel, novella, novelette and short story. Awards trophy.

SOCIETY OF CHILDREN'S BOOK WRITERS AND ILLUSTRATORS, 22736 Vanowen St., Suite 106, West Hills CA 91307. (818)888-8760. Chairperson, Board of Directors: Sue Alexander. Purpose of organization: to assist writers and illustrators working or interested in the field. Qualifications for membership: an interest in children's literature and illustration. Membership cost: $50/year. Different levels of membership include: full membership—published authors/illustrators; associate membership—unpublished writers/illustrators. Holds 30-40 events (workshops/conferences) around the country each year. Open to nonmembers. Publishes a newsletter focusing on writing and illustrating children's books. Sponsors grants for writers and illustrators who are members.

SOCIETY OF ILLUSTRATORS, 128 E. 63rd St., New York NY 10021. (212)838-2560. Director: Terrence Brown. Purpose of organization: to promote interest in the art of illustration for working professional illustrators and those in associated fields. Membership cost: Initiation fee—$250. Annual dues for Non-Resident members (those living more than 125 air miles from SI's headquarters) are $234. Dues for Resident Artist Members are $396 per year, Resident Associate Members $462. Different levels of membership: *Artist Members* "shall include those who make illustration their profession" and through which they earn at least 60% of their income. *Associate Members* are "those who earn their living in the arts or who have made a substantial contribution to the art of illustration." This includes art directors, art buyers, creative supervisors, instructors, publishers and like categories. "All candidates for membership are admitted by the proposal of one active member and sponsorship of four additional members. The candidate must complete and sign the application form which requires a brief biography, a listing of schools attended, other training and a résumé of his or her professional career." Candidates for *Artist* membership, in addition to the above requirements, must submit examples of their work. Sponsors "The Annual of American Illustration." Awards include gold and silver medals. Open to nonmembers. Deadline: October 1. Sponsors "The Original Art: The Best of Children's Book Illustration." Deadline: mid-July. Call for details.

SOCIETY OF MIDLAND AUTHORS, % SMA, P.O. 10419, Chicago IL 60610-0419. Purpose of organization: Create closer association among writers of the Middle West; stimulate creative literary effort; maintain collection of members works; encourage interest in reading and literature by cooperating with other educational and cultural agencies. Qualifications for membership: To be author or co-author of a book demonstrating literary style and published by a recognized publisher or author of published or professionally produced play and be identified through residence with Illinois, Indiana, Iowa, Kansas, Michigan, Minnesota, Missouri, Nebraska, North Dakota, Ohio, South Dakota or Wisconsin. Membership cost: $25/year dues. Different levels of membership include: regular—published book authors; associate, nonvoting—not published as above but having some connection with literature, such as librarians, teachers, publishers, and editors. Workshops/conferences: program meetings at 410 Club, Chicago, held 5 times a year, featuring authors, publishers, editors or the like individually or on panels. Usually second Tuesday of October, November, February, March and April. Also holds annual awards dinner at 410 Club, Chicago, in May. Publishes a newsletter focusing on news of members and general items of interest to writers. Non-member subscription: $5. Sponsors contests. "Annual awards in 7 catego-

The asterisk before a listing indicates the listing is new in this edition.

ries, given at annual dinner in May. Monetary awards for books published or plays which premiered professionally in previous calendar year. Send SASE to contact person for details." Categories include adult fiction, adult nonfiction, biography, juvenile fiction, juvenile nonfiction, poetry. No picture books. Contest open to non-members. Deadline for contest: January 1.

***THEATRE ASSOCIATION OF PENNSYLVANIA**, 1919 North Front St., Harrisburg PA 17102-2284. (717)232-9752. Fax: (717)232-9756. Executive Director: Al Franklin. "TAP, the only statewide service organization in Pennsylvania dedicated to theatre, was founded in 1969 to serve Pennsylvania theatre through support, promotion, education and advocacy. TAP, as Pennsylvania theatre's communication center and networking resource, plans and facilitates programs and projects for the 200 professional, community and academic member companies and for the 500 individual member theatre artists, craftsmen, educators and administrators." Membership cost: $30/year for individuals; $45-275/year for organizations (based on annual budget). Holds workshops/conferences. Publishes members-only newsletter focusing on theatre in Pennsylvania. Subscription free with membership. TAP sponsors an annual playwriting contest for members only. Membership may be obtained at time of submission. Awards include $500 and a public reading (sometimes including a workshop performance). Contest open to members only.

***VOLUNTEER LAWYERS FOR THE ARTS**, 1 E. 53rd St., 6th Floor, New York NY 10022-4201. (212)319-2787 (Administration); (212)319-2910 (Art Law Line) Fax: (212)752-6575. Executive Director: Daniel Y. Mayer. Purpose of organization: Volunteer Lawyers for the Arts is dedicated to providing free arts-related legal assistance to low-income artists and not-for-profit arts organizations in all creative fields. Over 800 attorneys in the New York area donate their time through VLA to artists and arts organizations unable to afford legal counsel. "There is no membership required for our services. Everyone is welcome to use VLA's Art Law Line, a legal hotline for any artist or arts organization needing quick answers to arts-related questions. VLA also provides clinics, seminars and publications designed to educate artists on legal issues which affect their careers. Membership is through donations and is not required to use our services." Members receive discounts on publications and seminars as well as other benefits.

WESTERN WRITERS OF AMERICA, INC., 1012 Fair St., Franklin TN 37064. (615)791-1444. Fax: (615)791-1444. Secretary/Treasurer: James A. Crutchfield. Purpose of organization: to further all types of literature that pertains to the American West. Membership cost: $60/year ($80 foreign). Different levels of membership include: Active and Associate—the two vary upon number of books published. Holds annual convention. Publishes bimonthly magazine focusing on market trends, book reviews, news of members, etc. Non-members may subscribe for $30 ($40 foreign). Sponsors contests. Spur awards given annually for a variety of types of writing. Awards include plaque, certificate, publicity. Contest open to nonmembers.

THE WRITERS ALLIANCE, 12 Skylark Lane, Stony Brook NY 11790. (516)751-7080. Executive Director: Kiel Stuart. Purpose of organization: "A support/information group for all types of writers." Membership cost: $10/year, payable to Kiel Stuart. A corporate/group membership costs $15. Sponsors conference. Publishes newsletter for all writers who use (or want to learn about) computers; features reviews, how-tos, computer information and market information. Nonmember subscription $10—payable to Kiel Stuart.

‡WRITERS CONNECTION, P.O. Box 24770, San Jose CA 95154-4770. (408)445-3600. Fax: (408)445-3609. Editor: Jan Stiles. Vice President/Program Director: Meera Lester. Purpose of organization: to provide services and resources for writers. Qualifications for membership: interest in writing or publishing. Membership cost: $45/year. Conferences: Selling to Hollywood and various genre conferences, including writing for children. Publishes a newsletter focusing on writing and publishing (all fields except poetry), how-to, markets, contests, tips, etc., included with membership. Subscription $25.

‡🍁WRITERS' FEDERATION OF NEW BRUNSWICK, Box 37, Station A, 103 Church St., Fredericton, New Brunswick E3B 4Y2 Canada. (506)459-7228. Project Coordinator: Anna Mae Snider. Purpose of organization: "to promote the work of New Brunswick writers and to help them at all stages of their development." Qualifications for membership: interest in writing.

Membership cost: $25, basic annual membership; $15, student/unemployed; $30, institutional membership; $100, sustaining member; $250, patron; and $1,000, lifetime member. Holds workshops/conferences. Publishes a newsletter with articles concerning the craft of writing, member news, contests, markets, workshops and conference listings. Sponsors annual literary competition (for New Brunswick residents). Categories: fiction, nonfiction, poetry, children's literature—3 prizes per category of $200, $100, $30; Alfred Bailey Prize of $400 for poetry ms, The Richards Prize of $400 for short novel, collection of short stories or section of long novel; The Sheree Fitch Prize for writing by young people (14-18 years of age). Contest open to nonmembers.

‡🍁WRITERS GUILD OF ALBERTA, 11759 Groat Rd., 3rd Floor, Percy Page Centre, Edmonton, Alberta T5M 3K6 Canada. (403)422-8174. Fax: (403)426-2663. Executive Director: Mr. Miki Andrejevic. Purpose of organization: to provide meeting ground and collective voice for the writers in Alberta. Membership cost: $55/year; $20 for seniors/students. Holds workshops/conferences. Publishes a newsletter focusing on markets, competitions, contemporary issues related to the literary arts (writing, publishing, censorship, royalties etc.). Nonmembers may subscribe to newsletter. Subscription cost: $55/year. Sponsors annual literary awards program in 7 categories (novel, nonfiction, short fiction, children's literature, poetry, drama, best first book). Awards include $500, leather-bound book, promotion and publicity. Open to nonmembers.

***‡WRITERS OF KERN**, P.O. Box 6694, Bakersfield CA 93386-6694. (805)871-5834. President: Debbie Bailey. Open to published writers and any person interested in writing. Dues: $18/year, discount for students. Types of Memberships: Professional, writers with published work; writers working toward publication, students. Monthly meetings held on the third Saturday of every month, except September which is our conference month, with speakers who are authors, agents, etc., on topics pertaining to writing; critique groups for several fiction genres, nonfiction and screenwriting which meet weekly or biweekly. Members receive a monthly newsletter with marketing tips, conferences and contests; access to club library; discount to annual conference. Annual conference held the third Saturday in September; annual writing contest held May-June with winners announced at the conference. Send SASE for information.

***‡THE YOUNG WRITERS CLUB**, Clubs for Kids™, P.O. Box 5504, Coralville IA 52241. (319)358-7923. Fax: (319)358-7923. E-mail address: kidsclub@aol.com. President: Amy Ruth. Purpose of organization: "to help kids 7-13 develop their skills as writers."

Clubs & Organizations/'95-'96 changes

The following listings were included in the 1995 edition of *Children's Writer's & Illustrator's Market* but do not have listings in this edition. The majority did not respond to our request to update their listings.

American Alliance for Theatre & Education
The Authors Guild
Children's Reading Round Table of Chicago
Christian Writers Guild
Florida Freelance Writers Association
Graphic Artists Guild
The Int'l Women's Writing Guild
League of Canadian Poets
The Nebraska Writers Guild
The Playwrights' Center
Society of Southwestern Authors

The double dagger before a listing indicates the contest or organization is open to students.

Conferences & Workshops

Writers and illustrators eager to expand their knowledge of the children's industry should consider attending one of the many conferences and workshops held each year. Whether you're a novice or seasoned professional, conferences and workshops are great places to pick up information on a variety of topics and network with experts in the publishing industry, as well as your peers.

Many conferences and workshops included here focus on juvenile writing or illustrating and related business issues. Others appeal to a broader base of writers or artists, but still provide information that can be utilized in creating material for children. Illustrators may be interested in painting and drawing workshops, for example, while writers can learn about techniques and meet editors and agents at general writing conferences. Workshops in this section which are open to student participants are marked with a double dagger (‡).

Artists can find a detailed directory of annual art workshops offered around the globe in the March issue of *The Artist's Magazine*. Writers should consult the May issue of *Writer's Digest* or *The Guide to Writers Conferences* (ShawGuides) for more general conferences.

Listings in this section provide details about what conference and workshop courses are offered, where and when they are held, and the costs. Some of the national writing and art organizations also offer regional workshops throughout the year. Write or call them for information.

AMERICAN CHRISTIAN WRITERS CONFERENCE, (formerly Arizona Christian Writers Conference), P.O. Box 5168, Phoenix AZ 85010. 1(800)21-WRITE or (602)420-1165. Director: Reg Forder. Writer and illustrator workshops geared toward beginner, intermediate and advanced levels. Classes offered include: fiction, nonfiction, poetry, photography, music, etc. Workshops held in a dozen US cities. Call or write for a complete schedule of conferences. 75 minutes. Maximum class size: 30 (approximate). Cost of conference: $99, 1-day session; $169, 2-day session; $229, 3-day session (discount given if paid 30 days advance).

ANTIOCH WRITERS' WORKSHOP, P.O. Box 494, Yellow Springs OH 45387. (513)866-9060. Director: Judy DaPolito. Writers' workshop geared toward all levels. Emphasizes "basic poetry, fiction, nonfiction—with some emphasis on genre and on screenwriting; 1995 workshop included a children's writing seminar with Marion Dane Bauer. Workshops held last week of July. Cost of workshop: $450; includes tuition. Room and board extra.

AUSTIN WRITERS' LEAGUE CONFERENCE WORKSHOP SERIES, 1501 W. Fifth St., Suite #E-2, Austin TX 78703. (512)499-8914. Fax: (512)499-0441. E-mail: awloffice@versa.com. Executive Director: Angela Smith. Writer and illustrator workshops and conferences geared toward all levels for children and adults. Sessions include writing children's books and marketing children's books. Annual conferences. Workshops usually held March, April and May; September, October and November. Weekend seminars are held during the summer. 3-6 hours for workshops; 1½-2 days for seminars. Registration limited to 200. Writing/art facilities available: none at workshop location, but "we do have facilities at the Austin Writers' League Resource Center/Library." Cost of workshop: $20-150 members, $35-195 non-members; includes tuition, registration, continental breakfasts, break refreshments, consultations. Write for more information. The Austin Writers' League has available audiotapes of past workshop programs.

BE THE WRITER YOU WANT TO BE—MANUSCRIPT CLINIC, Villa 30, 23350 Sereno Court, Cupertino CA 95014. (415)691-0300. Contact: Louise Purwin Zobel. Writer workshops geared toward beginner, intermediate, advanced levels. "Participants may turn in manuscripts at any stage of development to receive help with structure and style, as well as marketing advice. Manuscripts receive some written criticism and an oral critique from the instructor, as well as class discussion." Annual workshop. Usually held in the spring. Registration limited to 20-25. Cost of workshop: $40-65/day, depending on the campus; includes an extensive handout.

***CALIFORNIA WRITERS' CLUB CONFERENCE**, 4913 Marlborough Way, Carmichael CA 95608. (916)488-7094. Assistant Director: Nancy Elliott. Writer workshops geared toward beginner, intermediate, advance and professional levels. Features agents specializing in children's authors, book publishers who are interested in children's books, magazine editors who want fiction and nonfiction articles. Workshop held June or July. Registration limited to 500-550. Writing/art facilities available: large, well-lit meeting rooms that are fully equipped with audio/visual equipment. Cost of workshop: $350-400; includes workshops and all meals from Friday dinner through lunch on Sunday and a room at a convention center. Write for more information. A complete brochure is sent out 6 to 8 months prior to the event. Contest and critique services are available for a fee.

***CAPE COD WRITERS CONFERENCE**, Cape Cod Writers' Center, % The Conservatory, W. Barustable MA 02668. (508)375-0516. Contact: Executive Director. Writer workshops geared toward beginner, intermediate and professional levels. Annual workshop. Workshop held third week in August. Cost of workshop includes $80 to register; $90 per course (we offer 5); manuscript evaluation, $60; personal conference, $30. Write for more information.

CHILDREN'S LITERATURE CONFERENCE, 110 Hofstra University, U.C.C.E., 205 Davison Hall, Hempstead NY 11550. (516)463-5016. Fax: (516)463-4883. E-mail: dcelcs@vaxb.hofstra.edu. Writers/Illustrators Contact: Lewis Shena, Director, Liberal Arts Studies. Writer and illustrator workshops geared toward all levels. Emphasizes: fiction, nonfiction, poetry, submission procedures, picture books. Workshops held "usually in April." Registration limited to 35/class. Cost of workshop: approximately $55; includes 2 workshops, reception, lunch, 2 general sessions, and panel discussion with guest speakers, e.g. "What An Editor Looks For." Write for more information. Co-sponsored by the Society of Children's Book Writers and Illustrators.

***CLARION SCIENCE FICTION & FANTASY WRITING WORKSHOP**, Lyman Briggs School, E-185 Holmes Hall, Michigan State University, East Lansing MI 48825-1107. (517)355-9598. Administrative Assistant: Mary Sheridan. Writer's workshop geared toward intermediate levels. Emphasizes science fiction and fantasy. "An intensive workshop designed to stimulate and develop the talent and techniques of potential writers of speculative fiction. Previous experience in writing fiction is assumed. Approximately 17-20 participants will work very closely together over a six-week period, guided by a series of professional writers of national reputation." 1996 Workshop—June 2-July 13. Six weeks. Registration limited to 20. Cost of tuition (4 semester credits of upper-level course work): approximately $800. Lodging (single room) and meal costs are being negotiated. Submission of two mss (up to 5,000 words each) for review, and a completed application form with a $25 application fee required. Send SASE for more information.

***COLORADO CHRISTIAN WRITERS CONFERENCE**, 67 Seminole Court, Lyons CO 80540. (303)823-5718. Director: Debbie Barker. Writer workshops geared toward beginner, intermediate, advanced and professional levels. Emphasizes picture and board books, fiction for kids, nonfiction for kids, and understanding the children's book and magic market. Annual workshop. Workshop held first Thursday, Friday or Saturday of March. Cost of workshop: $100-130; includes choice of 8-12 workshops, 3-4 plenaries, lunches and 1 dinner, and appointments with editors and freelancers. Write for more information.

CRAFT OF WRITING, University of Texas at Dallas, Center for Continuing Education, P.O. Box 830688, CN1.1, Richardson TX 75083-0688. (214)690-2204. Fax: (214)883-2995. Director:

The asterisk before a listing indicates the listing is new in this edition.

Janet Harris. Writer workshops geared toward intermediate. Sessions include "Show and Tell: How to Balance and Pace Your Fiction," "Can I Say That?—A Writer's Guide to Copyright and Defamation Laws," "Finding the Right Agent for You," and "Getting Your Children's Book Published." Annual workshop. Workshop held every September. 2 days. Cost of workshop: $195; includes choice of among 28 workshops, manuscript contest, valuable tips for marketing yourself, discussion sessions conducted by editors and agents, participation in one of the manuscript clinics held both days, 1 lunch, reception and banquet. Write for more information. "In addition to a manuscript contest, the conference also offers critiquing sessions as well as a chance to meet and mingle with professional writers, agents and editors."

PETER DAVIDSON'S WRITER'S SEMINAR; HOW TO WRITE A CHILDREN'S PICTURE BOOK SEMINAR, 12 Orchard Lane, Estherville IA 51334. Seminar Presenter: Peter Davidson. "This seminar is for anyone interested in writing and/or illustrating children's picture books. Beginners and experienced writers alike are welcome. If participants have a manuscript in progress, or have an idea, they are welcome to bring it along to discuss with the seminar presenter." *Peter Davidson's Writer's Seminar* emphasizes writing fiction, nonfiction, magazine articles, poetry, scripts, children's work, personal experiences, etc. *How to Write A Children's Picture Book* is for those interested in both writing and illustrating children's material. Seminars are presented year round at community colleges. Even-numbered years, presents seminars in Minnesota, Iowa, South Dakota, Nebraska, Kansas, Colorado and Wyoming. Odd-numbered years, presents seminars in Illinois, Minnesota, Iowa, South Dakota, Missouri, Arkansas and Tennessee (write for a schedule). One day, 9 a.m.-4 p.m. Cost of workshop: varies from $39-59, depending on location; includes approximately 35 pages of handouts. Write for more information.

***DEEP SOUTH WRITERS CONFERENCE**, % English Dept. USL Box 44691, Lafayette LA 70504. (318)482-6918. E-mail: jwf4516@usl.edu. Professor, English: Sylvia Iskander. Writer workshops geared toward beginner and intermediate levels. Illustrator workshops geared toward beginner level. Topics offered include age-appropriateness, development of character and plot, and submission of mss (including query letter). Annual workshop. Workshop held third or fourth weekend in September. Registration limited to 10 people. Writing/art facilities available: special equipment can be made available if enough advanced notice is given. Cost of workshop: $40 and conference registration of $25-50, depending on status. Payment entitles workshop participants to workshop and all conference craft lectures and readings. Submit ms at least 3 weeks in advance (by end of August). Ms (not art) will be duplicated for all members of the workshop to critique. Write for more information.

***DOWN EAST MAINE WRITER'S WORKSHOPS**, P.O. Box 446, Stockton Springs ME 04981. (207)567-4317. Fax: (207)567-3023. E-mail: 6249304@mcimail.com. Director: Janet J. Barron. Writer workshops geared toward beginner and intermediate levels. We hold 1-, 2-, 3-, and 5-day workshops between spring and fall each year. 1996 workshops will include Writing for the Juvenile Market; Creative Writing (Basics of Fiction & Nonfiction); and How to Get Your Writing Published. Workshops held periodically from spring to fall each year. Cost of workshop: 1-day: $95; 2-day: $195; 3-day: $295; 5-day: $495. Accommodations and meals additional. Expert, individual personal practical instruction on how to write for publication. "We also offer a writer's clinic for writing feedback if students seek this type of guidance." No requirements prior to registration. Write for more information.

DRURY COLLEGE/SCBWI WRITING FOR CHILDREN WORKSHOP, Drury College, Springfield MO 65802. (417)873-7329. Fax: (417)873-7432. Assistant Director, Continuing Education: Lynn Doke. Writer and illustrator workshops geared toward all levels. Emphasizes all aspects of writing for children and teenagers. Classes offered include: "What Makes a Manuscript a Winner," "Writing & Illustrating Picture Books," "Nuts & Bolts for Beginners," "Non-fiction for Young Readers." All are geared toward writing for children and teenagers. One-day workshop held in October. 1 hour. Ms and portfolio consultations (by appointment only). $50 registration fee; individual consultations $25. Send SASE for more information.

***DUKE CREATIVE WRITER'S WORKSHOP**, Box 90702, Room 203, The Bishop's House, Durham NC 27708. (919)684-2827. Fax: (919)681-8235. E-mail: cashby@mail.duke.edu. Program Coordinator: Catherine Ashby. Writer workshops geared toward intermediate to advanced level. The Creative Writer's Workshop allows each participant to explore creative writing in-depth with the instructor of their choice. Each instructor focuses on a particular style or area of creative writing; for example, Short Fiction, Personal Narrative, Playwriting, Poetry and others. Annual workshop. Every summer there is a one-week session at the end of July. Registration limited to 50. All participants have access to University facilities including computer clusters, libraries and classrooms. Costs for 1995 were $700 for this one-week residential session. This cost includes room, board, activity and course expenses, special events and meals, and one camper T-shirt. Interested participants are requested to send a sample of their writing and a letter of introduction prior to registration. Write for more information.

DUKE UNIVERSITY WRITERS' WORKSHOP, P.O. Box 90703, Durham NC 27708-0703. Director: Georgann Eubanks. "There are various small groups based on level and genre." Writer workshops geared toward all levels. Classes offered include short short fiction, creative nonfiction, poetry, youth and young adult fiction, novel, etc. Annual workshop. Workshops held in June on the Duke campus. Registration limited to 10 in each small group. Cost of workshop: $350; includes registration, instruction materials, a few social meals. "Workshop sections are small; participants work intensively with their primary instructor in a genre. Write for brochure."

***‡DUKE YOUNG WRITER'S CAMP**, P.O. Box 90702, Room 203, The Bishop's House, Durham NC 27708. (919)684-2827. Fax: (919)681-8235. E-mail: cashby@mail.duke.edu. Program Coordinator: Catherine Ashby. Writer workshops geared toward beginner and intermediate levels. The Young Writer's Camp offers courses that help participants to increase their skills in Creative Writing, Expository Writing and Journalism. The courses are divided into lower and upper age groups. Specific examples of courses offered this summer for the older age group are: Writing the Short Story, Essays Made Fun and Magazine Production. Some examples of the lower age group classes are: Humor Writing, Children's Literature and Journal Writing. Annual Workshop. Every summer there are three two-week sessions in June and July. Registration limited to 140. All participants have access to University facilities including computer clusters, libraries and classrooms. Costs for 1995 were $1,115 for residential campers and $540 for day campers. The cost for residential campers includes room, board, activity and course expenses, one camp T-shirt, and one ticket for the end of session banquet. The cost for day campers includes all course expenses, one camp T-shirt, and one ticket for the end of session banquet. Write for more information.

***FISHTRAP, INC.**, P.O. Box 38, Enterprise OR 97828. (503)426-3623. Fax: (503)426-3281. Director: Rich Wandschneider. Writer workshops geared toward beginner, intermediate, advanced and professional levels. "We have offered workshops in the past: Illustrating the Children's Picture Book and Writing the Children's Picture Book. We will offer workshops this winter for teachers and writers of children's to young adults' books. Contact us for information." Annual workshop. Workshop held February 23-24, '96; July 7-10, '96; and up to three workshops during winter '96. Registration limited to 12. Cost of workshop: $40-200 for 1-4 days; includes workshop only. Food and lodging can be arranged. College credit is available for extra fee—usually $35/hour. Please contact Fishtrap for brochures of the Summer Gathering, July 7-14—theme: Sensuality and Nature. Also for information assorted winter workshops—times to be announced.

FLORIDA CHRISTIAN WRITERS CONFERENCE, 2600 Park Ave., Titusville FL 32780. (407)269-6702, ext. 202. Conference Director: Billie Wilson. Writer and illustrator workshops geared toward all levels. "We offer 48 one-hour workshops and 5 five-hour classes. Many of these are for the children's genre: Writing Children's Picture Books, Writing for Teens, Mysteries for Children Curriculum, etc. Annual workshop held in late January. We have 30 publishers and publications represented by editors teaching workshops and reading manuscripts from the

The double dagger before a listing indicates the contest or organization is open to students.

conferees. The conference is limited to 200 people. Usually workshops are limited to 25-30. Advanced or professional workshops are by invitation only via submitted application." Cost of workshop: $360; includes food, lodging and tuition. Write for more information.

FLORIDA SUNCOAST WRITERS' CONFERENCE, Department of English, University of South Florida, Tampa FL 33620. (813)974-1711. Directors: Ed Hirshberg and Steve Rubin. Writer workshops geared toward intermediate, advanced, professional levels. Workshops held first weekend in February. Class sizes range from 30-100. Cost of workshop: $95; $75 for students; includes all sessions, receptions, panels. Conference is held on St. Petersburg campus of USF.

***GILA WRITER'S CONFERENCE**, Western New Mexico University, Silver City NM 88062. (602)986-1399. Conference Director: Meg Files. Writer workshops geared toward beginner, intermediate and advanced levels. One or 2 sessions during the 5-day conference address writing for children and juveniles. Participants may have children's books critiqued by children's writers and agents. Annual Workshop held August, 1996. Cost of workshop: $200. Write for more information to Meg Files, 11012 E. Crescent Ave., Apache Junction AZ 85220. "The conference includes sessions on fiction, nonfiction, poetry, screenwriting and publishing, as well as readings and writing exercises."

GREEN LAKE CHRISTIAN WRITERS CONFERENCE, American Baptist Assembly, Green Lake WI 54941-9300. (800)558-8898. Writer workshops geared toward beginner, intermediate and advanced levels. Emphasizes poetry, nonfiction, writing for children, fiction. Classes/courses offered include: same as above plus 1-session or 2-session presentations on marketing, devotional writing and retelling Bible stories. Workshops held in early July—Saturday dinner through the following Saturday breakfast. Registration limited to 20/class. Writing and/or art facilities available: housing, conference rooms, etc. "No special equipment for writing." Cost of workshop: $80; includes all instruction plus room and meals as selected. Write for more information. "The conference focuses on helping writers to refine their writing skills in a caring atmosphere utilizing competent, caring faculty. This annual conference has been held every year since 1948."

***GREEN RIVERS WRITERS NOVELS-IN-PROGRESS WORKSHOP**, 11906 Locust Rd., Middletown KY 40243. (502)245-4902. President: Mary O'Dell. Writer workshops geared toward intermediate and advanced levels. Workshops emphasize novel writing. Format is 7 novelist instructors working with small groups (5-7 people); one of these novelists will be young adult novelist; "we can take only 5-7 young adult novelists in January '96 workshop." Workshop held January 7-14, 1996. Registration limited to 49. Participants will need to bring own computers, typewriters, etc. Private rooms are available for sleeping, working. No art facilities. Cost of workshop: $300; includes organization membership, registration, manuscript reading fee (60 pages approximately with outline/synopsis). Writers must supply 40-60 pages of manuscript with outline, synopsis or treatment. Write for more information. Conference held on Shelby Campus at University of Louisville; private rooms with bath between each 2 rooms. Linens furnished. $20 per night.

***THE HEIGHTS WRITER'S CONFERENCE**, Sponsored by Writer's World Press, P.O. Box 24684, Cleveland OH 44124-0684. (216)481-1974. Fax: (216)481-2057. Conference Director: Lavern Hall. Writer workshops geared toward beginner, intermediate, advanced and professional levels. "Our workshop topics vary yearly. We *always* have children's literature." Annual workshop. All-day workshop held May 4, 1996. Registration is open for seminars. The 2 teaching workshops are limited to 25 and pre-registration is a must. Cost of workshop: $68; includes continental breakfast, registration packet, lunch, seminars and/or workshops and networking reception at the end of the day. In 1996, Nancy McArthur will lead a seminar on "Writing a Children's Book from Idea to Finished Manuscript." Also presenting are Tom Clark, editor of *Writer's Digest* and Ralph Keyes (*The Courage to Write*), and others. SASE for brochure.

HIGHLAND SUMMER CONFERENCE, Box 7014 Radford University, Radford VA 24142. (703)831-5366. Director: Grace Toney Edwards. Assistant to the Director: Jo Ann Asbury. Writer workshops geared toward beginner, intermediate and advanced levels. Emphasizes Appalachian literature. Annual workshop. Workshop held June 17-28, 1996 (last 2 weeks in June annually).

Registration limited to 20. Writing facilities available: computer center. Cost of workshop: Regular tuition (housing/meals extra). Must be registered student or special status student. Write for more information. Past visiting authors include: Wilma Dykeman, Sue Ellen Bridgers, George Ella Lyons, Lou Kassem.

HIGHLIGHTS FOUNDATION WRITERS WORKSHOP AT CHAUTAUQUA, Dept. CWL, 814 Court St., Honesdale PA 18431. (717)253-1192. Fax: (717)253-0179. Conference Director: Jan Keen. Writer workshops geared toward those interested in writing for children; beginner, intermediate and advanced levels. Classes offered include: "Children's Interests," "Writing Dialogue," "Beginnings and Endings," "Rights, Contracts, Copyrights," "Science Writing." Workshops held July 13-20, 1996, at Chautauqua Institution, Chautauqua, NY. Registration limited to 100/class. Cost of workshop: $1,600; includes tuition, meals, conference supplies. Grants are available for first-time attendees. Write for more information.

HOFSTRA UNIVERSITY SUMMER WRITERS' CONFERENCE, 110 Hofstra University, UCCE, 205 Davison Hall, Hempstead NY 11550-1090. (516)463-5016. Director of Liberal Arts Studies: Lewis Shena. Writer workshops geared toward all levels. Classes offered include fiction, nonfiction, poetry, children's literature, stage/screenwriting and other genres. Children's writing faculty has included Pam Conrad, Johanna Hurwitz, Tor Seidler and Jane Zalben, with Maurice Sendak once appearing as guest speaker. Annual workshop. Workshops held July 10-21, 1995. Each workshop meets for 2½ hours daily for a total of 25 hours. Students can register for a maximum of 3 workshops, schedule an individual conference with the writer/instructor and submit a short ms (less than 10 pages) for critique. Enrollees may register as certificate students or credit students. Cost of workshop: certificate students enrollment fee is approximately $600 plus $26 registration fee; 2-credit student enrollment fee is approximately $800 undergraduate and $835 graduate; 4-credit student enrollment fee is approximately $1,500 undergraduate and $1,550 graduate. On-campus accommodations for the sessions are available for approximately $450/person. Certificate students may attend any of the 5 workshops, a private conference and special programs and social events. Credit students may attend only the workshops they have registered for (a maximum of 2 at 2 credits each) and the special programs and social events.

THE IUPUI NATIONAL YOUTH THEATRE PLAYWRITING SYMPOSIUM, 525 N. Blackford St., Indianapolis IN 46202. (317)274-2095. Literary Manager: W. Mark McCreary. "The purpose of the Symposium is to provide a forum in which we can examine and discuss those principles which characterize good dramatic literature for young people and to explore ways to help playwrights and the promotion of quality drama. Publishers, playwrights, directors, producers, librarians and educators join together to examine issues central to playwriting." Holds playwriting competition. Send SASE for guidelines and entry form. Deadline: September 1, 1996.

I'VE ALWAYS WANTED TO WRITE BUT—BEGINNERS' CLASS, Villa 30, 23350 Sereno Ct., Cupertino CA 95014. (415)691-0300. Contact: Louise Purwin Zobel. Writer workshops geared toward beginner, intermediate levels. "This seminar/workshop starts at the beginning, although the intermediate writer will benefit, too. There is discussion of children's magazine and book literature today, how to write it and how to market it. Also, there is discussion of other types of writing and the basics of writing for publication." Annual workshops. "Usually held several times a year; fall, winter and spring." Sessions last 1-2 days. Cost of workshop: $45-65/day, depending on the campus; includes extensive handout. Write for more information.

***LIGONIER VALLEY WRITERS CONFERENCE**, RR4 Box 8, Ligonier PA 15658. (412)238-5749. Director: Tina Thoburn. Writer and illustrator workshops geared toward intermediate level. Workshops are geared toward developing stories and characters that lend themselves to clear illustration. Annual workshop. Minimal facilities available. Cost of workshop: $250; includes tuition and a luncheon. Write for more information.

***JACK LONDON WRITERS' CONFERENCE**, 135 Clark Dr., San Mateo CA 94402-1002. (415)342-9123. Fax: (415)342-9155. Coordinator: Marlo Faulkner. Writer workshops geared toward beginner, intermediate, advanced and professional levels. Sample workshop subjects include queries, self-editing and poetry. Annual workshop. Workshop held the second weekend in

March. The conference is a program of speakers, panels and workshops—writing depends on the workshop leader. Cost of workshop: $75; includes continental breakfast, lunch, all programs and Ask a Pro sessions. Write for more information. One of the keynote speakers for 1996: Isabel Allende.

***MAKING WAVES WITH WRITERS**, Northern Arizona University, P.O. Box 6024, Flagstaff AZ 86011-6024. Workshop Director: Ray Newton. "While experiencing the elegance of MS Ryndam (commissioned in 1994) and the majesty that is Alaska, you'll have the unparalleled opportunity to enhance your ability in all facets of the writing and speaking profession. Among the noted editors and instructors eager to guide you to success are Thomas Clark, Editor-in-Chief, *Writer's Digest*; Caroll Shreeve, Gibbs/Smith Publishing; Carol O'Hara, Cat-Tails Press; and Robert Early, *Arizona Highways*." Workshop held September 22-29, 1996. Cost of workshop: $995-2,515; includes Alaskan cruise from Anchorage to Vancouver and workshop. Low-cost round-trip air fare from home city available. For more information, contact Carol O'Hara at (916)987-9489 or (800)979-3548, or Sue Cagle at (916)723-3355.

MANHATTANVILLE WRITERS' WEEK, Manhattanville College, 2900 Purchase St., Purchase NY 10577. (914)694-3425. Fax: (914)694-3488. Dean, Adult and Special Programs: Ruth Dowd. Writer workshops geared toward beginner, intermediate and advanced levels. Writers' week offers a special workshop for writers interested in children's/young adult writing. We have featured such workshop leaders as: Patricia Gauch, Patricia Horner, Elizabeth Winthrop and Lore Segal. Annual workshop held last week in June. Length of each session: one week. Cost of workshop: $560 (non-credit); includes a full week of writing activities, 5-day workshop on children's literature, lectures, readings, sessions with editors and agents, etc. Workshop may be taken for 2 graduate credits. Write for more information.

♣MARITIME WRITERS' WORKSHOP, Department Extension & Summer School, P.O. Box 4400, University of New Brunswick, Fredericton, New Brunswick E3B 5A3 Canada. (506)453-4646. Fax: (506)453-3572. Coordinator: Glenda Turner. Week-long workshop on writing for children geared to all levels and held in July. Annual workshop. 3 hours/day. Group workshop plus individual conferences, public readings, etc. Registration limited to 10/class. Cost of workshop: $300 tuition; includes tuition only. Meals and accommodations extra. 10-20 ms pages due before conference (deadline announced). Scholarships available.

‡MIDLAND WRITERS CONFERENCE, Grace A. Dow Memorial Library, 1710 W. St. Andrews, Midland MI 48640. (517)835-7151. Conference Chair: Katherine Redwine. Writer and illustrator workshops geared toward all levels. "We always have one session each on children's, poetry and basics." Classes offered include: how to write poetry, writing for youth, your literary agent/what to expect. Workshops held June 8, 1996. Length of each session: concurrently, 4 1-hour and 2-hour sessions. Maximum class size: 40. "We are a public library." Cost of workshop: $55; $45 seniors and students; includes choice of workshops and the keynote speech given by a prominent author. Write for more information.

***MIDSOUTH WRITERS FESTIVAL**, 5858 Sweet Oak Cove, Bartlett TN 38134-5545. (901)377-8250. Festival Director: Michael R. Denington. Writer workshops geared toward beginner, intermediate, advanced and professional levels. "We anticipate categories in children's literature for contests and awards. We have children's writers speak at the conference." Annual workshop held the second Saturday in May, 1996. Cost of workshop: $7 registration. Other costs are: awards banquet and entry fees for contest. Attendees must send mss and entry fees before the festival. Send SASE for more information. "Last year we had 20 categories/contests for participants to enter. We awarded over $1,800 for the categories of fiction, nonfiction, poetry and plays."

MIDWEST WRITERS' CONFERENCE, 6000 Frank Ave. NW, Canton OH 44720. (216)499-9600. Assistant Director: Debbie Ruhe. Writer workshops geared toward beginner, intermediate and advanced levels. Emphasizes markets, publications and selling your work. Annual workshop. Workshop held early October. Length of each session: 1 hour. Registration limited to 400 total people. Cost of workshop: $65; includes Friday afternoon workshops, keynote address, Saturday workshops, box lunch, up to 2-ms entries in contest. Write for more information.

***MIDWEST WRITERS WORKSHOP**, Dept. of Journalism, Ball State University, Muncie IN 47306. (317)285-2080. Fax: (317)285-7997. Director: Earl H. Conn. Writer workshops geared toward intermediate level. Topics include fiction and nonfiction writing. Annual workshop. Workshop held July 31-August 3, 1996. Registration tentatively limited to 135. Cost of workshop: $175; includes everything but room and meals. Write for more information.

***MILLS COLLEGE SUMMER INSTITUTE**, Mills College, NetWork Programs, 5000 MacArthur Blvd., Oakland CA 94613. NetWork Programs Coordinator: Roxi Sater. Writer workshops geared toward novice through published levels. This workshop is designed for writers of picture books through young adult novels. Writing techniques such as format, characterization and plotting are covered. Marketing and publishing issues are also covered. This is a dynamic, information filled week led by published authors. Annual workshop. Workshop held July 15-19, 1996. Registration limited to 20. Cost of workshop: $450 for the week; $50 ms critique fee is optional. Write for more information. "Mills offers on-going writing, illustrating and publishing classes through our Writing and Publishing Children's Books Certificate Program. These classes are small, 10-15 students, which allows for maximum personal attention. Open to beginners and published writers alike. Courses cover numerous topics including: Publishing and Marketing Issues, Writing & Illustrating Picture Books, Survey of Children's Literature, etc."

MISSISSIPPI VALLEY WRITERS CONFERENCE, Augustana College, Rock Island IL 61265. (309)762-8985. Conference Director: David R. Collins. Writer workshops geared toward all levels. Classes offered include Juvenile Writing—1 of 9 workshops offered. Annual workshop. Workshops held June 2-7, 1996; usually it is the second week in June each year. Length of each session: Monday-Friday, 1 hour each day. Registration limited to 20 participants/workshop. Writing facilities available: college library. Cost of workshop: $25 registration; $40 to participate in 1 workshop, $70 in 2, $30 for each additional; $25 to audit a workshop. Write for more information.

***MONTROSE CHRISTIAN WRITER'S CONFERENCE**, 5 Locust St., Montrose PA 18801-1112. (717)278-1001. Fax: (717)278-3061. E-mail: jfahring@epix.net Director: Jim Fahringer. Writer workshops geared toward beginner, intermediate and advanced levels. Annual workshop. Workshop held July 8-12, 1996. Cost of workshop: $70-85; includes tuition. Write for more information.

MOUNT HERMON CHRISTIAN WRITERS CONFERENCE, Mount Hermon Christian Conference Center, P.O. Box 413, Mount Hermon CA 95041. (408)335-4466. Fax: (408)335-9218. Director of Specialized Programs: David R. Talbott. Writer workshops geared toward all levels. Emphasizes religious writing for children via books, articles; Sunday school curriculum; marketing. Classes offered include: "Suitable Style for Children"; "Everything You Need to Know to Write and Market Your Children's Book"; "Take-Home Papers for Children." Workshops held annually over Palm Sunday weekend: March 29-April 12, 1996. 5-day residential conferences held annually. Registration limited 45/class, but most are 10-15. Conference center with hotel-style accommodations. Cost of workshop: $425-650 variable; includes tuition, resource notebook, refreshment breaks, full room and board for 13 meals and 4 nights. Write for more information.

THE NATIONAL WRITERS ASSOCIATION CONFERENCE, 1450 S. Havana, Suite 424, Aurora CO 80012. (303)751-7844. Executive Director: Sandy Whelchel. Writer workshops geared toward all levels. Classes offered include marketing, agenting, "What's Hot in the Market." Annual workshop. In 1996 the workshop will be held in Denver, Colorado, June 14-16. Write for more information.

***NEW ENGLAND WRITERS' WORKSHOP AT SIMMONS COLLEGE**, 300 The Fenway, Boston MA 02115. (617)521-2090. Fax: (617)521-3185. Assistant Director: Jean Welch. Writers' workshops geared toward intermediate and advanced levels. Writing workshops focusing on novels and short stories. We may be adding a children's literature section for 1996. Annual workshop. Workshop held mid-June, Monday-Friday. Registration limited to 45. Writing facilities available: computer labs and equipment in library. Cost of workshop: $525 (1995 rates); includes workshop, individual ms consultation. Write for more information.

CHRISTOPHER NEWPORT UNIVERSITY WRITERS' CONFERENCE, 50 Shoe Lane, Newport News VA 23606-2998. (804)594-7158. Coordinator: Terry Cox-Joseph. Director of Continuing Education: Dr. Sue Jones. Writer workshops geared toward beginner, intermediate, professional levels. Emphasizes all genres. Offers 4 awards: poetry, short stories, juvenile fiction, nonfiction. Call for guidelines and to be on mailing list. Workshop held April 12-13, 1996. Registration limited to 35/class. Cost of workshop: $69.

***NORTH CAROLINA WRITERS' NETWORK FALL CONFERENCE**, P.O. Box 954, Carrboro NC 27510. (919)967-9540. Fax: (919)929-0535. Writer workshops geared toward beginner, intermediate, advanced and professional levels. Sessions offered include Writing for Children, How to Get Published, etc. Annual workshop. Workshop held November 15-17, 1996 (Durham, NC). "We offer workshops and critiques in a variety of genres: fiction, poetry, children's, etc." Cost of workshop: approximately $110.

***NORTHWEST OKLAHOMA WRITERS WORKSHOP**, 219 N. 19th St., Enid OK 73701-4524. (405)237-3709. President of Enid Writers Club: Tracye White. Writer workshops geared toward beginner, intermediate, advanced and professional levels. Annual workshop. Workshop usually held in March. Cost of workshop: $40; includes registration, handouts. Write for more information. "Our workshops are not geared, per se, to children's writers. We generally have one speaker for the day. Past speakers were Mike McQuay (now deceased), Norma Jean Lutz, Deborah Bouziden, Anna Meyers (the only time we've had a children's writer) and Sandra Soli. The speaker for the 1996 workshop has not yet been determined."

***OUTDOOR WRITERS ASSOCIATION OF AMERICA ANNUAL CONTEST**, 2017 Cato Ave., Suite 101, State College PA 16801-2768. (814)234-1011. E-mail: 71340.303@compuserve.com. Meeting Planner: Eileen King. Writer workshops geared toward all levels. Annual workshop. Workshop held in June. Cost of workshop: $130; includes attendance at all workshops and most meals. Attendees must have prior approval from Executive Director before attendance is permitted. Write for more information.

OZARK CREATIVE WRITERS, INC. CONFERENCE, 6817 Gingerbread Lane, Little Rock AR 72204. (501)565-8889. Counselor: Peggy Vining. Writer's workshops geared to all levels. "All forms of the creative process dealing with the literary arts. We have expanded to songwriting." Always the second weekend in October (October 10-12, 1996) at Inn of the Ozarks in Eureka Springs AR (a resort town). Morning sessions are given to main attraction author . . . 6 1-hour satellite speakers during each of the 2 afternoons. Two banquets. "Approximately 125-150 attend the conference yearly . . . many others enter the creative writing competition." Cost of registration/contest entry fee approximately $50. "This does not include meals or lodging. We do block off 60 rooms prior to September 1 for OCW guests." Send #10 SASE for brochure. "Reserve early."

***PALM SPRINGS WRITERS' CONFERENCE**, 646 Morongo Rd., Palm Springs CA 92264. (619)864-9760. Fax: (619)322-1833. Co-director: Arthur Lyons. Writer workshops geared toward beginner, intermediate, advanced and professional levels. Emphasizes writing fiction and nonfiction for children and young adults. Annual workshop. Workshop held in May. Cost of workshop: $299-349; includes all classes, lectures, speakers, two meals, free one-on-one consultation with agents and editors. Write for more information.

***PENNWRITERS ANNUAL CONFERENCE**, RR2 Box 241, Middlebury Center PA 16935. (717)376-3361 or (717)376-2821. Fax: (717)376-2674. Conference Coordinator: C.J. Houghtaling. Writer workshops geared to all levels. Annual workshop. Workshop usually held first to second weekend in May. Cost of workshop: $110; includes 3 days of workshops, roundtables, critique sessions (Friday-Sunday) and a Saturday morning continental breakfast and Saturday lunch. Write for more information. Other workshops and 1-day seminars on writing for children as well as other category genre are held be Pennwriters throughout the year. For more information

Contact Pennwriter Secretary Joy Hopkins, 108 Jasper Way, Cannonsburg PA 15317.

PERSPECTIVES IN CHILDREN'S LITERATURE CONFERENCE, School of Education, 226 Furcolo Hall, University of Massachusetts, Amherst MA 01003. (413)545-4325 or (413)545-1116. Fax: (413)545-2879. E-mail: rudman@educ.umass.edu. Director of Conference: Masha K. Rudman. Writer and illustrator workshops geared to all levels. Emphasis varies from year to year. "We always have an editor who brings us up to date on the status of children's literature and we always have at least two illustrators. Next year one of them will be Ed Young. Presentors talk about how they broke into publishing and what guides them now." Next conference held May 11, 1996, 8 am-4 pm, 4 sessions approximately one hour each. Registration limited to 500. Cost of workshop: $50, $45 for SCBWI members; includes lunch, snacks and drinks, 10% discount on books purchased. $125 package for one academic credit also available; a one-page response to either two workshops or 1 workshop and one keynote speaker required.

PORT TOWNSEND WRITER'S CONFERENCE, Centrum, P.O. Box 1158, Port Townsend WA 98368. (206)385-3102. Director: Carol Jane Bangs. Writer workshops geared toward intermediate, advanced and professional levels. Emphasizes writing for children and young adults. Classes offered include: Jane Yolen master class; intermediate/advanced writing for children. Workshops held 10 days in mid-July. Registration limited to 20/class. Writing facilities available: classrooms. Cost of workshop: $400; includes tuition. Publication list for master class. Write for more information. $100 deposit necessary. Applications accepted after December 1 for following July; workshops fill by February.

***PUBLISH YOUR OWN BOOK: A ONE-DAY SEMINAR FOR SELF-PUBLISHERS**, P.O. Box 152281, Arlington TX 76015. (817)273-2581. Fax: (817)468-1172. Instructor: Mary Bold. Writer workshops geared toward beginner, intermediate, advanced and professional levels. Annual workshop. Workshop held August or September, 1996. Cost of workshop: $65-75. "Seminar includes a comprehensive look at self-publishing including editorial concerns, book production, basics of the business, book distribution and marketing. Bold emphasizes realistic budgeting and marketplace considerations. Past students refer to the seminar as reality therapy and credit Bold with alerting them to changes they needed to make in their projects." Text (*The Decision to Publish*) available at UTA Bookstore.

ROBERT QUACKENBUSH'S CHILDREN'S BOOK WRITING AND ILLUSTRATING WORKSHOP, 460 E. 79th St., New York NY 10021. Phone/fax: (212)744-3822. E-mail: naap95@aol.com. Contact: Robert Quackenbush. Writer and illustrator workshops geared toward all levels. Emphasizes picture books from start to finish. Also covered is writing fiction and nonfiction for middle grades and young adults, if that is the attendees' interest. Current trends in illustration are also covered. Workshops held fall, winter and summer. Courses offered fall and winter include 10 weeks each—1½ hour/week; July workshop is a full five day (9 a.m.-4 p.m) extensive course. Registration limited to 10/class. Writing and/or art facilities available; work on the premises; art supply store nearby. Cost of workshop: $650 for instruction. Cost of workshop includes instruction in preparation of a ms and/or book dummy ready to submit to 2 publishers. Attendees are responsible for arranging their own hotel and meals, although suggestions are given on request for places to stay and eat. "This unique five-day workshop, held annually since 1982, provides the opportunity to work with Robert Quackenbush, a prolific author and illustrator of children's books with more than 160 fiction and nonfiction books for young readers to his credit, including mysteries, biographies and song-books."

READER'S DIGEST WRITER'S WORKSHOP, Northern Arizona University, P.O. Box 5638, Flagstaff AZ 86011-5638. (602)523-3554. Workshop Director: Ray Newton. Writer workshops geared toward all levels. Classes offered include major emphasis on nonfiction magazine articles for major popular publications. Annual workshops in various locations in western US. Registration limited to 250. Cost of workshop: $150 registration fee; includes three meals. Does not include travel or lodging."Participants will have opportunity for one-on-one sessions with major editors, writers representing national magazines, including the *Reader's Digest*." Write for more information.

SAN DIEGO STATE UNIVERSITY WRITERS' CONFERENCE, The College of Extended Studies, San Diego CA 92182. (619)594-2514. Fax: (619)594-8566. E-mail: jwahl@mail.sdsu.edu. Extension Director: Jan Wahl. Writer workshops geared toward beginner, intermediate and advanced levels. Emphasizes nonfiction, fiction, screenwriting, advanced novel writing; includes session specific to writing and illustrating for children. Workshops held third weekend in January each year. Registration limited to 100/class. Cost of workshop: $194 if preregistered before January 15; includes Saturday reception, 2 lunches and all sessions. Write for more information.

SEATTLE PACIFIC CHRISTIAN WRITERS CONFERENCE, Humanities Department, Seattle Pacific University, Seattle WA 98119. (206)281-2109. Director: Linda Wagner. Writer workshops geared toward beginner, intermediate, advanced levels. Emphasizes "excellence in writing for the religious market. Stress on the craft of writing, usually includes some excellent workshops for children's writers." Workshops held fourth week of June. Length of each session: 70 minutes. Maximum class size: "varies—usually not more than 40." Cost of workshop: $200.

***SHENANDOAH VALLEY WRITERS' GUILD**, %Lord Fairfax College, P.O. Box 47, Middletown VA 22643. (540)869-1120. Faculty Liaison: Professor Cogan. Writer workshop geared toward beginner and intermediate levels. "We emphasize fiction, nonfiction and poetry, assuming that what is true of a genre will carry over to a specialization." Annual workshop. Workshop held in May. Cost of workshop: $40; includes all day workshop and luncheon. SASE for more information.

SOCIETY OF CHILDREN'S BOOK WRITERS—ALABAMA/GEORGIA REGION, 1616 Kestwick Dr., Birmingham AL 35226. E-mail: j.broerman@genie.geis.com. Regional Advisor: Joan Broerman. "The fall conference, 'Writing and Illustrating for Kids,' is always the third Saturday in October in Birmingham, and offers entry level and professional track workshops (i.e. 'Foundations of Writing and Submitting,' 'CD-ROM—Will It Change My Life?') as well as numerous talks on craft from early picture books through young adult novels." Cost of workshop: $50-60 for SCBWI members; $60-70 for nonmembers; ms critiques and portfolio review available for additional cost. Write for more information (include SASE). "Our spring conference, Springmingle!, is in different parts of the two-state region. The 1995 spring conference is in different parts of the two-state region. Springmingle '96! will be held at Gulf Shores, AL, February 23-25, 1996." Preregistration important for both conferences.

SOCIETY OF CHILDREN'S BOOK WRITERS AND ILLUSTRATORS—FLORIDA REGION, 2158 Portland Ave., Wellington FL 33414. (407)798-4824. Florida Regional Advisor: Barbara Casey. Writer and illustrator workshops geared toward beginner, intermediate, advanced and professional levels. Subjects to be announced. Workshop held second Saturday of September in the meeting rooms of the Palm Springs Public Library, 217 Cypress Lane, Palm Springs FL. Registration limited to 100/class. Cost of workshop: $45 for members, $50 for non-members. Special rates are offered through the West Palm Beach Airport Hilton Hotel for those attending the conference who wish to spend the night. Write for more information.

SOCIETY OF CHILDREN'S BOOK WRITERS AND ILLUSTRATORS—HAWAII, 98-688 Keikialii St., Aiea HI 96701. (808)486-4086. Fax: (808)486-4046. E-mail: 74250.357@compuserve.com or coste@uhunix3.uhcc.hawaii.edu. Regional Advisor: Marion Coste. Writer and illustrator conferences geared toward all levels. Conferences feature general topics—writing, illustrating, publishing and marketing; also specific skills workshops are offered such as "writing plays for children." Conferences are held in spring and fall; workshops in winter; retreat in fall. Cost varies. Reduced rate for SCBWI members. Open to nonmembers. Write for more information.

***SOCIETY OF CHILDREN'S BOOK WRITERS AND ILLUSTRATORS—HOUSTON; WRITE ON!**, SCBWI Conference, 2400 Old South Dr., #2501, Richmond TX 77469. Regional Advisor: Marj Gurasich. Writer and illustrator workshops geared toward beginner, intermediate and advanced levels. Emphasizes an editor's view of manuscripts, how to write chapter books and what makes a good picture book. Annual workshop. Cost of workshop: $65; includes all costs, handouts and lunch.

SOCIETY OF CHILDREN'S BOOK WRITERS AND ILLUSTRATORS—INDIANA SPRING WRITERS' CONFERENCE, P.O Box 36, Garrett IN 46738. E-mail: 70334.1145@compuserve.com. Conference Director: Lola M. Schaefer. Writer and illustrator workshops geared toward all levels. Workshop sessions include "Nuts and Bolts for Beginners," "Plotting the Middle-Grade Novel," "Lasting Themes in Picture Books" "Researching the Biography," and "Nonfiction for Children." All are geared toward children's writers and illustrators. Conference held annually in June. 1996 conference: June 29. Length of each session: 45 minutes to 1½ hours. Cost of workshop: approximately $95; includes meal and workshops. Write for more information. "Manuscript and portfolio critiques by published writers and illustrators will be offered at additional charge."

SOCIETY OF CHILDREN'S BOOK WRITERS AND ILLUSTRATORS—MINNESOTA, 7080 Coachwood Rd., Woodbury MN 55125. (612)739-0119. Minnesota Regional Advisor: Peg Helminski. Writer and illustrator workshops geared toward beginner, intermediate, advanced and professional levels. All of our workshops and conferences focus on the needs of children's writers and illustrators. Spring '95 topics included interactive CD storybooks, writing children's books and author/illustrator Debra Fraiser. Fall '95 topics include the young adult novel from both author and editor viewpoints, the middle grade novel from both author and editor perspectives, successful school visits, and how to successfully promote your children's book. Critique sessions and portfolio reviews are also available. We try to have one full day conference and one evening event per year. Twice a year workshop. Workshop held late April and early October. Cost of workshop: varies $20-85. Includes full day conferences include luncheon, coffee breaks and snack. Evening workshops include snack. SASE for more information 6 weeks prior to each event.

***SOCIETY OF CHILDREN'S BOOK WRITERS AND ILLUSTRATORS—NORCAL RETREAT AT ASILOMAR**, 1316 Rebecca Dr., Suisun CA 94585. (707)426-6776. Fax: (707)427-2885. Regional Advisor: Bobi Martin. Writer and illustrator workshops geared toward beginner, intermediate, advanced and professional levels. Emphasizes various topics from writing or illustrating picture books to young adult novels. Past speakers include agents, publishers, editors, published authors and illustrators. Annual workshop. Workshop generally held last weekend in February; Friday evening through Sunday lunch. Registration limited to 65. Rooms are shared with one other person. Desks available in most rooms. All rooms have private baths. Cost of workshop: $200 SCBWI members; $235 nonmembers; includes shared room, 6 meals, ice breaker party and conference. Registration opens October 1st and usually is full by October 31st. A waiting list is formed. SASE for more information. "This is a small retreat with a relaxed pace."

***SOCIETY OF CHILDREN'S BOOK WRITERS AND ILLUSTRATORS—NORTHWEST; WORKING WRITERS RETREAT**, P.O. Box 336, Noti OR 97461. (503)935-4589. Retreat Chair: Robin Koontz. Writer workshop geared toward intermediate, advanced levels. Illustrator workshop geared toward beginner, intermediate levels. "We have craft lectures with published authors who usually discuss how they got started, how they work and how they market. We also have an editor who usually discusses market trends. In the mornings, we have craft lectures. The afternoons are devoted to small groups where participants can critique manuscripts, exchange ideas or meet with the faculty." Retreat held at Silver Falls Conference Center. "We basically go all day. Although participants may choose to not attend everything." Registration limited to 40. Small groups are usually 5-10 people. Cost of workshop: 1991 prices: $295 (members of SCBWI-NW $10/year for membership), $280 (nonmembers); double occupancy room (single $70 more), 4 nights, all meals, all events.

***SOCIETY OF CHILDREN'S BOOK WRITERS AND ILLUSTRATORS—POCONO MOUNTAINS WRITERS' RETREAT**, 708 Pine St., Moscow PA 18444. Conference Director: Susan Campbell Bartoletti. Workshop held third weekend in April, depending upon Easter and Passover. Registration limited to 75. Cost of workshop: tuition about $125; room and board, $170. Send SASE for more information.

SOCIETY OF CHILDREN'S BOOK WRITERS AND ILLUSTRATORS—ROCKY MOUNTAIN CHAPTER SUMMER RETREAT, Franciscan Center, Colorado Springs CO 80919. Regional Advisor: Vivian Dubrovin. Writer workshop geared toward beginner, intermediate, advanced, professional levels. Annual workshop. Workshops held July 19-21, 1996. Friday-Sunday. Registration limited to 60. Cost of workshop: approximately $200; includes room, board and all sessions. Participants may submit writing to be critiqued by speakers (additional fee charged). Write for more information and dates and location for the SCBWI fall conference in Denver.

SOCIETY OF CHILDREN'S BOOK WRITERS AND ILLUSTRATORS—SAN DIEGO CHAPTER, Writing for Children, the Words and the Pictures, Society of Children's Book Writers and Illustrators/San Diego Chapter, 1238 Valencia Dr., Escondido CA 92025. (619)738-1629. E-mail: lpflueger@ucsd.edu. Conference Chairman: Lynda Pflueger. Writer and illustrator workshops geared toward all levels. Topics vary every year but emphasize writing and illustrating for children. Annual workshop. Workshop held on the second or third Saturday in March. Length: all day workshop with 6 1-hour sessions. Cost of workshop: $55-65; includes all day workshop and luncheon. Write for more information. "Meeting other writers, networking and marketing information is stressed during workshop."

SOCIETY OF CHILDREN'S BOOK WRITERS AND ILLUSTRATORS—SOUTHERN CALIFORNIA; ILLUSTRATORS DAY, 1937 Pelham Ave., #2, Los Angeles CA 90025. (310)446-4789. Regional Advisor: Judith Enderle. Illustrator workshops geared toward all levels. Emphasizes illustration and illustration markets. Conference includes: presentations by art director, children's book editor and panel of artists/author-illustrators. Workshops held annually in the fall. Length of session: full day. Maximum class size: 100. "Editors and art directors will view portfolios. We want to know if each conferee is bringing a portfolio or not." This is a chance for illustrators to meet editors/art directors and each other. Writers Day held in the spring. National conference for authors *and* illustrators held every August."

SOCIETY OF CHILDREN'S BOOK WRITERS AND ILLUSTRATORS—TENNESSEE SPRING CONFERENCE, Box 3342, Clarksville TN 37043-3342. (615)358-9849. Regional Advisor: Cheryl Zach. Writer workshop geared toward all levels. Illustrator workshops geared toward beginner, intermediate levels. Previous workshop topics have included Writing the Picture Book, Editors Look at First Pages, Historical Fiction and Nonfiction, Writing Poetry and Songs, Writing for Magazines, Illustrators' Workshops and more. Workshop held in the spring. 1 day. Cost of workshop: $50 SCBWI members, $55 nonmembers; includes all day of workshops and lunch. Registration limited to 100. Write for more information. "SCBWI-Tennessee's 1996 conference is scheduled for April 27 in Nashville." Write for information.

SOCIETY OF CHILDREN'S BOOK WRITERS AND ILLUSTRATORS—VENTURA/SANTA BARBARA FALL CONFERENCE, 22736 Vanowen, Suite 106, West Hills CA 91307. (818)888-8760. Regional Advisor: Alexis O'Neill. Writers conference geared toward all levels. "We invite editors, authors and author/illustrators and agents. We have had speakers on the picture book, middle grade, YA, magazine and photo essay books. Both fiction and nonfiction are covered." Conference held in October from 9:00 a.m.-4 p.m. on Saturdays. Cost of conference $55; includes all sessions and lunch. Write for more information.

SOCIETY OF CHILDREN'S BOOK WRITERS & ILLUSTRATORS—WISCONSIN ANNUAL FALL RETREAT, Rt. 1, Box 137, Gays Mills WI 54631. (608)735-4707. Regional Advisor: Patricia Pfitsch. Writer workshops geared toward all levels. Classes offered include: pre-publication secrets; post-publication problems; workshops on craft; author-editor dialogues on the revision process; working relationships; marketing. "The entire retreat is geared *only* to children's book writing." Annual workshop. Retreat held October 4-6, 1996, from Friday evening to Sunday afternoon. Registration limited to approximately 60. Cost of workshop: about $215 for SCBWI members, higher for nonmembers; includes room, board and program. "We strive to offer an informal weekend with an award-winning children's writer, an agent or illustrator and an editor from a trade house in New York in attendance." There's usually a waiting list by mid-July. Send SASE for flier.

***SOUTHEASTERN WRITER'S CONFERENCE**, Rt. 1, Box 102, Cuthbert GA 31740. (912)679-5445. Co-Director: Pat Laye. Writer workshops geared toward beginner and intermediate levels. Illustrator workshops geared toward beginner level. "We offer a 5-session juvenile writing class." Annual conference held on St. Simon's Island, CA. Registration limited to 100. Cost of workshops: $215; includes tuition only. "Attendees may submit one chapter of three different manuscripts for free professional critiques."

***SOUTHERN CALIFORNIA WRITERS CONFERENCE SAN DIEGO**, 2596 Escondido Ave., San Diego CA 92123. (619)273-2704. Director: Betty Abell Jurus. Writer workshops geared toward beginner, intermediate, advanced levels. Workshops offered include fiction, nonfiction, film and (marketing) business. Also speakers and agents' and editors' panels. Conference is annual on 4-day Martin Luther King weekend. Length of each session: Days, 2-hours; evenings, 2-4-hours. Cost of conference: Approx. $425, includes conference and hotel accommodations; approx. $250, conference without hotel. Write or phone for more information.

***SPACE COAST WRITERS GUILD CONFERENCE**, Box 804, Melbourne FL 32902. (407)727-0051. President: Dr. Edwin J. Kirschner. Writer workshops geared toward beginner, intermediate, advanced and professional levels. Annual workshop. Held 1st Friday and Saturday in November. Registration limited to 350. Cost of workshop: SCWG members and teachers, $50 both days; nonmembers, $65; students, $25. Price includes 2 days of workshops. Write for more information.

***SPLIT ROCK ARTS PROGRAM, University of Minnesota**, 306 Wesbrook Hall, 77 Pleasant St. SE, Minneapolis MN 55455. (612)624-6800. Fax: (612)625-2568. Registrar: Vivien Oja. Writer and illustrator workshops geared toward intermediate, advanced, professional levels. Workshops offered in writing and illustrating books for children and young people. 1996 workshops begin July 7 for 5 weeks. Two college credits available. Registration limited to 16 per class. Workshops held on the University of Minnesota-Duluth campus. Cost of workshop: $360; includes tuition and fees. Amounts vary depending on course fee, determined by supply needs, etc. "Moderately priced on-campus housing available." Complete catalogs available March 15. Call or write anytime to be put on mailing list. Some courses fill very early.

STATE OF MAINE WRITERS' CONFERENCE, 47 Winona Ave., P.O. Box 7146, Ocean Park ME 04063. (207)934-9806 (summer). (413)596-6734 (winter). Chairman: Richard F. Burns. Writers' workshops geared toward beginner, intermediate, advanced levels. Emphasizes poetry, prose, mysteries, editors, publishers, etc. Annual workshop held August 20-23, 1996. Cost of workshop: $75 ($40 for students 21 and under); includes all sessions and banquet, snacks, poetry booklet. Write for more information.

TRENTON STATE COLLEGE WRITERS' CONFERENCE, English Dept, Trenton State College, Hillwood Lakes CN 4700, Trenton NJ 08650-4700. (609)771-3254. Director: Jean Hollander. Writer workshops geared toward all levels. Workshops held April 6, 1995. Length of each session: 2 hours. Registration limited to 50. Cost of workshop: $50 (reduced rates for students); includes conference, workshop and ms critique. Write for more information.

MARK TWAIN WRITERS CONFERENCE, 921 Center St., Hannibal MO 63401. (314)221-2462 or (800)747-0738. Director: James C. Hefley. Writers' workshops geared toward beginner, intermediate and advanced levels. Workshops covering poetry, humor, Mark Twain, newspapers, freelancing, writing for children, the autobiography and working with an agent. Workshops held in June. Registration limited to 12-20/class. Writing facilities available: computers. Cost of workshop: $425; includes all program fees, room, meals and group photo. Write for more information.

UMKC/WRITERS PLACE WRITERS WORKSHOPS, (formerly New Letters Weekend Writers Conference), University of Missouri—Kansas City, 5100 Rockhill Rd., 215 55B, Kansas City

MO 64110-2499. (816)235-2736. Fax: (816)235-5279. Continuing Education Manager: Mary Ann McKinley. Writer and illustrator workshops geared toward intermediate, advanced and professional levels. Semi-annual workshops. Workshops held in fall and spring. Registration limited to 25. Writing facilities available on request. Cost of workshop: $65. "Credit fees vary depending on level. Write for more information.

‡✤VANCOUVER INTERNATIONAL WRITERS FESTIVAL, 1243 Cartwright St., Vancouver, British Columbia V6H 4B7 Canada. (604)681-6330. Fax: (604)681-8400. Producer: Alma Lee. "The mission of the Vancouver International Writers Festival is to encourage an appreciation of literature and to promote literacy by providing a forum where writers and readers can interact. This is accomplished by the production of special events and an annual Festival which feature writers from a variety of countries, whose work is compelling and diverse. The Festival attracts over 8,000 people and presents approximately 40 events in four venues during 5 days on Granville Island, located in the heart of Vancouver. The first 3 days of the festival are programmed for elementary and secondary school students." Held third week in October (5-day festival). All writers who participate are invited by the producer. The events are open to anyone who wishes to purchase tickets. Cost of events ranges from $10-15.

WELLS WRITERS' WORKSHOP, 69 Broadway, Concord NH 03301. (603)225-9162. Fax: (603)225-9162. E-mail: forbine@aol. Coordinator: Victor Andre Levine. Writer workshops geared toward beginner, intermediate levels. "Sessions focus on careful plot preparation, as well as on effective writing (characterization, dialogue and exposition), with lots of time for writing." Workshops which meet on Maine seacoast, are offered twice a year—May 20-25 and September 9-14. Registration limited to 5/class. Writing facilities available: space, electrical outlets, resident Mac computer. Cost of workshop: $950; includes tuition, room and board; some scholarship money available. Cost includes tuition, housing and food. Write for more information. "I invite interested writers to call or write. I'd be happy to meet with them if they're reasonably close by. Workshop stresses the importance of getting the structure right when writing stories for children."

WESLEYAN WRITERS CONFERENCE, Wesleyan University, Middletown CT 06459. (860)685-3604. Director: Anne Greene. Writer workshops geared toward all levels. "This conference is useful for writers interested in how to structure a story, poem or nonfiction piece. Although we don't always offer classes in writing for children, the advice about structuring a piece is useful for writers of any sort, no matter who their audience is." Classes in the novel, short story, fiction techniques, poetry, journalism and literary nonfiction. Guest speakers and panels offer discussion of fiction, poetry, reviewing, editing and publishing. Individual ms consultations available. Workshops held annually the last week in June. Length of each session: 6 days. "Usually, there are 100 participants at the Conference." Classrooms, meals, lodging and word processing facilities available on campus. Cost of workshop: tuition—$430, room—$95, meals (required of all participants)—$173. "Anyone may register; people who want financial aid must submit their work and be selected by scholarship judges." Write for more information.

WESTERN RESERVE WRITERS AND FREELANCE CONFERENCE, Lakeland Community College, 7700 Clocktower Dr., Mentor OH 44060. (216)943-3047 or (800)OLDHAM1. E-mail: fa837@cleveland.freenet.edu. Coordinator: Lea Leever Oldham. Writer workshops geared toward all levels. Emphasizes fiction, photography, greeting card writing, science fiction and fantasy writing, poetry. Classes offered include: copyright protection, picking a printer, target marketing. All-day conference. Cost of workshop: $49 plus lunch. Write for more information to 34200 Ridge Rd., Suite 110, Willoughby OH 44094. (216)943-3047.

WESTERN RESERVE WRITERS MINI CONFERENCE, 34200 Ridge Rd., #110, Willoughby OH 44094. (216)943-3047 or (800)OLDHAM1. E-mail: fa837@cleveland.freenet.edu. Coordi-

The maple leaf before a listing indicates that the market is Canadian.

nator: Lea Leever Oldham. Writer workshops geared toward beginner, intermediate and advanced levels. Topics include query letters, marketing, editing, grammar and other specifics about selling what you write. Quarterly workshop. Workshop held in March or early April at Lakeland Community College, Mentor OH. Cost of workshop: $39. Write for more information.

WILLAMETTE WRITERS ANNUAL WRITERS CONFERENCE, Suite 5A, 9045 SW Barbur Blvd., Portland OR 97219. (503)452-1592. Writer workshops geared toward all levels. Emphasizes all areas of writing. Opportunities to meet one-on-one with leading literary agents and editors. Workshops held in August.

***WRITE ON THE SOUND WRITERS CONFERENCE**, 700 Main St., Edmonds WA 98020. (206)771-0228. Contact: Edmonds Arts Commission. Writer workshops geared toward beginner, intermediate, advanced and professional levels. "In the past we have offered fiction and nonfiction writing for children. This year we had Ted and Gloria Rand (illustrator and writer) who have done children's books." Workshop held "usually the first weekend in October with two full days of a variety of lectures and workshops." Registration limited to 200. Cost of workshop: approximately $40/day, or $75 for the weekend, with optional boxed lunches available. Write for more information. "Brochures are mailed in August. Attendees must preregister. Write or call for brochure."

THE WRITERS' CENTER AT CHAUTAUQUA, Box 408, Chautauqua NY 14722. (716)357-2445 or (717)872-8337 (September through May). Director: Mary Jean Irion. Writer workshops geared toward beginner and intermediate levels. Emphasizes poetry, fiction, nonfiction, at least 1 week of which is devoted to writing for children; for example, the elements of writing, slanted for children's writers: setting, characters, plot, conflict, etc. In general, workshops are a combination of teaching and editing students' work. Workshop held sometime between June 22-August 25. Registration limited to 25. Cost of workshop: $60. "Often a leader will invite students to submit their work for class discussion or for comments by the leader, but this is never a requirement." Write for more information. September-May, mail should be addressed to 149 Kready Ave., Millersville PA 17551. "A $10 membership in The Writers' Center at Chautauqua includes full information on each season, mailed out in March, with registration blank."

WRITERS CONNECTION CONFERENCES, P.O. Box 24770, San Jose CA 95154-4770. (408)445-3600. Fax: (408)445-3609. Program Director: Meera Lester. Conferences are scheduled throughout the year and include "Writing for Children," "Literary Agents' Day," "Writing for Interactive Multimedia," "Selling to Hollywood" and other fiction, nonfiction and scriptwriting programs. Bookstore of writing, reference and how-to books. Monthly newsletter with membership, $45. Subscription only $25.

WRITERS' FORUM, 1570 E. Colorado Blvd., Pasadena CA 91106-2003. (818)585-7608. Coordinator of Forum: Meredith Brucker. Writer workshops geared toward all levels. "Last year Eve Bunting spoke on 'Writing the Picture Book.' " Workshop held March 9, 1996. Length of session: 1 hour and 15 minutes including Q & A time. Cost of workshop: $100; includes lunch. Write for more information to Community Education, Pasadena City College, 1570 E. Colorado Blvd., Pasadena CA 91106-2003.

WRITERS IN THE REDWOODS RETREAT, Alliance Redwoods, 6250 Bohemian Hwy., Occidental CA 95465. (707)874-3507. Guest Services Director: Bob Ward. Writer workshops geared toward beginner and intermediate levels. Topics include how freelancers can and do earn a living; how to write book proposals and get contracts; from idea to published novel; tricks of the trade to keep writing during dry spells. Annual workshop. Workshop held November 10-12, 1996. Registration limited to 100. Cost of workshop: $180-250; includes tuition, room and board, handouts, freebies. For information, write to Writers Information Network, P.O. Box 11337, Bainbridge Island WA 98110.

WRITERS STUDIO SPRING WRITERS CONFERENCE, 3403 45th St., Moline IL 61265. (309)762-8985. Coordinator, Pro Tem: David R. Collins. Writer workshops geared toward intermediate level. Emphasizes basic writing and mechanics. Workshops held annually in March or April. Workshop is free. Write for more information.

Conferences & Workshops/'95-'96 changes

The following listings were included in the 1995 edition of *Children's Writer's & Illustrator's Market* but do not have listings in this edition. The majority did not respond to our request to update their listings. If a reason was given for exclusion, it appears in parentheses after the listing's name.

The Art & Business of Humorous Illustration
Autumn Authors' Affair XI
Blue Ridge Writers Conference
The Brockport Writers Forum Summer Workshops
Cape Writing Workshops
Cedar Hills Christian Writers Weekend
Christian Writers' Institute Annual Writers' Conference
Christian Writers' Institute Florida Conference
Christian Writers' Institute Texas Conference
Creative Collaborative
Dillman's Creative Workshops
Education Writers Association National Seminar
Great Lakes Writer's Workshop
Heart of America Writers' Conference
International Women's Writing Guild (cancelled)
Maine Writers Workshop
Maple Woods Community College Writers' Conference
Oklahoma Fall Arts Institutes (per request)
101 Ways to Market Your Book
SCBWI Conference in Children's Literature
SCBWI—Mid-Atlantic Writers' Annual Conference
SCBWI—New England Conference
Southwest Writers Conference
Vassar Institute of Publishing and Writing: Children's Books in the Marketplace
Ventura/Santa Barbara Fall Workshop
Yachats Literary Festival

Helpful Books & Publications

The editor of *Children's Writer's & Illustrator's Market* suggests the following books and periodicals to keep you informed on writing and illustrating techniques, trends in the field, business issues and additional markets. Most are available in libraries or bookstores or may be ordered directly from their publishers.

Books

THE ARTIST'S FRIENDLY LEGAL GUIDE. By Floyd Conner, Peter Karlen, Jean Perwin and David M. Spatt. North Light Books, 1991.

CHILDREN'S WRITER'S WORD BOOK. By Alijandra Mogilner. Writer's Digest Books, 1992.

GETTING STARTED AS A FREELANCE ILLUSTRATOR OR DESIGNER. By Michael Fleishman. North Light Books, 1990.

HOW TO SELL YOUR PHOTOGRAPHS & ILLUSTRATIONS. By Elliott & Barbara Gordon. North Light Books, 1990.

HOW TO WRITE A CHILDREN'S BOOK & GET IT PUBLISHED. By Barbara Seuling. Charles Scribner's Sons, 1991.

HOW TO WRITE AND ILLUSTRATE CHILDREN'S BOOKS. Treld Pelkey Bicknell and Felicity Trotman, editors. North Light Books, 1988.

HOW TO WRITE AND SELL CHILDREN'S PICTURE BOOKS. By Jean E. Karl. Writer's Digest Books, 1994.

HOW TO WRITE, ILLUSTRATE, AND DESIGN CHILDREN'S BOOKS. By Frieda Gates. Lloyd-Simone Publishing Company, 1986.

MARKET GUIDE FOR YOUNG WRITERS. By Kathy Henderson. Writer's Digest Books, 1995.

THE WRITER'S ESSENTIAL DESK REFERENCE, Second Edition. Glenda Tennant Neff, editor. Writer's Digest Books, 1996.

A WRITER'S GUIDE TO A CHILDREN'S BOOK CONTRACT. By Mary Flower. Fern Hill Books, 1988.

WRITING AND ILLUSTRATING CHILDREN'S BOOKS FOR PUBLICATION: TWO PERSPECTIVES. By Berthe Amoss and Eric Suben. Writer's Digest Books, 1995.

WRITING & PUBLISHING BOOKS FOR CHILDREN IN THE 1990s. By Olga Litowinsky. Walker & Co., 1992.

WRITING BOOKS FOR YOUNG PEOPLE, Second Edition. By James Cross Giblin. The Writer, Inc., 1995.

WRITING FOR CHILDREN & TEENAGERS. By Lee Wyndham and Arnold Madison. Writer's Digest Books, 1985.

WRITING WITH PICTURES: HOW TO WRITE AND ILLUSTRATE CHILDREN'S BOOKS. By Uri Shulevitz. Watson-Guptill Publications, 1985.

Publications

BILLBOARD. Timothy White, editor-in-chief. 1515 Broadway, New York NY 10036. (800)745-8922. *Weekly music industry trade publication covering children's audio and video in biweekly "Child's Play" column. Subscription: $249/year. Available on newsstands for $5.50/issue.*

BOOK LINKS. Barbara Elleman, editor. American Library Association, 50 E. Huron St., Chicago IL 60611. (800)545-2433. *Magazine published six times a year (September-July) for the purpose of connecting books, libraries and classrooms. Features articles on specific topics followed by bibliographies recommending books for further information. Subscription: $17.95/year.*

CHILDREN'S BOOK INSIDER. Laura Backes, editor. P.O. Box 1030, Fairplay CO 80440-1030. (800)807-1916. E-mail: cbi@mindspring.com. World Wide Wed: http://www.mindspring.com/~cbi. *Monthly newsletter covering markets, techniques, and trends in children's publishing. Subscription: $29.95/year.*

CHILDREN'S WRITER. Susan Tierney, editor. The Institute of Children's Literature, 95 Long Ridge Rd., West Redding CT 06896-1124. (800)443-6078. *Monthly newsletter of writing and publishing trends in the children's field. Subscription: $24/year; special introductory rate: $15.*

THE FIVE OWLS. Susan Stan, editor. Hamline University Crossroads Center, MS-C1924, 1536 Hewitt Ave., St. Paul MN 55104. (616)644-7377. *Bimonthly newsletter for readers personally and professionally involved in children's literature. Subscription: $20/year.*

THE HORN BOOK MAGAZINE. The Horn Book, Inc., 11 Beacon St., Suite 1000, Boston MA 02108. (617)227-1555. *Bimonthly guide to the children's book world including views on the industry and reviews of the latest books. Subscription: $35/year.*

THE LION AND THE UNICORN: A CRITICAL JOURNAL OF CHILDREN'S LITERATURE. Jack Zipes and Louisa Smith, editors. The Johns Hopkins University Press—Journals Publishing Division, 2175 N. Charles St., Baltimore MD 21218-4319. (410)516-6987. *Biannual publication serving as a forum for discussion of children's literature featuring interviews with authors, editors and experts in the field. Subscription: $21/year.*

ONCE UPON A TIME. . . Audrey Baird, editor. 553 Winston Court, St. Paul MN 55118. (612)457-6223. *Quarterly magazine for children's writers and illustrators and those interested in children's literature. Subscription: $19/year.*

PUBLISHERS WEEKLY. Nora Rawlinson, editor-in-chief. Bowker Magazine Group, Cahners Publishing Co., 249 W. 17th St., New York NY 10011. (800)278-2991. *Weekly trade publication covering all aspects of the publishing industry; includes coverage of the children's field (books, audio and video) and spring and fall issues devoted solely to children's books. Subscription: $139/year. Available on newsstands for $3/issue. (Special issues are higher in price.)*

SOCIETY OF CHILDREN'S BOOK WRITERS AND ILLUSTRATORS BULLETIN. Stephen Mooser and Lin Oliver, editors. The Society of Children's Book Writers and Illustrators, 22736 Vanowen St., Suite 106, West Hills CA 91307. (818)888-8760. *Bimonthly organizational newsletter of SCBWI covering news of interest to members. Subscription with $50/year membership.*

Glossary

Advance. A sum of money a publisher pays a writer or illustrator prior to the publication of a book. It is usually paid in installments, such as one half on signing the contract; one half on delivery of a complete and satisfactory manuscript. The advance is paid against the royalty money that will be earned by the book.

All rights. The rights contracted to a publisher permitting the use of material anywhere and in any form, including movie and book club sales, without additional payment to the creator.

Anthropomorphization. The act of attributing human form and personality to things not human (such as animals).

ASAP. As soon as possible.

ASCAP. American Society of Composers, Authors and Publishers. A performing rights organization.

B&W. Black & white.

Backlist. A publisher's list of books not published during the current season but still in print.

Biennially. Occurring once every two years.

Bimonthly. Occurring once every two months.

Biweekly. Occurring once every two weeks.

BMI. Broadcast Music, Inc. A performing rights organization.

Book packager. A company which draws all elements of a book together, from the initial concept to writing and marketing strategies, then sells the book package to a book publisher and/or movie producer. Also known as book producer or book developer.

Book proposal. Package submitted to a publisher for consideration usually consisting of a synopsis, outline and sample chapters. (See Guide to Submitting Your Work.)

Business-size envelope. Also known as a #10 envelope. The standard size used in sending business correspondence.

Camera-ready. Refers to art that is completely prepared for copy camera platemaking.

Caption. A description of the subject matter of an illustration or photograph; photo captions include persons' names where appropriate. Also called cutline.

CD-ROM. Compact disc read-only memory. Non-erasable electronic medium used for digitalized image and document storage.

Clean-copy. A manuscript free of errors and needing no editing; it is ready for typesetting.

Concept books. Books that deal with ideas, concepts and large-scale problems, promoting an understanding of what's happening in a child's world. Most prevalent are alphabet and counting books, but also includes books dealing with specific concerns facing young people (such as divorce, birth of a sibling, friendship or moving).

Contract. A written agreement stating the rights to be purchased by an editor, art director or producer and the amount of payment the writer, illustrator or photographer will receive for that sale. (See Tips on Contracts & Negotiation.)

Contributor's copies. The magazine issues sent to an author, illustrator or photographer in which her work appears.

Co-op publisher. A publisher that shares production costs with an author, but, unlike subsidy publishers, handles all marketing and distribution. An author receives a high percentage of royalties until her initial investment is recouped, then standard royalties. Also called a joint-venture publisher.

Copy. The actual written material of a manuscript.

Copyediting. Editing a manuscript for grammar usage, spelling, punctuation and general style.

Copyright. A means to legally protect an author's/illustrator's/photographer's work. This can be shown by writing ©, the creator's name, and year of work's creation. (See Know Your Rights.)

Cover letter. A brief letter, accompanying a complete manuscript, especially useful if responding to an editor's request for a manuscript. May also accompany a book proposal. (See Guide to Submitting Your Work.)

Cutline. See caption.
Division. An unincorporated branch of a company.
Dummy. Handmade mock-up of a book.
E-mail. Electronic mail. Messages sent from one computer to another via a modem or computer network.
Final draft. The last version of a polished manuscript ready for submission to an editor.
First North American serial rights. The right to publish material in a periodical before it appears in book form, for the first time, in the United States or Canada. (See Know Your Rights.)
Flat fee. A one-time payment.
Galleys. The first typeset version of a manuscript that has not yet been divided into pages.
Genre. A formulaic type of fiction, such as horror, mystery, romance, science fiction or western.
Glossy. A photograph with a shiny surface as opposed to one with a non-shiny matte finish.
Gouache. Opaque watercolor with an appreciable film thickness and an actual paint layer.
Halftone. Reproduction of a continuous tone illustration with the image formed by dots produced by a camera lens screen.
Hard copy. The printed copy of a computer's output.
Hi-Lo. High interest, low reading level. Pertains mostly to books for beginning adult readers.
Imprint. Name applied to a publisher's specific line of books.
IRC. International Reply Coupon. Sold at the post office to enclose with text or artwork sent to a foreign buyer to cover postage costs when replying or returning work.
Keyline. Identification, through signs and symbols, of the positions of illustrations and copy for the printer.
Joint-venture publisher. See co-op publisher.
Layout. Arrangement of illustrations, photographs, text and headlines for printed material.
Line drawing. Illustration done with pencil or ink using no wash or other shading.
Mechanicals. Paste-up or preparation of work for printing.
Middle reader. The general classification of books written for readers ages 9-11.
Modem. A small electrical box that plugs into the serial card of a computer, used to transmit data from one computer to another, usually via telephone lines.
Ms (mss). Manuscript(s).
One-time rights. Permission to publish a story in periodical or book form one time only. (See Know Your Rights.)
Outline. A summary of a book's contents in 5-15 double-spaced pages; often in the form of chapter headings with a descriptive sentence or two under each heading to show the scope of the book.
Package sale. The sale of a manuscript and illustrations̄photos as a "package" paid for with one check.
Payment on acceptance. The writer, artist or photographer is paid for her work at the time the editor or art director decides to buy it.
Payment on publication. The writer, artist or photographer is paid for her work when it is published.
Photostat. Black & white copies produced by an inexpensive photographic process using paper negatives; only line values are held with accuracy. Also called stat.
Picture book. A type of book aimed at preschoolers to 8-year-olds that tells a story primarily or entirely with artwork.
Print. An impression pulled from an original plate, stone, block, screen or negative; also a positive made from a photographic negative.
Production house. A film company which creates video material including animation, special effects, graphics, filmstrips, slides, live action and documentaries.
Proofreading. Reading a manuscript to correct typographical errors.
Query. A letter to an editor designed to capture his interest in an article or book you propose to write. (See Guide to Submitting Your Work.)
Reading fee. An arbitrary amount of money charged by some agents and publishers to read a submitted manuscript.
Reprint rights. Permission to print an already published work whose first rights have been sold to another magazine or book publisher. (See Know Your Rights.)

Response time. The average length of time it takes an editor or art director to accept or reject a query or submission and inform the creator of the decision.

Rights. What are offered to an editor or art director in exchange for printing a manuscript, artwork or photographs. (See Know Your Rights.)

Rough draft. A manuscript which has been written but not checked for errors in grammar, punctuation, spelling or content. It usually needs revision.

Roughs. Preliminary sketches or drawings.

Royalty. An agreed percentage paid by a publisher to a writer, illustrator or photographer for each copy of her work sold.

SASE. Self-addressed, stamped envelope.

SCBWI. The Society of Children's Book Writers and Illustrators. (See listing in Club & Organizations section.)

Second serial rights. Permission for the reprinting of a work in another periodical after its first publication in book or magazine form. (See Know Your Rights.)

Semiannual. Occurring once every six months.

Semimonthly. Occurring twice a month.

Semiweekly. Occurring twice a week.

Serial rights. The rights given by an author to a publisher to print a piece in one or more periodicals. (See Know Your Rights.)

Simultaneous submissions. Material sent to several publishers at the same time. (See Guide to Submitting Your Work.)

Slant. The approach to a story or piece of artwork that will appeal to readers of a particular publication.

Slush pile. Editors' term for their collections of unsolicited manuscripts.

SOCAN. Society of Composers, Authors and Music Publishers of Canada. A performing rights organization.

Software. Programs and related documentation for use with a particular computer system.

Solicited manuscript. Material which an editor has asked for or agreed to consider before being sent by a writer.

Speculation (Spec). Creating a piece with no assurance from the editor or art director that it will be purchased or any reimbursements for material or labor paid.

Stat. See photostat.

Subsidiary rights. All rights other than book publishing rights included in a book contract, such as paperback, book club and movie rights. (See Know Your Rights.)

Subsidy publisher. A book publisher that charges the author for the cost of typesetting, printing and promoting a book. Also called a vanity publisher.

Synopsis. A brief summary of a story or novel. Usually a page to a page and a half, single-spaced, if part of a book proposal.

Tabloid. Publication printed on an ordinary newspaper page turned sideways and folded in half.

Tearsheet. Page from a magazine or newspaper containing your printed art, story, article, poem or photo.

Thumbnail. A rough layout in miniature.

Transparencies. Positive color slides; not color prints.

Unsolicited manuscript. Material sent without an editor's or art director's request.

Vanity publisher. See subsidy publisher.

Word processor. A computer that produces typewritten copy via automated typing, text-editing, and storage and transmission capabilities.

Young adult. The general classification of books written for readers ages 12-18.

Young reader. The general classification of books written for readers ages 5-8.

Age-Level Index

This index lists book and magazine publishers by the age-groups for which they publish material. Use it to quickly locate appropriate markets for your work. It's important to carefully read the listings and follow the specific guidelines of each publisher to which you submit. Use this index in conjunction with the Subject Index to further narrow your list of possible markets.

Book Publishers

Press; Hodder Children's Books; Holiday House Inc.; Holt & Co., Inc., Henry; Homestead Publishing; Honea Publishers, John; Houghton Mifflin Co.; Humanics Children's House; Huntington House Publishers; Hyperion Books for Children; Hyperion Press Limited; Ideals Children's Books; Jalmar Press; Jewish Publication Society; Jones University Press/Light Line Books, Bob; Just Us Books, Inc.; Kar-Ben Copies, Inc.; Knopf Books for Young Readers; Laredo Publishing Co. Inc.; Little, Brown and Company; Lodestar Books; Lothrop Lee & Shepard Books; Lucas/Evans Books Inc.; Lucky Books; McElderry Books, Margaret K.; Magination Press; Marlor Press, Inc.; Mayhaven; Meadowbrook Press; Messner, Julian; Millbrook Press, The; Morehouse Publishing Co.; Morgan Reynolds Publishing; Morris Publishing, Joshua; Northland Publishing; NorthWord Press, Inc.; Open Hand Publishing Inc.; Orca Book Publishers; Orchard Books; Our Child Press; Owen Publishers, Inc., Richard C.; Pacific Press; Pauline (St. Paul) Books and Media; Paulist Press; Peachtree Publishers, Ltd.; Peartree; Pelican Publishing Co. Inc.; Perspectives Press; Philomel Books; Planet Dexter; Players Press, Inc.; Polychrome Publishing Corporation; Price Stern Sloan, Inc.; Putnam's Sons, G.P.; Questar Publishers, Inc.; Random House Books for Young Readers; Read'n Run Books; Reidmore Books Inc.; Reynolds Publishing; Rizzoli Books For Children; Sasquatch Books; Scholastic Hardcover; Scientific American Books for Young Readers; Silver Moon Press; Simon & Schuster Books for Young Readers; Speech Bin, Inc., The; Sri Rama Publishing; Standard Publishing; Starburst Publishers; Stemmer House Publishers, Inc.; Sunbelt Media, Inc./Eakin Press; Sundance Publishing; Tricycle Press; Tyndale House Publishers, Inc.; University Classics, Ltd. Publishers; Victor Books; Victory Publishing; Walker And Co.; Weigl Educational Publishers; Weiss Associates, Inc., Daniel; Whitman & Company, Albert; WRS Publishing

Middle readers (9- to 11-year-olds). Advocacy Press; Africa World Press; African American Images; Aladdin Paperbacks; Alyson Publications, Inc.; American Bible Society; Archway/Minstrel Books; Atheneum Books for Young Readers; A/V Concepts Corp.; Avon Books; B&B Publishing, Inc.; Bantam Doubleday Dell; Barrons Educational Series; Beautiful American Publishing Company; Behrman House Inc.; Bess Press; Bethany House Publishers; Bethel Publishing; Blackbirch Press, Inc./Blackbirch Graphics, Inc.; Blizzard Publishing; Boingo Books, Inc.; Boyds Mills Press; Bright Ring Publishing; Broadman & Holman Publishers; Cambridge Educational; Candlewick Press; Carolrhoda Books, Inc.; Chariot Books; Chelsea House Publishers; Cherubic Press; Chicago Review Press; Children's Book Press; Childrens Press; Christian Ed. Publishers; Chronicle Books; Clarion Books; Cobblehill Books; Concordia Publishing House; Coteau Books Ltd.; Crossway Books; Crown Publishers (Crown Books for Children); Crumb Elbow Publishing; CSS Publishing; Davis Publications, Inc.; Denison Co. Inc., T.S.; Dial Books for Young Readers; Discovery Enterprises, Ltd.; Distinctive Publishing Corp.; Down East Books; Dutton Children's Books; E.M. Press, Inc.; Eerdmans Publishing Company, Wm. B.; Enslow Publishers Inc.; Farrar, Straus & Giroux; Fawcett Juniper; Feminist Press at The City University of New York, The; Fiesta City Publishers; Fitzhenry & Whiteside Ltd.; Franklin Watts; Free Spirit Publishing; Friends United Press; Friendship Press, Inc.; Geringer Books, Laura; Gibbs Smith, Publisher; Godine, Publisher, David R.; Golden Books; Grapevine Publications, Inc.; Greenhaven Press; Greenwillow Books; Grosset & Dunlap, Inc.; Gumbs & Thomas Publishers; HaChai Publishing; Harcourt Brace & Co.; Hendrick-Long Publishing Company; Herald Press; Highsmith Press; Hodder Children's Books; Holiday House Inc.; Holt & Co., Inc., Henry; Homestead Publishing; Honea Publishers, John; Houghton Mifflin Co.; Huntington House Publishers; Hyperion Books for Children; Hyperion Press Limited; Jalmar Press; Jewish Lights Publishing; Jewish Publication Society; Jones University Press/Light Line Books, Bob; Kar-Ben Copies, Inc.; Knopf Books for Young Readers; Laredo Publishing Co. Inc.; Lerner Publications Co.; Little, Brown and Company; Lodestar Books; Lorimer & Co., James; Lothrop Lee & Shepard Books; Lucas/Evans Books Inc.; Lucent Books; Lucky Books; McElderry Books, Margaret K.; Marlor Press, Inc.; Mayhaven; Meadowbrook Press; Meriwether Publishing Ltd.; Milkweed Editions; Millbrook Press, The; Misty Hill Press; Morehouse Publishing Co.; Morgan Reynolds Publishing; Morris Publishing, Joshua; Muir Publications, Inc, John; Open Hand Publishing Inc.; Orca Book Publishers; Orchard Books; Our Child Press; Pacific Press; Pacific-Rim Publishers; Pando Publications; Pauline (St. Paul) Books and Media; Paulist Press; Peachtree Publishers, Ltd.; Peartree; Pelican Publishing Co. Inc.; Philomel Books; Planet Dexter; Players Press, Inc.; Polychrome Publishing Corporation; Price Stern Sloan, Inc.; Putnam's Sons, G.P.; Questar Publishers, Inc.; Random House Books for Young Readers; Read'n Run Books; Reidmore Books Inc.; Reynolds Publishing; Rizzoli Books For Children; St. Anthony Messenger Press; Scholastic Hardcover; Scientific American Books for Young Readers; Silver Moon Press; Simon & Schuster Books for Young Readers; Speech Bin, Inc., The; Standard Publishing; Starburst Publishers; Stemmer House Publishers, Inc.; Sterling Publishing Co., Inc.; Sunbelt Media, Inc./Eakin Press; Sundance Publishing; Tambourine Books; Thistledown Press Ltd.; Tricycle Press; Tudor Publishers, Inc.; Tyndale House Publishers, Inc.; University Classics, Ltd. Publishers; Victor Books; Walker And Co.; Weigl Educational Publishers; Weiss Associates, Inc., Daniel; Whitman & Company, Albert; Wiley & Sons, Inc., John; WRS Publishing

Young adults (ages 12 and up). Africa World Press; African American Images; Aladdin Paperbacks; Alyson Publications, Inc.; American Bible Society; Archway/Minstrel Books; Atheneum Books for Young Readers; A/V Concepts Corp.; Avon Books; Bandanna Books; B&B Publishing, Inc.; Bantam Doubleday Dell; Barrons Educational Series; Behrman House Inc.; Berkley Publishing Group; Bess Press; Bethany House Publishers; Bethel Publishing; Blackbirch Press, Inc./Blackbirch Graphics, Inc.; Blizzard Publishing; Blue Sky Press; Boyds Mills Press; Broadman & Holman Publishers; Cambridge Educational; Candlewick Press; Chariot Books; Chelsea House Publishers; Chicago Review Press; Children's Book Press; Childrens Press; Chronicle Books; Clarion Books; Cobblehill Books; Concordia Publishing House; Crossway Books; Crumb Elbow Publishing; CSS Publishing; Davenport, Publishers, May; Davis Publications, Inc.; Dial Books for Young Readers; Discovery Enterprises, Ltd.; Distinctive Publishing Corp.; Down East Books; Dutton

Children's Books; E.M. Press, Inc.; Enslow Publishers Inc.; Farrar, Straus & Giroux; Fawcett Juniper; Feminist Press at The City University of New York, The; Fiesta City Publishers; Fitzhenry & Whiteside Ltd.; Franklin Watts; Free Spirit Publishing; Friends United Press; Friendship Press, Inc.; Geringer Books, Laura; Globe Fearon Educational Publisher; Godine, Publisher, David R.; Greenhaven Press; Greenwillow Books; Grosset & Dunlap, Inc.; Gumbs & Thomas Publishers; Harcourt Brace & Co.; Hendrick-Long Publishing Company; Herald Press; Highsmith Press; Hodder Children's Books; Holiday House Inc.; Holt & Co., Inc., Henry; Homestead Publishing; Honea Publishers, John; Houghton Mifflin Co.; Hunter House Publishers; Huntington House Publishers; Hyperion Books for Children; Jalmar Press; Jewish Publication Society; Jones University Press/Light Line Books, Bob; Knopf Books for Young Readers; Lerner Publications Co.; Lion Books, Publisher; Little, Brown and Company; Lodestar Books; Lorimer & Co., James; Lothrop Lee & Shepard Books; Lucas/Evans Books Inc.; Lucent Books; McElderry Books, Margaret K.; Mayhaven; Meriwether Publishing Ltd.; Milkweed Editions; Millbrook Press, The; Misty Hill Press; Morehouse Publishing Co.; Oliver Press, Inc., The; Open Hand Publishing Inc.; Orca Book Publishers; Orchard Books; Our Child Press; Pacific Press; Pacific-Rim Publishers; Pando Publications; Pauline (St. Paul) Books and Media; Paulist Press; Peachtree Publishers, Ltd.; Pelican Publishing Co. Inc.; Philomel Books; Players Press, Inc.; Polychrome Publishing Corporation; Price Stern Sloan, Inc.; Putnam's Sons, G.P.; Questar Publishers, Inc.; Read'n Run Books; Reidmore Books Inc.; Rizzoli Books For Children; Rosen Publishing Group, The; St. Anthony Messenger Press; Scholastic Hardcover; Scientific American Books for Young Readers; Silver Moon Press; Simon & Schuster Books for Young Readers; Speech Bin, Inc., The; Standard Publishing; Starburst Publishers; Sunbelt Media, Inc./Eakin Press; Sundance Publishing; Tambourine Books; Texas Christian University Press; Thistledown Press Ltd.; Tricycle Press; Tudor Publishers, Inc.; University Classics, Ltd. Publishers; Walker And Co.; Weigl Educational Publishers; Weiss Associates, Inc., Daniel; Wiley & Sons, Inc., John; WRS Publishing

Magazines

Picture-oriented material (preschoolers to 8-year-olds). Babybug; Bread for God's Children; Chickadee Magazine; Focus on the Family Clubhouse; Focus on the Family Clubhouse Jr.; Friend Magazine, The; Highlights for Children; Hodgepodge; Humpty Dumpty's Magazine; Ladybug; National Geographic World; Nature Friend Magazine; Science Weekly; Scienceland; Skipping Stones; Story Friends; Together Time; Totally Kids Magazine; Turtle Magazine

Young readers (5- to 8-year-olds). ASPCA Animal Watch; Bread for God's Children; Brilliant Star; Chickadee Magazine; Children's Playmate; Discoveries; Dynamath; Focus on the Family Clubhouse; Focus on the Family Clubhouse Jr.; Friend Magazine, The; Highlights for Children; Hodgepodge; Home Altar, The; Hopscotch; Jack and Jill; Lighthouse; My Friend; Nature Friend Magazine; Pockets; Primary Days; Racing for Kids; School Magazine (Blast Off!, Countdown, Orbit, Touchdown; School Mates; Science Weekly; Scienceland; Skipping Stones; Soccer Jr.; Spider; Story Friends; Straight; Totally Kids Magazine; U*S*Kids; Wonder Time; Writer's International Forum

Middle readers (9- to 11-year-olds). American Girl; ASPCA Animal Watch; Boys' Life; Bread for God's Children; Brilliant Star; Calliope; Child Life; Children's Digest; Cobblestone; Counselor; Cricket Magazine; Crusader; Current Health 1; Discoveries; Disney Adventures; Dolphin Log; Dynamath; Faces; Falcon Magazine; Field & Stream; Focus on the Family Clubhouse; Focus on the Family Clubhouse Jr.; Friend Magazine, The; Goldfinch, The; Guide Magazine; Guideposts for Kids; High Adventure; Highlights for Children; Home Altar, The; Hopscotch; Jack and Jill; Junior Scholastic; Junior Trails; KidSoft Magazine; Lighthouse; Magic Realism; My Friend; National Geographic World; Nature Friend Magazine; Odyssey; On the Line; OWL Magazine; PKA's Advocate; Pockets; Power and Light; Racing for Kids; R-A-D-A-R; Ranger Rick; School Magazine (Blast Off!, Countdown, Orbit, Touchdown; School Mates; Science Weekly; Shofar; Skipping Stones; Soccer Jr.; Superscience Blue; 3-2-1 Contact; Totally Kids Magazine; Touch; U*S*Kids; Venture; Writer's International Forum

Young Adults (ages 12 and up). AIM Magazine; Bread for God's Children; Calliope; Challenge; Cobblestone; Cricket Magazine; Crusader; Current Health 2; Dolphin Log; Dynamath; Exploring; Faces; For Seniors Only; Guide Magazine; High Adventure; Hobson's Choice; Hype Hair; Junior Scholastic; Lighthouse; Listen; Magic Realism; National Geographic World; Nature Friend Magazine; New Era Magazine; Odyssey; On Course; On the Line; OWL Magazine; PKA's Advocate; Racing for Kids; Scholastic Math Magazine; School Mates; Science Weekly; Seventeen Magazine; Sharing the Victory; Skipping Stones; Soccer Jr.; Street Times; Student Leadership Journal; Teen Life; 'Teen Magazine; Teen Power; 3-2-1 Contact; Touch; With; Writer's International Forum; Young Salvationist; Youth Update

Subject Index

This index lists book and magazine publishers by the subject area in which they publish. The index is divided into fiction and nonfiction needs. Use it to quickly locate appropriate markets for your work. It's important to carefully read the listings and follow the specific guidelines of each publisher to which you submit. Use this index in conjunction with the Age-Level Index to further narrow your list of possible markets.

Book Publishers: Fiction

Humor. American Education Publishing; Archway/Minstrel Books; Avon Books; Bantam Doubleday Dell; Barbour & Co., Inc.; Bess Press; Blizzard Publishing; Blue Sky Press; Boyds Mills Press; Charlesbridge; Cherubic Press; Children's Book Press; Childrens Press; Coteau Books Ltd.; Crossway Books; Crown Publishers (Crown Books for Children); Feminist Press at The City University of New York, The; Fitzhenry & Whiteside Ltd.; Freedom Publishing Company; Geringer Books, Laura; Gibbs Smith, Publisher; Grosset & Dunlap, Inc.; Hodder Children's Books; Holiday House Inc.; Honea Publishers, John; Houghton Mifflin Co.; Hyperion Books for Children; Ideals Children's Books; Little, Brown and Company; Lodestar Books; Mayhaven; Meriwether Publishing Ltd.; Milkweed Editions; Mondo Publishing; Morehouse Publishing Co.; Owen Publishers, Inc., Richard C.; Peachtree Publishers, Ltd.; Place In The Woods, The; Putnam's Sons, G.P.; Scholastic Canada Ltd.; Scholastic Hardcover; Simon & Schuster Books for Young Readers; Thistledown Press Ltd.; Time-Life for Children; TOR Books; Wild Honey

Multicultural. Advocacy Press; Africa World Press; African American Images; Barrons Educational Series; Bess Press; Blizzard Publishing; Blue Sky Press; Boyds Mills Press; Carolina Wren Press/Lollipop Power Books; Carolrhoda Books, Inc.; Charlesbridge; Children's Book Press; Childrens Press; Chronicle Books; Coteau Books Ltd.; Distinctive Publishing Corp.; Dorling Kindersley, Inc.; Dutton Children's Books; Feminist Press at The City University of New York, The; Fitzhenry & Whiteside Ltd.; Friendship Press, Inc.; Geringer Books, Laura; Gibbs Smith, Publisher; Globe Fearon Educational Publisher; Godine, Publisher, David R.; Gumbs & Thomas Publishers; Holiday House Inc.; Honea Publishers, John; Houghton Mifflin Co.; Humanics Children's House; Hyperion Books for Children; Ideals Children's Books; Just Us Books, Inc.; Kar-Ben Copies, Inc.; Laredo Publishing Co. Inc.; Lerner Publications Co.; Little, Brown and Company; Lodestar Books; Lorimer & Co., James; Mage Publishers Inc.; Magination Press; Milkweed Editions; Mondo Publishing; Morehouse Publishing Co.; Northland Publishing; Open Hand Publishing Inc.; Orchard Books; Our Child Press; Owen Publishers, Inc., Richard C.; Pacific Educational Press; Paulist Press; Peartree; Philomel Books; Place In The Woods, The; Polychrome Publishing Corporation; Ragweed Press; Read'n Run Books; Rizzoli Books For Children; Sasquatch Books; Scholastic Canada Ltd.; Simon & Schuster Books for Young Readers; Stemmer House Publishers, Inc.; Sundance Publishing; Thistledown Press Ltd.; TOR Books; Treasure Chest Books; Tricycle Press; Tudor Publishers, Inc.; Victory Publishing; Walker And Co.; Whitman & Company, Albert; Wild Honey; WRS Publishing

Nature/Environment. Advocacy Press; Barrons Educational Series; Beautiful American Publishing Company; Bess Press; Blizzard Publishing; Blue Sky Press; Carolrhoda Books, Inc.; Charlesbridge; Cherubic Press; Chronicle Books; Coteau Books Ltd.; Crown Publishers (Crown Books for Children); Dawn Publications; Dial Books for Young Readers; Distinctive Publishing Corp.; Dorling Kindersley, Inc.; Down East Books; Dutton Children's Books; E.M. Press, Inc.; Fitzhenry & Whiteside Ltd.; Geringer Books, Laura; Gibbs Smith, Publisher; Godine, Publisher, David R.; Grosset & Dunlap, Inc.; Hodder Children's Books; Houghton Mifflin Co.; Humanics Children's House; Ideals Children's Books; Knopf Books for Young Readers; Laredo Publishing Co. Inc.; Lerner Publications Co.; Little, Brown and Company; Lodestar Books; Lucky Books; Mayhaven; Milkweed Editions; Mondo Publishing; Morris Publishing, Joshua; NorthWord Press, Inc.; Orca Book Publishers; Orchard Books; Owen Publishers, Inc., Richard C.; Pacific Educational Press; Pando Publications; Paulist Press; Peachtree Publishers, Ltd.; Peartree; Philomel Books; Read'n Run Books; Sasquatch Books; Scholastic Canada Ltd.; Soundprints; Stemmer House Publishers, Inc.; Time-Life for Children; TOR Books; Treasure Chest Books; Tricycle Press; University Classics, Ltd. Publishers; Whitman & Company, Albert; Wild Honey

Poetry. Advocacy Press; Blue Sky Press; Boyds Mills Press; Candlewick Press; Chronicle Books; Clarion Books; Dial Books for Young Readers; Dutton Children's Books; Geringer Books, Laura; Godine, Publisher, David R.; Hyperion Books for Children; Laredo Publishing Co. Inc.; McElderry Books, Margaret K.; Meadowbrook Press; Orchard Books; Peachtree Publishers, Ltd.; Philomel Books; Rizzoli Books For Children; Scholastic Canada Ltd.; Simon & Schuster Books for Young Readers; Victory Publishing; Wild Honey

Problem novels. Avon Books; Barrons Educational Series; Berkley Publishing Group; Bess Press; Bethany House Publishers; Boyds Mills Press; Chronicle Books; Cobblehill Books; Dial Books for Young Readers; Eerdmans Publishing Company, Wm. B.; Geringer Books, Laura; HaChai Publishing; Harcourt Brace & Co.; Herald Press; Honea Publishers, John; Houghton Mifflin Co.; Hyperion Books for Children; Jewish Publication Society; Jones University Press/Light Line Books, Bob; Lerner Publications Co.; Lorimer & Co., James; Magination Press; Milkweed Editions; Orca Book Publishers; Philomel Books; Place In The Woods, The; Polychrome Publishing Corporation; Putnam's Sons, G.P.; Read'n Run Books; Royal Fireworks; Scholastic Hardcover; TOR Books; Tudor Publishers, Inc.; University Classics, Ltd. Publishers; Whitman & Company, Albert

Religious. Augsburg Fortress, Publishers; Barbour & Co., Inc.; Bethel Publishing; Concordia Publishing House; Crossway Books; CSS Publishing; Dial Books for Young Readers; Distinctive Publishing Corp.; E.M. Press, Inc.; Eerdmans Publishing Company, Wm. B.; Friends United Press; Friendship Press, Inc.; HaChai Publishing; Herald Press; Holiday House Inc.; Honea Publishers, John; Huntington House Publishers; Jewish Lights Publishing; Jewish Publication Society; Kar-Ben Copies, Inc.; Meriwether Publishing Ltd.; Morehouse Publishing Co.; Morris Publishing, Joshua; Our Sunday Visitor, Inc.; Pacific Press; Pauline (St. Paul) Books and Media; Paulist Press; Pelican Publishing Co. Inc.; Questar Publishers, Inc.; Read'n Run Books; Standard Publishing; Time-Life for Children; Tyndale House Publishers, Inc.; Victor Books

Romance. Archway/Minstrel Books; Avon Books; Berkley Publishing Group; Bethany House Publishers;

Cherubic Press; Fawcett Juniper; Harcourt Brace & Co.; Houghton Mifflin Co.; Hyperion Books for Children; Jewish Publication Society; Just Us Books, Inc.; Scholastic Hardcover

Science Fiction. Clarion Books; Dial Books for Young Readers; Dutton Children's Books; Fawcett Juniper; Harcourt Brace & Co.; Houghton Mifflin Co.; Hyperion Books for Children; Ideals Children's Books; Knopf Books for Young Readers; Little, Brown and Company; Lucky Books; Milkweed Editions; Mondo Publishing; Orchard Books; Pacific Educational Press; Royal Fireworks; Scholastic Canada Ltd.; Scholastic Hardcover; Walker And Co.

Special needs. Alyson Publications, Inc.; Blizzard Publishing; Carolrhoda Books, Inc.; Cherubic Press; Globe Fearon Educational Publisher; Houghton Mifflin Co.; Kar-Ben Copies, Inc.; Magination Press; Orca Book Publishers; Our Child Press; Paulist Press; Philomel Books; Putnam's Sons, G.P.; Sasquatch Books; Scholastic Hardcover; Speech Bin, Inc., The; University Classics, Ltd. Publishers; Whitman & Company, Albert

Sports. Archway/Minstrel Books; Avon Books; Bantam Doubleday Dell; Bess Press; Boyds Mills Press; Cherubic Press; Cobblehill Books; Dial Books for Young Readers; Distinctive Publishing Corp.; Feminist Press at The City University of New York, The; Fitzhenry & Whiteside Ltd.; Geringer Books, Laura; Godine, Publisher, David R.; Grosset & Dunlap, Inc.; Harcourt Brace & Co.; Honea Publishers, John; Houghton Mifflin Co.; Hyperion Books for Children; Ideals Children's Books; Jewish Publication Society; Jones University Press/Light Line Books, Bob; Knopf Books for Young Readers; Lerner Publications Co.; Mondo Publishing; Orchard Books; Place In The Woods, The; Random House Books for Young Readers; Read'n Run Books; Scholastic Canada Ltd.; Standard Publishing; Sunbelt Media, Inc./Eakin Press; Thistledown Press Ltd.; Time-Life for Children; Tudor Publishers, Inc.; Whitman & Company, Albert

Suspense/mystery. Archway/Minstrel Books; Avon Books; Bantam Doubleday Dell; Barrons Educational Series; Berkley Publishing Group; Bess Press; Bethany House Publishers; Cherubic Press; Christian Ed. Publishers; Cobblehill Books; Coteau Books Ltd.; Crocodile Books, USA; Crossway Books; Dial Books for Young Readers; Distinctive Publishing Corp.; Dutton Children's Books; E.M. Press, Inc.; Feminist Press at The City University of New York, The; Fitzhenry & Whiteside Ltd.; Freedom Publishing Company; Geringer Books, Laura; Harcourt Brace & Co.; Hodder Children's Books; Honea Publishers, John; Houghton Mifflin Co.; Hyperion Books for Children; Jewish Publication Society; Jones University Press/Light Line Books, Bob; Just Us Books, Inc.; Knopf Books for Young Readers; Lerner Publications Co.; Little, Brown and Company; Lodestar Books; McElderry Books, Margaret K.; Mayhaven; Milkweed Editions; Mondo Publishing; Morehouse Publishing Co.; Orca Book Publishers; Orchard Books; Place In The Woods, The; Putnam's Sons, G.P.; Random House Books for Young Readers; Read'n Run Books; Royal Fireworks; Scholastic Canada Ltd.; Scholastic Hardcover; Simon & Schuster Books for Young Readers; Standard Publishing; Thistledown Press Ltd.; Time-Life for Children; TOR Books; Tyndale House Publishers, Inc.; Victor Books; Whitman & Company, Albert

Book Publishers: Nonfiction

Activity Books. American Bible Society; American Education Publishing; Bess Press; Bright Ring Publishing; Cambridge Educational; Chicago Review Press; Crown Publishers (Crown Books for Children); Davenport, Publishers, May; Davis Publications, Inc.; Denison Co. Inc., T.S.; Dial Books for Young Readers; Dorling Kindersley, Inc.; Enslow Publishers Inc.; Evan-Moor Educational Publishers; Franklin Watts; Friendship Press, Inc.; Gibbs Smith, Publisher; Godine, Publisher, David R.; Grosset & Dunlap, Inc.; Highsmith Press; Hodder Children's Books; Humanics Children's House; Ideals Children's Books; Jewish Lights Publishing; Lion Books, Publisher; Little, Brown and Company; Lodestar Books; Lucky Books; Marlor Press, Inc.; Mayhaven; Meadowbrook Press; Meriwether Publishing Ltd.; Millbrook Press, The; Morris Publishing, Joshua; NorthWord Press, Inc.; Pacific-Rim Publishers; Pando Publications; Paulist Press; Peel Productions; Place In The Woods, The; Read'n Run Books; Rizzoli Books For Children; Sasquatch Books; Scholastic Canada Ltd.; Speech Bin, Inc., The; Sterling Publishing Co., Inc.; Sundance Publishing; Tricycle Press; Tyndale House Publishers, Inc.; University Classics, Ltd. Publishers; Victor Books; Victory Publishing; Wiley & Sons, Inc., John

Animal. American Education Publishing; Atheneum Books for Young Readers; Beautiful American Publishing Company; Blackbirch Press, Inc./Blackbirch Graphics, Inc.; Blue Sky Press; Boyds Mills Press; Candlewick Press; Carolrhoda Books, Inc.; Charlesbridge; Childrens Press; Chronicle Books; Clarion Books; Cobblehill Books; Crown Publishers (Crown Books for Children); Dawn Publications; Denison Co. Inc., T.S.; Dial Books for Young Readers; Distinctive Publishing Corp.; Dorling Kindersley, Inc.; Down East Books; Dutton Children's Books; Enslow Publishers Inc.; Franklin Watts; Golden Books; Grosset & Dunlap, Inc.; Harcourt Brace & Co.; Hodder Children's Books; Humanics Children's House; Ideals Children's Books; Jones University Press/Light Line Books, Bob; Knopf Books for Young Readers; Knopf Books for Young Readers; Lerner Publications Co.; Little, Brown and Company; Lodestar Books; Lucky Books; Mayhaven; Millbrook Press, The; Mondo Publishing; Morris Publishing, Joshua; Muir Publications, Inc, John; Northland Publishing; NorthWord Press, Inc.; Orca Book Publishers; Orchard Books; Owen Publishers, Inc., Richard C.; Pacific Educational Press; Pando Publications; Paulist Press; Peachtree Publishers, Ltd.; Place In The Woods, The; Random House Books for Young Readers; Read'n Run Books; Rhache Publishers, Ltd.; Sasquatch Books; Scholastic Canada Ltd.; Scholastic Hardcover; Simon & Schuster Books for Young Readers; Soundprints; Stemmer House Publishers, Inc.; Sterling Publishing Co., Inc.; Sunbelt Media, Inc./Eakin Press;

Time-Life for Children; Treasure Chest Books; University Classics, Ltd. Publishers; Walker And Co.; Whitman & Company, Albert; Wiley & Sons, Inc., John

Arts/crafts. Bright Ring Publishing; Cambridge Educational; Chicago Review Press; Childrens Press; Chronicle Books; Davis Publications, Inc.; Dorling Kindersley, Inc.; Fitzhenry & Whiteside Ltd.; Franklin Watts; Gibbs Smith, Publisher; Godine, Publisher, David R.; Grosset & Dunlap, Inc.; Humanics Children's House; Ideals Children's Books; Lerner Publications Co.; Lion Books, Publisher; Little, Brown and Company; Marlor Press, Inc.; Millbrook Press, The; Mondo Publishing; Muir Publications, Inc, John; Pacific Educational Press; Pando Publications; Paulist Press; Philomel Books; Read'n Run Books; Rhache Publishers, Ltd.; Sasquatch Books; Scholastic Canada Ltd.; Stemmer House Publishers, Inc.; Sterling Publishing Co., Inc.; Tricycle Press; University Classics, Ltd. Publishers; Victory Publishing; Wiley & Sons, Inc., John

Biography. Atheneum Books for Young Readers; Bandanna Books; B&B Publishing, Inc.; Barbour & Co., Inc.; Bess Press; Blackbirch Press, Inc./Blackbirch Graphics, Inc.; Blue Sky Press; Boyds Mills Press; Broadman & Holman Publishers; Candlewick Press; Carolrhoda Books, Inc.; Chelsea House Publishers; Childrens Press; Chronicle Books; Clarion Books; Crown Publishers (Crown Books for Children); Dial Books for Young Readers; Discovery Enterprises, Ltd.; Distinctive Publishing Corp.; Dutton Children's Books; Eerdmans Publishing Company, Wm. B.; Enslow Publishers Inc.; Evan-Moor Educational Publishers; Fitzhenry & Whiteside Ltd.; Franklin Watts; Globe Fearon Educational Publisher; Godine, Publisher, David R.; Greenhaven Press; Grosset & Dunlap, Inc.; Harcourt Brace & Co.; Hendrick-Long Publishing Company; Holiday House Inc.; Homestead Publishing; Jewish Publication Society; Jones University Press/Light Line Books, Bob; Just Us Books, Inc.; Knopf Books for Young Readers; Lee & Low Books, Inc.; Lerner Publications Co.; Lion Books, Publisher; Little, Brown and Company; Lodestar Books; McElderry Books, Margaret K.; Mayhaven; Milkweed Editions; Millbrook Press, The; Morehouse Publishing Co.; Morgan Reynolds Publishing; Muir Publications, Inc, John; Oliver Press, Inc., The; Pacific Educational Press; Pando Publications; Pauline (St. Paul) Books and Media; Paulist Press; Peachtree Publishers, Ltd.; Pelican Publishing Co. Inc.; Perfection Learning Corporation; Philomel Books; Putnam's Sons, G.P.; Random House Books for Young Readers; Read'n Run Books; Reynolds Publishing; Rhache Publishers, Ltd.; Rizzoli Books For Children; Royal Fireworks; Scholastic Canada Ltd.; Scholastic Hardcover; Scientific American Books for Young Readers; Simon & Schuster Books for Young Readers; Stemmer House Publishers, Inc.; Sundance Publishing; Texas Christian University Press; Tudor Publishers, Inc.; Walker And Co.; WRS Publishing

Careers. Advocacy Press; B&B Publishing, Inc.; Broadman & Holman Publishers; Cambridge Educational; Childrens Press; Crown Publishers (Crown Books for Children); Dial Books for Young Readers; Distinctive Publishing Corp.; Enslow Publishers Inc.; Fitzhenry & Whiteside Ltd.; Franklin Watts; Globe Fearon Educational Publisher; Hodder Children's Books; Lerner Publications Co.; Lodestar Books; Millbrook Press, The; Owen Publishers, Inc., Richard C.; Paulist Press; Perfection Learning Corporation; PPI Publishing; Read'n Run Books; Rhache Publishers, Ltd.; Rosen Publishing Group, The; Royal Fireworks; Scholastic Canada Ltd.; Tricycle Press; Walker And Co.; Weigl Educational Publishers; Whitman & Company, Albert

Concept. Africa World Press; American Education Publishing; B&B Publishing, Inc.; Barrons Educational Series; Bess Press; Blackbirch Press, Inc./Blackbirch Graphics, Inc.; Blue Sky Press; Cambridge Educational; Charlesbridge; Childrens Press; Clarion Books; Franklin Watts; Grosset & Dunlap, Inc.; Holiday House Inc.; Ideals Children's Books; Jalmar Press; Lerner Publications Co.; Little, Brown and Company; Lodestar Books; Magination Press; Millbrook Press, The; Muir Publications, Inc, John; Pando Publications; Paulist Press; Scholastic Canada Ltd.; Standard Publishing; Time-Life for Children; Tricycle Press; University Classics, Ltd. Publishers; Wiley & Sons, Inc., John; WRS Publishing

Cooking. Bright Ring Publishing; Chronicle Books; Fiesta City Publishers; Franklin Watts; Gibbs Smith, Publisher; Ideals Children's Books; Lerner Publications Co.; Little, Brown and Company; Mondo Publishing; Pacific Educational Press; Pando Publications; Paulist Press; Pelican Publishing Co. Inc.; Rhache Publishers, Ltd.; Rizzoli Books For Children; Sasquatch Books; Victory Publishing

Educational. Atheneum Books for Young Readers; Free Spirit Publishing; Planet Dexter

Geography. B&B Publishing, Inc.; Bess Press; Blackbirch Press, Inc./Blackbirch Graphics, Inc.; Boyds Mills Press; Cambridge Educational; Charlesbridge; Childrens Press; Chronicle Books; Denison Co. Inc., T.S.; Distinctive Publishing Corp.; Dorling Kindersley, Inc.; Down East Books; Evan-Moor Educational Publishers; Fitzhenry & Whiteside Ltd.; Franklin Watts; Friendship Press, Inc.; Holiday House Inc.; Lerner Publications Co.; Little, Brown and Company; Lodestar Books; Mayhaven; Millbrook Press, The; Oliver Press, Inc., The; Pando Publications; Perfection Learning Corporation; Reidmore Books Inc.; Sasquatch Books; Scholastic Canada Ltd.; Sterling Publishing Co., Inc.; Sundance Publishing; Time-Life for Children; TOR Books; Tricycle Press; Wild Honey; Wiley & Sons, Inc., John

Health. Boyds Mills Press; Childrens Press; Crown Publishers (Crown Books for Children); Denison Co. Inc., T.S.; Dial Books for Young Readers; Enslow Publishers Inc.; Fitzhenry & Whiteside Ltd.; Franklin Watts; Free Spirit Publishing; Freedom Publishing Company; Globe Fearon Educational Publisher; Hodder Children's Books; Hunter House Publishers; Ideals Children's Books; Lerner Publications Co.; Lucent Books; Magination Press; Millbrook Press, The; Paulist Press; Pelican Publishing Co. Inc.; Perfection Learning Corporation; PPI Publishing; Rhache Publishers, Ltd.; Scientific American Books for Young Readers; Speech Bin, Inc., The; Time-Life for Children; Tricycle Press; Tudor Publishers, Inc.; University Classics, Ltd. Publishers; Walker And Co.; Whitman & Company, Albert; Wiley & Sons, Inc., John; WRS Publishing

Hi-lo. Barrons Educational Series; Bess Press; Childrens Press; Fitzhenry & Whiteside Ltd.; Franklin Watts;

Globe Fearon Educational Publisher; Lerner Publications Co.; Lucky Books; Place In The Woods, The; Read'n Run Books; Read'n Run Books; Rosen Publishing Group, The

History. Africa World Press; Atheneum Books for Young Readers; Bandanna Books; B&B Publishing, Inc.; Barbour & Co., Inc.; Bess Press; Blackbirch Press, Inc./Blackbirch Graphics, Inc.; Blue Sky Press; Boyds Mills Press; Cambridge Educational; Candlewick Press; Carolrhoda Books, Inc.; Chelsea House Publishers; Childrens Press; Chronicle Books; Clarion Books; Crocodile Books, USA; Crown Publishers (Crown Books for Children); Denison Co. Inc., T.S.; Dial Books for Young Readers; Discovery Enterprises, Ltd.; Distinctive Publishing Corp.; Dorling Kindersley, Inc.; Dutton Children's Books; Eerdmans Publishing Company, Wm. B.; Enslow Publishers Inc.; Evan-Moor Educational Publishers; Feminist Press at The City University of New York, The; Fitzhenry & Whiteside Ltd.; Fitzhenry & Whiteside Ltd.; Franklin Watts; Friends United Press; Gibbs Smith, Publisher; Globe Fearon Educational Publisher; Godine, Publisher, David R.; Golden Books; Greenhaven Press; Grosset & Dunlap, Inc.; Harcourt Brace & Co.; Hendrick-Long Publishing Company; Holiday House Inc.; Homestead Publishing; Ideals Children's Books; Jewish Publication Society; Jones University Press/Light Line Books, Bob; Laredo Publishing Co. Inc.; Lerner Publications Co.; Lion Books, Publisher; Little, Brown and Company; Lodestar Books; Lucent Books; McElderry Books, Margaret K.; Mayhaven; Millbrook Press, The; Misty Hill Press; Mondo Publishing; Morgan Reynolds Publishing; Northland Publishing; Oliver Press, Inc., The; Open Hand Publishing Inc.; Orchard Books; Pacific Educational Press; Pando Publications; Paulist Press; Peachtree Publishers, Ltd.; Pelican Publishing Co. Inc.; Perfection Learning Corporation; Philomel Books; Place In The Woods, The; Polychrome Publishing Corporation; Putnam's Sons, G.P.; Random House Books for Young Readers; Reidmore Books Inc.; Reynolds Publishing; Rhache Publishers, Ltd.; Rizzoli Books For Children; Scholastic Canada Ltd.; Scholastic Hardcover; Simon & Schuster Books for Young Readers; Sunbelt Media, Inc./Eakin Press; Texas Christian University Press; Thorson & Associates; Time-Life for Children; TOR Books; Tudor Publishers, Inc.; Walker And Co.; Whitman & Company, Albert; Wild Honey

Hobbies. American Education Publishing; Avon Books; Bright Ring Publishing; Carolrhoda Books, Inc.; Chicago Review Press; Childrens Press; Crown Publishers (Crown Books for Children); Enslow Publishers Inc.; Fitzhenry & Whiteside Ltd.; Godine, Publisher, David R.; Harcourt Brace & Co.; Lerner Publications Co.; Lion Books, Publisher; Lucky Books; Millbrook Press, The; Mondo Publishing; Muir Publications, Inc, John; Pando Publications; Place In The Woods, The; Planet Dexter; Random House Books for Young Readers; Read'n Run Books; Rhache Publishers, Ltd.; Royal Fireworks; Scholastic Canada Ltd.; Scholastic Hardcover; Sterling Publishing Co., Inc.; Walker And Co.; Whitman & Company, Albert; Wiley & Sons, Inc., John

How-to. Barrons Educational Series; Cambridge Educational; Childrens Press; Freedom Publishing Company; Gibbs Smith, Publisher; Herald Press; Jalmar Press; Lerner Publications Co.; Lion Books, Publisher; Magination Press; Meriwether Publishing Ltd.; Mondo Publishing; Pando Publications; Place In The Woods, The; Planet Dexter; Rhache Publishers, Ltd.; Sasquatch Books; Scholastic Canada Ltd.; TOR Books; Tricycle Press; Victory Publishing; Wiley & Sons, Inc., John

Multicultural. Advocacy Press; Africa World Press; African American Images; American Bible Society; B&B Publishing, Inc.; Bess Press; Blackbirch Press, Inc./Blackbirch Graphics, Inc.; Blue Sky Press; Boyds Mills Press; Carolrhoda Books, Inc.; Charlesbridge; Chelsea House Publishers; Childrens Press; Chronicle Books; Clarion Books; Davis Publications, Inc.; Dutton Children's Books; Dutton Children's Books; Feminist Press at The City University of New York, The; Fitzhenry & Whiteside Ltd.; Franklin Watts; Free Spirit Publishing; Friendship Press, Inc.; Gibbs Smith, Publisher; Globe Fearon Educational Publisher; Godine, Publisher, David R.; Hendrick-Long Publishing Company; Humanics Children's House; Hunter House Publishers; Ideals Children's Books; Laredo Publishing Co. Inc.; Lee & Low Books, Inc.; Lerner Publications Co.; Lion Books, Publisher; Little, Brown and Company; Lodestar Books; Lucent Books; Mage Publishers Inc.; Magination Press; Millbrook Press, The; Mondo Publishing; Morgan Reynolds Publishing; Muir Publications, Inc, John; Northland Publishing; Open Hand Publishing Inc.; Orchard Books; Our Child Press; Owen Publishers, Inc., Richard C.; Pacific Educational Press; Pacific-Rim Publishers; Pando Publications; Paulist Press; Pelican Publishing Co. Inc.; Perfection Learning Corporation; Philomel Books; Place In The Woods, The; Polychrome Publishing Corporation; Putnam's Sons, G.P.; Read'n Run Books; Reidmore Books Inc.; Reynolds Publishing; Rizzoli Books For Children; Rosen Publishing Group, The; Sasquatch Books; Scholastic Canada Ltd.; Scholastic Hardcover; Simon & Schuster Books for Young Readers; Stemmer House Publishers, Inc.; Sundance Publishing; Tilbury House, Publishers; TOR Books; Treasure Chest Books; Tudor Publishers, Inc.; Walker And Co.; Weigl Educational Publishers; Whitman & Company, Albert; Wild Honey; WRS Publishing

Music/dance. Avon Books; Bright Ring Publishing; Candlewick Press; Crown Publishers (Crown Books for Children); Denison Co. Inc., T.S.; Dial Books for Young Readers; Fiesta City Publishers; Fitzhenry & Whiteside Ltd.; Franklin Watts; Godine, Publisher, David R.; Harcourt Brace & Co.; Humanics Children's House; Lerner Publications Co.; Lodestar Books; Millbrook Press, The; Mondo Publishing; Pacific Educational Press; Pacific-Rim Publishers; Pelican Publishing Co. Inc.; Philomel Books; Players Press, Inc.; Read'n Run Books; Rhache Publishers, Ltd.; Sasquatch Books; Stemmer House Publishers, Inc.; Sterling Publishing Co., Inc.; Walker And Co.; Whitman & Company, Albert; Wild Honey

Nature/environment. American Bible Society; Archway/Minstrel Books; B&B Publishing, Inc.; Beautiful American Publishing Company; Blue Sky Press; Boyds Mills Press; Bright Ring Publishing; Cambridge Educational; Candlewick Press; Carolrhoda Books, Inc.; Childrens Press; Chronicle Books; Clarion Books; Cobblehill Books; Crocodile Books, USA; Crown Publishers (Crown Books for Children); Dawn

Publications; Denison Co. Inc., T.S.; Dial Books for Young Readers; Dorling Kindersley, Inc.; Down East Books; Dutton Children's Books; Eerdmans Publishing Company, Wm. B.; Enslow Publishers Inc.; Evan-Moor Educational Publishers; Fitzhenry & Whiteside Ltd.; Franklin Watts; Gibbs Smith, Publisher; Globe Fearon Educational Publisher; Godine, Publisher, David R.; Golden Books; Greenhaven Press; Grosset & Dunlap, Inc.; Harcourt Brace & Co.; Homestead Publishing; Humanics Children's House; Ideals Children's Books; Jones University Press/Light Line Books, Bob; Knopf Books for Young Readers; Lerner Publications Co.; Little, Brown and Company; Lodestar Books; Lucent Books; Lucky Books; Mayhaven; Millbrook Press, The; Mondo Publishing; Morehouse Publishing Co.; Morris Publishing, Joshua; Muir Publications, Inc, John; NorthWord Press, Inc.; Orca Book Publishers; Orchard Books; Owen Publishers, Inc., Richard C.; Pacific Educational Press; Pando Publications; Paulist Press; Peachtree Publishers, Ltd.; Pelican Publishing Co. Inc.; Perfection Learning Corporation; Planet Dexter; PPI Publishing; Read'n Run Books; Reidmore Books Inc.; Rhache Publishers, Ltd.; Rizzoli Books For Children; Royal Fireworks; Sasquatch Books; Scholastic Hardcover; Scientific American Books for Young Readers; Simon & Schuster Books for Young Readers; Standard Publishing; Stemmer House Publishers, Inc.; Sterling Publishing Co., Inc.; Thorson & Associates; Time-Life for Children; TOR Books; Treasure Chest Books; Tricycle Press; University Classics, Ltd. Publishers; Walker And Co.; Whitman & Company, Albert; Wiley & Sons, Inc., John

Reference. American Bible Society; B&B Publishing, Inc.; Barrons Educational Series; Behrman House Inc.; Bess Press; Blackbirch Press, Inc./Blackbirch Graphics, Inc.; Childrens Press; Denison Co. Inc., T.S.; Fitzhenry & Whiteside Ltd.; Franklin Watts; Highsmith Press; Millbrook Press, The; Pacific Educational Press; Pando Publications; Read'n Run Books; Rhache Publishers, Ltd.; Scholastic Canada Ltd.; Sterling Publishing Co., Inc.; Thorson & Associates; Time-Life for Children; Tricycle Press; Tudor Publishers, Inc.; Wiley & Sons, Inc., John

Religious. American Bible Society; Augsburg Fortress, Publishers; Barbour & Co., Inc.; Bethany House Publishers; Bethel Publishing; Christian Ed. Publishers; Concordia Publishing House; Crown Publishers (Crown Books for Children); CSS Publishing; Dial Books for Young Readers; E.M. Press, Inc.; Eerdmans Publishing Company, Wm. B.; Franklin Watts; Friends United Press; Friendship Press, Inc.; Harcourt Brace & Co.; Herald Press; Holiday House Inc.; Huntington House Publishers; Jewish Lights Publishing; Jewish Publication Society; Kar-Ben Copies, Inc.; Meriwether Publishing Ltd.; Morehouse Publishing Co.; Morris Publishing, Joshua; Pacific Press; Pauline (St. Paul) Books and Media; Paulist Press; Pelican Publishing Co. Inc.; Questar Publishers, Inc.; St. Anthony Messenger Press; Scholastic Hardcover; Simon & Schuster Books for Young Readers; Standard Publishing; Starburst Publishers; Time-Life for Children; Tyndale House Publishers, Inc.; Walker And Co.

Science. American Education Publishing; A/V Concepts Corp.; B&B Publishing, Inc.; Blackbirch Press, Inc./Blackbirch Graphics, Inc.; Boyds Mills Press; Bright Ring Publishing; Cambridge Educational; Carolrhoda Books, Inc.; Charlesbridge; Chelsea House Publishers; Childrens Press; Chronicle Books; Clarion Books; Crown Publishers (Crown Books for Children); Discovery Enterprises, Ltd.; Dorling Kindersley, Inc.; Evan-Moor Educational Publishers; Feminist Press at The City University of New York, The; Franklin Watts; Globe Fearon Educational Publisher; Grosset & Dunlap, Inc.; Holiday House Inc.; Ideals Children's Books; Lerner Publications Co.; Lodestar Books; Millbrook Press, The; Mondo Publishing; Muir Publications, Inc, John; Pacific Educational Press; Pando Publications; Perfection Learning Corporation; Planet Dexter; Read'n Run Books; Rhache Publishers, Ltd.; Scholastic Canada Ltd.; Scientific American Books for Young Readers; Simon & Schuster Books for Young Readers; Sterling Publishing Co., Inc.; Thorson & Associates; Time-Life for Children; TOR Books; Tricycle Press; Victory Publishing; Walker And Co.; Wiley & Sons, Inc., John

Self Help. Advocacy Press; American Bible Society; A/V Concepts Corp.; Avon Books; Barrons Educational Series; Bethany House Publishers; Broadman & Holman Publishers; Cambridge Educational; Fiesta City Publishers; Free Spirit Publishing; Freedom Publishing Company; Herald Press; Hodder Children's Books; Humanics Children's House; Hunter House Publishers; Jalmar Press; Lerner Publications Co.; Little, Brown and Company; Paulist Press; Place In The Woods, The; PPI Publishing; Read'n Run Books; Rhache Publishers, Ltd.; Rosen Publishing Group, The; Royal Fireworks; Tudor Publishers, Inc.; University Classics, Ltd. Publishers; Wiley & Sons, Inc., John; WRS Publishing

Social Issues. Advocacy Press; African American Images; American Bible Society; Bandanna Books; B&B Publishing, Inc.; Barrons Educational Series; Bethany House Publishers; Broadman & Holman Publishers; Cambridge Educational; Carolrhoda Books, Inc.; Childrens Press; Chronicle Books; Clarion Books; Denison Co. Inc., T.S.; Distinctive Publishing Corp.; Dutton Children's Books; Fitzhenry & Whiteside Ltd.; Franklin Watts; Free Spirit Publishing; Freedom Publishing Company; Friendship Press, Inc.; Greenhaven Press; Herald Press; Hodder Children's Books; Hunter House Publishers; Jalmar Press; Lerner Publications Co.; Little, Brown and Company; Lodestar Books; Lucent Books; Millbrook Press, The; Mondo Publishing; Morehouse Publishing Co.; Morgan Reynolds Publishing; Muir Publications, Inc, John; Pacific Educational Press; Pando Publications; Paulist Press; Perfection Learning Corporation; Perspectives Press; Place In The Woods, The; PPI Publishing; Putnam's Sons, G.P.; Read'n Run Books; Reynolds Publishing; Simon & Schuster Books for Young Readers; Tricycle Press; Tudor Publishers, Inc.; Walker And Co.; WRS Publishing

Special Needs. American Bible Society; Blackbirch Press, Inc./Blackbirch Graphics, Inc.; Broadman & Holman Publishers; Carolrhoda Books, Inc.; Childrens Press; Davenport, Publishers, May; Franklin Watts; Free Spirit Publishing; Globe Fearon Educational Publisher; Lerner Publications Co.; Magination Press; Mayhaven; Our Child Press; Pando Publications; Paulist Press; Place In The Woods, The; Rosen Publishing

Magazines: Fiction

Seventeen Magazine; Shofar; Skipping Stones; Spider; Story Friends; Straight; Street Times; Teen Life; 'Teen Magazine; Teen Power; Touch; Turtle Magazine; U*S*Kids; Venture; With; Writer's International Forum; Zelos

Multicultural. AIM Magazine; American Girl; Brilliant Star; Chickadee Magazine; Counselor; Cricket Magazine; Crusader; Faces; Focus on the Family Clubhouse; Focus on the Family Clubhouse Jr.; Friend Magazine, The; Guideposts for Kids; Highlights for Children; Hodgepodge; Holidays & Seasonal Celebrations; Hopscotch; Humpty Dumpty's Magazine; Junior Trails; Ladybug; Pockets; Power and Light; Primary Days; Skipping Stones; Spider; Street Times; Student Leadership Journal; Teen Power; Turtle Magazine; U*S*Kids; With; Young Salvationist

Nature/Environment. Bread for God's Children; Chickadee Magazine; Children's Digest; Counselor; Cricket Magazine; Crusader; Focus on the Family Clubhouse; Focus on the Family Clubhouse Jr.; Guideposts for Kids; Highlights for Children; Hodgepodge; Holidays & Seasonal Celebrations; Hopscotch; Humpty Dumpty's Magazine; Junior Trails; Ladybug; Lighthouse; Listen; My Friend; PKA's Advocate; Pockets; Power and Light; Primary Days; R-A-D-A-R; Skipping Stones; Spider; Turtle Magazine; U*S*Kids; With; Wonder Time; Writer's International Forum

Problem-Solving. Boys' Life; Bread for God's Children; Brilliant Star; Chickadee Magazine; Child Life; Children's Digest; Counselor; Crusader; Discoveries; Friend Magazine, The; Guideposts for Kids; Highlights for Children; Home Altar, The; Hopscotch; Humpty Dumpty's Magazine; Jack and Jill; Junior Trails; Ladybug; Lighthouse; Listen; On the Line; PKA's Advocate; Pockets; Power and Light; Primary Days; R-A-D-A-R; Spider; Story Friends; Straight; Street Times; 'Teen Magazine; Teen Power; Touch; Turtle Magazine; U*S*Kids; With; Wonder Time

Religious. Brilliant Star; Counselor; Crusader; Discoveries; Faces; Friend Magazine, The; Guideposts for Kids; Home Altar, The; Junior Trails; My Friend; New Era Magazine; On Course; On the Line; Pockets; Power and Light; Primary Days; R-A-D-A-R; Seventeen Magazine; Shofar; Story Friends; Straight; Student Leadership Journal; Teen Life; Teen Power; Together Time; Touch; Venture; With; Wonder Time; Young Salvationist; Zelos

Romance. Lighthouse; New Era Magazine; PKA's Advocate; Seventeen Magazine; 'Teen Magazine; Touch

Sports. Boys' Life; Chickadee Magazine; Children's Digest; Children's Playmate; Disney Adventures; Focus on the Family Clubhouse; Focus on the Family Clubhouse Jr.; Highlights for Children; Hobson's Choice; Humpty Dumpty's Magazine; Ladybug; My Friend; New Era Magazine; PKA's Advocate; Ranger Rick; School Magazine (Blast Off!, Countdown, Orbit, Touchdown; Seventeen Magazine; Spider; With

Suspense/Mystery. American Girl; Boys' Life; Brilliant Star; Child Life; Children's Digest; Children's Playmate; Cricket Magazine; Crusader; Disney Adventures; Friend Magazine, The; Guideposts for Kids; Hodgepodge; Hopscotch; Humpty Dumpty's Magazine; Ladybug; Lighthouse; My Friend; On the Line; PKA's Advocate; R-A-D-A-R; School Magazine (Blast Off!, Countdown, Orbit, Touchdown; Seventeen Magazine; Spider; 'Teen Magazine; Turtle Magazine; U*S*Kids; Writer's International Forum

Magazines: Nonfiction

Animal. ASPCA Animal Watch; Boys' Life; Chickadee Magazine; Child Life; Children's Digest; Children's Playmate; Cricket Magazine; Crusader; Disney Adventures; Dolphin Log; Dynamath; Field & Stream; Focus on the Family Clubhouse; Focus on the Family Clubhouse Jr.; Friend Magazine, The; Girls' Life; Guide Magazine; Highlights for Children; Holidays & Seasonal Celebrations; Hopscotch; Humpty Dumpty's Magazine; Jack and Jill; Junior Trails; Ladybug; National Geographic World; Nature Friend Magazine; New Moon; On the Line; OWL Magazine; PKA's Advocate; R-A-D-A-R; Ranger Rick; react magazine; Scholastic Math Magazine; Scienceland; Seventeen Magazine; Skipping Stones; Spider; Superscience Blue; 3-2-1 Contact; TIME for Kids; Turtle Magazine; U*S*Kids; Venture

Arts/Crafts. Brilliant Star; Calliope; Chickadee Magazine; Child Life; Children's Digest; Children's Playmate; Cricket Magazine; Cricket Magazine; Crusader; Dynamath; Faces; Field & Stream; Focus on the Family Clubhouse; Focus on the Family Clubhouse Jr.; Friend Magazine, The; Girls' Life; Goldfinch, The; Highlights for Children; Holidays & Seasonal Celebrations; Hopscotch; Humpty Dumpty's Magazine; Ladybug; Listen; My Friend; New Moon; Odyssey; On the Line; PKA's Advocate; Primary Days; Scholastic Math Magazine; Scienceland; Spider; Street Times; TIME for Kids; Together Time; Turtle Magazine; U*S*Kids

Biography. Brilliant Star; Calliope; Child Life; Children's Digest; Children's Playmate; Cobblestone; Counselor; Cricket Magazine; Crusader; Disney Adventures; Focus on the Family Clubhouse; Focus on the Family Clubhouse Jr.; Friend Magazine, The; Girls' Life; Goldfinch, The; Guide Magazine; High Adventure; Highlights for Children; Holidays & Seasonal Celebrations; Hopscotch; New Era Magazine; Odyssey; On the Line; PKA's Advocate; Primary Days; Scienceland; Skipping Stones; Teen Power; TIME for Kids

Careers. American Cheerleader; Challenge; Child Life; Crusader; Florida Leader; For Seniors Only; Girls' Life; Highlights for Children; Hopscotch; Hype Hair; New Moon; On Course; PKA's Advocate; Scholastic Math Magazine; Scienceland; Seventeen Magazine; Street Times; 'Teen Magazine; TIME for Kids

Scholastic Math Magazine; Skipping Stones; Spider; Street Times; Student Leadership Journal; Teen Life; 'Teen Magazine; Teen Power; 3-2-1 Contact; TIME for Kids; Turtle Magazine; U*S*Kids; With; Young Salvationist

Nature/Environment. ASPCA Animal Watch; Boys' Life; Brilliant Star; Challenge; Child Life; Children's Digest; Counselor; Cricket Magazine; Crusader; Current Health 1; Current Health 2; Disney Adventures; Dolphin Log; Dynamath; Falcon Magazine; Field & Stream; Focus on the Family Clubhouse; Focus on the Family Clubhouse Jr.; Girls' Life; Guide Magazine; Guideposts for Kids; Holidays & Seasonal Celebrations; Junior Scholastic; Ladybug; Listen; My Friend; National Geographic World; Nature Friend Magazine; New Moon; On the Line; PKA's Advocate; Pockets; Primary Days; R-A-D-A-R; react magazine; Scholastic Math Magazine; Scienceland; Skipping Stones; Spider; Story Friends; Student Leadership Journal; Superscience Blue; 3-2-1 Contact; TIME for Kids; Turtle Magazine; U*S*Kids; Venture; With

Problem-solving. American Cheerleader; Bread for God's Children; Brilliant Star; Child Life; Counselor; Crusader; Current Health 2; Dynamath; Exploring; Friend Magazine, The; Girls' Life; Guide Magazine; Guideposts for Kids; Highlights for Children; Holidays & Seasonal Celebrations; Home Altar, The; Hype Hair; Jack and Jill; Junior Trails; Ladybug; Listen; My Friend; New Moon; On the Line; PKA's Advocate; Pockets; Primary Days; R-A-D-A-R; Skipping Stones; Spider; Straight; Street Times; Superscience Blue; 'Teen Magazine; Teen Power; TIME for Kids; Touch; With; Wonder Time; Young Salvationist

Religious. Bread for God's Children; Brilliant Star; Challenge; Counselor; Crusader; Faces; Friend Magazine, The; Guide Magazine; Guideposts for Kids; High Adventure; Home Altar, The; Junior Trails; My Friend; New Era Magazine; New Moon; On Course; Primary Days; Seventeen Magazine; Shofar; Skipping Stones; Straight; Student Leadership Journal; Teen Power; Touch; Venture; With; Wonder Time; Young Salvationist; Youth Update; Zelos

Science. Boys' Life; Challenge; Child Life; Counselor; Cricket Magazine; Crusader; Dolphin Log; Dynamath; Focus on the Family Clubhouse; Focus on the Family Clubhouse Jr.; Girls' Life; Guideposts for Kids; Highlights for Children; Hobson's Choice; Holidays & Seasonal Celebrations; Humpty Dumpty's Magazine; KidSoft Magazine; Ladybug; My Friend; New Moon; Odyssey; PKA's Advocate; R-A-D-A-R; react magazine; Scholastic Math Magazine; Science Weekly; Spider; Superscience Blue; 3-2-1 Contact; TIME for Kids; Turtle Magazine; U*S*Kids

Social Issues. Bread for God's Children; Challenge; Child Life; Choices; Counselor; Crusader; Dynamath; Florida Leader; Focus on the Family Clubhouse; Focus on the Family Clubhouse Jr.; For Seniors Only; Girls' Life; Guide Magazine; Guideposts for Kids; Highlights for Children; Junior Scholastic; New Era Magazine; New Moon; On Course; PKA's Advocate; react magazine; Scholastic Math Magazine; Seventeen Magazine; Street Times; Student Leadership Journal; Teen Life; 'Teen Magazine; Teen Power; TIME for Kids; U*S*Kids; Wonder Time; Young Salvationist

Sports. American Cheerleader; Boys' Life; Bread for God's Children; Brilliant Star; Challenge; Child Life; Children's Digest; Children's Playmate; Counselor; Cricket Magazine; Crusader; Disney Adventures; Dynamath; Field & Stream; Florida Leader; Focus on the Family Clubhouse; Focus on the Family Clubhouse Jr.; Focus on the Family Clubhouse; Focus on the Family Clubhouse Jr.; For Seniors Only; Friend Magazine, The; Girls' Life; Guide Magazine; Guideposts for Kids; Highlights for Children; Humpty Dumpty's Magazine; Listen; My Friend; National Geographic World; New Era Magazine; New Moon; On Course; PKA's Advocate; Primary Days; Racing for Kids; R-A-D-A-R; react magazine; Scholastic Math Magazine; Seventeen Magazine; Sharing the Victory; Skipping Stones; Teen Life; Teen Power; TIME for Kids; Turtle Magazine; U*S*Kids

Travel. Brilliant Star; Challenge; Chickadee Magazine; Child Life; Children's Digest; Children's Playmate; Cobblestone; Cricket Magazine; Crusader; Exploring; Faces; For Seniors Only; Girls' Life; Guideposts for Kids; Jack and Jill; National Geographic World; New Era Magazine; New Moon; OWL Magazine; PKA's Advocate; R-A-D-A-R; Scholastic Math Magazine; Skipping Stones; 'Teen Magazine; TIME for Kids; U*S*Kids

Photography Index

This index lists markets which buy photos from freelancers. It's divided into book publishers, magazines, and special markets (such as greeting card and puzzle producers). It's important to carefully read the listings and follow the specific guidelines of each publisher to which you submit.

Book Publishers

Magazines

Special Markets

General Index

U

V

W

Y

Z

1996 Insider Reports

Portrait Artist: Ann Barrow

J. Patrick Lewis
Poet
Page 48

Wendy Mass
Editor
Page 276

Denise Fleming
Illustrator/author
Page 88

William Wegman
Photographer
Page 96